1

Worlds Apart

Readings for a Sociology of Education

edited by
John Beck Chris Jenks Nell Keddie
Michael F D Young

Collier Macmillan
London

The Editors

JOHN BECK is Senior Lecturer in Education, Homerton College, Cambridge

CHRIS JENKS is Lecturer in Sociology, University of London, Goldsmiths College

NELL KEDDIE is an outreach worker in adult education and was formerly Lecturer in Sociology, University of London, Goldsmiths College

MICHAEL F D YOUNG is Senior Lecturer in Sociology of Education, University of London, Institute of Education

A Collier Macmillan book published by
CASSELL & COLLIER MACMILLAN PUBLISHERS LTD
35 Red Lion Square, London WC1R 4SG
Sydney, Auckland, Toronto, Johannesburg,
an affiliate of Macmillan Publishing Co. Inc.
New York

First published 1976

ISBN CASED 02 977260 5
     PAPER 02 977270 2

Filmset in 'Monophoto' Baskerville 10 on 12 pt by
Richard Clay (The Chaucer Press), Ltd, Bungay, Suffolk
and printed in Great Britain by
Fletcher & Son Ltd, Norwich

Contents

General Introduction   1

Part One
Childhood as a Social Construct   5

1 Otto Raum
Chaga Childhood   7
2 Camara Laye
Becoming a Man   22
3 Phillippe Ariès
Centuries of Childhood   37
4 George Eliot
School Time   48
5 Claude Brown
Growing Up in the Streets   56
6 Anthony Platt
Child-Savers   62
7 Frank Musgrove
Inventing the Adolescent   84

Part Two
Social Pathology Models and the Sociology of Education   91

8 C Wright Mills
The Professional Ideology of Social Pathologists   94
9 Robert Colquhoun
Values, Socialization and Achievement   105
10 Norman L Friedman
Cultural Deprivation: a commentary on the Sociology of Knowledge   120
11 Michael F D Young
On the Politics of Educational Knowledge   134

Part Three
Ability as a Social Construct 159

12 Hugh Mehan
Assessing Children's School Performance 161
13 Thomas Gladwin
Navigation and Logic on Puluwat Atoll 181
14 Aaron V Cicourel and John I Kitsuse
Educational Decision Makers 197
15 Bernard Coard
Educators' Theories and Pupil Identities 206
16 James Herndon
The Dumb Class 214
17 Lewis Anthony Dexter
On the Politics and Sociology of Stupidity 219
18 Barry Hines
The Employment Office 229

Part Four
Teacher–Pupil Relations 235

19 David Storey
New Boy 237
20 Jules Henry
Docility, or giving teacher what she wants 240
21 Harold Garfinkel
Conditions of Successful Degradation Ceremonies 250
22 Carl Werthman
Delinquents in Schools 258
23 Irving Piliavin and Scott Briar
Police Encounters with Juveniles 279
24 Erving Goffman
Rules of Conduct 292
25 Douglas Barnes
Classroom Language 297

Part Five
Perspectives on Learning 305

26 Joseph Gusfield and David Riesman
Styles of Teaching 307
27 Norman K Denzin
The Work of Little Children 316

28 Eleanor Leacock
Abstract versus Concrete Speech: a False Dichotomy   323
29 Robert Dumont and Murray Wax
Cherokee School Society and the Intercultural Classroom   334
30 Blanche Geer, Jack Hass, Charles V Vona, Stephen J
Miller, Clyde Woods and Howard S Becker
On the Job   346
31 Howard S Becker
History, Culture and Subjective Experience   353
32 Sol Worth and John Adair
Navajo Film Makers   364
33 Paulo Freire
Pedagogy of the Oppressed   374

Part Six

Knowledge as a Corpus   387

34 Raymond Williams
Rules for All Ranks and Food for Every Mind   389
35 Quintin Hoare
Education: Programmes or Men   405
36 Thomas S Kuhn
Text Book Knowledge   413
37 Charles Dickens
The One Thing Needful . . .   419
38 H F Ellis
Getting Rid of the Hypotenuse   425
39 Paul Radin
The Literature of Primitive Peoples   428
40 Charles Frake
How to Ask for a Drink in Subanum   453
41 Harold C Conklin
Hanunóo Color Categories   460
42 Alfred Schutz
Recipe Knowledge   466
43 Maxine Greene
Curriculum and Consciousness   470

Part Seven

Education and Rationality   489

44 Alan F Blum and Peter McHugh
The Social Ascription of Motives   491

45 Carlos Castenada
Finding Your Spot 510
46 C Wright Mills
Language, Logic and Culture 515
47 Ivan Illich
Deschooling Society 526
48 John Gay and Michael Cole
Mathematics and the Kpelle 528
49 Alfred Schutz
City Lives 544
50 Robin Horton
Neo-Tylorianism: Sound Sense or Sinister Prejudice? 548

Further Reading 561

General introduction

Collections of readings, like textbooks, all too easily become claims to define a field of enquiry, whatever their authors' intentions. This is no less true of collections claiming to be 'new perspectives' or 'new directions' than it is of those which are seen as representing a body of established knowledge. Such claims are as much features of what has passed for the sociology of education, as they are of sociological work that addresses other 'substantive' areas, like, for example, religion, industry or the family. It is the task of this brief introduction to try to specify our rather different intentions. We do not wish to give instructions to readers, but to emphasize our commitment to what we have collected; the papers and extracts we have chosen are largely those that we and our students have found useful in generating a sociology of education. More explicit reasons for inclusion are expressed in the part introductions, which offer *our* way of reading these materials, not *the* way.

We do not intend to provide a version of the history or development of the sociology of education, which by treating 'education' as somehow fixed or given would seem to pre-empt just those questions that we would wish to raise. Nor, just because many of what might be seen as the conventional sociology-of-education sources are absent, do we dismiss them; they are readily available. We hope therefore, readers will not come to see our collection as a competing paradigm or exclusive alternative; such conceptions quickly lead to closure and new orthodoxies rather than questions and new enquiries. For example, Part 2, which might be read as merely critical, is intended to open up a dialogue about certain ways of doing sociology of education that appear to have had, at least until recently, a wide and largely unquestioned acceptance.

We conceive of the task of our sociology of education as beginning by calling into question 'what might be taken as education'. This indicates not a move move to relativism, but an engagement in, and an invitation to the reader to engage in the on-going construction and exploration of what is to be questioned, or what is taken to be problematic.

We draw widely on writers who might typically be conceived of as philosophers, novelists and anthropologists, as well as on sociologists, and we bring together studies that do not explicitly address themselves to 'educational' questions. In so doing we wish to demonstrate certain possibilities of reflexive enquiry into those activities of teachers and pupils that come to be identified as educational practice. Particularly, we wish to show that such understandings need not be drawn only from the work of sociologists specifically concerned with 'education'. More strongly, there is, running through this collection, a suggestion that much work within the social sciences has confirmed, rather than opened up for enquiry, the ways in which childhood, ability, learning, etc have been and might be conceived.

The primary concern of this collection is to emphasize the possibilities of both suspending taken-for-granted categories and hierarchies of knowledge, and of displaying its contextual and situated character. This concern gives rise to such questions as 'who are the learners, the theorists, the abstract and rational thinkers?' As such we recognize the fundamentally political nature of our enterprise. It is explicitly political in directing attention to the socially constructed character of many of the 'absolutes' that make up the world of education. In raising questions about concepts of ability, knowledge and so on, we are inviting readers in their particular contexts to explore the possibilities of transcending or transforming them. Furthermore, we recognize that theorizing about our world or doing sociology, does not, as is often assumed, offer necessary remedies for existing practices (improving reading, increasing pupil involvement, etc) but offers, rather the potential of conceptualizing new possibilities. This potential does not reside in any particular institutional position, such as author, sociologist, teacher, or even adult, but in man's common humanity, his often unrealized capacity for changing as well as making his world. It is through this commitment to theorizing that we conceive of our work as different from other traditions, particularly that which has sought to uncover the rules which govern people's actions and bind them together as members of an ordered society.

The assembling of accounts which differ so widely serves to emphasize that our grounds for assembly are neither complete nor exclusive as ways of seeing. The grouping of the selections, therefore, is neither final nor exhaustive.

So pervasive in the educational literature is the notion that education is about doing things *to*, with, or *for* 'children', that Part 1 provides a graphic illustration of how we might make education, as an accomplishment, problematic. While all educational theories are premised on conceptions of childhood, such a category is a historical invention, and in different societies is so various as to defy description in the same terms. As regarded in 'educational' situations, childhood has come to be conceived as learnerhood. Theories of knowledge, in positing a body of knowledge external to the knower, parallel theories of learning with their models of the learner as one who does not 'know'. Such theories point to how our so-called knowledge of children, and thus our educational practice, is constructed by adults who rarely make explicit the grounds for the way they distinguish between adults and children. In pointing to what childhood might or might not be, we inevitably point to what education, school, and learning might be. It is here that we hope this collection may enable readers to begin.

Part One
Childhood as a Social Construct

In both the sociology of education and in the dominant branches of psychology the prevailing conceptions of childhood have been markedly ethnocentric, paying little regard to conceptions of childhood which have prevailed in other times and places. Indeed the constructions of childhood that we meet in literature may even differ in important respects from those current among many groups in our own society. To treat our concepts of childhood and adolescence as relative to our own normative values may allow us to see how the conceptions and categories which we take for granted are socially situated rather than to attribute to childhood an absolute status. By relative we do not mean that 'anything goes', but that concepts have coherence and are explanatory within the context in which they have currency and differ from those coherent in other social contexts. This may enable us to see more clearly how we conceptualize childhood in our own society. In particular, we may be wise to treat with extreme caution developmental schema whether they have a biological (eg Piaget, Bruner, Chomsky) or a sociological epistemology – (eg Durkheim and Parsons) especially when these are treated as containing universals which can legitimately be applied to children in other societies and to working-class children and the children of minority groups in our society.

A prime example of the way in which Western schema have been imposed on other societies is the preoccupation of anthropologists with Freudian constructs to explain 'socialization' processes in 'primitive' societies, constructs which have little relevance to members of those societies and serve no explanatory purpose for them. (For the implications of this kind of activity see Horton's 'Sound Sense or Sinister Prejudice' in this Reader). Frequently such accounts (for example, those of Mead and Wolfenstein) are so permeated with Freudian ideas that it is impossible to recover from their accounts what meaning their data had for the members of the culture studied. As Gladwin (1967) has pointed out anthropologists have been almost exclusively concerned with what is generally termed 'affective' development. It is a given maxim in the social sciences that people can be treated and understood as an amalgam of measurable attributes and the division between 'affective', 'cognitive' and 'social' development is ingrained in educational literature. One must assume the theoretical basis of such divisions is one of convenience which lacks a serious concern with the acquisition of human experience (Cicourel 1975) and an understanding of how it is acquired.

Our contention is that there are significant differences across social settings and that it is not the business of the sociologist either to rank such differences or to seek some universal explanatory scheme, but to try to understand members' accounts and practices in terms of the meaning they have for any given group's way of life. One pay-off this may have is to help us to understand how our beliefs about childhood in our own society are socially constructed.

The readings grouped in this section thus include historical and anthropological material which range from Ariès' contention that childhood as we understand it was an alien concept to medieval man to Musgrove's argument that adolescence was 'invented' in the eighteenth century. Necessarily all these writers use interpretive schema to provide for the sense of their data. Thus Musgrove uses an economic model which is hardly adequate to deal with the sources he uses, Raum uses an essentially functionalist model and so in a different tradition does Platt. The extracts from novels and autobiographies can suggest to us what it is like to be a member of a culture different from our own – they are also often all that is available in the area since social science studies are lacking or imbued with ethnocentricism. The extract from 'Mill on the Floss' may remind us that some of our educational practices are still the result of our particular notions of sexual differentiation and that Maggie's problems are central issues in the Newsome Report's comments on the education of girls.

References

A V CICOUREL ET AL, *Cognitive Sociology* – Language and Meaning in Social Interaction, Penguin Books, London 1973.

T GLADWIN, Culture and the Logical Process, 1967. Reprinted in N G Keddie (ed), *Tinker, Tailor: The Myth of Cultural Deprivation*, Penguin Books, 1975.

I

Chaga Childhood *

Otto Raum

Preliminary Methodological Remarks

Of all the sociological sciences, Education is the least advanced. The reasons for this are partly to be found in the past connexions of Education with Philosophy and partly in the educational situation itself. It is obviously difficult for an outsider to *observe* the educational process in a family fairly. This difficulty is increased among native peoples, as parental sensitiveness and the shyness of children are often fixed by tradition at a much higher pitch than in our society. It may, for instance, be assumed that the scarcity of observed cases of corporal punishment is partly due to this modifying factor.

Reliance on informants clearly suffers from the presence of many sources of error, such as the suggestibility of children, intentional bias in statements made by parents, and the unconscious colouring of reminiscences by natives who are neither parents nor children. Statistical methods, so useful in other sociological sciences, could therefore only be applied with great caution, and are in fact seldom or never used.

It is clear that the fundamental difficulty is the definition and classification of educational phenomena. From the educational point of view it is necessary to find an answer to the question of how a given people, such as the Chaga† deal with a certain educational situation, eg, how they treat a disobedient child. We would falsify our observations if we did not consider under the heading of disobedience the type of behaviour to which the Chaga themselves apply that word, but used European standards. Viewing it from this angle, the field-worker, by a careful combination of methods and by avoiding generalizations at an early stage of his study, will be able to collect

* Reprinted from *Journal of the Royal Anthropological Institute* **68**, 1938: 209–21, with permission of the author and of the Council of the Royal Anthropological Institute.

† The Chaga live on the slopes of Mount Kilimanjaro; aspects of their culture have been described by H Gutmann (1926 and 1932–35) and by C Dundas (1924).

adequate material on indigenous education.

Sociologically education can be defined as the relation between consecutive generations. This relationship, like all other social relations, possesses the characteristics of mutuality and reciprocity. It is usually assumed that in the educational process the child is subjected to a multiplicity of formative forces, eg, family, play group and tribal organization. If one tries to visualize the situation, one is easily led to imagine the child crushed by the action of many social forces. There are, however, three factors which restore the balance.

First, the sociological significance of the child is extraordinarily great and contrasts strongly with its biological dependence. The possession of a child raises the status of the parents among the Chaga. A young woman, who is called *mbora* from the time of her circumcision, receives the status of a *malyi* after the birth of her first child and that of *nka* after the arrival of her second. The status of her husband, too, is raised. His father gives a heifer to the young couple when the first child is born. On the other hand, barrenness in woman or man is considered a fault in character and leads to divorce. The death of a child is put down to the agency of sterile women or co-wives resorting to sorcery out of envy. Sociologically the Chaga child is therefore the founder of a stable marriage, just as marriage procures for the child the status of legitimacy.

Secondly, the psychological significance of the child for the parents must not be forgotten. Its trustfulness, simplicity, light-heartedness and fancifulness produce pleasurable emotional responses. Even the polygynous Chaga father cannot escape these influences. He fondles his baby, tickles it and addresses it respectfully by his father's name. The mother's lullabies have not only the purpose of quieting the child, but are an expression of her own experiences in adult society, as an examination of the texts reveals. Very significant in this respect are the names given to children. In many cases they embody a story, or hint at an event which is of importance to the parents.

Thirdly, the child is not a passive object of education. He is a very active agent in it. There is an irrepressible tendency in the child to become an adult, to rise to the status of being allowed to enjoy the privileges of grown-up Chaga. The child attempts to force the pace of his 'social promotion.' Thus, at five or six years of age, a little boy will surprise his mother one day by telling her that he wants to be circumcised. The mother will hear nothing of it and threatens to beat him if he repeats the request. But the demand will be made with increasing insistence as the child grows up. In former times it was the clamour and restiveness of the adolescents which decided the older section of Chaga society to start the formal education of the initiation camp.

The Child's Social Environment

The child's position in the Chaga family is determined by the fact that Chaga marriage is as a rule patrilocal, and not infrequently polygynous. Since the households of the wives do not form a kraal but are scattered over the district, this means that the father is only an occasional visitor to the child's home. The early intimacies between father and child are superseded by a period when the father is held up as a bugbear to the toddler by the mother. Later he comes to be feared for his disciplinary interventions. The mother's mediation prevents this fear from becoming a permanent mental state. But when the father departs from the compound the children cannot but make merry, and the mother joins in laughingly, saying: 'When the bull is gone, the lizards slip out to sun themselves!'

The child's attitude towards the mother is determined by the closeness and continuity of the contact. She knows the worries and troubles of her little flock. The sharing of trivial experiences in field and hut and her partial exclusion from affairs of court and community make a woman a member of the children's group. She stands out in it because of her wide knowledge, but the confidential relationship which she maintains with her children often makes it difficult for her to enforce discipline. She allies herself, therefore, to the father's authority and reports to him when the children have broken rules of conduct. As her mediation may, however, be favourable to a particular child, the children are ready to do their mother a good turn; eg, the boys, by taking a piece of roasted meat from the slaughtering place, circumvent for their mothers the taboo which prohibits them from cooking meat before the husband's return from the butchering party.

The Chaga family can thus be looked upon as having three layers of disciplinary authority. The bottom layer is formed by the children, for even among them the boys and the older girls rule the others. The top layer is represented by the father and the central one by the mother. She holds a crucial position, much more so than she can possibly do in a monogamous marriage, where the attempt is usually made for the parents to take up an identical attitude. The three layers find their expression in the rules of etiquette observed.

These rules can be sub-divided into terms of address and polite manners. Within the first two or three years a child learns all the names, proper, descriptive, and classificatory, of the members of the family group. The parents, notably the father, occasionally test the knowledge of the child as regards these names. The parents are differentiated from the children's group by the descriptive terms *awu* and *mai*, or the classificatory terms *baba* and *mama*, respectively. The latter

9

terms are used by smaller children, who also, when they want to confide something to one parent, use the proper name of the other parent.

The teaching of polite manners starts later than that of terms of address, as I was able to establish in my observation of Chaga family life during a number of years. It takes place between three and six years of age. The formalized kinds of behaviour comprise such acts as handing over things to older people with two hands and getting up from seats on the arrival of important persons. Polite manners to some extent imply the employment of a new and elaborate set of terms of address, involving the use of the clan name and other ceremonial phrases. Confusion with the ordinary set is unavoidable and is looked upon as normal. The method of training used is not one of attempting to ensure that 'right for the first time is right for all time', but rather of gradually restricting the originally vague boundaries of application to the appropriate persons.

Etiquette undoubtedly enhances the authority of the parents. Yet it is not a mere bolstering up of prestige, but a necessary factor in all family life, as it helps to create 'social distance' under the levelling conditions of close contact. That this is so is shown by the fact that parents observe some sort of etiquette towards the children, as they do, in turn, among themselves. The parents are particularly polite to the eldest son, and there is a formalized way of dealing with the youngest child. Again, the children, besides taking up a 'parental' attitude towards their younger brothers and sisters, address the eldest brother as *wawa* and habitually submit to his authority and give him precedence. This is not only of educational significance, but is an important element in the social organization of the Chaga. The classificatory application of the term *wawa* to eldest sibling, father, and paternal uncles implies potential identity of sociological function: if the father dies, the paternal uncle or the eldest brother assumes his position as regards ritual leadership and control of hereditaments.

The terms of address and manners which the child should adopt in its relations with grandparents, paternal and maternal uncles and aunts are first taught so early that the child cannot have the slightest idea of what it is all about. When the infant is a little more advanced, it is the members of the child's narrower family circle who comment on or check any misbehaviour in the presence of these relatives. The male members of the parental generation are all addressed as *baba*, the female ones as *mama*.

The attitude of the children towards the kindred has three components. First, according to native theory, the behaviour of the children towards their parents is also extended to uncles and aunts since they, on their part, exercise disciplinary authority like that of the parents over the children. To this corresponds the system of vocative terminology. Secondly, the general attitude towards the parental generation is modified in practice by the behaviour of the parents towards the individual members of the kindred group. The greater deference shown by the parents towards the senior mother's brother and father's brother, as well as the more confidential relationship between a man and his eldest sister, are reflected in the children's attitude and symbolized by indices of individuation, eg, the father's brother is called *awu o kawi*, 'second father'. Thirdly, special attitudes are ingrained towards those persons who are of ritual or social importance to the child, eg, the mother's brother who carried out the ear-piercing ceremony. Behaviour towards these relatives is less static than that examined so far. It looms large when the control of a relative becomes decisive to the child, eg, at the stage of initiation or marriage, and may weaken when the ties are not reinforced by social intercourse, eg, if spatial separation makes such intercourse difficult.

The relations of the children with their grandparents, especially the paternal ones, are very close. Frequent visits are paid to them. In fact, the parents' possessive rights in their children are restricted in favour of the grandparents. The first child is claimed by the paternal grandfather. The claim rests on the assistance which he rendered the young couple in setting up a household. The second child is claimed by the maternal grandfather. However, he must compensate its parents by the payment of a goat. If the first child is a girl and the second one a boy, the father usually insists on having his heir left with him. But the mother's people's claim is only postponed, not cancelled thereby. It appears from this and other factors that the system of child transference to kindred is different from what has been called fosterage, where children are sent to friends of their father's for their education. In fosterage a definite educational purpose is present, while in the Chaga system, as in the similar one reported of the Baganda, the emphasis lies on fulfilling a kinship obligation. Accordingly the claim of the maternal grandfather is inherited by the maternal uncle.

Children are generally sent to their paternal grandparents at the time of weaning. The grandmother attempts to console the child for the separation by cooking food which it likes, and care is taken not to beat it lest it be reminded of home. This laxity in grandparental education is said to result in rudeness of manners and stupidity. However, the statement may very well be only an expression of jealousy, as the boy who grows up with grandparents may inherit from them.

The relationship of cross- and parallel-cousins among the Chaga is not based on common play, but on more or less ceremonial meetings.

Thus when an animal has been butchered, the mother allows the children to invite their half-siblings and the children of the father's brothers to eat with them those parts of the animal which are reserved for children. The children of the other kindred are only invited if they happen to be neighbours. Similar children's parties take place at harvest time, and when a cow is newly in milk, for the beestings are consumed by children only. In adolescence the motive for meeting shifts gradually from the ceremonial to the utilitarian. It is especially paternal parallel-cousins who are bound together by the reciprocity of co-operation.

Within the cousin-group marriage is prohibited, with the exception that in certain circumstances marriage with the daughter of a mother's brother is allowed, but this is not a preferential marriage. It is only allowed after Ego's mother is dead. Cousin relationship, however, does not involve avoidance in play groups. Erotic elements enter very early into play imitative of married life. It sometimes happens that boys play such games with their sisters or cousins. When this is discovered the children are not scolded. They are asked in a sarcastic tone, 'Who would ever marry his sister?' As this happens at a time when the erotic impulse is vague, the boys' choice of playmates for wives becomes by degrees canalized, ie, limited to girls that stand outside the cousin relationship. Boys who ask their parents why one does not marry one's cousin are simply told, 'It is bad!'

In the foregoing sketch two types of relationships can be distinguished. First, the relationship to a definite individual, such as a mother or a father's father. This is the only type experienced by the smaller child. The primary relationships to members of the family are gradually extended to members of the kindred, and form a set of derived individual relationships. Secondly, there is the relationship of the child to a social unit as such. The older the child grows the more intimately his interests are interwoven with the welfare of the family. Through evasions of kinship obligations, through the fear experienced by the family as a whole regarding neighbours suspected of practising witchcraft, through petty quarrels between the different households of a polygynous family, loyalties are formed which have unique emotional value. By analogous processes the child finds its place in the play group, the clan and later the tribe.

The Parental Means of Education
The Chaga parent is fully aware of the process of education. There exists a great number of proverbs and tales concerning the effects of negligence, bias, harshness and other educational factors.

One of the most important means employed by parents is supervision of the smaller child. Infants are hidden in the 'sleeping corner' of the hut when anybody suspected of possessing the evil eye comes to call on the parents. This area is separated from the central passage by a beam which serves both as seat for the mother when cooking and as boundary for the infant in the crawling stage. The storage place for food and milk is forbidden territory to children of both sexes. For boys, in addition, it is considered a disgrace to touch a calabash. The Chaga child is prevented from handling the many implements which might injure it; they are tucked away out of reach in the thatch of the hut. A small child is also watched lest it come too near the open fire on the hearth.

However, the essential problem of education is how direct means of behaviour control, such as supervision, punishment and reward, which have only a temporary effect, can be superseded by an indirect mechanism which will determine the actions of the child in the absence of the parents and for a longer period than an ordinary command. This can only be done by the creation of a set of inhibitive factors in the mental make-up of the child itself. Accordingly, the older children are warned by terrifying, but quite probable, stories concerning the fate of disobedient children who kindled a fire or stole honey from the storage place.

In this indirect control of the child's behaviour magic plays an important role. If the mother wants the child to stop crying she calls the *irumbu*-spectre. If the baby does not drink its soup, a brother is sent behind the Dracaena hedge to produce the growl of his ghost. A loitering child is warned that the low-sailing clouds will carry it off. The speedy return of a child messenger is secured by spitting on the palm of his hand saying, 'If you are not back before the spittle is dried up, you will vanish like it!'

Taboos can be classed with this kind of magical behaviour control. The effect of these rules is to place the children into definite behaviour groups as they grow up, since the taboos differ according to age and sex. It is unnecessary to describe them in detail. It is of educational importance, however, to examine the way in which they are supposed to act. In general, the transgression is said either to have a detrimental effect on some person to whom the child is attached, usually the mother, or to react on the child itself by handicapping its future assumption of full adult status. Many food taboos are sanctioned by the threat that the mother will die, or that the transgressor will behave in a cowardly way during circumcision. Appeal is therefore made to the two most powerful sentiments, those centring round one's mother and one's own social aspirations. The educative function of these taboos consists thus in ensuring that the prescribed behaviour should appear to serve the interests of the children themselves.

A special class of sanctions, best called religious, threatens the child with death if it breaks certain rules. The mother tells the child in angry tones, 'If you won't obey, I shall call the spirits to kill you!' When the excitement has subsided, the parents usually repudiate the curse in a solemn manner. Of special efficacy are grandparental curses. Hence children who live with their grandparents are warned not to enrage them. Their nearness to death magnifies, in the eyes of the Chaga, their potentiality for interference.

Among the Chaga several kinds of punishment can be distinguished according to their nature, such as deprival of food, incarceration, disgrace, corporal punishment, and torture. But it is also possible to define them with reference to the situation from which the conflict ending in punishment arises. There is first the class of punishments which is inhibitive, conditioning or habituating. They occur mainly during the first half of childhood and can be easily observed. The kind of punishment most suitable for this purpose is a quick unexpected slap, and the Chaga mother makes frequent use of it, eg, when the child comes too near the fire, eats earth or dung, or refuses food when it is being weaned. When punishing, mothers act under an affective strain. Then the physiological exhaustion of the emotion of anger being complete, the opposite reaction is released. The mother who slapped her baby a minute ago proceeds to fondle and even lick it.

The other type of punishment is much more difficult to observe. It arises out of a conflict between the paternal and filial generations, and increases in frequency the older the boys grow. During the first six years there is little disciplinary differentiation between sons and daughters. Between eight and ten the girls enter into effective cooperation with their mother and gradually come to share all her burdens and rights, except marital ones. The occasions on which mother and daughters may fall out with each other are therefore limited to cases where the degree of diligence or thoroughness considered necessary for a particular job is in dispute. When the boys start looking after the cattle, however, the growing cleavage between mother and sons shows its effect in an increased disciplinary tension. It is at this time that boys become attached to a play group, and its influence makes the separation irrevocable. Moreover, the father deems it fit to inculcate in his sons a feeling of contempt for all womenfolk. But boys do not quarrel only with their mothers. Soon they will be passing out of their father's tutelage also, and at puberty a struggle ensues as to the time at which full adult status is to be granted to the striplings.

In this struggle deprival of liberty is a recognized form of punishment. Disobedient children may be shut up in an empty hut and left there without food for some time. Loiterers may be tied to the middle post of the hut and sometimes have to spend the whole night in this uncomfortable position. Deprival of food is common, probably because it lends itself to being administered in varying degrees. A lazy child does not get its share when an animal is slaughtered. The nurse who eats the baby's food may not get anything to eat for one or two days.

Degradation, the public deprival of one's honour, is not unknown as an educational method. A negligent herd-boy gets the excrements of a slaughtered animal smeared on his face in the presence of all the male members of the kinship group, who forgather on such an occasion. A persistent loiterer is given a goat's horn to drink out of during a carousal, a sign of utter disgrace. Quite distinct from degradation is humiliation, which is employed when the child has not given cause for complaint. For instance, a child that is being brought up in the home of his grandparents is made to remove their faeces from inside the hut without showing any signs of disgust. It is in this way that one earns the grandparents' blessing. Again when an elderly person emits wind, it is the child who is blamed for it. Children must not deny any such charge, because they are told that by their acquiescence they prevent the disgrace of their fathers.

Corporal punishment is also used as a means for settling disputes between father and son. A boy who loses a cow on the pasture gets 15 strokes with a stick, this being the traditional measure. In the exercise of their disciplinary rights, parents are subject to the control of the community in which they live. Cruelty is condemned and indulgence ridiculed. Individual cases are dealt with on their own merits. In spite of this check, the existence of stories of torture and the use made of them for intimidating a child into obedience suggest that they might in certain circumstances serve as justification for the summary punishment of young offenders.

When an interval is placed between the punishable act and the corrective reaction, opportunity is given for the elaboration of the punitive process. The necessity is felt, especially with adolescent children, for a confession to justify the punishment. When the child is young the reconcilation ritual may be a quite informal act, such as seizing the father's beard. But if the boy already possesses a semi-independent household of his own, the procedure is quite formal and takes place in the presence of the kindred, some of whom may act as mediators. Usually the ceremony consists in expressions of repentance, the handing over of a fine by the son to his father, and a symbolization of restored confidence on the father's part. It is important to notice that both the affective reconciliation noted above, and the ceremonial one, are initiated by the parent concerned. The explanation of this is the fact that not only the punishable act but also the punishment itself violates the principle of mutual assistance upon which family life is based. It is restored only if the parents resume the relations of affectionate attachment which amplify the biological bond existing between parents and children. These attempts at reconciliation clearly distinguish educational from legal punishment.

Rewards are, of course, extensively used by parents in their attempt to make the children conform to their standards. The technique of rewards implies the lavish use of promises, controlling child behaviour by anticipation. Thus when the mother goes to market, the children are promised a small present, such as a locust, a banana or a few beads, if they do not cry. The father who interests himself in his sons at a later stage deviates sometimes from the customary law of inheritance by assigning special gifts to a son who is obedient and exhibits good manners, thrift and diligence, and he ensures the carrying out of his will by a curse on anyone who should deprive his favourite of his claims.

A most important educational factor is training in work. It is impossible to distinguish play and work genetically. A great amount of childish energy is directed to the acquisition of techniques, and this is done spontaneously and in a style which differs little, if at all, from play activities. A condition of this state of affairs is the simplicity of the tools employed and the scarcity of toys. It is sometimes difficult to decide whether at a particular moment a child is using an implement as a tool or as a toy.

Actual training in work takes place at a much later date and consists chiefly in an impressive lesson in the necessity of diligence and thoroughness in work. From the above generalization professional training in one of the non-hereditary crafts must be excluded. This takes place after initiation and is surrounded by elaborate ceremonies to ensure the secrecy of the methods taught and to protect the teacher from future competition by the pupil.

As regards the content of training in work, the education of the girls is concluded much earlier than that of the boys. Both sexes learn first together all the domestic tasks of a Chaga household. At about eight years of age the division of labour is gradually imposed on this common base. For the girl this means continuation lessons in domestic tasks, with greater refinement and independence. For the boy this is the opening of a new chapter in life. As an informal process of social education he is taken to public meetings, where he gleans information about the political authorities, the distribution of wealth and influence, and legal procedure. He is also introduced to tasks reserved for men only, such as hunting and forest work.

We must next consider some of the methods employed in training for work. Extensive use is made of models. Oral explanation is rarely given, except to a very inquisitive child. The degree of skill attained in the basic tasks is ascertained, and proficiency made a pre-condition of advance in status. The training terminates in the handing over of some of the parental stock and land to the care and for the use of the adolescent child. The first-fruits of his labours are expected to be given to the parents, and later on annual gifts are the rule. Thus the adolescents grow into the adult system of kinship obligations.

Ceremonies hold a special position in the educational process. The Chaga *rites de passage* divide childhood into different stages. The infant has to undergo the rite of the 'First Tooth' and of receiving a name. From the time of the latter rite to the appearance of the second set of teeth the child is called a *mwana*, but thenceforward a *ndentewura*. About three years later the ear-piercing ceremony takes place and simultaneously the two lower incisors are knocked out, the child acquiring the status of a *ndaka*. At adolescence the boys form groups that loiter about and make a nuisance of themselves. In some districts a special *kisusa* rite is held to discipline the most forward of these stripling individuals. If the '*kisusa* spirit,' as the rebelliousness of youth is called, cannot be curbed, the demand for tribal initiation and the formation of a new age-class is raised before the chief.

The educational function of these rites has often been described. The special diet, the quaintness of the ceremonies and the tiring repetition of the ethical teaching all help to make the impression indelible. Yet if one has seen native children during the longer rites, haggard, drowsy, often insensible to what is going on around them, one doubts whether the educational importance of ritual lies entirely in its immediate effects. Much more important are, indeed, two other factors neglected hitherto. First, the anticipation of the rite influences childish behaviour long beforehand. Negatively this means that the parents make admission to the rite conditional on conformity to their demands, and positively that the child definitely strives to make himself worthy of acceptance. Secondly, the rites introduce the child into wider social circles. This rise in status, implying ever-increasing responsibilities, is the topic most discussed among the children. Their wish for social advancement is so strong that the children of third-generation Christian families are sometimes 'infected' by it and run away from their parents to take part in the rites, showing how effectively social pressure is still diffused in the society of the children.

The Self-Education of the Children

It is important that we should try to discover in what manner the society of the children reacts to the educational efforts of the parents. To some of them it makes a positive adjustment, others it dislikes because of the discrimination in status which they imply. It makes, in fact, an attempt to create in its play activities its own social life, with its own laws and cultural features.

It is possible to classify Chaga play activities into three groups. First, there is the playful exercise of the sensory and motor apparatus, resulting in the physical adaptation of the individual organism. Secondly, there is imitative play, consisting in an adaptation of adult life to the social needs and understanding of the children. Thirdly, there are competitive games, which test not only physical fitness but also intellectual and social qualities. These three groups follow one another in a rough time sequence, the first corresponding to infancy, the second to childhood, and the third to adolescence. Corresponding with this development there proceeds an increasing socialization of the children's group, and its gradual separation from adult society.

While the play of physical adaptation is performed by infants in isolation, the mimicry type of play draws the child into a community of players who enact the daily round, the activities of the annual cycle, and scenes from individual life-histories and the different social classes. In calling these play activities imitative, we must be careful to describe what we mean by this term. Imitation among people having the same status in society must clearly be distinguished from imitation which cuts across boundaries of status, such as is seen in the native's craze for European clothes and the child's copying of the adult. In the latter case the mental outlook of the imitator differs from that of the imitated, and the copy performs a different function from that of the original. For instance, in considering the mimicry of married life the fact must not be forgotten that most children know of the marriage ceremony only by hearsay, as they are forbidden to attend weddings. Much of the subject-matter of imitation is in fact relayed through the medium of speech only. This kind of imitation may therefore be described as 'blind,' ie, the children's performance is a free reconstruction of more or less imagined happenings.

It must also be noted that such imitative play is not a complete taking over of the example, but selective. Certain traits important or striking to the child are chosen from the adult pattern. This becomes apparent in the 'imitation' of so-called 'bride-lifting.' This practice has long fallen into desuetude. The reasons which caused this exceptional custom to be resorted to were in most cases economic. With children out on the pasture the economic justification for 'marriage by capture' obviously does not weigh. But it would also be an insufficient explanaton to call their imitation of this custom a survival, a mere form without meaning. As a matter of fact, the 'lifting' is to them a vital part of all play weddings, a symbol of marriage as they understand and practice it.

Having guarded against certain ambiguities arising from the use of the term 'imitation', it must be admitted that the accuracy of the copying process increases as the child grows up and approaches adult status. Younger children insist on the meticulous repetition of isolated bits of behaviour, which are taken as representative of the corresponding adult activities. But this insistence becomes less and less pronounced with increasing conceptual specialization in the minds of the children, which goes hand in hand with greater variation and realism in mimicry. This is the result of a mutually corrective process in which that child is accorded the approval of his associates who, by the standards of the play group, deviates least from the adult pattern.

The imitative play activities which copy family and tribal life also afford an opportunity for the exchange of experience regarding persons and institutions with which some children have little chance to become directly acquainted. The framework of social organization in its practical working is learned through the boys' participation in organizing the play group. This educates them to accept voluntarily a social system into which they would otherwise have to be forced when entering adult society. Besides, the element of secrecy which attaches to the copying of the more intimate scenes from the life of the parents and of the political authorities draws the boys into a close social unit with a sense of common interests and needs.

The play group on the pasture must be distinguished on the one hand from the very much smaller group of infants who meet in the yards and groves near the huts, and on the other hand from the age-class, an institution with a ritual and a significance which go beyond childish interests. The boys' group is altogether independent; it is not established by a ceremony controlled by adults, but is a spontaneous growth. While in the family and the tribal age-class a strict, authoritarian order prevails, the boys' group is an entirely democratic affair. Every boy enters it with equal chances of rising to a leading position. The qualities which decide his promotion are not the rank and wealth of his parents, but intelligence, physical prowess, and social adaptability. It is true that the chief's son is supposed to be treated with deference, and he has strict injunctions to be affable to his playmates; but his privileges count for little if he is a stupid or socially disagreeable fellow.

The methods by which the selection of the leaders in the boys' group is carried out begin with practical jokes and tests of endurance for the younger members. The tests later assume the form of competitive games, such as wrestling, fist-fights, bird-shooting and battles with a hard green fruit the size of an orange, exercises which resemble those which were part of the former military training of the Chaga. Besides competitive games, the distribution of food (originally supplied by the mother) is a means of obtaining at least temporary allegiance from others. Finally, the leadership in certain games, etc., is decided by mere chance, eg, by drawing straws or lots.

The Chief of the Pasture, if he has risen to his post through pluck and perseverance, often holds it for a considerable time. He appoints his henchmen and orders the other boys about on serious business. For instance, when during a heavy shower the boys have retired to the hut which they have built for themselves, he may command a boy to go out and look for the cattle, which often bolt into the bush on such an occasion. He also has a decisive voice in the choice and arrangement of the games and play activities. However, it is inherent in the democratic nature of the group that he may be superseded. His ascendancy may be resented by a number of boys whom he has defeated, and jealousy may develop into open conflict, serious fights, and his final deposition.

In assessing the position and function of the boys' group within the general scheme of Chaga society, we realised that the traditional system of play activities offers the children opportunities for obtaining more or less correct notions about married life and the social organization of the tribe. With the development of their own capabilities, this process assumes a more positive aspect and may well be described as an attempt by the children to create a society for themselves, keeping closely to the original from which they are still excluded. In a sense it is true to say that the children's society has its own culture, which on the one hand can be described as a system of instruments with which the children satisfy their needs, and on the other hand consists in the re-creation of the values possessed by the paternal generation. But the expressions 're-creation of values' and 'children's society' must not mislead us. In its fundamental nature the society of the children has not developed far from its adult prototype. The reasons for this are obvious. The time and capacities at the children's disposal in their striving towards independence are too limited to allow of the creation of something absolutely original, if such a thing were possible. And yet, within the cultural tradition, the function of play as an autonomous means of self-education seems to be fairly well established, for the children's society achieves a set of distinctive cultural features which are absent in adult culture.

With regard to language it is a well-known fact that children have what has been called 'age-dialects'. But over and above these natural developmental stages, the children evolve special secret languages, which resemble our 'Double Dutch,' by transposing syllables, inserting infixes and saying words backwards.

In the economic substratum of culture, the boys' group attempts to be independent by stealing food either at home or from strangers, and by bird-shooting and buck-hunting expeditions. Moreover, as they approach adolescence, boys and girls are given their own gardens and a few chickens and goats as a reward for having helped their parents. As regards material objects, the boys use bows and arrows, which are not employed by the Chaga warriors, and the children's tops, small toboggans used on grassy slopes, and other toys have no equivalents in the adult culture.

Concerning magic, taboos which are binding on grown-up men are not observed by the boys on the pasture. Chaga men are not allowed to eat fowls, but the boys relish them. Again the strong, unchecked desires of play-life lead the children to invent their own magic. Girls use wish-magic to make their breasts grow, and I know of a boy who, to ensure the capture of his hiding playfellows, cut himself in the finger. Also with regard to law and order the children's society has its own distinctive features, handed down by tradition in the play groups. Thus girls have an ordeal for detecting nurses who eat the food of their charges, while boys more frequently use more forceful methods, such as bombardment with missiles, to discipline a social misfit.

From the educational point of view it is very important to realise that the fundamental sentiments of loyalty to social groups and the authorities, upon which life in all its various kinds of organization depends, are not necessarily formed by teaching and the giving of instructions. They emerge naturally from the sentiments attaching to the 'imitative' institutions of childhood which are created through play activities.

2

Becoming a Man*

Camara Laye

Later on, I went through an ordeal much more frightening than Kondén Diara, this time a really dangerous ordeal whose nature is far removed from that of any game: circumcision.

I was then in my final scholarship year: I, too, was at last among the big boys, whom we had so detested when we were in the infants' class because they used to extort food and money from us and used to beat us; here we were taking their place, and the hardships we had endured at their hands were now happily abolished.

But it was not enough simply to be in the big boys' class: we had to be 'big' in every sense of the word, and that meant we had to become men. But I was still a child: I was considered not to have reached the age of discretion yet! Among my companions, most of whom were circumcised, I was still looked upon as a child. I suppose I was a little younger than they, or was it that my repeated visits to Tindican had delayed my initiation? I do not remember. Whatever the reason, I had now reached the age at which I, too, must be reborn, at which I, too, must abandon my childhood and my innocence, and become a man.

It was not without misgivings that I approached this transition from childhood to manhood; the thought of it really caused me great distress, as it did those who were to share the ordeal. Of course, the ceremony itself, the visible part of it at least, was familiar to us, for each year we would watch the candidates for circumcision dancing in the town's main square. But the important, the essential part of the ceremony remained a secret, and we only had a very vague notion of how it was carried out, though we knew that the operation itself was a painful one.

The public ceremony differs completely from the secret one. The public ceremony is one of rejoicing. It is the occasion of a great festival, a very noisy festival in which the whole town participates and which lasts several days. And it is almost as if by dint of noise and

---

* *The African Child*, pp 93–113, Fontana, 1959

activity and dancing and merry-making people were trying to make us forget our anxiety about the coming ordeal, and its very real physical pain.

But however great the anxiety, however certain the pain, no one would have dreamed of running away from the ordeal – no more than one would have dreamed of running away from the ordeal of the lions – and I for my own part never entertained such thoughts. I wanted to be born, to be born again. I knew perfectly well that I was going to be hurt, but I wanted to be a man and it seemed to me that nothing could be too painful if, by enduring it, I was to come to man's estate. My companions felt the same; like myself, they were prepared to pay for it with their blood. Our elders before us had paid for it thus; those who were born after us would pay for it in their turn. Why should we be spared? Life itself would spring from the shedding of our blood.

That year, I danced for a whole week in the main square at Kouroussa the dance of the *soli*, which is the dance of those who are to be circumcised. Every afternoon my companions and I would go to the dancing-place, wearing a cap and a boubou which reached to our heels, a much longer boubou than is generally worn, and split up the sides; the cap, a skull-cap, was decorated with a pompon that hung down at the back; and this was our first man's hat. The women and girls would come running to the gates of their compounds to watch us go by; then they would follow closely on our heels, decked in their holiday finery. The tom-tom would throb, and we would dance in the square until we were ready to drop. And as the week wore on, the dances grew longer and the crowds grew bigger.

My boubou, like that of my companions, was of a brownish-red colour, a colour on which bloodstains would not show too clearly. It had been specially woven for the ceremony, and had first of all been white; the masters of the ceremonies had then dyed it with dyes made from the bark of trees, after which they had plunged it into the muddy water of a brushwood pool. The boubou, in order to obtain the desired tone, had been left to soak for several weeks, perhaps because of some ritual reason which I forget. The cap, apart from the pompon, which remained white, had been treated in the same fashion.

We would dance, as I was saying, until we were out of breath; but we were not the only ones dancing: the whole town would dance with us! In our country, all dances have this cumulative tendency, because each beat of the tom-tom has an almost irresistible appeal. Soon those who were just spectators would be dancing too; they would crowd into the open space, and, though they did not mix with our group, they would take an intimate part in our revels, outdoing us in frenzy, men as well as women, women as well as girls; though the women and girls kept strictly apart from us in their dancing.

While I was dancing, my boubou, split from top to bottom at each side, would reveal the brightly-coloured silk handkerchief which I had knotted round my loins. I was quite aware of this and did nothing to prevent it; in fact I did all I could to show it off. This was because we each wore a similar handkerchief, more or less colourful, more or less ornate, which we had received from our acknowledged sweetheart. She would make us a present of it for the ceremony, and it was generally taken from her own head. As the handkerchief cannot pass unnoticed, as it is the one personal note that distinguishes the common uniform, and as its design, like its colour, makes it easily identified, there is in the wearing of it a kind of public manifestation of a relationship – a purely child-like relationship, it goes without saying – which the present ceremony may break for ever, or, as the case may be, transform into something less innocent and more lasting. Now if our so-called sweetheart was in the least pretty and consequently desirable, we would swing our hips with great abandon, the better to make our boubou fly from side to side, and thus show off our handkerchief to greater advantage. At the same time we would keep our ears open to catch anything that might be said about us, about our sweetheart and about our good fortune; but our ears caught very little, for the music was deafening; and there was extraordinary animation in the tightly-packed crowds all round the square.

From time to time a man would break through the crowd and come towards us. It would generally be an older man, often a person of some consequence who was on friendly terms with, or had obligations towards one of our families. The man would indicate that he wished to speak; the tom-toms would stop, and the dancing would stop, and the dancing would be interrupted for a moment. We would gather round him. Thereupon the man would address himself to one or the other of us in a very loud voice.

'O thou!' he would say, 'hearken unto me. Thy family has always been beloved of my family; thy grandfather is the friend of my father, thy father is my friend, and thou art the friend of my son. I come here this day that I may testify these things in public. Let every man here know that we are friends, and that we shall ever remain so. And as a symbol of this lasting friendship, and in order to show my gratitude for the goodwill that thy father and thy grandfather have always shown to me and mine, I make thee this gift of an ox on the occasion of thy circumcision.'

We would all applaud him; the entire assembly would applaud him. Many of the older men, all of them friends indeed, would come forward like this and make an announcement of what gifts they were going to present us with. Each one would make an offering in accordance with his means, and the spirit of rivalry would often make it beyond his means. If it was not an ox, it would be a sack of rice, or millet or maize.

For the great feast of the circumcision is the occasion of a great banquet attended by numerous guests; a banquet so enormous that, despite the number of guests, there is enough for days and days before the end is reached. Obviously this entails great expense. So, whoever is a friend of the family of the boy to be circumcised, or is bound to the family by bonds of obligation, makes it a point of honour to contribute to the banquet; and he will help both those who are in need of help and those who are not. That is why, at each circumcision, there is this sudden abundance of gifts and good things.

Did we enjoy this sudden shower of gifts? Not unreservedly; the ordeal that awaited us was not of the kind that whets the appetite. No, we would not be likely to have much appetite, when, the circumcision over, we were invited to take part in the banquet. Though we did not know it by actual experience, we were quite well aware that freshly-circumcised boys have a rather woebegone look.

This reflection would brutally recall our fears: we would be applauding the donor, and at the same time our thoughts would be returning to the ordeal before us. As I have said: this apprehension in the midst of the general excitement, an excitement in which we, through our dancing, took a major part, was not the least paradoxical aspect of those days. Were we not dancing to forget what we were all dreading? I can quite believe it. And in truth there were moments when we succeeded in forgetting it; but anxiety was never far away; there were always fresh occasions for it to spring to life again. Our mothers might make increased sacrifices on our behalf – and certainly they did not fail to do so – yet they were but sorry comfort.

Sometimes one of our mothers, or some other close relative, would join the dance, and often in dancing she would wave aloft the symbol of our class; it was generally a hoe – the peasant class in Guinea is by far the most numerous – and this was to show that the boy who was about to be circumcised was a good labourer.

This was when I saw my father's second wife make her appearance holding aloft an exercise-book and a fountain-pen. I must confess that this gave me no pleasure at all and rather than encouraging me it somewhat embarrassed me, although I knew quite well that my second mother was merely observing an old custom, and doing so with the best will in the world, since the exercise-book and the fountain-pen were the symbols of a profession which, in her eyes, was superior to that of a farmer or a mechanic.

My real mother was infinitely more discreet; she simply watched me from a distance; I even noticed that she tried to hide in the crowd. I am sure she was at least as anxious as I was, though she took the greatest trouble to conceal the fact. But for the most part the excitement was such, I mean so all-pervasive, that we had to bear the burden of our uneasiness on our own.

Need I mention that we ate rapidly and without relish? It goes without saying: everything centred on the dancing and on the preparations for the feast. We would go home foot-sore and weary and sleep like logs. In the morning, we could never get up, but lay in bed until the very last moment, when the tom-tom began to summon us. What did it matter if we had no proper meals? We barely had time to eat. We had to wash at top speed, fling on our boubous, jam our caps on our heads, run to the main square and dance. And each day we had to dance more; for we were all dancing now, the whole town was dancing, afternoon and evening – by torchlight in the evening – and on the eve of the ordeal, the town danced all day long, and all night long.

On this final day, we were all worked up into a strange kind of excitement. The men who perform this initiation, after having shaved our heads, gathered us together in a hut built apart from the compounds. This hut, which was very spacious, would henceforward be our dwelling-place; the spacious square in which it stood was fenced off by such tightwoven osiers that no inquisitive eyes could see through them.

When we entered the hut, we saw our boubous and caps spread on the ground. During the night our boubous had been stitched up the sides except for the armholes, so that they covered us completely. As for the caps, they had been transformed into tremendously high bonnets: the material which had originally hung loose had been stiffened by fixing it to a wicker framework. We slipped into our boubous, which made us look rather as if we were in tight sheaths; and now we looked even skinnier than we really were. Then when we had put our long, narrow bonnets on, we looked at each other for a moment; in any other circumstances, we would have certainly burst out laughing: we looked as long and as thin as bamboo poles.

'Go and walk outside for a while,' the men told us; 'you must get used to having your boubous sewn up.'

We took a little walk; but we could not take large strides, for the stitched-up boubous prevented it: it was as if we were in shackles.

We came back to the hut, sat down on the mats and remained there under the supervision of the men. We chattered among ourselves of one thing and another, concealing our uneasiness as best we could; but how could we banish from our minds the thought of tomorrow's ceremony? The uneasiness underlying all our chatter was obvious. The men who were with us were not unaware of this state of mind; whenever, in spite of ourselves, we gave vent to our anxiety, they would be at great pains to reassure us; and in this respect they were quite different from the big boys who performed the ceremony of the lions and who only wanted to frighten us as much as possible.

'Come, don't be afraid,' they said. 'This has happened to every man. Has it done any harm to them? It won't do you any harm either. Now that you are going to become men, conduct yourselves like men; drive away your fears. A man is afraid of nothing.'

But we were still children, all the same; all through that final day, and all through that final night, we would still be children. As I have said before: we were not even considered to have reached the age of discretion. And if that age is a long time in coming, if it does really come only after many years, our 'manhood' will seem all the more premature. We were still children. Tomorrow . . . But it was better to think of something else; to think, for example, of the whole town gathered in the main square and dancing happily. But what about us? Were not we, too, about to join the dance?

No. This time, we were going to dance on our own; we were going to dance, and the others were going to watch. At present we were not allowed to mix with other people; our mothers could not even speak to us, let alone touch us. We left the hut, swathed in our long sheaths, and with our enormous bonnets towering on our heads.

As soon as we appeared in the main square, the men ran to meet us. We advanced in single file between two rows of men. Kouyaté's father, a venerable old man with white beard and white hair, thrust through the ranks and placed himself at our head; it was his privilege to show us how to dance the *coba*, a dance kept, like the *soli*, for those who are about to be circumcised, and which is danced only on the eve of circumcision. Kouyaté's father, by virtue of his great age and good name, was the only one who had the right to strike up the chant which accompanies the *coba*.

I was walking behind him. He told me to put my hands on his shoulders, and then each of us placed his hands on the shoulders of the boy in front of him. When our Indian file had been linked up in this way, the tom-toms and drums suddenly ceased, and everyone was silent, everything became silent and still. Kouyaté's father then drew himself up to his full height, cast his eyes all round him – there was something imperious and noble in his attitude – and, as if it were a command, lifted up his voice in the *coba* chant:

'*Coba! Aye coba, lama!*'

At once the tom-toms and the drums shattered the silence and we all took up the phrase:

'*Coba! Aye coba, lama!*'

We were walking like Kouyaté's father, legs apart, as far apart as our boubous would allow, and naturally with very slow steps. As we chanted the words, we would turn our heads, as Kouyaté's father did, to the left, and then to the right; and our high bonnets extended this head movement in a curious way.

'*Coba! Aye coba, lama!*'

We had begun to dance round the square. The older men drew up in two rows as we advanced; and when the last of us had passed through their ranks, they went and formed their two rows again a little farther on for us to pass through. And because we were walking slowly with our legs wide apart, we looked rather like ducks waddling along.

The two ranks of men through which we were moving were thick and tightly packed. The women, behind, would scarcely see more than our high bonnets, and the children obviously even less than that. In previous years, I had only caught glimpses of the tops of the bonnets. But it was enough: the *coba* is a man's affair. The women . . . No, the women had no voice in this matter.

'*Coba! Aye coba, lama!*'

Finally we reached the spot where we had begun our dance. Then Kouyaté's father stopped, the tom-toms and drums fell silent, and we went back to our hut again. We had barely left the square before the dancing and shouting began again.

Three times that day we appeared in the main square to dance the *coba*; and three times again during the night, by torchlight; and each time the men enclosed us in a living hedge. We did not get any sleep; no one went to bed: the whole town stayed awake and danced all through the night. As we left our hut for the sixth time, dawn was breaking.

'*Coba! Aye coba, lama!*'

Our bonnets still moved in time to the rhythm, our boubous were still stretched over our straddling legs; but we were beginning to flag, our eyes were burning feverishly and our anxiety was mounting. If we had not been urged on, carried away by the tom-tom beat . . . But it urged us on, carried us away! And we danced on obediently, our heads curiously light from lack of sleep, curiously heavy, too, with thoughts of the fate that was to be ours.

'*Coba! Aye coba, lama!*'

As we came to the end of the dance, dawn began to lighten the main square. This time, we did not go back to our hut; we went immediately into the bush; we went a long way, to where there was no risk of our being disturbed. In the main square the dancing had stopped; the people had all gone home. Nevertheless, a few men followed us out. The rest awaited, in their huts, the ceremonial shots that would announce to all that one more man, one more Malinke, had been born.

We had reached a circular clearing, the ground completely bare. All round, grasses grew high, higher than the men's heads; it was the most secluded spot one could have wished to find. We were lined up, each of us in front of a stone. At the other end of the clearing, the men stood facing us. And we took off our clothes.

I was afraid, terribly afraid, and I needed all my willpower not to show it. All those men standing in front of us and watching us must see nothing of my fear. My companions showed themselves no less brave, and it was absolutely necessary that it should be so; among those men standing in front of us was perhaps our future father-in-law, or a future relative; we dared not let ourselves down now!

Suddenly the operator appeared. We had caught a glimpse of him the night before, when he had performed his dance in the main square. And now, also, I only caught a brief glimpse of him. I had hardly realized he was there, before I saw him standing in front of me.

Was I afraid? I mean, was I even more afraid, had I at that particular moment a fresh access of fear – for I had been beset by fears ever since I had entered the clearing? I did not have time to be afraid. I felt something, like a burn, and closed my eyes for a fraction of a second. I do not think I cried out. No, I cannot have cried out; I certainly did not have time to do that either. When I opened my eyes, the operator was bent over my neighbour. In a few seconds the dozen or so boys there were that year became men: the operator made me pass from one state to the other, with an indescribable rapidity.

Later, I learned that he was of the Dama family, my mother's family. He had a great reputation; and rightly so, for at the most important festivals he had often circumcised several hundreds of boys in less than an hour; this rapidity was very much appreciated, for it did not prolong the agony. So all parents, all the parents who could, had recourse to him, as he was the most skilful. He would be their guest for the evening, and the guest of the town's most important men, then would go back to the country, where he lived.

As soon as the operation was over, the guns were fired. Our mothers, our relatives in the compounds heard the reports. And while we were being made to sit on the stone in front of us, messengers rushed away, tore through the bush to announce the happy news, arriving bathed in sweat and gasping for breath, so much so that they could hardly deliver their message to the family that came running to meet them.

'Truly your son has been very brave,' they would shout at last to the mother of the circumcised boy.

And indeed we had all been very brave, we had all very carefully concealed our fear. But we were now perhaps not quite so brave, for the hæmorrhage that follows the operation is abundant, very long, and disturbing: all that blood lost! I watched my blood flowing away and my heart contracted. I thought: 'Is my body going to be entirely emptied of blood?' And I raised imploring eyes to our healer, the *sema*.

'The blood must flow,' said the *sema*. 'If it did not flow...'

He did not finish the sentence: he was looking at the wound. When he saw that the blood was finally beginning to flow a little less freely, he put on the first bandage. Then he went on to the others.

When the blood had finally ceased flowing, we were dressed in our long boubou again. Apart from a very brief undershirt, this was to be our only article of attire during the weeks of convalescence that were to come. We stood up awkwardly, light-headed and sick at our stomachs. Among the men who had been present at the operation, I saw several who, taking pity on our plight, turned their heads away to hide their tears.

In the town, our parents were making a fuss of the messenger, and loading him with gifts; and the celebrations began again: was it not an occasion for rejoicing over the fortunate outcome of our ordeal, for rejoicing over our new birth? Already friends and neighbours were crowding inside the compounds where the newly circumcised had their homes, and were beginning to dance the *fady fady* in our honour, the dance of manhood, until the enormous banquet was ready, which would be shared by all.

We, too, were naturally to receive a large share of the dishes. The young men who had conducted the ceremony and who were also our attendants as well as our supervisors, went to seek our share.

Alas! we had seen, and lost, too much blood – its unsavoury smell still seemed to linger in our nostrils – and, we all had a touch of fever: we were shaking. We could cast only sour looks on the succulent dishes; they did not tempt us at all, but filled us with revulsion. Of all that extraordinary abundance of viands assembled for our enjoyment we pecked with a ridiculously feeble appetite at only one or two dishes: we sat looking at them, sniffing at their savoury smells; we would take a mouthful, then turn our heads away.

At nightfall, we took the road back to town, escorted by the young men and by our healer. We walked with great care: we could not let the boubou rub against the wound. But sometimes, in spite of our precautions, it would do so, making us cry out with pain; we would stop for a moment, our faces drawn with suffering; the young men would hold us up. It took us a very long time to get back to our hut. When we finally reached it, we were at the end of our tether. We lay down at once on the mats.

We waited for sleep, but it was long in coming, as our fever kept us awake. Our eyes wandered sadly over the walls of the hut. At the thought that we were to live here until our period of convalescence was over – several weeks – in the company of these young men and our healer, we were seized by a kind of despair. Men! Yes, we were men at last, but what a price to pay!... At last we fell asleep. By the next morning our fever had abated, and we were able to laugh at the sombre thoughts of the night before.

Certainly the life we led in the hut was not the same as the life we led in the compounds; but it was not insupportable and it had its own delights, even though there was constant supervision and the discipline was rather strict, albeit wise and reasonable, with the sole aim of shielding us from anything that might retard our convalescence.

If we were watched closely day and night, and even more closely at night than during the day, it was because we were allowed to lie neither on our side nor on our face; as long as our wound was not properly healed, we could lie only on our backs, and, of course, we were absolutely forbidden to cross our legs. It goes without saying that when we were asleep it was difficult to remain constantly in one position; but if we so much as stirred the young men would intervene at once: they would rectify our position, as gently as they could, so as not to disturb our rest; they watched over us in relays so that we never for one second escaped their vigilant eyes.

But perhaps it would be better if I talked about their 'attendance' rather than their 'supervision'; they were more like nurses than supervisors. By day, when, weary of continually sitting or lying on our mats, we asked to be allowed to get up, they would help us; indeed, at every step we took they would be at our sides supporting us. They would go and collect our food, take news of our progress to our parents, and bring us news of them. Their task was no sinecure; we took their good nature for granted, and at times took advantage of it; but they never grumbled: they looked after us with boundless good-will.

Our healer was not so indulgent. He doubtlessly gave us the utmost devotion in his attendance upon us; but he was something of a disciplinarian, though not a harsh one; but he did not like us to pull a face when he was cleaning our wound.

'You are not little boys now,' he would tell us. 'Control yourselves.'

And we just had to control ourselves, if we did not want to be called hopeless little snivellers. So twice a day we would keep a stiff upper lip, for our healer used to clean our wound in the morning, then in the evening. He would use water in which certain kinds of bark had been steeping, and as he cleaned the wounds he would pronounce healing incantations. The task of teaching and initiating us also fell to him.

After the first week, which was passed entirely in the solitude of the hut, and whose monotony had been broken by a few visits from my father, we had recovered enough liberty of movement to be able to go for short walks in the bush, escorted by our healer.

As long as we remained in the immediate vicinity of the town, the young men would walk in front. They acted as scouts, so that, should some woman be found walking in our direction, they could warn her in time of our approach, and she could go some other way. Indeed we were not supposed to meet any women at all, until our wounds had properly healed. The rule is enforced simply to avoid any delay in the healing of the wound; I do not think any other explanation need be sought.

The teaching we received in the bush, far from all prying eyes, had nothing very mysterious about it; nothing, I think, that was not fit for ears other than our own. These lessons, the same as had been taught to all those who had gone before us, confined themselves to outlining the sort of conduct befitting a man: to be absolutely straightforward, to cultivate all the virtues that go to make an honest man, to fulfil our duties towards God, towards our parents, our superiors and our neighbour. And we had to tell nothing of what we learned, either to women or to the uninitiated; neither, had we to reveal any of the secret rites of circumcision. That is the custom. Women, too, are not allowed to tell anything about the rites of excision.

Should a non-initiate attempt later on to find out what we had been taught, and try to pass himself off as an initiate in order to do so, we were told how to expose him. The simplest, though not the least laborious way, was by using phrases with refrains that had to be whistled in a certain way. There are very many of these refrains; so many that should the impostor, by some extraordinary chance, have learned two or three, he will find himself baffled by the fourth or the tenth, if not by the twentieth. Always lengthy, always complicated, it is impossible to imitate these refrains unless they have been whistled time and time again, and patiently learnt by heart.

They really require very patient study, and an agile memory, if one is to retain them all, as we finally realized. Whenever our healer thought we were not learning them fast enough – and indeed we were not always very attentive – he would remind us sharply of our duty; he would avail himself of the pompom on our cap, with which he would belabour our backs. Thay would not hurt very much, you may say; but if the pompom is a large one, bound tightly with cotton and with something hard inside, it can be very painful.

By the third week, I was allowed to see my mother. When one of the younger men came and said my mother was at the door, I leapt to my feet.

'Here, not so fast,' he said, taking me by the hand. 'Wait for me.'

'All right, but hurry.'

Three weeks! Never before had we been separated from each other for so long. When I used to go on holiday to Tindican, I would seldom stay away longer than ten or fifteen days, and that was not to be compared with the length of our present separation.

'Well, are you coming?' I cried.

I was quivering with impatience.

'Listen,' said the young man. 'Listen first of all to what I have to say. You are going to see your mother, you are allowed to see her; but you must stand within the fence when speaking to her; you must not go beyond the fence.'

'I'll stay inside the fence,' I said. 'Just let me go.'

And I tried to shake off his hand.

'We'll go together,' he said.

He had not let go of my hand. We left the hut together. The gate in the fence was open. Several of the young men were sitting on the threshold; they signalled to me not to go beyond it. With a few swift strides I covered the few yards that separated me from the gate, and suddenly I saw my mother. She was standing in the dusty road a few steps away from the fence; she, too, was forbidden to come any closer.

'Mother!' I cried. 'Mother!'

And all at once I felt a lump in my throat. Was it because I could go no closer, because I could not hug my mother? Was it because we had already been separated so long, because we were still to be separated a long time? I do not know. All I know is that I could only say 'Mother!' and that after my joy in seeing her I suddenly felt a strange depression. Ought I to attribute this emotional instability to the transformation that had been worked in me? When I had left my mother, I was still a child. Now . . . But was I really a man now? Was I already a grown man? . . . I *was* a man! Yes, I was a grown man. And now this manhood had already begun to stand between my mother and myself. It kept us infinitely further apart than the few yards that separated us now.

'Mother!' I said again.

But this time I spoke it very low, like a lament, sadly, as if it were a lament for myself.

'Yes, here I am,' said my mother. 'I've come to see you.'

'Yes, you've come to see me.'

And suddenly I passed from sadness to joy. What was I worrying about? My mother was there. She was here in front of me. I only had to go a couple of steps, and I would be at her side; I would certainly have done so if there had not been that absurd order forbidding me to go beyond the gate.

'I am glad to see you,' went on my mother.

She smiled. At once I understood why she was smiling. When she came she had been a little uneasy, vaguely uneasy. Even though she had had news of my progress, even though my father himself had taken her news of me, and good news, nevertheless she had remained a little uneasy: how did she know that she was being told the truth? But now that she had been to see for herself, she had been able to judge for herself from how I looked that my convalescence was well under way, and she was really glad.

'I am really very glad,' she said.

Nevertheless, she did not say anything more; this casual reference was enough. One must not speak openly of anyone's return to health, especially ours; that would not be wise; it would be tempting hostile spirits to attack us.

'I brought you some kola nuts,' my mother said.

And she opened the little basket she held in her hand and showed me the nuts. One of the young men, who was sitting by the gate, went and took them and gave them to me.

'Thank you, Mother.'

'Now I must be getting back home,' she said.

'Say good-bye for me to my father, and to everyone.'

'Yes, I shall do so.'

'It won't be long now, Mother.'

'Not very long,' she replied.

Her voice was trembling a little. I went in at once. Our meeting had not lasted two minutes, but that was all we were allowed. And all the time between us there had been that space that could not be crossed. Poor dear little mother! She had not even held me in her arms. Nevertheless, I am sure she walked away with head held high, and with great dignity; she always used to hold herself very straight, and so appeared taller than she really was. I seemed to see her walking along the dusty road, her dress falling in noble folds, her waist-band neatly tied, her hair carefully plaited and drawn back on to the nape of her neck. How long those three weeks must have seemed to her!

I walked for a while in the yard before going back into the hut. I felt sad, I was feeling sad again. Had I, in losing my childhood, lost my carefree spirits too? I rejoined my companions, shared my nuts with them; their generally so pleasant bitterness, so refreshing to the palate, was now no more than the purest gall.

My father, of course, came often; he could visit me as often as he liked. But we did not have much to say to one another: those visits, in the midst of my companions, and the young men, had no real intimacy about them.

During the fourth week we were allowed more liberty. Our wounds had for the most part healed or else were making such good progress that there was no danger of set-backs to our convalescence. By the end of the week we had completely recovered. The young men took the framework out of our hats and unpicked our boubous. We were now wearing wide trousers, and we were, of course, very anxious to be seen again in public. We went for a walk in the town, very proud of ourselves, immensely proud of our new attire, and talking at the top of our voices, as if we were not already drawing enough attention to ourselves.

We still remained in a group, and it was again in this single group that we made a round of visits to the various compounds to which we belonged. We were fêted everywhere we went, and we did ample justice always to the banquet that awaited us; now that we were almost well again – several of us were in fact quite well again; I for my part, had completely recovered – we had wonderful appetites.

Whenever an uncircumcised boy came rather too close to our happy band, we would seize him and belabour him playfully with our pompoms. But we were still forbidden all contact with girls, and this was a ban which no one thought of breaking. I caught sight of Fanta, and she waved to me at a discreet distance; I answered her likewise by simply fluttering my eyelids. Was I still in love with her? I did not know. We had been so cut off from the world, we had become so different from what we had been, even though a mere month had elapsed between our childhood and our entry into manhood; we had become so indifferent to all that we had been before, that I no longer knew quite where I was. 'Time,' I thought, 'time will help me to settle down again.' But how? I had no idea.

Finally the time came when the healer considered us completely recovered and handed us over to our parents again. But I was still at school and I could no longer join in the excursions which my companions were going on among the neighbouring towns and villages. Nor could I take part in their labours in our healer's fields, work which they undertook to repay the care he had taken of us. My parents arranged with him for me to be exempted from it.

When I finally got back to my compound, the whole family was waiting for me. My parents held me tightly in their arms, particularly my mother, as if she was wanting secretly to proclaim that I was still her son, that my second birth had done nothing to alter the fact that I was still her son. My father watched us for a moment, then he said to me, almost regretfully:

'From now on, this is your hut, my son.'

The hut stood opposite my mother's.

'Yes,' said my mother, 'you will sleep there now. But as you can see, I am still within earshot.'

I opened the door of the hut; my clothes were laid out on the bed. I went up to it and took them in my hands one by one, then put them carefully back; they were men's clothes. Yes, the hut was opposite my mother's, I was still within earshot of her voice, but the clothes on the bed were men's clothes. I was a man!

'Are you pleased with your new clothes?' asked my mother.

Pleased? Yes, I was pleased; naturally I was pleased. At least I think I was pleased. They were fine clothes, they were... I turned towards my mother: she was smiling sadly at me. . . .

3

Centuries of Childhood*

Phillippe Ariès

Antiquo-medieval speculation had bequeathed to posterity a copious terminology relating to the ages of life. In the sixteenth century, when it was proposed to translate this terminology into French, it was found that the French language, and consequently French usage, had not as many words at its disposal as had Latin or at least learned Latin. The 1556 translator of *Le Grand Propriétaire de toutes choses* makes no bones about recognizing the difficulty: 'It is more difficult in French than in Latin, for in Latin there are seven ages referred to by various names, of which there are only three in French: to wit, childhood, youth and old age.'

It will be noted that since youth signifies the prime of life, there is no room for adolescence. Until the eighteenth century, adolescence was confused with childhood. In school Latin the word *puer* and the word *adolescens* were used indiscriminately. Preserved in the Bibliothèque Nationale are the catalogues of the Jesuit College at Caen, a list of the pupils' names accompanied by comments. A boy of fifteen is described in these catalogues as *bonus puer*, while his young schoolmate of thirteen is called *optimus adolescens*. Baillet, in a book on infant prodigies, admitted that there were no terms in French to distinguish between *pueri* and *adolescentes*. There was virtually only one word in use: *enfant*.

At the end of the Middle Ages, the meaning of this word was particularly extensive. It could be applied to both the *putto* (in the sixteenth century the *putti* room, the bedchamber decorated with frescoes depicting naked children, was referred to as 'the children's room') and the adolescent, the big lad who was sometimes also a bad lad. The word *enfant* ('child') in the *Miracles de Notre-Dame* was used in the fourteenth and fifteenth centuries as a synonym of other words such as *valets, valeton, garçon, fils* ('valet', 'varlet', 'lad', 'son'): 'he was a *valeton*' would be translated today as 'he was a good-looking lad' but

* Extracts from PHILLIPPE ARIÈS, *Centuries of Childhood*, 25-332, Vintage Books, New York

the same word could be used of both a young man ('a handsome *valeton*') and a child ('he was a *valeton*, so they loved him dearly ... *li valez* grew up'). Only one word has kept this very ancient ambiguity down to our times, and that is the word *gars* ('lad'), which has passed straight from Old French into the popular modern idiom in which it is preserved. A strange child, this bad lad who was 'so perverse and wicked that he would not learn a trade or behave as was fitting in childhood ... he kept company with greedy, idle folk who often started brawls in taverns and brothels, and he never came across a woman by herself without raping her'. Here is another child of fifteen: 'Although he was a fine, handsome son', he refused to go riding or to have anything to do with girls. His father thought that it was out of shyness: 'This is customary in children.' In fact, he was betrothed to the Virgin. His father forced him into marriage: 'The child became very angry and struck him hard.' He tried to make his escape and suffered mortal injuries by falling downstairs. The Virgin then came for him and said to him: 'Dear brother, behold your sweetheart.' And: 'At this the child heaved a sigh.' According to a sixteenth-century calendar of the ages, at twenty-four 'a child is strong and brave', and 'this is what becomes of children when they are eighteen.'

The same is true in the seventeenth century. The report of an episcopal inquiry of 1667 states that in one parish 'there is *un jeune enfant* ['a young child'] aged about fourteen who in the year or so he has been living in the aforementioned place has been teaching children of both sexes to read and write, by arrangement with the inhabitants of the aforementioned place.'

In the course of the seventeenth century a change took place by which the old usage was maintained in the more dependent classes of society, while a different usage appeared in the middle class, where the word 'child' was restricted to its modern meaning. The long duration of childhood as it appeared in the common idiom was due to the indifference with which strictly biological phenomena were regarded at the time: nobody would have thought of seeing the end of childhood in puberty. The idea of childhood was bound up with the idea of dependence: the words 'sons', 'varlets' and 'boys' were also words in the vocabulary of feudal subordination. One could leave childhood only by leaving the state of dependence, or at least the lower degrees of dependence. That is why the words associated with childhood would endure to indicate in a familiar style, in the spoken language, men of humble rank whose submission to others remained absolute: lackeys, for instance, journeymen and soldiers. A 'little boy' (*petit garçon*) was not necessarily a child but a young servant, just as today an employer or a foreman will say of a worker of twenty to

38

twenty-five: 'He's a good lad.' Thus in 1549, one Baduel, the principal of a college, an educational establishment, wrote to the father of one of his young pupils about his outfit and attendants: 'A little boy is all that he will need for his personal service.'

At the beginning of the eighteenth century, Furetière's dictionary gave an explanation of the usage: ' "Child" is also a term of friendship used to greet or flatter someone or to induce him to do something. Thus when one says to an aged person: "Goodbye, good mother" ['so long, grandma,' in the modern idiom] she replies: "Goodbye, my child" ['goodbye, lad']. Or she will say to a lackey: "Child, go and get me this or that." A master will say to his men when setting them to work: "Come along, children get to work." A captain will say to his soldiers: "Courage, children, stand fast." ' Front-line troops, those most exposed to danger, were called 'the lost children'.

At the same time, but in families of gentle birth, where dependence was only a consequence of physical infirmity, the vocabulary of childhood tended rather to refer to the first age. Its use became increasingly frequent in the seventeenth century: the expression 'little child' (*petit enfant*) began to take on the meaning we give it. The older usage had preferred 'young child' (*jeune enfant*), and this expression had not been completely abandoned. La Fontaine used it, and again in 1714, in a translation of Erasmus, there was a reference to a 'young girl' who was not yet five: 'I have a young girl who has scarcely begun to talk.' The word *petit* or 'little one' had also acquired a special meaning by the end of the sixteenth century: it referred to all the pupils of the 'little schools', even those who were no longer children. In England, the word 'petty' had the same meaning as in French, and a text of 1627 on the subject of school spoke of the 'lyttle petties', the smallest pupils.

It was above all with Port-Royal and with all the moral and pedagogic literature which drew its inspiration from Port-Royal (or which gave more general expression to a need for moral discipline which was widely felt and to which Port-Royal too bore witness), that the terms used to denote childhood became common and above all modern: Jacqueline Pascal's pupils at Port-Royal were divided into 'little ones', 'middle ones' and 'big ones'. 'With regard to the little children,' she wrote, 'they even more than all the others must be taught and fed if possible like little doves.' The regulations of the little schools at Port-Royal stated: 'They do not go to Mass every day, only the little ones.' People spoke in a new way of 'little souls' and 'little angels', expressions which foreshadowed the eighteenth century and Romanticism. In her tales, Mlle Lhéritier claimed to be addressing 'young minds', 'young people': 'These pictures probably lead young people to reflections which perfect their reasoning.' It can thus be seen that that seventeenth century which seemed to have scorned childhood, in fact brought into use expressions and phrases which remain to this day in our language. Under the word 'child' in his dictionary, Furetière quoted proverbs which are still familiar to us: 'He is a spoilt child, who has been allowed to misbehave without being punished. The fact is, there are no longer any children, for people are beginning to have reason and cunning at an early age.' 'Innocent as a new-born child.'

All the same, in its attempts to talk about little children, the French language of the seventeenth century was hampered by the lack of words to distinguish them from bigger ones. The same was true of English, where the word 'baby' was also applied to big children. Lily's Latin grammar in English, which was in use from the beginning of the sixteenth century until 1866, was intended for 'all lytell babes, all lytell chyldren'.

French was therefore reduced to borrowing from other idioms – either foreign languages or the slang used in school or trade – words to denote in French that little child in whom an interest was henceforth going to be taken. This was the case with the Italian *bambino* which became the French *bambin*. Mme de Sévigné also used in the same sense a form of the Provençal word *pitchoun*, which she had doubtless learnt in the course of one of her stays with the Grignans. Her cousin Coulanges, who did not like children but spoke of them a great deal, distrusted 'three-year-old *marmousets*', an old word which in the popular idiom would become *marmots*, 'brats with greasy chins who put a finger in every dish'. People also used slang terms from school Latin or from sporting and military academies: a little *frater*, a *cadet*, and, when there were several of them, a *populo* or *petit peuple*. Lastly the use of diminutives became quite common: *fanfan* is to be found in the letters of Mme de Sévigné and those of Fénelon.

In time these words would come to denote a child who was still small but already beginning to find his feet. There would still remain a gap where a word was needed to denote a child in its first months of life; this gap would not be filled until the nineteenth century, when the French would borrow from the English the word 'baby', which in the sixteenth and seventeenth centuries had denoted children of school age. This borrowing was the last stage of the story: henceforth, with the French word *bébé*, the very little child had a name.

*　　*.　　*

In the thirteenth-century Gospel-book of the Sainte-Chapelle, in an illustration of the miracle of the loaves and fishes, Christ and one of the Apostles are shown standing on either side of a little man who comes up to their waists: no doubt the child who carried the fishes. In the world of Romanesque formulas, right up to the end of the thirteenth century, there are no children characterized by special expression but only men on a reduced scale. This refusal to accept child morphology in art is to be found too in most of the ancient civilizations. A fine Sardinian bronze of the ninth century B.C. shows a sort of Pietà: a mother holding in her arms the somewhat bulky body of her son. The catalogue tells us: 'The little masculine figure could also be a child which, in accordance with the formula adopted in ancient times by other peoples, had been represented as an adult.' Everything in fact would seem to suggest that the realistic representation of children or the idealization of childhood, its grace and rounded charms, was confined to Greek art. Little Eroses proliferated in the Hellenistic period, but childhood disappeared from iconography together with the other Hellenistic themes, and Romanesque art returned to that rejection of the special features of childhood which had already characterized the periods of antiquity before Hellenism. This is no mere coincidence. Our starting-point in this study is a world of pictorial representation in which childhood is unknown; literary historians such as Mgr Calvé have made the same observation about the epic, in which child prodigies behave with the courage and physical strength of doughty warriors. This undoubtedly means that the men of the tenth and eleventh centuries did not dwell on the image of childhood, and that that image had neither interest nor even reality for them. It suggests too that in the realm of real life, and not simply in that of aesthetic transposition, childhood was a period of transition which passed quickly and which was just as quickly forgotten.

*   *   *

In 1600 the specialization of games and pastimes did not extend beyond infancy; after the age of three or four it decreased and disappeared. *From then on the child played the same games as the adult, either with other children or with adults.* We know this from the evidence furnished by an abundant iconography, for from the Middle Ages to the eighteenth century artists delighted in showing people at play: an indication of the place occupied by amusement in the social life of the ancien regime. We have already seen that from his earliest years, Louis XIII, as well as playing with dolls, also played tennis and hockey, which we nowadays consider as games for adolescents or adults. In an engraving by Arnoult of the late seventeenth century, we can see children playing bowls; children of good family, judging by the little girl's false sleeves. People had no objection to allowing children to play card games and games of chance, and to play for money. One of Stella's engravings devoted to the subject of *putti* at play gives a sympathetic picture of the child who has lost all his money. The Caravagesque painters of the seventeenth century often depicted bands of soldiers gambling excitedly in taverns of ill fame: next to the old troopers one can see some very young boys, twelve years old or so, who seem to be enthusiastic gamblers. A painting by S. Bourdon shows a group of beggars standing round two children and watching them playing dice. The theme of children playing games of chance for money obviously did not shock public opinion as yet, for the same theme is to be found in pictures portraying neither old soldiers nor beggars but Le Nain's solemn characters.

Conversely, adults used to play games which today only children play. A fourteenth-century ivory shows the frog-game: a young man sitting on the ground is trying to catch hold of the men and women who are pushing him around. Adélaïde de Savoie's book of hours, dating from the late fifteenth century, contains a calendar which is largely illustrated with pictures of games, and games which are not of a knightly character. (To begin with, the calendars depicted trades and crafts, except for the month of May, which was reserved for a court of love. Games were then introduced and occupied more and more space: knightly sports such as hunting, but also popular games.) One of these is the faggot-game: one person is playing the candle in the centre of a ring of couples in which each lady is standing behind her cavalier and holding him tightly round the waist. In another part of the calendar the whole population of the village is having a snow-ball fight: men and women, children and grown-ups. In an early sixteenth-century tapestry, some peasants and noblemen – the latter more or less convincingly dressed as shepherds – are playing hot cockles: there are no children. Several Dutch pictures of the second half of the seventeenth century also show people playing hot cockles. In one of them a few children appear, but they are mixed up with adults of all ages: one woman is standing with her head hidden in her apron and one hand held open behind her back. Louis XIII and his mother used to play hide-and-seek together. People played blind-man's buff at the Grande Mademoiselle's home, the Hôtel de Rambouillet. An engraving by Lepautre shows that adult peasants also played this game.

One can accordingly understand the comment which his study of the iconography of games and pastimes drew from the contemporary historian Van Marle: 'As for the games played by grown-ups, one cannot honestly say that they were any less childish than those played by children.' Of course not: they were the same!

*   *   *

In medieval society the idea of childhood did not exist; this is not to suggest that children were neglected, forsaken or despised. The idea of childhood is not to be confused with affection for children: it corresponds to an awareness of the particular nature of childhood, that particular nature which distinguishes the child from the adult, even the young adult. In medieval society this awareness was lacking. That is why, as soon as the child could live without the constant solicitude of his mother, his nanny or his cradle-rocker, he belonged to adult society. That adult society now strikes us as rather puerile: no doubt this is largely a matter of its mental age, but it is also due to its physical age, because it was partly made up of children and youths. Language did not give the word 'child' the restricted meaning we give it today: people said 'child' much as we say 'lad' in everyday speech. The absence of definition extended to every sort of social activity: games, crafts, arms. There is not a single collective picture of the times in which children are not to be found, nestling singly or in pairs in the *trousse* hung round women's necks, or urinating in a corner, or playing their part in a traditional festival, or as apprentices in a workshop, or as pages serving a knight, etc.

The infant who was too fragile as yet to take part in the life of adults simply 'did not count': this is the expression used by Molière, who bears witness to the survival in the seventeenth century of a very old attitude of mind. Argan in *Le malade imaginaire* has two daughters, one of marriageable age and little Louison who is just beginning to talk and walk. It is generally known that he is threatening to put his elder daughter in a convent to stop her philandering. His brother asks him: 'How is it, Brother, that rich as you are and having only one daughter, *for I don't count the little one*, you can talk of putting her in a convent?' The little one did not count because she could disappear.

*   *   *

The first concept of childhood – characterized by 'coddling' – had made its appearance in the family circle, in the company of little children. The second, on the contrary, sprang from a source outside the family: churchmen or gentlemen of the robe, few in number before the sixteenth century, and a far greater number of moralists in the seventeenth century, eager to ensure disciplined, rational manners. They too had become alive to the formerly neglected phenomenon of childhood, but they were unwilling to regard children as charming toys, for they saw them as fragile creatures of God who needed to be both safeguarded and reformed. This concept in its turn passed into family life.

In the eighteenth century, we find those two elements in the family, together with a new element: concern about hygiene and physical health. Care of the body was not ignored by seventeenth-century moralists and pedagogues. People nursed the sick devotedly (at the same time taking every precaution to unmask malingerers), but any interest shown in healthy bodies had a moral purpose behind it: a delicate body encouraged luxury, sloth, concupiscence – all the vices in fact!

General de Martange's correspondence with his wife gives us some idea of a family's private life and preoccupations about a century after Mme de Sévigné. Martagne was born in 1722 and married in 1754. He shows great interest in everything concerning his children's life, from 'coddling' to education; he watches closely over their health and even their hygiene. Everything to do with children and family life has become a matter worthy of attention. Not only the child's future but his presence and his very existence are of concern: the child has taken a central place in the family.

We have studied the beginnings and development of two views of childhood. According to the first, which was widely held, children were creatures to be 'coddled' and childhood was held to last hardly beyond infancy; the second, which expressed the realization of the innocence and the weakness of childhood, and consequently of the duty of adults to safeguard the former and strengthen the latter, was confined for a long time to a small minority of lawyers, priests and moralists. But for their influence, the child would have remained simply the *poupart* or *bambino*, the sweet, funny little creature with whom people played affectionately but with liberty, if not indeed with licence, and without any thought of morality or education. Once he had passed the age of five or seven, the child was immediately absorbed into the world of adults: this concept of a brief childhood lasted for a long time in the lower classes. The moralists and pedagogues of the seventeenth century, heirs of a tradition going back to Gerson, to the fifteenth-century reformers of the University of Paris, to the founders of colleges in the late Middle Ages, succeeded in imposing their considered concept of a long childhood thanks to the success of the educational institutions and practices which they guided and supervised. We find the same men, obsessed with educational questions, at the origins of both the modern concept of

44

childhood and the modern concept of schooling.

Childhood was extended beyond the years when the little man still walked on a 'leading-string' or spoke his 'jargon', when an intermediary stage, hitherto rare and henceforth more and more common, was introduced between the period of the robe with a collar and the period of the recognized adult: the stage of the school, of the college. The age groups in our societies are organized around institutions; thus adolescence, never clearly defined under the ancien regime, was distinguished in the nineteenth century and indeed already in the late eighteenth century by conscription and later by military service. The schoolboy or scholar or student – the terms were used interchangeably until the nineteenth century – of the sixteenth, seventeenth and eighteenth centuries was to a long childhood what the conscript of the nineteenth and twentieth centuries was to adolescence.

However, this demographic function of the school was not immediately recognized as a necessity. On the contrary, for a long time the school remained indifferent to the separation and distinction of the ages, because it did not regard the education of children as its essential aim. Nothing predisposed the medieval Latin school for this function of moral and social education. The medieval school was not intended for children: it was a sort of technical school for the instruction of clerics, 'young or old' as Michault's *Doctrinal* put it. Thus it welcomed equally and indifferently children, youths, adults, the precocious and the backward, at the foot of the magisterial rostrum.

Until the eighteenth century at least, a great deal of this mentality remained in school life and manners. We have seen how tardy was the division into separate and regular classes, and how the various ages remained mixed up within each class, with children between ten and thirteen sitting next to adolescents between fifteen and twenty. In common parlance, to say that someone was of school age did not necessarily mean that that person was a child, for school age could also be taken to mean the limit beyond which a pupil had small hope of success. That is how we must interpret the advice given by Theresa Panza to her husband Sancho as he sets off on an expedition with Don Quixote: 'Do not forget me or your children. Remember that our Sanchico is already fifteen and that it is time for him to go to school if it is agreed that his uncle the priest is going to make a churchman of him.' People went to school when they could, very early or very late. This way of looking at things continued throughout the seventeenth century, in spite of contrary influences. Sufficient traces of it would remain in the eighteenth century for the oldest pedagogues, after the Revolution, to remember it and to recall, in order to condemn it, the practice under the ancien regime of keeping old pupils on at school. It would not disappear for good until the nineteenth century.

This indifference shown by the school to the education of children was not characteristic simply of old-fashioned conservatives. It is important to note that the humanists of the Renaissance shared it with their enemies, the traditional schoolmen. Like the pedagogues of the Middle Ages, they confused education with culture, spreading education over the whole span of human life, without giving a special value to childhood or youth. As a result they exerted only a slight influence on the structure of the school, and their role has been grossly exaggerated by literary historians. The real innovators were the scholastic reformers of the fifteenth century, Cardinal d'Estouteville, Gerson, the organizers of the colleges and pedagogicas, and finally and above all the Jesuits, the Oratorians and the Jansenists in the seventeenth century. With them we see the appearance of an awareness of the special nature of childhood, knowledge of child psychology, and the desire to devise a method suited to that psychology.

The college under the ancien regime thus retained characteristics of its ancestor, the Latin cathedral school, for a very long time; many years passed before it became an institution specially intended for children.

*　　*　　*

If schooling in the seventeenth century was not yet the monopoly of one class, it remained the monopoly of one sex. Women were excluded. The result was that in their lives the habits of precocity and a brief childhood remained unchanged from the Middle Ages to the seventeenth century. 'Since the age of twelve, thanks to God whose life is eternal, I have taken a husband five times at the church porch.' Thus one of Chaucer's women in the fourteenth century. But at the end of the sixteenth century we find Catherine Marion marrying Antoine Arnauld at the age of thirteen. And she was sufficiently mistress of the house to give 'a slap to her first chambermaid, a girl of twenty, for not resisting a caress which someone gave her'. The person who wrote these lines, Catherine Lemaître, had herself been married at the age of fourteen. There was talk of marrying off her other sister, Anne, at the age of twelve, and only the little girl's religious vocation put a stop to this project. The suitor was in no hurry and was fond of the family for, so Catherine Lemaître tells us, 'not only did he delay marrying until she [Anne] had made her profession, but he even put off his marriage until he had seen the entry into religion of the youngest of the family, the little girl who, when his marriage to my sister Anne was being discussed, was a child of six'. At the most an engagement of four to six years. Moreover, by the age of ten, girls were already little women: a precocity due in part to an upbringing which taught girls to behave very early in life like grown-ups. 'At the age of ten, that little girl's mind was so developed that she ran the whole house for Mme Arnauld, who deliberately made her do this to train her in the work of a wife and mother, since that was to be her station in life.'

4

School Time*

George Eliot

If Tom had had a worse disposition, he would certainly have hated
the little cherub Laura; but he was too kind-hearted a lad for that –
there was too much in him of the fibre that turns to true manliness,
and to protecting pity for the weak. I am afraid he hated Mrs
Stelling, and contracted a lasting dislike to pale blond ringlets and
broad plaits, as directly associated with haughtiness of manner and a
frequent reference to other people's 'duty.' But he couldn't help playing with little Laura and liking to amuse her. He even sacrificed his
percussion-caps for her sake, in despair of their ever serving a greater
purpose, thinking the small flash and bang would delight her, and
thereby drawing down on himself a rebuke from Mrs Stelling for
teaching her child to play with fire. Laura was a sort of playfellow,
and oh, how Tom longed for playfellows! In his secret heart he
yearned to have Maggie with him, and was almost ready to dote on
her exasperating acts of forgetfulness; though, when he was at home,
he always represented it as a great favour on his part to let Maggie
trot by his side on his pleasure excursions.

And before this dreary half-year was ended Maggie actually came.
Mrs Stelling had given a general invitation for the little girl to come
and stay with her brother; so when Mr Tulliver drove over to King's
Borton late in October, Maggie came too, with the sense that she was
taking a great journey, and beginning to see the world. It was Mr
Tulliver's first visit to see Tom, for the lad must learn not to think too
much about home.

'Well, my lad,' he said to Tom, when Mr Stelling had left the room
to announce the arrival to his wife, and Maggie had begun to kiss
Tom freely, 'you look rarely. School agrees with you.'

Tom wished he had looked rather ill.

'I don't think I *am* well, father,' said Tom; 'I wish you'd ask Mr
Stelling not to let me do Euclid; it brings on the toothache, I think.'

* GEORGE ELIOT, *The Mill on the Floss*, **Book III**, chapter I, 'Tom's First
Half', 1860

(The toothache was the only malady to which Tom had ever been subject.)

'Euclid, my lad; why, what's that?' said Mr Tulliver.

'Oh I don't know. It's definitions and axioms, and triangles, and things. It's a book I've got to learn in; there's no sense in it.'

'Go, go!' said Mr Tulliver reprovingly; 'you mustn't say so. You must learn what your master tells you. He knows what it's right for you to learn.'

'*I'll* help you now, Tom,' said Maggie, with a little air of patronizing consolation. 'I'm come to stay ever so long, if Mrs Stelling asks me. I've brought my box and my pinafore – haven't I, father?'

'*You* help me, you silly little thing!' said Tom, in such high spirits at this announcement that he quite enjoyed the idea of confounding Maggie by showing her a page of Euclid. 'I should like to see you doing one of *my* lessons! Why, I learn Latin too! Girls never learn such things. They're too silly.'

'I know what Latin is very well,' said Maggie confidently. 'Latin's a language. There are Latin words in the dictionary. There's a bonus, a gift.'

'Now, you're just wrong there, Miss Maggie!' said Tom, secretly astonished. 'You think you're very wise: But "bonus" means "good," as it happens – bonus, bona, bonum.'

'Well, that's no reason why it shouldn't mean "gift," ' said Maggie stoutly. 'It may mean several things – almost every word does. There's "lawn" – it means the grass-plot, as well as the stuff pocket-handkerchiefs are made of.'

'Well done, little un,' said Mr Tulliver, laughing, while Tom felt rather disgusted with Maggie's knowingness, though beyond measure cheerful at the thought that she was going to stay with him. Her conceit would soon be overawed by the actual inspection of his books.

Mrs Stelling, in her pressing invitation, did not mention a longer time than a week for Maggie's stay; but Mr Stelling, who took her between his knees, and asked her where she stole her dark eyes from, insisted that she must stay a fortnight. Maggie thought Mr Stelling was a charming man, and Mr Tulliver was quite proud to leave his little wench where she would have an opportunity of showing her cleverness to appreciating strangers. So it was agreed that she should not be fetched home till the end of the fortnight.

'Now, then, come with me into the study, Maggie,' said Tom, as their father drove away. 'What do you shake and toss your head now for, you silly?' he continued; for though her hair was now under a new dispensation, and was brushed smoothly behind her ears, she seemed still in imagination to be tossing it out of her eyes. 'It makes you look as if you were crazy.'

'Oh, I can't help it,' said Maggie impatiently 'Don't tease me, Tom. Oh, what books!' she exclaimed, as she saw the bookcases in the study. 'How I should like to have as many books as that!'

'Why, you couldn't read one of 'em,' said Tom triumphantly. 'They're all Latin.'

'No, they aren't,' said Maggie. 'I can read the back of this – History of the Decline and Fall of the Roman Empire.'

'Well, what does that mean? *You* don't know,' said Tom, wagging his head.

'But I could soon find out,' said Maggie scornfully.

'Why, how?'

'I should look inside, and see what it was about.'

'You'd better not, Miss Maggie,' said Tom, seeing her hand on the volume. 'Mr Stelling lets nobody touch his books without leave, and *I* shall catch it if you take it out.'

'Oh, very well! Let me see all *your* books, then,' said Maggie, turning to throw her arms round Tom's neck, and rub his cheek with her small round nose.

Tom, in the gladness of his heart at having dear old Maggie to dispute with and crow over again, seized her round the waist, and began to jump with her round the large library table. Away they jumped with more and more vigour, till Maggie's hair flew from behind her ears, and twirled about like an animated mop. But the revolutions round the table became more and more irregular in their sweep, till at last reaching Mr Stelling's reading-stand, they sent it thundering down with its heavy lexicons to the floor. Happily it was the ground floor, and the study was a one-storied wing to the house, so that the downfall made no alarming resonance, though Tom stood dizzy and aghast for a few minutes, dreading the appearance of Mr or Mrs Stelling.

'Oh, I say, Maggie,' said Tom at last, lifting up the stand, 'we must keep quiet here, you know. If we break anything, Mrs Stelling'll make us cry peccavi.'

'What's that?' said Maggie.

'Oh, it's the Latin for a good scolding,' said Tom, not without some pride in his knowledge.

'Is she a cross woman?' said Maggie.

'I believe you!' said Tom, with an emphatic nod.

'I think all women are crosser than men,' said Maggie. 'Aunt Glegg's a great deal crosser than uncle Glegg, and mother scolds me more than father does.'

'Well, *you'll* be a woman some day,' said Tom, 'so *you* needn't talk.'

'But I shall be a *clever* woman,' said Maggie, with a toss.

'Oh, I dare say, and a nasty conceited thing. Everybody'll hate you.'

'But you oughtn't to hate me, Tom. It'll be very wicked of you, for I shall be your sister.'

'Yes, but if you're a nasty, disagreeable thing, I *shall* hate you.'

'Oh but, Tom, you won't! I shan't be disagreeable. I shall be very good to you, and I shall be good to everybody. You won't hate me really, will you, Tom?'

'Oh, bother, never mind! Come, it's time for me to learn my lessons. See here, what I've got to do,' said Tom, drawing Maggie towards him and showing her his theorem, while she pushed her hair behind her ears, and prepared herself to prove her capability of helping him in Euclid. She began to read with full confidence in her own powers; but presently, becoming quite bewildered, her face flushed with irritation. It was unavoidable: she must confess her incompetency, and she was not fond of humiliation.

'It's nonsense!' she said, 'and very ugly stuff, nobody need want to make it out.'

'Ah, there now, Miss Maggie!' said Tom, drawing the book away and wagging his head at her; 'you see you're not so clever as you thought you were.'

'Oh,' said Maggie, pouting, 'I dare say I could make it out, if I'd learned what goes before, as you have.'

'But that's what you just couldn't, Miss Wisdom,' said Tom. 'For it's all the harder when you know what goes before; for then you've got to say what definition 3 is, and what axiom V is. But get along with you now; I must go on with this. Here's the Latin Grammar. See what you can make of that.'

Maggie found the Latin Grammar quite soothing after her mathematical mortification, for she delighted in new words, and quickly found that there was an English Key at the end, which would make her very wise about Latin, at slight expense. She presently made up her mind to skip the rules in the Syntax – the examples became so absorbing. These mysterious sentences, snatched from an unknown context – like strange horns of beasts, and leaves of unknown plants, brought from some far-off region – gave boundless scope to her imagination, and were all the more fascinating because they were in a peculiar tongue of their own, which she could learn to interpret. It was really very interesting – the Latin Grammar that Tom had said no girls could learn, and she was proud because she found it interesting. The most fragmentary examples were her favourites. *Mors omnibus et communis* would have been jejune, only she liked to know the Latin; but the fortunate gentleman whom every one congratulated because he had a son 'endowed with *such* a diposition' afforded her a great deal of pleasant conjecture, and she was quite lost in the 'thick grove penetrable by no star' when Tom called out, –

'Now, then, Magsie, give us the Grammar!'

'O Tom, it's such a pretty book!' she said, as she jumped out of the large armchair to give it him; 'it's much prettier than the dictionary. I could learn Latin very soon. I don't think it's at all hard.'

'Oh, I know what you've been doing,' said Tom; 'you've been reading the English at the end. Any donkey can do that.'

Tom seized the book and opened it with a determined and business-like air, as much as to say that he had a lesson to learn which no donkeys would find themselves equal to. Maggie, rather piqued, turned to the bookcases to amuse herself with puzzling out the titles.

Presently Tom called to her, 'Here, Magsie, come and hear if I can say this. Stand at that end of the table, where Mr Stelling sits when he hears me.'

Maggie obeyed and took the open book.

'Where do you begin, Tom?'

'Oh, I begin at *"Appellativa arborum"* because I say all over again what I've been learning this week.'

Tom sailed along pretty well for three lines; and Maggie was beginning to forget her office of prompter in speculating as to what *mas* could mean, which came twice over, when he stuck fast at *Sunt etiam volucrum.*

'Don't tell me, Maggie; *Sunt etiam volucrum – Sunt etiam volucrum – ul ostrea, cetus –*'

'No,' said Maggie, opening her mouth and shaking her head.

'*Sunt etiam volucrum,*' said Tom, very slowly, as if the next words might be expected to come sooner when he gave them this strong hint that they were waited for.

'C, e, u,' said Maggie, getting impatient.

'Oh, I know; hold your tongue,' said Tom. '*Ceu passer, hirundo; Ferarum – ferarum –*' Tom took his pencil and made several hard dots with it on his bookcover – '*ferarum –*'

'Oh dear, oh dear, Tom,' said Maggie, 'what a time you are! *Ut –* '

'*Ut ostrea –* '

'No, no,' said Maggie; '*ut tigris –*'

'Oh yes, now I can do,' said Tom; 'it was *tigrie, vulpes* – I'd forgotten: *ut tigris, vulpes, et Piscium.*'

With some further stammering and repetition, Tom got through the next few lines.

'Now, then,' he said, 'the next is what I've just learnt for to-morrow. Give me hold of the book a minute.'

After some whispered gabbling, assisted by the beating of his fist on the table, Tom returned the book.

'*Mascula nomina in a,*' he began.

'No Tom,' said Maggie; 'that doesn't come next. It's *Nomen non creskens genittivo —*'

'*Creskens genittivo!*' exclaimed Tom, with a derisive laugh, for Tom had learned this omitted passage for his yesterday's lesson, and a young gentleman does not require an intimate or extensive acquaintance with Latin before he can feel the pitiable absurdity of a false quantity. '*Creskens genittivo!* What a little silly you are, Maggie!'

'Well, you needn't laugh, Tom, for you didn't remember it at all. I'm sure it's spelt so; how was I to know?'

'Phee-e-e-h! I told you girls couldn't learn Latin. It's *Nomen non crescens genitivo.*'

'Very well, then,' said Maggie, pouting. 'I can say that as well as you can. And you don't mind your stops. For you ought to stop twice as long at a semi-colon as you do at a comma, and you make the longest stops where there ought to be no stops at all.'

'Oh, well, don't chatter. Let me go on.'

They were presently fetched to spend the rest of the evening in the drawing-room, and Maggie became so animated with Mr Stelling, who, she felt sure, admired her cleverness, that Tom was rather amazed and alarmed at her audacity. But she was suddenly subdued by Mr Stelling's alluding to a little girl of whom he had heard that she once ran away to the gipsies.

'What a very odd little girl that must be!' said Mrs Stelling, meaning to be playful; but a playfulness that turned on her supposed oddity was not at all to Maggie's taste. She feared Mr Stelling, after all, did not think much of her, and went to bed in rather low spirits. Mrs Stelling, she felt, looked at her as if she thought her hair was very ugly because it hung down straight behind.

Nevertheless it was a very happy fortnight to Maggie, this visit to Tom. She was allowed to be in the study while he had his lessons, and in her various readings get very deep into the examples in the Latin Grammar. The astronomer who hated women generally caused her so much puzzling speculation that she one day asked Mr Stelling if all astronomers hated women, or whether it was only this particular astronomer. But, forestalling his answer, she said, —

'I suppose it's all astronomers; because, you know, they live up in high towers, and if the women came there, they might talk and hinder them from looking at the stars.'

Mr Stelling liked her prattle immensely, and they were on the best terms. She told Tom she should like to go to school to Mr Stelling, as he did, and learn just the same things. She knew she could do Euclid, for she had looked into it again, and she saw what A B C meant – they were the names of the lines.

'I'm sure you couldn't do it, now,' said Tom; 'and I'll just ask Mr Stelling if you could.'

'I don't mind,' said the little conceited minx. 'I'll ask him myself.'

'Mr Stelling,' she said, that same evening when they were in the drawing-room, 'couldn't I do Euclid, and all Tom's lessons, if you were to teach me instead of him?'

'No, you couldn't,' said Tom indignantly. 'Girls can't do Euclid – can they, sir?'

'They can pick up a little of everything, I dare say,' said Mr Stelling. 'They've a great deal of superficial cleverness; but they couldn't go far into anything. They're quick and shallow.'

Tom, delighted with this verdict, telegraphed his triumph by wagging his head at Maggie behind Mr Stelling's chair. As for Maggie, she had hardly ever been so mortified. She had been so proud to be called 'quick' all her little life, and now it appeared that this quickness was the brand of inferiority. It would have been better to be slow, like Tom.

'Ha, ha, Miss Maggie!' said Tom, when they were alone; 'you see it's not such a fine thing to be quick. You'll never go far into anything, you know.'

And Maggie was so oppressed by this dreadful destiny that she had no spirit for a retort.

But when this small apparatus of shallow quickness was fetched away in the gig by Luke, and the study was once more quite lonely for Tom, he missed her grievously. He had really been brighter, and had got through his lessons better, since she had been there; and she had asked Mr Stelling so many questions about the Roman empire, and whether there really ever was a man who said, in Latin, 'I would not buy it for a farthing or a rotten nut,' or whether that had only been turned into Latin, that Tom had actually come to a dim understanding of the fact that there had once been people upon the earth who were so fortunate as to know Latin without learning it through the medium of the Eton Grammar. This luminous idea was a great addition to his historical acquirements during this half-year, which were otherwise confined to an epitomized history of the Jews.

But the dreary half year *did* come to an end. How glad Tom was to see the last yellow leaves fluttering before the cold wind! The dark afternoons, and the first December snow, seemed to him far livelier than the August sunshine; and that he might make himself the surer about the flight of the days that were carrying him homeward, he stuck twenty-one sticks deep in a corner of the garden, when he was three weeks from the holidays, and pulled one up every day with a great wrench, throwing it to a distance with a vigour of will which would have carried it to limbo, if it had been in the nature of sticks to travel so far.

5

Growing Up in the Streets*

Claude Brown

Before I began going to school, I was always in the streets with Danny, Kid, and Butch. Sometimes, without saying a word, they would all start to run like hell, and a white man was always chasing them. One morning as I entered the backyard where all the hookey players went to draw up an activity schedule for the day, Butch told me that Danny and Kid had been caught by Mr Sands the day before. He went on to warn me about Mr Sands, saying that Mr Sands was that white man who was always chasing somebody and that I should try to remember what he looked like and always be on the look-out for him. He also warned me not to try to outrun Mr Sands, 'because that cat is fast'. Butch said, 'When you see him, head for a backyard or a roof. He won't follow you there.'

During the next three months, I stayed out of school twenty-one days, Dad was beating the hell out of me for playing hookey, and it was no fun being in the street in the winter, so I started going to school regularly. But when spring rolled around, hookey became my favorite game again. Mr Sands was known to my parents in the neighbourhood as the truant officer. He never caught me in the street, but he came by my house many mornings to escort me to class. This was one way of getting me to school, but he never found a way to keep me there. The moment my teacher took her eyes off me, I was back on the street. Every time Dad got a card from Mr Sands I got bruises and welts from Dad. The beatings had only a temporary effect on me. Each time, the beatings got worse, and each time I promised never to play hookey again. One time I kept that promise for three whole weeks.

The older guys had been doing something called 'catting' for years. That catting was staying away from home all night was all I knew about the term. Every time I asked one of the fellows to teach me how to cat, I was told I wasn't old enough. As time went on, I learned that guys catted when they were afraid to go home and that they slept

---

* CLAUDE BROWN, *Man child in the Promised Land*, Penguin, 1965

everywhere but in comfortable places. The usual places for catting were subway trains, cellars, unlocked cars, under a friend's bed, and in vacant newsstands.

One afternoon when I was eight years old, I came home after a busy day of running from the police, truant officer, and storekeepers. The first thing I did was look in the mailbox. This had become a habit with me even though I couldn't read. I was looking for a card, a yellow card. That yellow card meant that I would walk into the house and Dad would be waiting for me with his razor strop. He would usually be eating and would pause just long enough to say to me, 'Nigger, you got a ass whippin' comin'.' My sisters, Carole and Margie, would cry almost as much as I would while Dad was beating me, but this never stopped him. After each beating I got, Carole, who was two years older than I, would beg me to stop playing hookey. There were a few times when I thought I would stop just to keep her and Margie, my younger sister, from crying so much. I decided to threaten Carole and Margie instead, but this didn't help. I continued to play hookey, and they continued to cry on the days that the yellow card got home before I did.

Generally, I would break open the mailbox, take out the card, and throw it away. Whenever I did this, I'd have to break open two or three other mailboxes and throw away the contents, just to make it look good.

This particular afternoon, I saw a yellow card, but I couldn't find anything to break into the box with. Having some matches in my pockets, I decided to burn the card in the box and not bother to break the box open. After I had used all the matches, the card was not completely burned. I stood there getting more frightened by the moment. In a little while, Dad would be coming home; and when he looked in the mailbox, anywhere would be safer than home for me.

This was going to be my first try at catting out. I went looking for somebody to cat with me. My crime partner, Buddy, whom I had played hookey with that day, was busily engaged in a friendly rock fight when I found him in Colonial Park. When I suggested that we go up on the hill and steal some newspapers, Buddy lost interest in the rock fight.

We stole papers from newsstands and sold them on the subway trains until nearly 1 am. That was when the third cop woke us and put us off the train with the usual threat. They would always promise to beat us over the head with a billy and lock us up. Looking back, I think the cops took their own threats more seriously than we did. The third cop put us off the Independent Subway at Fifty-ninth Street and Columbus Circle. I wasn't afraid of the cops, but I didn't go back

57

into the subway – the next cop might have taken me home.

In 1945, there was an Automat where we came out of the subway. About five slices of pie later, Buddy and I left the Automat in search of a place to stay the night. In the center of the Circle, there were some old lifeboats that the Navy had put on display.

Buddy and I slept in the boat for two nights. On the third day, Buddy was caught ringing a cash register in a five-and-dime store. He was sent to a Children's Center, and I spent the third night in the boat alone. On the fourth night, I met a duty-conscious cop, who took me home. That ended my first catting adventure.

Dad beat me for three consecutive days for telling what he called 'that damn dumb lie about sleeping in a boat on Fifty-ninth Street'. On the fourth day, I think he went to check my story out for himself. Anyhow, the beating stopped for a while, and he never mentioned the boat again.

Before long, I was catting regularly, staying away from home for weeks at a time. Sometimes the cops would pick me up and take me to a Children's Center. The Centers were located all over the city. At sometime in my childhood, I must have spent at least one night in all of them except the one on Staten Island.

The procedure was that a policeman would take me to the Center in the borough where he had picked me up. The Center would assign someone to see that I got a bath and was put to bed. The following day, my parents would be notified as to where I was and asked to come and claim me. Dad was always in favor of leaving me where I was and saying good riddance. But Mama always made the trip. Although Mama never failed to come for me, she seldom found me there when she arrived. I had no trouble getting out of Children's Centers, so I seldom stayed for more than a couple of days.

When I was finally brought home – sometimes after weeks of catting – Mama would hide my clothes or my shoes This would mean I couldn't get out of the house if I should take a notion to do so. Anyway, that's how Mama had it figured. The truth of the matter is that these measures only made getting out of the house more difficult for me. I would have to wait until one of the fellows came around to see me. After hearing my plight, he would go out and round up some of the gang, and they would steal some clothes and shoes for me. When they had the clothes and shoes, one of them would come to the house and let me know. About ten minutes later, I would put on my sister's dress, climb down the back fire escape and meet the gang with the clothes.

If something was too small or too large, I would go and steal the right size. This could only be done if the item that didn't fit was not

58

the shoes. If the shoes were too small or large, I would have trouble running in them and probably get caught. So I would wait around in the backyard while someone stole me a pair.

Mama soon realized that hiding my clothes would not keep me in the house. The next thing she tried was threatening to send me away until I was twenty-one. This was only frightening to me at the moment of hearing it. Ever so often, either Dad or Mama would sit down and have a heart-to-heart talk with me. These talks were very moving. I always promised to mend my bad ways. I was always sincere and usually kept the promise for about a week. During these weeks, I went to school every day and kept my stealing at a minimum. By the beginning of the second week, I had reverted back to my wicked ways, and Mama would have to start praying all over again.

The neighborhood prophets began making prophecies about my life-span. They all had me dead, buried, and forgotten before my twenty-first birthday. These predictions were based on false tales of policemen shooting at me, on truthful tales of my falling off a trolley car into the midst of oncoming automobile traffic while hitching a ride, and also on my uncontrollable urge to steal. There was much justification for these prophecies. By the time I was nine years old, I had been hit by a bus, thrown into the Harlem River (intentionally), hit by a car, severely beaten with a chain. And I had set the house afire.

While Dad was still trying to beat me into a permanent conversion, Mama was certain that somebody had worked roots on me. She was writing to all her relatives in the South for solutions, but they were only able to say, 'that boy must have been born with the devil in him'. Some of them advised Mama to send me down there, because New York was no place to raise a child. Dad thought this was a good idea, and he tried to sell it to Mama. But Mama wasn't about to split up her family. She said I would stay in New York, devil or no devil. So I stayed in New York, enjoying every crazy minute.

Mama's favorite question was, 'Boy, why you so bad?' I tried many times to explain to Mama that I wasn't 'so bad'. I tried to make her understand that it was trying to be good that generally got me into trouble. I remember telling her that I played hookey to avoid getting into trouble in school. It seemed that whenever I went to school, I got into a fight with the teacher. The teacher would take me to the principal's office. After I had fought with the principal, I would be sent home and not allowed back in school without one of my parents. So to avoid all that trouble, I just didn't go to school. When I stole things, it was only to save the family money and avoid arguments or scoldings whenever I asked for money.

Mama seemed silly to me. She was bothered because most of the parents in the neighborhood didn't allow their children to play with me. What she didn't know was that I never wanted to play with them. My friends were all daring like me, tough like me, dirty like me. We took pride in being able to hitch rides on trolleys, buses, taxicabs and in knowing how to steal and fight. We knew that we were the only kids in the neighborhood who usually had more than ten dollars in their pockets. There were other people who knew this too, and that was often a problem for us. Somebody was always trying to shake us down or rob us. This was usually done by the older hustlers in the neighborhood or by storekeepers or cops. At other times, older fellows would shake us down, con us, or Murphy us out of our loot. We accepted this as the ways of life. Everybody was stealing from everybody else. And sometimes we would shake down newsboys and shoeshine boys. So we really had no complaints coming. Although none of my sidekicks was over twelve years of age, we didn't think of ourselves as kids. The other kids of my age were thought of as kids by me, I felt that since I knew more about life than they did, I had the right to regard them as kids.

I remember one time I hit a boy in the face with a bottle of Pepsi-Cola. I did it because I knew the older cats on 146th Street were watching me. The boy had messed with Carole. He had taken her candy from her and thrown it on the ground.

I came up to him and said, 'Man, what you mess with my sister for?'

All the older guys were saying 'That's that little boy who lives on Eighth Avenue. They call him Sonny Boy. We gon to see somethin' good out here now'.

There was a Pepsi-Cola truck there; they were unloading some crates. They were stacking up the crates to roll them inside. The boy who had hit Carole was kind of big and acted kind of mean. He had a stick in his hand, and he said, 'Yeah, I did it, so what you gon do about it?'

I looked at him for a while, and he looked big. He was holding that stick like he meant to use it, so I snatched a Pepsi-Cola bottle and hit him right in the face. He grabbed his face and started crying. He fell down, and I started to hit him again, but the man who was unloading the Pepsi-Cola bottles grabbed me. He took the bottle away from me and shook me. He asked me if I was crazy or something.

All the guys on the corner started saying 'You'd better leave that boy alone,' and 'Let go of that kid.' I guess he got kind of scared. He was white, and here were all these mean-looking colored cats talking about 'Let go of that kid' and looking at him. They weren't asking him to let me go; they were telling him. He let me go.

Afterward, if I came by, they'd start saying, 'Hey, Sonny Boy, how you doin'?' They'd ask me, 'You kick anybody's ass today?' I knew that they admired me for this, and I knew that I had to keep on doing it. This was the reputation I was making, and I had to keep living up to it every day that I came out of the house. Every day, there was a greater demand on me. I couldn't beat the same little boys every day. They got bigger and bigger. I had to get more vicious as the cats got bigger. When the bigger guys started messing with you, you couldn't hit them or give them a black eye or a bloody nose. You had to get a bottle or a stick or a knife. All the other cats out there on the streets expected this of me, and they gave me encouragement.

6

Child-Savers

Anthony Platt*

Studies of crime and delinquency have, for the most part, focused on their psychological and environmental origins. Correctional research has traditionally encompassed the relationship between prisoners and prison-management, the operation of penal programs, the implementation of the 'rehabilitative ideal' and, in recent years, the effectiveness of community-based corrections. On the other hand, we know very little about the social processes by which certain types of behaviour come to be defined as 'criminal' or about the origins of penal reforms.[1] If we intend rationally to assess the nature and purposes of correctional policies, it is of considerable importance to understand how laws and legislation are passed, how changes in penal practices are implemented, and what interests are served by such reforms.

This paper analyzes the nature and origins of the reform movement in juvenile justice and juvenile corrections at the end of the nineteenth century. Delinquency raises fundamental questions about the objects of social control, and it was through the child-saving movement that the modern system of delinquency-control emerged in the United States. The child-savers were responsible for creating a new legal institution for penalizing children (juvenile court) and a new correctional institution to accommodate the needs of youth (reformatory). The origins of 'delinquency' are to be found in the programs and ideas of these reformers, who recognized the existence and carriers of delinquent norms.

Images of delinquency

The child-saving movement, like most moral crusades, was characterized by a 'rhetoric of legitimization'[2], built on traditional values and imagery. From the medical profession, the child-savers borrowed the imagery of pathology, infection, and treatment; from the tenets of Social Darwinism, they derived their pessimistic views about the

* Annals of the American Academy (January 1969), 381, 21-38.

intractability of human nature and the innate moral defects of the working class; finally, their ideas about the biological and environmental origins of crime may be attributed to the positivist tradition in European criminology and to anti-urban sentiments associated with the rural Protestant ethic.

American criminology in the last century was essentially a practical affair. Theoretical concepts of crime were imported from Europe, and an indiscriminating eclecticism dominated the literature. Lombrosian positivism and Social Darwinism were the major sources of intellectual justification for crime workers. The pessimism of Darwinism, however, was counter-balanced by notions of charity, religious optimism, and the dignity of suffering which were implicit components of the Protestant ethic.

Before 1870 there were only a few American textbooks on crime, and the various penal organizations lacked specialized journals. Departments of law and sociology in the universities were rarely concerned with more than the description and classification of crimes. The first American writers on crime were physicians, like Benjamin Rush and Isaac Ray, who were trained according to European methods. The social sciences were similarly imported from Europe, and American criminologists fitted their data to the theoretical framework of criminal anthropology. Herbert Spencer's writings had an enormous impact on American intellectuals, and Cesare Lombroso, perhaps the most significant figure in nineteenth-century criminology, looked for recognition in the United States when he felt that his experiments had been neglected in Europe [3].

Although Lombroso's theoretical and experimental studies were not translated into English until 1911, his findings were known by American academies in the early 1890's, and their popularity, like that of Spencer's works, was based on the fact that they confirmed popular assumptions about the character and existence of a 'criminal class'. Lombroso's original theory suggested the existence of a criminal type distinguishable from noncriminals by observable physical anomalies of a degenerative or atavistic nature. He proposed that the criminal was a morally inferior human species, characterized by physical traits reminiscent of apes, lower primates, and savage tribes. The criminal was thought to be morally retarded and, like a small child, instinctively aggressive and precocious unless restrained [4]. It is not difficult to see the connection between biological determinism in criminological literature and the principles of 'natural selection'; both of these theoretical positions automatically justified the 'eradication of elements that constituted a permanent and serious danger' [5].

Nature versus nature

Before 1900, American writers were familiar with Lombroso's general propositions but had only the briefest knowledge of his research techniques[6]. Although the emerging doctrines of preventive criminology implied human malleability, most American penologists were preoccupied with the intractability of the 'criminal classes'. Hamilton Wey, an influential physician at Elmira Reformatory, argued before the National Prison Association in 1881 that criminals were 'a distinct type of human species', characterized by flat-footedness, asymmetrical bodies, and 'degenerative physiognomy'[7].

Literature on 'social degradation' was extremely popular during the 1870's and 1880's, though most such 'studies' were little more than crude polemics, padded with moralistic epithets and preconceived value judgments. Richard Dugdale's series of papers on the Jukes family, which became a model for the case-study approach to social problems, was distorted almost beyond recognition by anti-intellectual supporters of hereditary theories of crime[8]. Confronted by the evidence of Darwin, Galton, Dugdale, Caldwell and many other disciples of the biological image of man, correctional professionals were compelled to admit that 'a large proportion of the unfortunate children that go to make up the great army of criminals are not born right'[9]. Reformers adopted the rhetoric of Darwinism in order to emphasize the urgent need for confronting the 'crime problem' before it got completely out of hand. A popular proposal was the 'methodized registration and training' of potential criminals, 'or these failing, their early and entire withdrawal from the community'[10].

The organization of correctional workers through national representatives and their identification with the professions of law and medicine operated to discredit the tenets of Darwinism and Lombrosian theory. Correctional workers did not think of themselves merely as custodians of a pariah class. The self-image of penal reformers as doctors rather than guards and the domination of criminological research in the United States by physicians helped to encourage the acceptance of 'therapeutic' strategies in prisons and reformatories. As Arthur Fink has observed[11]:

> The role of the physician in this ferment is unmistakable. Indeed, he was the dynamic agent. . . . Not only did he preserve and add to existing knowledge – for his field touched all borders of science – but he helped to maintain and extend the methodology of science.

Perhaps what is more significant is that physicians furnished the official rhetoric of penal reform. Admittedly, the criminal was 'pathological' and 'diseased', but medical science offered the possibility of miraculous cures. Although there was a popular belief in the existence of a 'criminal class' separated from the rest of mankind by a 'vague boundary line', there was no good reason why this class could not be identified, diagnosed, segregated, changed, and controlled[12].

By the late 1890's, most correctional administrators agreed that hereditary theories of crime were over-fatalistic. The superintendent of the Kentucky Industrial School of Reform told delegates to a national conference on corrections that heredity is 'unjustifiably made a bugaboo to discourage efforts at rescue. We know that physical hereditary tendencies can be neutralized and often nullified by proper counteracting precautions'[13]. E R L Gould, a sociologist at the University of Chiago, similarly criticized biological theories of crime for being unconvincing and sentimental. 'Is it not better', he said, 'to postulate freedom of choice than to preach the doctrine of the unfettered will, and so elevate criminality into a propitiary sacrifice?'[14]

Charles Cooley was one of the first sociologists to observe that criminal behaviour depended as much upon social and economic circumstances as it did upon the inheritance of biological traits. 'The criminal class,' he said, 'is largely the result of society's bad workmanship upon fairly good material'. In support of this argument, he noted that there was a 'large and fairly trustworthy body of evidence' to suggest that many 'degenerates' could be converted into 'useful citizens by rational treatment'.[15]

Urban disenchantment

Another important influence on nineteenth-century criminology was a disenchantment with urban life – an attitude which is still prevalent in much 'social problems' research. Immigrants were regarded as 'unsocialized', and the city's impersonality compounded their isolation and degradation. 'By some cruel alchemy,' wrote Julia Lathrop, 'we take the sturdiest of European peasantry and at once destroy in a large measure its power to rear to decent livelihood the first generation of offspring upon our soil.'[16] The city symbolically embodied all the worst features of industrial life. A member of the Massachusetts Board of Charities observed[17]:

> Children acquire a perverted taste for city life and crowded streets;
> but if introduced when young to country life, care of animals and
> plants, and rural pleasures, they are likely to be healthier in mind
> and body for such associations.

Programs which promoted rural and primary group concepts were encouraged because slum life was regarded as unregulated, vicious, and lacking social rules. Its inhabitants were depicted as abnormal and maladjusted, living their lives in chaos and conflict[18]. It was consequently the task of social reformers to make city life more wholesome, honest and free from depravity. Beverely Warner told the National Prison Association in 1898[19] that philanthropic organizations all over the country were

> making efforts to get the children out of the slums, even if only once a week, into the radiance of better lives. . . . It is only by leading the child out of sin and debauchery, in which it has lived, into the circle of life that is a repudiation of things that it sees in its daily life, that it can be influenced.

Although there was a wide difference of opinion among experts as to the precipitating causes of crime, it was generally agreed that criminals were abnormally conditioned by a multitude of biological and environmental forces, some of which were permanent and irreversible. Biological theories of crime were modified to incorporate a developmental view of human behavior. If, as it was believed, criminals are conditioned by biological heritage and brutish living conditions, the prophylactic measures must be taken early in life. Criminals of the future generations must be reached. 'They are born to crime,' wrote the penologist Enoch Wines in 1880, 'brought up for it. They must be saved.'[20]

Maternal justice

The 1880's and 1890's represented for many middle-class intellectuals and professionals a period of discovery of the 'dim attics and damp cellars in poverty-stricken sections of populous towns' and of 'innumerable haunts of misery throughout the land'[21]. The city was suddenly discovered to be a place of scarcity, disease, neglect, ignorance, and 'dangerous influences'. Its slums were the 'last resorts' of the penniless and the criminal'; here humanity reached its lowest level of degredation and despair[22].

The discovery of problems posed by 'delinquent' youth was greatly influenced by the role of feminist reformers in the child-saving movement. It was widely agreed that it was a woman's business to be involved in regulating the welfare of children, for women were considered the 'natural caretakers' of wayward children. Women's claim to the public care of children had some historical justification during the nineteenth century, and their role in child-rearing was considered paramount. Women were regarded as better teachers than men and were also more influential in child-training at home. The fact that public education also came more under the direction of women teachers in the schools increased the predominance of women in the raising of children[23].

Child-saving was a predominantly feminist movement, and it was regarded even by antifeminists as female domain. The social circumstances behind this appreciation of maternalism were women's emancipation and the accompanying changes in the character of traditional family life. Educated middle-class women now had more leisure time but a limited choice of careers. Child-saving was a reputable task for women who were allowed to extend their house-keeping functions into the community without denying antifeminist stereotypes of woman's nature and place. 'It is an added irony,' writes Christopher Lasch in his study of American intellectualism,[24]

> that the ideas about women's nature to which some feminists still clung, in spite of their opposition to the enslavement of woman in the home, were these very deep clichés which had so long been used to keep her there. The assumption that women were morally purer than men, better capable of altruism and self-sacrifice, was the core of the myth of domesticity against which the feminists were in revolt. . . . (F)eminist and antifeminist assumptions seemed curiously to coincide.

Child-saving may be understood as a crusade which served symbolic and status functions for native, middle-class Americans, particularly feminist groups. Middle-class women at the turn of the century experienced a complex and far-reaching status revolution. Their traditional functions were dramatically threatened by the weakening of domestic roles and the specialized rearrangement of family life.[25] One of the main forces behind the child-saving movement was a concern for the structure of family life and the proper socialization of young persons, since it was these concerns that had traditionally given purpose to a woman's life. Professional organizations – such as settlement houses, women's clubs, bar associations and penal organizations – regarded child-saving as a problem of women's rights, whereas their opponents seized upon it as an opportunity to keep women in their proper place. Child-saving organizations had little or nothing to do with militant supporters of the suffragette movement. In fact, the new role of social worker was created by deference to antifeminist stereotypes of a 'woman's place'.

A woman's place

Feminist involvement in child-saving was endorsed by a variety of penal and professional organizations. Their participation was usually justified as an extension of their housekeeping functions so that they did not view themselves, nor were they regarded by others, as competitors for jobs usually performed by men. Proponents of the 'new penology' insisted that reformatories should resemble home life, for institutions without women were likely to do more harm than good to inmates. According to G E Howe, the reformatory system provided 'the most ample opportunities for woman's transcendent influence'[26].

Female delegates to philanthropic and correctional conferences also realized that correctional work suggested the possibility of useful careers. Mrs W P Lynde told the National Conference of Charities and Correction in 1879 that children's institutions offered the 'truest and noblest scope for the public activities of women in the time which they can spare from their primary domestic duties'[27]. Women were exhorted by other delegates to make their lives meaningful by participating in welfare programs, volunteering their time and services, and getting acquainted with less privileged groups. They were told to seek jobs in institutions where 'the woman-element shall pervade . . . and soften its social atmosphere with motherly tenderness'[28].

Although the child-savers were responsible for some minor reforms in jails and reformatories, they were more particularly concerned with extending governmental control over a whole range of youthful activities that had previously been handled on an informal basis. The main aim of the child-savers was to impose sanctions on conduct unbecoming youth and to disqualify youth from enjoying adult privileges. As Bennett Berger has commented, 'adolescents are not made by nature but by being excluded from responsible participation in adult affairs, by being rewarded for dependency, and penalized for precocity'[29].

The child-saving movement was not so much a break with the past as an affirmation of faith in traditional institutions. Parental authority, education at home, and the virtues of rural life were emphasized because they were in decline at this time. The child-saving movement was, in part, a crusade which, through emphasizing the dependence of the social order on the proper socialization of children, implicitly elevated the nuclear family and, more especially, the role of women as stalwarts of the family. The child-savers were prohibitionists, in a general sense, who believed that social progress depended on efficient law enforcement, strict supervision of children's leisure and recreation, and the regulation of illicit pleasures. What seemingly began as a movement to humanize the lives of adolescents soon developed into a program of moral absolutism through which youth was to be saved from movies, pornography, cigarettes, alcohol, and anything else which might possibly rob them of their innocence.

Although child-saving had important symbolic functions for preserving the social prestige of a declining elite, it also had considerable practical significance for legitimizing new career openings for women. The new role of social worker combined elements of an old and partly fictitious role – defenders of family life – and elements of a new role – social servant. Social work was thus both an affirmation of cherished American values and an instrumentality for women's emancipation.

Juvenile court

The essential preoccupation of the child-saving movement was the recognition and control of youthful deviance. It brought attention to, and thus 'invented', new categories of youthful misbehaviour which had been hitherto unappreciated. The efforts of the child-savers were institutionally expressed in the juvenile court, which, despite recent legislative and constitutional reforms, is generally acknowledged as their most significant contribution to progressive penology.

The juvenile-court system was part of a general movement directed towards removing adolescents from the criminal-law process and creating special programs for delinquent, dependent, and neglected children. Regarded widely as 'one of the greatest advances in child welfare that has ever occurrred', the juvenile court was considered 'an integral part of total welfare planning'[30]. Charles Chute, an enthusiastic supporter of the child-saving movement, claimed[31]:

No single event has contributed more to the welfare of children and their families. It revolutionized the treatment of delinquent and neglected children and led to the passage of similar laws throughout the world.

The juvenile court was a special tribunal created by statute to determine the legal status of children and adolescents. Underlying the juvenile-court movement was the concept of *parens patriae* by which the courts were authorized to handle with wide discretion the problems of 'its least fortunate junior citizens'[32]. The administration of juvenile justice differed in many important respects from the criminal-court processes. A child was not accused of a crime but offered assistance and guidance; intervention in his life was not supposed to carry the stigma of criminal guilt. Judicial records were not generally available to the press or public, and juvenile-court hearings were conducted in relative privacy. Juvenile-court procedures were typically informal and inquisitorial. Specific criminal safeguards of due process were not applicable because juvenile proceedings were defined by statute as civil in character[33].

The original statutes enabled the courts to investigate a wide variety of youthful needs and misbehavior. As Joel Handler has observed, 'the critical philosophical position of the reform movement was that no formal, legal distinctions should be made between the delinquent and the dependent or neglected[34]. Statutory definitions of 'delinquency' encompassed (1) acts that would be criminal if committed by adults; (2) acts that violated county, town, or municipal ordinances; and (3) violations or vaguely defined catch-alls – such as 'vicious or immoral behavior', 'incorrigibility' and 'truancy' – which 'seem to express the notion that the adolescent, if allowed to continue, will engage in more serious conduct'[35].

The juvenile-court movement went far beyond a concern for special treatment of adolescent offenders. It brought within the ambit of governmental control a set of youthful activities that had been previously ignored or dealt with on an informal basis. It was not by accident that the behaviour selected for penalizing by the child-savers – sexual license, drinking, roaming the streets, begging, frequenting dance halls and movies, fighting, and being seen in public late at night – was most directly relevant to the children of lower-class migrant and immigrant families.

The juvenile court was not perceived by its supporters as a revolutionary experiment, but rather as a culmination of traditionally valued practices[36]. The child-saving movement was 'antilegal', in the sense that it derogated civil rights and procedural formalities, while relying heavily on extra-legal techniques. The judges of the new court were empowered to investigate the character and social life of the predelinquent as well as delinquent children; they examined motivation rather than intent, seeking to identify the moral reputation of problematic children. The requirements of preventive penology and child-saving further justified the court's intervention in cases where no offense had actually been committed, but where, for example, a child was posing problems for some person in authority such as a parent or teacher or social worker.

The personal touch

Judges were expected to show the same professional competence as doctors and therapists. The sociologist Charles Henderson wrote[37]:

> A careful study of individuals is an essential element in wise procedure. The study must include the physical, mental and moral peculiarities and defects of the children who come under the notice of the courts. Indeed we are likely to follow the lead of those cities which provide for a careful examination of all school children whose physical or psychical condition is in any way or degree abnormal, in order to prevent disease, correct deformity and vice, and select the proper course of study and discipline demanded by the individual need.

Juvenile court judges had to be carefully selected for their skills as expert diagnosticians and for their appreciation of the 'helping' professions. Miriam Van Waters, for example, regarded the juvenile court as a 'laboratory of human behaviour' and its judges as 'experts with scientific training' and specialists in 'the art of human relations'. It was the judge's task to 'get the whole truth about a child' in the same way that a 'physician searches for every detail that bears on the condition of a patient'[38].

The child-savers' interest in preventive strategies and treatment programs was based on the premise that delinquents possess innate or acquired characteristics which predispose them to crime and distinguish them from law-abiding youths. Delinquents were regarded as constrained by a variety of biological and environmental forces, so that their proper treatment involved discovery of the 'cause of the aberration' and application of 'the appropriate corrective or antidote'[39]. 'What the trouble is with the offender,' noted William Healy, 'making him what he is, socially undesirable, can only be known by getting at his mental life, as it is an affair of reactive mechanisms.'[40]

The use of terms like 'unsocialized', 'maladjusted' and 'pathological' to describe the behaviour of delinquents implied that 'socialized' and 'adjusted' children conform to middle-class morality and participate in respectable institutions[41]. The failure empirically to demonstrate psychological differences between delinquents and nondelinquents did not discourage the child-savers from believing that rural and middle-class values constitute 'normality'. The unique character of the child-saving movement was its concern for predelinquent offenders – children who occupy the debatable ground between criminality and innocence – and its claim that it could transform potential criminals into respectable citizens by training them in 'habits of industry, self-control and obedience to law'[42]. This policy justified the diminishing of traditional procedures in juvenile court. If children were to be rescued, it was important that the rescuers be free to provide their services without legal hindrance. Delinquents had to be saved, transformed and reconstituted. 'There is no essential difference', said Frederick Wines, 'between a criminal and any other sinner. The means and methods of restoration are the same for both.'[43]

The reformatory system

It was through the reformatory system that the child-savers hoped to demonstrate that delinquents were capable of being converted into law-abiding citizens. The reformatory was initially developed in the United States during the middle of the nineteenth century as a special form of prison discipline for adolescents and young adults. Its underlying principles were formulated by Matthew Davenport Hill, Alexander Maconchie, Walter Crofton and Mary Carpenter. If the United States did not have any great penal theorists, it at least had energetic penal administrators who were prepared to experiment with new programs. The most notable advocates of the reformatory plan in the United States were Enoch Wines, Secretary of the New York Prison Association; Theodore Dwight, the first Dean of Columbia Law School; Zebulon Brockway, Superintendent of Elmira Reformatory in New York; and Frank Sanborn, Secretary of the Massachusetts State Board of Charities.

The reformatory was distinguished from the traditional penitentiary by its policy of indeterminate sentencing, the 'mark' system, and 'organized persuasion' rather than 'coercive restraint'. Its administrators assumed that abnormal and troublesome individuals could become useful and productive citizens. Wines and Dwight, in a report to the New York legislature in 1867 [44], proposed that the ultimate aim of penal policy was reformation of the criminal, which could only be achieved by placing the prisoner's fate, as far as possible, in his own hand, by enabling him, through industry and good conduct to raise himself, step by step, to a position of less restraint; while idleness and bad conduct, on the other hand, keep him in a state of coercion and restraint. But, as Brockway observed at the first meeting of the National Prison Congress in 1870, the 'new penology' was tough-minded and devoid of 'sickly sentimentalism. . . . Criminals shall either be cured, or kept under such continued restraint as gives guarantee of safety from further depredations' [45].

Reformatories, unlike penitentiaries and jails, theoretically repudiated punishments based on intimidation and repression. They took into account the fact that delinquents were 'either physically or mentally below the average'. The reformatory system was based on the assumption that proper training can counteract the impositions of poor family life, a corrupt environment, and poverty, while at the same time toughening and preparing delinquents for the struggle ahead. 'The principle at the root of the educational method of dealing with juvenile crime', wrote William Douglas Morrison, 'is an absolutely sound one. It is a principle which recognizes the fact that the juvenile delinquent is in the main, a product of adverse individual and social conditions.' [46]

The reformatory movement spread rapidly through the United States, and European visitors crossed the Atlantic to inspect and admire the achievements of their pragmatic colleagues. Mary Carpenter, who visited the United States in 1873, was generally satisfied with the 'generous and lavish expenditures freely incurred to promote the welfare of the inmates, and with the love of religion'. Most correctional problems with regard to juvenile delinquents, she advised, could be remedied if reformatories were built like farm schools or 'true homes'. At the Massachusetts Reform School, in Westborough, she found an 'entire want of family spirit', and, in New York, she complained that there was no 'natural life' in the reformatory. 'All the arrangements are artificial', she said; 'instead of the cultivation of the land, which would prepare the youth to seek a sphere far from the dangers of large cities, the boys and young men were being taught trades which will confine them to the great centers of an over-crowded population.' She found similar conditions in Philadelphia where 'hundreds of youth were there congregated under lock and key', but praised the Connecticut Reform School for its 'admirable system of agricultural training'.[47] If she had visited the Illinois State Reformatory at Pontiac, she would have found a seriously overcrowded 'minor penitentiary' where the inmates were forced to work ten hours a day manufacturing shoes, brushes, and chairs.

To cottage and country

Granted the assumption that 'nurture' could usually overcome most of nature's defects, reformatory-administrators set about the task of establishing programs consistent with the aim of retraining delinquents for law-abiding careers. It was noted at the Fifth International Prison Congress, held in Paris in 1895, that reformatories were capable of obliterating hereditary and environmental taints. In a new and special section devoted to delinquency[48], the Congress proposed that children under twelve years:

> should always be sent to institutions of preservation and unworthy parents must be deprived of the right to children. . . . The preponderant place in rational physical training should be given to manual labor, and particularly to agricultural labor in the open air, for both sexes.

The heritage of biological imagery and Social Darwinism had a lasting influence on American criminology, and penal reformers continued to regard delinquency as a problem of individual adjustment to the demands of industrial and urban life. Delinquents had to be removed from contaminating situations, segregated from their 'miserable surroundings' instructed and 'put as far as possible on a footing of equality with the rest of the population'.[49]

The trend from congregate housing in the city to group living in the country represented a significant change in the organization of penal institutions for young offenders. The family or cottage plan differed in several important respects from the congregate style of traditional prisons and jails. According to William Letchworth, in an address delivered before the National Conference of Charities and

Correction in 1886[50]:

> A fault in some of our reform schools is their great size. In the congregating of large numbers, individuality is lost. . . . These excessive aggregations are overcome to a great extent in the cottage plan. . . . The internal system of the reformatory school should be as nearly as practicable as that of the family, with its refining and elevating influences; while the awakening of the conscience and the inculcation of religious principles should be primary aims.

The new penology emphasized the corruptness and artificiality of the city; from progressive education, it inherited a concern for naturalism, purity, and innocence. It is not surprising, therefore, that the cottage plan also entailed a movement to a rural location. The aim of penal reformers was not merely to use the countryside for teaching agricultural skills. The confrontation between corrupt delinquents and unspoiled nature was intended to have a spiritual and regenerative effect. The romantic attachment to rural values was quite divorced from social and agricultural realities. It was based on a sentimental and nostalgic repudiation of city life. Advocates of the reformatory system generally ignored the economic attractiveness of city work and the redundancy of farming skills. As one economist cautioned reformers in 1902[51]:

> Whatever may be said about the advantages of farm life for the youths of our land, and however much it may be regretted that young men and women are leaving the farm and flocking to the cities, there can be no doubt that the movement city-ward will continue . . . There is great danger that many who had left home (that is reformatory), unable to find employment in agricultural callings, would drift back to the city and not finding there an opportunity to make use of the technical training secured in the institution, would become discouraged and resume their old criminal associations and calling.

The 'new' reformatory suffered, like all its predecessors, from overcrowding, mismanagement, 'boodleism', under-staffing, and inadequate facilities. Its distinctive features were the indeterminate sentence, the movement to cottage and country, and agricultural training. Although there was a decline in the use of brutal punishments, inmates were subjected to severe personal and physical controls: military exercise, 'training of the will', and long hours of tedious labour constituted the main program of reform.

Summary and conclusions

The child-saving movement was responsible for reforms in the ideological and institutional control of 'delinquent' youth. The concept of the born delinquent was modified with the rise of a professional class of penal administrators and social servants who promoted a developmental view of human behavior and regarded most delinquent youth as salvageable. The child-savers helped to create special judicial and correctional institutions for the processing and management of 'troublesome' youth.

There has been a shift during the last fifty years or so in official policies concerning delinquency. The emphasis has shifted from one emphasizing the criminal nature of delinquency to the 'new humanism' which speaks of disease, illness, contagion, and the like. It is essentially a shift from a legal to a medical emphasis. The emergence of a medical emphasis is of considerable significance, since it is a powerful rationale for organizing social action in the most diverse behavioral aspects of our society. For example, the child-savers were not concerned merely with 'humanizing' conditions under which children were treated by the criminal law. It was rather their aim to extend the scope of governmental control over a wide variety of personal misdeeds and to regulate potentially disruptive persons[52]. The child-savers reforms were politically aimed at lower-class behavior and were instrumental in intimidating and controlling the poor.

The child-savers made a fact out of the norm of adolescent dependence. 'Every child is dependent,' wrote the Illinois Board of Charities in 1899, 'even the children of the wealthy. To receive his support at the hands of another does not strike him as unnatural, but quite the reverse.'[53] The juvenile court reached into the private lives of youth and disguised basically punitive policies in the rhetoric of 'rehabilitation'.[54] The child-savers were prohibitionists, in a general sense, who believed that adolescents needed protection from even their own inclinations.

The basic conservatism of the child-saving movement is apparent in the reformatory system which proved to be as tough-minded as traditional forms of punishment. Reformatory programs were unilateral, coercive, and an invasion of human dignity. What most appealed to correctional workers were the paternalistic assumptions of the 'new penology', its belief in social progress through individual reform, and its nostalgic preoccupation with the 'naturalness' and intimacy of a preindustrial way of life.

The child-saving movement was heavily influenced by middle-class women who extended their house-wifely roles into public service. Their contribution may also be seen as a 'symbolic crusade' in defense of the nuclear family and their positions within it. They regarded themselves as moral custodians and supported programs and institutions dedicated to eliminating youthful immorality. Social service was an instrumentality for female emancipation, and it is not too unreasonable to suggest that women advanced their own fortune at the expense of the dependency of youth.

This analysis of the child-saving movement suggests the importance of (1) understanding the relationship between correctional reforms and related changes in the administration of criminal justice, (2) accounting for the motives and purposes of those enterprising groups who generate such reforms, (3) investigating the methods by which communities establish the formal machinery for regulating crime, and (4) distinguishing between idealized goals and enforced conditions in the implementation of correctional reforms.

Implications for corrections and research

The child-saving movement illustrates a number of important problems with the quality and purposes of correctional research and knowledge. The following discussion will draw largely upon the child-saving movement in order to examine its relevance for contemporary issues.

Positivism and progressivism

It is widely implied in the literature that the juvenile court and parallel reforms in penology represented a progressive effort by concerned reformers to alleviate the miseries of urban life and to solve social problems by rational, enlightened, and scientific methods. With few exceptions, studies of delinquency have been parochial and inadequately descriptive, and they show little appreciation of underlying political and cultural conditions. Historical studies, particularly of the juvenile court, are, for the most part, self-confirming and support an evolutionary view of human progress.[55]

The positivist heritage in the study of social problems has directed attention to (1) the primacy of the criminal actor rather than the criminal law as the major point of departure in the construction of etiological theory, (2) a rigidly deterministic view of human behavior, and (3) only the abnormal features of deviant behavior.[56] The 'rehabilitative ideal' has so dominated American criminology that there have been only sporadic efforts to undertake sociological research related to governmental invasion of personal liberties. But, as Francis Allen has suggested[57]:

Even if one's interests lie primarily in the problems of treatment of offenders, it should be recognized that the existence of the criminal presupposes a crime and that the problems of treatment are derivative in the sense that they depend upon the determination by law-giving agencies that certain sorts of behavior are crimes.

The conservatism and 'diluted liberalism'[58] of much research on delinquency results from the fact that researchers are generally prepared to accept prevailing definitions of crime, to work within the premises of the criminal law, and to concur at least implicitly with those who make laws as to the nature and distribution of a 'criminal' population. Thus, most theories of delinquency are based on studies of convicted or imprisoned delinquents. As John Seeley has observed in another context, professional caution requires us 'to *take* our problems rather than *make* our problems, to accept as constitutive of our "intake" what is held to be "deviant" in a way that concerns people in that society enough to give us primary protection'[59]. Money, encouragement, co-operation from established institutions, and a market for publication are more easily acquired for studies of the socialization or treatment of delinquents than for studies of how laws, law-makers, and law-enforcers, contribute to the 'registration' delinquency.

Law and its implementation have been largely dismissed as irrelevant topics for inquiry into the 'causes' of delinquency. According to Herbert Packer, it is typical that the National Crime Commission ignored the fundamental question of: 'What is the criminal sanction good for?'[60] Further research is needed to understand the dynamics of the legislative and popular drive to 'criminalize'.[61] Delinquency legislation for example, as has been noted earlier, was not aimed merely at reducing crime or liberating youth. The reform movement also served important symbolic and instrumental interests for groups who made hobbies and careers out of saving children.

Policy research

Correctional research in this country has been dominated by persons who are intimately concerned with crime and its control. The scholar-technician tradition in corrections, especially with regard to delinquency, has resulted in the proliferation of 'agency-determined' research whereby scholarship is catered to institutional interests[62]. Much of what passes under the label of 'research' takes the form of 'methods engineering', produced in the interest of responsible officials and management[63]. It is only rarely, as in Erving Goffman's study of 'total institutions', that sympathetic consideration is given to the perceptions and concerns of subordinates in the correctional hierarchy[64].

There are many historical and practical reasons why corrections has been such a narrow and specialized field of academic interest. First, corrections has been intellectually influenced by the problematic perspective of scholar-technicians, which limits the scope of 'research' to local, policy issues. In the last century especially, penology was the exclusive domain of philanthropists, muckrakers, reformers, and missionaries. Secondly, the rise of the 'multiversity' and of federal-grant research has given further respectability to applied research in corrections, to the extent that social science and public policy are inextricably linked[65]. Nevertheless, such research is minimal when compared, for example, with that done under the auspices of the Defense Department.[66] It is quite true, as the National Crime Commission reports, that research in corrections has been unsystematic, sporadic, and guided primarily by 'intuitive opportunism'.[67] Thirdly, it should be remembered that correctional institutions are politically sensitive communities which resist intrusions from academic outsiders unless the proposed research is likely to serve their best interests.[68] Research which undermines policy is generally viewed as insensitive and subversive, aside from the fact that it helps to justify and harden administrators' suspicions of 'intellectuals'. The lack of critical research is, no doubt, also due to the reluctance of scholars to address the specific problems faced by those charged with the perplexing task of controlling and rehabilitating offenders'.[69]

Politics and corrections
Correctional institutions have been generally regarded as distinct, insulated social organizations. Their relationship to the wider society is viewed in a bureaucratic, civil-service context, and their population is defined in welfare terms. Prisons and their constituency are stripped of political implications, seemingly existing in an apolitical vacuum. Corrections as an academic specialization has focused on the prison community to the neglect of classical interest in the relationship between political decision-making and social policies. As Hans Matick has observed[70]:

> There is very little appreciation . . . that this 'contest between good and evil', and the whole 'drama of crime', is taking place within the larger arena of our political system and this, in part, helps to determine public opinion about the nature of crime, criminals and how they are dealt with.

As the gap between social deviance and political marginality narrows, it becomes increasingly necessary to examine how penal administrators are recruited, how 'new' programs are selected and implemented, and how local and national legislatures determine correctional budgets. The crisis caused by white racism in this country also requires us to appreciate in what sense prisons and jails may be used as instrumentalities of political control in the 'pacification' of black Americans. Similarly, it furthers our understanding of 'delinquency' if we appreciate the motives and political interests of those reformers and professionals who perceive youth as threatening and troublesome.

Faith in reform

The child-saving movement further illustrates that corrections may be understood historically as a succession of reforms. Academics have demonstrated a remarkably persistent optimism about reform, and operate on the premise that they can have a humanitarian influence on correctional administration. As Irving Louis Horowitz has observed, to the extent that social scientists become involved with policy-making agencies, they are committed to an elitist ideology[71]:

They come to accept as basic the idea that men who really change things are at the top. Thus, the closer to the top one can get direct access, the more likely will intended changes be brought about.

There is little evidence to support this faith in the ultimate wisdom of policy-makers in corrections. The reformatory was not so much an improvement on the prison as a means of extending control over a new constituency; probation and parole became instruments of supervision rather than treatment; halfway houses have become a means of extending prisons into communities rather than democratically administered sanctuaries; group therapy in prisons has justified invasion of privacy and coercive treatment on the dubious grounds that prisoners are psychologically unfit; community-based narcotics programs, such as the nalline clinic, disguise medical authoritarianism in the guise of rehabilitation. Nevertheless, the optimism continues, and this is nowhere more apparent than in the National Crime Commission's Task Force Report on Corrections, which reveals that, in Robert Martinson's words, correctional policy consists of 'a redoubling of efforts in the face of persistent failure'.[72]

Finally, we have neglected to study and appreciate those who work in corrections. Like the police and, to an increasing extent, teachers and social workers, correctional staffs are constrained by the ethic of bureaucratic responsibility. They are society's 'dirty workers', technicians working on people. As Lee Rainwater has observed[73]:

The dirty-workers are increasingly caught between the silent middle class, which wants them to do the dirty work and keep quiet about it, and the objects of that dirty work, who refuse to continue to take it lying down. . . . These civilian colonial armies find their right to respect from their charges challenged at every turn, and often they must carry out their daily duties with fear for their physical safety.

Correctional workers are required to accommodate current definitions of criminality and to manage victims of political expediency and popular fashion – drug users, drunks, homosexuals, vagrants, delinquents and 'looters'. They have minimal influence on law-makers and rarely more than ideological rapport with law enforcers. They have no clear mandate as to the purpose of corrections, other than to reduce recidivism and reform criminals. They have to live with the proven failure of this enterprise and to justify their role as pacifiers, guards, warehouse-keepers and restrainers[74]. They are linked to a professional system that relegates them to the lowest status in the political hierarchy but uses them as a pawn in electoral battles. They are doomed to annual investigations, blue-ribbon commissions, ephemeral research studies, and endless volumes of propaganda and muckraking. They live with the inevitability of professional mediocrity, poor salaries, uncomfortable living conditions, ungrateful 'clients', and tenuous links with established institutions. It is understandable that they protect their fragile domain from intrusive research which is not supportive of their policies.

Notes

[1] This perspective is influenced by HOWARD S BECKER, *Outsiders; Studies in Sociology of Deviance*, Collier-Macmillan, 1963.

[2] This term is used by DONALD W BALL, 'An abortion clinic ethnography', *Social Problems*, **14**, 1967, 293–301.

[3] See LOMBROSO's 'Introduction' to ARTHUR MACDONALD, *Criminology*, Funk and Wagnall, New York, 1893.

[4] MARVIN E WOLFGANG, CESARE LOMBROSO, in *Pincers in Criminology* ed HERMANN MANNHEIM, Stevens, London 1960, 168–227.

[5] LEON RADZINOWICZ, *Ideology and Crime*, Heinemann Education Books, London 1966, 55.

[6] See, for example, ARTHUR MACDONALD, *Abnormal Man*, U.S. Government Printing Office 1893, Washington DC; and ROBERT FLETCHER, *The New School of Criminal Anthropology*, Judd and Detwiler, Washington DC 1891.

[7] HAMILTON D WEY, 'A plea for physical training of youthful criminals', in National Prison Association, *Proceedings of the Annual Congress, (Boston 1888)*, 181–193.

[8] RICHARD L DUGDALE, 'Hereditary pauperism, as illustrated in the "Jukes" family' in Annual Conference of Charities, *Proceedings (Saratoga 1877)*, 81–99; *The Jukes; A Study in Crime, Pauperism, Disease and Heredity*, G P Putnam, New York 1877.

[9] SARAH B COOPER, 'The kindergarten child-saving work', in National Conference of Charities and Correction, *Proceedings (Madison 1883)*, 130–138.

[10] I N KERLIN, 'The moral imbecile', in National Conference of Charities and Correction, *Proceedings (Baltimore 1890)*, 244–250.

[11] ARTHUR E FINK, *Causes of Crime; Biological Theories in the United States, 1800–1915*, Perpetua 1926, 247.

[12] See, for example, Illinois. Board of State Commissioners of Public Charities, *Second Biennial Report*, State Journal Steam Print, Springfield, 1873, 195–196.

[13] PETER CALDWELL, 'The Duty of the State to Delinquent Children',

National Conference of Charities and Correction, *Proceedings* (*New Haven 1895*), 134–143.

[14] E R L GOULD, 'The statistical study of hereditary criminality', National Conference of Charities and Correction, *Proceedings* (*New Haven 1895*), 134–143.

[15] CHARLES H COOLEY, 'Nature v. nurture' in making of social careers, National Conference of Charities and Correction, *Proceedings* (*Grand Rapids, Michigan 1896*), 399–495.

[16] JULIA LATHROP, 'The Development of the probation system in a large city', *Charities*, **13** (January 1905), 348.

[17] CLARA T LEONARD, 'Family homes for pauper and dependent children', Annual Conference of Charities, *Proceedings* (*Chicago 1897*), 174.

[18] WILLIAM FOOTE WHYTE, 'Social disorganization in the slums', *American Sociological Reviews*, **8** (1943), 34–39.

[19] BEVERLEY WARNER, 'Child-saving', in National Prison Association, *Proceedings of the Annual Congress* (*Indianapolis 1898*), 377–378.

[20] ENOCH C WINES, *The State of Prisons and of Child-Saving Institutions in the Civilized World*, Harvard University Press, Cambridge, Mass, 1880, 132.

[21] WILLIAM P LETCHWORTH, 'Children of the state', National Conference of Charities and Correction, *Proceedings* (*St Paul, Minn 1886*), 138. The idea that intellectuals *discovered* poverty as a result of their own alienation from the centers of power has been fully treated by RICHARD HOFSTADTER, *The Age of Reform*, Cape 1962; and CHRISTOPHER LASCH, *The New Radicalism in America*, 1889–1963; *The Intellectual as a Social Type*, (Chatto & Windus 1966).

[22] R W HILL, 'The children of Shinbone Alley', National Conference of Charities and Correction, *Proceedings* (*Omaba 1887*), 231

[23] ROBERT SUNLEY, 'Early nineteenth-century American literature on child-rearing', in MARGARET MEAD and MARTHA WOLFENSTEIN (eds) *Childhood in Contemporary Cultures*, 152, University of Chicago Press 1955; see also ORVILLE G BRIM, *Education for Child-Rearing*, Collier-Macmillan 1965, 321–49.

[24] LASCH, *op cit* 53–54.

[25] TALCOTT PARSONS and ROBERT F BALES, *Family; Socialization and Interaction Process*, Routledge & Kegan Paul 1956, 3–33.

[26] G E HOWE, 'The family system', National Conference of Charities and Correction, *Proceedings* (*Cleveland 1880*), 212–213.

[27] W P LYNDE, 'Prevention in some of its aspects', Annual Conference of Charities, *Proceedings* (*Chicago 1879*), 167.

[28] CLARA T LEONARD, 'Family homes for pauper and dependent children', in *ibid*, 175.

[29] BENNETT BERGER, review of FRANK MUSGROVE, 'Youth and the Social Order,' *American Sociological Review*, **32**, 1021.

[30] CHARLES L CHUTE, 'The juvenile court in retrospect, *Federal Probation*, **13**, September 1949, 7; HARRISON A DOBBS, 'In defense of juvenile courts', *ibid* 29.

[31] CHARLES L CHUTE, 'Fifty years of the juvenile court', in *National Probation and Parole Association Yearbook* (*1949*), 21.

[32] GUSTAV L SCHRAMM, 'The juvenile Court Idea', *Federal Probation*, **13**, (September 1949), 21.

[33] CONRAD G PAULSEN, 'Fairness to the juvenile offender', *Minnesota Law Review*, **41**, (1957), 547–67. Note: 'Rights and rehabilitation in juvenile courts', *Columbia Law Review*, **67** (1967), 281–341.

[34] JOEL F HANDLER, 'The juvenile court and the adversary system: problems

of function and form', *Wisconsin Law Review (1965)*, 281–341.

[35] JOEL F HANDLER AND MARGARET K ROSENHEIM, 'Privacy and welfare; public assistance and juvenile justice', *Law and Contemporary Problems*, **31** (1966), 377–412.

[36] A reform movement, according to Herbert Blumer, is differentiated from a revolution by its inherent respectability and acceptance of an existing social order. 'The primary function of the reform movement is probably not so much the bringing about of a social change, as it is to reaffirm the ideal values in a given society.' HERBERT BLUMER, 'Collective behavior', in ALFRED MCLUNG LEE (ed) *Principles of Sociology*, Barnes and Noble, New York, 1963, 212–213.

[37] CHARLES R HENDERSON, 'Theory and practice of juvenile courts', National Conference of Charities and Correction, *Proceedings (Portland 1904)*, 358–359.

[38] MIRIAM VAN WATER, 'The socialization of juvenile court procedure', *Journal of Criminal Law and Criminology*, **12**, (1922), 61, 69.

[39] Illinois, Board of State Commissioners of Public Charities, *First Biennial Report* (Springfield: Illinois Journal Printing Office 1871), 180.

[40] WILLIAM HEALY, 'The psychology of the situation: a fundamental for understanding and treatment of delinquency and crime', in Jane Addams (ed), *The Child, The Clinic and The Court* New Republic Inc. New York 1925), 40.

[41] C WRIGHT MILLS, 'The professional ideology of social pathologists', in BERNARD ROSENBERG, ISRAEL GERVER and F WILLIAM HOWTON (eds), *Mass Society in Crisis* (Collier-Macmillan 1964), 92–111.

[42] Illinois, Board of State Commissioners of Public Charities, *Sixth Biennial Report* (Springfield: H W Rokker 1880), 104.

[43] FREDERICK H WINES, 'Reformation as an end in prison discipline', National Conference of Charities and Correction, *Proceedings* (Buffalo 1888), 198.

[44] MAX GRUNHUT, *Penal Reform*, Clarendon Press 1948, 90.

[45] This speech is reprinted in ZEBULON REED BROCKWAY, *Fifty Years of Prison Service*, Charities Publication Committee 1912, 389–408.

[46] WILLIAM DOUGLAS MORRISON, *Juvenile Offenders*, Appleton, New York, 1967, 274–5.

[47] MARY CARPENTER, 'Suggestions on reformatory schools and prison discipline, founded on observations made during a visit to the United States', National Prison Reform Congress, *Proceedings, St Louis*, 157–73.

[48] NEGLEY K TEETERS, *Deliberations of the International Penal and Penitentiary Congresses*, 1872–1935, Temple University Book Store, Philadelphia, 1949, 97–102.

[49] MORRISON, *op cit*, 60, 276.

[50] WILLIAM P LETCHWORTH, 'Children of the State', National Conference of Charities and Correction, *Proceedings (St Paul, Minnesota 1886)*, 151, 156.

[51] M B HAMMOND's comments at Illinois Conference of Charities (1901), reported in Illinois, Board of State Commissioners of Public Charities, *Seventeenth Biennial Report*, Phillips Brothers, 1902, 232–3.

[52] This thesis is supported by a European study of family life, PHILLIPE ARIES, *Centuries of Childhood*, Cape 1962.

[53] Illinois, Board of State Commissioners of Public Charities, *Fifteenth Biennial Report*, Phillips Brothers, Springfield, 1899, 62–72.

[54] FRANCIS A ALLEN, *The Borderland of Criminal Justice*, University of Chicago Press, 1964, *passim*.

[55] See, for example, HERBERT H LOU, *Juvenile Courts in the United States*, University of North Carolina, Chapel Hill, 1927; NEGLEY K TEETERS and JOHN OTTO REINEMANN, *The Challenge of Delinquency*, Prentice-Hall, New York, 1950; KATHERINE L BOOLE, 'The juvenile court: its origin, history and procedure' unpublished doctoral dissertation, University of California, Berkeley, 1928. One notable exception is PAUL W TAPPAN, *Delinquent Girls in Court*, Columbia University Press, 1947.

[56] DAVID MATZA, *Delinquency and Drift*, Wiley 1964.

[57] ALLEN, *op cit*, 125.

[58] This phrase and its perspective are taken by C WRIGHT MILLS (ed) *Images of Man*, George Braziller, New York, 1960, 5.

[59] JOHN R SEELEY, 'The making and taking of problems: Toward an ethical stance', *Social Problems*, **14**, 1967, 384–5.

[60] HERBERT L PACKER, 'A patchy look at crime', New York Review of Books, **17**, October 12, 1967.

[61] SANFORD H KADISH, 'The crisis of over-criminalization', *Annals of the American Academy*, **374**, November 1967, 157–70.

[62] HERBERT BLUMER, 'Threats from agency-determined researching: the case of Camelot, in IRVIN LOUIS HOROWITZ (ed), *The Rise and Fall of Project Camelot*, MIT Press, Cambridge, Mass. 1967, 153–74.

[63] See, for example, DANIEL GLASER, *The Effectiveness of a Prison and Parole System*, Bobbs-Merrill, New York, 1964.

[64] ERVING GOFFMAN, *Asylums* (New York: Anchor Books, 1961).

[65] CLARK KERR, *The Uses of the University* (New York: Anchor Books 1961).

[66] 'Approximately 15 per cent of the Defense Department's annual budget is allocated for research, compared with one per cent of the total federal expenditure for crime control.' – US President's Commission on Law Enforcement and Administration of Justice (National Crime Commission), *The Challenge of Crime in a Free Society* (the General Report) (Washington, DC: US Government Printing Office 1967), 273.

[67] US President's Commission on Law Enforcement and Administration of Justice (National Crime Commission), *Task Force Report: Corrections*, US Government Printing Office, 1967, 13.

[68] Controversial studies of official institutions run the risk of hampering further academic investigations, as was apparently the case with JEROME SKOLNICK's study of a California police department, *Justice without Trial* (Wiley 1966).

[69] *The Challenge of Crime in a Free Society*, 183.

[70] HANS W MATTICK (ed), 'The Future of Imprisonment in a Free Society', *Key Issues*, **2** (1965), 5.

[71] HOROWITZ (ed), *op cit*, 353.

[72] ROBERT MARTINSON, 'The age of treatment: some implications of the custody treatment dimension', *Issues in Criminology*, **2** (Fall 1966), 291.

[73] LEE RAINWATER, 'The Revolt of the Dirty-Workers', *Trans-action*, **5** (November 1967), 2.

[74] HENRY MCKAY's 'Report on the Criminal Careers of Male Delinquents in Chicago' concludes that 'the behavior of significant numbers of boys who become involved in illegal activity is not redirected toward conventional activity by the institutions created for that purpose.' – US President's Commission on Law Enforcement and Administration of Justice (National Crime Commission), *Task Force Report; Juvenile Delinquency and Youth Crime* (Washington, DC US Government Printing Office 1967), 113.

7

Inventing the Adolescent *

Frank Musgrove

The adolescent was invented at the same time as the steam-engine. The principal architect of the latter was Watt in 1765, of the former Rousseau in 1762. Having invented the adolescent, society has been faced with two major problems: how and where to accommodate him in the social structure, and how to make his behaviour accord with the specifications. For two centuries English society has been involved in the problem of defining and clarifying the concept of precocity.

Rousseau defined the adolescent, but he evaded the problem of his location in society by consigning him with his tutor to the wilderness. He belittled childhood as a phase of development: the first twelve years of life could be abandoned to 'negative education'. But puberty, he claimed, 'is the second birth I spoke of; then it is that man really enters upon life; henceforth no human passion is a stranger to him. Our efforts (in education) so far have been child's play, now they are of the greatest importance. The period when education is usually finished is just the time to begin...'

The tailor, the publisher, the social reformer and the educator came to Rousseau's assistance: they began in the late eighteenth and early nineteenth centuries to cater for a specific age-group of 'young persons', neither children nor adults. Instead of wearing imitation-adult clothing, young people at the end of the eighteenth century had their distinctive uniform, including 'long trousers', which actually anticipated the grown-up fashions of the future. School stories such as *Tom Brown* (1856) and *Eric, or Little by Little* (1858), *The Boys' Own Paper* (from 1879) and *Stalky and Co.* (1903) addressed themselves to, and helped to create, a specifically (middle-class) adolescent world.

Reforms of the penal system and of factory conditions also distinguished 'young persons' from children on the one hand and from adults on the other. Mary Carpenter argued strenuously that young persons should be distinguished from adults by the law courts, should

---

* Excerpt from: *Youth and the Social Order*, published by Routledge & Kegan Paul, 1964. Pp 33–37 and 76–79.

suffer penalties appropriate to their years, and receive corrective treatment in special, juvenile reformatories. The Youthful Offenders Act of 1854 enabled magistrates to treat young offenders and adult criminals differently. The Factory Acts of 1833 and 1847 distinguished the age-group 13–18 as needing protection from the full rigours of the adult world and restricted their hours of labour.

Social legislation and changing social conventions *made* the adolescent. Areas of experience and knowledge were now designated 'adult', from which the less-than-adult must be shielded. The early acquaintance with birth and especially with death were no longer considered essential to a child's education: these were adult matters from which the young should be carefully excluded. The young were now kept from the room in which confinement or death occurred: more spacious and elaborate architecture made it possible to segregate the young from such adult concerns.

And yet before his redefinition in the nineteenth century the adolescent had not necessarily been wholly integrated into the life of the adult world – or at least, in the case of upper-class children, into the world of adults who were their social equals. Indeed, it was the great achievement of the eighteenth century to rescue middle- and upper-class youth from the world of their social inferiors. For a time, at the end of the century, there was a powerful middle- and upper-class movement to save them from relegation to the marginal world of menials and domestic servants and to bring them more intimately into the lives of their own families. This experiment was incongruous with the needs of a rapidly changing social order; and in the nineteenth century upper-class youths were again ejected from their families – but now into the protected world of the public school.

In the later eighteenth century adolescence was not only redefined, as a distinct phase of the life cycle, but socially reclassified. Little distinction had been made hitherto between older children and adolescents: they sat together in the schools and were subject to similar discipline. They were not distinguished in dress, in the games they played, in the books they read. Formerly the upper-class young had been classed with servants and apprentices – often, indeed, they *were* apprentices, if they were younger sons. They were socially and often geographically remote from their elders; the elaboration of domestic architecture had made it possible to seclude them from the orbit of adult affairs, in the children's parlour or the 'Red Room'; although, as they advanced in years, they were more often to be found at the stable door. The tutor or governess who might supervise their lives was a menial, treated as such, a member of the servants' hall, as many have bitterly testified in their memoirs.

The infants of upper- and middle-class families were suckled by the wives of peasants and labourers. Powerful voices testified to, and attacked, this practice: Defoe criticized the upper-class mother on this score, as did Priestley, Whitchurch and Rousseau. David Williams described her as 'the most unnatural brute in creation'.

But older children were also permitted an easy relationship and familiarity with servants. Locke was issuing a warning against a widespread situation when he advised the parent to keep his child free 'from the taint of servants'. 'And there is another great inconvenience, which children receive from the ill examples which they meet with, among the meaner servants. They are wholly, if possible, to be kept from such conversation: for the contagion of these ill precedents, both in civility and virtue horribly infects children, as often as they come within reach of it. They frequently learn from unbred and debauched servants such language, untowardly tricks and vices, as otherwise they would possibly be ignorant of all their lives.' Defoe similarly complained of the country squire who 'educates his sons at the stable door, instead of the grammar school, and his huntsman is Head Tutor'. But even when he educated them at the grammar or public school he was unperturbed by the social mixture they would encounter. It was not until the middle of the nineteenth century that the 'social difficulty' which the Taunton Commission described caused the decay of grammar schools as the middle classes withdrew their sons from inferior social contacts.

The young were consigned to the company of servants because they were socially classified with servants. This was not a situation peculiar to England. Ariès has pointed to the similarity of conditions in France and England: 'Le *Book of Common Prayer* de 1549 fait une obligation aux chefs de famille de veiller à l'instruction religieuse de tous les enfants de la maison, c'est-à-dire aux *children, servants and prentices*. Les serviteurs et apprentis sont assimilés aux enfants de la famille. Ils s'amusaient entre eux à des jeux de gamins.'

The relegation of the young to the world of their social inferiors (and often to inferior living quarters and even an inferior diet) was commented on adversely by some seventeenth- and eighteenth-century writers. Locke reproved parents for their aloofness towards their children, for a 'constant stiffness, and a mien of authority to them all their lives.' He complained: 'And why those, who live in the country, should not take them (their children) with them, when they make visits of civility to their neighbours, I do not know'. Locke's recommendations were clearly of a revolutionary nature.

A century later the same complaints were still being made. David Williams asserted that in the homes of the gentry 'The father's attention is divided by the mercenary politics of parties, and the qualities of brutes: mothers are occupied by frivolous plans of fatiguing dissipation; by anxiety to give point or wit to cards, for insipid, importunate visitors, or messages for the health of dogs. But of their children they know only their persons, and reputation in the house.' Williams complained of fathers who knew their dogs better than their children; he commented acidly on the formalized, ritualistic separation of child and adult worlds. 'In almost all the families I know' – and as a private tutor his acquaintance was extensive – 'children are ushered to their parents at appointed hours and with certain ceremonies.' The contact was not only formal but of exceedingly brief duration.

Child and adult worlds briefly converged and made nominal contact each day by special arrangement. The children were attired for a ceremonial appearance each evening in the drawing-room. 'We had to be dressed out for the occasion, in coloured silk slips, and muslin frocks, which were very suitable, as the moment we entered the drawing-room, after our formal curtsies, we had to sit up all in a row, and we were constantly told, "be silent, and look pretty, as children should be seen and not heard".' The children were not long detained in this alien sphere. 'After a while, at a bow to the governess from my mother, we again made our curtsies at the door, and were marched off to our part of the house, to our great delight.' . . .

*　　*　　*

Between the 1780s and the 1860s young people, particularly the working-class young, were able to approximate to adult status because of their importance to the economy. Superfluous apprenticeship was an artifice which kept a diminishing proportion in unmerited subordination, particularly in the regions of most rapid social change; in 1863, before the National Association for the Promotion of Social Science, its remaining vestiges were roundly attacked as 'a species of slavery', 'incompatible with the free institutions of this country', which, 'unsuited to the present advanced state of society', 'should be discontinued as a worn-out vestige of the past . . .' These were not strictures on 'parish apprenticeship', but on normal apprenticeship for which high premiums might be charged, which might require seven years' training for 'what might be acquired by a sharp lad in three or four.' The early nineteenth century offered youth a dominant and not a subordinate economic role. The young, in their 'teens, could attain an independence which gave them virtually adult status, a situation reflected in, and further confirmed by, the tendency to early marriage.

The independence and early marriage of young industrial workers were severely disapproved of by (middle-class) social commentators and legislators. The resentment of the high status of the young (and of employed women) echoed through the parliamentary debates on the regulation of factory employment. Social workers were surprised that people who worked long hours under conditions which the middle class would have found distasteful did not feel sorry for themselves. Fanny Herz found young women factory workers 'exceeding tenacious of the independence and jealous to a surprising degree of even the appearance of condescension or patronage in the conduct of those who would approach them with the kindest intentions... Lord Ashley, in the course of the debates on the Ten Hours Bill, wished to regulate the conditions whereby women were 'gradually acquiring all those privileges which are held to be the proper portion of the male sex' and which promoted a 'perversion as it were of nature which has the inevitable effect of introducing into families disorder, insubordination and conflict.

Early marriage, the reflection and confirmation of the high status of young industrial workers, was generally deplored. Factory work was condemned for the young not because wages were low, but because they were high. 'From the same cause, namely high wages, very many early and improvident marriages take place.' 'The Census returns of 1861', runs a typical lament of the period, 'show that among the population of Bolton, 45 husbands and 172 wives were coupled at the immature age of "15 or under"; in Burnley there were 51 husbands and 147 wives; in Stockport 59 husbands and 179 wives in the same category.'

This tendency to early marriage dated from the later eighteenth century and has been attributed to the breakdown of traditional apprenticeship with its requirement of celibacy, to changes on the organization of farming, particularly to the decline of the custom of labourers 'living in', to the higher earnings of the young, and, more doubtfully, to the system of poor-law allowances. Because of the few hindrances to early marriage and the high birth rate of the period the later eighteenth century and the early nineteenth have been described as 'an almost, if not quite, unique epoch in the history of the human race.'

These circumstances prevailed in Ireland equally with England; and the social history of Ireland illustrates even more vividly than the history of England the close connection between the status of the young and the amount of marriage among them. The contrast between the Ireland of the later eighteenth century which Arthur Young described in his *Tour of Ireland* (1780) and the Ireland which American anthropologists described in the 1930's is between a country with independent youth and early marriage and a country with subordinate youth and remarkably belated marriage.

Arthur Young was impressed by the independence of young people and the early age at which they married. The reclamation of waste land and the subdivision of land were important economic circumstances behind these developments. 'There is no doubt at all that in the late-eighteenth and early-nineteenth centuries the Irish married while unusually young.' But whereas in 1841 only 43 per cent of males aged 25 to 35 were unmarried, in 1926 the percentage was 72. In the meantime the economic circumstances that had made early marriage possible had dramatically changed; in particular the shift from tillage to livestock production after the Famine, and the virtual cessation of the subdivision of land after 1852. By the 1920's, while 45 per cent of England males aged 25 to 30 were unmarried, 39 per cent of American, and 49 per cent of Danish, 80 per cent of Irish males of this age were still single.

Wherever social and economic institutions restrict the freedom of young people past puberty to marry, their social standing is depressed. The institutions may be as varied as protracted compulsory schooling, apprenticeship, exclusion from employment, the dowry, the bride-price, the monopoly of wives by elderly polygynists, or exchange-marriage. A bride-price or a dowry which is paid by parents enables the latter to regulate and impede the progress of youth towards adult status; exchange-marriage, whereby a man could marry only when his father supplied him with one of his daughters to give in exchange for a bride, was practiced by the Tiv of Nigeria until 1927 and effectively diminished the status of the young.

Arensberg and Kimball have described how in County Clare in the 1930's farmers arranged their children's marriages with a keen eye to economic advantage. Marriage conferred status, and until marriage, whatever his chronological age, a man remained a 'boy'. 'Even at 45 or 50, if the old couple have not yet made over the farm, the countryman remains a 'boy' in respect to farm work and in the rural vocabulary.' 'It goes without saying that the father exercises his control over the whole activity of the 'boy'. It is by no means confined to their work together.' Groups of 'young' (ie unmarried) men, unlike the 'cuaird' of older men, discuss no serious adult concerns; their main activity together is gambling. They have been effectively reduced to a condition of social subordination and irresponsibility. . . .

Part Two

Social Pathology Models and the Sociology of Education.

The first reading in this section, C Wright Mills' paper *The Professional Ideology of Social Pathologists*, is a classic statement of the procedures for making manifest the latent value assumptions and tacit theoretical presuppositions underlying a tradition of sociological enquiry. In his discussion of textbooks in the field of social disorganization (or social pathology), Mills remarks:

'Even though the perspectives of these texts are usually not explicit, the facts selected for treatment are not "random". One way to grasp the perspective within which they do lie is to analyse the scope and character of their problems.'

The remaining readings grouped in this section are devoted to critical analysis, very much in the spirit of Mills, of the presuppositions which have informed the dominant tradition of research and enquiry in the sociology of education since the Second World War. Although this tradition was itself rooted in genuinely egalitarian concerns and although, as Burns (T Burns, 1967) has emphasized, it was authentically critical of the optimistic assumptions of the champions of post-war educational reform, it nevertheless lacked an adequately critical and explicit theoretical perspective. Rather, a 'weak' structural-functionalist orientation (B Bernstein, 1972) provided a framework for a body of research strongly influenced by the imperatives of educational and social *policy* requirements. In consequence, those working within this tradition remained largely unaware of the ethnocentric character of their own (and educators') conceptions of 'normal' education and 'normal' schooling. Schools were implicitly treated as neutral institutions devoted to the 'transmission' of self-evidently 'worthwhile' aspects of a mainstream cultural heritage. (N G Keddie, 1973.) In these institutions the more educable children succeeded and the less educable failed, owing fundamentally to the influence of more or less favourable 'factors' in the family and social-class backgrounds from which the children came. In Bartholomew's words: 'Generally the research on educational performance measures properties of those who succeed in education and takes these as criteria of educability. By contrast, it shows the lack of these properties [educability] in those who do not succeed.' (J Bartholomew, 1972.)

Missing from this tradition of enquiry is sustained recognition that educators' categories of social-class, academic ability and worthwhile educational knowledge, form part of the social situation in which children's educational identities are constructed and assessed and that this everyday form of assessment is inescapably part of the social process by which rates of educational achievement are produced.

It is a hall mark of ethnocentric thinking that it remains unconscious of the normative nature of its own presuppositions while being simultaneously both evaluative and prescriptive on the basis of these presuppositions. This characteristic is very evident in the portrait of the 'less educable' pupil which has emerged as a product of sociological (and psychological) research into the origins of educational failure. The inferior educational performance of such pupils is explained, not by reference to features of the educational settings within which such failure occurs, but rather as the result of the influence of various pathological features which are *imputed* to the family and social class backgrounds of such children. The positivist methodologies of researchers within this tradition have facilitated the construction of accounts of lower-class and ethnic minority subcultures which provide more insights into the normative and prescriptive nature of the *researchers' categories* ('low level of parental interest', 'deferred gratification', 'restricted code', 'cultural deprivation', 'compensatory education'), than insights into the lived experience of members of such sub-cultures. It is a fundamental contention shared and developed by the authors of the papers which follow in this section, that such 'social pathology' assumptions are not confined to those studies which explicitly employ the concepts of cultural and verbal deprivation; rather they are regarded as informing, albeit in varying degrees, a substantial proportion of the contributions to this entire research tradition.

References

J BARTHOLOMEW, 'The Teacher as Researcher – a Key to Innovation and Change', *Hard Cheese – a Journal of Education*, **1**, 1972.

B BERNSTEIN, 'Sociology and the Sociology of Education: Some Aspects', *Open University Course Unit, E.282, Unit 17*, Open University Press, Bletchley, England, 1972.

T BURNS, 'Sociological Explanation', *British Journal of Sociology*, **xviii**, 1967.

N G KEDDIE [Ed] 'Tinker, Tailor ... The Myth of Cultural Deprivation', Penguin Education, 1973.

8

The Professional Ideology of Social Pathologists *

C Wright Mills

An analysis of textbooks in the field of social disorganization reveals a common style of thought which is open to social imputation. By grasping the social orientation of this general perspective we can understand why thinkers in this field should select and handle problems in the manner in which they have.

By virtue of the mechanism of sales and distribution, textbooks tend to embody a content agreed upon by the academic group using them. In some cases texts have been written only after an informal poll was taken of professional opinion as to what should be included, and other texts are consulted in the writing of a new one. Since one test of their success is wide adoption, the very spread of the public for which they are written tends to insure a textbook tolerance of the commonplace. Although the conceptual framework of a pathologist's textbook is not usually significantly different from that of such monographs as he may write, this essay is not concerned with the 'complete thought' or with the 'intentions' of individual authors; it is a study of a professional ideology variously exhibited in a set of textbooks. Yet because of its persistent importance in the development of American sociology and its supposed proximity to the social scene, 'social pathology' seems an appropriate point of entry for the examination of the style of reflection and the social-historical basis of American sociology.

The level of abstraction which characterizes these texts is so low that often they seem to be empirically confused for lack of abstraction to knit them together. They display bodies of meagerly connected facts, ranging from rape in rural districts to public housing, and intellectually sanction this low level of abstraction. The 'informational' character of social pathology is linked with a failure to consider total social structures. Collecting and dealing in a fragmentary way with scattered problems and facts of *milieux*, these books are not focused on larger stratifications or upon structured wholes. Such an omission may not be accounted for merely in terms of a general

* *American Journal of Sociology*, 49, 2, 1943 (and C W Mills' estate).

'theoretical weakness'. Such structural analyses have been available; yet they have not been attended to or received into the tradition of this literature. American sociologists have often asserted an interest in the 'correlation of the social sciences'; nevertheless, academic departmentalization may well have been instrumental in atomizing the problems which they have addressed. Sociologists have always felt that 'not many representatives of the older forms of social science are ready to admit that there is a function for sociology'. However, neither lack of theoretical ability nor restrictive channeling through departmentalization constitutes a full explanation of the low level of abstraction and the accompanying failure to consider larger problems of social structure.

If the members of an academic profession are recruited from similar social contexts and if their backgrounds and careers are relatively similar, there is a tendency for them to be uniformly set for some common perspective. The common conditions of their profession often seem more important in this connection than similarity of extraction. Within such a generally homogeneous group there tend to be fewer divergent points of view which would clash over the meaning of facts and thus give rise to interpretations on a more theoretical level.

The relatively homogeneous extraction and similar careers of American pathologists is a possible factor in the low level of abstraction characterizing their work. All the authors considered (except one, who was foreign born) were born in small towns, or on farms near small towns, three fourths of which were in states not industrialized during the youth of the authors. The social circles and strata in which they have severally moved are quite homogeneous; all but five have participated in similar 'reform' groups and 'societies' of professional and business classes. By virtue of their being college professors (all but three are known to have the Ph.D.), of the similar type of temporary positions (other than academic) which they have held, of the sameness of the 'societies' to which they have belonged and of the social positions of the persons whom they have married, the assertion as regards general similarity of social extraction, career and circles of contact seems justified.

A further determinant of the level of abstraction and lack of explicit systematization (beyond which the mentality we are examining does not easily or typically go) is the immediate purpose and the type of public for which they have presumably written. They have been teachers and their specific public has been college students: this has influenced the content and direction of their intellectual endeavors. Teaching is a task which requires a type of systematization to which the textbook answers. Most of the 'systematic' or 'theoretical' work in 'social pathology' has been performed by teachers. The fact that sociology often won its academic right to existence in opposition to other departments may have increased the necessity for *textbook* systematization. Such systematization occurs in a context of presentation of justification rather than within a context of discovery. The textbook-writing and the academic profession of the writers thus figure in the character and function of systematic theory within the field. Systematization of facts for the purpose of making them accessible to collegiate minds is one thing; systematization which is oriented toward crucial growing-points in a research process is quite another. An attempt to systematize on the level of the text-book makes for a taxonomic gathering of facts and a systematization of them under concepts that have already been logically defined. The research possibilities of concepts are not as important as is the putting of the accumulated factual details into some sort of order.

But, even though the perspectives of these texts are usually not explicit, the facts selected for treatment are not 'random'. One way to grasp the perspective within which they do lie is to analyze the scope and character of their problems. What, then, are the selecting and organizing principles to be extracted from the range and content of these texts? What types of fact come within their field of attention?

The direction is definitely toward particular 'practical problems' – problems of 'everyday life'. The ideal of practicality, of not being 'utopian', operated, in conjunction with other factors, as a polemic against the 'philosophy of history' brought into American sociology by men trained in Germany; this polemic implemented the drive to lower levels of abstraction. A view of isolated and immediate problems as the 'real' problems may well be characteristic of a society rapidly growing and expanding, as America was in the nineteenth century and, ideologically, in the early twentieth century. The depictive mode of speech and the heavy journalistic 'survey' are intellectual concomitants of an expanding society in which new routines are arising and cities are being built. Such an approach is then sanctioned with canons of what constitutes real knowledge; the practice of the detailed and complete empiricism of the survey is justified by an epistemology of gross description. These norms of adequate knowledge linger in an academic tradition to mold the work of its bearers. The emphasis upon fragmentary, practical problems tends to atomize social objectives. The studies so informed are not integrated into designs comprehensive enough to serve collective action, granted the power and intent to realize such action.

One of the pervasive ways of defining 'problems' or of detecting 'disorganization' is in terms of *deviation from norms*. The 'norms' so used are usually held to be the standards of 'society'. Later we shall see to what type of society they are oriented. In the absence of studies of specific norms themselves this mode of problematization shifts the responsibility of 'taking a stand' away from the thinker and gives a 'democratic' rationale to his work. Rationally, it would seem that those who accept this approach to 'disorganization' would immediately examine these norms themselves. It is significant that, given their interest in reforming society, which is usually avowed, these writers typically assume the norms which they use and often tacitly sanction them. There are few attempts to explain deviations from norms in terms of the norms themselves, and no rigorous facing of the implications of the fact that social transformations would involve shifts *in them*.

The easy way to meet the question of why norms are violated is in terms of biological impulses which break through 'societal restrictions'. A paste-pot eclectic psychology provides a rationale for this facile analysis. Thus, more comprehensive problematization is blocked by a biological theory of social deviation. And the 'explanation' of deviations can be put in terms of a requirement for more 'socialization'. 'Socialization' is either undefined, used as a moral epithet, or implies norms which are themselves without defintion. The focus on 'the facts' takes no cognizance of the normative structures within which they lie.

The texts tend either to be 'apolitical' or to aspire to a 'democratic' opportunism. When the political sphere is discussed, its pathological phases are usually stated in terms of 'the anti-social', or of 'corruption', etc. In another form the political is tacitly identified with the proper functioning of the current and unexamined political order; it is especially likely to be identified with a legal process or the administration of laws. If the 'norms' were examined, the investigator would perhaps be carried to see total structures of norms and to relate these to distributions of power. Such a structural point of sight is not usually achieved. The level of abstraction does not rise to permit examination of these normative structures themselves, or of why they come to be transgressed, or of their political implications. Instead, this literature discusses many kinds of apparently unrelated 'situations'.

About the time W I Thomas stated the vocabulary of the situational approach, a social worker was finding it congenial and useful. In M E Richmond's influential *Social Diagnosis* (1917) we gain a clue as to why pathologists tend to slip past structure to focus on isolated situations, why there is a tendency for problems to be considered as problems of individuals, and why sequences of situations were not seen as linked into structures:

> Social diagnosis ... may be described as the attempt to make as exact a definition as possible of the situation and personality of a human being in some social need – of his situation and personality, that is, in relation to the other human beings upon whom he in any way depends or who depend upon him, and in relation also to the social institutions of his community.

This kind of formulation has been widely applied to isolated 'problems' addressed by sociologists. And the 'situational approach' has an affinity with other elements which characterize their general perspective.

Present institutions train several types of persons – such as judges and social workers – to think in terms of 'situations'. Their activities and mental outlook are set within the existent norms of society; in their professional work they tend to have an occupationally trained incapacity to rise above series of 'cases'. It is in part through such concepts as 'situation' and through such methods as 'the case approach' that social pathologists have been intellectually tied to social work with its occupational position and political limitations. And, again, the similarity of origin and the probable lack of any continuous 'class experience' of the group of thinkers decrease their chances to see social structures rather than a scatter of situations. The mediums of experience and orientation through which they respectively view society are too similar, too homogeneous, to permit the clash of diverse angles which, through controversy, might lead to the construction of a whole.

The paramount fact of immigration in American culture, with each wave of immigrants displacing the lower-class position of former waves and raising the position of the earlier immigrants also tends to obscure structural and class positions. Thus, instead of positional issues, pathologists typically see problems in terms of an individual, such as an immigrant, 'adjusting' to a milieu or being 'assimilated' or Americanized. Instead of problems of class structure involving immigration, the tendency has been to institute problems in terms of immigration involving nationalist assimilation of individuals. The fact that some individuals have had opportunities to rise in the American hierarchy decreases the chances fully to see the ceilings of class. Under these conditions such structures are seen as fluctuating and unsubstantial and are likely to be explained not in terms of *class position* but in terms of *status attitudes*.

Another element that tends to obviate an analytic view of structure is the emphasis upon the 'processual' and 'organic' character of society. In Cooley, whose influence on these books is decisive, one gets a highly formal, many-sided fluidity where 'nothing is fixed or independent, everything is plastic and takes influence as well as gives it'. From the standpoint of political action, such a view may mean a reformism dealing with masses of detail and furthers a tendency to be apolitical. There can be no bases or points of entry for larger social action in a structureless flux. The view is buttressed epistemologically with an emotionalized animus against 'particularism' and with the intense approval of the safe, or colorless, 'multiple-factor' view of causation. The liberal 'multiple-factor' view does not lead to a conception of causation which would permit points of entry for broader types of action, especially political action. No set of underlying structural shifts is given which might be open to manipulation, at key points, and which, like the fact of private property in a corporate economy, might be seen as efficacious in producing many 'problems'. If one fragmentalizes society into 'factors', into elemental bits, naturally one will then need quite a few of them to account for something, and one can never be sure they are all in. A formal emphasis upon 'the whole' plus lack of total structural consideration plus a focus upon scattered situations does not make it easy to reform the status quo.

The 'organic' orientation of liberalism has stressed all those social factors which tend to a harmonious balance of elements. There is a minimization of chances for action in a social milieu where 'there is always continuity with the past, and not only with any one element only of the past, but with the whole interacting organism of man'. In seeing everything social as continuous process, changes in pace and revolutionary dislocations are missed or are taken as signs of the 'pathological'. The formality and the assumed unity implied by 'the mores' also lower the chances to see social chasms and structural dislocations.

Typically, pathologists have not attempted to construct a structural whole. When, however, they do consider totalities, it is in terms of such concepts as 'society', 'the social order', or 'the social organization', 'the mores and institutions', and 'American culture'. Four things should be noted about their use of such terms: (a) The terms represent undifferential entities. Whatever they may indicate, it is systematically homogeneous. Uncritical use of such a term as 'the' permits a writer the hidden assumption in politically crucial contexts of a homogeneous and harmonious whole. The large texture of 'the society' will take care of itself, it is somehow and in the long run harmonious, it has a 'strain toward consistency' running through it; or, if not this, then only the co-operation of all is needed, or perhaps even a right moral feeling is taken as a solution. (b) In their formal emptiness these terms are commensurate with the low level of abstraction. Their *formality* facilitates the empirical concern with 'everyday' problems of (community) milieu. (*c*) In addition to their 'descriptive' use, such terms are used normatively. The 'social' becomes a good term when it is used in ethical polemics against 'individualism' or against such abstract moral qualities as 'selfishness', lack of 'altruism', or of 'antisocial' sentiments. 'Social' is conceived as a 'co-operative' 'sharing' of something or as 'conducive to the general welfare'. The late eighteenth-century use of 'society' as against 'state' by the rising bourgeoisie had already endowed 'society' with a 'democratic' tinge which this literature transmits. (*d*) There is a strong tendency for the term 'society' to be practically assimiliated to, or conceived largely in terms of, primary groups and small homogeneous communities. Such a conception typically characterizes the literature within our purview. In explaining it, we come upon an element that is highly important in understanding the total perspective.

The basis of 'stability', 'order', or 'solidarity' is not typically analyzed in these books, but a conception of such a basis is implicity used and sanctioned, for some normative conception of a socially 'healthy' and stable organization is involved in the determination of 'pathological' conditions. 'Pathological' behavior is not discerned in a *structural sense* (ie, as incommensurate with an existent structural type) or in a *statistical* sense (ie, as deviations from central tendencies). This is evidenced by the regular assertion that pathological conditions *abound* in the city. If they '*abound*' therein, they cannot be 'abnormal' in the statistical sense and are not likely to prevail in the structural sense. It may be proposed that the norms in terms of which 'pathological' conditions are detected are 'humanitarian ideals'. But we must then ask for the social orientation of such ideals. In this literature the operating criteria of the pathological are typically *rural* in orientation and extraction.

Most of the 'problems' considered arise because of the urban deterioration of certain values which can live genuinely only in a relatively homogeneous and primary rural milieu. The 'problems' discussed typically concern urban behavior. When 'rural problems' are discussed, they are considered as due to encroaching urbanization. The notion of disorganization is quite often merely the absence of that *type* of organization associated with the stuff of primary-group communities having Christian and Jeffersonian legitimations.

Cooley, the local colorist of American sociology, was the chief publicist of this conception of normal organization. He held 'the great historical task of mankind' to be the more effective and wider organization of that moral order and pattern of virtues developed in primary groups and communities. Cooley took the idealists' absolute and gave it the characteristics of an organic village; all the world should be an enlarged, Christian-democratic version of a rural village. He practically assimiliated 'society' to this primary-group community, and he blessed it emotionally and conceptually. 'There is reflected here,' says T V Smith of Cooley – and what he says will hold for the typical social pathologist – 'what is highly common in our culture, an ideal of intimacy short of which we do not rest satisfied where other people are concerned. Social distance is a dire fate, achieved with difficulty and lamented as highly unideal, not to say as immoral, in our Christian traditions. It is not enough to have saints; we must have "communion" of the saints. In order to have social relations, we must nuzzle one another.'

The aim to preserve rurally oriented values and stabilities is indicated by the implicit model which operates to detect urban disorganization; it is also shown by the stress upon *community* welfare. The community is taken as a major unit, and often it sets the scope of concern and problematization. It is also within the framework of ideally democratic communities that proposed solutions are to be worked out. It should be noted that sometimes, although not typically or exclusively, solutions are conceived as dependent upon abstract moral traits or democratic surrogates of them, such as a 'unanimous public will'.

'Cultural lag' is considered by many pathologists to be the concept with which many scattered problems may be detected and systematized. Whereas the approach by deviation from norms is oriented 'ideologically' toward a rural type of order and stability, the cultural-lag model is tacitly oriented in a 'utopian' and progressive manner toward changing some areas of the culture or certain institutions so as to 'integrate' them with the state of progressive technology. We must analyze the use made by pathologists of 'lag' rather than abstract formulations of it.

Even though all the situations called 'lags' *exist* in the present, their functional realities are referred back, away from the present. Evaluations are thus translated into a time sequence; cultural lag is an assertion of unequal 'progress'. It tells us what changes are 'called for', what changes 'ought' to have come about and didn't. In terms of various spheres of society it says what progress is, tells us how much we have had, ought to have had, didn't have, and when and where we didn't have it. The imputation of 'lag' is complicated by the historical judgment in whose guise it is advanced and by the programmatic content being shoved into pseudo-objective phrases, as, for example, 'called for'.

It is not enough to recognize that the stating of problems in terms of cultural lag involves evaluations, however disguised. One must find the general loci of this kind of evaluation and then explain why this form of evaluation has been so readily accepted and widely used by pathologists. The model in which institutions lag behind technology and science involves a positive evaluation of natural science and of orderly progressive change. Loosely, it derives from a liberal continuation of the enlightenment with its full rationalism, its messianic and now politically naive admiration of physical science as a kind of thinking and activity, and with its concept of time as progress. This notion of progress was carried into American colleges by the once prevalent Scottish moral philosophy. From after the Civil War through the first two or three decades of the twentieth century the expanding business and middle classes were taking over instruments of production, political power, and social prestige; and many of the academic men of the generation were recruited from these rising strata and/or actively mingled with them. Notions of progress are congenial to those who are rising in the scale of position and income.

Those sociologists who think in terms of this model have not typically focused upon the conditions and interest groups underlying variant 'rates of change' in different spheres. One might say that in terms of the rates of change at which sectors of culture *could* move, it is technology that is 'lagging', for the specific reason of the control of patents, etc, by entrenched interests. In contrast to the pathologists' use, Veblen's use of 'lag, leak, and friction' is a structural analysis of industry versus business enterprise. He focused on where 'the lag' seemed to pinch; he attempted to show how the trained incapacity of legitimate businessmen acting within entrepreneurial canons would result in a commercial sabotage of production and efficiency in order to augment profits within a system of price and ownership. He did not like this 'unworkman-like result', and he detailed its mechanism. In the pathologists' usage the conception has lost this specific and structural anchorage: it has been generalized and applied to everything fragmentarily. This generalization occurs with the aid of such blanket terms as 'adaptive culture' and 'material culture'. There is no specific focus for a program of action embodied in the application of such terms.

Another model in terms of which disorganizations are instituted is that of 'social change' itself. This model is not handled in any one typical way, but usually it carries the implicit assumption that human beings are 'adjusted' satisfactorily to any social condition that has existed for a long time and that, when some aspect of social life changes, it may lead to a social problem. The notion is oriented ideologically and yet participates in assumptions similar to those of cultural lag, which, indeed, might be considered a variant of it. Such a scheme for problematization buttresses and is buttressed by the idea of continuous process, commented on above; but here the slow, 'evolutionary' pace of change is taken explicitly as normal and organized, whereas 'discontinuity' is taken as problematic. The orientation to 'rural' types of organization should be recalled. In line with the stress on continuous process, the point where sanctioned order meets advisable change is not typically or structurally drawn. A conception of 'balance' is usual and sometimes is explicitly sanctioned. The question, 'Changes in what spheres induce disorganization?' is left open; the position taken is usually somewhere between extremes, both of which are held to be bad. This comes out in the obvious fact that what a conservative calls *dis*-organization, a radical might well call *re*organization. Without a construction of total social structures that are actually emerging, one remains caught between simple evaluations.

Besides deviation from norms, orientation to rural principles of stability, cultural lag, and social change, another conception in terms of which 'problems' are typically discussed is that of adaptation or 'adjustment' and their opposites. The pathological or disorganized is the maladjusted. This concept, as well as that of the 'normal', is usually left empty of concrete, social content; or its content, is in effect, a propaganda for conformity to those norms and traits, ideally associated with small-town, middle-class *milieux*. When it is an individual who is thought to be maladjusted, the 'social type' within which he is maladjusted is not stated. Social and normal elements are masked by a quasi-biological meaning of the term 'adaptation' with an entourage of apparently socially bare terms like 'existence' and 'survival', which seem still to draw prestige from the vogue of evolutionism. Both the quasi-biological and the structureless character of the concept 'adjustment' tend, by formalization, to universalize the term, thus again obscuring specific social content. Use of 'adjustment' accepts the goals and the means of smaller community *milieux*. At the most, writers using these terms suggest techniques or means believed to be less disruptive than others to attain the goals that are given. They do not typically consider whether or not certain groups or individuals caught in economically underprivileged situations can possibly obtain the current goals without drastic shifts in the basic institutions which channel and promote them. The idea of adjustment seems to be most directly applicable to a social scene in which, on the one hand, there is a society and, on the other, an individual immigrant. The immigrant then 'adjusts' to the new environment. The 'immigrant problem' was early in the pathologist's center of focus, and the concepts used in stating it may have been carried over as the bases for a model of experience and formulations of other 'problems'. *The Polish Peasant* (1918), which has had a very strong influence on the books under consideration, was empirically focused upon an immigrant group.

In approaching the notion of adjustment, one may analyze the specific illustrations of maladjustment that are given and from these instances infer a type of social person who in this literature is evaluated as 'adjusted'. The ideally adjusted man of the social pathologists is 'socialized'. This term seems to operate ethically as the opposite of 'selfish' it implies that the adjusted man conforms to middle-class morality and motives and 'participates' in the gradual progress of respectable institutions. If he is not a 'joiner', he certainly gets around and into many community organizations. If he is socialized, the individual thinks of others and is kindly toward them. He does not brood or mope about but is somewhat extrovert, eagerly participating in his community's institutions. His mother and father were not divorced, nor was his home ever broken. He is 'successful' – at least in a modest way – since he is ambitious; but he does not speculate about matters too far above his means, lest he become 'a fantasy thinker', and the little men don't scramble after the big money. The less abstract the traits and fulfilled 'needs' of 'the adjusted man' are, the more they gravitate toward the norms of independent middle-class persons verbally living out Protestant ideals in the small towns of America.

9

Values, Socialization and Achievement: Aspects of Positivism in the Sociology of Education *

Robert Colquhoun

To understand existing sociological approaches to the study of education, it is important to examine and make explicit the assumptions and value-judgements implicit in sociological theory in general. My contention here is that sociological theories are what Dawe[1] has called 'doctrines' – combinations of judgements of value as well as of fact, containing social philosophies as well as systems of propositions and concepts. That is, sociological theories are normative: in John Horton's terms[2], they define and explain behaviour from socially situated value positions. They are shaped by the professional and political ideologies of sociologists.

Though one might not realize it from a glance at the textbooks in the sociology of education, there are competing doctrines in sociology. The dominant one has been the 'order' doctrine. One of the few theses about which there has been considerable agreement in debate about sociological theory is that sociology developed in response to the 'problem of order', as defined by Hobbes: if a war of all against all is inevitable, as he maintained, in view of the scarcity of goods available and the lack of means to attain them, how is social order possible? Sociology developed in the nineteenth century as a reaction to what Dawe has termed the subversive rationalism of the Enlightenment, the traumatic disorder of the French Revolution, and the destructive egoism of the Industrial Revolution – three historical movements which appeared to confirm Hobbes' view of man. It was, for example, Durkheim's view that in the face of such forces tending to the destruction of social order, a new source of order and constraint was necessary: 'Society', reified – made, that is, into a 'thing' – with an exist-

* This paper is based on a dissertation for the MA in the Sociology of Education, University of London Institute of Education, 1970. I am particularly grateful to Michael F D Young for his encouragement. Copyright Robert Colquhoun. Goldsmiths College, University of London.

ence independent of that of its members, a reality set over and above the individual, which would curb his ungoverned desires. 'Society' is invested with a 'central value system' which is the ultimate source of moral authority for its members. Through it, 'society' imposes a common meaning and order upon them.

How? Take the dominant tradition in sociological theory, stemming from Durkheim and clearly visible in Parsons and his followers, which postulates a 'consensus' model of society. Crudely oversimplifying, in this perspective society is a relatively stable, persistent and well-integrated 'structure' of elements; every element in a society has a 'function' which contributes to the 'system's' maintenance or equilibrium or survival; and every functioning social structure is based on a consensus of values among its members. For those who adopt this 'structural-functionalist' perspective or 'systems' approach, a key concept is that of social 'role': members of a society 'occupy' roles which contribute to the functioning of the social system and its various 'subsystems' – the family, the education system, the economic system, the political system, the value system etc [3]. But members of a society also have certain acquired dispositions towards the roles 'laid down' for them by 'society' and embodied in the 'expectations' of society's members – dispositions which they have internalized through processes of socialization, which becomes another central concept.

Thus, on this view, the teacher has a 'role' in the educational system, which in its turn has 'functions' which contribute to the maintenance of the social system. In this sense he is a 'socializer' of pupils into the values and norms of the social system and the roles necessary for its 'functioning'. This is the perspective adopted in most sociological studies of so-called 'teaching'. The pupil, on the other hand, is viewed in terms of the dispositions he brings to the school as a consequence of his prior socialization within the home and the degree to which these facilitate or hinder the teacher in his role as a socializer.

Where members of a society hold competing definitions of their 'roles' or have acquired dispositions which are not shared by others, this is accounted for in terms of differing sub-cultural traditions which deviate from the established consensus. Such deviations from the norm are characterized as failures of socialization, a concept and process which, on this view, become the central concern of the sociology of education. Thus, the apparently well-documented social-class differences in educational achievement are explained in terms of the prior socialization of the pupil. The middle-class pupil is successful at school because he has been successfully socialized in terms of the values, child-rearing practices and especially the language patterns of the home. On the other hand, it is said, the working-class pupil fails at school because of his inadequate socialization in terms of the dominant value of achievement, linguistic code etc.

There is no place in this model for the possibility that man may give meanings to his existence which are not those of the 'central value system', nor for the view that he may act in spite of the constraints imposed by the 'social system'. For subjective meanings are supposedly laid down for him; they are derived from the central value or normative or cultural system. They are not only meant to, but they actually do, control behaviour. As for a person's actions, it is said that, because of the assumption of consensus, these may be deduced from a knowledge of his 'role' and his acquired disposition to that role, since his disposition supposedly determines his behaviour in all social situations. In other words, in order to 'solve' the problem of order, the actor is thought of as merely 'reflecting' the social system, and meaning as 'reflecting' the cultural system. Neither action itself nor meaning are, therefore, of interest to the sociologist – on this view. Paradoxically, of no one is this more true than Parsons, who claims to have reinstated the actor in a systems perspective; for, in spite of his assertions to the contrary, there is no action in the Parsonian model of man in society. 'Behaviour' is 'explained' in terms of prior dispositions; 'action' disappears, to be replaced by perpetual 'orientation'[4].

On this argument, the methodological consequences which flow from the structural-functionalist or consensus model are clear. The model is behaviourist. Man is simply a passive object to which things just happen, like the objects studied by natural scientists. The behaviour of man in society may therefore be studied, it is said, through methods analogous to those of the natural sciences, and it is upon them that the logic of sociological enquiry should be based. On this view, in order to understand human behaviour, predispositional 'factors' or 'variables' are singled out and statistically correlated. Those correlations become the data which have to be explained. In time, as a cumulative body of knowledge is amassed, and concepts and methodological techniques become ever more refined, the level of prediction will improve, it is hoped, and ultimately result in a necessary and sufficient set of conditions – a 'cause', long the official trademark of the scientist.

For the sociology of education, therefore, in time statistical correlations will be established between such 'factors' as social-class values, achievement motivation, and linguistic code, sufficient for us to be able to say that we have arrived at a causal explanation of pupil behaviour in the school.

107

The above, it will be argued, have been some of the assumptions implicitly made by those researchers whose work has dominated the sociology of education in the USA and Britain in the 1950's and 1960's. More concretely, and with conscious but not, it is hoped, unfair oversimplification, their thesis may be stated as follows:

It is possible to discern in American and, by inference, British society the existence of a dominant 'value-orientation' towards 'achievement'. Members of those societies tend to be characterized by a high degree of 'achievement motivation', or a high 'need for achievement'. However, it is argued, such values and motives are not present in all social groups to an equal degree: the middle classes, for example, are said to value 'achievement' more highly than the working classes – witness their occupational aspirations – and also to rate more highly on scores of achievement motivation. It is claimed that this largely, if not wholly, 'explains' the apparently well-documented social-class differences in educational achievement to be found in Britain and America. Finally, in an effort to explain how these social-class differences in achievement values and motivation are generated, researchers have tried to investigate the ways in which parental child-rearing practices 'determine', or at any rate influence, the development of children's values and motivation to succeed at school.

As the field is a complex one, it will be considered for analytical purposes under three headings, though in the literature no sustained attempt is made to maintain such distinctions. The three headings are: the achievement value-orientation, achievement motivation, and child-rearing practices.

The achievement value-orientation

The claim that it is possible to discern a dominant value-orientation towards achievement in American society can be traced back to the writings of the anthropologist, Florence Kluckhohn. For example, her typology of what she calls 'basic human problems and their possible solutions' is set out in Banks[7]. Yet it is worth looking closely at some of the writings in which she puts forward this kind of claim[8]: the poverty of the evidence she offers, in support of her broad generalizations about these basic human problems and the personality types to which they allegedly give rise, would be almost laughable if her claims had not been taken so seriously by sociologists of education[9].

More generally, however, there are a number of difficulties in Kluckhohn's account and the inferences drawn from it. There is, first, the problem of establishing the existence of anything which might be called a 'societal value' – such as the value of 'achievement' – about which there is general consensus. In our complex kind of society, which is characterized more by conflict and change than consensus and stability, it is difficult to find any overriding values about which the members of all social groups are in general agreement. Second, to talk in terms of the existence of 'the achievement value-orientation' is too general to be of much help in understanding human action. It is reasonable to suppose that if people do want to 'achieve', it is unlikely that they want to achieve in any and every area – that is, it would seem more useful to specify the areas in which people value achievement highly, instead of talking about a generalized achievement value. Third, even if we were to succeed in establishing that such values exist, there is still the problem of making inferences from values to actions[10]. It is not self-evident that, in their everyday life situations, people's actions follow 'automatically' or 'inevitably' from their values. In the situations of everyday life, they may have so many differing or competing purposes and be subject to so many conflicting pressures that it is hazardous to say that, for example, a pupil is working hard at Chemistry because he values achievement highly. His reasons may be much more mundane; his father may have promised him a bike if he gets a good report; he may be engaged in some competition over marks with his best friend; the teacher may have threatened to punish anyone who gets under half-marks on the test; or the pupil may simply like doing Chemistry.

However, the problems are not eased to any appreciable extent by those who have argued that social classes differ in certain of the values held by their members, especially achievement values as manifested by 'ambition' and 'educational aspirations'. This is the dominant view in the sociology of education. Stemming largely from Kluckhohn's theoretical framework and relying on the use of questionnaires, interviews and to a lesser extent controlled experimental situations, this claim has been built up over the years and been given legitimation through the work of Hyman[11] (using 'the accumulated findings of public opinion surveys'), Rosen[12] (using questionnaires)' Kahl[13] (four thousand questionnaires and twenty-four interviews) and Strodtbeck[14] (one thousand questionnaires, then forty-eight questionnaires and recorded discussions of them) – to name only some of the more well-known American studies. Kahl, in a later paper[15], summarizes the position nicely:

'Each of the field studies reported here had its own purpose, and accordingly devised its own measurements. Samples included high-school boys, adult men, and adult women. Yet the studies all came from the same theoretical stance, and their results proved to be comparable and parallel. Simple attitude items were devised to measure abstract values about certain social relationships and behaviour connected with achievement orientation, and they produced scales that 'worked' in two senses; the same items clung together to define given scales, despite the distances of time, geography and language that divided the field studies; and the correlations of the scales with an outside variable, socioeconomic status, were stable.'

Here Kahl takes for granted precisely those issues which should be treated as problematic [16]: the possibility of devising 'simple attitude items . . . to measure abstract values'; the dubious relationship, discussed above, between actual 'behaviour' and achievement orientation; the assumption that it is possible to divorce items in a scale from the contexts in which researchers generated them ('the distances of time, geography and language that divided the field studies'); and the implicit, though unexplicated, inference that correlations between social-class membership and attitude scales somehow signify a causal relationship between the two 'variables'.

In this country, Kluckhohn's theoretical stance was adopted by a number of researchers in the 1960's, most notably perhaps by Swift and Sugarman. Swift, as a result of his review of the literature [17], suggests that there are two ideal-types of family which produce academically successful children. The first is the middle-class, supportive, 'democratic' family which encourages self-confidence in the children and satisfaction with self-accepted rather than externally-imposed values. The second is the lower middle-class/upper working-class family in which the father is pessimistic about his prospects for upward social mobility and seeks to compensate for this by placing emphasis on his children's academic success and consequent upward mobility. But unlike the middle-class family in which, Swift contends, education is valued intrinsically for its liberating qualities for the individual, in the second type of family education is viewed instrumentally as a process of certificate-collecting.

Having constructed his hypothesis, Swift set about testing it and reported his findings in a later paper [18]. On the basis of 132 interviews about which he says not a word in terms of schedules, direct quotation, or his interpretation and coding of responses, he found his hypothesis confirmed. However, because Swift makes no attempt to recreate the context of the research for other sociologists, the reader can only judge the validity of Swift's 'findings' in terms of what is left unsaid about his research procedures [19].

Also in this country, Sugarman [20] has attempted to verify the existence of social-class differences in values in terms of three of Kluckhohn's value-orientation dimensions: the future/present time-

orientation; activism/being; and individualism/collectivism. He himself gave a questionnaire to all the fourth-year boys (540) in four
London boys' secondary schools (one grammar, two secondary
modern, and one comprehensive school). The following is an example
of his methodology:

'Pupils responded "agree", "disagree", or "don't know" to a list
of statements, some phrased so as to affirm one of the supposed
middle-class values and some in the opposite direction. Thus, to
score highly on *future orientation* pupils would have to disagree with
statements such as "There is no sense in worrying about the future
so long as you are doing all right now" and they would have to
agree to statements such as "You have to give up having a good
time now to do well later on" and "Most times it is better to be
tactful and diplomatic instead of saying just what you think". To
score highly on *activism* they would have to reject statements like
"One must learn to take life as it is without always trying to improve things", and "The greatest source of happiness in life is to be
satisfied with whatever you have." To get high scores for the third
value, *individualism*, they would have to reject statements like "It is
best to be like everyone else and not stand out from the rest", and
endorse others like "Nowadays you have to look out for yourself
before helping your parents".'

Again there is the assumption of shared meanings between respondent, researcher and reader; the assumption that there is no problematic gap between words and deeds[21]; and the assumption that a
response elicited in a questionnaire situation holds in the context of
everyday life situations. Sugarman's hypothesis was broadly
confirmed.

In constructing their theories, hypotheses and ideal types, Banks,
Swift, Sugarman and other British sociologists in this tradition draw
on well-known studies carried out in this country which do not employ a Kluckhohnian typology of value-orientations but which nevertheless appear to support the theory. Such studies include those of
Floud, Halsey and Martin[22], Douglas[23] and the Plowden Report's
National Survey[24]. For example, much is made of apparent social-
class differences in the 'attitudes' which parents show towards education, the 'interest' they display in their children's schooling, and the
'encouragement' with which they provide them. Yet the procedures
by which such 'findings' are produced are rarely questioned. Floud,
Halsey and Martin, for example, in trying to determine the 'attitudes'
of the parents in their sample, carried out interviews about which we
are told absolutely nothing. The move from respondents' statements –
we are given no examples of these – to researcher's interpretation and

coding of the responses is made without commentary.

Again, Douglas has come to the following conclusion: 'The middle-class parents take more interest in their children's progress at school than the manual working-class parents do, and they become relatively more interested as their children grow older'. But there are considerable problems in moving from statements of 'fact' about, for example, the number of books on the shelves at home or the number of visits a parent pays to a school, to the making of inferences about attitudes, interest and dispositions to, in this case, schooling. Again, the researcher is making the assumption that his interpretation of a 'fact' is shared by the respondent and the reader. Similar problems are raised by the well-known finding of the Plowden Report's National Survey that 'variation in parental attitudes can account for more of the variation in children's school achievement than either the variation in home circumstances or the variation in schools'[25].

But another word of warning, about American studies of this kind, has been sounded by Turner[26]. He suggests that a close examination of the studies of social-class differences in values reveals that the relationships claimed are often quite modest – a fact often under-played by researchers who tend to report only significant measures. Furthermore, the characterization of social-class groups in terms of alleged differences in the values they hold is likely to result in the creation by sociologists of mere caricatures of middle- and working-class people, such that any resemblance to living persons is purely coincidental[27].

The danger is perhaps best illustrated by the notions of middle-class 'deferred gratification' and working-class 'immediate gratifica-tion'[28]. These concepts reveal the ideological assumptions which underlie much of the research in this area: what the middle-class do is conceived as the norm, while the working-class are viewed merely as failing to do what the middle-class can do. In other words, such notions contain value judgements which need to be made explicit. The implicit model used is a cultural or social pathology model of working-class behaviour: the working-class are seen as sick, diseased, pathological because they are allegedly unable to 'defer gratification'.

One of the problems, however, is that data about people's 'gratifi-cation patterns' are usually gathered by questionnaire and interview. It is the researcher who, on the basis of such data, attributes to the respondent a willingness, or otherwise, to defer gratification. How-ever, the researcher usually fails to observe the social member in particular situations to find out what he actually does and how the member, rather than the researcher, interprets what he does. Unlike the researcher, the social member may not interpret a given action in a specific situation as having anything to do with the immediate satisfying or deferring of his 'gratifications'.

Achievement motivation

Achievement values are said to be one component of what has been called the 'achievement syndrome'. The other component is 'achievement motivation' or the 'need for achievement' – a psychological concept developed by McClelland and his associates in the early 1950's and defined as underlying 'persistent striving activity, aimed at attaining a high goal in some area involving competition with a standard of excellence'[29].

Although the concept was psychological in origin, sociologists quickly showed an interest in it, particularly in response to the early suggestion that achievement values 'define and implement' achievement motivation[30]. Basically, achievement motivation is measured in two ways. Subjects undergo Thematic Apperception Tests in which they are shown pictures (perhaps of a boy sitting at a desk in a classroom) and asked to say what they represent. Their responses are then scored for achievement motivation imagery in a highly complex way. Alternatively, subjects are given questionnaires designed to test achievement motivation.

However, there are a number of criticisms which might be made of work in this tradition[31]. First, as with the achievement value-orientation, the concept of achievement motivation is too general: it seems necessary to take into account that people presumably differ in the areas in which they want to 'achieve' and in the meanings they give to the term. Second, it is important to study people in their actual situations in everyday life (eg pupils in school contexts) rather than present them with the contrived situations provided by McClelland's pictures and questionnaires. Third, there are considerable problems – which McClelland's associates do not deny – in scoring the tests. Fourth, the contention that an achievement 'syndrome' exists is doubtful. Although achievement values are supposed to 'define and implement' achievement motivation, the evidence is in fact contradictory: at best there is a positive, but low, correlation between scores on tests of achievement value and motivation. However, it does seem surprising that two factors which are supposedly components in a syndrome should appear to bear so little relationship to one another. Finally, numerous attempts have been made to relate achievement motivation to school performance[32]. Where the Thematic Apperception Tests have been used, there is no relation between the two; but where questionnaires are used, there is some degree of correlation. However, the much sought-after 'causal' relation has certainly not been established.

Child-rearing practices.

In an effort to explain alleged social-class differences in achievement values and motivation, sociologists and psychologists have tried to investigate the ways in which parents from different social classes bring up their children. Researchers have doubtless been encouraged in this endeavour by statements like that of Parsons[33]:

> 'There is room to believe that, among the learned elements of personality, in certain respects the stablest and most enduring are the major value-orientation patterns, and there is much evidence that these are "laid down" in childhood and are not on a large scale subject to drastic alteration during adult life. There is good reason to treat these patterns of value-orientation . . . as the core of what is sometimes called "basic personality structure" '.

There are a number of questionable assumptions here. The view that there is such a thing as 'basic personality' which is largely explicable as the product of interpersonal relations in early childhood and remains constant throughout life is a psychologism which has been persuasively challenged by Becker[34] – to name only one of a number of critics. This is not to deny that important learning does take place in the early years of a person's life; but it is to say that early socialization is not necessarily *all*-important: much learning takes place after the early years of childhood, in primary and secondary school and in adult life, as many people would probably attest from their own biographies.

On the relation between child-rearing practices and the development of achievement values and motivation, the evidence is – frankly – a mass of anomalies and inconsistencies. Some of these are discussed by Banks[35], who is generally sympathetic to the work done in this field, and more critically and in greater detail by Colquhoun[36]. In this connection, even Bernstein's research into socialization and language, which to many has been by far the most interesting, persuasive and influential work in this area, has been under attack in the writings of Coulthard[37], Labov[38], and Rosen[39]. Furthermore, as Friedman[40] and Baratz and Baratz[41] have argued, it is particularly in the area of socialization that the social pathology model of working-class behaviour is most damagingly evident.

The above is a characterization, necessarily highly simplified, of the dominant paradigm in the sociology of education. Yet it would, of course, be wrong to suggest that the conception of man and society which it implies has gone wholly unopposed. As Dawe[42] has argued, historically sociology did not simply originate in answer to the 'problem of order'; an alternative source from which sociology developed lay in the problem posed by thinkers of the Enlightenment – the 'problem of control': how could human beings regain *control* over man-made institutions and historical situations? The thinkers of the Enlightenment put forward a human construction of the ideal – the creative imposition of a human (as opposed to a supra-human) meaning upon the actual. Thus, in this perspective, three central concepts emerge: the first is *action*, which is the 'attempt to exert control over existing situations, relationships and institutions'. To this is joined a second concept, *meaning*: 'to control a situation is to impose meaning upon it by acting upon it'. To this may be added a third concept, *interaction*, in that 'to control a situation is (also) to impose one's definition upon the other actors in that situation'.

On this view, human action is not the product of factors which play on or through the human actor – 'factors' such as values, norms, cultural prescriptions and 'needs'. The human being is more than a 'medium' or 'forum' for the operation of factors which produce behaviour. Rather, human action is viewed as constructed by the actor; it is not just response elicited from some kind of pre-formed organization within him. Action is not simply released from a pre-existing psychological structure, but is built up by the actor as he copes with his world[43].

It is this 'human capacity for the construction of meaning' which distinguishes the subject-matter and the logic of sociological enquiry from that of the natural sciences. The facts, data and events in the natural scientist's field of observation do not 'mean' anything to the molecules, atoms and electrons he observes; but the facts, data and events of the world observed by the sociologist *do* have meaning for the human beings who live, think and act within it[44]. Thus it may be possible to view the phenomena investigated by the natural sciences as passive objects, for which the events of that world have no meaning; but such a view is not applicable to the study of man, since being human implies subjectivity – man subjectively interprets the events of his world in order to make sense of them and give them meaning. Man living in his social world is not like the objects of the physical world – to which things just happen. To compare man to object is to suggest that he is merely passive and reactive; it is to ignore his activity, his consciousness, his intentionality, and his attempts to transcend and not merely succumb to the circumstances that supposedly constrain him. To liken man to object is to fail to take into account that his world is not simply created for him: he creates his own reality[45].

To think otherwise is, in Marxist terms, to be alienated and to reify 'the world'. If alienation is 'the process by which man forgets that the world he lives in has been produced by himself'[46], then reification is the moment in the process of alienation in which what man produces is, literally, made into a thing, conceived of as having an objective reality. Reification may take place on a theoretical level, as in the sociological concept of role. Action is reified when we say that the actor did something *because* he is such and such a *type* of person. Actions are conceived as roles, and actors as embodiments of roles: that is, role-playing *replaces* existence. Roles, not people, become the prime reality. This mystifies actual situations and eliminates human intentionality and choice. People act as they do, and may come to see themselves as acting, 'because' they 'have no choice'. Such reifications, it could be argued, are reifications of the values and motives of dominant groups in society – a means of exercising effective social control by imposing their definitions and meanings on others. 'Achievement value-orientation' and 'achievement motivation' are further examples of reified theoretical constructs.

What can be done, sociologically, about such reified sociology? The essential problem is that 'Sociology has lost its own subject-matter. A sociology which retains a grasp of itself and its subject-matter must be a continuing clarification of everyday life. The fulfilling of this task entails a critique of consciousness, which is the very stuff of everyday life'[47]. In other words, any understanding of human action which lays claim to sociological validity must begin with an understanding of how human beings interpret, and act in, their everyday life situations[48].

It must be pointed out, therefore, that both the role studies of the teacher which have proliferated in the sociology of education[49], and the attempts to explain pupils' learning in terms of the dispositions they bring to the school, are not studies of the activities of teaching and learning in the classroom. For reasons already discussed, neither sociologists in general nor sociologists of education in particular have thought it necessary to discuss the human actor in his everyday life settings; mistakenly, they have not begun, in Goffman's terms – 'where the action is'[50] – in this case, in the classroom and, more generally, in the school itself.

Becker's paper 'Becoming a marihuana user'[51] provides an illustration of this thesis. Explanations of why people smoke marihuana are usually given in terms of some psychological disposition, such as a 'need to escape from the "real" world'. But Becker argues that there is a problematic gap to be crossed between being willing to do a thing and actually doing it. He deliberately starts with the person willing to try marihuana, but suggests that there are still a number of stages which the person goes through if he is to smoke marihuana for pleasure: learning the technique, learning to perceive the effects and learning to enjoy them. Each of these is problematic to the learner and involves redefinition by him usually in the course of interaction with others. Becker in fact argues that in his study the actor 'develops a disposition or motivation to use marihuana which was not and could not have been present when he began use, for it involves and depends on conceptions of the drug which could only grow out of the . . . actual experience of using it. In other words, in this case, deviant motives actually develop in the course of the deviant activity . . .: instead of the deviant motives leading to the deviant behaviour, it is the other way round; the deviant behaviour in time produces the deviant motivation'.

Can we generalize from this to other forms of activity? Might it not be that for the pupil in the school, his motives are formed not as dispositions prior to schooling, but involve conceptions of school knowledge which he builds up in the course of interaction with teachers and other pupils? In other words we must, I suggest, focus our attention on the context and process by which 'a subject is *converted* to conduct novel for him but already established for others'[52]; we must consider the context and the process by which the novice may be 'turned on' or 'out'. What is involved, then, is a shift in perspective and emphasis from 'must' to 'may', from the traditional view that a form of behaviour is passively caught like a contagious disease to the idea that man may be converted and may become committed to one of several competing forms of action against which he has to choose.

But although on this view man is endowed with the possibility of choice, it is important to bear in mind that the forms of behaviour made available to him, from which he may choose, are not limitless: the alternatives offered to him will have been produced by other men and therefore exist to varying degrees as social constraints upon his action. Hence the importance of examining, for example, the institutionally organized character of the knowledge which teachers make available in schools – a question traditionally unexamined by sociologists of education, as Young has argued[53].

In short, the pupil must, as it were, be followed as he moves through the school, for there is considerable evidence that in interaction with teachers and pupils within the school itself, and not simply within the home and the community, the pupil's willingness and ability to be 'educated' may be both formed, maintained, modified and even transformed[54].

Notes

[1] A DAWES, 'The two sociologies', *BJS*, **21**, 1970.

[2] J HORTON, 'Order and conflict theories of social problems as competing ideologies'. *AJS*, **71**, 1966.

[3] Cotgrove's well-known textbook provides a clear illustration of these themes. S COTGROVE, *The Science of Society*.

[4] DAWES, *op cit*.

[5] The literature in this tradition has been lucidly summarized in O BANKS, *The Sociology of Education*, Batsford, 1968, chapters 4 and 5.

[6] See, eg, BANKS, *op cit*, chapter 3.

[7] BANKS, *op cit*, chapter 4.

[8] See, eg F R KLUCKHOHN, *Variations in the basic values of family systems*. In D F SWIFT (ed), Basic Readings in the Sociology of Education. RKP 1970.

[9] For a detailed critique, see R F COLQUHOUN, MA dissertation, 1970. University of London Institute of Education Library.

[10] See, eg H S BECKER, *Outsiders*, Free Press, 1963, chapter 7.

[11] H H HYMAN, 'The value system of different classes', in R BENDIX and S LIPSET, (eds) *Class, Status and Power*. RKP 1954.

[12] B C ROSEN, 'The achievement syndrome.' *ASR* **21**, 1956.

[13] J A KAHL, 'Common man boys'. In A H HALSEY ET AL (eds) *Education, Economy and Society*, Free Press, 1961.

[14] F L STRODTBECK, 'Family integration, values, and achievement', in HALSEY ET AL, *op cit*.

[15] J A KAHL, 'Some measurements of achievement orientation'. *AJS* **70**, 1965.

[16] A V CICOUREL, *Method and Measurement in Sociology*. Free Press, 1964.

[17] D F SWIFT, 'Social class and achievement motivation', in SWIFT (ed) *op cit*.

[18] D F SWIFT, 'Social class, mobility-ideology and eleven-plus success', *BJS*, **18**, 1967.

[19] Cf CICOUREL, *op cit*.

[20] B N SUGARMAN, 'Social class and values as related to achievement and conduct in school'. *Sociological Review*, **14**, 1966.

[21] I DEUTSCHER, 'Words and deeds', *Social Problems*, **13**, 1966.

[22] J FLOUD, A H HALSEY and F M MARTIN, *Social Class and Educational Opportunity*, Heinemann, 1956.

[23] J W B DOUGLAS, *The Home and the School*, MacGibbon and Kee, 1964.

[24] Report of the Central Advisory Council for Education (England), *Children and their Primary Schools*, HMSO, 1967.

[25] *Ibid.* 2, Appendix 4, p. 184. For a critique of this conclusion see B BERNSTEIN and B DAVIES. Some sociological comments on Plowden. In R S PETERS (ed) *Perspectives on Plowden*. RKP 1969.

[26] R H TURNER, *The Social Context of Ambition*, 213, Chandler, 1964.

[27] It could be argued that this is the tendency to be found in, eg, J KLEIN, *Samples from English Cultures*. RKP, 1965.

[28] L SCHNEIDER and S LYSGAARD, 'The deferred gratification pattern', ASR, **18**, 1953.

[29] B C ROSEN, *op cit*.

[30] *Ibid.*

[31] See, eg, I KATZ, 'The socialization of academic motivation in minority group children', in D Levine, (ed) *Nebraska Symposium on Motivation*, 1967.

[32] D E LAVIN, *The Prediction of Academic Performance*, Russell Sage Foundation, 1965.

[33] T PARSONS, *The Social System*, RKP, 1951, 208.

[34] H S BECKER. 'Personal change in adult life', in B R COSIN ET AL (eds) *School and Society*, RKP 1971.

[35] BANKS, *op cit*.

[36] R F COLQUHOUN, *op cit*.

[37] M COULTHARD, A discussion of restricted and elaborated codes, in A CASHDAN and E GRUGEON (eds) *Language in Education*, RKP, 1972.

[38] W LABOV, *The logic of nonstandard English*, *ibid*.

[39] H ROSEN, *Language and Class*, Falling Wall Press, 1972.

[40] N L FRIEDMAN, 'Cultural deprivation: a commentary in the sociology of knowledge'. *Journal of Educational Thought*. **I**. 1967.

[41] S S BARATZ and J C BARATZ, 'Early childhood intervention: the social science base of institutional racism', *Harvard Educational Review*, **40**, 1970.

[42] A DAWES, *op cit*.

[43] H BLUMER, 'Sociological implications of the thought of George Herbert Mead,' in B R COSIN ET AL, *op cit*.

[44] A SCHUTZ, *Collected Papers*, **I**, ch 1, Martinus Nijhoff, The Hague, 1967.

[45] D MATZA, *Becoming Deviant*, Prentice-Hall, 1969.

[46] P L BERGER and S PULLBERG, 'Reification and the sociological critique of consciousness'. *New Left Review*, **35**, 1966.

[47] *Ibid*.

[48] *Cf* J D DOUGLAS (ed) *Understanding Everyday Life*, RKP, 1971.

[49] See M COULSON, *Role: a redundant concept in sociology?* in J A JACKSON (ed) *Role*, Cambridge UP 1972.

[50] E GOFFMAN, *The Presentation of Self in Everyday Life*. Doubleday Anchor, 1957.

[51] H S BECKER, 'Becoming a marihuana user'. In his *Outsiders*. Free Press, 1963. Also in COSIN ET AL, *op cit*. I am grateful to John Hayes of the University of London Institute of Education for first drawing my attention to the possible relevance of Becker's paper for the sociology of education.

[52] D MATZA, *op cit*.

[53] M F D YOUNG (ed) *Knowledge and Control*, ch 1, Collier-Macmillan, 1971.

[54] An attempt is made in the early units (eg nos 1.12) of the Open University's School and Society Course to give the neglected situation in the school itself some of the emphasis it merits.

10

Cultural Deprivation: a commentary on the Sociology of Knowledge *

Norman L Friedman

'Culturally deprived' children and 'cultural deprivation' are terms that have been extensively used and heard in recent years. Perhaps enough time has now passed to warrant an examination of and reflection upon the idea of cultural deprivation in the tradition of the sociology of knowledge – looking into its nature, social and cultural context, development, impact, and interest group support and opposition[1]. The years from about 1955 through early 1967 will be surveyed, with emphasis upon the 1960's[2].

Development

In 1955, the presidential address at the School Psychology division of the annual meetings of the American Psychological Association dealt with 'Cultural Deprivation and Child Development'. The president, a psychologist with the Bureau of Educational Research of the Board of Education of New York City, attempted to discuss those aspects of the anthropological and sociological literature about cultural and social class differences that would be of greatest relevance to school psychologists. References were made to 'deprived homes', 'deprived areas', and the 'emotional deprivation' of some children. Describing an experimental study of a group of lower-class New York City school children, she reported that an attitude syndrome of 'cultural deprivation', based upon environmental limitations and handicaps, could be identified: low self conceptions, guilt and shame feelings, distrust, and family problems. Such experiences adversely affected a child's motivation and functioning in school and even impaired school adjustment before entry. The address was subsequently published in *High Points*, the journal of the New York City Board of Education[3].

The notions of 'cultural deprivation' and 'culturally deprived' children and youth caught on, particularly within the mammoth New

* *Journal of Educational Thought*, 1 (2) 1967, pp 88–99.

York City school system. By 1958, another psychologist with the Board's Bureau of Educational Research, in an article which contrasted homes of 'cultural deprivation' with 'culturally privileged' homes, could use these terms as a matter of course, in an almost self-evident fashion[4].

New York City became a pioneer in experimental efforts to improve the education of so-called culturally deprived learners through the Demonstration Guidance Project and Higher Horizons Program, 1956–62. The orientations towards 'compensatory' practices designed to alleviate cultural deprivation – special guidance, 'cultural enrichment', smaller classes, additional services – became models for similar improvement projects subsequently launched in other cities and states.

While experimental and demonstration projects increased, a cumulative body of literature about cultural deprivation developed. It emphasized the cognitive and linguistic problems of the children, and indicated that deprivation deficits caused them to fall more and more behind as they proceeded through school. A new classification of 'cultural deprivation' was added to *The Education Index*, beginning with 21 entries in volume 13, July 1961 – June 1963;[5] by volume 15, July 1964–June 1965, the number had grown to 122 entries[6].

The following is a fairly typical illustration of the widespread portrait of the culturally deprived child that had emerged by the first third of the 1960's:

> . . . he is essentially the child who has been isolated from those rich experiences that should be his. This isolation may be brought about by poverty, by meagerness of intellectual resources in his home and surroundings, by the incapacity, illiteracy, or indifference of his elders or of the entire community. He may have come to school without ever having had his mother sing him the traditional lullabies, and with no knowledge of nursery rhymes, fairy stories, or the folklore of his country. He may have taken few trips – perhaps his only one the cramped, uncomfortable trip from the lonely shack on the tenant farm to the teeming, filthy slum dwelling – and he probably knows nothing of poetry, music, painting, or even indoor plumbing[7].

Meanwhile, an important new twist was added to thought and experimentation about cultural deprivation in the 1960s: the pre-school emphasis. Psychologists postulated that the 'critical' pre-school years, especially ages three and four, were the most effective and strategic stage of life to administer a diet of compensatory 'planned enrichment'[8]. This would function as a counteractive 'antidote' for the 'experiental inadequacies' of cultural deprivation, and afford lower-class children some familiarity with pre-school experiences and objects common in the lives of middle-class children:

> ... cultural deprivation may be seen as a failure to provide an opportunity for infants and young children to have the experiences required for adequate development of those semi-autonomous central processes demanded for acquiring skill in the use of linguistic and mathematical symbols and for the analysis of casual relationships. The difference between the culturally deprived and the culturally privileged is, for children, analogous to the difference between cage-reared and pet-reared rats and dogs.[9]

Pre-school programmes designed to teach about objects, concepts, shapes, colours, and animals, such as Baltimore's Early School Admissions Project (begun in 1963), followed.

By 1964, the cultural deprivation concept had become recognized by many as an important addition to educational knowledge; 'gross and undifferentiated . . . however, . . . the concept points in a very promising direction[10]'. In a broad way it offered a theoretical explanation for the fact that the lower-class student tended to perform inadequately in schools, a description of this type of child's environmental circumstances and personal style, and an initial prescription for pre- and regular school remedies. A group of prominent scholars, mainly psychologists and educationists, met that year at the University of Chicago for a Research Conference on Education and Cultural Deprivation. The published results of the conference, *Compensatory Education for Cultural Deprivation*[11], set forth a consensus position on the nature, causes, characteristics of, and remedial measures designed for culturally deprived students. By 1964, then, the cultural deprivation idea had decidedly emerged as a theoretical concept fashioned by numerous psychological and educational researchers. But it was also potentially something more: a popular image.

Public Response

In the growing public concern in the 1950's and 1960's for the education of lower-class children, three books (or at least their titles), stimulated and influenced the popular imagination: the novel (and film) *The Blackboard Jungle*[12] in the 1950's, Conant's *Slums and Suburbs*[13] in the early 1960's, and (probably third in impact) psychologist Frank Riessman's *The Culturally Deprived Child*,[14] published in 1962.

As to its social impact, *The Culturally Deprived Child* was probably less important for its specific contents than for its title, which reinforced and broadened the use of the term. After some initial reservations, *culturally deprived* was employed throughout the book, 'because it is the term in current usage'[15]. This no doubt added greatly to the wide popularization of the concept and image. The book became one of those few volumes that is written for a smaller, specialized audience but for one reason or another attracts the interest and attention of a much wider audience of intelligent laymen. In this regard *The Culturally Deprived Child* was selected as one of the 'notable books of 1962' by the American Library Association.

Popular interest in culturally deprived children was stimulated after 1963 by the federal government's 'war on poverty' and the increased drive of the civil rights movement. Education became viewed by many as a major means of improving the plight of poor people and minority groups. In the Kennedy-Johnson era of the 1960's, the poverty programme's Economic Opportunity Act 1964 sought to aid the education of the poor through the pre-school Operation Head Start programme, Project Upward Bound, and the Job Corps. The Elementary and Secondary Education Act of 1965 authorised over one billion dollars expressly to strengthen elementary and secondary school programmes for culturally deprived students. The winds of policy making and implementation had obviously picked up the cultural deprivation theme.

What seems to have happened was that the idea of culturally deprived children was successful as a trigger for legislative action because it possessed an extensive and flexible image appeal to a broad spectrum of persons and publics of various ideological persuasion. To the social and political liberals of the Kennedy-Johnson era, cultural deprivation as explanatory theory and popular image seemed to be a valid and reasonable interpretation of the scholastic retardation of lower-class children in slum schools, and pre- and regular school compensatory programmes presented hopeful possible solutions for this condition. A dynamic educational programme also seemed to liberals to be an important way to advance the progress of minority groups.

Even to political and social conservatives, nationally supported educational programmes held out the hope of 'straightening out' and 'keeping straight' lower-class children, of helping to make and keep them good, respectable, solid citizens, and of preventing the 'social dynamite' in the slums from exploding or re-exploding. Such an orientation was not new in American history. Education has frequently served as America's major and most popular instrument of social reform and as a presumed cure-all for social and political ills. In the nineteenth century, support from conservatives for the establishment of universal public education was sought on the grounds that an educated citizenry would not run wild or foment revolutions, but would be taught to maintain and preserve the status quo[16]. Christopher Jencks has suggested that the War on Poverty in the 1960's has also been basically conservative in the same sense that it primarily aims not only to make over the poor by educating them, but also by changing their 'wrong skills', places of residence, personality traits, and fertility patterns, and to provide 'character building' in the lower-middle-class virtues:[17] '. . . this approach has met with enthusiastic support from those middle-class Americans who feel that if "they" were just more like "us", everything would be all right'.[18]

An example of the above tendencies was the official response to the riots by Los Angeles Negroes in the summer of 1965. The subsequent report on the riots by the governor's moderate/conservative McCone Commission turned to cultural deprivation theory and image as its major explanation for the lower achievement of students in 'disadvantaged areas' and proposed extensive pre-school education as an antidote:

> Children in disadvantaged areas are often deprived in their pre-school years of the necessary foundations for learning. They have not had the full range of experiences so necessary to the development of language in the pre-school years, and hence they are poorly prepared to learn when they enter school. Their behaviour, their vocabulary, their verbal abilities, their experience with ideas, their view of adults, of society, of books, of learning, of schools, and of teachers are such as to have a negative impact on their school experience. Thus, the disadvantaged child enters school with a serious educational handicap, and because he gets a poor start in school, he drops further behind as he continues through the grades. His course towards academic failure is already set before he enters school, it is rooted in his earliest childhood experiences. The Commission concludes that this is the basic reason for low achievement in the disadvantaged areas.[19]

Opposing views

In recent years, several writers have expressed opposition to the cultural deprivation idea. It has been criticized on the grounds of being conceptually inaccurate and theoretically inadequate, of being an incorrect explanation of massive scholastic retardation, of being an obstacle to active civil rights progress, and of being a device to force a questionable middle-class culture on lower-class students.

Riessman early pointed out that culturally deprived was an inappropriate usage, since lower-class children do possess a culture of their own, however different from middle-class culture.[20] Obviously many who originally used the designation must have conceived of 'culture' in the popular sense of 'high culture', rather than in the broader anthropological sense. This is seen in the frequent use made of the educationist's concept of 'cultural enrichment' as a response to those who allegedly are deprived of (high) culture.

Bernard Mackler and M G Giddings, researchers with New York City's Center for Urban Education, observed that the cultural deprivation idea is theoretically inadequate, because it assumes that a certain kind of deprivation leads to a certain universal reaction, without explaining away the variety of different reactions and adaptations: 'an adequate theory of deprivation must eventually explain why certain pupils succeed and others do not, given the same social background'.[21]

As discussed previously, the cultural deprivation idea has been the most widely used and accepted explanation for the comparative scholastic retardation (as measured in IQ and achievement tests) of slum school students. Such explanations, like that quoted earlier from the McCone Commission Report, have stressed the devastating impact of community and neighbourhood environmental conditions upon the slum child. Kenneth B Clark, former head of Harlem Youth Opportunities Unlimited, contended to the contrary that there is no overwhelming evidence that cultural deprivation is the major reason for this retardation. He reported that studies in Harlem showed that the attitude of teachers towards their students emerged as the crucial explanatory factor:

> The evidence . . . seems to indicate that a child who is expected by the school to learn does so; the child of whom little is expected produces little. Stimulation and teaching based upon positive expectation seem to play an even more important role in a child's performance in school than does the community environment from which he comes.[22]

Clark also asserted that the culturally deprived label too often is used as an 'alibi' to cover up the educational ineffectiveness of teachers and schools.[23]

The cultural deprivation idea has also been criticized as an obstacle to active civil rights progress, in that it has helped to promote a negative stereotype of Negroes and has conservatively directed attention away from the more basic problem of *de facto* segregation. Mackler and Giddings suggested that the term persists because it implies that Negroes have an inferior and deprived culture and thereby perpetuates the 'myth' that Negro and lower-class children are of inherent, inferior ability in comparison with middle-class children.[24]

Cultural deprivation has therefore been accused of being a notion that focuses all attention upon the alleged failings of minority members, rather than the shortcomings and cruelties of the dominant society.[25] A psychologist presented this argument quite emphatically:

> The new ideology, accepted now even by some liberals would make it seem that unemployment, poor education and slum conditions result from family breakdown, 'cultural deprivation', and lack of 'acculturation' of Southern rural migrants.

> To sustain this ideology, it is necessary to engage in the popular new sport of Savage Discovery and, to fit the theory, savages are being discovered in great profusion in the Northern ghetto. The all time favourite 'Savage' is the promiscuous mother who produces a litter of illegitimate brats in order to profit from AFDC. Other triumphs of savage discovery are the child who cannot read because, it is said, his parents never talk to him, and the 'untenant-able' Negro family (apparently a neologism for 'unbearable') that is reputed to throw garbage out the window.

> . . . we are told the Negro's condition is due to his 'pathology', his values, the way he lives, the kind of family life he leads. . . . It is all rather painful as well as fallacious. For the fact is that *the Negro child learns less not because his mother doesn't subscribe to* The Reader's Digest *and doesn't give him coloured crayons for his third birthday, but because he is miseducated in segregated slum schools* . . . The Negro is more often unemployed because he is last hired and first fired . . . the condition of housing is more easily explained by the neglect of slum landlords, and the crowding caused by the criminal shortage of decent low-income housing.[26] (Author's italics)

By the same token, it has been argued that cultural deprivation, with its emphasis on change in individual life-styles, detracts from the need for large-scale structural changes in education, such as an end to *de facto* segregation. The McCone Commission Report has been criticized for ignoring the problem of *de facto* segregation, while high-lighting cultural deprivation and pre-school enrichment, and thus playing up Negro cultural backgrounds rather than the educational inequalities and imbalances maintained by the white power groups.[27]

A final source of opposition to the cultural deprivation idea, per-haps still more potential than actual, is the view that programmes designed to upgrade and 'enrich' the lives of culturally deprived students are unfortunate in the sense that they attempt to impose the sickness, inadequacy, inhumanity and hypocrisy of the dominant middle-class society upon lower-class youngsters. A full-blown view along these lines still awaits elaboration, possibly in conjunction with some more specific future application of the New Left's critique of contemporary American society to the educational problems of lower-class children. One glimpse of the possible shape of things to come in this respect, however, is in the writings of educational sociologist Edgar Friendenberg. He has generally taken the position that public education all too successfully moulds American youth into the stultification, evil and absurdity of the dominant middle-class adult culture. Thus lower-class dropouts, who are genuinely sincere and loyal human beings, are driven out because of 'moral revulsion from the middle-class life of the school'.[28]

School practitioners

What about the influence upon and reactions of school practitioners, especially the teachers who deal daily with so-called culturally deprived students? As a result of transmission of knowledge from researchers to practitioner, the *NEA Journal*, publication of the National Education Association and received by all its members, carried its first article with the term 'culturally deprived child' specifically in the title in April, 1961.[29] It was written by a New York City school administrator. The April 1963 issue of the *NEA Journal* devoted fifteen pages and seven articles to discussions of approaches to and programmes for culturally deprived students. Riessman's *The Culturally Deprived Child* was written '. . . to provide teachers . . . with a picture of the deprived individual, including his psychology and culture, that will enable them to work with this individual in a fruitful, non-patronizing manner'.[30] Other writings[31] have subsequently also intended to inform, aid and advise practitioners concerning strategies by which they can more effectively 'reach' and communicate with lower-class students.[32] Moreover, numerous large city school systems, in addition to participating in experimental programmes, have sponsored special faculty sessions or formal communications concerning urban educational problems and cultural deprivation. Some schools of education have recently initiated special courses about culturally deprived learners.

The kind and extent of influence that such writings and activities have had on teachers is not precisely known. One survey found that 294 elementary school teachers in a California city 'agreed a good deal more than they disagreed' with Riessman's observations in *The Culturally Deprived Child*, but the procedures employed prevented much real depth-of-insight into the matter.[33] In the absence of more precise information, the writer will offer some speculative suggestions, based upon personal experiences as an interviewer of public school teachers in social research and as an instructor of pre-service and in-service school teachers.

His first personal contact with the cultural deprivation idea came in early 1963. At that time, he was interviewing teachers in a central city public junior college located in a border state metropolitan area. Alarmed at the growing number of Negro students in their college since the desegregation decision in 1954, and the increase in remedial English sections and students on probation, a number of teachers, without being asked, stressed to the interviewer that many of their students, particularly the Negroes, were, as they put it, 'culturally deprived'. The idea of cultural deprivation, which had been formally diffused throughout that larger public school system during the 1962–63 academic year, seemed to many of these junior college teachers to be a satisfactory and logical conceptualization that explained what they felt was lacking in their troublesome low achievement, lower-class students.

The writer has had subsequent experiences at a California university, transmitting some of the cultural deprivation literature to education students through readings and the classroom. It seems that many of the in-service teachers with some experience in slum schools have seriously questioned and often rejected what they have read, particularly when it seemed to contradict their own experiences, to 'over-romanticize' culturally deprived students, or to be highly critical of the effectiveness of slum school teachers.

One student, for example, reacting in a written critique to Riessman's emphasis upon the 'positive strengths' of the culturally deprived child's extended family life and sense of humour,[34] responded (according to Riessman) that:

There is more equalitarianism, informality, warm humour and security found in the extended family . . . it is in this area that I question his theory. For several years I worked in Harlem, New York and was not aware of these strengths which Riessman speaks of. It is true that in most of the cases the families were large and had an assortment of relatives living in the apartment. However, rather than noticing a strong feeling of cooperation and security it seemed to me that there was very little of this and the individuals went their separate ways, without too much concern for the other members of the family. If the social worker wanted to do something for the child, that was OK but nobody seemed to care too much and there seemed to be a general feeling of apathy. I do not doubt that there was informality in the family but the warm humour and friendly give and take which Riessman stresses were not qualities that I noticed.

In similar vein, in a published article a New York City high school teacher wrote that '. . . the college professor who reads . . . Riessman's *The Culturally Deprived Child* is mistaken if he thinks he can tell us why our schools have failed'.[35] The teacher then argued that the environmental problems of students are so enormous that they make even the most devoted and energetic teacher's effectiveness low in the face of bad discipline, poor reading, and sordid self-images:

> As a teacher in a ghetto school, it is not surprising that I have dared voice the foregoing opinions. I feel, in fact, that I am saying things that many teachers believe though few find it expedient to say.[36]

The above illustrations have been used to formulate the following speculative suggestions: teachers have tended to find cultural deprivation a suitable explanation and conceptualization for what they feel is either troubling or lacking in their lower-class students; by the same token, they are somewhat skeptical of these aspects of the cultural deprivation literature that view such students in a more favourable and positive light or that indicate that the primary responsibility for the ineffectiveness of slum school education rests upon the shoulders of teachers.

Concluding observations

The cultural deprivation idea began to be developed in the mid-1950's by various psychologists and educators, particularly in the New York City area. Most of the researchers and scholars centrally involved in both the development of and opposition to the idea have been psychologists (school, educational, developmental and social). As an explanatory theory, it was largely psychological in its (a) emphasis upon the technical problems of learning; (b) use of such terms as 'deprivation', 'cage-reared and pet-reared rats and dogs', 'cognitive deficit'; (c) great stress upon the lifelong importance of experiences during the first four years of life; (d) sometimes amateurish and erroneous misuse of sociological and anthropological concepts as they were grafted on to psychological assumptions and pre-conceptions in education. (Of course at the time the idea originated, the New York City school system employed more than one hundred psychologists but no sociologists).[37] Consequently, when a sociologist has been called in to participate in interdisciplinary research on the 'sociological aspects' of cultural deprivation, he often has found the central core of the topic so permeated with psychological suppositions that his own efforts have of necessity been at the periphery of the problem as defined.

The pattern of knowledge diffusion in this case was that of origination and early growth in New York City and a later fanning out to other parts of the country. Is this typical? Does this reflect the concentration of a larger quantity and higher quality of intellectual resources in New York City, or perhaps an inevitably earlier response to the greater intensity and pathology of problems associated with lower-class students in New York City, or some other factor?

School practitioners who deal with culturally deprived students have probably tended to agree with the idea as an explanation of their students' scholastic retardation, but have resented assertions that the ineffectiveness of slum school practitioners is largely responsible for this lack of achievement.

The idea, particularly as a popular image, eventually attracted widespread public interest and support in connection with the issues of poverty and civil rights. It turned out to be one of those rare societally important ideas that, for various reasons, possessed an image appeal to a broad spectrum of persons and publics of various ideological persuasions – conservative, moderate and liberal. Bennett Berger has described a similar occurrence in regard to the idea of 'suburbia' in the 1950s:

> . . . the myth of suburbia conveniently suited the ideological pur-poses of several influential groups . . . Realtor-Chamber-of-Commerce interests and the range of opinion represented by the Luce magazines could use the myth of suburbia to affirm the American Way of Life; city planners, architects, urban design people and so on could use the myth of suburbia to warn that those agglomerations of standardized, vulgarized, mass-produced cheer-fulness which masqueraded as homes would be the slums of tomor-row. Liberal and left-wing culture-critics could (and did) use the myth of suburbia to launch an attack on complacency, conformity and mass culture . . . the *descriptive* accuracy of the myth of subur-bia went largely unchallenged because it suited the *prescriptive* desires of such a wide variety of opinion. . .[38]

Cultural deprivation was a popular image that was able to rally the support of varied interests in order to produce needed legislation and experimental programmes. Whether in the long run its alleged de-trimental effect as a negative stereotype will outweigh its utility as an image that seems able to bring about worthwhile programmes of action, remains to be seen. And 'culturally disadvantaged', a similar label that appears to be displacing 'culturally deprived' in academic (though not yet in popular) usage in 1967, and that is almost as technically inaccurate and descriptively derogatory, may or may not prove as successful as an action-producing popular image.

Along with recent criticisms on the grounds of theoretical inadequacy, explanatory inaccuracy, and negative stereotyping, the idea has been opposed as one based upon a piecemeal, patchwork, conservative-oriented approach to change. The bulk of writing and action in regard to cultural deprivation (and 'cultural disadvantage' as well) does seem to have rested upon the following 'self-evident' underlying assumptions: (*a*) our formal educational system, particularly in its success with middle-class students, and in its practices since Sputnik, is essentially sound; (*b*) the educational improvement of culturally deprived children in the large cities is a worthwhile effort that can succeed even within the existing situation of *de facto* segregation; and (*c*) much progress can come about by giving head starts and special attention to individual children and categories of children, so that they will be helped to overcome some of the adverse conditions of their daily lives. In a society that might have been occupied and concerned during the past several years, on the other hand, with a serious questioning of the direction of contemporary life and the related aims of education, with a frontal attack on *de facto* segregation, and with large-scale, far reaching change in the economic and social conditions of minorities and the poor (rather than in their individual behaviour)'[39] cultural deprivation would probably not have developed into the focal idea of recent educational thought.

References
[1] LOUIS WIRTH's 'Preface' to KARL MANNHEIM (1949) *Ideology and Utopia*, Harcourt, Brace & Co., New York, xxix–xxx.

[2] For a brief summary of the major facets of the pre-1955 literature dealing with the education of lower-class children, see HOWARD S BECKER, 'Education and the Lower-Class Child', in *Modern Sociology by* A V GOULDNER and H P GOULDNER (1963) Harcourt, Brace and World, NY 244–250.

[3] JUDITH KRUGMAN, 'Cultural Deprivation and Child Development', *High Points*, **38** (November, 1956), 5–20.

[4] J W WRIGHTSTONE, 'Discovering and Stimulating Culturally Deprived Talented Youth', *Teachers College Record* **60**, October, 1958, 23–7.

[5] M A SENG (ed) (1963) *The Education Index*, The H W Wilson Company, **13**, New York, 233.

[6] M A SENG (ed) (1965) *The Education Index*, The H W Wilson Company, **15**, New York, 165–167.

[7] CHARLOTTE K BROOKS, 'Some approaches to Teaching English as a Second Language', in *The Disadvantaged Learner*, edited by S W WEBSTER, San Francisco, Chandler Publishing Co 1966 516–517.

[8] MARTIN DEUTSCH, 'Facilitating Development in the Pre-School Child: Social and Psychological Perspectives', *Merrill-Palmer Quarterly* **10** (April, 1964) 256.

[9] J MCVICKER HUNT, 'The Psychological Basis for Using Pre-School Enrichment as an Antidote for Cultural Deprivation', *Merrill-Palmer Quarterly* **10** (July, 1964), 236.

[10] *Ibid*, p. 236.

[11] BENJAMIN S BLOOM, DAVIS, ALLISON, and ROBERT HESS (1965) *Compensatory Education for Cultural Deprivation*, Holt, Rinehart and Winston, New York.

[12] EVAN HUNTER, *The Blackboard Jungle*, Simon & Schuster, New York, 1954.

[13] JAMES B CONANT, *Slums and Suburbs: A Commentary on Schools, in Metropolitan Areas*, McGraw-Hill Book Company, New York, 1961.

[14] FRANK RIESSMAN, *The Culturally Deprived Child*, Harper and Row, New York, 1962.

[15] *Ibid*, 3.

[16] These views are convincingly developed in RUSH WELTER, (1962) *Popular Education and Democratic Thought in America*, Columbia University Press, New York, also see chapter 3 of MERLE CURTI, *The Social Ideas of American Educators*, Littlefield, Adams and Company, Patterson, New Jersey, 1959.

[17] CHRISTOPHER JENCKS, 'Johnson vs Poverty', *New Republic* **150** (March 28, 1964), 15–18.

[18] CHRISTOPHER JENCKS, 'The Moynihan Report', *The New York Review of Books*, **5** (October 14, 1965), 39. By 1967, the least criticized program in the War on Poverty was the pre-school Operation Head Start, probably because even the most rigid and financially-cautious conservative was reluctant to violate the 'American Spirit of Fair Play' by depriving cute little four-year old tots of a little better chance in life.

[19] 'Violence in the City – An End or a Beginning?' *Report by the Governor's Commission on the Los Angeles Riots*, Los Angeles, College Book Store, 1965, 57–8.

[20] RIESSMAN, *op cit*, 3.

[21] BERNARD MACKLER and M G GIDDINGS, 'Cultural Deprivation: A Study in Mythology', *Teachers College Record*, **66** (April, 1965), 610.

[22] KENNETH B CLARK, (1965) *Dark Ghetto: Dilemmas of Social Power*, Harper and Row, New York, 132.

[23] *Ibid*, 131.

[24] MACKLER AND GIDDINGS, *op cit*, 611.

[25] An indignant Puerto Rican, probably equating 'culture' with 'civilization', has asked just whose civilization is more deprived: 'Is a culture that has for four centuries been able to maintain the individual dignity, value and worth of all its members (despite differences in race and class) a deprived or disadvantaged culture when compared with one that has been striving to achieve these values and has as yet not been able to do so?' Quoted in PATRICIA CAYO SEXTON, (1965) *Spanish Harlem*, Harper and Row, New York, 61.

[26] WILLIAM RYAN, 'Savage Discovery: The Moynihan Report', *Nation*, **201** (November 22, 1965), 383. This article was written in reaction to a controversial government report on the Negro family written by DANIEL P MOYNIHAN. For further exchanges in the Moynihan/Ryan controversy, see LEE RAINWATER, and WILLIAM L YANCEY 'Black Families and the White House', *Trans-action*, **3** (July/August, 1966), 6–11, 48–53; replies by WILLIAM RYAN and DANIEL P MOYNIHAN in *Trans-action*, **4** (January/February, 1967), 62–3; and DANIEL P MOYNIHAN, 'The President and the Negro: The Moment Lost', *Commentary*, **43** (February, 1967), 31–45.

[27] ROBERT BLAUNER, 'Whitewash over Watts', *Trans-action*, **3** (March/April, 1966), 5; RUSTIN BAYARD 'The Watts "Manifesto" and the McCone Report', *Commentary*, **41** (March, 1966), 33–34. For an exchange between Rustin and an author of the education section of the McCone Commission report, see *Commentary*, **42** (August, 1966), 6–14.

[28] EDGAR Z FRIEDENBERG, 'An Ideology of School Withdrawal', in *The School Dropout*, edited by DANIEL SCHREIBER, National Education Association, Washington, DC, (1964), 36.

[29] MORRIS KRUGMAN, 'The Culturally Deprived Child in School', *NEA Journal*, **50** (April, 1961), 23–24.

[30] RIESSMAN, *op cit*, xiii.

[31] L D CROW, W I MURRAY and H H SMYTHE, (1966) *Educating the Culturally Disadvantaged Child*, New York, David McKay Company; J L FROST and G R HAWKES (ed), (1966) *The Disadvantaged Child; Issues and Innovations*, Boston, Houghton Mifflin Company; S W WEBSTER (ed.) (1966) *The Disadvantaged Learner*, San Francisco, Chandler Publishing Company.

[32] EDGAR Z FRIEDENBERG has commented that he views such writings as 'offensive' because they are designed to aid in a more expert manipulation and exploitation of student clientele, based upon assumptions and goals that are questionable at best. See his *Coming of Age in America: Growth and Acquiescence*, Random House, New York, 1965, 195–196.

[33] PATRICK J GROFF, 'Culturally Deprived Children: Opinions of Teachers on the Views of Reissman', *Exceptional Children*, **31** (October, 1964), 61–65.

[34] RIESSMAN, *op cit*, pp.25–48.

[35] ALLAN C ORNSTEIN, 'Effective Schools for Disadvantaged Children', *Journal of Secondary Education*, **40** (March, 1965), 105.

[36] *Ibid*, 108.

[37] ORVILLE G BRIM JR., *Sociology and the Field of Education*, Russell Sage Foundation, New York 77–78, 1958.

[38] BENNETT M BERGER, 'Suburbia and the American Dream', *The Public Interest*, **1** (Winter, 1966), 82–83.

[39] In the latter half of 1966, two events occurred which may affect future trends relating to these matters. A large-scale survey for the federal government, the 'Coleman Report', empirically pointed not only to factors of family background and teacher characteristics, but especially to the social class mix of classroom peers as a critically important variable related to academic achievement. See JAMES S COLEMAN, (1966) *Equality of Educational Opportunity*, (Washington DC, U.S. Government Printing Office 1966. From a sociology of knowledge perspective, it will be interesting to observe the possible future impact of the Coleman Report on official, academic and popular thought and policy-making. The second event in late 1966 was the election of governors and United States congressmen, the results of which seemed to reflect a public desire for at least some temporary slow-down in the pace of domestic social change.

On the Politics of Educational Knowledge *

Michael F D Young

Introduction

A weakness of much sociological research and 'theorizing' about education has been that it has failed to treat as problematic the categories used by educators. This implies that a sociological approach to education needs to begin by treating definitions of education as the product of social arrangements. More specifically, 'subjects' (Musgrove 1968) and schools (Cicourel and Kitsuse 1963) are viewed not as fact but as the products of the activities of educational personnel, and the language of education (with its terms like ability, achievement, motivation, innovation, etc.), becomes viewed as a vocabulary of motives (Mills 1940) used in particular contexts.

A further implication, that is central to the issues raised in this paper, is the assumptions that 'education' is a label with political and ideological connotations[1]. Thus all 'educational' issues are viewed as 'political' in that they involve decisions (or non-decisions [Bachrach and Baratz 1963]) about priorities in contexts where there is differential access to resources, both of economic support and cognitive legitimacy[2]. Most educators[3] do not perceive educational matters as political in this sense, and in their writings and public statements appear concerned to emphasize a distinction between 'educational' and 'political'[4], and the need to decide things on 'educational grounds'[5]. Such statements are conceived here as claims for the legitimacy of particular definitions of 'educational' made by those in a position to assert their 'non political' character.

The purpose of this paper therefore is to explore the implications of these proposals and some of the research questions they give rise to. It is divided into two main parts.

1 Some comments on existing approaches to the 'control' of education, which serve to emphasize the necessity of focusing on definitions of educational knowledge that are maintained in particular settings, followed by a brief account of some features of a

* Abridged from *Economy and Society* (1972), **1** (2), 194–215.

particular setting, the Schools Council [6]. A statement of the rationale for treating it as a potentially critical case leads on to an
examination of the assumptions underlying the one available account of its development and activities in Manzer's (1970) study of
the National Union of Teachers.

2 An alternative perspective that is developed from the preceding
critique, which leads to a focus on three main issues underlying
both specific questions about Schools Council and more general
questions concerning the political character of education:

(i) Teacher autonomy and control.
(ii) Curriculum project styles and the legitimation of educational
knowledge.
(iii) definitions of 'types of child' and their implications for the
differentiation of curricula.

The 'control of education': some existing approaches

Research into the control [7] of education is still, as Banks (1968)
reported, almost non-existent. In the way she, and more recently
Musgrove (1971), set up the discussion, we are not taken much further with suggestions about how it might develop. Banks focuses on
the very general issue of the degree of decentralization of decision-
making but does not point to the specific issues about which
'decisions' are made or the process involved that might be open to
empirical enquiry. This question might be explored fruitfully in a
comparative study of say, French and English teachers. The former
participate in a system that is highly centralized, but which at least
one case study suggests allows considerable areas of discretion (Wylie
1961). The latter as will be referred to later, participate in a formally
decentralized system. However, the extent of this 'decentralization',
in practice, would appear to be limited by the way English teachers
perceive the examination systems and accept existing academic and
institutional hierarchies. This was eloquently demonstrated to me
recently when a group of teachers were complaining about their CSE
Board (*a teacher-based* exam system, but no one present knew who the
teachers on the Board were or how they were selected) [8].

Musgrove (1971), in asserting that 'contemporary research reveals
the impotence of schools', and defining the problem (whose problem?)
as the expansion of their power, evades both the substantive question
of 'power to do what?', and the theoretical and empirical problems of
what might be meant either to the sociologist or the teacher by the
notion of 'impotence'.

An alternative approach, which did not take as a 'given' particular definitions of educational knowledge, is suggested in the latter section of this paper. This focuses on how priorities for 'curriculum development' are defined which would involve exploring the definitions of educational knowledge that are held by different groups. One can view these priorities as constituted in the interaction, in particular settings, of agents of educational support (primarily those from business, local government and the Ministry, who are in a position to allocate resources), and of educational practice (teachers). One such setting is the Schools Council. It is suggested that an enquiry of this kind might point to how one might explore linkages between the financing, control and practice of education more generally, which at present can only be hinted at[9].

The Schools Council
In spite of its annual reports, monthly newsletter and voluminous publications, remarkably little is known beyond 'official histories' of how it operates. However there are certain features which are worth emphasizing at this stage, which give some indication of what its significance might be.

Firstly, it is an agency which has spent £4·3m since its inception in 1964, at present spends on both 'projects' and administration approximately £1m a year, and increasingly as the Nuffield Foundation has withdrawn from research in education, has become the *only* source of funds for curriculum development projects in primary and secondary schools. Furthermore, it not only has significant advisory powers over the forms of CSE and GCE 'O' level examining[10], but it is able to veto any new proposals for courses to be examined at 'A' level[11]. Thus in a very real sense the Schools Council activities define educational priorities and the limits of certain kinds of educational change. Secondly, of the 111 projects reported in the Schools Council document, *Projects*, in June 1971, seventy-six were situated in Universities, eleven in Colleges of Education and two in schools. It would be unjustified to infer too much from figures such as these, but they would seem to be an indication of at least one largely unquestioned assumption, 'educational research is best done in Universities'. A third point to note from the Schools Council's Annual Reports is that of the £3m spent by the Schools Council up to 1970; £660 500 was committed to proposals in which particular ability-groupings are *explicitly* referred to, but only £97 000 was committed to projects *specifically* referring to 'mixed ability' teaching. These figures are at least some indication that a change towards curricula based on non-hierarchical conceptions of ability is not a high Schools Council priority. Each of these features of Schools Council activity, linked to the questions raised in the last part of the paper concerning teachers' autonomy, the legitimation of 'subjects' and institutional hierarchies, and the assumptions made about 'types of children', are no more than possible illustrations of potential areas of enquiry.

A critique of Manzer's model of 'educational politics', and its application to the Schools Council

In view of the little interest shown by sociologists or political scientists in the politics of education, it is not surprising that Manzer's (1970) study of 'educational politics'[12] should have become so widely quoted, well received and in 'educational circles' almost definitive. What is more significant is the way in which his own analysis appears to be an explication of many of the shared understandings held by educational personnel. This becomes apparent when one reads an account such as Nisbet's (1971)[13]. Though containing none of the familiar concepts of the 'systems theory' used by Manzer, the implicit model of explanation is very similar. It is therefore primarily because it makes it possible to examine the tacit assumptions of both official histories and educationalists' accounts that it seems useful to begin by looking in some detail at Manzer's theoretical framework, before making some tentative alternative suggestions.

Manzer's book is a study of British education after 1944 as a 'political system', and in particular the role of the National Union of Teachers in this system. The section of the book of major concern for this paper is his account of the origins and development of the Schools Council as a case study in 'educational politics'. His theoretical framework (drawn from the 'political system' theorists – such as Easton (1953)) and the assumptions implicit in it can be outlined as follows:

Political culture is seen as a relatively persistent set of common values. Manzer characterizes the values of the British political culture as 'support of evolutionary changes', 'hesitant support for innovation', 'education as a good', 'commitment to maintaining a public education system', and governmental right to 'interpret community needs'. The problem arises when the 'common values' referred to are postulated and then used as an explanation of the maintenance of a particular order. If one moves from the very general level of 'support of evolutionary changes', to more substantive values, these can only be seen as constructed and legitimated by groups with common concerns in particular historical contexts; these have *to be explained* not used as explanations.

Political structure. The British political structure is conceived as a 'pluralist', which implies sets of relatively autonomous 'subgovernments' of education, housing, health, etc. These structures represent agreed definitions of the limits of 'educational (or housing) politics'. They are seen as serving to translate in a relatively unproblematic way changing 'demands for education' (inputs), which are generated through wider social and economic changes, into 'educational policies' (outputs) [14]. However, the assumptions on which such a 'pluralistic' view of English politics rely are as dogmatic and naive assertions as the idea of some conspiratorial ruling class. Each remains closed to questions about the origins and persistence of particular definitions of 'educational politics', and of the distinctions between 'educational' and 'political' in terms of which educators want 'education kept out of politics'. Furthermore an input/output model of education is just as vulnerable in relation to the Schools Council as Cicourel and Kitsuse (1963) have shown it to be in connection with the social class determinants of college-going in the USA. In the latter case it was demonstrated that the high proportion of college achievers among upper class groups was 'produced' through the routine practices of high school personnel. Similarly it would be necessary in the case of the Schools Council to show the processes of interaction involved among the different groups, and not just assume an unproblematic translation of assumed 'demand' into 'policy'.

The 'educational sub-government' (teachers, local authorities and Ministry) is described as acting as a self-regulating 'adaptive' system', with the major concerns of the three groups being to maintain any existing power balance within the values defined by the 'educational culture'. Thus, 'educational politics' are removed from macropolitics', and analysed as an autonomous system. Manzer views the values of the educational culture as the expression of the wider political culture that defines the legitimate rights of the three main interest groups referred to above. As with his concept of political culture, values are imputed and used as explanations. If, however, one views a belief in professional autonomy, not as an expression of the 'educational culture' with a relatively fixed meaning, but as a product of teachers' particular historical and social circumstances, then this also becomes a topic of enquiry rather than an explanation of teachers' corporate actions.

In terms of Manzer's model, the origin and development of the Schools Council is viewed as a process of 'structural differentiation' which can be summarized as follows:

1 The central government initiative in forming the Curriculum Study Group [15], which Manzer 'accounts for' in terms of 'demands' external to the system. As this was perceived by local authority associations and teachers' unions [16] as illegitimate interference, the system

138

'adapted' and a new structure was created (the Schools Council).

2 This structure through the limits of its sphere of action (only powers to 'recommend'), its legal autonomy from central government, and the teacher majorities built into its constitution, recognized both the 'new needs' of the society and the traditional rights of the members of the 'educational subgovernment'. The formally defined objectives of the Council were to 'keep under review curricula, teaching methods and examinations. . . . It should produce recommendations which were agreed by all member interests concerned. But they would still be *recommendations . . .*' (HMSO 1964) (author's italics).

Like all functional analyses, we are presented with an account that seems plausible enough and is accepted to a large extent though not explicitly in the Nisbet report already referred to and by the 'member interests', whether in DES reports, statements by teacher unions, local authority representatives, or Council officials (Caston 1971). Everything is made to seem understandable and non-problematic, provided you accept the original assumptions.

Let us look briefly at three critical elements of Manzer's account:

a The assumed 'adaptation' processes
If one does not, like Manzer, start from an equilibrium model of an educational system, the Ministry's ready 'adaptations' to criticisms of the Curriculum Study Group by forming the Schools Council raises quite different questions which he does not consider. If the 'reality' of a teacher-controlled curriculum was in question, then the Schools Council might in this situation serve to maintain this 'reality'. One can only speculate on the implications of teachers, pupils and parents finding that perhaps 'what was taught was *not* really decided by teachers (except in a very limited way), and politics *did* enter in'. Conceivably the response might be an attempt to assert collective influence through which each group might come to question the whole hierarchical structure of English curricula.

b His characterization of 'teacher politics' between the wars.
The period between 1920 and 1940 is described by Manzer as one in which teachers as a group were 'responsible', 'idealistic', and 'autonomous'. Except that it provides a neat contrast to his pathological model of contemporary education, one is led to ask what kind of account this might be. In apparently equating a lack of union militancy with responsibility, a concern for the 'underprivileged' with 'idealism,' and for protecting 'professional rights' with 'autonomy', we are told more about the values implicit in Manzer's perspective

139

than about the activities of teachers in their discussions about curricula. Manzer relies on this account to be able to claim that changes were little more than the formalizing of existing processes of negotiation about curricula. However, terms like 'negotiation' and 'cooperation' hide just the processes that need to be understood, and evade the issues about how 'demands' like 'more scientists' and 'less specialization in the VIth form' come to be defined. A description of discussions about the curriculum in English education prior to the creation of the Schools Council is one of the informal processes of consultation that Manzer refers to. As suggested, it is important to his account, and would seem to be a characteristic of the biological analogy underlying structural differentiation models of change, that what appears like a change is in fact a modification and elaboration of what was already there. In this case the informal processes still go on, but in a new context (the Schools Council).

c Accounts of the influence of 'demand' on 'policy'
Manzer claims to describe the influence of increases in the demand for education on policies. However, persistences and changes in curricula and examinations remain just as much a mystery as before, and the expenditure priorities of the Schools Council of about £1m per annum are left unexplained. They are presumably a product of some inevitable process or of a series of 'acts of faith, followed by trial and error', as Wrigley (1970) puts it. Manzer's plausible 'redescription' creates problems even within its own terms as it cannot account for the differences and lack of consensus on 'desirable policies' among teachers and administrators. He is thus led to a kind of 'social pathology' model to account for what he calls the 'sickness' of British education. The 'causes' of the 'illness' are primarily lack of leadership, in the Ministry and among the unions (pp 52 and 149–150— lack of leadership is reflected in the irresponsibility of salary claims, imposed on the leadership by union members). Its symptoms are a failure to 'go far enough fast enough to do more than gradually shift the balance of English Education to the needs of a more technologically oriented society' (p 161). Again the familiar, rather naive, technological determinism is apparent, a characteristic of functionalist accounts of change ably criticized by Goldthorpe (1964).

The basic weakness of Manzer's approach is characteristic of the 'systems' perspective that he uses, that is not uncommon among those who write about education. He manages to make problems unproblematic and thus fails to raise questions for research or the hypotheses that require data to support them that might generate new enquiries. I would suggest that it is the uncritical though, doubtless not con-

140

scious, acceptance of assumptions like Manzer's that has contributed to the aridness of much discussion about the Schools Council. It has either been criticized for being 'power hungry' (usually by the unions), or defensive and lacking a coherent policy (usually by academics). Again such criticisms are more informative about the critics than about how competing priorities in education come to be defined or resolved.

The advantage of presenting the functional analysis in some detail is that it enables one to see what has to be taken for granted or 'given', for such an approach to be accepted as an explanation at all. If one conceives of the assumptions implicit in such concepts as 'political culture', etc, as 'produced conditions' rather than 'given', then one can begin to see why such a model of explanation is so limited and how a whole set of questions that might have been raised are not. Questions about the content of education which provided the context in which discussions about curricula were given meaning are avoided, as are the particular economic circumstances of the time. It would be valuable, for instance, to examine why the legitimacy of various conceptions of hierarchically differentiated education do not appear to have been questioned. The 'informal consultations', which were the precursors of the Schools Council, presupposed as 'given' these definitions of education and academic knowledge which were themselves historical products.

An alternative perspective

Much of this paper so far has been concerned with an elaboration of a critique of the functionalist model of 'change' in education as used in a particular case. The thrust of the argument can be summarized by a claim that sociological questions for research in education (or politics or industry for that matter) can only be posed by not accepting the ideas and institutions of the system that those involved in it are constrained to take for granted. This is as true for an institution like the Schools Council as it is for categories like teacher and pupil or even what counts as education, ability and achievement. An alternative perspective to the system model is implicit in the critique, and one of the limitations of this paper is that it is only hinted at, rather than made explicit.

It must incorporate the way those involved in 'education' give meaning to their activities and to the curricular material that they construct or that is made available. These meanings will vary with the context, from classroom to staff meeting or union conference to Schools Council committee. However, this is not enough; classrooms, staff meetings, union conferences and Council committees as contexts of interaction, all in part *take their meaning* from wider social and economic contexts.

It was suggested at the beginning of this paper, that we consider what counts as education as socially and historically constructed. This process points to an analysis of what are perceived as the dominant definitions of educational knowledge by different groups at particular times. This takes us back to the political nature of education, and the opportunity of some groups to restrict access to the records or information that would be necessary for this kind of research. This question would have to be asked within a broader framework that treated as 'to be explained' the definitions of 'political' and 'legitimate autonomy', which gave meaning, to quote one of Manzer's sources to 'the actual as well as inalienable right of teachers to teach what they liked, how and when'. One problem that might be explored, assuming this to be a view widely held by practising teachers and not just an example of union rhetoric, is to question how it is possible that the university-dominated Examination Boards are accepted by teachers as legitimate definers of 'what ought to be taught' and are not seen as posing a threat to this 'inalienable right'. A remaining difficulty not recognized by Manzer and to some extent evaded in this paper is that teachers are not a homogeneous group and the meaning of 'rights' is likely to be very different when say a Grammar School teacher involved primarily in VIth form work is compared to a middle school general subjects teacher.

An examination of the ways in which different groups have been involved in attempts to redefine what counted as education might shed light on one of the more significant aspects of the Schools Council's priorities. Its projects have, to a large extent reflected an acceptance of the academic/non-academic distinction as characterizing two kinds of knowledge, suitable for two distinct groups of children and associated with fairly distinct occupational rewards. This is illustrated not so much in the early priority given by the Council to problems of 'the extra year' and the 'Newsom Child', but in how these problems were defined. If one conceives of the 'early leaver' or 'Newsom child', not in terms of this group of children's 'characteristics', but as 'products' of the dynamics of the school system of a particular society, quite different 'problems' are raised. One gets some indications from the 'Young School Leavers' working papers, whether in science, mathematics of the humanities, and in Nisbet's comment that 'the increasing numbers of pupils in full time education . . . resulted in a situation where the traditional curriculum was unsuited to *many* secondary school pupils' (author's italics).

If we draw together the strands of the argument of this section so far, an alternative perspective, which focuses on the socially constructed character of educational knowledge, will direct our attention to three questions which have largely gone unasked up till now:

1 What is the political or social meaning of teachers 'having control' over what they teach or 'being controlled'?
2 How are existing educational hierarchies (both 'subject' and institutional) maintained and legitimated?
3 What are the assumptions implicit in distinctions made between different types of child and different 'curricula'?

We shall take these questions, in the context of the Schools Council though clearly they have much wider implications.

1 Teacher control and autonomy

It is worth exploring the possible meanings of 'teacher autonomy' in relation to the Schools Council. The Nisbet Report documents what is at least the rhetoric of the rights of teachers to decide the content of what they teach, and how it has been supported not only by teachers, but by local authorities, Schools Council personnel, and civil servants. However, what it actually means is uncertain, and in the absence of research one can only raise some questions.

On the evidence of NUT policy statements it would appear that the Union, and therefore presumably its representatives on the Schools Council, while having specific policies on the abolition of the 11 + and on examinations, does not have any policies at all on curricula, streaming or the form of organization of secondary education. The implication is that professional autonomy involves having a union policy in what is seen as an area of professional expertise (an example is whether or not children should take a selection test or an examination). Whether however, the issue concerns the individual teacher selecting syllabuses, textbooks, etc, or the individual headmaster planning the grouping of children and timetable of his school, then for the Union to have a policy would itself be an infringement of professional autonomy. This is a highly individualistic notion of autonomy, and is expressed in such public statements of teachers' unions as that 'the Schools Council should not be able to legislate to teachers what they should teach'. If teacher members of the Schools Council do attach this meaning to autonomy, it would seem to raise questions about the significance of the teacher majorities on committees, which will be taken up in more detail later; in particular it would seem doubtful whether in terms of this notion of autonomy they can do more than respond to initiatives from elsewhere. This may well leave teachers, while 'in theory' protected from imposition by the Schools Council (or anyone else), 'in practice' accepting that the initiative for developing new courses and materials comes from project directors, Schools Council officials, academics, and publishing companies. Some reference has already been made, and one finds frequent mention in public statements, to the 'teacher majorities' on all the Schools Council committees except the Finance Committee[17]. However the power that these majorities are assumed to imply depends on what may often be a very heterogeneous group of teachers from different unions voting as a block[18]. It is equally possible that they may see themselves as union representatives first[19] and teachers (independently of what and who they teach) second[20]. Furthermore if the meaning of autonomy is defined by the teachers, as has been suggested earlier, primarily as defending teachers' right *not* to use Schools Council material, then the consequences for committee members who have to generate priorities, make recommendations, and provide rationales for particular projects would appear uncertain. What, we would need to ask, are the legitimizing categories that members use to accept or reject proposals? It may be appropriate here to raise some of the problems associated with the term autonomy which have recurred in this paper. Prior to an empirical enquiry into the areas where different groups of teachers perceive differing areas of discretion over their activities and the accounts of the constraints that they give, it might be better to dispense with the term though not with the questions it raises. Like most school systems, English education is pervaded with various constraints which teachers may not perceive as such, as they are seen as 'legitimate'. 'Expert' knowledge (as will be taken up later), respect for 'academics' as selectors of students, and the relative 'fairness' of the examination system are examples. I would suggest that it is in the inter-relations of social and economic circumstances and the context these have provided for the development of beliefs in these legitimacies that the problematic nature of what has been referred to as the 'freedom of the teacher', or 'teacher autonomy' might be best examined.

An alternative approach to the problem of the nature and origin of curricular initiatives, would be to start by examining empirically what is seen to count as an 'initiative' or 'innovation'. This would suggest that the Schools Council, by making recommendations within currently accepted definitions of knowledge and ability, may either be disregarded or be perceived by teachers as one of the constraints on change not unlike the Examination Boards. The sanctions available in this case are not the power to 'fail' pupils, but the control of resources which enables members of the Schools Council to become in effect, definers of what is to count as innovation. A more satisfactory answer to this whole question could only be found through having much more direct access to the Schools Council at work. Whatever the other advantages, the limitations in this context of the appointment of a part-time research professor are apparent when one looks at what is no more than another 'official' account that he provides (Wrigley 1970). If we take the question of teacher control out of the context of the Schools Council, we find a Ministry memorandum (MOE 1962) justifying some form of intervention in the following way:

'The tradition of substantial *laissez-faire* in curriculum matters . . . becomes a means whereby . . . teachers are forced to respond to events they cannot control.'

The implied question then becomes, who does control the events referred to? The implication of this, theoretically, is a view of curricula as 'political products', in the sense that 'what is taught' is an expression of current legitimacies as to what is valued knowledge, and how they are distributed. To take an extreme case, it would only need the assertion of teachers' 'inalienable right' to, say, 'not teach maths', for the *constraints* on the teacher to be more apparent than his *freedom*. However it is only by rejecting the widely-held tacit consensus that 'education is good' and 'we all know what education ought to be', that social or political constraints can be distinguished from legal, traditional or constitutional freedoms. This does not necessarily imply that all teachers subscribe to similar definitions of 'a good education', but it does suggest that rights and freedoms are socially defined in terms of particular definitions of education, and that in terms of alternative definitions, notions of freedom and autonomy may have a very restricted meaning.

In order to examine the possible nature of the constraints on teachers who may believe that they have 'rights' as traditionally defined, it becomes necessary to question what is taken for granted in most educational practice, writing and research. This is not only that 'schooling is good', but that 'we all know what a good school is'[21]. It is through starting from the opposite assumption 'that all schooling as we know it is harmful' that Illich (1971) is able to raise fundamental questions about the 'political' character of contemporary education.

A revealing quotation from a Schools Council official addressing a group of headmasters suggests links between the question of teacher control of the Schools Council and the legitimation of kinds of knowledge. The official is quoted in Nisbet's report as saying 'the Council has *no authority over teachers*. It may – and indeed I hope it does sometimes carry a certain amount of professional consensus, and *a great deal of the kind of authority which comes with organized knowledge*' (my italics). The question that this raises is that the speaker appears to be tacitly assuming that he and his audience all know and agree what 'organized knowledge' is and that the legitimacy of its authority is unquestioned. What the quotation does suggest is the kind of data one might look for to illustrate how the activities of the Schools Council are but one example of the hierarchical assumptions about what counts as knowledge that are held by educational personnel. A further illustration can be found in the Foreword to Working Paper 33 'Choosing a Curriculum for the Young School leaver'. The writer states '*At the outset* there was no firm intention of producing a report of the conference for publication: there were no *authoritative* speakers present, *only* people working on development projects' (author's italics). Questioning the legitimacy of 'curriculum development projects' as 'organized knowledge', and linking this to the concepts that teachers have of their autonomy, would seem an important way to begin to explore the meaning of teacher participation in the work of the Schools Council. We know little of the processes through which teachers get selected through unions and other sources for the Council's committees. A study of the career patterns of teachers who have been involved in projects, working parties and committees would seem an important extension of this; one might also study types of project sponsorship as a way of approaching the social and economic basis of particular definitions of education. Similarly, we know little of the processes by which projects become legitimized as '*organized*' knowledge, through the support of local authorities and industry or being 'housed' by universities, and through the elevation of project directors to professorial status.

2 Legitimation of 'subject' and 'institutional' hierarchies

Most accounts of Schools Council activities see one of its purposes as a centre for discussion and debate. However this, as so often, while on a general level true, begs just the question that needs to be asked; what are the legitimate alternatives that define the terms of the discussion? For no one would suggest they are not limited (see note 21). One would want to know how far the various conferences of 'academic educators' (Hirst and Peters, among others), which are 'written up' as working papers, provide guide lines for the defining of 'problems' and 'priorities' (see Schools Council Working Paper 12). Perhaps the age and subject distinctions of the *Steering* and *Advisory* Committees provide institutional constraints on what is developed or discussed and for whom[22]. In having official representatives from 'subject associations', whose 'right to speak about their subject', would appear to be largely accepted, the Schools Council structure contributes to the maintenance of 'subjects' as 'educational realities'[23], and defines

146

the distinctions in terms of which debates about 'integration'[24] and 'the slow learner' are likely to take place. Clearly one would need to know something of the educational background and ideas of participants in various conferences and working parties – as well as the characteristics of the Council as a particular institutional context (how do practising teachers act in relation to 'academics', HMI's, and Ministry personnel?), in order to begin an explanation of what is debated and what is not, and the possible meanings of such debates in terms of maintaining academic legitimacies.

The question of 'academic legitimacy' leads us to one of the more neglected sets of social processes, which Bourdieu (1968) discusses and to which an enquiry into types of curriculum project might contribute. The problem is how various kinds of intellectual activity gain and maintain institutional support. It is related to the question, opened up by Horton (1967), but hardly considered by sociologists, of the relation between what is treated as 'theoretical' and 'practical' knowledge, how in different contexts the legitimation of 'theory' or 'practice' is called on, and also how 'theoretical' or 'practical' knowledge may be defined as legitimate for different types of child (see (3) later). Nisbet, in the report already referred to, distinguishes two broad classes of Schools Council development projects, based on what I shall call 'academic expertise' and those based on 'good practice'. It is not suggested that all of the hundred projects sponsored by the Schools Council can be classed as one or the other, or that it may not be possible to develop other more sophisticated classifications. However the distinction does appear to have two advantages. Firstly it is simple and appears to be based on what the practitioners think they are doing. Secondly it does suggest ways of asking questions about the educational philosophies and epistemologies underlying the projects. More specifically it raises questions about 'the range of specific meanings given to the intuitively understood elements that make up the components of schooling'[25].

The distinction, then points not only to how particular projects are legitimated in different contexts, but also to the relation between the social position and occupational career of those involved and their conceptions of 'what a curriculum development project is.'

The 'academic expertise' style characterizes those projects, particularly in the sciences and mathematics which draw on university 'subject experts', who start with a fairly explicit idea of 'what ought to be learnt'. In these projects the fundamental 'structure' of 'what is to be learnt' is not in question, because the academic experts involved in the project are also in a position to be the definers of this 'structure'[26]. The typical project therefore consists of developing teaching and learning materials which reflect these ideas and using field trials in schools to modify them in light of how teachers find they 'work'. In contrast to this 'style' is the 'good practice' style, which appears to draw on an older English educational tradition carried out earlier almost entirely by the Inspectorate. These projects (the Middle School Curriculum, English in the Middle Years, and Social Studies (8–13) are examples) rely on those involved having some implicit notion of 'good practice', with which they can identify such practices in schools. The project therefore consists of collecting together and ordering samples of 'good practice' for dissemination to the schools. The possible differences and similarities in the underlying assumptions can only be hinted at here without a detailed investigation of particular projects.

The 'academic expertise' style depends on a fairly explicit definition of the 'structure of a subject'; it rests on a clear distinction between knower and known, and therefore between *what* has to be taught and *how* it is taught. The model of the teacher, then, is a kind of technologist (used in a very general sense). The criteria used to define those aspects of the child, such as age and measured 'ability', that are explicitly taken account of in the construction of teaching materials, are limited and fairly specific.

As criteria of success are fairly rigorously 'subject-defined', failure will be likely to be seen in terms either of the materials' unsuitability for particular children (Nuffield Science), or in terms of attributes of the children. It is entailed in these subject-defined criteria that such projects will operate with typically hierarchical concepts of knowledge and ability, and though they appear to be likely where practitioners make claims for fairly explicit 'logics', as in mathematics and science, investigation might well suggest similar philosophies underlying projects in other fields, particularly for the 'less able'. There is a paradox indicated in how this style has been characterized, that would be worth exploring empirically. It has been implied that the assumptions about knowledge of the 'academic expertise' style define what is seen as relevant knowledge 'of' and 'by' the pupils in the construction of project material; relevant knowledge 'of' the pupils would be restricted to age and 'future studies' (for example a major criterion of relevance for the new 'integrated science' project has been, 'will pupils be able to go on to single subjects (physics, chemistry and biology) at 'A' level?'). Pupil science, for example, is only 'relevant' when incorporated into 'subject' science. However, one would speculate that the failure or inappropriateness of these projects may be explained by those involved, whether project developers or teachers, by drawing on 'knowledge' that has no explicit subject definitions of relevance. This suggests that this style does in practice carry with it a model of the child that incorporates many features that are not made formally explicit.

I am suggesting, that, although in the new 'O' level science syllabuses one finds few explicit references to what might be significant or relevant to different children's own non-school experience, implicit in the activity of construction of 'suitable' teaching materials is a concept of the kind of child the materials will be suitable for.

Focusing on the model of the typical child or children held by those involved in this style of project, could be one way of raising more general questions about social and political definitions of knowledge. It may not be without significance, to take an example, that the early working papers that formed the basis of the Nuffield 'O' levels in Physics, Chemistry and Biology were drawn up by members of the then Science Masters Association (now the Association for Science Education), which was founded by a group of Eton Science masters and has drawn its membership largely from independent, voluntary aided and direct grant grammar schools.

The underlying assumptions, particularly the notion of what counts as knowledge, of the 'good practice' style are less easy to postulate, partly because they are far less explicit. With its major emphasis on the exemplar of good practice, this style necessarily entails less emphasis on the cognitive aspects of 'practice', and more on the personal involvement of the learner[27], and an educational philosophy that is pragmatic and empiricist. The questions any enquiry would ask then are, firstly, what are the exemplars of 'good practice', and what are the tacit criteria used to identify them? If they cannot, as has been suggested, be made formally explicit, how are the 'ropes' of good practice learnt by pupils and student teachers? The second point is to consider the implications of the definitions of knowledge characteristic of the 'academic expertise' style, where the 'knowledge', not the teacher, is treated as the exemplar; how different in this context is the process of learning or not learning the 'academic ropes'? With the exception of one study (Reisman *et al*, 1970), sociological enquiry into education hardly seems to have raised these questions. Furthermore, an understanding of the processes involved in 'reconstructing' the 'good practice' of a sample of teachers' logics in use (to borrow Kaplan's distinction) which are then made available to other teachers would need much more detailed investigation.

It would not be surprising, given the common social and economic context in which they are generated, if there were significant similarities as well as the differences in educational philosophies of the two project styles that have been referred to. The 'academic expertise' style takes for granted the basic structure of academic 'subjects' while the 'good practice' style does not question the practice of 'good' teachers. Thus each makes implicit assumptions about the autonomy of educational knowledge from the society of which the educational institutions are a part. In this way both project styles may contribute to maintaining for educators the 'reality' of 'something that really *is* education' and the 'non-political' character of education.

To be able to suggest any explanations about how Schools Council priorities might be determined would seem premature without any access to records or committees. Council officials tend to claim that decisions rest on 'the quality of the proposals', and that they represent no balance across subjects, or age groups. However, though it is not easy to infer from the patterns of expenditure an alternative explanation, it would appear somewhat naive to accept at face value such statements from officials of an organization so strongly committed to not having a policy. This does not imply that such statements were not believed to be true, or that given the categories that they were working with (Languages, Science, English, Mathematics, Humanities, etc) they were not true. The point is that we would want to try and ask how are the categories themselves constituted,[28] and how might they influence the conception of available alternatives.

3 Types of child and types of knowledge

The Schools Council has had explicit priorities for projects specifically directed to 'the young school leaver'. Furthermore in Geography, Science and Maths, there are two separate projects, that can be broadly characterized as for the 'academic' and for the 'non-academic' child.

The features of the 'slow learning child' which are claimed to ground such 'projects for the majority' are well illustrated in the Schools Council's 'Science for the young school leaver'; the picture they present, in summary, is of a child who does not see relationships spontaneously, has difficulty in generalizing, is likely to be confused by open-endedness, and needs ideas repeated in successive guises. Such a view of the 'non-examination child' is reaffirmed in the more recent Bulletin (1970) which says that for these children 'reasons for doing the work must either be apparent to the pupils or explained . . . Materials, therefore deal with aspects of science which are important in the present lives of the pupils'. The curious notion one is left with is of the 'examination child', presumably, as one who needs no reasons for doing work (in this case science), and who works with materials that are of no importance to him. Therefore different kinds of courses with different kinds of examinations must be organized for different kinds of children. The maintenance of these distinctions has been a central if unpublicized aspect of the Schools Council activity; it has links to the two previous questions discussed, and implications both within the schools system and outside it. A glance at the teaching materials or working papers in the 'Young School Leaver' series (and a detailed analysis would be an important task for the sociologist) would suggest that whatever use teachers may make of such documents, the authors claim to be contributing to what they see as a critical 'teacher problem'[29] – the control and occupying of time of increasing numbers of children who would rather not be in school at all. Even if they are not made specific use of in the schools they confirm and legitimate the distinctions on which they are based, and thus also provide legitimacy for existing subject and institutional hierarchies and the assumptions about competence and ability that they imply. Within the schools the distinct courses make the feasibility of mobility between courses seem 'for all practical purposes' to be impossible. Outside of schools the distinction becomes (at the extreme) between those courses that are qualifcations for further schooling or particular jobs, and those courses that are qualifications for jobs that do not require qualifications, or no jobs. It is suggested therefore that the Schools Council, through its legitimation of curricula that might be characterized in Bourdieu's terms as based on 'class cultures', together with the schools, maintain the class structure of which they are a reflection. The task of a politics of educational knowledge, is then, in the context of this paper, not only the empirical study of such legitimations as 'academic expertise' and 'good practice', but also the construction of possible alternative models reflecting different assumptions about knowledge, learning and ability.

Conclusion

To conclude then, an attempt has been made to examine some of the implications of recognizing the political character of education by drawing on a sociology of knowledge perspective and focusing on a particular institution, the Schools Council. Some readers of this paper, whether they be teachers or sociologists or both, may well ask: why bother with the Schools Council? – it does not have any influence anyway. Whether or not this is true is beside the point, though the sale of over half a million copies of *Mathematics in the Primary School* – its first curriculum bulletin – and the increasing numbers of commercial companies signing contracts to publish Schools Council material would suggest that it is not. What is important, and in the widest sense what this paper is about, is to try to show how enquiries that start by considering education as a social category cannot be separated from a perspective which conceives of what is taught as a 'political' question. The former treat as problematic, and thefore as topics for enquiry, the social meanings that make the interaction between educational personnel in different contexts possible. The latter emphasizes the distribution of power which limits access to some contexts and some meanings and not others. Thus not only education, but educational research is political; to put it crudely, dossiers on children are available, but Department of Education and Schools Council minutes are not; teachers in classrooms are observable, the Programme Committee of the Schools Council is not. It is not surprising therefore that in this, as in other fields of sociological enquiry, we get detailed information about the subordinate group (in this case children), but only speculation or official histories of the activities of those who control their educational destinies. The parallel with recent criticisms of research into race relations is not hard to see. It has frequently been suggested that the separation of the sociology of knowledge from the sociological study of education has impoverished both. Perhaps a further suggestion is that a similar impoverishment has been a product of maintaining the distinction between education and politics, whether in sociology or anywhere else. However these speculations about the control and accessibility of knowledge may raise even more fundamental questions that are implicit, if not central to the sociological enquiries suggested in this paper. What kind of model of education is implicit is an alternative to one based on agreed definitions of expertise and good practice? What kind of model of society is implied where all or none are experts or good practitioners and there is no differential opportunity to avoid 'being researched', when, as it were, the researchers and controllers are researched?

Notes

[1] This point is a major focus of the work of Paulo Freire (1972a; 1972b).

[2] This term is taken from Bourdieu (1967; 1968), who in a series of papers has examined the relationship between kinds of educational institution and the structures implicit in various kinds of intellectual activity and modes of thought.

[3] The use of this 'global' term is not intended to imply any necessary consensus among a very heterogeneous group. It is merely a convenient way of referring to those who have a direct and officially defined responsibility for educational matters – teachers, union officials, administrators and academics.

[4] Paradoxically this was also true of the overtly political debate between the Black Paper supporters (Cox and Dyson 1969) and their opponents Rubinstein and Stoneman (1970) (among others), most of whom limit the terms of political debate to 'who gets education?' rather than the political character of education itself.

[5] That there are such grounds is very much part of the 'vocabulary of motives' (Mills 1940), referred to earlier, of those who write about, administer and practise education. The 'reality' of 'educational grounds' forms part of the tacit assumptions of all government reports and recent discussions about examinations and secondary school reorganization. They enable those involved to perceive their discussions as insulated from the political and economic context in which they take place.

[6] The Schools Council for Curriculum and Examinations was established in October 1964, on the lines recommended by the Lockwood Report (Ministry of Education 1964), with representatives from the teachers' unions, local authority associations and others. Details of its constitution, official policy and the scope of the projects it has sponsored can be found in its Annual Reports (Schools Council 1969; 1970).

[7] Banks (1968) in her chapter, 'Who controls our schools?', avoids making explicit what is meant by control. In this paper I shall use it in the way discussed in the introduction to Young (1971) when I draw explicitly on the ideas of Dawes (1970). It points to questions about how and by whom is meaning given to education.

[8] It would be naive to suppose that classroom teachers, in effect, ever thought they would control the Certificate of Secondary Education, in spite of its constitution which emphasized its regional basis, independence from the universities, and the process of nomination to the regional Boards through the teacher unions. This examination system was specifically set up for those children not able to reach General Certificate of Education (the university controlled system) standards. The fact, therefore that it maintained rather than questioned existing academic legitimacies with regard to the crucial question of access to higher education, may account for the universities' lack of active interest. Whether they will remain similarly detached during the projected discussions about amalgamating the two exam systems remains to be seen.

[9] Whether, and what it means to say that the Schools Council has *influenced* educational practice remains an empirical question. The lack of follow-up research and the inaccessibility of the Council to 'being researched' will be taken up later in the paper. Two points are worth mentioning here:

i The concern of the Council with the raising of the school leaving age has enabled schools to have a new claim on resources, though which section of the school population are in practice the beneficiaries remains to be seen.

ii The fate 'in the schools' of projects like the Humanities Curriculum Project (which was explicitly set up to provide material for 'children of average and below average ability') is uncertain, though the willingness of local authorities to sponsor in-service courses on the project material may be significant. The wider question this raises is whether some projects are more actively 'sponsored' than others.

[10] Not only does the Council have specific committees (see n 17) concerned with GCE and CSE examining, but 36 per cent (85) of the references to Schools Council projects refer to examining, mostly CSE (Schools Council 1971).

[11] Nisbet (1971) mentions that 20 of the 84 'A' Level syllabuses considered between 1968–70 were not approved, though we have no information as to the criteria of approval used.

[12] It is important to distinguish between Manzer's (1970) use of the term politics and that used in this paper, referred to earlier. The use in this paper is more akin to that of Dexter (1964) and Postman (1970), while Manzer's definition 'politics is the process by which social values are authoritatively allocated' (op cit, p 1) presupposes the consensus on values that it is the aim of this paper to treat as problematic.

[13] I am very grateful to Professor Nisbet for lending me a copy of his report prior to publication. Though it reads rather like an 'official history', it is useful in being carefully documented often from not readily accessible sources.

[14] By implication, what counts as 'education' is not questioned.

[15] A small group of 'experts', drawn mainly from the Ministry and the Inspectorate and set up in 1962.

[16] It would be more accurate to say the leaders of the teachers' unions and local authority associations, as Manzer is only able to document *their* public statements.

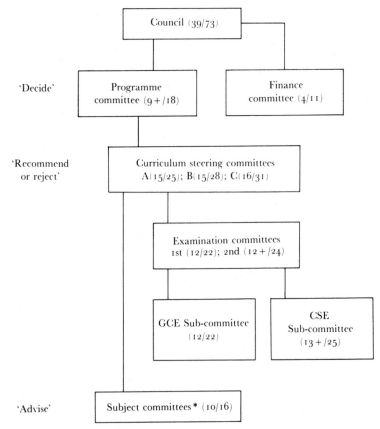

(* Art, classics, craft, English, geography, history, home economics, modern languages, music, physical education, maths, religious education, science, social science, general studies.)

¹⁷ The Constitution of the Schools Council lays down that all committees except the Finance Committee should have a majority of teacher representatives. The significance of the distinction made concerning the Finance Committee is uncertain, though Schools Council personnel would undoubtedly see it as subordinate to the 'teacher controlled' Programme Committee. A summary picture of the Council's formal structure is presented opposite and is adapted from *Dialogue*, no 1, the Schools Council's Newsletter.

Note Numbers refer to proportions of *teacher union* representatives.
Two points are worth mentioning here:
i Each potential 'project' is considered twice at each level, but can be rejected on the first or second 'round' by the Programme Committee.
ii The teacher majorities are in all cases small, so for the committees to be at least 'formally' teacher-controlled, a high level of teacher attendance is assumed.

¹⁸ For instance the nine teacher 'representatives' on the key Programme Committee come from five different unions, which in other contexts are competing for legitimacy and new members.

¹⁹ The question still remains as to how 'representative' the teachers' representatives are. They may tend to be union office holders, or potential office holders, and therefore in this context what 'representativeness' means remains uncertain.

²⁰ After a year or more of meetings they may even come to see themselves as primarily 'Schools Council men'. A possibility suggested by the most recent 'official' account of the aims and activities of the Schools Council (Caston 1971).

²¹ The 'Raising of the School Leaving Age' programme illustrates this. The whole question of compulsory school attendance for all for 11 years from 5–16 has only been discussed in terms of finding activities that are 'relevant' for the 'young school leaver' (itself an unexamined social category). More specific examples are how Working Paper 33, 'Choosing a curriculum for the Young School Leaver', and the Welsh Committee's 'Another Year – to endure or enjoy?' have an image of the characteristics and future occupational position of the 'type' of child under discussion, a point taken up in the final section in this paper.

²² The Steering Committees are the three Curriculum Committees referred to in n 17. They are distinguished by overlapping age categories which define their responsibilities (A from 8–13; B from 11–16; C from 14–18). B and C also supervise the examination Committees responsible, respectively for CSE and 'O' level, and 'A' level. One might speculate that members come to conceive of their groups of children as, partly, separate problems, with C Committee members being predominantly concerned with 'academic' children and B Committee members with 'non-academic' children. The Advisory Committees are those associated largely with the traditional subjects of the curriculum (see n 23).

²³ A very crude index of support for this can be obtained from an analysis of the Schools Council Project list produced by its Library and Information Centre. There are 161 references to what are usually called school subjects. Of these 84 (52 per cent) refer to science, English and maths, 28 (17 per cent) refer to geography, history and French, but only 7 (4 per cent) to home economics, technical drawing, health and handicraft.

²⁴ The conference in June 1971 on the Integration of the Social Sciences in the Sixth Form at Norwich, whatever its outcome, reflected in its conception

the group of 'subject' representatives that are represented on the Schools Council 'Social Science' Advisory Committee, and so, what one might call the Schools Council definition of 'Social Science'.

[25] The quotation is taken from Westbury and Steiner's (1971) paper, where they make an interesting comparison between the assumptions of two quite different approaches to curriculum development; Bereiter and Engelman's 'compensatory education' programme, and Dennison's (1969) description of his First Street School.

[26] This notion of structure was first used by Bruner (1960). Its implications have been examined by Kleiband (1964), who suggests that it has become a source of legitimacy for various 'subject associations' to gain economic support; he also suggests how the idea of 'structure' is related to an unquestioned acceptance of the disjunctions between school and non-school knowledge.

[27] For example in the 1969–70 Schools Council report, the reference to the 'Middle Years of Schooling' project emphasized the 'needs of the children . . . and ease of transition from primary to secondary education' (13); likewise in Working Paper 33, the project 'Arts and the Adolescent' emphasized the intention to 'study art education to pinpoint key factors effecting *success in terms of pupil response*', p. 33 (my italics).

[28] To view these categories as 'normative orders' (Blum 1970), is only to pose the problem. Empirically it would lead to an enquiry into what members of different committees take for granted in making these distinctions appear 'obvious'.

[29] That such ways of titling children are not restricted to writers of Schools Council papers is indicated by Townsend (1971) who describes his 'special child' in similar terms:

'He is unable to communicate suitably either verbally or literally.

His ability to read and write is far below what it should be. . . .

He has limited powers of concentration. . . .

Any given teaching method – however novel – soon loses its initial attraction for him

His powers of retention, as shown by regurgitation of facts, are poor.

His clothing and home background are of a low standard.

He lacks self confidence, and continually seeks reassurance. . . .'

In treating the 'causes' (home background and inter-marriage of kin as possibly leading to a low genetic pool') and 'characteristics' as relatively fixed, he goes on to propose a 'relevant science, within his capacity, specially designed to meet his needs', through which he argues 'we can offer our special child a valuable moral lesson'.

References

P BACHRACH and M S BARATZ. 'Decisions and non-decisions; an analytical framework'. *American Political Science Review*, **57** (3), 1963.

OLIVE BANKS, *The Sociology of Education*, Batsford, London, 1968.

ALAN BLUM, 'The corpus of knowledge as a normative order,' in *Theoretical Sociology*, ed J MCKINNEY and E TIRYAKIAN. Appleton Century Croft, New York, 1970. Also in MICHAEL F D YOUNG, 1971.

PIERRE BOURDIEU, 'Systems of education and systems of thought', *International Social Science Journal*, **19** (3), 1967.

PIERRE BOURDIEU, 'Intellectual field and creative project'. *Social Science Information*, **8**, (2) (both papers available in MICHAEL F D YOUNG, 1971).

JEROME S BRUNER, *The Process of Education*, Harvard University Press and Random House Vintage Books, New York, 1960.

GEOFFREY CASTON, 'The Schools Council in context'. *Journal of Curriculum Studies*, **3**, May.

A V CICOUREL and J I KITSUSE, *The Educational Decision Makers*, Bobbs Merrill, Indianapolis.

C E COX and A E DYSON, 'Black Papers 1 and 2', *Critical Quarterly*, 1969.

ALAN DAWES, 'The two sociologies', *British Journal of Sociology*, **21** (2), 1970.

LEWIS DEXTER, 'The politics and sociology of stupidity', in *The Other Side*, ed, HOWARD S BECKER, Free Press, New York.

GEORGE DENNISON, *The Lives of Children*. Random House, New York, 1969.

DAVID EASTON, *The Political System*, Alfred A Knopf, New York, 1953.

PAULO FREIRE, *Cultural Action for Freedom*, Penguin Books, 1972.

PAULO FREIRE, *Pedagogy of the Oppressed*, Penguin Books, 1972.

JOHN GOLDTHORPE, 'Social stratification in industrial societies', in *Sociological Review Monograph*, no 8, ed P Halmos.

Report of the Working Party on Schools Curricula and Examinations. HMSO 1964.

ROBIN HORTON, 'African traditional thought and Western science', *Africa*, **67**, and in MICHAEL F D YOUNG, 1971.

IVAN ILLICH, *Deschooling Society*, Penguin Books, London, 1971.

H KLEIBAND, 'Structure of the disciplines as an educational slogan', *Teachers College Record*, **66**.

R A MANZER, *Teachers and Politics*, Manchester University Press, 1970.

C W MILLS, 'Situated actions and vocabularies of motive'. *American Sociological Review*, **4** (5), 1940.

F W MUSGROVE, 'The sociologist's contribution to the curriculum', in J KERR, (ed), *Changing the Curriculum*, Unibooks, London, 1968.

F W MUSGROVE, *Patterns of Power and Authority in English Education*, Methuen London.

J NISBET, *The Schools Council*, unpublished report for the OECD, 1971.

NEIL POSTMAN, 'The politics of reading', *Harvard Educational Review*, **40** (2), 1970.

D REISMAN, J GUSFIELD and Z GAMSON, *Academic Values and Mass Education*, Doubleday, New York, 1970.

D RUBINSTEIN and C STONEMAN (eds), *Education for Democracy*, Penguin Books, 1970.

SCHOOLS COUNCIL, Schools Council Projects; Information Centre/Library (mimeographed), 1971.

I TOWNSEND, 'Science for the special child, part I.' *School Science Review*, **183**, 768–71, 1971.

I WESTBURY and W STEINER, 'A discipline in search of its problems.' *School Review*, February. 1971.

LAWRENCE WYLIE, *Village in the Vaucluse*, Harvard University Press, 1961.

J WRIGLEY, 'The Schools Council' in J BUTCHER and H B PONT (eds) *Educational Research in Britain*, **2**, University of London Press, 1970.

MICHAEL F D YOUNG (ed) *Knowledge and Control: New Directions for the Sociology of Education*. Collier-Macmillan, London, 1971.

157

Part Three

Ability as a Social Construct

It is ironic that despite the origins of psychometric intelligence testing in the context of attempts to devise more impartial instruments of educational selection, and in spite of the acknowledgement by some psychologists (eg D O Hebb, 1949) of the 'operational' and in that sense 'circular' character of psychometric definitions of intelligence, there can nevertheless be little doubt that constructs such as Mental Age and IQ have contributed to the widespread plausibility in Western educational settings of what Esland (Esland G M 1971) has called 'a psychometric model of intelligence,' – a model which 'endows the child with *an* intelligence, a capacity of given power within which his thinking develops'. As Mehan points out in the first reading in this section, it is typically the case that although 'the child's performance on standardized tests and his performance in class and out of school are seldom formally compared, test performance is', nevertheless, 'taken as an unquestioned, non-problematic measure of the child's underlying ability' and 'the authority of the test to meas-ure the child's "real" ability is not challenged'. Such reified notions of ability, however, as well as the more developmental conceptions of intelligence such as those proposed by Piaget, all presuppose and perhaps take for granted the culturally specific and socially con-stituted nature of the settings in which 'intelligent' activity is displayed, recognized and measured.

Mehan's paper subverts all reified conceptions of intelligence by restoring us to an awareness of the socially situated character of any attempt to measure human abilities. More particularly, he examines some of the ways in which 'the socially organized features of testing procedures' can be viewed as themselves contributing to the child-ren's performance on such tests. The outstanding merit of the read-ing by Gladwin is that it examines intellectual functioning in relation to particular cultural contexts and activities and yet suggests that, despite differences of a substantive kind, the *processes* of thought, theorizing, abstraction and inference found both in primitive cultures and in ethnic and social class sub-cultures are not inherently different

159

from the cognitive processes of members of 'academic' cultures in industrial societies. (N G Keddie, 1973) However, differences of 'idiom' (R Horton, 1967) may prevent such unfamiliar modes of cognitive functioning from being *recognized* as intelligent, and this may be a particular danger in formal educational settings. For example, children who are cultural strangers (A Schutz, 1964) in relation to 'normal' school activities, may be viewed by their teachers as cognitively deficient rather than simply as culturally different. Moreover, the scores of such children on tests of intelligence may be interpreted as a 'scientific' confirmation of such judgements. The possibility of such mistaken interpretations being made suggests that it is important to study teachers' *common-sense* assumptions and theories about their pupils' cognitive capacities, since such practical theories may well have consequences for children's educational careers. This concern is central to the extracts from the book by Cicourel and Kitsuse and the polemical paper by Bernard Coard.

The readings by Herndon, Dexter and Hines are united by a recognition which is most explicit in the paper by Dexter, that 'ability' is the basis of a cardinal *moral* status in Western societies, which implies the existence of social penalties for those who are judged deficient.

References

G M ESLAND 'Teaching and Learning as the Social Organization of Knowledge', in M F D YOUNG (ed) *Knowledge and Control*, 1971, Collier-Macmillan, London.

D O HEBB *The Organization of Behaviour*, Chapman-Hall, London.

R HORTON 'African Traditional Thought and Western Science', in M F D YOUNG (ed) *Knowledge and Control*, 1971, Collier-Macmillan, London.

N G KEDDIE, *Tinker, tailor . . . the Myth of Cultural Deprivation*, Penguin, London, 1973.

A SCHUTZ, 'The Stranger', in *Collected Papers*, **II**, Martinus Nijhoff, The Hague, 1964.

Assessing Children's School Performance*

Hugh Mehan

Socialization and Education

The conventional American school is a major socializing agency in the United States. Compulsory education laws place the child in school most of his waking hours nine months of the year from the age of six until sixteen or eighteen. The school has assumed responsibility for instructional activities which were previously accomplished informally or at home, including the transmission of cultural values, and the acquisition of the skills and abilities considered necessary for competent societal membership.

The conventional American school is a classic example of a bureaucratically organized institution. Its governance is hierarchically arranged, and responsibility is allocated among highly trained specialists. A superintendent is in charge of a school system composed of a number of schools, each of which is directed by a principal. The principal is in charge of an administrative and a teaching staff. The administrative staff is responsible for budgetary, custodial, and business matters, while the teaching staff is concerned with instructing the pupils. Work and responsibility is further divided within the teaching staff. Some teachers specialize in teaching at the primary grade level, others at the secondary level. Some teachers are subject matter specialists, teaching maths, science, history, etc, exclusively.

Performance Assessment in Elementary Schools

Specialization and compartmentalization also characterize the way subject matter is presented to pupils and the way in which the pupil's academic performance is evaluated. Lessons are generally taught in compartments of equal physical size during periods of equal temporal length. A concern for objective evaluation has led to the use of standardized educational tests to assess the child's performance. The

* H P Dreitzel (ed) *Recent Sociology no 5, Childhood and Socialization*, Collier Macmillan Canada Ltd 1973.

child's performance on reading, IQ, and language development tests, among others, inform decisions which school officials make to promote or retain children, and to place them in certain 'tracks' or 'skill groups' within classes. Children's test results are also used by school superintendents and state education officials to gauge the quality of teachers' performances and to evaluate and compare schools and school districts.

Although the teacher in the classroom has daily, personal contact with the children in her[1] class, sees them in a wide variety of teaching-learning situations, at various motivational and performance levels, she does not have well documented reports of her children's achievement and progress. Consider the classroom situation. There are often more than thirty children constantly making demands on the teacher. She has to keep track of each child's rate of progress, remember current interests and peculiar problems. Often she has to involve many different children in diverse activities simultaneously. While she is explaining a math problem to one child, another may be seeking help with his art work. The teacher must be able to encourage both without discouraging either. If the teacher decides to work closely with a small group of children, she must also monitor from a distance the rest of the children who may be playing, working alone, or with a teaching aid.

Because often more than 30 children make constant demands on the teacher's attention, and because educational activities blend into each other without 'time out' or breaks in between, the teacher is not able to write out a detailed progress report for each child's performance in such subjects as arithmetic, spelling, and science each day or after each lesson. Instead she has vague, loosely assembled impressions about each child in her class which are subject to constant change as the child's performance varies from lesson to lesson and day to day. The teacher takes time once or twice a semester to write reports about each child which are placed in his cumulative record, perhaps sent home to the child's parents, or are discussed with them if they visit the school for 'parent-teacher' conferences. In preparing the report, the teacher is faced with the problem of transforming the swarm of impressions she has had about each child into a coherent and orderly form. The teacher produces descriptions like 'Johnny seems to have trouble with fine motor control'; 'Suzie has mastered initial consonants, short vowels, initial digraphs, initial blends, and is ready for elementary readers'; 'Max is unable to make left-right discriminations which hinders him when he reads' which, in their abbreviated, summary form, are far removed, high level glosses of the moment to moment, day to day changes in attention, interest, and performance which led to those formulations.

Parents complain that such descriptions are uninformative and meaningless, and do not explain the 'successes' or 'troubles' their child is having in school. Teachers who read such descriptions about the children they inherit each year complain that they are unreliable and do not instruct them on how to construct the child's program of learning.

Because teachers often do not have documents to support their claims about the child's performance, and because the documents they do have are considered vague and unreliable, teachers and other school officials turn to standardized intelligence and achievement tests to measure the child's ability and to assess his academic progress. Standardized tests have all the features found lacking in teachers' subjective reports. They can be uniformly, simply, and neatly applied; all children are examined on the 'same' material. Each child receives a score which can be compared to 'national norms' and scores of other children.

Although the use of standardized tests seems to have solved the problem of subjective and non-uniform teacher evaluation, the child's performance on standardized tests and his performance in class and out of school are seldom formally compared. Test performance is taken as an unquestioned, non-problematic reflection of the child's underlying ability. When informal comparisons of children's classroom performance and test results are made (teachers constantly make remarks like 'I thought Johnny was smarter than that IQ test showed' and 'I didn't think Max was as good as that test showed, but I guess he must be smart after all'), the authority of the test to measure the child's 'real' ability is not challenged. The evaluation of the child's ability obtained by test measurement is accepted by teachers and other school officials, while teachers' evaluations which contradict test results are dismissed by principals (and soon by the reporting teachers) as biased, subjective, and inaccurate.[2]

Contrastive Performance Assessment

As part of a larger sociolinguistics study[3], I investigated the school performance of elementary school children in contrasting educational environments by videotaping and analyzing adult-child interaction in the classroom, in testing encounters, and the home (MEHAN, 1971).

One of the Southern California schools used a series of psycholinguistic tests to evaluate the child's language skills. Children's results on these tests contributed to decisions made to place children in one of the three first grade classrooms (see LEITER, in CICOUREL, ET AL, in preparation.) The children who scored lowest on the diagnostic tests were all placed in one classroom. Their poor test performance, coupled with their low SES (and often Chicano origin) seemed to make these children prime examples of the 'culturally deprived child'[4] placed in a special classroom designed to accelerate their academic progress.

One of these children's sources of trouble on the school's diagnostic tests was an inability to respond correctly to questions asking for discriminations about sentences with prepositional phrases which express locational reference. Because the children had had difficulty with prepositions and other grammatical forms, the teacher presented them with 'language development' lessons to teach them the requisite grammatical forms. My informal comparison of the children's responses on the Fall diagnostic test with their work in early language development lessons showed that some children gave correct responses in one situation but not the other. The children's differential performances on tests and lessons prompted me to examine those situations to see whether the socially organized features of the interrogation procedure itself contributed to the children's performance and the school official's evaluations of it.

Examining the Assumptions of the Formal Test

The educational test is constructed with the following assumptions about (1) the nature of cognitive abilities, (2) the meaning of test items, (3) the basis of the respondent's performance, and (4) the testing situation.

(1) The educational test, though not always an IQ test, incorporates the assumptions about the nature of mental abilities which originated in intelligence testing theory. Spearman (1923) proposed that each individual possesses a general intelligence factor (g). Intelligence is viewed as a fixed mental capacity 'of the individual to act purposefully, to think rationally, to deal effectively with his environment' (Wechsler, 1944:3). The implication is that intelligence is an underlying mental ability. Underlying mental abilities are composed of previously learned experiences, accumulated knowledge, and skills. Simply stated, if learning opportunities and all other factors are equal, those persons who learn the most and perform the best probably have greater innate mental capacity than those who learn and perform most poorly' (Mercer, 1971:322–23). Tests measure these experiences learned in the past.

(2) The tester assumes that the meaning of instructions, questions, and answers is obvious to the test taker and is shared among the test constructor, test taker, and test administrator. The test items serve as unambiguous stimuli which tap the respondents' underlying attitudes

about or knowledge of certain factors.

Each test item is considered to be clear and unambiguous because the test constructor assumes that persons taking the test have had experience with the test items, whether they be words, pictures, or objects, and that the test experience will be the same as the prior experiences he has had with these items. Because of this assumed similarity of experience, test takers will interpret the items in the same way the test constructor did when he compiled the items. Because each test item will be interpreted only in the way intended by the test constructor, the test taker's reasons or purposes for making certain choices, or for giving certain explanations are assumed to match the purposes of the tester.

Each question asked has a correct answer which consists of a connecting link between stimulus instruction and test item. The respondent who answers questions properly is assumed to have searched for and found the intended connection between questions and materials. While correct answers to questions are seen as products of correct search procedures, incorrect answers are seen as the products of faulty reasoning, or the lack of underlying ability, knowledge or understanding.

(3) The educational tester makes the same assumptions about the measurement of behavior that the experimental psychologist makes: 'A psychological experiment, then, can be symbolized by S-O-R, which means that E (understood) applies a certain stimulus (or situation) to O's receptors and observes O's response' (Woodworth and Schlosberg, 1954:2). The test taker, like the experimental subject, responds to the stimulus, and his response is a direct and sole result of the 'stimulus acting at that moment and the factors present in the organism at that moment' (Woodworth and Schlosberg, 1954:3).

(4) The respondent's behavior is considered to be the sole result of his underlying abilities and stimulus application because other factors and variables which might be influential are able to be standardized and controlled.

Standardization implies uniformity of procedure in administering and scoring the test. . . . Such standardization extends to the exact materials employed, time limits, oral instructions to subjects, preliminary demonstrations, ways of handling queries from subjects, and every other detail of the testing situation (Anastasi, 1968:23).

The tester (or experimenter) is supposed to present the stimulus while holding other factors in the situation constant. The test is supposed to be standardized in its presentation of stimuli so that all respondents face the same conditions which make comparisons of performances and replications possible.

The assumptions made by the formal test include: (1) the abilities being tested are the products of past experience, (2) cultural meanings are shared in common by tester and respondent, (3) the respondent's performance is an exclusive function of underlying abilities and stimulus presentation, (4) stimuli are presented to respondents in standardized ways, extraneous variables in the testing situation are controlled, and (5) the tester passively records the respondent's performance.

The structure of the testing encounter was examined in two ways. First, six of the first grade children who took the Spring test were videotaped. After the test was over, I informally interrogated the children about their perceptions and understandings of the testing materials. Second, versions of the formal test which systematically altered its features were presented to the first grade children.

The language development tests employed by the school are picture indentification tasks in which children are asked to identify the grammatical forms represented by a series of pictures by pointing to the one that correctly characterizes it. Instead of using only one kind of stimulus, I used three alternative versions of the picture identification task. I had children demonstrate their knowledge of orientational prepositions by manipulating their hands, manipulating small objects, and by drawing pictures in response to the instructions I gave. I contrasted the formal testing characteristic of a strange and unfamiliar environment by presenting the 'orientations tasks' to children in the less formal surroundings of the classroom, and (to a few) in the familiar settings of their homes. To examine the 'common culture' assumption, the general research design required that one test be presented in Spanish to those children familiar with that language, and that all children's definitions and conceptions of testing materials be analyzed. Six classroom and six home testing encounters were videotaped[5].

Results of Children's Performances
The results of the children's performances on the two sessions of school administered tests and the 'orientations tasks' appear in Table 1. A table of scores like this one, or a more general comment like: 'Adam has command of preopositions,' or 'Sarah does not comprehend the negative or the orientational preposition' is characteristically provided to teachers after a testing session and is entered into the child's school record. I will now examine this table of scores to see that it reports about the child's abilities and the manner in which

Table 1 RESULTS OF LANGUAGE TESTING IN THREE FIRST GRADES

Part A: Individual Results

| | School Tests | | Variations | |
Child	Fall	Spring	Class	Home
1 (Jean)	73	69	93	100
2 (Clare)	10	50	86	86
3 (Lesli)	46	76	44	65°
4 (Lora)	10	25	33	60°
5	50	61	86	
6	52	54	77	
7	75	85	75	
8	65	70	80	
9	60	75	75	
10	40	50	50	
11	15	25	37	
12	60	75	55	
13	35	70	75	
14	55	85	87	
15	35	65	67	
16	63	77	80	
17	50	54	60	85°
18	85	95	93	
19	56	86	55	75°
20	10	35	33	
21	85	95	95	
22	35	50	45	
23	75	85	85	
	1140	1512	1566	

° Tested in Spanish at home.

Part B: Results by Classroom

| | School Tests | | Classroom |
Classroom	Fall	Spring	Variations
# 1	49·5	65·7	68·0
# 2	73·0	87·0	
# 3	77·0	82·0	

results are reported. Such a table of scores or a general descriptive statement (1) obscures the child's understanding of the materials and task, (2) does not capture the child's reasoning abilities and (3) does not show the negotiated, contextually bound measurement decisions which the tester makes while scoring the child's behavior as 'correct' or 'incorrect.'

The Child's Conception of the Task

One question on the school language test (the Basic Concept Inventory, Englemann, 1967, henceforth BCI) asks the respondent to decide which child in a group is the tallest. Because the heads of the children are obscured, the child taking the test is supposed to reply that he can't make that judgment. However, many children examined selected one of the children in the picture as the tallest. When I interviewed the children after they took the Spring test, and I asked them why they chose that boy, they replied that he was the tallest boy because 'his feet are bigger.' Investigating the thread of reasoning used by the children, then, showed that they understood the *intent* of the question – to discriminate and compare – but they were not using the same criteria as the tester. Because they were not using the criteria *intended* (but never explicated), answers which indicated that one child was taller than another were marked wrong. However, in this case, a wrong answer does not index a lack of ability, but rather the use of an alternative scheme of interpretation.

Another question on the BCI asks the child to decide which of two boxes a ball is in after the tester has told him which box the ball is *not* in. The child is expected to point to the box which the tester hasn't touched. The question following that on the BCI asks the child to decide which of *three* boxes a ball is in after the tester has told the child which box does not contain the ball. The child is expected to say the problem can't be solved. Many children failed to answer this question correctly; they chose one or sometimes both, of the remaining two boxes. In a follow-up interview, when I asked the children why they chose one of the other boxes (instead of saying the problem could not be solved) they replied: 'You said it's not in that one.' I think children find it untenable to doubt an adult's word. An adult has told the child that a state of affairs actually exists: 'There is a ball in one of these three boxes.' He has been told that the ball isn't in one, so, he reasons: 'It must be in one of the other two because the adult said do.' That is, these children's answers may have been wrong, but not necessarily because they didn't have the proper reasoning ability; rather, they lacked the sophistication necessary to doubt an adult's word.

A question from another language development test instructs the child to choose the 'animal that can fly' from a bird, an elephant, and a dog. The correct answer (obviously) is the bird. Many first grade children, though, chose the elephant along with the bird as a response to that question. When I later asked them why they chose that answer they replied: 'That's Dumbo.' Dumbo (of course) is Walt Disney's flying elephant, well known to children who watch television and read children's books as an animal that flies.

On another BCI question the child is asked to 'find the ones that talk' when presented pictures of a man, a boy, a dog, and a table. Children frequently include the dog along with the man and the boy as an answer to this question. For those children who have learned to say their pets 'speak' or 'talk' that is not an unlikely choice. Deciding that the child doesn't know how to use the verb 'talk' correctly would, in this case, be erroneous, for that decision would have resulted from an unexamined assumption that both adult and child attribute the same characteristics to objects or are attending to them in the same way.

For a question from another language development test, children are presented a picture of a medieval fortress – complete with moat, drawbridge, and parapets – and three initial consonants: D, C, and G. The child is supposed to circle the correct initial consonant. C for 'castle' is correct, but many children choose D. After the test, when I asked those children what the name of the building was, they responded 'Disneyland.' These children used the same line of reasoning intended by the tester, but they arrived at the wrong substantive answer. The score sheet showing a wrong answer does not document a child's lack of reasoning ability; it only documents that the child indicated an answer different from the one the tester expected.

These descriptions demonstrate that the child can exist simultaneously in a number of different 'realities' or worlds (Schutz, 1962:207–59), ie, the 'factual' world of everyday life and the world of fantasy. The child who says that animals can fly and talk is (from the adult point of view) mixing and blending the characteristics of fantasy and everyday worlds. The test, however, assumes the child is attending to stimulus items only from the viewpoint of the everyday world where dogs do not talk and elephants do not fly. The test assumes further that the child keeps the world of play, fantasy, and television out of the testing situation. Yet, as these anecdotes demonstrate, the child of age 4–6 does not always keep his realities sequentially arranged. Because the child may be operating simultaneously in multiple realities, valid interrogations must examine why a child answers questions as he does and must determine what children 'see' in educational materials; they must not use test results exclusively.

In sum, a document of the children's correct and incorrect responses, such as Table 1, does not show the variation in the children's answers across materials, test, and languages of interrogation. Conventional testing techniques cannot determine if a child's wrong answers are due to his lack of ability or are due to his equally valid alternative interpretations. Differences in tester and child meaning of educational materials does not lend support for the 'common culture' assumption of the educational test.

The Test Assembly Process

A table of correct answers (eg, Table 1) is a static display which does not capture the contextually bound, fluid and dynamic activities which constitute its production.[6] When I re-examined the videotape of the testing sessions which produced Table 1, I found that these results were not as unequivocal as they appeared in tabular form.

Testers deviated from the requirements of a mechanical, uniform presentation of instructions and stimuli to respondents. The school test required a series of pictures to be presented to respondents, each with the instruction 'look at the picture'. The following variations on that introductory comment are just some of those recorded during the school administered testing session which I videotaped. (Similar deviations occurred in the informal tests that I presented and may be observed in any interrogation) (cf, Friedman, 1968, who documents the same phenomenon in social-psychological experiments.)

FT[7]	1:7	Look at that picture and show a find . . .
	4:17	Y'see all the things in that picture
	8:1	Let's look at that one
	11:1	Now you look at those pictures
	3:3	I want you to look at that picture and tell me what you see by looking at the picture
	1:8	Look at this picture now
	5:9	See all those pictures?
	5:10	What those?
	5:11	Okay, now I want you to find the right ones

Under the criteria of the formal test, test takers are supposed to respond only to stimulus materials presented to them, but these respondents are not receiving the same stimulus instructions. Some are being told to look and find the correct pictures; others are being told just to look. No child, however, is told what constitutes a correct answer. The child is expected to operate without this information.

When I re-examined the testing videotapes, I found that when children were asked a question, they presented many displays. If I looked at one of the other displays the children presented, rather than those originally scored, a substantially different evaluation of each child's performance would have been obtained. In cases where a child had been marked wrong, an instance of the correct display was apparent in his actions, and vice versa. If that display, rather than the one noted by the tester had been recorded, the child's overall score would have changed.

When answering questions, the child is supposed to touch that picture or part of it that best answers the question asked. Often the children either did not touch any part of the objects represented in the picture, or covered more of the picture than was required by the question. Because the child's response was ambiguous, the tester had to determine the boundaries of the answering gesture to the stimulus picture. Depending on which picture the space between the pictures was assigned to, the tester either marked the child right or marked him wrong.

When the children touched two or more pictures in succession, the tester had to decide which of the movements was intended by the child as his answer. On a number of occasions, the children began to answer before the complete question was asked. Regardless of whether or not the correct picture was touched, the tester did not count the action as an answer. It seemed that the responses had to be given *after* questions had been completely asked in order to be considered answers-to-questions.

Some children touched the page of pictures with both of their hands simultaneously, and also laid their palms flat on the page while answering a question. In these cases, one hand touched an 'incorrect' part of the page while the other hand touched the 'correct' part. To count the child's answer as correct in these cases, the tester had to assign the status of 'hand indicating an answer' to one hand and not the other.

The following example is representative of the way in which the tester assigned the status of 'answer' during the orientations tasks. In the hand manipulation phase of the orientations task, after I finished my instruction: 'Put your hand below the table,' Clare placed his hand in the air:

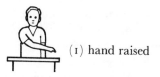

(1) hand raised

I repeated the substance of the instruction: 'Below the table,' and Clare modified his initial response. He lowered his hand slowly until it was parallel with and off the side of the table top:

(2) hand off to the side

He paused there, and I said nothing. His hand continued in the arc he had been circumscribing until it was as far down below the table as it would go:

 (3) hand underneath, but not touching the underside of the table.

At that point, realizing that I had, in fact, influenced his behavior and thereby modified his answer, I attempted to neutralize this influence by saying, 'Put it anywhere you want.' Clarc left his hand in the last position (3), and I scored that 'final' placement 'correct.' But note, there are at least three separate displays given in response to the question asked. The production of multiple responses was obviously influenced by the challenges I made of the child's responses. With each challenge, the child modified his behavior until his arm could literally go no further under the table. Had I recorded either of his first two displays as his 'answer' rather than challenging those displays, the child would have been considered wrong for this question.

The protocol conditions of the formal testing procedures are violated in other ways. In the school tests, the child is supposed to touch the correct picture as soon as the question is read. Often more than one picture is to be touched in response to a question. Ideally, the child is supposed to touch all pictures as soon as the question is read. Often the child only touches one. When this occurs, a tester employs various practices to elicit further answers from the child. A tester may prompt the child with verbal cues like 'that one,' or 'is that the only one?' These cues tell the child to continue searching for more answers in the series. A similar cue is provided non-verbally when the tester pauses after a response and does not immediately go on to the next question. The pause serves as a cue to the child to keep looking for a correct answer. When the tester provides a commendatory comment like 'good', 'fine', or goes immediately on to the next question, the child is prohibited from providing any more responses or changing answers he has already given.

Not only do testers contribute to respondents' productions, but respondents interrupt and thereby contribute to their interrogation. During a test, the tester is supposed to ask questions and the respondent is supposed to answer them. But if a respondent asks the tester a question instead of just answering the tester's question, the adult is forced to respond to the demand made of him by the respondent, ie, the adult/tester has to respond to the demand made of him by the child/respondent *before* the child answers the original test question.[8] The tester can ignore the child's request and repeat the original question, he can pause and say nothing, or he can provide a 'neutral' comment like 'do whatever you think is best.' Regardless of the tester's reaction to the child's request, though, the child gains further information that influences his interpretation of the original request made of him.

The following interchange exemplifies the manner in which the child gains supplemental information from a tester's responses to his questions. A child was asked to draw a circle above the line. She placed her pencil on the paper at a point slightly above the diagonal line she had drawn and asked: 'Above?' 'Right here?'

I interpreted the child's action as a request for information about the suitability of an answer which she was considering giving. She had not yet committed herself to producing a particular answer, but was asking for confirmation of a possible answer in advance of its production.

That request for information required me to respond in some way. Regardless of my action, the child would learn something about the suitability of the answer she was proposing. I chose to repeat the question as a way out of the dilemma posed by her question. The child then reviewed the entire paper. Her pencil wandered all around the area of the line – both above and below it. She finally settled on this point:

While performing this act, she asked: 'Right here?' Perhaps exasperated, perhaps convinced that she now 'knew' the answer, perhaps unable to restrain myself, I said 'Okay.' The child drew a circle at the second point and got the question right.

Summary
This examination of testing interactions shows test assumptions are not met in practice. Stimulus items are not presented in standardized ways. Test materials do not always have the same meaning for tester

and child. The child's performance is not just the result of his ability and the stimulus presented but is also influenced by contextually provided information. The respondent's answers are not the product of the tester's passive record keeping; they emerge from the tester's interpretive assessment of the child's actions.

The tester is not just examining and recording the child's response. He is actively engaged in assigning the status of 'answer' to certain portions of the child's behavioral presentation. The tester is according differential status to similar behavioral displays produced by the child as answers-to-questions because the tester is not seeing the child's display in isolation from other aspects of the testing situation. The fingers used to point and the hand laid on the page are included in a perceptual field and are seen against a constantly changing background of features which includes the questions asked, the child's restlessness, his performances on previous questions, teachers' reports about him, and the tester's expectations for the child's performance on any particular question. Therefore, the 'same' behavioral display, seen against different backgrounds, is interpreted differently; it obtains a different reading. In short, test taking and test scoring are interpretive interactional processes which should be approached and studied as such.

Educational Implications

Performance in Different Interrogation Contexts

I have suggested that examining only educational test results makes it impossible to determine the child's understanding of test materials, and prohibits comparison of his test performance with his daily experiences. When I assessed first grade children's abilities in different situations and with different materials, their performances varied. Comparing the results of the children's performances on two sessions of school administered tests with my informal variations (Table 1) shows that the children scored better on the informal tests than on the formal tests.

These results are consistent with other studies which examine the child's performance in different contexts of interrogation. Labov (1969) and Lewis (1970) have shown how Black children produce more vivid, complex, and spontaneous utterances in peer centred, unstructured situations than they do in the power relationship of adult over child, Abrahams (1970), Mitchell-Kernan (1969), and Ward (1971) give numerous examples of the Black child's oral expressiveness outside the classroom. Phillips (1970) documents the reluctance of Indian children from the Warmsprings Reservation to participate in classroom verbal interaction when it is competitive, adult organized, and controlled, in contrast to the eagerness of these same children to speak out when activity is unstructured, unsupervised, and group centered. These results suggest that the structure of the interrogation encounter influences the assessment of the child's abilities. Cultural deprivation proponents say the minority child's school failure is the function of the child's lack of language and culture. These studies demonstrate that the minority child possesses language and culture, but his are often different than that demanded in the white middle-class oriented classroom. Therefore, it seems that the minority child's poor school performance may be due to the inability of current educational interrogation methods to assess the child's abilities and may not be the result of the minority child's lack of ability, language, or culture.

Language and Meaning in Educational Testing

The scores of the children tested who speak both Spanish and English show they scored higher when question were asked of them in Spanish than when questions were asked of them in English at school. If this difference in performance were shown to be systematic across all bilingual children, it could lead to the conclusion that these children understand instructions better when they are presented in their native language, which, in turn can lead to the recommendation to instruct and test bilingual children in their native language.

Due to the difficulties inherent in developing 'culture free' and 'culture specific' tests[9], educational tests have commonly been modified by translation in response to the problems raised by the need to test children from different cultures (Mercer, 1971). Darcy (1963) summarized the bilingualism testing literature. The consistent findings reported were (1) bilingual subjects received significantly lower scores than comparable monolinguals, (2) bilinguals received lower scores when tested in their native language than when they were tested in English, (3) bilinguals scored lower on verbal tests than they did on non-verbal tests. The second result was explained by the fact that the children were instructed in English, while their native language training stopped, for all intents and purposes, when the children entered primary school; thus, the translated version of the formal test probably differed significantly from the native language familiar to the children.

Translating assessment materials will not solve the school problems of the lower class or bilingual child because the content of the entire interrogation encounter, not just the words of the test, is culture bound. Questions, materials, and referents reflect the content of the culture in which the test was developed. Simply translating the content of a test designed for persons socialized in one culture into the language of another does not eliminate culture differences.

Furthermore, the respondent's performance and the observer's evaluation of that performance is an interpreted and negotiated process. Although my analysis of interrogation encounters is not finely enough calibrated to decide which particular situational features available to a child contribute to his answer on a given occasion, I have shown that much more than just the presentation of stimulus items serves as the source of the child's answer. Although the tester assumes variations in stimulus presentation and his intervening activity do not contribute to the child's understanding of testing materials and are unimportant features in his evaluation of the respondent's performance, I have shown the child is not attending to stimulus items in isolation and the tester is not passively recording 'answers.' The questions and materials appear against a background composed of the negotiated aspects of the question-answer sequence, verbal and non-verbal cues. Because the respondent has to interpret the entire interrogation setting, the translation of materials, or the substitution of one mode of interrogation for another, does not solve the respondent's test taking problems, for he must interpret the materials against a situationally provided background. Simple translation and the exclusive reliance on any single kind of instrument to evaluate competence is limited, for such practices fail to recognize that each communicative encounter is self-organizing (Zimmerman and Pollner, 1970:94–100), and each question-answer sequence imposes its own perceptual demands and interpretive requirements on respondents and evaluators.

In short, each encounter between interrogator and respondent has its own social organization and unique features which produce different (not necessarily better) evaluations of a respondent. Therefore, instead of searching for a single best test or a best single learning environment, the recommendation being made here is to study the interpretive process in any educational environment, and to examine a child's performance in different situations so that the encounter best suited to the child's experience can be utilized.

Notes
[1] The feminine pronoun is used to reflect the high proportion of women teachers in public schools.

[2] A number of writers, eg, Dennison (1969), Friere (1970), Holt (1964), Kozol (1968), Illich (1970), have criticized the prevailing structure and organization of conventional schools. The research of which this report is a part is focusing on the procedures used to evaluate the child's performance

and is attempting to point out the practical problems facing the teacher in the classroom regardless of organizational structure.

[3] The overall contrastive study of language acquisition, language use, and school performance utilized data gathered in 1969–1970 from two elementary schools in Southern California. Cicourel is studying the demands that multiple sources of information make on teachers' and children's information processing. Jennings and Jennings are studying the interactional aspects of the psycholinguistic assessment of the child's acquisition of syntactic structures. Leiter is analyzing the decision-making processes school officials use to place children in elementary school classrooms. MacKay is contrasting teachers' and children's conceptions of classroom and testing materials. Roth is examining the conception of the child's abilities which intelligence tests provide educators (see Cicourel, et al, in preparation). In related studies, Boese (1971) described the deaf child's acquisition and use of natural sign language, and Shumsky (1972) describes the structure of interpretations of an encounter group session.

[4] Lower class American Indian, Black, Chicano, Puerto Rican, and other 'minority' children perform poorly in school by comparison with their middle class school mates. This poor performance has been said to be the result of a cultural or hereditary deficiency by some educators and researchers (see Jensen, 1969; Hernstein, 1971; Bereiter and Englemann, 1966; Hunt, 1964; Deutsch, 1964). The *hereditary* deprivation argument, defended primarily by Jensen and Hernstein, is explained and critically examined by Roth in this volume. The *culturally* deprived child is said to be the product of an impoverished environment. It is argued that overcrowded facilities, infrequent social contact, inconsistent discipline, absence of cultural artifacts provide limited opportunities for the lower class child to be verbally expressive, develop cooperative, perceptual, and attitudinal skills. As a result, the child is said to possess an impoverished language and has few of the skills and experiences required by the middle class oriented school.

The two forms of the cultural deprivation explanation of the lower class child's school failure have been attacked by linguists, sociologists, and anthropologists (see, for example, Laboy, 1969; Gumperz, 1972; and a collection of essays in Williams, 1970), who argue that the lower class child does not come from a *deprived* environment or speak a *degraded* language, but rather possesses a *different* culture and speaks a language which has some different grammatical rules and rules for social usage. These cultural and linguistic differences produce anomalies for the lower class child in the classroom as he is expected to perform in ways he has not been taught.

Care must be taken in saying the Black, Chicano, or other minority child possesses a different culture. Although many proponents of the 'difference' thesis recognize the existence of alternate cultures, it is possible that the child's behavior which is called culturally different may be treated in the same way as behavior which is called culturally deficient: as behavioral attributes to be eradicated. A third proposal, called 'bi-cultural' by Valentine (1971) and others recognizes and seeks to preserve the ethnic child's unique cultural identity while allowing him to develop skills which allow him to operate in the white middle class culture if he so chooses.

Although the 'deficit' rather than the 'difference' or 'bicultural' thesis has been the dominant view among educators during the last two decades, the 'deprived' child's 'impoverished' cultural or linguistic system has not been shown to inhibit actual classroom interaction. Instead the academic and behavioral difficulties of the 'deprived' child have been documented by the use of data, gathered from formal tests conducted outside the classroom. This report, then, is in part an examination of the 'deficiency' thesis which advertises its findings without a critical examination of the methods used to assess the child's abilities.

5 This is obviously not the first critical examination of educational tests. Educators, psychologists, and sociologists have long been concerned with the accuracy and fairness of educational tests. Previous criticisms of testing, however, have dealt only with the *product* and *results* of testing, ie, the test scores of different groups of children have been compared. When differences in test scores (read: ability) have been found, attempts have been made to make tests 'culture free' (eg, Goodenough draw-a-man, David-Eel's games, the Raven Progressive Matrices), or to develop culture-sensitive tests (eg, by translating tests into the respondent's native language, eg, the Peabody Picture Vocabulary Test, the Stanford-Binet, and the WISC). (Mercer, 1971 presents a concise summary of this literature.) The examination of tests reported here differs from previous ones in that testing is treated as an interactional accomplishment. The meaning of the testing situation, the source of the respondent's answer, and the tester's scoring are examined from within ongoing testing situations.

6 The way in which production procedures and practices are said to constitute socially organized settings is explained by Garfinkel (1967), Garfinkel and Sacks (1970), Cicourel (1968b, 1969, 1970, and forthcoming), and Zimmerman and Pollner (1970).

7 Numbers refer to the full transcript of the school administered testing session; transcripts which are part of this study may be examined upon request.

8 Sacks (1967–1970) and Schegloff (1968, 1971) have proposed that when one question follows another in conversation, the question asked second is answered before the one asked first. Schegloff (1971) calls this an 'embedded question' sequence:

Turn	Speaker	Response
1	Tester	question———
2	Child	question——
3	Tester	answer——
4	Child	answer——

9 From its appearance in 1926, Goodenough's 'draw-a-man' test was considered a possible culture-free test of intelligence because it was non-verbal, presumably not subject-matter related, and the referent drawn was universal. Recent testing has shown, however, that Goodenough's scores correlate highly with the presence, familiarity, and encouragement of representative art in a society, a factor which seems to be a function of a society's degree of modernization (Dennis, 1966). These kinds of findings have led Goodenough to say:

> The present writers would like to express the opinion that the search for a culture free test, whether of intelligence, artistic ability, personal-social characteristics, or any other measurable trait is illusory, and that the naive assumption that mere freedom from verbal requirements renders a test equally suitable for all groups is no longer tenable (Goodenough and Harris, 1950: 339).

References

ROGER ABRAHAMS, *Deep Down in the Jungle*, Aldine, Chicago, 1970.

ANNE ANASTASI, *Psychological Testing*, Macmillan, New York, 1968.

CARL BEREITER and SIEGFRIED ENGLEMANN, *Teaching Disadvantaged Children in the Preschool*, Prentice-Hall, Englewood Cliffs, New Jersey, 1966.

ROBERT BOESE, *Natural Sign Language and the Acquisition of Social Structure*, Unpublished PhD Dissertation, University of California, Santa Barbara, 1971.

AARON V CICOUREL, *Method and Measurement in Sociology*, The Free Press, New York, 1974.

The Social Organization of Juvenile Justice, Wiley, New York, 1968a.

'Verso una Sociologia Evoltiva del Linguaggio e del Significato.' *Rassegna Italiana di Sociologia* **9**:211–258. 1968b. Reprinted 1970 as: 'The Acquisition of Social Structure Towards a Developmental Sociology of Language and Meaning.' in JACK DOUGLAS (ed) *Understanding Every Day Life*, Aldine, Chicago.

'Generative Semantics and the Structure of Social Interaction' in *International Days of Sociolinguistics*, Luigi Sturzo Institute, Rome, 1969.

'Basic and Normative Rules in the Negotiation of Status and Role' in HANS P DREITZEL (ed) *Recent Sociology*, **2**, 'Patterns of Communicative Behavior', Macmillan, New York, 1970.

Forthcoming 'Ethnomethodology', to appear in THOMAS A SEBEOK (ed) *Current Trends in Linguistics*, **XII**, Mouton, The Hague.

AARON V CICOUREL, KENNETH JENNINGS, SYBILLYN JENNINGS, KENNETH LEITER, ROBERT MACKAY, HUGH MEHAN and DAVID ROTH, (in preparation) *Language Acquisition and Use in Testing and Classroom Settings*, Seminar Press, New York.

NATALIE T DARCY, 'Bilingualism and the Measurement of Intelligence', *Journal of Genetic Psychology*, **103**, 259–282, 1963.

GEORGE DENISON, *Lives of Children*, Random House, New York, 1969.

WAYNE T DENNIS, 'Goodenough Scores, Art Experience, and Modernization', *Journal of Social Psychology*, **68**, 211–288, 1966.

MARTIN DEUTSCH, *Teaching the Disadvantaged Child*, Prentice-Hall, Englewood Cliffs, New Jersey, 1964.

SIEGFRIED ENGLEMANN, *The Basic Concept Inventory*, Follet, Chicago, 1967.

NEIL FRIEDMAN, *The Social Nature of Psychological Research*, Basic Books, New York, 1968.

PAOLO FRIERE, *Pedagogy of the Oppressed*, Herder and Herder, New York, 1970.

HAROLD GARFINKEL, *Studies in Ethnomethodology*, Prentice-Hall, Englewood Cliffs, New Jersey, 1967.

HAROLD GARFINKEL and HARVEY SACKS, 'The Formal Properties of Practical Actions, in JOHN C MCKINNEY and EDWARD A TIRYAKIAN (eds) *Theoretical Sociology*, Appleton-Century-Crofts, New York, 1970.

FLORENCE GOODENOUGH and D L HARRIS, 'Studies in the Psychology of Children's Drawings' *Psychological Bulletin*, 369–433, 1950.

JOHN J GUMPERZ, *Language in Social Groups*, Stanford University Press, Palo Alto, 1972.

JOHN HOLT, *How Children Fail*, Putnam, New York, 1964.

J MCVEICH HUNT, *Intelligence and Experience*, 1964.

IVAN ILLICH, *Deschooling Society*, Harper and Row, New York, 1970.

ARTHUR JENSEN, 'How Much Can We Boost IQ and Scholastic Achievement', Harvard Educational Review, **39**, 1–123, 1969.

JONATHAN KOZOL, *Death at an Early Age*, Houghton Mifflin, Boston, 1969.

WILLIAM LABOV, 'The Logic of Non-Standard English,' in GEORGE ALATIS (ed) *Linguistics and Language Study*, Monograph Series 22. Georgetown University Press, Washington DC, 1969.

LOUISA LEWIS, 'Culute and Social Interaction in the Classroom' Working Paper 38, Language Behavior Research Lab, University of California, Berkeley.

HUGH MELAN, *Accomplishing Understanding in Educational Settings*, unpublished PhD Dissertation, University of California, Santa Barbara.

PAUL MELMED, *Black English Phonology*, Monograph 1, Language-Behavior Research Lab, University of California, Berkeley, 1971.

JANE R MERCER 'Institutionalized Anglocentricism' in PETER ORLEANS and WILLIAM R ELLIS, Jr (eds) *Race, Change and Urban Society*, Russell Sage, Publishers, New York, 1971.

CLAUDIA MITCHELL-KERNAN, *Language Behavior in a Black Urban Community*, unpublished PhD Dissertation, University of California, Berkeley. Working Paper 23, Language-Behavior Research Lab, University of California, Berkeley, 1969.
Also Monograph 2, Language, Behavior Research Lab, 1971.

SUSAN PHILLIPS, 'Acquisition of Rules for Appropriate Speech Usage' in GEORGE ALATIS (ed) *Linguistics and Language Study*, Monograph Series 23, Georgetown University Press, Washington DC, 1970.

HARVEY SACKS, *Unpublished Lecture Notes*, UCLA, UC Irvine, 1967–70.

EMMANUEL A SCHEGLOFF, 'Sequencing in Conversational Openings', *American Anthropologist* **70** (6), 1075–1095.

ALFRED SCHÜTZ, Collected Papers **I**: *The Problem of Social Reality*, Martinus Nijhoff, The Hague, 1962.

DAVID L SHORES (ed) *Contemporary English*, Lippincott, Philadelphia, 1972.

MARSHALL SHUMSKY, *Encounter Groups: A Forensic Science*, PhD Dissertation, University of California, Santa Barbara.

CARL SPEARMAN, *The Nature of Intelligence and the Purposes of Cognition*, Macmillan, London, 1923.

CHARLES A VALENTINE, 'Deficit, Difference, and Bi-Cultural Models of Afro-American Behavior', *Harvard Educational Review*, **41**, 137–158, 1971.

MARTHA COONFIELD WARD, *Them Children*, Holt, Rinehart, Winston, New York, 1971.

DAVID WECHSLER, *The Measurement of Adult Intelligence*, Williams and Wilkens, Baltimore, 1944.

FREDERICK WILLIAMS (ed) *Language and Poverty*, Markham, Boston, 1970.

THOMAS P WILSON, 'Conceptions of Interaction and Forms of Sociological Explanation'. *American Sociological Review* **35** (4), 697–709, 1970.

ROBERT S WOODWORTH and HAROLD SCHLOSBERG, *Experimental Psychology*, Holt, New York, 1954.

DON H ZIMMERMAN and MELVIN POLLNER, 'The Everyday World as a Phenomenon' in JACK DOUGLAS (ed) *Understanding Every Day Life*, Aldine, Chicago, 1970.

13

Navigation and Logic on Puluwat Atoll*

Thomas Gladwin

The theory of canoe design on Puluwat is by no means confined to the sail and rigging, where causal relations are fairly obvious and immediate. Earlier in this chapter a number of relations of balance, rigidity, clearance, and strength were mentioned with respect to the outrigger and lee platform. Each of these statements was drawn directly from explanations made by one or another canoe-builder on Puluwat. However, in Puluwat design theory the most complex and the most critical relations exist within the contours of the hull itself.

The manner in which the major measurements of the hull are laid out has already been described. They depend largely upon halving and halving again the length of the keel, with the use of measuring lines. These dimensions are traditional, with minor variations between two schools of boatbuilders, and they are essentially uniform. The system of dimensioning taken together with the size and shape of the available breadfruit tree from which the keel piece is hewn determines the principal proportions of the hull. It is only after these major proportions are established that theory and deliberate individual variation come into play. It will be possible here to outline only the broader aspects of design which occupy the attention of the master canoe builder. For me to have learned the more subtle relations would have required constant attention and inquiries throughout the many months which are required for the building of a large sailing canoe. Much of the final design of a hull on Puluwat as elsewhere depends upon the refined judgment of a practiced eye. Ask a man as he decides upon each next step why he made that particular decision and he can probably tell you. Ask him later how a canoe is designed and he will have forgotten that he ever made the decision. . . .

Surprisingly, the very end of the boat, which meets the water first, is not only rather blunt, but variations in its width and shape are not

* Thomas Gladwin *East is a Big Bird*, Harvard University Press, 1971, 118–119, 122–123, 127–132, 141–142, 214–225

believed to play a critical role in the performance of the canoe. Sometimes the flat surfaces are the same width on both sides, sometimes one side is wider; the latter is true only of hulls with an asymmetrical plan, and the wide side is then on the more curved or outrigger side of the hull. This bluntness and variability is surprising for two reasons. At a naive level one expects a hull to be sharp in cleaving the water, not blunt, and most small Western boats are built this way. It is surprising too, however, because the bluntness conforms to principles which have been worked out as preferable only in recent years in tow tanks and model basins in the United States and elsewhere. Furthermore, this research has indicated that a wide range in the amount of bluntness frequently makes little difference in performance, precisely as the Puluwatan builders contend. That they are right is attested to also by the very small bow wave which the Puluwat sailing canoe produces despite its bluntness even when it is travelling quite fast.

Whether all the principles through which the canoe-builders guide their work would prove out as fully as the design of the hull ends cannot be established. It did not prove feasible to obtain lines from the hulls, lines which could be translated into models and tested. A tabulation was made of some dimensions and some characteristics of all the interisland sailing canoes, along with ratings of the relative performance of each under different conditions. However, the simple measurements and observations which could be recorded in this way did not show any significant correlation with the performance ratings for the canoes. Even such obvious things as the width of the hull (measured at the top) relative to its length did not seem to predict either speed or load-carrying ability. However, since some men, most notably Ikuliman, can consistently build canoes of outstanding performance, and have reasons for doing what they do each time even if I was not able to understand and record them all, the conclusion is inescapable that there are principles which predictably govern performance and my tabulation was simply too crude to capture them.*

. . . Navigation is not easy to learn. The senior navigators often dis-

* Since the publication of *East is a Big Bird*, further work on Puluwat canoe design by Dr Edwin Doran Jr, has indicated an error in Dr Gladwin's interpretation of the design parameters. Doran's work has demonstrated that the blunt ends of the canoe hull do *not* ease its passage through the water; rather, they slow it down. Their purpose is to prevent the canoe from being driven into a steep wave, especially in a following sea. Similar compromises are reflected in all design considerations.

It is important to note, however, that this information in no way invalidates Dr Gladwin's general argument; if anything, it provides stronger support for that argument.

courage young men from trying because they are fairly sure they will not make it. For the same reason many young men never even volunteer to try. Presumably too some do not actually care enough to bother with the long grind. Although on Puluwat this may seem improbable, there is perhaps no culture in which a central activity, no matter how heavily favored and rewarded, is uniformly embraced by everyone eligible to participate. In some cultures it is more difficult than others to avoid joining in. On Puluwat it is easy. Although the role of navigator brings rich rewards of virtuosity and membership in a distinguished elite, the many who for whatever reason are not so accomplished are never publicly criticized. This is true whether they tried and failed to learn or never cared to try.

Despite the several ways in which young men can be deterred from entering training, of those who do undertake it less than half, probably substantially less than half, complete the course and achieve recognition as master navigators. Others, having completed their training, are known as navigators but are also known never to have achieved the skill and precision of judgment necessary to complete long trips. They too make only short trips or travel in convoy even though in point of years many are quite senior. Because of the rich satisfaction and prestige which reward the master navigator, failure even though private must come very hard. Despite our relationship of complete trust, Hipour would not identify for me any men of whose failures he was aware, and he was sure there were many more about whom he had never heard. Failure of anyone in the study of navigation is not a decent subject for discussion.

Navigation is taught both at sea and on land. In a sense every Puluwat man has had some instruction in navigation at sea because every man travels on canoes. Whether or not he is destined to study navigation, he is bound to learn how the canoe feels as it rides over the waves, and how this feel alters with changes in course, in wind, or in weather. He acquires skill in steering, and perhaps in handling the sheet. He becomes familiar with the different kinds of seabirds, and with the habits of those which can guide a canoe to its destination. He comes to know how a canoe handles, how fast it travels under different conditions, how it drifts with the sail down, and the differences between various canoes. Nowadays he may learn a little about the compass, especially if a navigator is thinking of taking him into instruction. He can detect reefs many fathoms down by subtle changes in the color of the water and in the character of waves on the surface, and he learns to see them under all kinds of sky and conditions of the sea. No man can avoid being exposed to all these things and learning them all if he lives the life which is the heritage of birth on Puluwat. Some learn them better than others, and this can have an important bearing on their eligibility for instruction as navigators.

Formal instruction begins on land. It demands that great masses of factual information be committed to memory. This information is detailed, specific, and potentially of life-or-death importance. It is taught by a senior navigator to one or several students, some young, some older. Often they sit together in the canoe house, perhaps making little diagrams with pebbles on the mats which cover the sandy floor. The pebbles usually represent stars, but they are also used to illustrate islands and how the islands 'move' as they pass the canoe on one side or the other.

In the past instruction was very secret. There was much magic and esoteric knowledge which could be known only by the privileged few. Some of it could be used against the navigator in sorcery if others knew it. In addition the navigational skills were and still are valuable property, willingly passed on to relatives but taught to non-relatives only for a stiff price. It is even said that a few crucial elements of navigation were often explained to non-relatives in somewhat garbled form despite their having paid well for their instruction. This was especially true of the component of navigational knowledge referred to in the next chapter as 'sealife'. Suffice it to say here that sealife is one of those tantalizing examples of a body of esoteric knowledge which from our 'rational' Western point of view we cannot believe a reasonable man would take seriously. Yet even now with the passing of belief in the supernatural, sealife is still learned and cherished with deadly earnestness and is still highly valued, with a conviction that one day it may save a navigator's life. However, it is no longer considered any more critical than the other arts of navigation. All are still intrinsically so valuable that instruction must remain somewhat confidential. You do not give away something which you could sell. However, some parts are more carefully protected than others.

Although the divisions are not rigorously maintained, distinguishable subsystems exist within the overall system of navigation. Some of these subsystems are separately named and taught as separate courses in a larger curriculum, while others are considered more in the nature of general knowledge to be taught whenever they seem to fit in. At the heart of the whole system, which will be described in detail in the next chapter, are the stars, specifically the points or directions where certain stars rise and set around the horizon. The identities and positions of these stars are so basic to travel at sea that everyone claims to know them, although it turned out that when non-navigators were asked, their identifications invariably contained some discrepancies. The stars are taught by placing a circle of pebbles on the ground, each standing for a star which the student must learn to name. This placement in a circle is itself interesting because earlier German accounts from Puluwat describe arranging the pebbles in a square, and this is still done on some of the islands to the west. On Puluwat, however, the instructors have apparently long since adopted the circular shape of a compass card even though compasses were quite rare until recent postwar years. The points of a compass are even identified with the same names as the navigation stars.

Next come the star courses. These are the courses, with respect to the rising or setting of stars, which are sailed in order to get from one island to another. They must be learned for every pair of islands between which a navigator might conceivably find himself sailing. When it is borne in mind that there are at least twenty-six separate islands or atolls to which living Puluwat navigators have sailed, plus a number more for which a navigator is expected to know the sailing directions so he could sail there if called upon to do so (for example, Hipour's trip to Saipan), and furthermore that nominally one could sail from any one of these islands to any other, the number of possible island pairs between which star courses must be learned grows to formidable size. The directions for fifty-five commonly made journeys were recorded (one hundred and ten if return routings are included) and the more remote islands add as many more.

This is a body of knowledge which is not kept secret, but there is scarcely any need to do so. No one could possibly learn it except through the most painstaking and lengthy instruction, so no outsider could pick it up merely by occasional eavesdropping. Instead it is taught and memorized through endless reiteration and testing. The learning job is not complete until the student at his instructor's request can start with any island in the known ocean and rattle off the stars both going and returning between that island and all the others which might conceivably be reached directly from there. Although this recitation of a sequence of stars between a given island and all the other islands around it is occasionally used even by an accomplished navigator to refresh his memory, it is not a litany memorized by rote. Not only did my instructor Hipour state flatly that it was not (I suggested to him an analogy between this recital of stars and prayers chanted in church), but in addition a navigator the moment he is asked can usually give at will not only the star course but also a lot of other information about sailing between any two islands. In other words, all this information is learned so that each item is discretely available, as it were floating on the surface of the navigator's mind rather than embedded in a long mnemonic chain. This is a long task, and one which requires patient commitment by both instructor and student.

After the star courses, or frequently along with them, come the many other subjects which will occupy us in the chapter to follow. These include knowledge of currents and other special conditions affecting travel between each of the many island pairs; *etak* (eh-tack), the system used for keeping track of distance traveled; how to read several kinds of information from the waves; navigation in storms, including keeping track of position while drifting; navigation when tacking upwind; techniques for locating, even in the dark, passes through the reefs of various islands; forecasting the weather through an almanac of rising and setting stars (not the navigation stars) and the moon; sealife; star courses, and sometimes long sequences of star courses, for remote and occasionally mythological islands; and, in the past, spells of magic and divination and the taboos governing the work of the sea.

Hipour showed no curiosity about matters of history. Unlike many Trukese of my earlier experience he never asked any questions about the role of Japan or the United States in World War II, even though Puluwat was seriously dislocated by the building and operation of a fighter strip on Allei. As another example he had a compass, a great heavy affair obviously designed for use on a ship of some size. It had been given by a Spanish priest on Truk to a great-uncle of Hipour's who gave it to his nephew, who in turn passed it on to Hipour. It had been made by Plath in Hamburg and carried a serial number, so I offered to see if I could trace its history and let him know. Although he was polite he was completely uninterested.

In contrast he was very interested in a star chart, as were a number of other men. This interest surprised me since seeing stars on paper could add nothing to his already complete knowledge of the heavens. However, it illustrated well the flexibility and insight of Puluwatans in perceiving spatial relationships. *Bernard's Nautical Star Chart*, published in Glasgow, is a schematic diagram designed solely for the use of Western celestial navigators. It is laden with conventions and symbols. The stars are shown as five-pointed, magnitude is represented by size, the stars listed in nautical almanacs are in red while the rest are black, lines are drawn between those which are linked in the constellations of our European folklore, the projection is Mercator's with gross distortion of the polar regions, and finally east and west are reversed so the chart must be held over the head to look 'right'. It is doubtless fine for a Scottish mariner but one would think its many cabalistic signs would render it utterly incomprehensible to a Puluwatan. Far from it. After my first lesson in star identifications I could point to a few stars on the chart by their Puluwat names.

Hipour at once understood what I was demonstrating. After puzzling over the whole chart scarcely a minute he began pointing to other stars and naming them. I got out the list of equivalents given by Goodenough (1953) and all the identifications agreed. I later tried this with some other men. The navigators in particular understood the chart with no more trouble than Hipour. Tawaru was so delighted he insisted I leave the chart with him on my departure. I did so even though I felt sure he knew more than the chart did. I was also personally delighted because this saved me many late nights of peering into the heavens to verify star identifications.

Another example of Hipour's presumably not unique spatial and angular sophistication followed upon my turning over to him, shortly before my departure, the chart we had both been using of the islands around Puluwat. This was laminated in flexible plastic for protection, and had the familiar circles which show degrees of bearing and magnetic deviation. After taking the chart along on a trip to Pikelot, Hipour brought it back to me and inquired how to transfer a line of bearing between two islands on the chart to an adjacent bearing circle. He believed that if he could do this, even though he could not read the bearing numbers he could count divisions on the circle on the chart and thus transfer readings to his compass. Unfortunately in the last days before I left the United States I had been unable to purchase the parallel rulers which are customarily used for this purpose and instead had brought along an adjustable protractor. The protractor was especially inconvenient because it moved only through a 45-degree span and had to be turned around to complete the 90-degree sector. All in all the process was so complicated and confusing that I put it aside for use only if in an emergency I had to navigate myself. No such emergency arose and I forgot it. So I got out the protractor and did my best to explain it to Hipour. To my amazement he soon said he understood, and showed me by applying the device a couple of times in ways that seemed appropriate. I was not on the island long enough thereafter to follow up and determine if he really had mastered the protractor, but he was at least enthusiastic and delighted to have it. . . .

Perspectives on Thinking

We have now before us a complex and organized body of knowledge, Puluwat navigation, and a somewhat less explicit and more intuitive theory of canoe design. We are ready at last to move into the psychological domain, treating navigation no longer as technology but rather as a sample of purposeful thinking in another culture. Before undertaking this, however, it will be well to restate the rationale for doing so, and particularly for making the comparisons promised earlier between the logic of Puluwat navigators and that of poor people in the United States.

Much more than just style of logic is associated with being poor, as there is more to be said about a navigator than to describe the way he thinks. The navigator is proud, assured, respected. A poor American is likely to be hungry, powerless, weak from poor health, his spirit crushed by hopelessness, in addition to whatever difficulties he may experience in solving the logical problems people ask him to solve. Just being 'intelligent' is far from enough to assure that a poor person can escape the suffocating constraints of poverty. Yet if the child of a poor family is seen as not 'intelligent', which means particularly he is not able to do well on psychological tests and with the tasks presented to him in school, he is almost certainly doomed to the lifelong misery which is the lot of the poor.

In the Western world, and throughout the world wherever change and modernization is valued, doing well in school is an almost inescapable requirement for moving upward into the ranks of privilege. Although persons who have not gone far or done well in school may regularly perform tasks which are objectively quite complex and difficult, the jobs they do are rarely accorded high prestige, and advancement is usually difficult or impossible. Furthermore, it is by now universally recognized that economically poor children generally make academically poor students. Thus any knowledge we can gain about why poor people do or do not perform well in school is relevant to the role of education as an avenue of escape from poverty.

Obviously, one important element in determining school performance is the way in which students use their minds, that is, the cognitive abilities and strategies they are able to bring to bear upon the problems presented to them in school. Many other factors are involved, especially for poor children, but there is general agreement that a child's way of going about solving intellectual problems has a major effect on his classroom achievement, and that poor children are generally less able to solve the problems presented both in class and on tests than are their more privileged fellows. Yet surprisingly little is reliably known about the nature of the logical processes which go on in the heads of children from underprivileged families, or in the minds of the undereducated and disadvantaged adults into which such children are too often transformed.

Part of the reason for this lack is doubtless that cognitive psychologists, like their colleagues in other areas of psychology, generally use as subjects for research and experimentation persons who are readily available and with whom they can communicate easily, which usually means college students or college graduates. Yet because those in our society who have been reared in poverty tend to do badly in school, they generally do not get into college. The consequence is that poor people and their style of thinking have not had a chance to play any significant role as subjects of basic research on cognition and the structure of human intellect.

This is not to ignore the large amount of research which has been done on learning deficits of poor people in the United States. The difficulty with this research, however, is that, instead of exploring the foundations of logical thinking as they are laid down in different environments, it has more commonly focused on how lower-class intellectual handicaps are manifested and distributed relative to income level, type of school, and so on. It is perhaps historically inevitable that research on cognition in poor people should emphasize contrasts with middle-class thinking. Not only did social class differences in cognitive style first become evident through recognition of consistently poor lower-class school performance, a quantitatively defined deficit which evaluative research now seeks to specify and delimit, but in addition the research tools available for this purpose are principally measurement techniques derived from concepts of intelligence developed within educational settings. Thus, rather than trying at the outset to discover qualities of thinking in underprivileged populations, researchers seek to *quantify* divergences from the psychological baselines used by educators, baselines rooted in middle-class intellectual culture. Emphasis is therefore on measurement, with the *qualities* to be measured accepted as given. The possibility is thereby largely foreclosed of exploring other dimensions of thinking beyond those which are traditionally recognized within educational psychology. Stodolsky and Lesser succinctly state the limiting effect this has on research in lower-class cognition: 'The types of achievement and intelligence tests which are most often used can have only limited value in describing the cognitive functioning of children. In almost all instances, we are concerned with scratchings on an answer sheet, not with the ways in which a student arrived at a conclusion. No matter how much we may think we know by looking at scores on such psychometric procedures, unless tests are constructed deliberately to reveal reasoning processes, these processes will not be identified.' Under these circumstances it is not surprising that despite a formidable amount of research, psychology has thus far failed to create any real strategic breakthroughs in educational technology for deprived populations. Research findings point either toward broadly maladaptive personality characteristics in poor children or to contrasts between the environments of home and school so wide that they are almost unbridgeable. Programs to prevent or remedy these conditions have been forced to adopt strategies equally broad and unfocused. Lasting successes have been correspondingly rare.

In reviewing this body of research one has the sense of many people groping about, trying out their familiar tools and strategies in infinitely varied ways in the hope of stumbling upon the effective cause of a deficit which all agree exists. Failing in the search, they are forced back upon old inadequate remedies and ever more precise but not very helpful tabulations of symptoms and cases. One is reminded of some of the dramatic searches for causes of deadly diseases which at intervals have illuminated the history of public health epidemiology. The successful quest for the cause of beriberi (Williams, 1961), now known to result from vitamin deficiency, could provide a hopeful prototype for the present research. Beriberi was recognized as a distinct syndrome at a time when germ theory was revolutionizing the practice of medicine and of public health. Persistent efforts were made to isolate sources of beriberi 'infection', especially on ships where mass outbreaks occurred, and to investigate the effect of the treatments then available for dealing with infections. No answer was found. Finally Western medicine turned to another area of the world, Asia. There, as we now know, eating polished versus unpolished rice can by itself make the difference between an adequate diet and thiamine deficiency, with resultant beriberi. In the Philippines a shrewd United States Army doctor, Edward B Vedder, noting the striking differences in incidence of beriberi among troops on different diets, concluded that something left in unpolished grains of rice prevented the disease. From there to the isolation and synthesis of thiamine the road was long, but straight. Such can be the rewards of going to unfamiliar settings to seek the answer to overly familiar problems.

Thirty years ago a similar challenge confronted students of an area in psychology closely related to the focus of this book, that of personality research. Clinical studies of that time, especially in psychoanalysis, seemed to demonstrate that some aspects of personality characterized not only individuals but also sub-groups in our society. Behaviors and emotions which appeared bizarre in some settings could be normal in others. The initial question raised by these seeming differences in group characteristics was whether they were real, and if so what their nature might be. Edward Sapir proposed that the first step should be to determine which aspects of personality are likely to be shaped by cultural forces and which are more idiosyncratic. To this end, he contended, one should begin with studies of people of markedly different cultures and then, enlightened by these dramatic perspectives, return to an examination of differences within one's own society. This insight inspired a research interest in culture and personality which continues to the present. Whatever their scientific merits, the resulting studies have helped clinicians discriminate between aspects of personality which are likely to be culturally determined and those which are individual or even accidental in origin. It is precisely this sort of clarification which is needed now with respect to styles of thinking and problem solving in different social groups.

There are already in existence numerous comparative studies of cognition in different cultures. However, with but a few rare exceptions these have been concerned with the frameworks within which information is organized for use, frameworks which have been variously called cognitive maps, semantic frames, or ethnoscience. Yet the differences in cognition between middle-class and poor people in the United States seem to lie more in the way information is processed and manipulated than in the way in which it is categorized and organized. If this is true, the critical differences should be sought in styles of thinking, problem-solving, and planning. For this reason an information-processing system such as navigation seemed more appropriate than one principally devoted to classifying hierarchies of information.

It scarcely need be added that a comparison of this sort, taken between two widely different cultures, can only lead to highly speculative conclusions. To the degree that constructs derived from one culture seem to fit plausibly phenomena found in another, the comparison has at least a measure of face validity. If the constructs in addition provoke further inquiry the effort can be judged worthwhile. It may in the end even lead to some change for the better in the human condition, in which event it must be viewed as very worthwhile. However, the goal of this book, and particularly of this chapter, is far more modest. It is only to seek and suggest new avenues of investigation in a crucial field of research, a field which seems at times to be approaching stagnation.

When we relate Puluwat navigation as a way of thinking to our own culture it is not because we think we are looking at a similar pathology, like beriberi, in both settings. Rather it is because we can look at a comparable process, like personality development, which is common to both but probably different enough in each to provide illuminating contrasts. This process is the use of one's intelligence in the solving of important problems.

Puluwat navigation is unquestionably intelligent behavior, but Puluwatans do not necessarily think of it this way. It is an obvious feat of intellect to travel far across the ocean and arrive at a tiny island through the use of nothing but one's mind and senses. We in the Western world value intelligence highly. For this reason we respect the Puluwat navigator. Puluwatans also respect their navigators, but not primarily because they are intelligent. They respect them because they can navigate, because they can guide a canoe safely from one island to another. There is, it is true, a Puluwat word one can translate as 'intelligent,' and in these terms navigators are considered intelligent, but etymologically it refers only to having a good memory. There are furthermore many useful ways to use one's mind in addition to remembering technical information. A Puluwatan who is asked to identify people who think well or use their minds effectively is likely to select those whose decisions are wise, who are moderate and statesmanlike in discussion, not the technicians. This does not mean that the statesman is more important than the navigator. On Puluwat nothing is more important than navigation. It means that whereas *we* can recognize and respect navigation as a pre-eminently intelligent activity, this is not its significant quality for the Puluwatan. Because navigation is in our terms intelligent, it can provide useful perspectives on intelligence in our own culture. In thinking of navigation in this way, however, we must not slip into the assumption that Puluwatans view their navigators as highly intelligent. They do not. They view them as navigators.

In the description of navigation in the preceding chapter two qualities emerged to characterize it logically, or cognitively, in addition to its technological dimensions. It is on the one hand comprised of systems of explicit theory, and on the other hand works with a limited array of predetermined alternatives of acceptable input and output. Examined more closely, from some of our traditional perspectives on intelligence, these qualities could be seen as contradictory. First, Puluwat navigation (and canoe design) can be said to be cast in theoretical terms because it is explicitly taught and conceptualized as a set of principles governing relationships between phenomena. The phenomena are sometimes directly observed but at other times are only inferred, as in the case of star-compass bearings when the course star is not in position to be directly observed. These relationships and these inferences are unquestionably abstractions. Some, for example *etak*, are abstractions of a rather high order. The concept in *etak* of a specified but invisible island moving under often invisible navigation stars is not only an abstraction. It is also a purposefully devised logical construct by the use of which data inputs (rate and time) can be processed to yield a useful output, proportion of the journey completed. Abstract thinking is therefore a pervasive characteristic of Puluwat navigation.

The second characteristic, that all inputs of information and outputs of decision are so to speak prepackaged or predetermined, means that within the navigation system there is little room or need for innovation. Navigation requires the solution of no unprecedented problems. The navigator must be judicious and perceptive, but he is never called upon to have new ideas, to relate things together in new ways.

The contradiction, if there is one, derives from our custom in psychology in the United States of relating both these qualities, abstract thinking and innovative problem-solving to a third, superior intelligence. More particularly all three of these qualities are often attributed to middle-class intelligence, and said to be lacking in the 'concrete' style of thinking of poorly educated lower-class persons. True, statements of this order are usually descriptive rather than analytic and therefore do not, for example, stipulate a causal or inevitable relationship such that innovative thinking must always be abstract, or vice versa. An association between the three is, however, so consistently noted that one is inclined to think of them as regularly occurring together. Although Puluwat navigation can 'prove' nothing about cognitive styles in the United States, we may at least say with respect to one of these associations that on Puluwat abstract thinking exists as a dominant mode in the absence of any requirement for solving new problems or solving old problems in new ways.

Although it may not be contradictory in a literal sense to say that Puluwat thinking as reflected in navigation is at once intelligent, abstract, and not innovative, this appears to contrast with the conventional wisdom regarding thinking styles as related to social class in the United States. We must therefore examine the relationships more closely. The associations here are: middle class: high IQ, abstraction, innovation; lower class: low IQ, concreteness, little innovation. Perhaps these associations are real. It is equally possible, however, that they result from a lack of precision in our definition of the terms used. It is the latter question to which this chapter is principally directed. What are the significant dimensions of intelligence, innovation, or abstraction to which we should be addressing ourselves when we make comparisons across cultural lines, whether these are between social classes or between the United States and Puluwat?

Let us look first at the abstract-concrete continuum. Abstract thinking as it is usually conceived by psychologists in the United States deals with properties of things which are not usually obvious. Often a quality must be inferred, or its significance sought through its being shared in other things which would not otherwise be seen as related. At one extreme abstractions may consist in simple qualities such as color or size which link objects together into classes. From there they range into far more complex logical constructs embracing phenomena of several diverse orders in complex relationships. *Etak* with its moving island is a good example from Puluwat. So is a canoe-builder who makes statements about the unobservable flow of water around the lower part of a hull. He is dealing with abstractions about forces and movements of water which he can only infer from surface waves, sounds, and the comparative performance of different hulls. In contrast with such abstractions, concrete thinking is concerned entirely with the immediately perceived qualities of an object or situation. Once something has been observed and its distinguishing characteristics noted, this observation leads without further intellectual manipulation toward one or a very few possible responses.

Since we have already established that there is in Puluwat navigation a reliance on abstractions, we must now inquire about concrete thinking in the same context. Each observation a navigator makes of waves, stars, or birds is related directly without any logical reordering or interpretation to a conclusion about position, direction, or weather. Each such conclusion in turn permits of only one or at most two or three clearly defined alternative responses. Some of the observations are based on perceptions we (but not the Puluwatans) would consider extraordinarily acute, and some of the responses are complex, but once the initial observation has been made the steps which follow upon it are unequivocal. Is this concrete thinking? Few psychologists would argue otherwise. Not only is it concrete but direct pathways of this sort between observation and response comprise the principal operational mode of the entire navigation system. In other words, Puluwat navigation is a system which simultaneously employs fairly high orders of abstraction and yet is pervaded by concrete thinking.

If these two kinds of cognitive operations, abstract and concrete, can so intimately coexist in the working mind of a Puluwat navigator, how can these same qualities of thinking in the United States provide a basis of contrast and comparison between classes of people? In the United States the abstract-concrete, middle-class-lower-class distinctions have been elevated to particular prominence in the critically important context of remedial educational programs for poor children. Yet it is ironic to discover that the authors who originally defined the contrast never proposed that these qualities should be used at all to discriminate between people, especially normal people. In their classic monograph on the subject Goldstein and Scheerer (1941) on the first page, before they even define the two terms, insist that abstract and concrete 'attitudes' (as they call them) are mutually interdependent within each total personality. They are levels of intellectual operation differentially utilized by every person for different tasks, not necessarily differentially utilized by different people. Nor did they propose these concepts in relation to social class-determined behaviors. Their concern was better to understand the thinking of persons whose brains were damaged or who were psychotic. Although they argue effectively that both abstract and concrete thinking occur as major modalities in the cognitive processes of all persons, it is doubtful that they would have selected this particular distinction for emphasis were it not especially germane to their interests in psychopathology. However, they did. Not only that but they devised a number of tests and tasks to be used to assess these thinking styles. In time the tests were tried out on different populations from those for which they were initially designed and applied to different problems. Then, as so often happens in psychology – intelligence tests are the classic case – results of the tests came to stand for the thing they were said to measure. Thereupon all manner of distinctions became possible, including that between lower- and middle-class thinking.

Rather than test results, let us examine an example of another kind of problem-solving, an example from real life which offers significant comparisons with Puluwat navigation. There is in the United States an occupation not unlike navigation, but one which frequently engages people who are poor, have dropped out of school, and presumably cannot handle the kind of thinking usually required on intelligence tests. This is driving, specifically driving taxis or delivery trucks in a city. Not all taxi drivers or deliverymen are school dropouts or even poor, but enough are to demonstrate that this kind of driving falls within the capability of undereducated persons. Furthermore, in many (but not all) cities driving is a fairly open occupation in which a start can be made with minimum skill, education, or cash investment. Where this is true it provides an avenue leading out of poverty for many who have little more than the initiative to pursue it. To become a successful driver getting better runs, hours, and more income requires, however, the learning of new skills. It is the nature of these skills which interests us here.

What does the driver do? In some respects he responds in immediate and concrete ways to the things which happen as he moves through the traffic. He makes concrete but accurate judgments of timing and speed (his own and others'), somewhat less concrete inferences about such matters as the traction of road surfaces or the condition of the brakes on an old car next to him, and acute discriminations such as picking out the traffic light from among a welter of red and green neon signs. More than this he plans a route through the maze of city streets which will not only be as short as possible but will also take into account which streets are one-way, where the bottle-necks are, when and where rush-hour traffic will build up, and any temporary obstacles such as new construction. To do this he must have in his mind a plan of the city which is not only detailed and complete but has superimposed upon it the flux of traffic as this is governed by the time of day and day of the week. He must be able to superimpose himself on this dynamic map and project his course from start to finish upon it. Can one call this image of the city with which the driver must work anything but an abstraction? What of the infer-ences about other cars whose inner machinery he cannot see at all, or about what a policeman in a car is going to concern himself with next? All the specifics of what the driver does differ from the work of the navigator who in addition, with a crew aboard and no phone booth to stop at if he gets lost, bears a far more awesome responsib-ility. Yet in many ways both think alike: concretely, yet abstractly, and acutely. Both did a great deal of thinking while they were learn-ing, but now both can do their work and reach their decisions with a minimum of conscious deliberation. What is so obvious in both, how-ever, is that they are dealing constantly in complex abstractions, abstractions so essential to their tasks that they almost literally could not move without them, while at the same time responding concretely and immediately to most of the relevant observations they make.

If the driver and the navigator both do what they have to do in accordance with similar cognitive strategies, is it possible there are also significant things which neither does? More specifically, are there kinds of thinking which are not required for the routine tasks of either the navigator or the driver? In Chapter 5 it was pointed out that there were two distinctive cognitive characteristics of the navigation system on Puluwat. We have considered the explicit theoretical con-structs in it and called them abstractions. The second characteristic of the system is a lack of necessity for making innovations within it. This leads to concrete thinking, but its significance goes beyond con-creteness alone.

Innovation here means thinking about new things, finding new solutions to new problems. I have said the navigator does not do this because he does not have to.

14

Educational Decision Makers

Aaron V Cicourel and John I Kitsuse

The school curriculum provides courses for students of three broad capability categories: honours courses for those with consistently high performance on tests and/or course grades; regular courses for students classified as 'low-average, average, and slightly better than average'; and 'opportunity' courses for students with consistently low performance on tests and course grades. Students are classified into ability groups on the basis of their SCAT and STEP scores.*

In assigning students to the ability-grouped sections of the various courses, the chairman of each department is authorized to interpret the student's capability and to place him in the appropriate section. In this assignment process, the student's past performance in junior high school and the recommendations of his eighth-grade treachers as well as his SCAT (Scholastic and College Aptitude Test) and STEP (Sequential Test of Educational Progress) scores are reviewed. Two levels of honors sections are provided for the best students – advanced honors and honors – in English, history, mathematics, science, and foreign languages. Students are invited to enroll in the advanced honors courses, an invitation which they or their parents may decline. Enrollment in honors courses, on the other hand, is by assignment and is not optional. Students with poor records may be assigned to the 'opportunity' sections of any or all of the courses in their program.

Several organizational features of ability grouping are specifically relevant for the assignment of freshmen to the three types of course programs discussed previously. First, biology is open to freshmen as an honors or advanced honors course; there are no 'regular' or 'opportunity' sections of this course. A second feature of the ability-grouping procedure is that there are no 'opportunity' sections of algebra or foreign languages. Thus, students who are considered to have low ability are automatically excluded from those courses which differentiate the college from non-college course programs. The exclusion of students who have declared college-going intentions from

* Bobbs-Merrill Co Inc Indianapolis, 1963, 53–55, 73–75, 142–148.

enrollment in college credit courses depends heavily upon the department chairman's judgment of the students capabilities and the importance he assigns to the reliability and validity of the records and other information on which his judgment is based.

A third organizational feature to be noted about the ability-grouping practice is that the performance of students in the several sections of a course is evaluated and graded with reference to the ability range of the students enrolled and the level of the materials presented in the course. In order to adjust the 'bias' against the students in honors courses that results from their competing for grades with peers in the high-ability group, course grades are differentially weighted by the administration in the computation of grade-point averages. Thus, a given grade in an honors course should contribute more to the grade-point average than does the same grade in a regular or opportunity course.

Finally, ability grouping as practiced at Lakeshore High School generally places restrictions upon the grade-point level that a student can attain. Since performance is evaluated and graded relative to the presumed ability range for which the course is designed, a student who is the top performer in an opportunity course would not be accorded the same grade as the best student in an average or honors course. (Theoretically, the former student should be transferred out of the opportunity course to a higher ability section before the end of the semester.) The corollary of this feature of ability grouping should also obtain: The student who performs poorly relative to his peers in an honors course is generally not assigned the lowest absolute grade but one that takes into account the level of the course and the level of the competition. Thus, in practice, there is an implicit 'ceiling' and 'floor' for grades assigned to students in the various ability sections. The combined effect of the differential *weighting* of grades and the restriction on the *range* of grades assigned is that the high-ability students presumably enjoy an advantage while the low-ability students bear a disadvantage in the competition for grades and academic rank. (Schools that do not prepare a weighted average would tend to create the opposite effect.) . . .

The discussion may be summarized as follows:

1. The relation between student and parental college-going aspirations and their implementation of those aspirations must be viewed as problematic. We have stressed the point that, given the formal declaration of such aspirations, the implementation of the declaration is contingent upon the organizational procedures that launch freshmen students toward their educational goals. These contingencies are created by the educational doctrines of the school, the organization of

its curriculums, and the routines of bureaucratic procedures in which 'objective' and 'subjective' criteria are combined in the processing of students through the system. The question we have explored is not how the school does or does not manage to process students independently of the students' declared educational aspirations. Rather, we have been concerned with how the school as a bureaucratic organization incorporates in its rules and procedures the processes by which the aspirations of students are recorded, their ability assessed, and their performance evaluated.

2. We have presented materials to illustrate the diffuse character of the criteria used in assigning students to types of programs and courses, and we have discussed the implications of this assignment procedure for the progress of students toward their declared educational goals. Our materials indicate also that the criteria used to evaluate the subsequent performance of students are equally diffuse and that the evaluation process makes the realization of those goals problematic. We have illustrated how the rationale of ability grouping organizationally produces and defines instances of SCAT/ grade-point discrepancies as 'problems' to be identified and classified by the counselor. In addition to the 'objective' data of the SCAT/grade-point discrepancy, the counselor must somehow decide the relevance of a variety of noncomparable factors for her evaluation of the students' performance. Such factors as the comments of teachers concerning students, the expressed concern of parents regarding the prospects of realizing their plans for sending their children to college, information about a student's 'delinquent' activities, and the like may implicitly or explicitly enter into her evaluations. The limitations of resources and time do not allow the counselor to 'objectively' weigh and give weightings to the variety of information considered relevant for the evaluation. The task of 'objectifying' the bases of such decisions is clearly a difficult if not an impossible one.

3. We have suggested that the differentiation of students produced by the evaluation process is directly related to the organizational effort to identify and develop talent, because the categories of differentiation are defined in terms of a presumed relationship between ability and performance. The classification of students differentiates those who are and are not 'having trouble'. The evaluation of student performance and the classification it produces has more than nominal significance for the future educational, occupational, and life careers of students. In a bureaucratically organized school such as Lakeshore High, the classification of students routinely initiates organizational actions that may progressively define and limit the development of such careers. From this perspective, the criteria employed in the

evaluation process, the information considered relevant and recorded, the interpretations made of such information, and the organizationally defined categories by which students are classified are important for an understanding of how the school produces senior students who are or are not qualified for college entrance, 'highly recommended' or 'poor prospects', 'well-rounded personalities' or 'maladjusted'.

In view of the strategic importance of educational organizations for the transmission and implementation of democratic values, the doctrines, policies, and practices of such organizations should be continually examined and subjected to the test of democratic ideals. As sociologists, we have focused attention on the practiced and enforced rules of organizational procedures at Lakeshore High School. As the subject of objective inquiry, the everyday workings of social organizations are not matters to be condemned as immoral, expedient, idealistic, or cynical. Our study was not designed to condemn the modern comprehensive high school as one in which educational standards are confused, criteria of decisions are arbitrary or commonsensical, and sponsorship is based on considerations other than ability and performance. The school system we have studied reveals the patterned deviations from bureaucratic procedures that sociologists have found in other large bureaucracies such as professional, industrial, military, and governmental organizations.

Our interest in the organization and functioning of the school system cannot be described as purely scientific, for field research makes it difficult to separate our roles as social scientists from our roles as private citizens. In the course of the research we both reacted to material which suggested that the bureaucratization of the school system would leave no place for the student to 'hide' – specifically, that the day-to-day management of the student's academic, personal, peer, and family problems by school personnel would limit individual variations in self development and social and occupational careers.

It would be presumptuous to issue a set of recommendations concerning the goals of education, the re-organization of existing institutions, and the methods by which those goals might be realized. We propose instead to limit our comments to four organizational features of the school studied that, in our judgment, deserve serious consideration by those concerned with the education of youth.

1 The emphasis upon the recognition and rewarding of ability and achievement is, of course, consistent with the American ideology of

equal opportunity for individuals of equal ability. Our study of Lakeshore High School, however, suggests that objective measures of ability may be supplemented by difficult-to-measure attributes. The existence of such cases and the consequences that follow from such misclassifications obviously bring into question the assumption that equal educational opportunities for students of equal capability are insured by the use of testing devices. The use of tests commits the organization to the scores that are produced by those tests as objective bases for decisions and actions vis-à-vis the processing of students. Yet in specific cases, when those results are considered to be inconsistent with other information, the reliability or validity of the test scores may be questioned and taken into account in deciding various courses of action. But if the reliability and validity of the test score in one case are questioned, for whatever reason, the test scores of all cases might also be called into question. The fact that in many cases the test scores are considered to be consistent with other information does not alter the logical implications of attributing less validity or reliability to some test scores than to others.

The problem of insuring equal opportunity, however, is not merely a matter of increasing the reliability and validity of the tests. Rather, the effective realization of equal opportunity is a problem of organizational implementation. However efficient the instruments of identifying capability may be, the distribution of opportunities among students of different levels of ability depends upon whether or not students are in fact organizationally processed with reference to their tested scores.

2 In our discussion of the differential interpretation of test scores and course grades, we barely touched upon the question of the degree to which social class is related to this organizational contingency. In this regard we may ask if Hollingshead's Elmtown study, which underlined the determinant effect of the student's social-class membership on the way he was handled within the school system, is pertinent to the analysis of the social organization of Lakeshore High, and more generally of large comprehensive high schools in metropolitan areas. We suggest that the organizational accommodation of disputes between parents and counselors highlights the changing relation between the family and school system, and by implication the relation between social-class membership and the organizational processes of the high school. In the current 'crisis in education' and the search for talent it has organized, the high school has received increased support from civic and professional groups to create a program that will maximize the development of

talent. Such support has tended to increase the autonomy and authority of the school system and to insulate it against the complaints and pressures of middle- and upper-class families.

But the major criterion of the effectiveness of the high school's program for the development of talent is the proportion of its graduates who are admitted to colleges. The proportion of college-*qualified* graduates that a high school produces is limited by the number of students who declare their college-going intentions, whatever their capability. The declaration may be, in the general case, a necessary condition for producing a student who is qualified for college at the end of his high school career. The proportion of graduates who do in fact *register* in colleges is limited by the number of students (again, somewhat independent of their test capability) whose families are able to provide financial support for part or all of their college education (excluding the small number of 'complete-expenses' scholarship students). Such conditions would lead high school administrators and their personnel to spend more time with the processing of middle- and upper-class students for college entrance, for it is the students from these social classes who have the best means at hand to validate the effectiveness of the high school's program of developing the talent.

Thus, we suggest that the influence of social class upon the way students are processed in the high school today is reflected in new and more subtle family-school relations than the direct and often blatant manipulation of family class pressure documented by Hollingshead. In one sense, the influences of social class on the treatment accorded students has become a built-in feature of the organizational activities of the modern comprehensive high school, particularly those with highly developed counseling programs. Insofar as the high school is committed to the task of identifying talent and increasing the proportion of college-going students, counselors will tend to devote more of their time and activities to those students who plan and are most likely to go to college and whose parents actively support their plans and make frequent inquiries at the school about their progress – namely, the students from the middle and upper social classes. Thus, as between two students of equal ability, who are reported as failing in their courses, if one is a college-going upper-middle-class student and the other a non-college working-class student, how is the counselor likely to handle them? If our assumption is valid, the upper-middle-class student will be called to a conference, inquiries will be made among his teachers, and his parents will be informed of his problems, while the lower-class student, unless he is considered exceptionally bright, may be ignored. The differential attention given students of middle and upper social classes is not here seen as a result of direct class pressures applied by parents, but as an effect of the counselor's conceptions of the type of student who should be doing better, who 'won't make it if he doesn't apply himself', whose parents 'will be very upset if he isn't accepted at x University', and so on.

3 One of the consequences of the disproportionate attention given to college-going students in the organizational effort to develop talent is that the recognition and exploration, by students as well as school personnel, of the range and variety of talent are limited if not precluded. We do not refer here simply to the frequently discussed problem of the discriminatory effects imposed by academically oriented high schools upon students who do not plan to go to college. We refer to the consequences of the organizational emphasis on talent upon the development of the full range of individuality among the student population, and most particularly among the college-going students. The high school as a 'talent farm' that attempts to accommodate parents, colleges, and the demands of the larger society may produce seniors who are college-qualified but not interested in a broad educational experience. The differentiation of college-going and non-college-going students defines the standards of performance by which they are evaluated by the school personnel and by which students are urged to evaluate themselves. It is the college-going student more than his non-college-going peer who is continually reminded by his teachers, counselor, parents, and peers of the decisive importance of academic achievement to the realization of his ambitions and who becomes progressively committed to this singular standard of self-evaluation. He becomes the future-oriented student interested in a delimited occupational specialty, with little time to give thought to the present or to question the implications of his choice and the meaning of his strivings.

We are not subscribing to the notion that the high school should provide a period of mindless fun and games to distract adolescents from the presumed confusions of their period of personal growth. American adolescents have too long been victims of their own publicity, which describes them as a population given to performing personal rituals with extravagant enthusiasm or hopeless despair. In this respect, the search for talent in the high school has generated an atmosphere in which academic achievement provides a meaningful basis for esteem and prestige within the peer group as well as the school system. We are concerned, however, that the organizational emphasis upon talent and the pursuit of narrow specialties virtually ignores the significance of adolescence as a period during which individuals may explore the alternatives of personal style, interests, and identity. With the diffusion of specialized educational programs from the graduate school through colleges into the lower school systems, the adolescent is forced to make decisions and declare choices from a range of alternatives he can hardly be expected to know.

4 Some may argue that although the contemporary educational system has (perhaps unnecessarily) pushed the college/non-college decision into the freshman year in high school, the college-going alternative is open to all students. What we take to be the serious issue is that the college/non-college decision has become *the* decision with reference to which the student is assigned to courses, evaluated as to performance, and organizationally processed. It should certainly be no surprise that counselors find in the course of their counseling activities that students are concerned with a variety of personal problems other than whether or not they are achieving up to their ability. Indeed, how can we doubt that they are troubled by feelings of uncertainty, inadequacy, futility, self-pity, and so on when they are continually reminded that their present actions are fraught with consequences for the future?

In a high school geared to the development of talent, however, the student discusses such feelings at his peril, for they are not viewed as simply normal manifestations of adolescence compounded by the stresses generated by the organization itself. It would not be an exaggeration to state that high school as a 'talent farm' produces its own problems, and that it has developed a 'clinic' to deal with them. The sense in which the high school has become a 'clinic' in the name of developing talent has, in our judgment, ramifications that extend far beyond providing counseling and guidance services to the student population. Suspending the questions of the validity of interpretations of student problems made by the counseling personnel and the modes of treatment that are prescribed and practiced, the issue which must be addressed is whether or not the school is or should be authorized to engage in such activities. We do not doubt that from a psychiatric point of view the behavior of some students may be diagnosed as serious problems that call for specialized treatment, but these students must certainly represent a small fraction of the student population. We do question, however, the propriety of a procedure that routinely assigns students to counselors who not only monitor their progress but actively seek and probe for 'problems'. This is an invasion of privacy, however disguised it may be by an ideology of service and 'help', and an invasion during a period when maintaining the privacy of unique personal experience may be critical for the adolescent's awareness of his own individuality. What is even more disturbing is the prospect that this solicitous treatment will produce a new generation of youth socialized to the practice of easy confessions and receptive to 'professional' explanations of who they are and what they aspire to become.

In this volume, we have advanced the view that the modern comprehensive high school is characterized by a highly organized effort, implemented by bureaucratic procedures, to identify and develop the talent distributed among its student population. We do not question the relevance or legitimacy of the high school's current concern and involvement in this effort. Clearly, the search for talent is not simply a manifestation of the 'crisis in education' but a consequence of the more general demands imposed upon the educational system by a society increasing in scale and complexity. The American school systems have responded to these demands with actual and suggested re-organization of curriculums, experimentation with new methods of teaching, institution of long-range research programs, and other efforts. In this study we have attempted to explore how organizational accommodations to scale and complexity have transformed the conception and function of the school system, and how the consequences of this transformation might affect the socialization of the student population as individuals and as members of the adult society.

15

Educators' Theories and Pupil Identities*

Bernard Coard

The Attitude of the Teacher

From what has been said already, it is quite clear that large numbers of West Indian children are failing to perform to the best of their abilities, or even averagely. They are falling behind in their classroom work, and they get low scores on tests, relative to their true abilities. There are many reasons for this, and it is important to know what they are if we are to do anything to alter the situation.

Prejudice and Patronization

There are three main ways in which a teacher can seriously affect the performance of a Black child: by being openly prejudiced; by being patronizing; and by having low expectations of the child's abilities. All three attitudes can be found among teachers in this country. Indeed, these attitudes are widespread. Their effect on the Black child is enormous and devastating.

That there are many openly prejudiced teachers in Britain is not in doubt in my mind. I have experienced them personally. I have also consulted many Black teachers whose experiences with some white teachers are horrifying. Two West Indian teachers in South London have reported to me the cases of white teachers who sit smoking in the staff-room, and refuse to teach a class of nearly-all-Black children. When on one occasion they were accosted by one of the Black teachers, they stated their refusal to teach 'those niggers'. These incidents were reported to the head teachers of the schools, who took no action against the teachers concerned. In fact, the heads of these schools had been trying to persuade the children to leave school when they had reached the school-leaving age, even though their parents wished them to continue their education, in some cases in order to obtain CSE's and 'O' levels, and in other cases because they thought the children could benefit from another year's general education.

* *How the West Indian Child is made Educationally Subnormal in the British School System*, Beacon Press, 1971.

Therefore the teachers in this case conspired to prevent these Black children from furthering their education by simply refusing to teach them.

There are many more teachers who are patronizing or condescending towards Black children. These are the sort who treat a Black child as a favourite pet animal. I have often overheard teachers saying: 'I really like that coloured child. He is quite bright for a coloured child'! One teacher actually said to me one day, in a sincere and well-meaning type of voice: 'Gary is really quite a nice boy considering he is Black.' There are other teachers who won't press the Black child too hard academically, as 'he isn't really up to it, poor chap.' Children see through these hypocritical and degrading statements and attitudes more often than adults realize, and they feel deeply aggrieved when anyone treats them as being inferior, which is what patronization is all about. They build up resentment, and develop emotional blocks to learning.

When the teacher does not expect much from the child

Most teachers absorb the brainwashing that everybody else in society has absorbed – that Black people are inferior, are less intelligent, etc, than white people. Therefore the Black child is expected to do less well in school. The IQ tests which are given to the Black child, with all their cultural bias, give him a low score only too often. The teachers judge the likely ability of the child on the basis of this IQ test. The teacher has, in the form of the IQ test results, what she considers to be 'objective' confirmation of what everybody in the society is thinking and sometimes saying: that the Black children on average have lower IQs than the white children, and must consequently be expected to do less well in class. Alderman Doulton of the Education Committee in the Borough of Haringay has expressed this view, and it is probably fair to say that the banding of children in Haringay for supposedly achieving equal groups of ability in all the schools was really a clever plot to disperse the Black children in the borough throughout the school system. The notorious Professor Jensen, the Enoch Powell of the academic world, has added credence to the myth of Black inferiority by openly declaring that Black people are inherently less intelligent than whites, and therefore Black children should be taught separately. In these circumstances, it is not surprising that most English teachers expect less from the Black child than from the white child.

In a study done in London, 118 epileptic children were given an IQ test. Their teachers, not knowing the results of the test, were then asked to give their assessment of the children's intelligence by stating whether a child was 'average', 'above average', 'well above average', etc, from their knowledge of each child. It is important to mention at this stage that epileptic children suffer a lot of prejudice directed against them by the general society, similar to that Black children face – but obviously not as great. Teachers also tend to think of them as being less intelligent than ordinary children – again similar to what the Black child faces.

In twenty-eight cases, the teachers seriously underestimated the child's true ability. This means that a *quarter* of the children were wrongly assessed! In one case a thirteen-year-old girl with an IQ of 120 (which is university level!) had failed her 11 + examination and was in the 'D' stream of a secondary modern school. Her teacher considered that she was of 'below average' intelligence! (average intelligence = 100). Another child with family problems and very low income got an IQ score of 132 (which is exceedingly high). Her teachers, however, all rated her as being 'low-stream' material!

This sort of information is shocking, because now that most schools are either comprehensive or going comprehensive, it is the assessment of the teachers and head teachers which decides which stream a child is placed in – which in turn influences what is expected of him academically. If these teachers who are supposed to know the children make serious mistakes in a *quarter* of the cases concerning epileptic children, against whom there is *some* prejudice, can you imagine how many wrong assessments are made by teachers when Black children are involved?!

What the British School System does to the Black Child

Some time ago a white boy of thirteen in the school for Educational Subnormal children where I teach, asked my permission to draw a picture of me. I had been his class teacher for one year. I had a very good relationship with him, and he was very fond of me. He enjoyed drawing. The picture he did of me was quite good. He had included my spectacles, which he always teased me about, and he also drew my moustache and beard while he made great jokes about them. When he was finished, he passed me the paper with the portrait of myself, looking very pleased with himself at having drawn what he considered a near-likeness. I said to him: 'Haven't you forgotten to do something?'

'What?' he said, looking curious and suspicious.

'You forgot to colour my face. My face, cheeks, etc – they are not white, are they?'

'No, no! I can't do that!' he said, looking worried.

'Well, you said you were painting a picture of me. Presumably you wanted it to look like me. You painted my hair, moustache and beard, and you painted them Black – which they are. So you have to paint my face dark brown if it is to look like me at all.'

'No! I can't. I can't do that. No. No,' he said, looking highly embarrassed and disturbed. He then got up and walked away, finding himself a hammer to do woodwork with in the corner of the room far away from me.

This same boy, along with one of his white school friends, had waited outside the school gate for me one afternoon the previous week. When I approached, one of them said: 'People are saying that you are coloured, but you aren't, sir, are you?' This was a rhetorical question on their part. They both looked very worried that 'some people' should be calling me 'coloured', and wanted my reassurance that I was not. They both liked and admired me, and hated thinking that I might be coloured! I explained to them then, as I *had* done many times before in class, that I *was* Black, that I was from the West Indies, and that my forefathers came from Africa. They obviously had mental blocks against accepting me as being Black.

The white boy, who did not even know who 'coloured people' were, obviously had the most fearful image of what Black people were supposed to be like, even though his favourite teacher was Black, and one of his closest friends in class was a Black child. I happened to know that his house mother at the children's home where he lives has never discussed race with him, and does not display any open prejudice to Black people. In fact she has, over the years, been an excellent foster-mother to two West Indian boys. Yet he picked up from somewhere a sufficiently adverse image of Black people, that he couldn't bear to have his favourite teacher be 'coloured', and could not bring himself to draw me as I was – a Black man. He had to have my face white.

This experience of mine gave me an idea; if this was how two white boys in the class felt about me, then perhaps they felt the same way about their close friend, Desmond, a Black boy of eleven from Jamaica. So I gathered together all the drawings and paintings which the children had done of each other, and sure enough, Desmond got painted white by all the white children! What's worse, Desmond and the other four Black children had painted each other white also!

A week later, Desmond, the West Indian boy, asked me to draw a picture of him. I drew the outline, as he watched, making critical comments from time to time. Having completed the outline, I began shading his face Black. He immediately said: 'What – what are you doing? You are *spoiling* me!'

I said: 'No, of course not, I am painting you as you are – Black; just like *I* am. Black *is* beautiful, you know. You aren't ashamed of that, are you?'

At that he calmed down, and I completed shading his face Black,. Then I did his hair. His hair was Black, short, and very African in texture. I drew it exactly as his hair really was. When he saw it, he jumped out of his chair and shouted: 'You painted me to look like a golliwog! You make me look just like a golliwog!' and he was half about to cry, half about to pounce on me for having done so terrible a thing as to have drawn his hair like it was, instead of making it long, straight and brown, as he had drawn himself in the past!

After I had calmed him down, again by pointing out that my hair was exactly the same as his, and that *I* liked mine, he decided to retaliate by drawing one of me. He drew my hair Black and African-like, he drew my moustache and beard, but he, like the white boy before, refused to shade my face dark brown or Black even though I had done his that way. When I asked him to draw my face the colour it really was, rather than leaving it white, he said very emotionally: 'You do it yourself', and walked out of the room.

Obviously in an English classroom it is terrible to be Black. The white child is concerned lest his best friend be considered Black, and the Black child is more than concerned that he should be considered Black!

And this is what this society, with the aid of the school system, is doing to our Black children!

The examples I have given above are not isolated ones. There is the Indian girl in my class who wears Indian clothes to school and whose mother wears her caste-marks and sari when going anywhere, and yet this girl once denied she was Indian when speaking to her English friends in class. Or there is the case of the Jamaican girl in my class who pretended not to know where Jamaica was, and stated indignantly that she was not from 'there' when speaking to some of the other children one day. Both conversations I overheard by accident. I could give case after case, for they are endless. In fact, none of the West Indian children whom I taught and ran clubs for over a period of three years, have failed to reveal their feelings of ambiguity, ambivalence, and at times despair, at being Black. Many have been made neurotic by their school experience.

How the System Works

The Black child's true identity is denied daily in the classroom. In so far as he is given an identity, it is a false one. He is made to feel inferior in every way. In addition to being told he is dirty and ugly and 'sexually unreliable', he is told by a variety of means that he is intellectually inferior. When he prepares to leave school, and even before, he is made to realize that he and 'his kind' are only fit for manual, menial jobs.

The West Indian child is told on first entering the school that his language is second rate, to say the least. Namely, the only way he knows how to speak, the way he has always communicated with his parents and family and friends; the language in which he has expressed all his emotions, from joy to sorrow; the language of his innermost thoughts and ideas, is 'the wrong way to speak'.

A man's language is part of him. To say that his language and that of his entire family and culture is second rate, is to accuse him of *being* second rate. But this is what the West Indian child is told in one manner or another on his first day in an English school.

As the weeks and months progress, the Black child discovers that all the great men of history were white – at least, those are the only ones he has been told about. His reading-books show him white children and white adults exclusively. He discovers that white horses, white rocks and white unicorns are beautiful and good; the word 'Black' is reserved for describing the pirates, the thieves, the ugly, the witches, etc. This is the *conditioning effect* of what psychologists call *word association* on people's minds. If every reference on TV, radio, newspapers, reading-books and story-books in school shows 'Black' as being horrible and ugly, and everything 'white' as being pure, clean and beautiful, then people begin to think this way on racial matters.

Several months ago in my class I was reading one of S K McCullagh's story-books for children, *The Country of the Red Birds*. This author is world famous, and she has written numerous story-books and reading series for children, used in schools in many parts of the world. She is actually a lecturer in psychology. In this story, these two white children went out to the 'island of Golden Sands'. They got to the 'white rock', where the very helpful 'white unicorn' lives. When they met the unicorn, 'the first thing that they saw was a Black ship, with Black sails, sailing towards the white rock.

"The Black pirates! The Black pirates!" cried the little unicorn. "They'll kill us! Oh, what shall we do?" '

Finally they escaped from the white rock, which the 'Black pirates' had taken over, and went to the island of the 'red birds'. There, 'a Black pirate stood on the sand, with a red bird in his hand', about to kill it. The white boys and the white unicorn, along with the other red birds, managed to beat off the Black pirate, and the red birds in gratitude to the white boys and white unicorn state: ' "We will do anything for you, for you have saved a red bird from the Black pirates." '

For those who may be sceptical about the influence of word association on people's minds, it is interesting to note that when I said 'Black pirates' in the story, several of the white children in the class turned their heads and looked at the Black children, who in turn looked acutely embarrassed.

When the pictures, illustrations, music, heroes, great historical and contemporary figures in the classroom are all white, it is difficult for a child to identify with anyone who is not white. When in addition the pictures of Blacks are golliwog stereotypes, about whom filthy jokes are made; when most plays show Black men doing servant jobs; when the word 'Black' in every story-book is synonymous with evil, then it becomes impossible for the child to want to be Black. Put another way, it would be unnatural of him not to want to be white. Does this not explain why Desmond and the other Black children draw themselves as white? Can you blame them?

But this is not the end of the picture, unfortunately, for the Black children know they are Black. Whenever they might begin in their fantasy to believe otherwise, they are soon reassured on this score by being told they are 'Black bastards' whenever there is a row in the playground – and even when there isn't.

The children are therefore made neurotic about their race and culture. Some become behaviour problems as a result. They become resentful and bitter at being told their language is second-rate, and their history and culture is non-existent; that they hardly exist at all, except by grace of the whites – and then only as platform sweepers on the Underground, manual workers, and domestic help.

The Black child under these influences develops a deep inferiority complex. He soon loses motivation to succeed academically, since, at best, the learning experience in the classroom is an elaborate irrelevance to his personal life situation, and at worst it is a racially humiliating experience. He discovers in an amazingly short space of time the true role of the Black man in a white-controlled society, and he abandons all intellectual and career goals. Remember the four-year-old Black girl in America, mentioned earlier, who said to Mary Goodman: 'The people that are white, they can go up. The people that are brown, they have to go down.' When two other psychologists in America 'Radke and Trager' investigated 'Children's perception of the social roles of Negroes and White', the 'poor house' was assigned to Negroes and the 'good house' to White by the great majority of white and Negro children aged five to eight years.

Conclusion

The Black child acquires two fundamental attitudes or beliefs as a result of his experiencing the British school system: a low self-image, and consequently low self-expectations in life. These are obtained through streaming, banding, bussing, ESN schools, racist news media, and a white middle-class curriculum; by totally ignoring the Black child's language, history, culture, identity. Through the choice of teaching materials, the society emphasizes who and what it thinks is important – and by implication, by omission, who and what it thinks is unimportant, infinitesimal, irrelevant. Through the belittling, ignoring or denial of a person's identity, one can destroy perhaps the most important aspect of a person's personality – his sense of identity, of who he is. Without this, he will get nowhere.

16

The Dumb Class *

James Herndon

One afternoon during our free seventh period someone looked around and said 'This faculty is the Dumb Class'.

It was so. Given the community or the entire country as a school – reversing the usual image of the school as mirror of society to make society the mirror of the school – and given that community as one which is tracked or ability-grouped into high, high-average, average, low-average, high-low, low and low-low, the faculty or faculties, teachers, *educators*, are the dumb class.

We are the dumb class because we cannot learn. Cannot achieve. Why not? Cannot concentrate, have a low attention span, are culturally deprived, brain-damaged, non-verbal, unmotivated, lack skills, are anxiety-ridden, have broken homes, can't risk failure, no study habits, won't try, are lazy . . . ? Those are the reasons *kids* are in the dumb class, supposing we don't say it's because they are just dumb. But the characteristic of the dumb class is that it cannot learn how to do what it is there to do. Try as one may, one cannot make the dumb class learn to do these things, at least not as long as it is operating together as a dumb class. Even if those things are completely obvious, the dumb class cannot learn them or achieve them.

Is it so that what the dumb class is supposed to achieve is so difficult that only superior individuals can achieve it, and then only with hard work, endless practice? Is it so mysterious and opaque that only those with intelligence and energy enough to research and ferret out the mysteries of the universe can gain insight into it? Eighth period I was involved with this dumb class which was supposed to achieve adding and subtracting before it got out of the eighth grade and went to high school. Could the class achieve it? No sir. Given an adding problem to add, most of the dumb class couldn't add it. Those who did add it hadn't any notion of whether or not they'd added it correctly, even if they had. They asked me: Is this right? Is this right? This ain't right, is it? What's the answer? If you don't know whether

---

* *How to Survive in your Native Land*, Bantam Edition, 1972, 92–97.

it's right or not, I'd say, then you aren't adding it. Is this right? screamed four kids, rushing me waving papers. Boy, this dumb class can't learn, I'd say to myself. Not a very sophisticated remark, perhaps.

For a while I would drop in on the Tierra Firma bowling alley, since Jay and Jack were always dying to go there. One day I ran into the dumbest kid in the dumb class. Rather, he came up to us as we were playing this baseball slot machine. Jay and Jack were not defeating the machine, to say the least, and as a result had to put in another dime each time they wanted to play again. Well the dumb kid showed us how to lift the front legs of the machine in just the right way so that the machine would run up a big score without tilting, enough for ten or so free games, all by itself. After it did that, he told us you could go ahead and really play it for fun. Jay and Jack were pretty impressed; they thought this dumb kid was a genius. Those big kids in your school sure are smart, was how Jack put it.

Well, as Jay and Jack happily set out to strike out and pop-up to the infield on the machine for those free games, the dumb kid and I walked around and watched the bowlers and had a smoke and talked. In the end, of course, I asked him what he was doing around there. He was getting ready to go to work, he told me. Fooling around until five, when he started. What did he do? I keep score, he told me. For the leagues. He kept score for two teams at once. He made fifteen bucks for a couple of hours. He thought it was a great job, making fifteen bucks for something he liked to do anyway, perhaps would have done for nothing, just to be able to do it.

He was keeping score. Two teams, four people on each, eight bowling scores at once. Adding quickly, not making any mistakes (for no one was going to put up with errors), following the rather complicated process of scoring in the game of bowling. Get a spare, score ten plus whatever you get on the next ball, score a strike, then ten plus whatever you get on the next two balls; imagine the man gets three strikes in a row and two spares and you are the scorer, plus you are dealing with seven other guys all striking or sparing or neither one . . . The bowling league is not a welfare organization nor part of Headstart or anything like that and wasn't interested in giving some dumb kid a chance to improve himself by fucking up their bowling scores. No, they were giving this smart kid who had proved to be fast and accurate fifteen dollars because they could use a good scorer.

I figured I had this particular dumb kid now. Back in eighth period I lectured him on how smart he was to be a league scorer in bowling. I pried admissions from the other boys, about how they had paper routes and made change. I made the girls confess that when they went to buy stuff they didn't have any difficulty deciding if those shoes cost $10.95 or whether it meant $109.50 or whether it meant $1.09 or how much change they'd get back from a twenty. Naturally I then handed out bowling-score problems and paper-route change-making problems and buying-shoes problems, and naturally everyone could choose which ones they wanted to solve, and naturally the result was that all the dumb kids immediately rushed me yelling: Is this right? I don't know how to do it! What's the answer? This ain't right, is it? and What's my grade? The girls who bought shoes for $10.95 with a $20 bill came up with $400.15 for change and wanted to know if that was right? The brilliant league scorer couldn't decide whether two strikes and a third frame of eight amounted to eighteen or twenty-eight or whether it was one hundred eight and one half.

The reason they can't learn is because they are the dumb class. No other reason. Is adding difficult? No. It is the dumb class which is difficult. Are the teachers a dumb class? Well, we are supposed to teach kids to 'read, write, cipher and sing', according to an old phrase. Can we do it? Mostly not. Is it difficult? Not at all. We can't do it because we are a dumb class, which by definition can't do it, whatever it is.

Yet what we are supposed to do is something which, like adding, everyone knows how to do. It isn't mysterious, nor dependent on a vast and intricate knowledge of pedagogy or technology or psychological tests or rats. Is there any man or woman on earth who knows how to read who doesn't feel quite capable of teaching his own child or children to read? Doesn't every father feel confident that his boy will come into the bathroom every morning to stand around and watch while the father shaves and play number games with the father and learn about numbers and shaving at the same time? Every person not in the dumb class feels that these things are simple. Want to know about Egypt? Mother or father or older brother or uncle or someone and the kid go down to the public library and get out a book on Egypt and the kid reads it and perhaps the uncle reads it too, and while they are shaving they may talk about Egypt. But the dumb class of teachers and public educators feel that these things are very difficult, and they must keep hiring experts and devising strategies in order that they can rush these experts and strategies with their papers asking: Is this right? and What's my grade?

Yet, released from the dumb class to their private lives, teachers are marvelous gardeners, they work on ocean liners as engineers, they act in plays, win bets, go to art movies, build their own houses, they are opera fans, expert fishermen, champion skeet shooters, grand golfers, organ players, oratorio singers, hunters, mechanics . . . all just as if they were smart people. Of course it is more difficult to build a house or sing Bach than it is to teach kids to read. Of course if they operated in their lives outside of the dumb class the same way they do in it, their houses would fall down, their ships would sink, their flowers die, their cars blow up.

This very morning in the San Francisco *Chronicle* I read a scandalous report. The reporter reports the revelations of a member of the board of education, namely that 45 per cent of the *Spanish-surname children* (that is how we put it in the paper these days) who are in mentally retarded classes have been found, when retested in Spanish, to be of average or above-average intelligence. The board member thought that 'the Spanish-speaking kids were shunted into classes for the mentally retarded because they did not understand English well enough to pass the examinations they were given'. He figured that, just like if he was told that a bowler had a spare on the first frame and got eight on his next ball, he'd figure that the bowler's score in the first frame ought to be eighteen. Well, in this matter assume that the board member is the teacher in a dumb class. He's trying to tell the school administrators something obvious. Does the administrator learn, now he's been told it, that ten and eight are eighteen? No, the assistant superintendent for special services says that 'the assumption was that they understood English well enough to be tested by the English versions of the Stanford-Binet and the WISC intelligence tests'. He thought that 'it wasn't so much the fault of the test as it was the cultural deprivation of the child at the time of testing' which caused these smart kids to be retarded. Asked if these smart retarded Spanish-surname kids were now going to be moved into the regular program, he *revealed* that no, that wasn't the case, for they were '*still working* with the elementary division to seek a proper *transitional* program, since these children were still *functional retardates*' no matter what their IQ.

The reporter, acting in his role as critical parent, found out that the tests *were* available in Spanish but that Spanish-speaking kids *weren't* tested, therefore, in Spanish (because of the above assumption). The tests *weren't* available in 'Oriental', and 'Oriental' kids *weren't* tested, therefore, in 'Oriental'. Well, that made sense; so the reporter pried out the information that the school district got $550 extra a year for each kid in mentally retarded classes. The reporter implied cynically that they were doing it for the money and that if they let all these bright retarded Spanish kids out there might be a shortage of $550 kids to be retarded.

But it is the dumb class we are concerned with. Here this administrator is told something obvious, told to learn it, told to achieve this difficult knowledge that them Spanish-speaking kids are only dumb if they are tested in a language they don't understand. But being in the dumb class, he don't learn it. He may be the smartest man in the world, able to keep score for league bowling, read *The Book of the Dead*, go water skiing, make bell curves. But in the dumb class he can't learn anything, and there is no reason to expect that he ever will as long as he is in there.

17

On the Politics and Sociology of Stupidity*

Lewis Anthony Dexter

Why are the high grade retarded – and more generally the 'dull' and stupid, slow learners of all sorts – regarded as one of the great problem groups of our society? Why is a special association devoted to mental deficiency and another set up chiefly for parents of retarded children? This inquiry is part of an effort[1] to determine whether application of a prevailing point of view in the study of social problems may be useful in thinking about stupidity. Our concern here is with what Josiah Royce[2] has described as 'regulative principles of research [which may] provide the larger ideas of guidance [to] empirical investigation [but which are not in themselves subject to] precise, empirical tests; which, if they happen to prove coherent and illuminating, may provide the basis for more specific hypotheses which can be empirically tested'. This prevailing point of view about social problems is based on the postulate that 'social problems' are not properly or adequately defined in terms of the obvious and manifest rationalizations or explanations of them by those who experience them. Thus, Myrdal,[3] for instance, demonstrated that the problem of 'race', so-called, could best be understood by analysis of *conflicting* moral values; while Wirth[4] similarly was able to show that the common-sense 'explanation' of the housing dilemma in the United States in the 1930's omitted the significant *social* factors; and Davis[5] that the stigma imposed upon illegitimacy in most Western societies is subtly interrelated to neglected social institutions.

Generally, problems, ideas, and institutions are taken as given and their consequences seen as self-evident facts of nature. For decades, as is well known, many people, white *and* Negro, saw the issues of 'race relations' as self-evident. Similarly, for a century or more, statesmen and thinkers alike adopted a version of *laissez-faire* economics which made mass unemployment seem absolutely natural in an industrial society. Ultimately, within the last generation, Keynesian economics

* H Becker (ed), *The Other Side*, Free Press of Glencoe, 1964 (37–45, 48–49).

clarified the conception that the 1929 type of depression is a consequence of systems and institutions, rather than a necessary product of the nature of man in industrial society. This revision of economic thought forced those of us whose economic ideas were learned before 1935 to *un*learn a good deal. A similar effort at rethinking the problems of mental deficiency may be worth while.

An Analogy: Gawkiness as a Cardinal Social Defect

An easy way to indicate how we might reinterpret mental deficiency along these lines is by means of an analogy. Let us imagine a society in which the major target group of social discrimination is composed of the clumsy people, the so-called 'gawkies'. Let us assume that this is because such a society stresses grace and style in movement *as* we stress intellectual skill. Let us assume that people are taught to abhor clumsiness as many people in our society are taught to abhor stupidity. Let us suppose, to put the analogy on all fours, that there has been invented a system of writing in that society which can only be mastered by those who are graceful; and that the technology of the society is such that a high degree of grace and skill are necessary to run its machines. This will be so, *not* because of the inherent necessities of industrial processes, but because the engineers and businessmen of the society arrange to have things done in a way which takes grace – as a matter of course.

The schools in such a social system would stress movement, dancing, rhythmics, etc. The psychometric institutes of the society would develop an elaborate vocabulary and even more elaborate testing mechanisms for distinguishing between *manifest* grace and inherent *potentiality* for grace of movement. A considerable literature would develop about the 'pseudo-clumsy' – and in many cases, parents and schools would be so embarrassed and bothered by the presence of gawky children that they would send them to special custodial institutions where they would not be a constant reminder of parental or pedagogical inadequacy.

Naturally, under such circumstances, the marginally clumsy, permitted to remain at large in the community, would always be conscious of having two strikes already called against them. They would be liable to be institutionalized if they did anything unusual. Naturally, too, clumsy children would become social rejects and isolates, and instead of the moron jokes, beloved in this country[6], there would probably develop pantomime jokes, directed against the gawky.

Some academic iconoclast might raise considerable doubts as to his own accuracy and academic probity by reporting that, in fact, once out of school and in those economic activities where grace of movement was not really imperative, many persons with a subnormal grace quotient (GQ) could earn their own living and even make an economic contribution. There would be great surprise when it was reported that some superficially or evidently clumsy persons could hunt effectively, walk competently, even play games successfully; those reporting such findings would be under considerable pressure to 'explain them away'. And a scholar, giving a paper with such findings at the National Association on Clumsiness, would find that the news report on her paper made her the target of many scurrilous letters, much as though she had written a Kinsey-type book[7].

Nevertheless, under the circumstances just described, clumsiness would be regarded as pathological. And these circumstances are analogous to Western European and American attitudes toward stupidity. In making such an assertion, there is no intention to deny the reality of the social problem created by mental deficiency. In the first place, mental deficiency is a problem, or creates problems, because, in fact, there are many activities in our society which *demand* a substantial degree of verbal intelligence. As our analogy suggests, it is probable that some of these activities could be reorganized so as to lessen the problems attendant upon mental deficiency. Nevertheless, mental deficiency would still remain a problem.

But even more significantly in terms of our hypothesis, and going back to the analogy for the moment, clumsiness in our imaginary society would be a real social problem with real social consequences, for as W I Thomas[8] has pointed out, the way situations are defined by the society as a whole is for the people in that society the realest of realities. The mother of twins in a society which regards twin-bearing as wicked and repulsive, cannot escape from that 'reality' (nor can the mother of twins in a society which regards twin-bearing as a noble act escape from that reality either!)[9] In our imaginary society, clumsiness would be a real social problem with real consequences. It is necessary to emphasize this because it sometimes happens that if we raise questions about the one-factor strictly physiological explanation of a social problem, we are interpreted as denying its reality.

But Are the Stupid Really Discriminated Against and Despised?

Articles by Strickland[10] and by Johnson and Kirk[11] and such studies as that by Wolfstein[12] seem to the writer to demonstrate that indeed they are. There is also the experience which may be observed over and over again of the denial of employment, of legal rights, of a fair hearing, of an opportunity, to the stupid because they are stupid (eg, have a low IQ or show poor academic performance), *and not because the stupidity is relevant to the task, or claim, or situation.* A comment by one student of social problems[13] suggests that because discrimination against stupidity *per se* rarely comes to the attention of middle-class people, they ordinarily are quite unaware of it.

This objectively demonstrable, gross discrimination is of great significance. Within the actual life of most readers of these pages, however, the more subtle forms of 'discrimination' against stupidity are more likely to be experienced; by analogy, few US sociologists are likely to observe the type of crude anti-Semitism which occurred in medieval Europe or modern Germany: but most of them have seen gestures of withdrawal, listened to anti-Semitic jokes, etc. Unfortunately, no systematic, empirical study of attitudes toward cleverness or dullness is known to exist. As hypothesis, it is suggested that many influential people in our society – including particularly classroom teachers (the carriers *par excellence* of public, middle-class culture) – show more repugnance (eg, frown and scold more often) toward stupidity than toward anything else except dirtiness.

A change appears to have taken place in these attitudes toward 'stupidity' in recent years. At one time, the stupid were simply objects of derision or scorn: 'Simple Simon met a pieman. . . .' Then, in the first two decades of the twentieth century, in the United States and Great Britain at least (concurrently with the growth of mass education), the stupid were regarded with genuine fear and apprehension; 'moron' became a synonym for rapist. Both attitudes closely resemble feelings which people have displayed toward foreigners: foreigners are either ridiculous *or* frightening and wicked. But nowadays, in the era of foreign aid and Point IV programs, we believe in teaching foreigners 'democracy', modern technology, and other aspects of 'our way of life'. And, just as some of us are willing to spend a good deal of money on foreign aid, we are willing to do so on teaching the stupid *not* to be stupid.

But the one thing we often find it hard to tolerate about the foreigner is his remaining *fundamentally* alien *and wishing to do so*; and so, similarly, many with a deep interest in mental defectives, are concerned *only* to make them less defective, less stupid. This is a truism which is so obvious as to 'go without saying', but since hardly anybody says it we do not perhaps fully realize its consequences.

Clearly, the hypotheses just advanced could be better tested by study of verbal expression, of gesture, of manner, than by analyses of overt ideology. The sophisticated modern, familiar with cultural differentiation, may not *express* his distaste for foreign ways of doing things, but he will manifest in withdrawal or frown exactly the distaste he is trying to conceal, and perhaps *is* concealing from himself[14].

The analogy with reactions to stupidity is apparent. What needs to be determined is the degree to which the stupid are aware of the slights, contempt, and scolding to which they are exposed and how far they are affected by them in developing a self-image. On the basis of available knowledge, the most plausible hypothesis seems to be that intellectual skill – skill at handling abstract conception – is not related to ability to perceive that one is the object of contempt; stupid people are quite as likely to suffer psychologically from contempt as are the more intelligent[15].

The School, the Democratic Dogma and the Glorification of Intellectual Aptitudes

But, in most societies, the stupid are not victims of the same overt discrimination as in our society. For in other societies, race, clan-membership, ancestry, religion, status, physical prowess, and probably appearance, play more of a part in determining what rewards one gets and what values one is deprived of than in ours. A stupid person with the right ancestry, for instance, can 'get by' better than with us. A society which increasingly focuses on 'excellence', meaning thereby intellectual excellence[16], as does ours, tends more and more to discriminate against stupidity. This is not logically defensible. Because intellectual excellence is required of atomic physicists or for students of sociology is no reason to require intellectual prowess from people in most occupations and activities. In athletics, we admire skilled performance; but we do not[17] discriminate much more against the very incompetent athlete than against the merely mediocre performer. It seems probable that the attitude and response toward stupidity, characteristic of our society, is a function of the common school and of two interrelated ideologies which affect that school. These ideologies are: (1) the post-Renaissance emphasis upon achievement in certain lines of activity as a justification of one's righteousness, The Protestant Ethic, and (2) the radical aspect of democratic thought, identified particularly with the French Revolution and, later, with Jacksonian democracy, with its emphasis on the rights and obligations of equality.

For our present purposes, it is needless to recapitulate the extensive literature on The Protestant Ethic, and its secular variants, as expressed for instance in *Poor Richard's Almanac*[18]. It is sufficient to point out that the impact of that ethic upon those affected by it was to lead them to regard stupidity as a sin, rather than as a common human failing. For, it led to failure; and failure was a manifestation of

Heavenly displeasure.

The French Revolutionary notion of equality, as it spread to the American frontier and, later, to Soviet Russia, involved not only the *opportunity* to be equal, but the *obligation* to take advantage of the opportunity to be equal. Equal opportunity for education tended to result in compulsory education; and this notion of compulsory equality was embedded in the institution of the public or common school. As Sarason and Gladwin[19] make clear, the school and its demands and instruments – the intelligence test, for instance – play a substantial part in making the high-grade retarded a problem to themselves and to society. The public school has become, under the inspiration of egalitarian democracy, the central sacred institution of the community to a good many people in our society – more in the suburbs than in the slums, more among the tepidly religious than among the fundamentalists, more for some occupations and temperaments than others.

The high-grade retarded become, in such an interpretation of the school, heretics – unwilling heretics, heretics despite themselves, but heretics nevertheless. By merely being what they are, they challenge and cast doubt upon the system through which most people have gone. If, as many of them do, they succeed in earning their own living and getting along well in the community, they are even more puzzlingly unorthodox than those who accommodate to the system by cheating their way through. For the cheat, like the medieval penitent, admits the rightness of the system by his short-cut method of conforming to it. But the stupid who get along well cast doubt on the alleged secular justification of the system – that it helps people succeed. It is repulsive for some to believe that mental defectives can support themselves, no matter how much evidence is amassed to this effect, because, if so, how can we justify the discomforts and sacrifices and anguish of schooling? And when a scholar reported that some mental defectives have been more successful than non-defective counterparts, it is not surprising that she received fifty or so scurrilous attacks; she was denying the sacred[20].

Community Reorganization and the Social Problem Status of the Retarded and Stupid: A Wholesaler's Approach to Vocational Placement of the Retarded

It follows from what has just been said that if 'society' were re-organized the social problem and the individual problems of the retarded would be much less serious. Clearly, 'society' taken as a whole, is not going to be reorganized. But it may help to clarify the sociological nature of the problem of retardation by making the following conceivable assumption. Suppose that a community were to be planned on the assumption that approximately 25 per cent of its adults would be 'feeble-minded'. How should it differ from the towns and cities we actually know?

First: we would underline the point that there is no evidence that such a community would have any great economic difficulty. Verbal intelligence is necessary for administrators, accountants, attorneys, and engineers, for instance; but this intelligence is not necessary for all employees in manufacturing and service occupations *as such*. (It is, of course, necessary for these individuals as citizens, and as consumers, in the *modern* world, but it is precisely these peripheral necessities we wish to reconsider.)

The widespread use of secondary symbols – for purposes of legal contract and for borrowing money, even for such mechanical activities as reading road signs – is the heart of the problem of the stupid in our world. Accordingly, we would attempt to reorganize matters so that such symbols become less significant[21].

In such a society, we would, necessarily, abandon our present pattern of education and even compulsory literacy. We would have to change patterns of voting and limit seriously the right to borrow and to lend on credit for consumer purchases. We would probably reorganize certain activities so that they would be conducted more on a group basis and less by individuals than is currently the case; a stupid woman, as one nursemaid among several caring for children, may do an excellent job, but she lacks the adaptability and initiative to care for them *by herself*. In many old-fashioned villages, mothers, aunts, and cousins, on the whole, cared for children as a joint enterprise, so one particularly stupid woman did not necessarily cause too much trouble. Day-care centers could make it possible for our imaginary community to make similar good use of stupid, good-hearted, affectionate women to care for young children[22].

The proposal is not purely speculative. If constitutional barriers could be overcome[23], the organization of such a town or city (ideally on some isolatable spot, such as St Croix or Martha's Vineyard) would permit us to find out how much of a handicap mental retardation really is (and vice versa, where verbal intelligence is essential). But even if the idea remains in the realm of speculation, it would be extremely valuable if specialists on retardation and backwardness worked out in detail what it would involve if put into practice, because this would permit us to 'think out' the social meaning of these conditions in a way which has never been done.

225

Directions of Research

Usually, when research is started on social problems, it is based upon common-sense assumptions. The history of knowledge suggests, however, that common-sense assumptions are frequently inadequate or erroneous. Until fundamental assumptions have been critically examined, and alternatives postulated and explored, much talent and ingenuity may be wasted. The entire argument of the present paper rests on the assertion that perhaps the common-sense assumptions about mental deficiency need more criticism than they have received. One way to criticize them is to suggest alternative ways of looking at the issues as in the examples of the 'gawkies' above, or the proposal in the last section for setting up a community with 25 per cent retarded adults. It is very likely that the last approach is unworkable; but this is not the major point. So long as effort is devoted to formulating alternative constructions [24] and alternative formulations of the issues, there is a better prospect of resolving our problems successfully than there is if we simply stick to elementary common-sense [25]. In other words, the greatest current need in mental deficiency research is the search for new, unorthodox perspectives; they can help to test the value and appropriateness of the prevailing doctrines.

Notes

[1] Other articles in the series include: LEWIS A DEXTER, 'Research on Problems of Mental Subnormality', *American Journal of Mental Deficiency*, **64** (1960), 835–838. LEWIS A DEXTER, 'A Social Theory of Mental Deficiency', *ibid*, **62** (1958), 920–928 (bibliog). LEWIS A DEXTER, 'Towards a Sociology of Mental Deficiency', *ibid*, **61** (1956), 10–16. LEWIS A DEXTER, 'The Sociology of Adjudication: Who Defines Mental Deficiency?' *American Behavioral Scientist*, **4** (October 1960), 13–15. LEWIS A DEXTER, 'Heredity and Environment Re-explored', *Eugenics Quarterly*, **3** (1956), 88–93. LEWIS A DEXTER, 'A Note on Selective Inattention in Social Science', *Social Problems*, **6** (1958), 176–182.

[2] JOSIAH ROYCE, 'Introduction' to HENRI POINCARÉ, *The Foundations of Science*, Science Press, New York, 1921, xiv–xxi.

[3] G MYRDAL, *American Dilemma*, Harper's, New York, 1944.

[4] L WIRTH, *Contemporary Social Problems*, Second Edition, University of Chicago Press, Chicago, 1940.

[5] K DAVIS, 'Illegitimacy and the Social Structure', *American Journal of Sociology*, **45** (1939), 215–233.

[6] M WOLFENSTEIN, *Children's Humor, a Psychological Analysis* (esp the chapter on the moron joke), The Free Press of Glencoe, New York, 1954.

[7] This actually happened in the field of mental deficiency.

[8] W I THOMAS and F ZNANIECKI, *Polish Peasant in Europe and America*, Knopf, New York, 1927.

[9] W I THOMAS, *Primitive Behavior*, McGraw-Hill, New York, 1937, 9–18. (The three articles by Dexter, cited in footnote 1, which were published in

American Journal of Mental Deficiency, expand the relevance of Thomas' theory of 'definition of the situation' to the social role of the retarded.)

[10] C STRICKLAND, 'The Social Competence of the Feeble-Minded', *American Journal of Mental Deficiency*, **53** (1949), 504–515.

[11] G O JOHNSON and S KIRK, 'Are Mentally Handicapped Children Segregated in The Regular Grades?' *Journal of Exceptional Children*, **17** (1950), 65–68.

[12] *Op cit.*

[13] On my article dealing with the judicial treatment of alleged mental defectives, *American Behavioral Scientist, op cit.*

[14] EDWARD T HALL, *The Silent Language*, Doubleday, Garden City, 1959, shows how unspoken Latin-American and Anglo-American reactions to the *embrazo*, for instance, and the degree of physical distance it is appropriate to maintain, color many transcultural relationships. The type of analysis which underlies Hall's entire argument could most profitably be applied to the sphere of disapproval.

[15] A particularly perceptive social scientist who has had some contact with retardates, was much surprised at this hypothesis: he had assumed that sensitiveness to slight *and* intelligence go together. No doubt, the definition or recognition of slights depends upon intelligence: a stupid person may notice the praise and not the damnation in being 'damned with the faint praise,' but this and similar facts do not in all probability permit the stupid to live according to the widely accepted stereotype of 'the happy moron . . . who does not give a damn.'

[16] Many stupid would be better off if we attached more weight to *moral* excellence: 'Be good, sweet child, let who will be clever.'

[17] Some groups of young males may, in fact, make such a distinction; but it is not a norm for the society as a whole.

[18] M WEBER, *Protestant Ethic and the Spirit of Capitalism*, Scribner's, New York, 1948.

[19] S SARASON and T GLADWIN, 'Psychological and Biological Problems in Mental Subnormality: A Review of Research,' *American Journal of Mental Deficiency*, **63** (1958), 1115–1307 (reprinted from *Genetic Psychology Monographs*, 1958, and in S SARASON, *Psychological Problems of Mental Deficiency,* Third Edition, Harper's, New York, (1959).

[20] Fortunately for the stupid, the eccentric and the unorthodox, we are not consistent in our acceptance of the sacredness of schooling. There are reservations and ambiguities which permit loopholes for escape and accommodation. This is presumably always true of attitudes toward the sacred.

[21] See LEWIS A DEXTER, *American Journal of Mental Deficiency*, 1958, *op cit.*

[22] Another example: in the nineteenth century, in a large house with several servants, one *stupid* maid might be very useful. Nowadays, most large houses have only one maid, and she is expected to write down telephone messages, cope with door-to-door salesmen, and otherwise manifest verbal intelligence.

[23] Real barriers *are* constitutional, and for the idea to become practical, a very careful study of constitutional law as it affects proposals of this sort would have to be made. This fact is extremely ironic, because in reality, as I have pointed out in my article in *American Behavioral Scientist, op cit* (and as the National Council for Civil Liberties has demonstrated in great detail in Great Britain), under present circumstances, retardates do not receive the

benefits of due process. Nevertheless, we can be reasonably certain that a formal proposal of the sort here made would, in the present temper of the Courts and especially of the US Supreme Court, be regarded as depriving stupid citizens of essential rights (even though these citizens do not, in practice, get the opportunity to exercise many of these rights).

[24] The ideas in the present paper were in part stimulated by the theory of postulation by the theory of naming and by the transactional approach of the late ARTHUR F BENTLEY in his *An Inquiry into Inquiries*, Beacon Press, Boston, 1954, and also *Behavior . . . Knowledge . . . Fact*, Principia Press, Bloomington, 1935. Mr Bentley in correspondence with me indicated that he thought the present effort a satisfactory application of his approach.

[25] It may very well be that there is a brain damage affecting all mental defectives, not otherwise physiologically abnormal, and that this will ultimately be ascertained. Even supposing this to be so, the brain damage is not necessarily the important point. To the medieval leper, the sociology of leprosy was often more important than its pathology; to the contemporary homosexual, employed by a Federal agency, the sociology of attitudes toward homosexuality is far more significant than the physiological basis (if any) of his deviation; and so, to the 'garden variety' mental defective, attitudes toward his affliction may matter more than its genesis. It might, indeed, also be literally true that the exceptionally clumsy or awkward also suffer from some form of brain damage; but, in our imaginary society, postulated above, the social psychology affecting clumsiness would be far more vital to them than the physiology of their situation.

18

The Employment Office*

Barry Hines

There were four chairs outside the medical room. A woman and a
boy occupied the two nearest the door. Billy sat down, leaving an
empty chair between them. The boy leaned forward and nodded at
him across the front of the woman. The woman glanced round, then
turned back to the boy.

'And don't be sat there like a dummy when you get in there.'

The boy blushed and looked across at Billy again. Billy sat staring
straight ahead, top teeth working across his bottom lip, squeezing it
white.

'Tell him that you're after a good job, an office job, summat like
that.'

'Who's after an office job?'

'Well what are you after then? A job on t'bins?'

'I wish you'd shut up.'

'An' straighten your tie.'

The boy held the knot and pulled the back tag. The knot slid up
and covered the top button of his clean white shirt. 'I wish you'd stop
nagging.'

'Somebody's to nag.'

The door opened. The woman stood up and practised a smile down
at herself. A boy emerged, followed by a woman smiling back into the
room. The women smiled at each other. Their boys grinned. They
crossed. The door closed, and the interviewed couple walked away,
close in conversation. They stepped in accord, but the clip of high-
heels predominated, and their echo preceded them down the corridor. Billy watched them go, then propped his face in his hands and
stared down between his legs.

The floor was covered with red and green vinyl tiles set in a check
pattern. Their surfaces were mottled white, seeking a marble effect.
On some tiles the mottling was severe, on others a mere fleck, and
where a series of heavily mottled tiles had been laid together, the

---

* *A Kestrel for a Knave*, Michael Joseph 1968, (Penguin Edition 135–140).

white dominated the basic colours as though something had been spilt there.

Billy placed his feet parallel over two edges of the red tile directly between his legs. They just failed to span the tile's length. He eased his heels back to the corner, increasing the space at his toes. Then he eased them forward, decreasing the toe space, but introducing a growing space at his heels. He wriggled his toes, trying to stretch his feet, his pumps rippling like caterpillars. But the space remained constant, so he lifted his feet and perched them out of sight on the stretcher under the chair.

The white marking of the red tile, and the markings of the adjoining green ones never matched up; they all missed slightly, like a fault in a stratum of rock. The only strokes that did cross the dividing lines were skid marks made by rubber-soled shoes. These skid marks scarred all the tiles, and ranged from blunt scuffs to long sabres. They all pointed lengthways down the corridor, but were so different in form that they were never quite parallel to each other, or to the lanes formed by the edges of the tiles.

Billy sat back and lifted his head. On the opposite wall, directly across from the Medical Room door, was a fire alarm. Underneath it, in red capitals, were the instructions, IN CASE OF FIRE BREAK GLASS. The case of the alarm was red painted metal. The glass was round, like a big watch face. Billy sat and stared at it. A woman laughed close by. He turned instinctively towards the sound, then stood up and walked across to the alarm. Behind the glass, almost touching it, was a knob. Billy ran a finger round the rim, gathering dust under the nail. He breathed on the glass, drew a Union Jack in the vapour, then rubbed it up with his cuff. The glass shone. He tinked it with his nails, tapped it with a knuckle, then rapped it with his knuckles. The noise made him step back and glance up and down the corridor. All quiet. Nobody there. Then the door opened. Billy swung round. Boy. Woman. Man at desk behind, between them. 'Good afternoon.' Left masking the alarm, looking across, in at the bald crust of a man writing. He looked up, out at Billy.

'Are you next?'

Billy looked in, not moving.

'Well come in, lad, if you're coming, I haven't got all day.'

Billy walked in, closed the door and crossed the room.

'Sit down, Walker.'

I'm not Walker.'

'Well who are you then? According to my list it should be Gerald Walker next.'

He checked his name list.

'Oliver, Stenton, then Walker.'

'I'm Casper.'

'Casper. O yes. I should have seen you earlier, shouldn't I?' He flicked through the record cards. 'Casper. . . . Casper. . . . here we are,' placed it on top, then replaced the stack on the blotting square. 'Mmm.'

While he studied Billy's card, Billy studied his scalp. The crown was clean and pink. Hair, cut short and neat, grew round the back and sides, and a few greased strands had been carefully combed across the front to disguise the baldness. But they failed, like a trap covered with inadequate foliage.

'Now then, Casper, what kind of job had you in mind?'

He shunted the record cards to one side, and replaced them with a blank form, lined and sectioned for the relevant information. CASPER WILLIAM, in red on the top line. He copied age, address and other details from the record card, then changed pens and looked up.

'Well?'

'I don't know, I haven't thought about it right.'

'Well you should be thinking about it. You want to start off on the right foot, don't you?'

'I suppose so.'

'You haven't looked round for anything yet then?'

'No, not yet.'

'Well what would you like to do? What are you good at?'

He consulted Billy's record card again.

'Offices held . . . Aptitudes and Abilities . . . right then . . . would you like to work in an office? Or would you prefer manual work?'

'What's that, manual work?'

'It means working with your hands, for example, building, farming, engineering. Jobs like that, as opposed to pen pushing jobs.'

'I'd be all right working in an office, wouldn't I? I've a job to read and write.'

The Employment Officer printed MANUAL on the form, then raised his pen hand as though he was going to print it again on the top of his head. He scratched it instead, and the nails left white scratches on the skin. He smoothed his fingers carefully across the plot of hair, then looked up. Billy was staring straight past him out of the window.

'Have you thought about entering a trade as an apprentice? You know, as an electrician, or a bricklayer or something like that. Of course the money isn't too good while you're serving your apprenticeship. You may find that lads of your own age who take dead end jobs will be earning far more than you; but in those jobs there's no satisfaction or security, and if you do stick it out you'll find it well worth your while. And whatever happens, at least you'll always have a trade at your finger tips won't you? . . .

'Well, what do you think about it? And as you've already said you feel better working with your hands, perhaps this would be your best bet. Of course this would mean attending Technical College and studying for various examinations, but nowadays most employers encourage their lads to take advantage of these facilities, and allow them time off to attend, usually one day a week. On the other hand, if your firm wouldn't allow you time off in the day, and you were still keen to study, then you'd have to attend classes in your own time. Some lads do it. Some do it for years, two and three nights a week from leaving school, right up to their middle twenties, when some of them take their Higher National, and even degrees.

'But you've got to if you want to get on in life. And they'll all tell you that it's worth it in the end. . . . Had you considered continuing your education in any form after leaving? . . . I say, are you listening, lad?'

'Yes.'

'You don't look as though you are to me. I haven't got all day you know, I've other lads to see before four o'clock.'

He looked down at Billy's form again.

'Now then, where were we? O, yes. Well if nothing I've mentioned already appeals to you, and if you can stand a hard day's graft, and you don't mind getting dirty, then there are good opportunities in mining . . .'

'I'm not goin' down t'pit.'

'Conditions have improved tremendously . . .'

'I wouldn't be seen dead down t'pit.'

'Well what do you want to do then? There doesn't seem to be a job in England to suit you.'

He scrutinized Billy's record card again as though there might be a hint of one there.

'What about hobbies? What hobbies have you got? Do you like gardening, or constructing Meccano sets, or anything like that?'

Billy shook his head slowly.

'Don't you have any hobbies at all?'

Billy looked at him for a moment, then stood up quickly.

'Can I go now?'

'What's the matter with you, lad? Sit down, I haven't finished yet.'

Billy remained standing. The Youth Employment Officer began to fill in the blanks on the form, quickly and noisily.

'Well I've interviewed some lads in my time, but I've never met one like you. Half the time you're like a cat on hot bricks, the other half you're not even listening.'

He turned the form face down on the blotter and ran the sides of his fist along it, continuing the stroke off the blotter and pinching a blue leaflet off a wad at the front of the desk.

'Here, take this home and read it. It gives you all the relevant information concerned with school leaving and starting work. Things like sickness benefits, National Insurance, etcetera. At the back,' he turned it over and pointed at it, 'there's a detachable form. When you want your cards, fill it in and send it in to the office. The address is given at the top. Have you got that?'

Billy stared at the leaflet and nodded.

'Well take it then. . . . And if you do have trouble getting fixed up, don't forget, come in and see me. All right?'

The pamphlet was entitled LEAVING SCHOOL. The text on the cover page was built around a sketch which showed a man in square glasses shaking hands across a desk with a strapping youth in blazer and flannels. Their mouths were all teeth. Through the window behind the man was a tree, and a flying V bird.

'Right, Casper, that's all. Tell the next boy to come in.'

When he got out he started to run. He ran straight out of school and all the way home.

Part Four

Teacher-Pupil Relations

The activities of teachers and pupils in 'formal learning situations' has produced a seemingly well defined category of empirical phenomena that in the sociology of education is referred to as 'classroom interaction'. Given that the one intention of this collection of readings is to pose the notion of 'education' itself as a problematic, it should be apparent that a closing of concern by sociologists is inevitably produced by concentrating attention on the practices of particular culturally situated actors (teachers and pupils) within certain locations (namely schoolrooms). We would claim that such a closure can provide us with little further insight into the deeper question of the significant features of teaching-learning situations.

Having stressed this point it should be clear that the readings in this section have not been selected with reference to what they can tell us about social exchanges taking place within classrooms, but with reference to education-in-the-doing (whatever form that might take). We are directed then to a concern with members' (and observers') rules for the constitution of successful 'teaching' and 'learning' and ultimately of successful 'social situations' as 'educational situations'.

Other sections of this book critically address the taken-for-granted status of concepts like 'ability' and 'learning' which are crucial features of the vocabulary of teacher-pupil relations. In this section Werthman's paper offers us an instance of the negotiated production of pupils' ability (as grading) and thus of his educational identity; in doing so it involves us with a rendering by pupils of the teacher as an instance of a 'valid' or 'acceptable' authority.

The studies from outside the obvious context of 'education' provide us with ways of seeing processes potentially at work in interactional situations. Piliavin and Briar display the possibility of social typing by agencies of control providing for 'social types' (as deviants); a view of labelling theory with obvious parallels. Likewise Garfinkel's paper considers the situated apportioning of shame, that is, the negotiated conditions of constructing an individual's identity as an aspect of his status within a community. Both papers together with Goffman's consideration of the rules of conduct bestowing personal 'sacredness' on members, enable us to conceptualize teacher-pupil relations as being, foremost, contexted sequences of action, not essentially dissimilar from all social encounters.

Certain peculiar constructs of the teaching-learning situation are highlighted by Henry's paper which considers a particular pedagogical style as producing pupil docility as a feature of its own method; the teacher's acceptance of the pupils provides for a particular social setting. In the extracts from Barnes' partial analysis of pupil-teacher talk, we see his construction of a special language of 'knowledge transmission'; this, although constituted by Barnes as a member's problem is perhaps more relevant to us as a theoretical problem.

This section hopefully suggests some of the ways in which we may begin to theorize about the teacher-pupil relations and in passing illuminates the paucity and inadequacy of previous work in the field. It is anticipated that we may, as sociologists, be led to address more theoretic questions about 'what constitutes a teaching-learning situation' – or what are the grounds (members' but ultimately theorists') by which such situations are seen to be constituted.

19

New Boy *

David Storey

The Headmaster brought the new boy into the classroom several weeks after the term had begun. He stood alone, the centre of the children's curiosity, as the class-teacher, a squat, kindly-faced matron, talked quietly with the Headmaster by the open door. At first he returned the solemn gaze of the children, but as the time passed he began to blush and look urgently away, the stares slowly changing to open expressions of amusement. Eventually several of the children burst out laughing at his plaintive isolation.

He was a small boy, very slight with an intense, Spanish kind of face, narrowly featured and pale, and with eyes of such a dark liquidity that they suggested an almost permanent expression of condolence. It was the kind of bland transparency seen in people of little sophistication or self-assertion, and in certain peripheral conditions of idiocy. He had thick, straight black hair and thick black eyebrows which, in private moments of despair such as this, gave his face the imitative irony of a mask. It was as if he guyed his own emotions. It amused the children intensely.

Eventually the Headmaster gave the teacher a certificate and a letter which had been flapping in his hand, and left the room. The teacher closed the door and came back to her desk. The class watched in silence as the new boy responded to her instructions, walking quickly to her chair and standing stiffly beside it while she ordered them to work. She sat down and, turning to him with a sympathetic smile, began to ask him the relevant questions.

His full name was Leonard Radcliffe, he was nine years and seven months old, and had been transferred from a private school in the centre of town. His father was a caretaker. As she copied down this final piece of information in the Register under the heading 'Father's Occupation' the teacher paused, and glanced at the boy then put down her pen and wrote the word in pencil. The gesture itself, made almost absent-mindedly, caused a fresh suffusion of blood to creep up

---

* *Radcliffe*, Longmans Green, 1964, Penguin 1965, 7–10.

his face, and after looking hurriedly at the class he stared down at his feet in confusion.

He was given a place at the front, close to the teacher's own desk, until he should become more familiar with his surroundings. But as the weeks passed, his single desk, protruding irregularly from the set pattern behind, tended to confirm that isolation, a nervous shyness and detachment, which the children had instinctively recognized, and been amused by, when he first came into the room. Yet he was an alert boy, with an anxious alacrity, and a condoling, private kind of humour, so that when the teacher was belabouring some child at the back of the class he would twist round, his arm crooked over his chair, and watch with a slight smile of consolation. Frequently, as the teacher came to recognize his unusual if erratic intelligence, he was called upon almost as her accomplice to provide those answers which the children themselves had been unable to suggest.

One day, shortly after his arrival, the teacher had glanced meaningfully at the class then out of the large windows of the room, and pointing her broad, slightly inflamed arm, said, 'Why do you think it is that chimneys, *factory* chimneys, are so tall?' It was a question characteristic in its simplicity of her relationship with the children, as if she sought some way of antagonizing them, or of suggesting the preposterous nature of knowledge itself. She was that not unusual paradox in her profession, a sympathetic yet didactic person at heart.

Radcliffe's hand had risen immediately; but not satisfied with this response she searched round the class for others, prompting them by name and even by drawing a chimney and a factory, roughly, on the blackboard. The question defeated them: there were so many tall chimneys visible at that moment through the classroom windows, their black streamers furled over the ranked houses of the estate. Chimneys *were* tall. Eventually, as if acknowledging her oblique success, she turned to Radcliffe. 'Well, Leonard? Can you tell us?'

'They're tall so that they can carry the dirty smoke well away from the ground.'

Someone laughed; it was as if this simplicity confirmed the teacher's own eccentricity. She looked up amusedly.

'Well? Can anyone else think of a better reason?'

She sought a sudden and ironical confederacy in Radcliffe whenever she was opposed by the class, and as if stimulated by their amusement she turned to a large, muscular boy at the back of the room and posed a similarly disarming question: 'Why are roofs pointed and not flat like in the pictures in the Bible?' And when he could give no hope of an answer she moved towards the class, coming to a stop by Radcliffe's desk, and asked the large boy to stand up.

Tall and thickset, with dark, tightly curled hair and a frank, unwittingly surly face, he stood facing the teacher as if the question demanded some physical retaliation. His muscular figure was set in an instinctively aggressive pose. Then his eyes rolled slowly upwards in search of the answer.

Radcliffe, his head close to the teacher's thighs, had twisted round to stare almost grievedly at the boy as though his enforced furtiveness were directly his fault.

'Now, Tolson . . . *Victor*,' the teacher said as if his inability served as a further illustration in her didactic pursuit of the class. 'Do you know?'

He nodded, continuing his search of the ceiling while a gradual blush lit his powerful cheekbones. And, as though disregarding his male pride, or out of some innate desire to take advantage of such an exposed muscular confusion, the teacher pressed her inquisition. 'Well, come on, then Victor. Let us all hear.' A deeper look of humiliation gave way to one of helplessness. The boy suddenly stared round guiltily at the class.

'Perhaps there's no reason for Victor to think at all. We already know where he's going to end up, don't we?' She gestured at the factory chimneys outside about which Radcliffe had already been so articulate. 'There are places waiting for him out there already. Well, never mind. Just you stand there a moment, *Vic*, and let me see you paying attention and listening.'

She left him exposed in his quaint destitution and continued her questioning further, but more superficially, round the rest of the class.

'Well, Leonard. Can you tell us?' she said eventually, almost revengefully.

'No.' He shook his head, blushing.

'Are you sure?'

He shook his head again, looking down at his desk.

'Now, you're not going to let me down?'

He looked away in confusion. Then he said hurriedly, almost inaudibly, 'So that the rain can run off.' His look continued across the room until it reached the muscular boy at the back of the class. Their eyes met. The boy's expression was one of such incoherent humiliation, half-blinded with reproach, that Radcliffe swung round to stare fixedly at his desk, his face red and peculiarly tortured.

'Roofs are pointed so that the rain can run off,' the teacher said, wiping her hands free of chalk on her smock.

*　　*　　*

20

Docility, or giving teacher what she wants *

Jules Henry

This essay deals with one aspect of American character, the process whereby urban middle-class children in elementary school acquire the habit of giving their teachers the answers expected of them. Though it could hardly be said that I deal exhaustively with this matter, what I do discuss, using suggestions largely from psychoanalysis and communications theory, is the signaling process whereby children and teacher come to understand each other or, better, to pseudo-understand each other, within the limited framework of certain schoolroom situations.

I think it will be readily understood that such a study has intercultural significance and interesting biosocial implications. The smooth operation of human interaction, or 'transaction', if one prefers the Dewey and Bentley decor, requires that in any culture much of the give and take of life be reduced to a conventional, parsimonious system of quickly decipherable messages and appropriate responses. These messages, however, are different in different cultures, because the give and take of life is different in different cultures. At a simple level, for example, a Pilaga Indian paints his face red when he is looking for a sexual affair with a woman, whereas were an American man to paint his face red, the significance of this to other Americans would be quite different. Behaviors that have been variously called signal, cue, and sign are as characteristic of the animal world as they are of the human, and in both groups tend to be highly specific both with respect to themselves (signs, signals, cues) and with respect to the behavior they release in those for whom they are intended. Since, furthermore, each culture tends to standardize these, it would seem that any study of such behaviors, or rather behavior systems, in humans in any culture would throw light on two problems: (1) What the signal-response system is; and (2) How humans learn the system.

Since in humans the mastery of a signal-response system often

* *Journal of Social Issues*, **2** (1955) 33–41

involves the emotional life, and since in this paper on docility I am dealing with urban American middle-class children, it will readily be seen that a study of the manner in which they learn the signal-response system called docility carries us toward an understanding of the character of these children.

When we say a human being is docile we mean that, without the use of external force, he performs relatively few acts as a function of personal choice as compared with the number of acts he performs as a function of the will of others. In a very real sense, we mean that he behaves mostly as others wish him to. In our culture this is thought undesirable, for nobody is supposed to like docile people. On the other hand, every culture must develop in its members forms of behavior that approximate docility; otherwise it could not conduct its business. Without obedience to traffic signals transportation in a large American city would be a mess. This is a dilemma of our culture: to be able to keep the streets uncluttered with automotive wrecks, and to fill our armies with fighting men who will obey orders, while at the same time we teach our citizens not to be docile.

It is to be supposed that, although the basic processes as outlined are universal, every culture has its own way of creating the mechanism of docility. It will be the purpose of the rest of this paper to examine the accomplishment of docility in some American middle-class schoolrooms. The study was carried out by several of my graduate students and me. Names of persons and places are withheld in order to give maximum protection to all concerned.

In the following examples I shall be concerned only with demonstrating that aspect of docility which has to do with the teacher's getting from the children the answers she wants; and I rely almost entirely on verbal behavior, for without cameras it is impossible to record non-verbal signals. The first example is from the second grade.

1 The children have been shown movies of birds. The first film ended with a picture of a baby bluebird.

Teacher: Did the last bird ever look like he would be blue?

The children did not seem to understand the slant of the question, and answered somewhat hesitantly: Yes.

Teacher: I think he looked more like a robin, didn't he?

Children, in chorus: Yes.

In this example one suspects that teacher's intonation on the word 'ever' did not come through as a clear signal, for it did not create enough doubt in the children's minds to bring the right answer, 'No'. The teacher discovered that her signal had not been clear enough for these seven year-olds, so she made it crystal clear the second time, and got the 'right' response. Its correctness is demonstrated by the unanimity of the children's response, and the teacher's acceptance of it. Here the desire of the teacher, that the children shall acknowledge that a bird looks like a robin, is simple, and the children, after one false try, find the correct response.

In the next example we see the relation of signal to cultural values and context:

2a A fourth grade art lesson. Teacher holds up a picture.
Teacher: Isn't Bobby getting a nice effect of moss and trees?
Ecstatic Ohs and Ahs from the children. . . .
2b The art lesson is now over.
Teacher: How many enjoyed this?
Many hands go up.
Teacher: How many learned something?
Quite a number of hands come down.
Teacher: How many will do better next time?
Many hands go up.

Here the shifts in response are interesting. The word 'nice' triggers a vigorously docile response, as does the word 'enjoy'. 'Learned something', however, for a reason that is not quite clear, fails to produce the desired unanimity. On the other hand, the shibboleth, 'better next time' gets the same response as 'enjoyed'. We see then that the precise triggering signal is related to important cultural values; and that the value-signal must be released in proper context. One suspects that the children's resistance to saying they had learned something occurred because 'learned something' appeared out of context. On the other hand, it would be incorrect to describe these children as perfectly docile.

3 The children have just finished reading the story, *The Sun, Moon, and Stars Clock*.

Teacher: What was the highest point of interest – the climax?

The children tell what they think it is. Teacher is aiming to get from them what she thinks it is, but the children give everything else but. At last Bobby says: When they capture the thieves.

Teacher: How many agree with Bobby?
Hands, hands, hands.

In this example the observer was not able to record all the verbal signals, for they came too fast. However, it is clear that hunting occurred, while the children waited for the teacher to give the clear signal, which was '(I) agree with Bobby'.

In all the examples given thus far, the desired answer could be indicated rather clearly by the teacher, for the required response was relatively unambiguous. Even so, there was some trouble in obtaining most of the answers. In the example that follows, however, the entire situation becomes exceedingly ambiguous because emotional factors in the children make proper interpretation of teacher's signals difficult. The central issue is that teacher and children are seen to have requirements that are complementary on one level, because teacher wants the children to accept her point of view, and they want to be accepted by her; but these requirements are not complementary on a different level, because the children's emotional organization is different from the teacher's. Hence exact complementarity is never achieved, but rather a pseudo-complementarity which enables teachers and pupils to extricate themselves from a difficult situation. The example comes from a fifth-grade schoolroom:

4 This is a lesson on 'healthy thoughts' for which the children have a special book that depicts specific conflictful events among children. There are appropriate illustrations and text, and the teacher is supposed to discuss each incident with the children in order to help them understand how to handle their emotions.

One of the illustrations is of two boys, one of whom is griping because his brother has been given something he wants himself – a football, I think. The other is saying his brother couldn't help being given it – they'll both play with it.

(Observer is saying that this sibling pair is illustrated by three boys: (1) The one who has received the ball. (2) The one who is imagined to react with displeasure. (3) The one who is imagined to react benignly and philosophically, by saying: My brother couldn't help being given the football; we'll use it together.)

Teacher: Do you believe it's easier to deal with your thoughts if you own up to them, Betty?

Betty: Yes it is, if you're not cross or angry.

Teacher: Have you any experience like this in the book, Alice?

Alice tells how her brother was given a watch and she envied him and wanted one too, but her mother said she wasn't to have one until she was fifteen, but now she has one anyway.

Teacher: How could you have helped – could you have changed your thinking? How could you have handled it? What could you do with mean feelings?

Alice seems stymied; she hems and haws.

Teacher: What did Susie (a character in the book) do?

Alice: She talked to her mother.

Teacher: If you talk to someone you often feel that 'It was foolish of me to feel that way. . . .'

Tommy: He says he had an experience like that. His cousin was given a bike, and he envied it. But he wasn't ugly about it. He asked if he might ride it, and his cousin let him, and then I got one myself;

and I wasn't mean or ugly or jealous.

Here the process of signal development is intricate, and children and teacher do not quite manage to arrive at a mutually intelligible complex of signals and behavior. The stage is set by the presentation of a common, but culturally unacceptable situation: A child is pictured as envious of the good luck of his sibling. Since American culture cannot accept two of its commonest traits, sibling rivalry and envy, the children are asked by teacher to acknowledge that they are 'bad', and to accept specific ways of dealing with these emotions. The children are thus asked to fly in the face of their own feelings, and, since this is impossible, the little pigeons never quite get home. This is because teacher and pupil wants are not complementary.

It will have been observed that at first Alice does well, for by docilely admitting that it is good to own up to evil, she correctly interprets the teacher's wish to hear her say that the ancient ritual of confession is still good for the soul; and she continues docile behavior by giving a story of her own envy. However, eventually she muffs the signal, for she says she was gratified anyway; she did get a watch. And the reason Alice muffs the signal is that her own impulses dominate over the signals coming in from the teacher. Teacher, however, does not reject Alice's story but tries, rather, to get Alice to say she could have 'handled' her thoughts by 'owning up' to them and talking them over with someone. Alice, however, stops dead because she cannot understand the teacher. Meanwhile Tommy has picked up the signal, only to be misled by it, just as Alice was. By this time, however, the matter has become more complex: Tommy thinks that because teacher did not reject Alice's story it is 'correct'. Teacher's apparent acceptance of Alice's story then becomes Tommy's signal; therefore he duplicates Alice's story almost exactly, except that a bike is substituted for a watch. Like Alice he is not 'mean' or 'ugly' or 'jealous', not because he 'dealt with' his thoughts in the culturally approved-but-impossible manner, but because he too got what he wanted. So far, the only part of the message that is getting through to the children from the teacher is that it is uncomfortable – not wrong – to be jealous, etcetera. Thus the emotions of the children filter out an important part of the message from the teacher.

We may summarize the hypotheses up to this point as follows:

1 By virtue of their visible goal-correcting behavior the pupils are trying hard to be docile with respect to the teacher.

2 They hunt for signals and try to direct their behavior accordingly.

3 The signals occur in a matrix of cultural value and immediate circumstance.

4 This fact at times makes interpretation and conversion into action difficult.

5 A basis in mutual understanding is sought, but not quite realized at times.

6 The children's internal signals sometimes conflict with external ones and thus 'jam the receiver'.

7 Both children and teacher want something. At present we may say that the children want acceptance by the teacher, and teacher wants acceptance by the children.

8 However it is clear, because of the mix-up that may occur in interpreting signals, as in the lesson on healthy thoughts, that the desires of teacher and pupil are sometimes not quite complementary.

9 Teacher must avoid too many frustrating (painful) failures like that of Alice, otherwise lessons will break down.

As we proceed with this lesson, we shall see how teacher and pupils strive to 'get on the same wave length', a condition never quite reached because of the different levels of organization of teacher and pupil; and the unawareness of this fact on the part of the teacher.

Two boys, the 'dialogue team', now come to the front of the class and dramatize the football incident.

Teacher, to the class: Which boy do you think handled the problem in a better way?

Rupert: Billy did, because he didn't get angry . . . It was better to play together than to do nothing with the football.

Teacher: That's a good answer, Rupert. Has anything similar happened to you, Joan?

Joan can think of nothing.

(Observer notes: I do not approve of this business in action, though I have not yet thought it through. But I was intermittently uncomfortable, disapproving and rebellious at the time.)

Sylvester: I had an experience. My brother got a hat with his initials on it because he belongs to a fraternity, and I wanted one like it and couldn't have one; and his was too big for me to wear, and it ended up that I asked him if he could get me some letters with my initials, and he did.

Betty: My girl-friend got a bike that was 26-inch and mine was only 24; and I asked my sister what I should do. Then my girl-friend came over and was real nice about it, and let me ride it.

Teacher approves of this, and says: Didn't it end up that they both had fun without unhappiness? (Observer notes: Constant questioning of class, with expectation of affirmative answers: that wasn't this the right way, the best way, etc to do it?)

Here we note that the teacher herself has gone astray, for on the one hand her aim is to get instances from the children in which they themselves have been yielding and capable of resolving their own jealousy, etc, while on the other hand, in the instance given by Betty, it was not Betty who yielded but her friend. The child immediately following Betty imitated her since Betty had been praised by the teacher:

Matilde: My girl-friend got a 26-inch bike and mine was only 24; but she only let me ride it once a month. But for my birthday my mother's getting me a new one, probably (proudly) a '28'. (Many children rush in with the information that '28' doesn't exist.) Matilde replies that she'll probably have to raise the seat then, for she's too big for a '26'.

This instance suggests more clearly, perhaps, than the others, another possible factor in making the stories of the children end always with their getting what they want: the children may be afraid to lose face with their peers by acknowledging they did not get something they wanted.

As we go on with this lesson, we shall see how the children's need for substitute gratification and their inability to accept frustration prevent them from picking up the teacher's message. As we continue, we shall see, how, in spite of the teacher's driving insistence on her point, the children continue to inject their conflicts into the lesson, while at the same time they gropingly try to find a way to gratify the teacher. They cannot give the right answers because of their conflicts; teacher cannot handle their conflicts because she cannot perceive them. The lesson goes on:

Teacher: I notice that some of you are only happy when you get your own way. (Observer noticed too, horrified.) You're not thinking this through, and I want you to. Think of an experience when you didn't get what you want. Think it through. (Observer wonders: Are the children volunteering because of expectations: making desperate efforts to meet the expectation, even though they do not quite understand it?)

Charlie: His ma was going to the movies and he wanted to go with her; and she wouldn't let him; and she went off to the movies; and he was mad; but then he went outside and there were some kids playing baseball, so he played baseball.

Teacher: But suppose you hadn't gotten to play baseball? You would have felt hurt because you didn't get what you wanted. We can't help feeling hurt when we are disappointed. What could you have done? How could you have handled it? (Observer notes: Teacher is not getting what she wants, but I am not sure the kids can understand. Is this a function of immaturity, or of spoiling by parents? Seems to me the continued effort to extract an idea they have not encompassed may be resulting in reinforcement for the one they have got – that you eventually get the watch, or the bicycle, or whatever.)

Charlie: So I can't go to the movies; so I can't play baseball; so I'll do something around the house.

Teacher: Now you're beginning to think! It takes courage to take disappointments. (Turning to the class) What did we learn? The helpful way. . . .

Class: is the healthy way!

Thus the lesson reaches this point on a note of triumphant docility, but of pseudo-complementarity. If the teacher had been able to perceive the underlying factors that made it impossible for these children to accept delayed gratification or total momentary frustration, and had handled that problem, instead of doggedly sticking to a text that required a stereotyped answer, she would have come closer to the children and would not have had to back out of the situation by extracting a parrot-like chorusing. The teacher had to get a 'right' answer, and the children ended up giving her one, since that is what they are in school for. Thus on one level teacher and pupils were complementary, but on another they were widely divergent. This is the characteristic condition of the American middle-class schoolroom.

If we review all the verbal messages sent by the teacher, we will see how hard she has worked to get the answer she wants; how she has corrected and 'improved' her signaling in response to the eager feedback from the children:

1 Do you believe it's easier to deal with your thoughts if you own up to them, Betty?

2 Have you any experience like this in the book, Alice?

3 What could you do with mean feelings?

4 What did Susie (in the book) do?

5 (Rupert says that Billy, the character in the book, handled the problem in the better way because he did not get angry.) That's a good answer, Rupert.

6 (Betty tells how nice her girl-friend was, letting her ride her bike.) Teacher approves of this and says: Didn't it end up that they both had fun without unhappiness?

7 I notice that some of you are happy only when you get your own way.

8 What could you have done (when you did not get your own way)?

9 Now you're beginning to think. It takes courage to take disappointments. What did we learn? The helpful way. . . . and the class

responds, is the healthy way.

Discussion and conclusions

This paper has been an effort to describe the mental docility of middle-class American children *in their classrooms*. It says nothing about the home or the play group. The analysis shows how children are taught to find the answer the teacher wants, and to give it to her. That they sometimes fail is beside the point, because their trying so hard is itself evidence of docility; and an understanding of the reasons for failure helps us to see why communication breaks down and pseudo-understanding takes its place. When communication breaks down it is often because complementarity between sender (teacher) and receivers (pupils) is not exact; and it is not exact because teacher and pupils are at different levels of emotional organization.

We may now ask: Why are these children, whose phantasies our unpublished research has found to contain so many hostile and anxious elements, so docile in the classroom? Why do they struggle so hard to gratify the teacher and try in so many ways, as our protocols show, to bring themselves to the teacher's attention?

We might, of course, start with the idea of the teacher as a parent-figure, and the children as siblings competing for teacher's favor. We could refer to the unresolved dependency needs of children of this age, which make them seek support in the teacher, who then man-ipulates this seeking and the children's sibling rivalry in order, as our unpublished research suggests, to pit the children against each other. Other important factors, however, that appear in the middle-class schoolrooms, ought to be taken into consideration. For example, our research shows the children's tendency to destructively criticize each other, and the teacher's repeated reinforcement of this tendency. We have taken note, in our research, of the anxiety in the children as illustrated in the stories they tell and observed that these very stories are subjected to carping criticism by other children, the consequence of which would be anything but an alleviation of that anxiety. Hence the schoolroom is a place in which the child's underlying anxiety may be heightened. In an effort to alleviate this he seeks approval of the teacher, by giving right answers, and by doing what teacher wants him to do under most circumstances. Finally, we cannot omit the teacher's need to be gratified by the attention-hungry behavior of the children.

A word is necessary about these classrooms in middle class. The novel *Blackboard Jungle*, by Evan Hunter, describes schoolroom behavior of lower-class children. There we see them solidly against the teacher, as representative of the middle class. But in the classes we have observed we see the children against each other, with the teacher abetting the process. Thus, as the teacher in middle-class schools directs the hostility of the children toward one another (particularly in the form of criticism), and away from herself, she reinforces the competitive dynamics within the middle class itself. The teacher in the lower-class schools, on the other hand, appears to become the organizing stimulus for behavior that integrates the lower class, as the children unite in expressing their hostility to the teacher.

In conclusion, it should be pointed out that the mental docility (or near docility) achieved in these middle-class schoolrooms is a peculiar middle-class kind of docility. It is not based on authoritian control backed by fear of corporal punishment, but rather on fear of loss of love. More precisely, it rests on the need to bask in the sun of the teacher's acceptance. It is not fear of scolding or of physical pain that makes these children docile, but rather fear of finding oneself outside the warmth of the inner circle of teacher's sheltering acceptance. This kind of docility can be more lethal than the other, for it does not breed rebellion and independence, as struggle against authoritarian controls may, but rather a kind of cloying paralysis; a sweet imprisonment without pain. Looking at the matter from another point of view, we might say that were these children not fearful of loss of love they would be indifferent to the teacher's messages. In a sense what the teacher's signals are really saying is: 'This is the way to be loved by me; and this is the way I want you to love me'.

Conditions of Successful Degradation Ceremonies *

Harold Garfinkel

Any communicative work between persons, whereby the public identity of an actor is transformed into something looked on as lower in the local scheme of social types, will be called a 'status degradation ceremony'. Some restrictions on this definition may increase its usefulness. The identities referred to must be 'total' identities. That is, these identities must refer to persons as 'motivational' types rather than as 'behavioral' types,[1] not to what a person may be expected to have done or to do (in Parsons' term,[2] to his 'performances') but to what the group holds to be the ultimate 'grounds' or 'reasons' for his performance.[3]

The grounds on which a participant achieves what for him is adequate understanding of why he or another acted as he did are not treated by him in a utilitarian manner. Rather, the correctness of an imputation is decided by the participant in accordance with socially valid and institutionally recommended standards of 'preference'. With reference to these standards, he makes the crucial distinctions between appearances and reality, truth and falsity, triviality and importance, accident and essence, coincidence and cause. Taken together, the grounds, as well as the behavior that the grounds make explicable as the other person's conduct, constitute a person's identity. Together, they constitute the other as a social object. Persons identified by means of the ultimate 'reasons' for their socially categorized and socially understood behavior will be said to be 'totally' identified. The degradation ceremonies here discussed are those that are concerned with the alteration of total identities.

It is proposed that only in societies that are completely demoralized, will an observer be unable to find such ceremonies, since only in total anomie are the conditions of degradation ceremonies lacking.

---

* Reprinted by permission of the author and *The American Journal of Sociology*, **61** (March, 1956), 420–424. Copyright, 1956, The University of Chicago. All rights reserved.

Max Scheler[4] argued that there is no society that does not provide in the very features of its organization the conditions sufficient for inducing shame. It will be treated here as axiomatic that there is no society whose social structure does not provide, in its routine features, the conditions of identity degradation. Just as the structural conditions of shame are universal to all societies by the very fact of their being organized, so the structural conditions of status degradation are universal to all societies. In this framework the critical question is not whether status degradation occurs or can occur within any given society. Instead, the question is: Starting from any state of a society's organization, what program of communicative tactics will get the work of status degradation done?

First of all, two questions will have to be decided, at least tentatively: *What are we referring to behaviorially when we propose the product of successful degradation work to be a changed total identity?* And *what are we to conceive the work of status degradation to have itself accomplished or to have assumed as the conditions of its success?*

I

Degradation ceremonies fall within the scope of the sociology of moral indignation. Moral indignation is a social affect. Roughly speaking, it is an instance of a class of feelings particular to the more or less organized ways that human beings develop as they live out their lives in one another's company. Shame, guilt, and boredom are further important instances of such affects.

Any affect has its behavioral paradigm. That of shame is found in the withdrawal and covering of the portion of the body that socially defines one's public appearance – prominently, in our society, the eyes and face. The paradigm of shame is found in the phrases that denote removal of the self from public view, ie, removal from the regard of the publicly identified other: 'I could have sunk through the floor; I wanted to run away and hide; I wanted the earth to open up and swallow me'. The feeling of guilt finds its paradigm in the behavior of self-abnegation – disgust, the rejection of further contact with or withdrawal from, and the bodily and symbolic expulsion of the foreign body, as when we cough, blow, gag, vomit, spit, etc.

The paradigm of moral indignation is *public* denunciation. We publicly deliver the curse: 'I call upon all men to bear witness that he is not as he appears but is otherwise and *in essence*[5] of a lower species.'

The social affects serve various functions both for the person as well as for the collectivity. A prominent function of shame for the person is that of preserving the ego from further onslaughts by withdrawing entirely its contact with the outside. For the collectivity shame is an 'individuator'. One experiences shame in his own time.

Moral indignation serves to effect the ritual destruction of the person denounced. Unlike shame, which does not bind persons together, moral indignation may reinforce group solidarity. In the market and in politics, a degradation ceremony must be counted as a secular form of communism. Structurally, a degradation ceremony bears close resemblance to ceremonies of investiture and elevation. How such a ceremony may bind persons to the collectivity we shall see when we take up the conditions of a successful denunciation. Our immediate question concerns the meaning of ritual destruction.

In the statement that moral indignation brings about the ritual destruction of the person being denounced, destruction is intended literally. The transformation of identities is the destruction of one social object and the constitution of another. The transformation does not involve the substitution of one identity for another, with the terms of the old one loitering about like the overlooked parts of a fresh assembly, any more than the woman we see in the department-store window that turns out to be a dummy carries with it the possibilities of a woman. It is not that the old object has been overhauled; rather it is replaced by another. One declares, '*Now*, it was otherwise in the first place'.

The work of the denunciation effects the recasting of the objective character of the perceived other: The other person becomes in the eyes of his condemners literally a different and *new* person. It is not that the new attributes are added to the old 'nucleus'. He is not changed, he is reconstituted. The former identity, at best, receives the accent of mere appearance. In the social calculus of reality representations and test, the former identity stands as accidental; the new identity is the 'basic reality'. What he is now is what, 'after all', he was all along.[6]

The public denunciation effects such a transformation of essence by substituting another socially validated motivational scheme for that previously used to name and order the performances of the denounced. It is with reference to this substituted, socially validated motivational scheme as the essential grounds, ie, the *first principles*, that his performances, past, present, and prospective, according to the witnesses, are to be properly and necessarily understood.[7] Through the interpretive work that respects this rule, the denounced person becomes in the eyes of the witnesses a different person.

II

How can one make a good denunciation?[8]

To be successful, the denunciation must redefine the situations of those that are witnesses to the denunciation work. The denouncer, the party to be denounced (let us call him the 'perpetrator'), and the thing that is being blamed on the perpetrator (let us call it the 'event') must be transformed as follows: [9]

1 Both event and perpetrator must be removed from the realm of their everyday character and be made to stand as 'out of the ordinary'.

2 Both event and perpetrator must be placed within a scheme of preferences that shows the following properties:

A The preferences must not be for event A over B, but for event of *type* A over event of *type* B. The same typing must be accomplished for the perpetrator. Event and perpetrator must be defined as instances of a uniformity and must be treated as a uniformity throughout the work of the denunciation. The unique, never recurring character of the event or perpetrator should be lost. Similarly, any sense of accident, coincidence, indeterminism, chance, or momentary occurrence must not merely be minimized. Ideally, such measures should be inconceivable; at least they should be made false.

B The witnesses must appreciate the characteristics of the typed person and event by referring the type to a dialectical counterpart. Ideally, the witnesses should not be able to contemplate the features of the denounced person without reference to the counterconception, as the profanity of an occurrence or a desire or a character trait, for example, is clarified by the references it bears to its opposite, the sacred. The features of the mad-dog murderer reverse the features of the peaceful citizen. The confessions of the Red can be read to teach the meanings of patriotism. There are many contrasts available, and any aggregate of witnesses this side of a complete war of each against all will have a plethora of such schemata for effecting a 'familiar', 'natural', 'proper', ordering of motives, qualities, and other events.

From such contrasts, the following is to be learned. If the denunciation is to take effect, the scheme must not be one in which the witness is allowed to elect the preferred. Rather, the alternatives must be such that the preferred is morally required. Matters must be so arranged that the validity of his choice, its justification, is maintained by the fact that he makes it. [10] The scheme of alternatives must be such as to place constraints upon his making a selection 'for a purpose'. Nor will the denunciation succeed if the witness is free to look beyond the fact that he makes the selection for evidence that the correct alternative has been chosen, as, for example, by the test of empirical consequences of the choice. The alternatives must be such that, in 'choosing', he takes it for granted and beyond any motive for doubt that not choosing can mean only preference for its opposite.

3 The denouncer must so identify himself to the witness that during the denunciation they regard him not as a private but as a publicly known person. He must not portray himself as acting according to his personal, unique experiences. He must rather be regarded as acting in his capacity as a public figure, drawing upon communally entertained and verified experience. He must act as a *bona fide* participant in the tribal relationships to which the witnesses subscribe. What he says must not be regarded as true for him alone, not even in the sense that it can be regarded by denouncer and witnesses as matters upon which they can become agreed. In no case, except in a most ironical sense, can the convention of true-for-reasonable-men be invoked. What the denouncer says must be regarded by the witnesses as true on the grounds of a socially employed metaphysics whereby witnesses assume that witnesses and denouncer are alike in essence.[11]

4 The denouncer must make the dignity of the supra-personal values of the tribe salient and accessible to view, and his denunciation must be delivered in their name.

5 The denouncer must arrange to be invested with the right to speak in the name of these ultimate values. The success of the denunciation will be undermined if, for his authority to denounce, the denouncer invokes the personal interests that he may have acquired by virtue of the wrong done to him or someone else. He must rather use the wrong he has suffered as a tribal member to invoke the authority to speak in the name of these ultimate values.

6 The denouncer must get himself so defined by the witnesses that they locate him as a supporter of these values.

7 Not only must the denouncer fix his distance from the person being denounced, but the witnesses must be made to experience their distance from him also.

8 Finally, the denounced person must be ritually separated from a place in the legitimate order, ie, he must be defined as standing at a place opposed to it. He must be placed 'outside', he must be made 'strange'.

These are the conditions that must be fulfilled for a successful denunciation. If they are absent, the denunciation will fail. Regardless of the situation when the denouncer enters, if he is to succeed in degrading the other man, it is necessary to introduce these features.[12]

Not all degradation ceremonies are carried on in accordance with publicly prescribed and publicly validated measures. Quarrels which seek the humiliation of the opponent through personal invective may achieve degrading on a limited scale. Comparatively few persons at a time enter into this form of communion, few benefit from it, and the fact of participation does not give the witness a definition of the other that is standardized beyond the particular group or scene of its occurrence.

The devices for effecting degradation vary in the feature and effectiveness according to the organization and operation of the system of action in which they occur. In our society the arena of degradation whose product, the redefined person, enjoys the widest transferability between groups has been rationalized, at least as to the institutional measures for carrying it out. The court and its officers have something like a fair monopoly over such ceremonies, and there they have become an occupational routine. This is to be contrasted with degradation undertaken as an immediate kinship and tribal obligation and carried out by those who, unlike our professional degraders in the law courts, acquire both right and obligation to engage in it through being themselves the injured parties or kin to the injured parties.

Factors conditioning the effectiveness of degradation tactics are provided in the organization and operation of the system of action within which the degradation occurs. For example, timing rules that provide for serial or reciprocal 'conversations' would have much to do with the kinds of tactics that one might be best advised to use. The tactics advisable for an accused who can answer the charge as soon as it is made are in contrast with those recommended for one who had to wait out the denunciation before replying. Face-to-face contact is a different situation from that wherein the denunciation and reply are conducted by radio and newspaper. Whether the denunciation must be accomplished on a single occasion or is to be carried out over a sequence of 'tries', factors like the territorial arrangements and movements of persons at the scene of the denunciation, the numbers of persons involved as accused, degraders, and witnesses, status claims of the contenders, prestige and power allocations among participants, all should influence the outcome.

In short, the factors that condition the success of the work of degradation are those that we point to when we conceive the actions of a number of persons as group-governed. Only some of the more obvious structural variables that may be expected to serve as predictors of the characteristics of denunciatory communicative tactics have been mentioned. They tell us not only how to construct an effective denunciation but also how to render denunciation useless.

References

[1] These terms are borrowed from ALFRED SCHUTZ, 'Common Sense and Scientific Interpretation of Human Action,' *Philosophy and Phenomenological Research*, **XIV**, No 1 (September, 1953).

[2] TALCOTT PARSONS and EDWARD SHILS, 'Values, Motives, and Systems of Action,' in PARSONS and SHILS (Eds), *Toward a General Theory of Action*, Harvard University Press, Cambridge, 1951.

[3] Cf the writings of KENNETH BURKE, particularly *Permanence and Change*, Hermes Publications, Los Altos, Calif, 1954, and *A Grammar of Motives*, Prentice-Hall, Inc, New York, 1945.

[4] RICHARD HAYS WILLIAMS, 'Scheler's Contributions to the Sociology of Affective Action, with Special Attention to the Problem of Shame,' *Philosophy and Phenomenological Research*, **II**, No 3 March 1942.

[5] The man at whose hands a neighbor suffered death becomes a 'murderer'. The person who passes on information to enemies is really, ie, 'in essence', 'in the first place', 'all along', 'in the final analysis', 'originally', an informer.

[6] Two themes commonly stand out in the rhetoric of denunciation: (1) the irony between what the denounced appeared to be and what he is seen now really to be where the new motivational scheme is taken as the standard and (2) a re-examination and redefinition of origins of the denounced. For the sociological relevance of the relationship between concerns for essence and concerns for origins see particularly Kenneth Burke, *A Grammar of Motives*.

[7] While constructions like 'substantially a something' or 'essentially a something' have been banished from the domain of scientific discourse, such constructions have prominent and honored places in the theories of motives, persons, and conduct that are employed in handling the affairs of daily life. Reasons can be given to justify the hypothesis that such constructions may be lost to a group's 'terminology of motives' only if the relevance of socially sanctioned theories to practical problems is suspended. This can occur where inter-personal relations are trivial (such as during play) or, more interestingly, under severe demoralization of a system of activities. In such organizational states the frequency of status degradation is low.

[8] Because the paper is short, the risk must be run that, as a result of excluding certain considerations, the treated topics may appear exaggerated. It would be desirable, for example, to take account of the multitude of hedges that will be found against false denunciation; of the rights to denounce; of the differential apportionment of these rights, as well as the ways in which a claim, once staked out, may become a vested interest and may tie into the contests for economic and political advantage. Further, there are questions centering around the appropriate arenas of denunciation. For example, in our society the tribal council has fallen into secondary importance; among lay persons the denunciation has given way to the complaint to the authorities.

[9] These are the effects that the communicative tactics of the denouncer must be designed to accomplish. Put otherwise, in so far as the denouncer's tactics accomplish the reordering of the definitions of the situation of the witnesses to the denunciatory performances, the denouncer will have succeeded in effecting the transformation of the public identity of his victim. The list of conditions of this degrading effect are the determinants of the effect. Viewed in the scheme of a project to be rationally pursued, they are the adequate means. One would have to chose one's tactics for their efficiency in accomplishing these effects.

[10] Cf GREGORY BATESON and JURGEN RUESCH, *Communication: The Social Matrix of Psychiatry* (New York: W W Norton & Co, 1951), 212–27.

[11] For bona fide members it is not that these are the grounds upon which

we are agreed but upon which we are *alike*, consubstantial, in origin the same.

[12] Neither of the problems of possible communicative or organizational conditions of their effectiveness have been treated here in systematic fashion. However, the problem of communicative tactics in degradation ceremonies is set in the light of systematically related conceptions. These conceptions may be listed in the following statements:

1 The definition of the situation of the witnesses (for each of discourse we shall use the letter S) always bear a time qualification.

2 The S at t_2 is a function of the S at t_1. This function is described as an operator that transforms the S and t_1.

3 The operator is conceived as communicative work.

4 For a successful denunciation, it is required that the S at t_2 show specific properties. These have been specified previously.

5 The task of the denouncer is to alter the S's of the witnesses so that these S's will show the specified properties.

6 The 'rationality' of the denouncer's tactics, ie, their adequacy as a means for effecting the set of transformations necessary for effecting the identity transformation, is decided by the rule that the organizational and operational properties of the communicative net (the social system) are determinative of the size of the discrepancy between an intended and an actual effect of the communicative work. Put otherwise, the question is not that of the temporal origin of the situation but always and only how it is altered over time. The view is recommended that the definition of the situation at time 2 is a function of the definition at time 1 ,where this function consists of the communicative work conceived as a set of operations whereby the altered situation at time 1 is the situation at time 2. In strategy terms the function consists of the program of procedures that a denouncer should follow to effect the change of state S_{t_1} to S_{t_2}. In this paper S_{t_1} is treated as an unspecified state.

22

Delinquents in schools *

Carl Werthman

In the recent sociology on juvenile delinquents, the school is characterized as the major instrument and arena of villainy. Cloward and
Ohlin suggest that lower class delinquents suffer from unequal 'access
to educational facilities',[1] Cohen points to their 'failures in the classroom',[2] and Miller and Kvaraceus argue that a 'conflict of culture'
between school administrators and lower-class students is precipitating delinquent behavior.[3] Although there are many differences between contemporary sociological portraits of the lower-class juvenile
delinquent, the same model of his educational problem is used by all
authors. Regardless of whether the delinquent is ambitious and capable,[4] ambitious and incapable,[5] or unambitious and incapable,[6] the
school is sketched as a monolith of middle-class personnel against
which he fares badly.

Yet data collected by observation and interviews over a two-year
period on the educational performances and classroom experiences of
lower-class gang members suggest that pitting middle-class schools
against variations in the motivation and capacity of some lower-class
boys is at best too simple and at worst incorrect as a model of the
problems faced by the delinquents.

First, during middle adolescence when the law requires gang members to attend school, there seems to be no relationship between
academic performance and 'trouble'. Gangs contain bright boys who
do well, bright boys who do less well, dull boys who pass, dull boys
who fail, and illiterates. To cite a single example, the grades of thirty
'core' members of a Negro gang, the Conquerors, were equally

* Berkeley Journal of Sociology (1963), **8** (1), 36–60.
This paper is part of a larger research project down with Irving Piliavin on
delinquent street gangs in San Francisco. The project was initiated by the
survey Research Center at the University of California on a grant from the
Ford Foundation and was later moved to the Center for the Study of Law
and Society where funds were made available from the Delinquency Studies
Program sponsored by the Department of Health, Education, and Welfare
under Public Law 87–274.

distributed in the sophomore and junior years of high school. Four of the gang members are illiterate (they cannot read, write, or spell the names of the streets they live on); twelve consistently receive Ds and Fs on their report cards; and fourteen consistently receive Cs or better. Four are on the honor roll. Yet all thirty were suspended at least once a semester during the tenth and eleventh grades, and the average number of suspensions received per semester was above two. There was a general tendency for the illiterate and dull boys to get into more trouble than the better students, but none of them was immune from difficulty. Twenty-two of these thirty regular members spent some time in jail during this period. Differences in access, success, and failure thus did not seem to have a determinate effect on 'trouble' in school – at least among the Conquerors.

Second, difficulties occur only in some classes and not others. Good and bad students alike are consistently able to get through half or more of their classes without friction. It is only in particular classes with particular teachers that incidents leading to suspension flare up. This suggests that schools are not as monolithic as most contemporary sociologists have argued. Moreover, it suggests that something more specific about teachers than being 'middle class' produces problems, just as something more specific than being 'lower class' about gang members produces the response.

The problem

For events in high school classrooms to proceed smoothly, students must grant teachers some measure of authority. Although teachers are in a position to overlook a great deal of extra-curricular student activity in classrooms, they cannot ignore everything. Some modicum of order must be maintained if anything resembling a process of education is to take place. Most teachers thus find themselves in the position of having to act on definitions of improper behavior and hope that students will stop. The authority of teachers is put to a test in this act of communication.

Authority becomes a stable basis for interaction only when those to whom commands are issued voluntarily obey.[7] Students in classrooms, like all parties judging claims to authority made by others, must therefore decide whether treatments received at the hands of teachers are based on grounds that can be considered legitimate.

Most students accept the authority of teachers to pass judgment on practically all behavior that takes place in classrooms. The teacher is seen as a person who can pay legitimate official attention to everything that happens inside the physical confines of a school plant[8]. Since the authority of teachers is accepted at face value, most students can make sense of the specific actions teachers take towards them. Any specific action is interpreted as an instance in which this general rule is being applied.

This is why, for example, most students do not question the grades they receive. They accept the norm that teachers have the authority to grade them. This authority is more or less traditional. A report card signed by the teacher is accepted on much the same basis as are proclamations of war signed by kings. Neither are required by their subjects to give strict accounts of the decisions they make because the prerogative to make them has been granted in advance of the act.

Gang members understand the treatments they receive in no such way. They do not *a priori* accept the authority of any teacher. Final judgment on the conferral of legitimacy is suspended until it is discovered whether or not authority is being exercised on suitable grounds and in a suitable way. The burden of proof lies with the teacher.

Since teachers exercise authority in a variety of ways, becoming a 'delinquent' depends in large measure on whether these various claims are accepted. This is why gang members are frequently 'delinquent' in one class and ordinary students in the adjoining room. This paper analyses accounts of classroom situations in which gang members received unacceptable treatments, refused to recognize the authority of teachers, and were labelled 'delinquent'. These accounts are compared to classroom situations in which the treatments received were considered soundly based, the authority of teachers was accepted, and gang members remained ordinary students[9].

Gang members make decisions to accept or reject the authority of teachers on the basis of four criteria. First, they evaluate the jurisdictional claims made by teachers. Some teachers not only insist on the physical presence of students but also expect a measure of intellectual and spiritual 'attention' as well. These teachers frequently take issue with behavior such as sleeping on desks, reading comic books, talking to neighbors, passing notes, gazing out of the window, turning around in chairs, chewing gum, and eating peanuts. Gang members do not *a priori* grant teachers the right to punish this behavior although good reasons for ceasing these activities are often accepted.

Second, under no conditions can race, dress, hair styles, and mental capacities receive legitimate official attention. Failures on the part of teachers to accept these rules of irrelevance often contribute to denial of authority[10].

Third, gang members are extremely sensitive to the style in which authority is exercised. The frequent and consistent use of the imperative is perceived as an insult to the status and autonomy of those to whom this form of address is directed. Teachers who 'request' conformity are more likely to achieve desired results.

Ultimately, however, the decision to accept or reject the authority of teachers is made on the basis of a weightier concern. Teachers who consistently violate conceptions of proper jurisdiction, irrelevance rules, and modes of address will not find gang members particularly co-operative architects of authority. But the grounds on which teachers make their formal and semi-public evaluations of students tell a more important tale. Grades can be based on a number of criteria, not all of which gang members find legitimate. Moreover, the fact that they get a grade tells them nothing about the basis on which the judgment was made. They must discover the general rule used by particular teachers to assign grades with only a single application of the rule to go on.

Gang members thus find themselves in a rather serious bind. They *must* figure out the general basis on which teachers are assigning grades because their future behavior depends on what they discover. They cannot walk away from the claims made by teachers to possess authority.

Hypotheses

Their task, however, is not hopeless. Gang members do know *something* about the basis on which a grade might have been assigned. In fact, given what they know about their situation, they reduce the rules teachers might be using to four.

First, the grades might be given out fairly. Although as a rule gang members have no idea how much knowledge they possess relative to other students, they have a general idea of how 'smart' they are relative to others. They judge the intelligence of the boys and girls they know personally, and they estimate the intelligence of strangers from the contributions they make in class. They thus generate a set of expected frequencies on the basis of the hypothesis that bright boys will do better than dull boys.

(Is there any relationship between getting into trouble in school and getting good grades?) Naw. Take likes Charles. He in my classes. He bad outside, and he doing well in school. There ain't no difference. Let's put it like this. Friday, Saturday, Sunday, that's the nights for fucking, drinking, driving, fighting, killing, doing the shit you want to do. There's a lot of guys like Charles in my classes that gets A's on their report cards in school, but when they on the outside, the hell, they bad! They crazy! Dice, drink, shoot people. (How about the ex-President of the Club? How does he do in your classes?) Johnny's smart. Johnny's got a good brain. He doing good. Everytime I see Johnny, he always got his books. He goes to the bathroom – smokes cigarettes and shoots dice like all of us – but you don't see that man cutting no classes. I swear to God, I think he really got a swell mental brain. (How about the rest of the club?) It just that some people lazier than others. Just like Donald. He in my classes. I ain't got no more brains than that man. I may know a little more than he do from the past things, but as far as that class is related and all, I don't know no more than him. The class is just as new to me as it is to him. Now if I can pass that class, he can pass that class. He didn't pass this time. He flunked. He got a F. He got a F in all his classes. I passes those classes with flying colors, with a C. That's average. I always get average grades. I don't look for no A's and B's. (Do you think you could get A's if you tried?) I doubt it. I don't see racking my brains to death to get no A on no paper. Cause I feel like a A ain't nothing. A C will get you just as far. I mean truthfully I think the highest grade I could ever get was a D. (How about Carson?) He's not smart. He dumb. I mean he goofy. He just ain't got it up here, period. We gonna get kicked out. (What for?) Fighting, gamblin, cutting classes, nasty attitude. (How about the guys who don't get in trouble. How do they do?) Just like us. Some of them smart, some of them stupid. I mean there's a couple dudes in my classes that's born to be somebody, people with straight A's like Johnny, and then there's the real stupid ones. They just sit there all quiet, get to class on time, never gamble, smoke or nothing and they flunk. You might say we got smart ones and they got smart ones just like we got average ones and they got average ones and we got dumb ones and they got dumb ones. Everybody born on this earth ain't got the same brains.

Second, their response to the presumed authority of the teacher may enter into the grade they receive. They are conscious that the grade is a source of power, and they understand that it may be used as a weapon against them. When teachers use grades as sanctions in this way, gang members perceive it as discrimination. On the basis of the behavior observed in class, gang members divide their fellow students into those who *a priori* take as legitimate the claims to authority made by teachers and those who do not. (As a rule, the latter category is filled with friends.) Expected frequences are thus generated under this condition also. The distinction between scientists and sell-outs lies at the heart of what gang members consider the essential difference between their kind of person and 'squares'.

There's some teachers that treats everybody differently. He always get wise with the studs that ain't gonna take no shit, and they real nice to the people that just sit there, the people that kiss ass behind him. He give the good grades to the ass-kissers and he give us bad grades cause we ain't gonna suck up to him. (Are there many kinds in class who kiss up to teachers?) Yeah. There's enough. Like this one girl, she's kiss behind everybody, and the President of the school! He'll eat you if you ask him to! The bad teachers give the kiss-asses good grades and make us eat shit. They always looking for the ones that run errands, shit like that. (What kind of people are the ass-kissers? Do they wear any special kind of clothes?) Some of them come looking like a farmer or something. Jeans. Or maybe they were a tie or something. They not like us. We come to have a good time in school as well as sometimes learn something. Some of those boys don't even enjoy parties and things like that. They allergic to girls. They just poopbutts.

The third dimension that may affect a grade is the amount of power possessed by particular students. The sources of this power stem from the possibilities of physical assault on teachers and an ability to keep a class in constant turmoil. Delinquents thus hypothesize that teachers may award grades on this basis. The boys define this possibility as 'bribery'.

(Are there any teachers who give you good grades because they are afraid of you?) Yeah. Like Mr F. He say, 'Aw, come on, why don't you go give us a break or something.' And all the lady teachers, I won't let them go with nothing. Like these teachers say, 'You do me a favor and I do you one. You straighten up in class and I'll make your grade better.' Shit like that. If you control that class, you gonna get a good grade. They afraid of you or they want you to stop fucking up the class. I control a lot of those classes. (What do you do when the teacher tries to make a deal with you?) I don't take shit. That way they gotta keep giving me a good grade. They try to con me, but I ain't going for it. Like that stud that kicked me out of class yesterday? He tell me, 'Come on, why don't you be a good guy? I'll give you a good grade if you be quiet. Why don't you go on and give me a break?' I said, 'I sure will, right on your neck!' When you get a good grade, sometimes you know the teacher is afraid of you. That's why he give it to you.

The final alternative is that grades are randomly distributed. This is a distinct possibility in large classes such as gym where teachers cannot possibly interact personally with all participants. Some students become visible of course, either as athletes, delinquents, or 'funkies'. But it is quite possible for a particular boy to be graded on the basis of the way his name happens to strike the teacher when he sees it printed on the report card.

When I think I deserve a C and I get a D? That's when I'm gonna bitch. I'm really gonna have something to say about it. Cause when I feel like I got a better grade? And get something lower? I feel like that teacher either prejudiced or he just, you know, he just don't give a damn. He just go down, read your name and everybodies' name, and go A, B, C, – A, B, C. He get to a special name. 'Well, I don't like this fellow, I'll give him a C. I don't like him. I'll give him a D.' You know, so on and so on. Shit. That's like they do in gym, seem like to me. Every damn time it seem like my report card came up to be a C. I don't mind a C if I have to get it, but I seen the gym teacher, you know, in the office. They have a whole stack of report cards. Now how a gym teacher gonna look at your name and go straight down the line, just put a grade on? Like he going A, B, C, – A, B, C, – A, B, C. And he just throw them away! And if he run across a name he know real good? Somebody that, you know, real tight with him? Go out for all the sports? You know, he flunky for him. Work around the gym. Shit like that. You know you gonna give him a B or something. Somebody that deserve a B, he gonna give a C or D. All kinda shit like that.

Thus before grades are handed down, gang members construct four alternative hypotheses or rules about the basis on which teachers evaluate them. Given what they know about the student population being graded, they make predictions about how fellow class members will be marked under three of the four alternative conditions. They know that the grade they receive will be a single case of one of these four classes of rules, but the single grade they receive will not tell them *which* rule the teacher is using. Their problem is to discover it.

Methods

As soon as the grade is handed down, gang members behave like good social scientists. They draw a sample, ask it questions, and compare the results with those predicted under alternative hypotheses. The unit of analysis is a *set* of relevant grades. The one received by a particular student is only a single member. No interpretation of a grade can be made before the others are looked at.

The sample is not selected randomly from the class. The class contains types of students constructed from the knowledge on which the predictions were based. Gang members thus divide the class into four basic sub-groups: bright students who recognize the authority of teachers; duller students who recognize the authority of teachers; bright students withholding judgment about teachers; and dull students withholding judgment about teachers. The latter two types are like himself. They are his friends. If the gang member conducting the inquiry possesses power, this dimension will also be of concern.

264

As soon as the grades are delivered to the students in class, representatives of all types are sampled. First, gang members typically ask their friends what they received, and then others in the rest of the class are interviewed. Most of the 'poopbutts', 'sissies' or 'squares' will usually show a gang member their report card. Refusals to reveal grades are often dealt with sharply.

(How do you know how the teacher is grading you?) Sometimes you don't man. You don't know whether the stud bribing you with a grade, whether he giving you a bad one cause you don't kiss behind him, or whether he straight. Or maybe he like the gym teachers that give out the grades any which way. (But how do you find out what basis the teacher is using?) Well, you gotta ask around the class. Find out what other kids got. Like when I get my report card? I shoot out and ask my partners what they got. Then I go ask the poopbutts what they got. (Do they always let you look at their report cards?) They can't do nothing but go for it. Like they got to go home sometime. I mean we shoot them with a left and a right if they don't come across. I mean this grade shit is important. You gotta know what's happening. (Why?) Well, shit, how you gonna know what the teacher like? I mean if he straight or not.

After the grades have been collected, the process of analysing data begins. Final conclusions can be reached at this point, however, only if the teacher has previously provided an account of the grounds being used to grade. Some teachers voluntarily provide these accounts and others do not. Although there is considerable variation in this behavior among teachers, the variation is not random. Teachers who believe that their authority in the classroom should be accepted *a priori* are less likely to volunteer the basis on which they judge students. In fact they are less likely to offer explanations of any action they take. Claims to authority are often demonstrated by not having to account for all decisions made.

On the other hand, some teachers are careful to make visible at all times the basis on which they grade. These teachers understand that they have certain students who will not accept authority in advance of proof that it is being legitimately exercised.

(What made this teacher fair?) He'd give the class an equal chance to be graded. Like he'd say, 'How'd you like to be graded on this? Class average, individual, or what?' And you know, let's say half the class want to be graded on class average and the other half on individual. He just take the group out like that, you know, and he would grade you as such if that's the way you want to be graded. I mean I felt that the teacher real fair. See, after the first report card, after he see the grades wasn't too good? He asked us how we would like him to grade, and what we would like him to do. (The grades from the first report weren't very good?) No, they weren't so hot. Cause, you know, he wanted to see how his approach did and how we would react to it. Anyway, the results wasn't so hot. Anyway, he gave us a choice. So I felt that was helping them, helping me, and that he seemed fair.

In addition, teachers who attempt to bribe certain students will also signal the basis on which they behave in advance of the grade. If a gang member receives a better grade than the one he expected relative to other students, he suspects a 'con'. He thus reviews his previous relationship with the teacher. If the teacher has offered him a good grade in return for good behavior, he has sufficient grounds to conclude that the grade he received was based on his power to control the class.

(How do you know when you get a good grade whether you deserved it or whether the teacher is trying to buy you off?) When they tell you personally. You know, we was in the class by ourself when they told me I could get a good grade if I stop being a troublemaker. Like Mrs C. Like in class she told the whole class, 'If you be quiet you get a good grade!' You know, everybody get a C or something on their report card. But she told me privately, I guess maybe cause I was such a troublemaker. When I see what everybody else got? And I see that they all fail or get something else? I know I got the grade cause I control the class.

Similarly, if the teacher has recently left him alone in class regardless of what he has done, he concludes that the teacher is afraid of him. In this case also he thinks that the teacher is trying to buy control.

(How do you know when you get a good grade because the teacher is afraid of you?) After you ask around the class, you know, you see everybody that shoulda done bad done bad and shit like that. And you got a good grade? Well, sometimes that teacher just leave you alone. I mean you be talking and everything and they won't say nothing. Then you know he afraid of you and he afraid you'll fire on him [slug him] if you get a bad grade.

If teachers provide the rules used to grade students in advance of the grading period, regardless of whether they are using fair criteria, bribing, or discriminating, gang members do not need to request information in order to find out what is going on. As soon as they receive their grade and compare it to others, they 'know what's happening'.

But if gang members need more information to discover the rule being used and it has not been provided in advance of the marking period, they will go to the teacher and ask for an account of the grade they received. This event typically takes place a day or two after report cards have been handed out.

If a gang member is given a grade he thinks he deserves relative to others, he suspects that the grades have been awarded fairly. But his suspicions are based only on the perceived relationship between grades and mental capacity. He can only confirm his suspicions by checking with the teacher. Moreover, if the gang member suspects that the grade is fair, his request to have the grade explained is uniformly polite.

The teacher's response to a request is crucial information to the gang member. If he receives an account of his grade and the account is at all reasonable, he concludes that the teacher is grading fairly. The very fact that the teacher provides a reason at all predisposes him to conclude that the criteria being used to pass and fail students are on the 'up and up'.

After we got our compositions back I went up to him you know. I asked him about my composition. I got a D over F and I ask him what I did wrong. He told me that he could tell by the way I write that I could do better than what I did. And he explained it to me, and he showed me what I need to improve. And he showed me, if I correct my paper, I would get a D, a straight D instead of that F. OK. And I got the D for half the work. But anyway he showed me how I could get a regular D and pass his class. I mean I feel like that teacher was helping me. I mean he was showing me a way I could pass the class and how he was grading everybody. I mean the way he explained everything to me, I knew he was straight, that he was grading fairly.

Similarly, if a gang member receives a lower grade than expected, he suspects that teachers are using grades as a weapon to award those who accept their authority and punish those who reject it. Again, he can come to no final conclusions about the rule being used to give grades until he checks with the teacher.

If the gang member feels there is a possibility he is being discriminated against, he *demands* an account of the grade. He typically asks, 'What the *hell* did I get this for?' Moreover, since each gang member is in a slightly different position with respect to mental capacity and power, they all approach the teacher alone instead of in groups, even though they compare notes carefully after the encounter has passed.

See, me and that man, we always be fighting. Maybe because of my attitude. See, a lot of teachers grade you on your attitude toward them and not your work. And like sometimes you be talk-

ing, you know, and he say, 'Why don't you hush! Shut up! I told you once or twice already not to be saying that in class!'
Everybody else be talking.
He say, 'Trying to get smart with me?'
'No,' I say, 'I ain't trying to get smart with you.'
He say, 'What are you trying to do? Start an argument?'
And you know, I get tired of copping pleas.
'Hell yeah I'm trying to start an argument!'
So he say, 'If you keep fooling around I'm going to lower your grade.'
On the report card, the dude give me a D. I told that son of a bitch today, I know damn well my work better than a D! Cause all my tests have been C's, you know, and everybody else getting a C. I'm hip to shit like that, man.
Then he gonna tell me, 'Well, I grade on the notes and the home-work more than I do the tests.'
I say, 'Well, what kind of a teacher are you? What bull shit you got on your mind?' I cussing at him all the time. That man don't move me! He bore me! He get on my damn nerves! He look up at me. 'You trying to start a fight?'
I say, 'I'm gonna start the biggest fight you ever seen! I want my grade changed!'
And he say, 'Why don't you go sit down?'
'No man, I ain't gonna sit down till you straighten my grade out! You show me my grade in the book and I show you. I know I got a C!'
And he just say, 'Go on and sit down before I call the boys' dean to come up here and get you.' I say to myself, 'I can't get suspended no more. If I get suspended again, I fucked. I never pass.' So I went and sit down. That nasty ass motherfucker just don't like bloods.

If a gang member receives a bad grade and finds the teacher frightened and apologetic, he concludes that grades have been awarded randomly. The gang member reasons that if the teacher is frightened during the encounter and grades had not been given ran-domly, he probably would have received a better one.

Like my gym teacher today. That fucking freak! F? Aw hell no! Nobody get no F in gym. And I stripped every day! My gym suit wasn't clean every Monday. That's just three points minus. All right. Six weeks times three is eighteen. Right? Eighteen points minus out of a hundred. How the hell you gonna get a F? And I stripped every day. All right then. So I went in there and told Mr C. I say, 'Now look here, the man gave me a F! I stripped every day. My gym suit wasn't clean every Monday. I took a shower after class every day. Now why I get a F?'

He looked in the book. 'Oh, I guess he made a mistake. I'm not sure cause I wasn't with you all during the six weeks so I give you a D.'

So I say, 'Look, man, I don't think a D's fair either. I think I ought to get a B or C just like everyone else.'

'Well, I'll give you a D and you'll get a better grade next time.'

All the time I was talking to him he had his head in a book, and when he looked up it seemed like you could see in his eyes that he was almost scared. You know, Didn't want to say too much. It seem like almost everything you say, he agrees with you and make you look like a ass. 'Yeah. Yeah. That's right, that's right.' Stuff like that. And you know that some of the things you be saying you know is wrong. You'd be expecting him to say, 'No, that's wrong.' You know. And he'd be agreeing with everything you say. He just say, 'Well, do things right next time and I'll go on and give you a better grade.' Something like that. Then he say, 'I sorry.' He apologize to you. Shit like that. That's how you know a teacher is scared of you, and if he scared of you, he going to give you a better grade than you deserve, not a worse one! That gym man! They don't know what they give you. They just hand them out as they come up.

I finally say, 'OK. Fuck it!' You know. I didn't want no F so I took the D. And I say, 'Well look here, man, I hope to hell I don't have your stupid ass for a gym teacher next term!'

If he is dealing with a teacher who believes it is not necessary and in fact demeaning to explain decisions to students, the gang member may receive no answer at all. His search is then frustrated, and he has been directly insulted. This frustration and anger is typically reflected in loud and obscene outbursts directed at the teacher. This is a 'classic' scene in the folklore of a delinquent gang. After blowing up at the teacher and storming from the classroom, he comes to the conclusion that he is being discriminated against, regardless of whether or not this is in fact true.

(How did Tyrone get kicked out of school?) Putting down the teachers. He didn't feel that he was given adequate grades for a term paper or work that he had passed in. He went up and told the teacher to get fucked. She went up to the Dean of Boys, and he tell Tyrone that he'd have to let him go. (Were you in his class?) Yeah. (Did you see him tell off the teacher?) Yeah. I was standing right behind him. (What happened?) Well, see we get these papers back and Tyrone, he start asking everybody what they got. So he go up to this one stud, Art, and he say, 'You see Mrs G., that bitch, she gave me a F. What's the story?'

Art say, 'She gave me a passing grade.'

Tyrone say, 'Shit. You don't do a damn thing. How come you pass and I don't?'

Art say, 'I don't know, man. Maybe she don't like you.'

So Tyrone goes up to her. He said, 'What the hell's going on here? Why I get that F? I felt the answer to this question was right! I think it's right!'

She said, 'Well, no, it isn't. I'm sorry.'

He say, 'Why ain't it right?'

She say, 'I corrected it the way I saw fit.'

He say, 'Well shit! Why ain't it right?'

She say, 'Uh, would you stop using so much profound [*sic*] language. I'll have to tell the Dean.' He say, 'Tell the fucking Dean! He ain't nobody! Aw fuck you!'

She told the Dean, and the Dean kicked him out.

It is important to point out that not all gang members are able to learn something about the rules teachers use to grade by using this procedure. The illiterates or relatively dull students who expect Fs even under the fair condition, and the bright gang members who expect As and Bs, are in a further bind. The F students cannot distinguish between the fair case and the case of discrimination, and the A student cannot distinguish between the fair case and the case of being 'bribed'. Unlike the F student, however, the A student will be particularly sensitive to discrimination. Gang members who fall in these two categories use other grounds to decide whether or not to co-operate with teachers. The procedure being discussed here thus works best for average students, those who can learn something by receiving As and Fs. Most boys, including gang members, however, fall into this category – at least while they are attending school.

Conclusions

Once gang members have either requested or demanded accounts from teachers, they have all the materials needed to come to a conclusion. The accounts that teachers give or fail to give furnish warranted grounds for understanding one aspect of what goes on in the classroom. The gang member has discovered the class or rule being used to grade and thus can understand the single grade he received. Once having discovered the rule, however, he then faces the question of what to do about it. It is in the decisions he makes about his future course of action that we discover the essence of the delinquent.

If he concludes that he is being either discriminated against, bribed, or treated randomly, he does not modify his behavior. Even though he becomes aware that 'kissing ass' will get him a better grade, he does not avail himself of the technique. He is prevented by his sense of morality. The tactic is considered illegitimate. After all, he reasons, 'If I go for that shit I might as well stick to the streets and pull some big-time action!'

(So you know your attitude toward the teacher gets you bad grades sometimes?) Yeah, sometimes it does. (Why don't you change your attitude?) I wouldn't go kiss up to them motherfucking teachers for nothing! Shit! They prejudiced or they gonna hit you over the head with that fucking grade so you gonna kiss up to them? Well no! We supposed to be graded on what we know. Right? Ain't that supposed to be how it is? Damn teachers are something. I tell you they ain't got shit but a racket going, man. Motherfuckers get down there and kiss them God damn principals' asses, the bosses' asses. That's the last motherfucking thing I do! I wouldn't go kiss that damn horse's ass for nothing! I wouldn't do shit for that man. If I go running over there, I'm gonna feel funny. Cause I'm always getting in trouble. What if I go running over there and ask him, 'Look man, why don't you help me out in gym. Tell this man to kinda lighten up on me cause he kinda fucking my grades around. I ain't for all this shit. I know I'm doing right.' You know. Shit like that. He gonna say, 'Lee, you always want favors, but you never want to do nothing in return. You're always messing up in class.' And this and that and the other shit. I'd rather be raped, man. If I go for that shit I might as well stick to the streets and pull some big time action! Shit! If I gonna be corrupt? If I gonna get me a racket going like that, shit, I ain't gonna waste my time sucking up to no teachers! I gonna pull some big time shit.

Practical applications

How do gang members act in classroom once they decide that a teacher's claims to authority are illegitimate? While gang members remain in school, either before graduating or before being kicked out, they do not comply with the grounds teachers use to treat them. This fact explains much of their delinquency in the classroom. If they feel that a teacher is discriminating against them because his claims to authority are not being granted, they are careful to avoid all behavior that implicitly or explicitly recognizes this authority. Raising a hand in class, for example, is a gesture used by students to present themselves as candidates for speaking. Implicit in the gesture is an understanding that the student may not be called on. The gesture implies further that the teacher has the authority to grant speaking privileges in class. If a student raises his hand, he thus implicitly makes the authority of the teacher legitimate. This is why gang members refuse to raise their hands in some classes and prefer interjecting comments without being recognized. This behavior would no doubt be treated by some theorists as a rude and unruly by-product of 'lower-class culture'. Lower-class or not, the behavior has its reasons.

I'm not the quiet type in that class [California history]. Like when we're having a discussion or something? I don't go for all that raising your hand. Cause everybody else on the other side of the room might – while the teacher asking you a question – well the one that just went by, people probably still discussing it. And you might want to get in on that. And you just come on out and say something, and he tell you to get out of class. Well that shit ain't no good, man. So you know that kinda get on my nerves. But I don't mind getting kicked out of class. That ain't no big thing. I feel like – that class I got now? – if I try hard I can pass. My citizenship may not be worth a damn, but I can pass the class. (Do you always forget to raise your hand?) Hell no! I raise my hand in Civics and some of the other classes. That's interesting. But California history ain't shit. It's easy. It's simple. It's just that teacher. He a punk! He just ain't used to us. He just don't understand bloods [Negroes]. I don't raise my hand for that freak! I just tell the dude what's on my mind.

The time and circumstances that surround entering and leaving class also have implications for the implicit acceptance or rejection of authority. If a student consistently comes to class on time, he implicitly gives teachers grounds to assume that he accepts both their authority and the legitimacy of school rules. This is why gang members frequently make it a point to arrive five minutes late to class. It is no accident that gang members are suspended most frequently for tardiness. Not only is tardiness an affront to the authority of teachers but it also flaunts the claims to authority made by the school system as a whole.

We came in late to class today because he threatened us. He see us between fifth and sixth period when he was supposed to be going to one class and coming from another. We was on our way to his class. I was standing by my locker. My locker right next to his class. So he come up to me and say, 'Lee, you tell Wilson that if you two come late to class I'm gonna get you both kicked out of school.' So I went and told Billy, and we made it our business to be late. We walked in about five minutes late. Knocked on the door. He opened the door. Just went in and sat down. I looked him in the eye. Would have put a ring around it if he'd said too much. The door comes in through the back. We made a little bit of noise sitting down to make sure he sees us. We giggled and laughed a little bit to make sure he noticed we were there. We try to remind him that he suppose to kick us out. It was almost to the end of the period before he kicked us out.

Gang members also have the choice of leaving class before the bell is rung, when the bell is ringing, or when the class is formally dismissed by the teacher. When they occasionally leave class before the bell is rung, they flaunt the authority of both the teacher and the school.

(What do you do when you discover that the teacher has been grading you unfairly?) Lots of times we just get up and walk out. Like you say, 'Oh man, I'm tired of this class.' You just jump up and walk out and shut the door. (What do the teachers do?) Mostly they just look at us and then resume with the rest of the class and don't say nothing. (Why don't they report you?) I guess they be glad for us to be out of their class.

More frequently, however, they wait until the bell rings to leave class instead of waiting for a sign of dismissal from the teacher. This act implicitly accepts the authority of the school while explicitly rejecting the authority of the teacher. When this happens teachers who feel they have authority to protect often take action.

After class, as soon as the bell rang, everybody jumped up. The teacher said, 'Everybody sit back down! You're not leaving right now!'

So Alice jumped up. She starts walking out.

He say, 'Alice, go sit down!'

Alice say, 'Who the hell you talking to! I'm tired of school. I'm going home!'

She walked to the door. He grabbed her. She looked at him. 'I'm gonna count to three, and if you don't get your hands off me . . . No, I ain't even gonna count! Take your hands off me!'

He took his hands off. He say, 'We're going to the office this minute!'

She say, 'You going to the office by yourself unless you get somebody else to go down there with you!'

And so she walked away. So she was down talking to some other girls, and he say, 'Alice, would you please come!'

She say, 'No! And stop bugging me! Now get out of here!'

I didn't see all of the argument. I just went off and left. When I passed him I said, 'Man, you ain't nothing!'

He looked at me. Then he say, 'One of these days you gonna get yours.'

In addition, gang members are careful never to use forms of address that suggest deference. 'Yes Sir' and 'No Sir' are thus self-consciously stricken from the vocabulary.

And you know like in some classes the teacher tell you you don't say 'Yes' and 'No'. It's 'Yes Sir' and 'No Sir'. They would have to whip my ass to make me say that. I don't go for it. Shit. They don't call me Mr Lee! Teacher once tried to tell me to say, 'Yes M'am'. I say, 'All right, you call me Mr Lee.' I don't like it. I feel if I did, I'd probably feel funny saying 'Yes Sir' and 'No Sir' to somebody. (How would you feel?) I'd feel like I was a little old punk or something.

But of all the techniques used by gang members to communicate rejection of authority, by far the most subtle and most annoying to teachers is demeanor. Both white and Negro gang members have developed a uniform and highly stylized complex of body movements that communicate a casual and disdainful aloofness to anyone making normative claims on their behavior. The complex is referred to by gang members as 'looking cool', and it is part of a repertoire of stances that include 'looking bad' and 'looking tore down'. The essential ingredients of 'looking cool' are a walking pace that is a little too slow for the occasion, a straight back, shoulders slightly stooped, hands in pockets, and eyes that carefully avert any part to the interaction. There are also clothing aides which enhance the effect such as boot or shoe taps and a hat if the scene takes place indoors.

This stance can trigger an incident if a teacher reacts to it, but it is the teacher who must make the first overt move. The beauty of the posture resides in its being both concrete and diffuse. Teachers do not miss it, but they have a great deal of difficulty finding anything specific to attack. Even the mightiest of educators feels embarrassed telling high school students to 'stand up straight'. As the following episode suggests, teachers typically find some other issue on which to vent their disapproval.

The first day I came to school I was late to class so this teacher got smart with me. He didn't know me by name. See a lot of people have to go by the office and see what class they in or something. Like there was a lot of new people there. So you know I was fooling around cause I know nothing gonna happen to you if you late. Cause all you tell them, you tell them you got the program mixed or something.

When I came into the class you know I heard a lot of hollering and stuff. Mr H was in the class too. He's a teacher, see. I guess he had a student teacher or something, you know, because he was getting his papers and stuff. So Mr H went out. Well this new teacher probably wonder if he gonna be able to get along with me or something. Cause when I came in the class, you know, everybody just got quiet. Cause the class was kinda loud. When I walked in the class got quiet all of a sudden. Like they thought the Principal was coming in or something.

So I walk into class and everybody look up. That's natural, you know, when somebody walk into class. People gonna look up at you. They gonna see who it is coming in or something. So I stopped. You know, like this. Looked around. See if there was any new faces. Then a girl named Diane, she say, 'Hey Ray!' You know, when I walk into class they start calling me and stuff. They start hollering at me.

I just smile and walk on. You know. I had my hands in my pocket or something cause I didn't have no books and I just walk into class with my hands in my pockets a lot of times. I mean I have to walk where I can relax. I'm not going to walk with my back straight. I mean you know I relax. (What were you wearing?) About what I got on now. I had a pair of black slacks and a shirt on but they weren't real high boots. They came up to about here.

Then I looked over at the teacher. I see we had a new teacher. He was standing in front of the desks working on some papers and doing something. He looked at me. I mean you enter by the front of the classroom so when you walk into the classroom he's standing right there. You gotta walk in front of him to get to the seats. So then I went to sit down. Soon as I passed his desk he say, 'Just go sit down', just like that. So I stop. I turn around and look at him, then I went and sat down. (What kind of look did you give him?) You might say I gave him a hard look. I thought you know he might say something else. Cause that same day he came he got to hollering at people and stuff. I don't like people to holler at me. He was short, you know, about medium build. He might be able to do a little bit. So I say to myself, 'I better sit down and meditate a little bit.'

So I went and sat down. I sat in the last row in the last seat. Then he say, 'Come sit up closer.' So I scoot up another chair or two. Then he tell me to come sit up in the front. So I sat up there. Then you know a lot of people was talking. A lot of people begin telling me that he be getting smart all day. You know Studdy? He a big square but he pretty nice. He told me how the teacher was. And Angela start telling me about how he try to get smart with her. He say, 'This is where you don't pick out no boy friend. You come and

275

get your education.' I mean just cause you talk to a boy, that don't mean you be scheming on them or nothing. It just that you want to be friends with people.

Then he say something like, 'You two shut up or I'll throw you out on your ear.' So he told me he'd throw me out.

So I say, 'The best thing you can do is ask me to leave and don't tell me. You'll get your damn ass kicked off if you keep messing!'

Then he told me to move over on the other side. See I was talking to everybody so he told me to move away from everybody. And so I moved to the other side. He told me to move three times! I had to move three times! And then he got to arguing at somebody else. I think at somebody else that came in the class. You know, a new person. So while he was talking to them, I left out. I snuck out of class.

So I walked out the class. Went out in the yard and started playing basketball. We were supposed to turn in the basketball out there so I took the ball through the hall on the way back in. I was gonna go back out there and play some more. See I had the ball and I passed by his class and I looked in. I seen him with his back turned and I didn't like him. That's when I hit him. I hit him with the ball. Got him! I didn't miss. Threw it hard too. Real hard!

It is easier for teachers to attack the demeanor of students directly if the encounter is formal and disciplinary. If a gang member is 'sent' to someone for punishment, the teacher or principal he appears before often makes demeanor an issue. In the following incident, a gang member is suspended for ten days ostensibly because he faced the music with his hands in his pockets and the touch of a smile on his face.

Miss W, she sent me to Mr M cause I cussed at her. When I came to class he was talking to some gray boys [white boys] and he called me in. He talked at me like he gonna knock me out. Talked about fifteen minutes. He wasn't coming on nice. He got right down to the point. 'I think you know what you're in here for. I think you know what you did fourth period concerning Miss W.'

I say, 'Yeah, I know what I done.'

And so he just sat down and went on and talked. He told me to sit down. I was already sat down. I had my hands in my pockets. He told me to take my hands out of my pockets. (Why?) I guess he wanted my attention. I was looking down at the floor and he told me to look at him. I look at him and look down at the floor again. He didn't say nothing then. And I walked out the woodship and I just smiled. And he say, 'Come on back here! I want to talk to you again.' So I went back there. 'What was that smile for? That little

276

smile you gave.'

I say, 'Ain't nobody can tell me if I can smile.'

He said, 'You smiling as if you gave me a bad time. You didn't. I gave you a bad time!'

So he told me to go on down to the Principal. He told me the Principal was gonna suspend me for ten days. (Did he?) Yup.

Yet when gang members are convinced that the educational enterprise and its ground rules are being legitimately pursued, that a teacher is really interested in teaching them something, and that efforts to learn will be rewarded, they consistently show up on time, leave when the class is dismissed, raise their hands before speaking, and stay silent and awake.

I mean I feel like that teacher was helping me. I mean he was showing me a way I could pass his class. And then all the time he was telling me, you know, he was leaving me with confidence that I could do better if I wanted to. Like I mean he'd be up in front of the class you know, and he'd give the class an equal chance to be graded. I mean I felt that the teacher was real fair. Cause some of the people that were slow, he would help. I mean he wouldn't take off time just for that few little people but he would help you. He'd give you confidence. Tell you you can do better. That man used to have a desk full of people. Everyday after class you know there be somebody up there talking to him. Everybody passed his class too. He let you know that you wasn't in there for nothing.

Notes

[1] RICHARD A CLOWARD and LLOYD E OHLIN, *Delinquency and Opportunity* (Routledge & Kegan Paul 1961), **102**.

[2] ALBERT K COHEN, *Delinquent Boys: The Culture of the Gang* (Routledge & Kegan Paul 1956), **115**.

[3] WALTER B MILLER and WILLIAM C KVARACEUS, *Delinquent Behavior: Culture and the Individual*, National Educational Association of the United States 1959, **144**. See also WALTER MILLER, 'Lower-class culture as a generating milieu of gang delinquency', *Journal of Social Issues* (1958), **14** for a more explicit statement of this position.

[4] CLOWARD and OHLIN, *op cit*.

[5] COHEN, *op cit*

[6] MILLER, *op cit*.

[7] CHESTER I BARNARD, *The Functions of the Executive* (Cambridge, Mass: Harvard University Press 1938), **163**.

[8] This assumption is widely shared by both sociologists and gang members. Hopefully we will some day put it to a test.

[9] This model of events is based on the assumption that regardless of how students are behaving in class, they can only misbehave if a rule about proper conduct is invoked by teachers. It is in this sense that 'social groups create deviance by making the rules whose infraction constitutes deviance, and by

applying those rules to particular people'. See HOWARD S BECKER, *Outsiders* (Collier-Macmillan 1963), **9**.

[10] For a general discussion of the problems created by contingent or purposive infraction of irrelevance rules see ERVIN G GOFFMAN, *Encounters* (Indianapolis: Bobbs-Merrill 1961), 17–85.

23

Police Encounters with Juveniles * †

Irving Piliavin and Scott Briar

As the first of a series of decisions made in the channeling of youthful offenders through the agencies concerned with juvenile justice and corrections, the disposition decisions made by police officers have potentially profound consequences for apprehended juveniles. Thus arrest, the most severe of the dispositions available to police, may not only lead to confinement of the suspected offender but also bring him loss of social status, restriction of educational and employment opportunities, and future harassment by law-enforcement personnel[1]. According to some criminologists, the stigmatization resulting from police apprehension, arrest, and detention actually reinforces deviant behavior[2]. Other authorities have suggested, in fact, that this stigmatization serves as the catalytic agent initiating delinquent careers[3]. Despite their presumed significance, however, little empirical analysis has been reported regarding the factors influencing, or consequences resulting from, police actions with juvenile offenders. Furthermore, while some studies of police encounters with adult offenders have been reported, the extent to which the findings of these investigations pertain to law-enforcement practices with youthful offenders is not known[4].

The above considerations have led the writers to undertake a longitudinal study of the conditions influencing, and consequences flowing from, police actions with juveniles. In the present paper findings will be presented indicating the influence of certain factors on police actions. Research data consist primarily of notes and records based on nine months' observation of all juvenile officers in one police department[5]. The officers were observed in the course of their regular tours of duty[6]. While these data do not lend themselves to quantitative assessments of reliability and validity, the candor

* Reprinted from *American Journal of Sociology*, **69** (September, 1964), 206–214, by permission of the authors and The University of Chicago Press, Copyright 1964 by The University of Chicago Press.

† This study was supported by Grant MH-06328-02, National Institute of Mental Health, United States Public Health Service.

shown by the officers in their interviews with the investigators and their use of officially frowned-upon practices while under observation provide some assurance that the materials presented below accurately reflect the typical operations and attitudes of the law-enforcement personnel studied.

The setting for the research, a metropolitan police department serving an industrial city with approximately 450 000 inhabitants, was noted within the community it served and among law-enforcement officials elsewhere for the honesty and superior quality of its personnel. Incidents involving criminal activity or brutality by members of the department had been extremely rare during the ten years preceding this study; personnel standards were comparatively high; and an extensive training program was provided to both new and experienced personnel. Juvenile Bureau members, the primary subjects of this investigation, differed somewhat from other members of the department in that they were responsible for delinquency prevention as well as law enforcement, that is, juvenile officers were expected to be knowledgeable about conditions leading to crime and delinquency and to be able to work with community agencies serving known or potential juvenile offenders. Accordingly, in the assignment of personnel to the Juvenile Bureau, consideration was given not only to an officer's devotion to and reliability in law enforcement but also to his commitment to delinquency prevention. Assignment to the Bureau was of advantage to policemen seeking promotions. Consequently, many officers requested transfer to this unit, and its personnel comprised a highly select group of officers.

In the field, juvenile officers operated essentially as patrol officers. They cruised assigned beats and, although concerned primarily with juvenile offenders, frequently had occasion to apprehend and arrest adults. Confrontations between the officers and juveniles occurred in one of the following three ways, in order of increasing frequency: (1) encounters resulting from officers' spotting officially 'wanted' youths; (2) encounters taking place at or near the scene of offenses reported to police headquarters; and (3) encounters occurring as the result of officers' directly observing youths either committing offenses or in 'suspicious circumstances'. However, the probability that a confrontation would take place between officer and juvenile, or that a particular disposition of an identified offender would be made, was only in part determined by the knowledge that an offense had occurred or that a particular juvenile had committed an offense. The bases for and utilization of non-offenses related criteria by police in accosting and disposing of juveniles are the focuses of the following discussion.

280

Sanctions for Discretion

In each encounter with juveniles, with the minor exception of officially 'wanted' youths[7], a central task confronting the officer was to decide what official action to take against the boys involved. In making these disposition decisions, officers could select any one of five discrete alternatives:

1 outright release
2 release and submission of a 'field interrogation report' briefly describing the circumstances initiating the police-juvenile confrontation
3 'official reprimand' and release to parents or guardian
4 citation to juvenile court
5 arrest and confinement in juvenile hall.

Dispositions 3, 4, and 5 differed from the others in two basic respects. First, with rare exceptions, when an officer chose to reprimand, cite, or arrest a boy, he took the youth to the police station. Second, the reprimanded, cited, or arrested boy acquired an official police 'record', that is, his name was officially recorded in Bureau files as a juvenile violator.

Analysis of the distribution of police disposition decisions about juveniles revealed that in virtually every category of offense the full range of official disposition alternatives available to officers was employed. This wide range of discretion resulted primarily from two conditions. First, it reflected the reluctance of officers to expose certain youths to the stigmatization presumed to be associated with official police action. Few juvenile officers believed that correctional agencies serving the community could effectively help delinquents. For some officers this attitude reflected a lack of confidence in rehabilitation techniques; for others, a belief that high case loads and lack of professional training among correctional workers vitiated their efforts at treatment. All officers were agreed, however, that juvenile justice and correctional processes were essentially concerned with apprehension and punishment rather than treatment. Furthermore, all officers believed that some aspects of these processes (eg, judicial definition of youths as delinquents and removal of delinquents from the community), as well as some of the possible consequences of these processes (eg, intimate institutional contact with 'hard-core' delinquents, as well as parental, school, and conventional peer disapproval or rejection), could reinforce what previously might have been only a tentative proclivity toward delinquent values and behavior. Consequently, when officers found reason to doubt that a youth being confronted was highly committed toward deviance, they were inclined to treat him with leniency.

Second, and more important, the practice of discretion was sanctioned by police-department policy. Training manuals and departmental bulletins stressed that the disposition of each juvenile offender was not to be based solely on the type of infraction he committed. Thus, while it was departmental policy to 'arrest and confine all juveniles who have committed a felony or misdemeanor involving theft, sex offense, battery, possession of dangerous weapons, prowling, peeping, intoxication, incorrigibility, and disturbance of the peace', it was acknowledged, that 'such considerations as age, attitude and prior criminal record might indicate that a different disposition would be more appropriate'[8]. The official justification for discretion in processessing juvenile offenders, based on the preventive aims of the Juvenile Bureau, was that each juvenile violator should be dealt with solely on the basis of what was best for him[9]. Unofficially, administrative legitimation of discretion was further justified on the grounds that strict enforcement practices would overcrowd court calendars and detention facilities, as well as dramatically increase juvenile crime rates – consequences to be avoided because they would expose the police department to community criticism[10].

In practice, the official policy justifying use of discretion served as a demand that discretion be exercised. As such, it posed three problems for juvenile officers. First, it represented a departure from the traditional police practice with which the juvenile officers themselves were identified, in the sense that they were expected to justify their juvenile disposition decisions not simply by evidence proving a youth had committed a crime – grounds on which police were officially expected to base their dispositions of non-juvenile offenders[11] – but in the *character* of the youth. Second, in disposing of juvenile offenders, officers were expected, in effect, to make judicial rather than ministerial decisions[12]. Third, the shift from the offense to the offender as the basis for determining the appropriate disposition substantially increased the uncertainty and ambiguity for officers in the situation of apprehension because no explicit rules existed for determining which disposition different types of youths should receive. Despite these problems, officers were constrained to base disposition decisions on the character of the apprehended youth, not only because they wanted to be fair, but because persistent failure to do so could result in judicial criticism, departmental censure, and, they believed, loss of authority with juveniles[13].

Disposition Criteria

Assessing the character of apprehended offenders posed relatively few difficulties for officers in the case of youths who had committed serious crimes such as robbery, homicide, aggravated assault, grand theft, auto theft, rape, and arson. Officials generally regarded these juveniles as confirmed delinquents simply by virtue of their involvement in offenses of this magnitude[14]. However, the infraction committed did not always suffice to determine the appropriate disposition for some serious offenders[15]; and, in the case of minor offenders, who comprised over 90 per cent of the youths against whom police took action, the violation *per se* generally played an insignificant role in the choice of disposition. While a number of minor offenders were seen as serious delinquents deserving arrest, many others were perceived either as 'good' boys whose offenses were atypical of their customary behavior, as pawns of undesirable associates or, in any case, as boys for whom arrest was regarded as an unwarranted and possibly harmful punishment. Thus, for nearly all minor violators and for some serious delinquents, the assessment of character – the distinction between serious delinquents, 'good' boys, misguided youths, and so on – and the dispositions which followed from these assessments were based on youths' personal characteristics and not their offenses.

Despite this dependence of disposition decisions on the personal characteristics of these youths, however, police officers actually had access only to very limited information about boys at the time they had to decide what to do with them. In the field, officers typically had no data concerning the past offense records, school performance, family situation, or personal adjustment of apprehended youths[16]. Furthermore, files at police headquarters provided data only about each boy's prior offense record. Thus both the decision made in the field – whether or not to bring the boy in – and the decision made at the station – were based largely on cues which emerged from the interaction between the officer and the youth, cues from which the officer inferred the youth's character. These cues included the youth's group affiliations, age, race, grooming, dress, and demeanor. Older juveniles, members of known delinquent gangs, Negroes, youths with well-oiled hair, black jackets, and soiled denims or jeans (the presumed uniform of 'tough' boys), and boys who in their interactions with officers did not manifest what were considered to be appropriate signs of respect tended to receive the more severe dispositions.

Other than prior record, the most important of the above cues was a youth's *demeanor*. In the opinion of juvenile patrolmen themselves the demeanor of apprehended juveniles was a major determinant of their decisions for 50–60 per cent of the juvenile cases they processed[17]. A less subjective indication of the association between a youth's demeanor and police disposition is produced by Table 1, which

Table 1 SEVERITY OF POLICE DISPOSITION BY YOUTH'S DEMEANOR

Severity of Police Disposition	Youth's Demeanor		
	Co-operative	Unco-operative	Total
Arrest (most severe)	2	14	16
Citation or official reprimand	4	5	9
Informal reprimand	15	1	16
Admonish and release (least severe)	24	1	25
Total	45	21	66

presents the police dispositions for sixty-six youths whose encounters with police were observed in the course of this study[18]. For purposes of this analysis, each youth's demeanor in the encounter was classified as either co-operative or unco-operative[19]. The results clearly reveal a marked association between youth demeanor and the severity of police dispositions.

The cues used by police to assess demeanor were fairly simple. Juveniles who were contrite about their infractions, respectful to officers, and fearful of the sanctions that might be employed against them tended to be viewed by patrolmen as basically law-abiding or at least 'salvageable'. For these youths it was usually assumed that informal or formal reprimand would suffice to guarantee their future conformity. In contrast, youthful offenders who were fractious, obdurate, or who appeared nonchalant in their encounters with patrolmen were likely to be viewed as 'would-be tough guys' or 'punks' who fully deserved the most severe sanction: arrest. The following excerpts from observation notes illustrate the importance attached to demeanor by police in making disposition decisions.

1 The interrogation of 'A' (an 18-year-old upper-lower-class white male accused of statutory rape) was assigned to a police sergeant with long experience on the force. As I sat in his office while we waited for the youth to arrive for questioning, the sergeant expressed his uncertainty as to what he should do with this young man. On the one hand, he could not ignore the fact that an offense had been committed; he had been informed, in fact, that the youth was prepared to confess to the offense. Nor could he overlook the continued pressure from the girl's father (an important political figure) for the police to take severe action against the youth. On the other hand, the sergeant had formed a low opinion of the girl's moral character, and he considered it unfair to charge 'A' with statutory rape when the girl was a willing partner to the offense and might even have been the instigator of it. However, his sense of

injustice concerning 'A' was tempered by his image of the youth as a 'punk', based, he explained, on information he had received that the youth belonged to a certain gang, the members of which were well known to, and disliked by, the police. Nevertheless, as we prepared to leave his office to interview 'A', the sergeant was still in doubt as to what he should do with him.

As we walked down the corridor to the interrogation room, the sergeant was stopped by a reporter from the local newspaper. In an excited tone of voice, the reporter explained that his editor was pressing him to get further information about this case. The newspaper had printed some of the facts about the girl's disappearance, and as a consequence the girl's father was threatening suit against the paper for defamation of the girl's character. It would strengthen the newspaper's position, the reporter explained, if the police had information indicating that the girl's associates, particularly the youth the sergeant was about to interrogate, were persons of disreputable character. This stimulus seemed to resolve the sergeant's uncertainty. He told the reporter, 'unofficially', that the youth was known to be an undesirable person, citing as evidence his membership in the delinquent gang. Furthermore, the sergeant added that he had evidence that this youth had been intimate with the girl over a period of many months. When the reporter asked if the police were planning to do anything to the youth, the sergeant answered that he intended to charge the youth with statutory rape. In the interrogation, however, three points quickly emerged which profoundly affected the sergeant's judgment of the youth. First, the youth was polite and co-operative; he consistently addressed the officer as 'sir', answered all questions quietly, and signed a statement implicating himself in numerous counts of statutory rape. Second, the youth's intentions toward the girl appeared to have been honorable; for example he said that he wanted to marry her eventually. Third, the youth was not in fact a member of the gang in question. The sergeant's attitude became increasingly sympathetic, and after we left the interrogation room he announced his intention to 'get "A" off the hook', meaning that he wanted to have the charges against 'A' reduced or, if possible, dropped.

2 Officers 'X' and 'Y' brought into the police station a seventeen-year-old white boy who, along with two older companions, had been found in a home having sex relations with a fifteen-year-old girl. The boy responded to police officers' queries slowly and with obvious disregard. It was apparent that his lack of deference toward the officers and his failure to evidence concern about his situation were irritating his questioners. Finally, one of the officers

turned to me and, obviously angry, commented that in his view the boy was simply a 'stud' interested only in sex, eating, and sleeping. The policemen conjectured that the boy 'probably already had knocked up half a dozen girls'. The boy ignored these remarks, except for an occasional impassive stare at the patrolmen. Turning to the boy, the officer remarked, 'What the hell am I going to do with you?' And again the boy simply returned the officer's gaze. The latter then said, 'Well, I guess we'll just have to put you away for a while'. An arrest report was then made out and the boy was taken to Juvenile Hall.

Although anger and disgust frequently characterized officers' attitudes toward recalcitrant and impassive juvenile offenders, their manner while processing these youths was typically routine, restrained, and without rancor. While the officers' restraint may have been due in part to their desire to avoid accusation and censure, it also seemed to reflect their inurement to a frequent experience. By and large, only their occasional 'needling' or insulting of a boy gave any hint of the underlying resentment and dislike they felt toward many of these youths [20].

Prejudice in Apprehension and Disposition Decisions

Compared to other youths, Negroes and boys whose appearance matched the delinquent stereotype were more frequently stopped and interrogated by patrolmen – often even in the absence of evidence that an offense had been committed [21] – and usually were given more severe dispositions for the same violations. Our data suggest, however, that these selective apprehension and disposition practices resulted not only from the intrusion of long-held prejudices of individual police officers but also from certain job-related experiences of law-enforcement personnel. First, the tendency for police to give more severe dispositions to Negroes and to youths whose appearance corresponded to that which police associated with delinquents partly reflected the fact, observed in this study, that these youths also were much more likely than were other types of boys to exhibit the sort of recalcitrant demeanor which police construed as a sign of the confirmed delinquent. Further, officers assumed, partly on the basis of departmental statistics, that Negroes and juveniles who 'look tough' (eg, who wear chinos, leather jackets, boots, etc) commit crimes more frequently than do other types of youths [22]. In this sense, the police justified their selective treatment of these youths along epidemiological lines: that is, they were concentrating their attention on those youths whom they believed were most likely to commit delinquent acts. In the words of one highly placed official in the department:

> If you know that the bulk of your delinquent problem comes from kids who, say, are from 12 to 14 years of age, when you're out on patrol you are much more likely to be sensitive to the activities of juveniles in this age bracket than older or younger groups. This would be good law enforcement practice. The logic in our case is the same except that our delinquency problem is largely found in the Negro community and it is these youths toward whom we are sensitized.

As regards prejudice *per se*, eighteen of twenty-seven officers interviewed openly admitted a dislike for Negroes. However, they attributed their dislike to experiences they had, as policemen, with youths from this minority group. The officers reported that Negro boys were much more likely than non-Negroes to 'give us a hard time,' be unco-operative, and show no remorse for their transgressions. Recurrent exposure to such attitudes among Negro youth, the officers claimed, generated their antipathy toward Negroes. The following excerpt is typical of the views expressed by these officers:

> They (Negroes) have no regard for the law or for the police. They just don't seem to give a damn. Few of them are interested in school or getting ahead. The girls start having illegitimate kids before they are 16 years old and the boys are always 'out for kicks'. Furthermore, many of these kids try to run you down. They say the damnedest things to you and they seem to have absolutely no respect for you as an adult. I am prejudiced now, but frankly I don't think I was when I began police work.

Implications

It is apparent from the findings presented above that the police officers studied in this research were permitted and even encouraged to exercise immense latitude in disposing of the juveniles they encountered. That is, it was within the officers' discretionary authority, except in extreme limiting cases, to decide which juveniles were to come to the attention of the courts and correctional agencies and thereby be identified officially as delinquents. In exercising this discretion policemen were strongly guided by the demeanor of those who were apprehended, a practice which ultimately led, as seen above, to certain youths (particularly Negroes [23] and boys dressed in the style of 'toughs'), being treated more severely than other juveniles for comparable offenses.

But the relevance of demeanor was not limited only to police disposition practices. Thus, for example, in conjunction with police crime statistics the criterion of demeanor led police to concentrate their surveillance activities in areas frequented or inhabited by Negroes. Furthermore, these youths were accosted more often than others by officers on patrol simply because their skin color identified them as potential troublemakers. These discriminatory practices – and it is important to note that they are discriminatory, even if based on accurate statistical information – may well have self-fulfilling consequences. Thus it is not unlikely that frequent encounters with police, particularly those involving youths innocent of wrongdoing, will increase the hostility of these juveniles toward law-enforcement personnel. It is also not unlikely that the frequency of such encounters will in time reduce their significance in the eyes of apprehended juveniles, thereby leading these youths to regard them as 'routine.' Such responses to police encounters, however, are those which law-enforcement personnel perceive as indicators of the serious delinquent. They thus serve to vindicate and reinforce officers' prejudices, leading to closer surveillance of Negro districts, more frequent encounters with Negro youths, and so on in a vicious circle. Moreover, the consequences of this chain of events are reflected in police statistics showing a disproportionately high percentage of Negroes among juvenile offenders, thereby providing 'objective' justification for concentrating police attention on Negro youths.

To a substantial extent, as we have implied earlier, the discretion practiced by juvenile officers is simply an extension of the juvenile-court philosophy, which holds that in making legal decisions regarding juveniles, more weight should be given to the juvenile's character and life-situation than to his actual offending behavior. The juvenile officer's disposition decisions – and the information he uses as a basis for them – are more akin to the discriminations made by probation officers and other correctional workers than they are to decisions of police officers dealing with non-juvenile offenders. The problem is that such clinical-type decisions are restrained by mechanisms comparable to the principles of due process and the rules of procedure governing police decisions regarding adult offenders. Consequently, prejudicial practices by police officers can escape notice more easily in their dealings with juveniles than with adults.

The observations made in this study serve to underscore the fact that the official delinquent, as distinguished from the juvenile who simply commits a delinquent act, is the product of a social judgment, in this case a judgment made by the police. He is a delinquent because someone in authority has defined him as one, often on the basis of the public face he has presented to officials rather than of the kind of offense he has committed.

References

[1] RICHARD D SCHWARTZ and JEROME H SKOLNICK, 'Two Studies of Legal Stigma', *Social Problems*, **X** (April, 1962), 133–42; SOL RUBIN, *Crime and Juvenile Delinquency* (Oceana Publications, New York, 1958); B F MCSALLY, 'Finding Jobs for Released Offenders', *Federal Probation*, **XXIV** (June, 1960), 12–17; HAROLD D LASSWELL and RICHARD C DONNELLY, 'The Continuing Debate over Responsibility: An Introduction to Isolating the Condemnation Sanction', *Yale Law Journal*, **LXVIII** (April, 1959), 869–99.

[2] RICHARD A CLOWARD and LLOYD E OHLIN, *Delinquency and Opportunity* (Free Press, New York, 1960), 124–30.

[3] FRANK TANNENBAUM, *Crime and the Community* (Columbia University Press: New York, 1936), 17–20; HOWARD S BECKER, *Outsiders: Studies in the Sociology of Deviance* (Free Press of Glencoe, New York, 1963), chaps i and ii.

[4] For a detailed accounting of police discretionary practices, see JOSEPH GOLDSTEIN, 'Police Discretion Not To Invoke the Criminal Process: Low Visibility Decisions in the Administration of Justice', *Yale Law Journal*, **LXIX** (1960), 543–94; WAYNE R LAFAVE, 'The Police and Non-enforcement of the Law—Part I.' *Wisconsin Law Review*, January, 1962, 104–37; S H KADISH 'Legal Norms and Discretion in the Police and Sentencing Processes,' *Harvard Law Review*, **LXXV** (March, 1962), 904–31.

[5] Approximately thirty officers were assigned to the Juvenile Bureau in the department studied. While we had an opportunity to observe all officers in the Bureau during the study, our observations were concentrated on those who had been working in the Bureau for one or two years at least. Although two of the officers in the Juvenile Bureau were Negro, we observed these officers on only a few occasions.

[6] Although observations were not confined to specific days or works shifts, more observations were made during evenings and weekends because police activity was greatest during these periods.

[7] 'Wanted' juveniles usually were placed under arrest or in protective custody, a practice which in effect relieved officers of the responsibility for deciding what to do with these youths.

[8] Quoted from a training manual issued by the police department studied in this research.

[9] Presumably this also implied that police action with juveniles was to be determined partly by the offenders' need for correctional services.

[10] This was reported by beat officers as well as supervisory and administrative personnel of the Juvenile Bureau.

[11] In actual practice, of course, disposition decision regarding adult offenders also were influenced by many factors extraneous to the offense *per se*.

[12] For example, in dealing with adult violators, officers had no disposition alternative comparable to the reprimand-and-release category, a disposition which contained elements of punishment but did not involve mediation by the court.

[13] The concern of officers over possible loss of authority stemmed from their belief that court failure to support arrests by appropriate action would cause policemen to 'lose face' in the eyes of juveniles.

[14] It is also likely that the possibility of negative publicity resulting from the failure to arrest such violators – particularly if they became involved in further serious crime – brought about strong administrative pressure for their arrest.

[15] For example, in the year preceding this research, over 30 per cent of the juveniles involved in burglaries and 12 per cent of the juveniles committing auto theft received dispositions other than arrest.

[16] On occasion, officers apprehended youths whom they personally knew to be prior offenders. This did not occur frequently, however, for several reasons. First, approximately 75 per cent of apprehended youths had no prior official records; second, officers periodically exchanged patrol areas, thus limiting their exposure to, and knowledge about, these areas; and third, patrolmen seldom spent more than three or four years in the juvenile division.

[17] While reliable subgroup estimates were impossible to obtain through observation because of the relatively small number of incidents observed, the importance of demeanor in disposition decision appeared to be much less significant with known prior offenders.

[18] Systematic data were collected on police encounters with seventy-six juveniles. In ten of these encounters the police concluded that their suspicions were groundless, and consequently the juveniles involved were exonerated; these ten cases were eliminated from this analysis of demeanor. (The total number of encounters observed was considerably more than seventy-six, but systematic data-collection procedures were not instituted until several months after observations began.)

[19] The data used for the classification of demeanor were the written records of observations made by the authors. The classifications were made by an independent judge not associated with this study. In classifying a youth's demeanor as co-operative, or unco-operative, particular attention was paid to: (1) the youth's responses to police officers' questions and requests; (2) the respect and deference – or lack of these qualities – shown by the youth toward police officers; and (3) police officers' assessments of the youth's demeanor.

[20] Officers' animosity toward recalcitrant or aloof offenders appeared to stem from two sources: moral indignation that these juveniles were self-righteous and indifferent about their transgressions, and resentment that these youths failed to accord police the respect they believed they deserved. Since the patrolmen perceived themselves as honestly and impartially performing a vital community function warranting respect and deference from the community at large, they attributed the lack of respect shown them by these juveniles to the latters' immorality.

[21] The clearest evidence for this assertion is provided by the overrepresentation of Negroes among 'innocent' juveniles accosted by the police. As noted, of the seventy-six juveniles on whom systematic data were collected, ten were exonerated and released without suspicion. Seven, or two-thirds of these ten 'innocent' juveniles were Negro, in contrast to the allegedly 'guilty' youths, less than one-third of whom were Negro. The following incident illustrates the operation of this bias: One officer, observing a youth walking along the street, commented that the youth 'looks suspicious' and promptly stopped and questioned him. Asked later to explain what aroused his suspicion, the officer explained. 'He was a Negro wearing dark glasses at midnight.'

[22] While police statistics did not permit an analysis of crime rates by appearance, they strongly supported officers' contentions concerning the delinquency rate among Negroes. Of all male juveniles processed by the police department in 1961, for example, 40·2 per cent were Negro and 33·9 per cent were white. These two groups comprised at that time, respectively, about 22·7 per cent and 73·6 per cent of the population in the community studied.

[23] An unco-operative demeanor was presented by more than one-third of the Negro youths but by only one-sixth of the white youths encountered by the police in the course of our observations.

24

Rules of Conduct *

Erving Goffman

A rule of conduct may be defined as a guide for action, recommended not because it is pleasant, cheap, or effective, but because it is suitable or just. Infractions characteristically lead to feelings of uneasiness and to negative social sanctions. Rules of conduct infuse all areas of activity and are upheld in the name and honor of almost everything. Always, however, a grouping of adherents will be involved – if not a corporate social life – providing through this a common sociological theme. Attachment to rules leads to a constancy and patterning of behavior; while this is not the only source of regularity in human affairs it is certainly an important one. Of course, approved guides to conduct tend to be covertly broken, side-stepped, or followed for unapproved reasons, but these alternatives merely add to the occasions in which rules constrain at least the surface of conduct.

Rules of conduct impinge upon the individual in two general ways: directly, as *obligations*, establishing how he is morally constrained to conduct himself; indirectly, as *expectations*, establishing how others are morally bound to act in regard to him. A nurse, for example, has an obligation to follow medical orders in regard to her patients; she has the expectation, on the other hand, that her patients will pliantly cooperate in allowing her to perform these actions upon them. This pliancy, in turn, can be seen as an obligation of the patients in regard to their nurse, and points up the interpersonal, actor-recipient character of many rules: what is one man's obligation will often be another's expectation.

Because obligations involve a constraint to act in a particular way, we sometimes picture them as burdensome or irksome things, to be fulfilled, if at all, by gritting one's teeth in conscious determination. In fact, most actions which are guided by rules of conduct are performed unthinkingly, the questioned actor saying he performs 'for no reason' or because he 'felt like doing so'. Only when his routines are blocked may he discover that his neutral little actions have all along

* 'Deference and Demeanor'. Reprinted by permission of *American Anthropologist*, **58**, June 1956.

been consonant with the proprieties of his group and that his failure to perform them can become a matter of shame and humiliation. Similarly, he may so take for granted his expectations regarding others that only when things go unexpectedly wrong will he suddenly discover that he has grounds for indignation.

Once it is clear that a person may meet an obligation without feeling it, we can go on to see that an obligation which *is* felt as something that *ought* to be done may strike the obligated person either as a desired thing or as an onerous one, in short, as a pleasant or unpleasant duty. In fact, the same obligation may appear to be a desirable duty at one point and an undesirable one at another, as when a nurse, obliged to administer medication to patients, may be glad of this when attempting to establish social distance from attendants (who in some sense may be considered by nurses to be not 'good enough' to engage in such activity), yet burdened by it on occasions when she finds that dosage must be determined on the basis of illegibly written medical orders. Similarly, an expectation may be perceived by the expectant person as a wanted or unwanted thing, as when one person feels he will deservedly be fired. In ordinary usage, a rule that strikes the actor or recipient as a personally desirable thing, apart from its propriety, is sometimes called a right or privilege, as it will be here, but these terms have additional implications, suggesting that special class of rules which an individual may invoke but is not required to do so. It should also be noted that an actor's pleasant obligation may constitute a recipient's pleasant expectation, as with the kiss a husband owes his wife when he returns from the office, but that, as the illustration suggests, all kinds of combinations are possible.

When an individual becomes involved in the maintenance of a rule, he tends also to become committed to a particular image of self. In the case of his obligations, he becomes to himself and others the sort of person who follows this particular rule, the sort of person who would naturally be expected to do so. In the case of his expectations, he becomes dependent upon the assumption that others will properly perform such of their obligations as affect him, for their treatment of him will express a conception of him. In establishing him as the sort of person who treats others in a particular way, he must make sure that it will be possible for him to act and be this kind of person. For example, with certain psychiatrists there seems to be a point where the obligation of giving psychotherapy to patients, *their* patients, is transformed into something they must do if they are to retain the image they have come to have of themselves. The effect of this transformation can be seen in the squirming some of them may do in the early phases of their careers when they may find themselves employed to do research, or administer a ward, or give therapy to those who would rather be left alone.

In general then, when a rule of conduct is broken we find that two individuals run the risk of becoming discredited: one with an obligation, who should have governed himself by the rule; the other with an expectation, who should have been treated in a particular way because of this governance. Both actor and recipient are threatened.

An act that is subject to a rule of conduct is, then, a communication, for it represents a way in which selves are confirmed – both the self for which the rule is an obligation and the self for which it is an expectation. An act that is subject to rules of conduct but does not conform to them is also a communication – often even more so – for infractions make news and often in such a way as to disconfirm the selves of the participants. Thus rules of conduct transform both action and inaction into expression, and whether the individual abides by the rules or breaks them, something significant is likely to be communicated. For example, in the wards under study, each research psychiatrist tended to expect his patients to come regularly for their therapeutic hours. When patients fulfilled this obligation, they showed that they appreciated their need for treatment and that their psychiatrist was the sort of person who could establish a 'good relation' with patients. When a patient declined to attend his therapeutic hour, others on the ward tended to feel that he was 'too sick' to know what was good for him, and that perhaps his psychiatrist was not the sort of person who was good at establishing relationships. Whether patients did or did not attend their hours, something of importance about them and their psychiatrist tended to be communicated to the staff and to other patients on the ward.

In considering the individual's participation in social action, we must understand that in a sense he does not participate as a total person but rather in terms of a special capacity or status; in short, in terms of a special self. For example, patients who happen to be female may be obliged to act shameless before doctors who happen to be male, since the medical relation, not the sexual one, is defined as officially relevant. In the research hospital studied, there were both patients and staff who were Negro, but this minority group status was not one in which these individuals were officially (or even, in the main, unofficially) active. Of course, during face-to-face encounters individuals may participate officially in more than one capacity. Further, some unofficial weight is almost always given to capacities defined as officially irrelevant, and the reputation earned in one capacity will flow over and to a degree determine the reputation the individual earns in his other capacities. But these are questions for more refined analysis.

In dealing with rules of conduct it is convenient to distinguish two classes, symmetrical and asymmetrical. A symmetrical rule is one which leads an individual to have obligations or expectations regarding others that these others have in regard to him. For example, in the two hospital wards, as in most other places in our society, there was an understanding that each individual was not to steal from any other individual, regardless of their respective statuses, and that each individual could similarly expect not to be stolen from by anyone. What we call common courtesies and rules of public order tend to be symmetrical, as are such biblical admonitions as the rule about not coveting one's neighbor's wife. An asymmetrical rule is one that leads others to treat and be treated by an individual differently from the way he treats and is treated by them. For example, doctors give medical orders to nurses, but nurses do not give medical orders to doctors. Similarly, in some hospitals in America nurses stand up when a doctor enters the room, but doctors do not ordinarily stand up when a nurse enters the room.

Students of society have distinguished in several ways among types of rules, as for example, between formal and informal rules; for this paper, however, the important distinction is that between substance and ceremony. A substantive rule is one which guides conduct in regard to matters felt to have significance in their own right, apart from what the infraction or maintenance of the rule expresses about the selves of the persons involved. Thus, when an individual refrains from stealing from others, he upholds a substantive which primarily serves to protect the property of these others and only incidentally functions to protect the image they have of themselves as persons with proprietary rights. The expressive implications of substantive rules are officially considered to be secondary; this appearance must be maintained, even though in some special situations everyone may sense that the participants were primarily concerned with expression.

A ceremonial rule is one which guides conduct in matters felt to have secondary or even no significance in their own right, having their primary importance – officially anyway – as a conventionalized means of communication by which the individual expresses his character or conveys his appreciation of the other participants in the situation. This usage departs from the everyday one, where 'ceremony' tends to imply a highly specified, extended sequence of symbolic action performed by august actors on solemn occasion when religious sentiments are likely to be invoked. In wanting to stress the common element in such practices as tipping one's hat and a coronation, I will neglect what many anthropologists would see as overriding differences.

In all societies rules of conduct tend to be organized into codes which guarantee that everyone acts appropriately and receives his due. In our society the code which governs substantive rules and substantive expressions comprises our law, morality, and ethics, while the code which governs ceremonial rules and ceremonial expressions is incorporated in what we call etiquette. All of our institutions have both kinds of codes, but in this paper attention will be restricted to the ceremonial one.

The acts or events, that is, the sign-vehicles or tokens which carry ceremonial messages, are remarkably various in character. They may be linguistic, as when an individual makes a statement of praise or depreciation regarding self or other, and does so in a particular language and intonation; gestural, as when the physical bearing of an individual conveys insolence or obsequiousness; spatial, as when an individual precedes another through a door, or sits on his right instead of his left; task-embedded, as when an individual accepts a task graciously and performs it in the presence of others with aplomb and dexterity; part of the communication structure, as when an individual speaks more frequently than the others, or receives more attentiveness than they do. The important point is that ceremonial activity, like substantive activity, is an analytical element referring to a component or function of action, not to concrete empirical action itself. While some activity that has a ceremonial component does not seem to have an appreciable substantive one, we find that all activity that is primarily substantive in significance will nevertheless carry some ceremonial meaning, provided that its performance is perceived in some way by others. The manner in which the activity is performed, or the momentary interruptions that are allowed so as to exchange minor niceties, will infuse the instrumentally-oriented situation with ceremonial significance.

All of the tokens employed by a given social group for ceremonial purposes may be referred to as its ceremonial idiom. We usually distinguish societies according to the amount of ceremonial that is injected into a given period and kind of interaction, or according to the expansiveness of the forms and the minuteness of their specification; it might be better to distinguish societies according to whether required ceremony is performed as an unpleasant duty or, spontaneously, as an unfelt or pleasant one.

Ceremonial activity seems to contain certain basic components. As suggested a main object of this paper will be to delineate two of these components, deference and demeanor, and to clarify the distinction between them.

25

Classroom Language *

Douglas Barnes

Both the 1966 and the 1967 lessons provided many examples of what the investigators came to call 'pseudo-questions', since they appeared open but were treated by the teacher as closed. For example, in Lesson L (the 1967 science lesson) the teacher asked:

T   What can you tell me about a bunsen burner, Alan?

P1   A luminous and a non-luminous flame.

T   A luminous and a non-luminous flame . . . When do you have a luminous flame?

P1   When there's . . . there's oxygen.

T   When the airhole is closed . . . When is it a non-luminous flame, Gary?

P2   When . . . when the airhole is open.

T   Right . . . good . . .

The original question requires the pupil to abstract from all possible statements about the bunsen burner, that one which the teacher's unstated criterion finds acceptable. He is presumably helped to do this by memories of a former lesson on the topic. Our samples suggest that it is not unusual for teachers to ask children to conform to an unstated criterion; children might participate better if the criteria were explicit.

Another group of 'pseudo-questions' appears to relate to classroom procedure but should perhaps be reckoned as 'social' in function. For example, in Lesson F (1966; grammar school; chemistry lesson) has several such questions:

T   Now what we want is a method whereby we can take off this . . . um . . . green material . . . this green stuff off the grass and perhaps one or two of you can suggest how we might do this . . . Yes?

P1   Boil it.

T   Boil it? What with?

* *Language, Learner and the School*, Penguin Books, 24–25, 28–29, 43–44, 48–49.

P1   Some water in a beaker and . . .

T   Yes, there's that method . . . we could do it and . . . um . . . I think probably you could guess how we might be able to do it by what we've already got out in the laboratory. How do you think we might do it?

(Pestle and mortar on on bench.)

P2   Could pound it . . .

T   Pound it up with water . . . and that's exactly what we're going to do.

The teacher having, perhaps necessarily, predetermined the method to be used, asks the question in order to involve his pupils more personally into the activity. But this forces him (a) to interrupt a pupil who is thinking aloud ('some water in a beaker and . . .') and (b) to reject that pupil's reasonable suggestion. It could be argued that both of these are to be avoided for pedagogical reasons.

The teacher in Lesson F (1966; chemistry; grammar school) might have described the following as 'discussion'. He was explaining that milk is an example of the suspension of solids in a liquid:

T   You get the white . . . what we call casein . . . that's . . . er . . . protein . . . which is good for you . . . it'll help to build bones . . . and the white is mainly the casein and so it's not actually a solution . . . it's a suspension of very fine particles together with water and various other things which are dissolved in water . . .

P1   Sir, at my old school I shook my bottle of milk up and when I looked at it again all the sides was covered with . . . er . . . like particles and . . . er . . . could they be the white particles in the milk . . .?

P2   Yes, and gradually they would sediment out, wouldn't they, to the bottom . . .?

P3   When milk goes very sour though it smells like cheese, doesn't it?

P4   Well, it is cheese, isn't it, if you leave it long enough?

T   Anyway can we get on . . . We'll leave a few questions for later.

What is happening here? The teacher talks about milk, using his specialist language to help him perceive it as an exemplar of the category 'suspension', and to free him from all other contexts and categories it might appear in. But for his pupils 'milk' collocates not with 'suspension' but with 'cheese', 'school', 'shook', 'bottle'; they perceive it in that context and his use of 'casein' and 'fine particles' signals to only two of them that some different response is expected. Pupil 1 recognizes 'particles' and, searching his experience, comes up with lumps of curd. Trying to conform to the teacher's expectation, he manages 'the side was covered with . . . like particles', his uncertainty finding its expression in the deprecatory 'like'. Pupil 2 follows this line of thought and, associating the idea of sedimentation with suspended particles, tries 'they would sediment out'. These two pupils are beginning to use the language of science to make the specifically scientific abstraction from the experience. But Pupils 3 and 4, although *they are attentive to what the teacher appears to be saying* are unable to make this abstraction; the words the teacher has used do not signal to them which aspects of the 'milk' experience should be abstracted. Far from helping them to bridge the gulf between his frame of reference and theirs, the teacher's language acts as a barrier, of which he seems quite unaware. They are left with their own first-hand experience – 'it smells like cheese'. The state of the other less articulate members of the class can only be guessed at. The teacher, frightened by his sudden glimpse of the gulf between them, hastily continues with the lesson he has planned.

This teacher teaches within his frame of reference; the pupils learn in theirs, taking in his words, which 'mean' something different to them, and struggling to incorporate this meaning into their own frames of reference. The language which is an essential instrument to him is a barrier to them. How can the teacher help his pupils to use this language as he does? Certainly not by turning away from the problem.

* * *

A quite different kind of explicitness was sought by the teacher of Lesson D (1966; geography; girls' grammar school). The class was looking at a photograph of sand dunes:

T Sand dunes. They're usually in an unusual . . . a specific shape . . . a special shape . . . Does anybody know what shape they are? Not in straight lines . . .
P They're like hills.
T Yes, they're like low hills.
P They're all humpy up and down.
T Yes, they're all humpy up and down.
P They're like waves.
T Good, they're like waves.
P They're like . . .
T They're a special shape.
P They're like boulders . . . sort of go up and down getting higher and higher.
T I don't know about getting higher and higher.
P Something like pyramids.

T   Mm . . . wouldn't call them pyramids, no.

P   They're in a semi-circle.

T   Ah, that's getting a bit nearer. They're often in a semi-circle and nearly always . . . we call them . . . well, it's part of a semi-circle . . . What do we call part of a semi-circle? You think of the moon . . . perhaps you'll get the shape.

P   Water.

T   No, not shaped like water . . . Yes?

P   An arc.

T   An arc . . . oh, we're getting ever so much nearer.

P   Crescent.

T   A crescent shape. Have you heard that expression . . . a crescent shape? I wonder if anybody could draw me a crescent shape on the board. Yes, they're nearly all that shape.

Although the teacher seems from the first to have been looking for the verbal label, 'crescent', in the course of searching for it language was used in quite other ways than in merely offering a series of labels for rejection or acceptance. At first the girls, who had a picture (and probably some personal experience) to start from, took the question as an invitation to *make this experience explicit*. Thus we have 'like hills', 'like waves', 'sort of go up and down getting higher and higher', and the strikingly evocative 'all humpy up and down'. They are not taking the shared experience of shape as given and finding a name for it; they are exploring *what meaning any agreed name should have*. But 'like pyramids' turns the class towards the labelling function of language, so that 'in a semi-circle', having earned the teacher's approval, directs the class towards 'arc' and 'crescent'.

Would the class have gained as much if the name 'crescent' had come as an immediate answer to the first question? What did they gain? Why is this the only case in twelve lessons when the personal meaning of a word was explored? Does this represent a significant lack in the learning experience of younger secondary pupils, or is this merely a chance bias of the small sample? What function has language like 'all humpy up and down' for the child who used it? Is it the vestige of something to come? This single example can raise these questions but not answer them.

*   *   *

Indeed, in many of the twenty-two examples examined it is hard to say what value could come either from defining a term or in providing a term for a concept which pupils had already verbalized successfully. An extreme case occurred in Lesson F:

T   We're going to cut the grass into small pieces and then we're going to put it into the . . . what we call a mortar . . . this is what we call a mortar . . . this bowl . . . and anyone know what we call the other thing which we're going to pound it in?

The act of giving a technical name seems for many teachers to have taken on a value of its own in separation from its utility; in this case the naming activity is totally irrelevant to the process which it interrupts.

Later in the same lesson the teacher, his attention upon purposeless name teaching, fails to notice a pupil whose reply shows his incomprehension.

T   Now I don't know whether any of you could jump the gun a bit and tell me what actually is this green stuff which produces green colour . . .

P   Er . . . um . . . water.

T   No . . . Have you heard of chlorophyll?

The pupil's reply should have warned the teacher that there were children in the class to whom he was communicating nothing. (When seen in the total context of the lesson, the child's reply must mean no less than this.)

This makes the teacher's wish to teach the word 'chlorophyll' doubly irrelevant. His desire to teach terminology prevents him from perceiving his true tasks.

In Lesson E (1966; biology; comprehensive school) also, the biological terminology seems to take a value of its own:

T   Where does it go then?

P   To your lungs, Miss.

T   Where does it go before it reaches your lungs? . . . Paul.

P   Your windpipe, Miss.

T   Down the windpipe . . . Now can anyone remember the other word for windpipe?

P   The trachea.

T   The trachea . . . good . . . After it has gone through the trachea where does it go then? . . . There are a lot of little pipes going into the lungs . . . what are those called? . . . Ian?

P   The bronchii.

T   The bronchii . . . that's the plural . . . What's the singular? What is one of these tubes called? . . . Ann.

P   Bronchus.

T   Bronchus . . . with 'us' at the end . . . What does 'inspiration' mean . . .?

This too is an extreme case, which underlines an assumption shared in some degree by six of the twelve teachers; the teaching of terminology is seen as part of the task. It is clear from the substitution of 'trachea' for 'windpipe' that it is not merely the referential function of the word that is valued; the teacher is valuing that of the two synonyms which carries with it (for her, not the pupils, of course) the stronger suggestion of a strictly biological context.

* * *

It is the teacher of Lesson G (1966; physics; comprehensive school) who makes the most consistent effort to use language which will carry precise meaning to his pupils without building a wall of formality between them. 'The tin box only moves a tiny bit so the pointer has got to move a big lot', and 'Why does the tin have crinkly edges?' and 'It would be really squashed-in-like'. Some teachers feel that this is a betrayal of standards, but this is probably not justifiable. Although the reader cannot tell whether 'crinkly' means 'serrated' or 'corrugated' or something else, this must have been clear enough in the lesson. Nor can the colloquial 'like' be objected to except upon grounds of social propriety. The language serves its purpose well: it directs the pupils' attention to the appropriate aspect of the apparatus, when the very unfamiliarity of technical terms might discourage attentiveness. If it is argued that pupils will later require a more specialized register at least for their written work, this may well be conceded. Yet this teacher, by encouraging pupils to talk about this subject matter in terms which they already possessed, was probably helping them more effectively towards this, than a teacher who threw his pupils in at the deep end of his own adult language. Because of an inadequate recording it is impossible to give any lengthy quotations of the kind of participation by the pupils which this teacher's informality made possible. Some impression of their contributions can, however, be gained from isolated questions such as: 'Please sir, if you go up a high mountain when you get near the top you feel sick', and 'Sir, if you climbed a high height in the car would the engine stop?' These are quite different from the contributions of any other class, even in the same school. It is easier to illustrate the teacher's style:

T   This is almost the same as that one . . . a slightly different arrangement . . . cut in half . . . you see it? . . . little tin can . . . silver thing in the middle . . . silver thing with circles on it? . . . that's that tin can . . . tin can just like that one . . . all right . . . on a good day then what is going to happen to the shape of that? Is it going to go . . . down? . . . Do you know? . . . See what happens to the pointer. Well that pointer's got to be connected . . .

It seems reasonable to assume that this teacher's unusual language, informal and yet exactly adjusted to the apparatus, is related to his

302

pupils' equally unusual degree of active participation in the lesson. This is not, of course, to argue that pupils should not eventually be asked to write in a more formal way about this material, once they have mastered it.

Part Five
Perspectives on Learning

When Koch (1969)[1] wrote that in spite of all the 'theoretical formulations, rational equations, mathematical models . . . (and) thousands of research studies . . . our actual insight into the learning processes . . . has not improved one jot', he could as well have been reflecting on the state of sociology as of psychology. This is perhaps not so surprising when one considers that such enquiries rarely treat as their problem what is to constitute 'learning' (or what they claim to be theorizing about). This also seems to be a feature of the protagonists of both sides in the current debate on 'active' and 'passive' theories of learning – or as it is usually referred to, 'socialization', that catch-all explanatory concept of so much social science.

In their very different ways the readings in this section offer the possibility of rethinking the conceptions about learning (and by implication, of teaching) on which most educational research and practice are so uncritically based. The first four readings (Reisman and Gusfield, Denzin, Leacock, and Dumont and Wax) suggest that learning is not so much a property of particular activities, but rather the ascription of particular meanings by some, usually teachers and other adults, to the actions of others, usually children or students. Geer and her associates highlight the complexities of any so-called 'formal' learning situations: what it is important to know and what can be learnt may be quite different from what is made available in the 'official' hierarchy of teacher and taught. Though Becker and Worth and Adair's accounts deal respectively and very specifically with LSD-users and film-makers, in doing so they raised fundamental questions about models of education that are very much part of the tradition that is classically exemplified in the writing of Durkheim. In recognizing that 'learning' cannot be conceived as a separate activity, distinguished in some objectively definable way from the interpretive work we are engaged in all the time, these readings point to the untenability of the pervasive notion of education as 'cultural transmission'. Likewise the notion of 'education as initiation' can best be seen as an all too plausible myth, for how could the supposedly 'uninitiated' Navajo make films? The possibility both as a teaching and a research enterprise of exploring, as Worth and Adair do, how people use the knowledge they have in novel contexts, seems considerable.

All the studies point to the importance of recognizing that 'learning' is always and irremediably an essential feature of being human, but that many of the possibilities of being human are not recognized as 'learning' in the contexts people find themselves in, not the least significant of such contexts being school. The final extract from Freire emphasizes the project of any sociology of education to authenticate the possibilities of all men as learners, and as such, not to digest the knowledge of others but to 'name their world'.

References

[1] S KOCH, 'Psychology cannot be a coherent science', *Psychology Today* **3**, 1969.

26

Styles of Teaching

Joseph Gusfield and David Riesman *

Evocative and Didactic Styles

Let us begin with illustrations. At Elmswood we visited a psychology class in which the topic was 'Research on Small Groups'. Some thirty or thirty-five students sat in rows of separate light armchairs. (The seats were moveable and could have been arranged in seminar fashion, and were so arranged on another occasion in a section meeting of the Western Civilization course.) The class began at the sound of the bell. The instructor had mimeographed a number of sociometric matrices and had put the same table on the blackboard. He then proceeded to show how Robert Bales, using such data, had derived his typology of leaders of small groups. The instructor, moving about the room, standing, and sitting on the desk, managed to convey a great deal of his own excitement about the elegance and clarity of Bales' ideas. He lectured without a break for questions and comments, the students paid attention, most of them taking notes. (On another day, the instructor set aside time for specific questions concerning materials.) About two minutes before the end of the fifty-minute class, many of the students began to put away their books. The lecture seemed extremely well organized as well as contagious in communicating the lecturer's excitement and pleasure about research on small groups. As far as we could tell, the students were diligent, although there was no way of gauging their involvement in the material.

We have termed such a style of teaching *didactic*. It was labeled a lecture rather than a discussion, although in principle there could be lectures which are more evocative and less didactic than this one, and there could be discussions that would also be didactic: oriented towards pleasing the teacher through finding the right answers. A didactic class takes for granted the instructor's greater knowledge and authority, and invites students into the material on terms set by the instructor, terms often set by his academic guild. The initiative lies entirely in the instructor's hands: the class is a production in which he

* R. Morrison (ed), *The Contemporary University in the USA*, Houghton Mifflin, 1965, 249–257

is the producer, the director, the writer, while the students act at his direction and are the ultimate audience. Even if the actors are allowed to play bit parts, this does not greatly change the mode of production.

Another class we attended was a social science discussion section at Hawthorne in which, as it happened, small groups were also the topic. In a classroom used by the School of Education, six girls and three boys were entertaining themselves by reading the children's literature on the bookshelves while awaiting the instructor who was ten minutes late for his nine o'clock class. A group of wooden tables were arranged to form a U pattern, and the six girls all sat on one side opposite the boys. The instructor stood at the open end of the U during the entire period, sometimes walking to the blackboard and sometimes standing at the table.

He began the class by quoting from the syllabus. After reading a quotation proposing that the next logical step after studying 'relations' was to study 'small groups', he asked, 'Why is the study of small groups the next logical step?' Variations on this question comprised the content of the period. He wrote on the blackboard the terms describing the major topics studied during this term in the social-science sequence, namely: relation, small groups, socialization, differentiation, pattern. 'What we want to do is get the logical connection between "relations" and "small groups".'

He proceeded by asking questions and soliciting answers from the students until he received an answer he regarded as satisfying. Students also volunteered, and he called on them, at times ignoring some of the volunteers. He managed to draw out the point that moving from relation to small group was an increase in depth and a decrease in extensiveness.

The participation of the class grew as the hour went on and most of the students volunteered at some time. The instructor's questions set up tensions of finding the 'right' answer, tensions which would be dissipated when he moved on to the next point. Several times a student interrupted to make suggestions, but the instructor did not encourage him. This same student, at another time, proposed a logical, but false, solution to a problem; the instructor shrugged his shoulders, said 'maybe', and passed on to others in his quest for the answer he wanted. Occasionally, dialogue would develop among students. The instructor would sit back and listen, and then return to the earlier point at issue. Five minutes before the hour's close, the instructor himself began to answer the major questions with which he had opened. He said that the relation among the various terms or headings was not additive. Then he stated the original question again and read the answer from the syllabus, explaining each term, such as locus and constellation.

It would seem on the surface that this second class was more evocative than the first one. Perhaps it was. Certainly it was overtly participative. Many students might well feel that they took a more active part when they raised their voices than when they were silent. But such an assumption would neglect both the vicarious evocativeness that is possible in a lecture and the over-controlled activism of a discussion where the prime task of the student is to fill in the blanks on a diagram already given. One could say that, in this second classroom, both students and teacher were subordinate to the syllabus, but the responsibility for the proper outcome remained almost entirely in the instructor's hands. The latter saw the task as getting the students to understand the syllabus, to 'cover ground', or to get across a certain content. In fact, though he brought the students in as props, he conveyed somewhat less enthusiasm for his subject than did the instructor at Elmwood.

Our notes on another social-science class at Hawthorne may illuminate the differences here. This also took place in a borrowed classroom, too large for the five boys and six girls constituting the class. Here, the students clustered together at one end of a U-shaped arrangement of the tables, and the instructor sat close to the students; the effect was that of a small group huddling together in the corner of a large room. The class began with a question from one of the boys, asked just before the bell rang. Erving Goffman's article, 'On Face-Work,' had been assigned in the week's reading, and the student wanted to know if the article related to the concept of 'patterns'. The instructor responded to this as a prelude. Then he began the class by asking the group, 'What impressed you most in this section?' One of the girls responded, 'The article on the dyad.' (She was referring to an essay by Georg Simmel on numbers and social groups which was also part of the assignment.) A boy commented, 'We know these things ourselves, but we have never realized them before.' A middle-aged woman asked if this article on the dyad was sociology or philosophy, and the instructor said, 'Let's defer the question until we find out more about the idea of relation.'

The concept of relation then occupied much of the discussion. The middle-aged woman talked of this in the light of her personal experiences, and an exchange developed between this woman and a girl sitting next to her, who disagreed with her conclusions. This exchange became heated, but the instructor did not interfere. Then he asked if a relation ends when a person dies. He mentioned a primitive tribe in which the death of a person was followed by the adoption of a child to replace the relative. The older woman compared this to a Jewish custom, that of naming a child after a dead person. One of the students responded to this, as the instructor did also.

Only when the topic seemed to have exhausted itself did the instructor move on to something else. 'What did you think of Orwell's essay, "Shooting an Elephant"?' This elicited a few reactions, how a person might be led to an action violating his own ethical norms. The irrepressible woman said that one might be put into a position of feeling obligated to comply with another's demands. A boy entered the discussion in very general terms, using the word 'relation' pretentiously in an apparent effort to impress the instructor. The instructor did not respond to this but sought instead to get students to talk about their own lives as a way of illustrating his questions about the Orwell essay. He asked whether any of them had ever felt themselves in a situation where, as in 'Shooting an Elephant', there was only one thing to do in the light of the expectations of others.

By this time, half the class time had elapsed, and most of the eleven students had participated. The instructor tried different ways of escaping the domination of the middle-aged woman, sometimes ignoring her and sometimes encouraging others to speak in order to shunt her out of the discussion. In the remaining time, the discussion turned to dyadic and triadic relations, and students drew on their own relationships with friends and relatives for illustration. After the bell had rung, the instructor suggested they write a paper on face-work and dating behavior. Someone asked if it could be a personal experience, and the instructor said it could.

Chaotic as this class may have seemed to those accustomed to more structure classroom situations, the instructor was in charge at all times. But his effort was less to cover ground or to convey ideas than to get the students to connect what they were reading with their own experience, even at the cost of a certain fuzziness of outline. What he rewarded was never the correct answer – nor did he actually propose 'correct' answers – but rather the effort by students to draw on personal observation and to gain a new purchase on it through the reading and discussion. Mere slinging of terms uncoupled with experience was negatively sanctioned. In considerable measure, what happened was not in the script. For one thing, the older, talkative woman could only barely be kept in control; she was indeed meeting the payroll of personal experience, only too much of it. (In one of the classes we visited at Elmwood, just such an older woman, neither innocent nor docile, was of immense help in breaking the ice in a rather frozen discussion where that was what the instructor wanted.) At the same time, the class was not permissive or 'student-centred' in the way those terms are often used, for the instructor was not seeking experience alone and uninterpreted, nor was he allowing students to assault or invade each other under the guise of candor or therapy. We could see that he must have already gone a long way toward reducing the barriers of age and rank. He appeared to use the class to evoke the experiences generated by the materials.

He did not do this in isolation, for a climate of evocativeness was consciously sought for at Hawthorne. And while it might seem that classes in the more 'social' social sciences (or in some of the humanities) would lend themselves more readily to this, we found a similar climate in a class in the natural sciences.

This was a class of about half a dozen students, scheduled for eight o'clock. On the morning we visited it, the instructor arrived about eight minutes late, and the students had already begun asking each other questions about the material. The instructor came in and sat down at the head of the table; and, after the students had handed in their outlines (their reading concerned the historical development of atomic theory), he began the discussion by asking what had led chemists (Davies and Berzelius) to propose a dualistic theory of matter. How did one of the experiments bearing on the idea of elements support the received theory as against new theory? In the state of the art at that time, molecules were thought to repel, while atoms must attract to make up a molecule. The discussion proceeded in question-and-answer fashion in an attempt to develop explanations or theories for the facts that were known at that time.

The instructor at one point referred to an experiment in their readings where, with electrodes and water, there was a separation of water into hydrogen at one pole and oxygen at the other. The problem then became one of developing theory which would resolve the problem of repulsion and attraction. One of the girls made a suggestion, which the instructor restated and then diagrammed on the board. Another student criticized this. The instructor agreed with the criticism and pointed out the grounds for his view. Then the girl tried to defend her original idea against the criticism. The instructor rejected this, explaining in detail why he did so. Then he gave a hint as to how the problem had been solved historically, saying that the ideas of this girl were indeed on the right track. One had to think in terms of a 'mechanical' answer (by which he meant an answer in terms of what atoms were thought to look like). Two members of the class volunteered their own ideas, and the same girl who had presented an idea earlier now proposed an ingenious model of molecules in which the atoms were arranged as on a color wheel. At one point, her model of complementary colors or atoms became complex, and the instructor said she had lost him. She then went to the board and made a diagram of it. The instructor added a new condition to the discussion to see if she could integrate this into her model. One of the boys asked if the model really did explain the facts of the experiment, and those known at the time. Much discussion then focused on the girl's model and its potential usefulness, and another student sought to add to the model. Most of the class entered in.

At this point the instructor pointed out what was unclear in the model and what it failed to take into account, and also indicated the reasons why it would have been rejected in the historical period under consideration. Another boy then suggested a new model. As the hour drew to a close, the instructor himself suggested still another model and pointed out how the girl's model had come close to meeting the problem.

In this class, as compared with the one just described in the social sciences, the emphasis is somewhat more on readings that are to be understood than on experiences that may be shared. Even so, the instructor was not especially concerned with eliciting the correct answer, and what he rewarded in students was the contribution of something interesting, whether or not correct; the materials were a means to elicit the class, to involve it in problem-solving. To be sure, when dealing with the history of science, the instructor could count on less knowledge than when talking about dyads and human relations. But he did his best to erase differences of age and knowledge so that the students would feel free to talk and make mistakes.

One might wonder whether the examinations would provide any control over the instructor's balancing act between conveying context and creating an experience of discovery for the student. To a certain extent, the entire staff in the social sciences and the natural sciences at Hawthorne shared an ideology about their methods of teaching and the kinds of examinations they gave. These could be answered without a premium on factual accuracy or clarity of outline. But beyond that, a certain looseness pervaded the examination system itself, especially in the social sciences, where students were permitted to take examinations over again and erase previous failures and where, in any case, in the casual climate of a state university, students did not feel that they must graduate in a four-year lockstep. Hawthorne opposed premature specialization, and, to the degree that its students in fact wanted to prepare themselves as undergraduates for specific careers or to acculturate themselves in a specialty, they could do so on the larger campus outside Hawthorne. This allowed Hawthorne to maintain its sense of mission through its tension with that larger campus. In the Hawthorne ideology, didactic teaching was considered suitable for the development of specialists and 'mere technicians', but not conducive to meeting the kinds of intellectual and personal issues which could prepare a student emotionally for academic life, or for comparable professional goals.

In this ideology, in our judgment, an error is sometimes made in seeing didactic teaching not only as authoritative, but also as authoritarian. This psychological transposition is not automatically justified. In our observations at Hawthorne, we saw a good many classes in which the instructor appeared to be merely one of the boys, sitting on the desk with his coat off, swinging his legs and talking in hipster argot, drawing on his own experiences in order to evoke those of the students. But such a procedure, as any student of transference realizes, can be quite intrusive and oppressive, stifling to a student who wants to maintain his distance and even his individuality. Conversely, a didactic class can be conducted with genuine warmth, simply recognizing and employing the instructor's greater knowledge and experience.

Nevertheless, we are inclined to think that in dealing with the sort of student body drawn to both institutions, didactic styles of teaching have certain limitations which would perhaps be less evident in elite colleges where the students come already conversant with ideas and prepared to enjoy the play of the mind.

Our misgivings can be suggested by an experience on one of our early visits to Elmwood. We had been observing classes and talking with some faculty members about the diligence of the students, their readiness to work extremely hard. There was some surprise at this, for the young faculty had been recruited from leading institutions and had come expecting to be faced with Midwestern philistinism and a 'collegiate' withdrawal of effort. It appeared that the students, coming as isolated commuters, had not formed themselves in a cohesive student culture to resist faculty demands even though these were exorbitant in the light of previous high-school experience. Yet, some of the faculty were vaguely dissatisfied. They told us about what had occurred when, a few days earlier, the students in the required Western Civilization course had been asked to see a showing of *Henry V*, the Laurence Olivier film, in an effort to lend vividness and excitement to materials currently being read. To the faculty's dismay, the students had attended *Henry V* as they would have attended a lecture, with assiduity rather than delight. Anxiously and effortfully, they had sought to grasp what it was about and what they were expected to get out of it. Indeed, the film had not been required, as became evident when many other voluntary cultural events were offered at the College, the great majority of students would not have gone to the film but would have attended to their required reading, to their part-time jobs, to the families with whom they lived, or to the bursts of relaxation they deemed owing to them.

Experiences of the sort typified by the showing of *Henry V* suggested to some Elmwood faculty members the limits of a didactic program even for preparing specialists. To become, for instance, a professor of English, one needs to possess more than a force-fed knowledge of Elizabethan drama, although how much more is an open question. Mere diligence is unlikely to carry a student through the rigor, boredom, and uncertainty of graduate school; some additional motivation, some at least rudimentary interest in the topic, some connection between the topic and one's inner life may also be required. To be sure, all of us know many men and women in academic life who have suffered an attrition of interest and simply go through the motions, as they might in some other bureaucratic or entrepreneurial post. But we are dealing here with students who, until they arrived at Elmwood or Hawthorne, in almost no case would have imagined becoming a professor; a school-teacher, yes, for that was a familiar role, or an engineer, or some vaguely defined respectable white-collar job. Both colleges did, in fact, in their very first years, produce a number of converts to the academic life, who have gone on to leading graduate schools, legitimizing the possibility for later generations of students. But, when they entered as freshmen, most of them were scarcely aware of the fields of knowledge into which they are now going. A number of students we have interviewed or talked with informally have given us the impression that it was an evocative rather than a didactic type of instructor who furnished the original inspiration and impetus.

Who Is a Good Teacher?

In addition to sitting in on classes we asked faculty members in both colleges what it was that made them feel they had done a good job of teaching. Here again one could see a range between the didactic and the evocative, between the communication of content and the communication of commitment or involvement. The former style is illustrated by the response of a mathematician at Elmwood to the question, 'What is a good class? When do you feel you've done a good job of teaching?'

'When you teach mathematics and teach something difficult and feel that the students are getting it – you can sense the reaction. A good day is when I feel I've had difficult concepts and have gotten them across.'

Another Elmwood mathematician placed his emphasis less on the clarity of communication and more on the creation of an affective stance toward the subject:

'I feel I've done a good job with these students in this class. Everyone distrusted mathematics when we began and dared me to get them to like it. Now they are interested. They are reading and getting together. There is a difference between active and passive students though . . . (like the active theater-goer) the active student must be part of the process . . . A good teacher is going to create this atmosphere.'

An anthropologist at Hawthorne talked at length about this horror of distant and didactic teaching in large, impersonal settings. For him, a good class was one which was responsive to itself; he continued:

'When no one addresses himself to anyone else's point it's a poor discussion . . . when it gets off the ground there is a certain sense of excitement, talking to each other. The instructor becomes a part of the group.'

In contrast he described a bad class:

'As I was more directive, they were more silent. The class became polarized into a student-against-family situation . . . the students began to get the idea that they shouldn't participate, that, like high school, they should play it cool.'

In this interview, nothing was said about content; and, when we observed the classes of this same instructor, it was clear that he made efforts to erase any symbols of authority that came from his knowledge and rank. For him and for others in the markedly evocative group of teachers, the idea was a classroom in which they were, at most, first among equals, following the line of the students' own interests as brought in from outside the readings, and seeking as an outcome insight and involvement rather than skill or finesse.

Sitting in on such a classroom, the observer might suppose that no demands were being made on the students who were being encouraged or permitted to trade personal anecdotes with the instructor. Such an interpretation would overlook the demands these evocative instructors (more dominant at Hawthorne, but not wholly absent at Elmwood) made upon the students for adopting a certain style of intellectual-emotional involvement; indeed, the insistent encouragement to become an intellectual, critical of received patterns and ideas, was often extended by quite charismatic instructors who underestimated their impact, seeing themselves as only a member of the peer group. In another form of corruption, the student adopts this style of response of his instructors but not the substance of experience which the style connotes.

315

27

The Work of Little Children *

Norman K Denzin

Societies and people organize themselves into interacting moral orders: families and schools, rich people and poor people, the educated and the uneducated, the child and the adult. Relationships between them are grounded in assumptions which justify the various social evaluations. Thus, it is taken as right and proper that the rich should have more privileges than the poor, or that children cannot engage in adult activities. These assumptions are institutionalised and routinely enforced, so that those people who are judged to be less competent are kept in their place. In this article, I want to look at some of the ideologies that surround the adult-child relationship. I shall present data from an on-going field study of young children in 'pre-school', in recreational areas and in families, which challenge the view of children that is taken for granted, at least in America.

Childhood is conventionally seen as a time of carefree, disorganized bliss. Children find themselves under constant surveillance. They are rewarded and punished so that proper standards of conduct can be instilled in their emergent selves. The belief goes that they enjoy non-serious, play-directed activities. They avoid work and serious pursuits at all costs. It is the adult's assignment to make these non-serious selves over into serious actors. In America, this belief lasts at least until the child enters the world of marriage and gainful employment.

There is a paradox in these assumptions. Even if a child or adolescent wants to take part in serious concerns he may find himself excluded. Thus, when the state of California recently passed a law, along the lines already adopted in Britain, giving the vote to 18 year olds, members of the Assembly refused to accord them drinking privileges, and one argument held that eighteen year olds were not yet competent enough to incur debts and assume adult responsibilities (like signing contracts).

The paradox extends beyond exclusion. Even when children go so far as to act in adult-like ways, these actions are usually defined as

* *New Society*, January 1971, 12-14.

unique, and not likely to occur again unless an adult is there to give guidance and direction. This assumption serves to justify the position of the educator. If children could make it on their own, there would be no place for the teacher. This fact is best seen in American pre-schools, where instructors assume that little children have short atten-tion or concentration spans. The belief is quite simple. If left to their own ingenuity, little children become bored. Time structures must be developed, so that the child does not become bored. In California, these timetables typically go as follows:

9–9.15	Hang up coats and say 'Good morning' to other child-ren.
9.15–10:	Play inside on solitary activities (painting, puzzles, toys).
10–10.30:	Go outside for group activities on swing, in sandbox, dancing, making things.
10.30–11:	Juice and biscuit time in small groups around tables.
11–11.20:	Quiet time: small groups around instructors where instructor reads a story.
11.20–11.30:	Get coats and jackets and prepare to be picked up by parents.
11.30:	Session over; instructors relax and have coffee and cigarettes.

When there are clashes over timetable – if, for example, a child refuses to come in for juice and biscuits – an instructor will be dispatched to inform him that it is time to come in.

These timetables are revealing and serve several functions. They tell the instructor what he will be doing at any given moment. They give instructors control over the children. They state that children, if left on their own, could not organize their own actions for two and a half hours.

Another paradox is evident. Although children are systematically informed of their incompetence, and rewarded for the quality of their non-serious conduct, adults appear to assume that something import-ant is happening at these early ages. In fact, it is something so serious that normal, everyday adults cannot assume responsibility for what occurs. As rapidly as possible, the child is taken from the family setting and placed in any number of child-care, educational and baby-sitting facilities.

My interviews with, and observations of, 100 American parents, who delivered their children to a co-operative and experimental pre-school, revealed two assumptions. Firstly, the school was a cheap and effective baby-sitter. The parents had no fears for their child's safety when he was there. Second, if the child was an only child, or if the parents lived in a neighbourhood where there were no other play-mates, the pre-school would expand and cultivate the child's skill at getting on with other children. These parents feared that their child would appear later in kindergarten, and not know how to interact with other children. Because pre-schools do not formally assess how a child is doing, the parents felt fairly safe. They transferred the function of looking after their child's sociability from themselves to a neutral party – the pre-school teacher.

The school, then, gave the parents a year to get the child ready for his first encounter with formal education. The task of the pre-school was to shape up the child's speech and to teach him or her how to be polite and considerate to others. A side function was to give painting, say, which many parents defined as too messy for their homes. Economically stable families with several children were less likely to send their child to the pre-school. Brothers and sisters performed the sociability function of the pre-school.

Let me now note a final paradox. Observers like Iona and Peter Opie – in their *Lore and Language of Schoolchildren*[1] and their *Children's Games in Street and Playground*[2] – have found that, when left on their own, children produce complex societies and social orders.

The fact that many children's games are often spontaneously produced, yet are passed on from generation to generation, and that their songs and stories are made to fit special selves, must indicate the child's ability to be a serious, accountable actor.

An example from the Opies' study of children's games reveals the serious character of play. Here the game is 'playing school':

'The most favourite game played in school is Schools.' says an Edinburgh nine year old. 'Tommy is the headmaster. Robin is the schoolteacher, and I am the naughty boy. Robin asks what are two and two. We say they are six. He gives us the belt. Sometimes we run away from school and what a commotion! Tommy and Robin run after us. When we are caught we are taken back and everyone is sorry.'

In their attendant analysis of this game, the Opies observe:

'Clearly, playing Schools is a way to turn the tables on real school: a child can become a teacher, pupils can be naughty, and fun can be made of punishments. It is noticeable, too, that the most demure child in the real classroom is liable to become the most talkative when the canes are make-believe.'

Urie Bronfenbrenner's recent study[3] of child-rearing practices in the Soviet Union shows, too, that Russians take the games of their young children quite seriously. Such games are used to instill self-reliance and collective respect on the part of the child. Here is one instance:

Kolya started to pull at the ball Mitya was holding. The action was spotted by a junior staff member who quickly scanned the room and then called out gaily: 'Children, come look! See how Vasya and Marusya are swinging their teddy bear together. They are good comrades.' The two offenders quickly dropped the ball to join the others in observing the praised couple, who now swung harder than ever.

Bronfenbrenner notes that such co-operation is not left to chance. From pre-school on, Soviet children are encouraged to play co-operatively. Group games and special toys are designed to heighten this side of self-development.

The point I want to make is that when they are left on their own, young children do not play, they work at constructing social orders. 'Play' is a fiction from the adult world. Children's work involves such serious matters as developing languages for communications; presenting and defending their social selves in difficult situations; defining and processing deviance; and construction rules of entry and exit into emergent social groups. Children see these as serious concerns and often make a clear distinction between their play and their work. This fact is best grasped by entering those situations where children are naturally thrown together and forced to take account of one another.

Many specialists have assumed that young children lack well-developed self-conceptions. My observations show, on the contrary, that as early as four a child can stand outside his own behaviour and see himself from another's perspective. I carried out intensive interviews with fifteen four year olds. These revealed support for the general hypothesis that a person's self-concept reflects the number of people he interacts with. The more friends a child had, or the larger his network of brothers and sisters, the more elaborate his self-conception.

Keith, who was four years seven months old at the time of the interview, described himself as follows:

1 My name is Keith—.

2 I am a boy who plays at a nursery school.

3 If I was asked 'What do you like to play best?' I would say 'I like to dance to my favourite records'! (*What are your favourite records?*) 'Yummy, Yummy'; 'Bonnie and Clyde.'

4. If someone asked me, 'Where do you live?' I'd say, '(Name of street).'

5 If someone said, 'Do you know how to do cartwheels?' I'd say 'No.'

6 If someone said, 'What kind of picture can you draw?' I'd say 'I can draw my favourite things. I like to draw a man's head.' (*Why?*) 'Because so much can be added to it. I'd put hair, a chin, eyes, a forehead, a nose, a mouth, and a chin on it.'

Keith was a leader of the boys' group at the pre-school, had nine good friends, and was one of a family that had two other children. Nancy, on the other hand, was an isolate, having only four acquaintances at school. However, her family also had two other children. Her low integration in the social netowrk of the school is reflected in the fact that she could only give two self-descriptions:

1 I'm at school.

2 I live in (name of city).

As extremes, Keith and Nancy point to a basic feature of life at the pre-school. Insofar as a child is a member of the social life of the pre-school, the more adult-like will be his, or her, behaviour. The social life of the school, then, makes the child into a small adult.

Name games – which take many forms – reveal another side of the child's serious self. Children may reverse or switch names. On a Hallowe'en afternoon, I saw three girls, all aged four, who were sitting around a table mixing pumpkin muffins, systematically assign to themselves and all newcomers the name of the child next to them. The rule was quite simple. Each child was assigned every name in the group but their own. One girl resisted and said: 'That's a mistake! My name isn't Kathy. I'm Susan.' Kathy replied: 'We know your name isn't mine, silly; we're just pretending. We don't mean it.'

There was a clear separation of play, fantasy and serious activity in this eposide. Each girl knew her name. The sequence merely solidified their self-identity. Martha Wolfenstein, in a study of children's humour[4], has observed that inevitably some child will find these games disturbing, refusing to accept the identity that goes with the new name. Probably such children are not yet firmly committed to the identity designated by their proper name.

Name calling is another game. Here, the child's proper name is dropped and replaced by either a variation on that name, or by an approving/disapproving term. Martha Wolfenstein noted names like 'Heinie', 'Tits', 'Freeshow', 'Fuckerfaster', and 'None-of-your-business'. In name-calling games the child's real identity is challenged. He or she is singled out of the group and made a special object of abuse or respect. (Parenthetically, it must be noted that adults also engage in such games. Special names for sports and political figures are examples.)

A more severe game is where the child has his name taken away. The other children simply refuse to interact with him. By taking away his name, they effectively make him a non-person, or non-self. In nameless games the child may be referred to as a member of a social category (young child, honkie, brat, dwarf). In these moments his essential self, as a distinct person is denied.

The Opies have described another name game, which is called 'Names', 'Letters in Your Name' or 'Alphabet'. Here, a child calls out letters in the alphabet, and contestants come forward every time a letter contained in their name is called.

All of these name games reflect the importance children assign to their social lives. A name is a person's most important possession simply because it serves to give a special identity.

In pre-schools, the children are continually constructing rules to designate group boundaries. In those schools where sexual lines are publicly drawn, boys and girls may go so far as to set off private territories where members of the opposite sex are excluded. One observer working with me noted boys and girls in a four-year-old group, carrying posters stating that they were 'Boys' or 'Girls'. On another occasion I observed the creation of a 'Pirate Club' which denied entry to all females and all males who did not have the proper combination of play money for paying their membership dues. This group lasted for one hour. At juice and biscuit time, it was disbanded by the instructor and the boys were made to sweep out their tree house. Adult entry into the club seemed to reduce its interest for the boys.

The study of early childhood conversations reveals several similarities to adult speech. Like adults, young children build up special languages. These languages are silent and gestural. What a child says with his eyes or hands may reveal more than his broken speech. As children develop friendships, 'private' terms and meanings will be employed. To grasp the conversations of young children, it is necessary to enter their language communities and learn the network of social relationships that bind them together. Single words can have multiple meanings. 'Baby' can cover a younger brother or sister, all small children, or contemporaries who act inappropriately. To understand what the word 'baby' means for the child, it is necessary to (a) understand his relationship to the person called a baby, (b) the situation where he uses the word, and (c) the activity he is engaging in at the moment.

Neologisms are especially crucial in the development of new relationships. The involved children attempt to produce a word that outsiders cannot understand. Its use sets them off from the other children; it serves to give a special designation to the newly formed relationship. I observed two girls, aged three, who had suddenly discovered one another. Within an hour they had developed the word 'Buckmanu'. With smiles on their faces they came running inside the pre-school, holding hands and singing their new word. After several repetitions of 'Buckmanu' they came over for juice, and a mother asked them what they were saying. They ignored her and suddenly switched the word to 'Manubuck'. And then, with precision and correct enunciation, they said, 'Manuel bucked us off!' Manuel was the name of a pre-school instructor. They had taken one of his actions (playing horseback) and his name, and forged the two into a new word. Once they revealed the name to the mothers, they ceased using it.

References

[1] IONA AND PETER OPIE, *The Lore and Language of Schoolchildren*, Oxford University Press, 1959.

[2] IONA AND PETER OPIE, *Children's Games in Street and Playground*, Oxford University Press, 1969.

[3] URIE BRONFENBRENNER, *Two Worlds of Childhood: US and USSR*, Russell Sage, New York, 1970.

[4] MARTHA WOLFENSTEIN, 'Children's humour; sex, names, and double meanings' in TOBY TALBOT (ed) *The World of the Child*, Anchor Books, 1968.

28

Abstract versus Concrete Speech: A False Dichotomy *

Eleanor Leacock

Concepts of 'Abstract' and 'Concrete'

Various strategies of speech have been subjected to analysis, particularly in the 'street-corner society' of the ghetto, and consciously elaborated and constantly proliferating terminologies for social situations, personality types, and psychological states have been defined that are no less 'abstract' than the scientific or academic terminologies utlilized (part of the time) by various sections of the white middle-class world. Furthermore, the marked use of metaphor as a form of analytic description, which has been noted among working-class people in general and black people in particular, involves a high order of abstraction. In order to explicate this point, it is first necessary to examine the terms 'abstract' and 'concrete' and their spurious designation as apposing forms of speech or thought, one said to be 'higher', one 'lower'.

Our intellectual tradition that 'abstract' thought is separable from and superior to thinking about 'concrete' things and situations stems, of course, from Plato's statement of the ideal 'form' as the ultimately true, good, and beautiful. Over the centuries the tradition has been reinforced by the generally superior position of the educated man to the manual laborer, and the strong emphasis of education upon philosophy. Yet it was none other than G W F Hegel, one of the more abstruse among nineteenth-century philosophers, who some hundred years ago poked fun at the touting of the 'abstract'.

In a short article entitled 'Who Thinks Abstractly', Hegel spoke of the prejudice for abstract thinking, and wrote:

That everybody present should know what thinking is and what is abstract is presupposed in good society, and we certainly are in good society. The question is merely *who* thinks abstractly? (1966, p 115).

* C CAZDEN ET AL (eds), *Functions of Language in the Classroom*, Teachers College Press, 1972, 121–134.

Not the educated, he answered, but the uneducated, and he continued, 'Good society does not think abstractly because it is too easy, because it is too lowly . . .' (p 116). To illustrate his point, Hegel describes a murderer being led to execution. Ladies may comment that he looks strong, handsome, and interesting; and an insightful person may wonder about the source of the crime in the individual's life history. The populace is horrified. 'How can one think so wickedly and call a murderer handsome?' – or how can one want to excuse him for his crime? Hegel points out:

> This is abstract thinking: to see nothing in the murderer except the abstract fact that he is a murderer, and to annul all other human essence in him with this simple quality (pp 116–117).

If one is driven to argue that such abstraction is not worthy of the name, that it is a mere low-level 'stereotype', one has changed the terms of the discussion, from the relative presence or absence in different groups of abstracting behavior, to a concern with the form and purpose of the abstraction. One must then ask, as Hegel of course intended, what *is* an abstraction, or, conversely, what is it to be 'concrete'?

According to Webster, who as might be expected is not altogether unambiguous on the matter, there seem to be four main notions involved in the term 'abstract': intangibility, generality, separation, and essence. To form a general idea about some intangible but essential quality separated from any context is the epitome of abstraction. To abstract is 'to think of [a quality] apart from any particular instance or material object that has it; form [a general idea] from particular instances.' Interestingly enough, in its etymological meaning, 'to draw from' or 'separate', it has also meant 'to take dishonestly', 'to purloin'.

As long as 'concrete' refers to some immediately experienced specific event or tangible object, it appears to be altogether different from 'abstract'. But the matter is not so simple, and elements of intangibility, generality, separation, and essence all creep in at some point. The etymological meaning of concrete is 'to unite or coalesce into a mass', and a term that designates not only a thing but 'a class of things' may still be concrete if these are things that 'can be perceived by the senses, as opposed to naming a quality or attribute'. One can have a 'concrete idea'. According to Webster, 'man' is a concrete term, 'human' is abstract.

It would be concrete, then, according to Webster, to have an idea of 'tables', but abstract to have an idea of 'tableness'. The question is, is the first possible without the second? The linguist Eric Lenneberg suggests that it is not. He writes:

324

In all languages of the world *words label a set of relational principles* instead of being labels of specific objects. Knowing a word is never a simple association between an object and an acoustic pattern, but the successful operation of those principles, or application of those rules, that lead to using the word 'table' or 'house' for objects never before encountered (1960, p 641; italics added).

Thus the simplest act of naming involves abstracting certain features of an object (both formal and functional – where precisely do tables, desks, and bureaus begin and end?), generalizing on the basis of these features, and referring to the object by a series of stylized sounds. This is 'symboling', or the act that differentiates human from animal behavior. To say as Graham does that any group of people does not find meaning in 'verbal symbols', is utter nonsense. In a criticism of Vernon's work (1969), the sociolinguist Joshua Fishman writes that when such a person, 'himself not a specialist in language theory, language data, or language analysis', relies on studies by others 'who also lack adequate sophistication in these respects':

it is quite predictable that he will regress to crude Whorfianisms ... which describe entire languages or language varieties – and, therefore, their speakers – as characterized by 'necessary' deficiencies in abstractness, flexibility, and so on (1969, p 1108).

One might also question how far one can take such elegant and widely accepted 'abstractions' as beauty, truth, honesty, piety, and so on, without some notion of specific contexts within which they apply. Not far, if one really *thinks* about them, instead of merely parroting them with appropriate remarks or definitions, as happens all too often in our classrooms. Thinking about such notions, 'taken dishonestly' from their contexts, necessarily involves moving back and forth between them and various of their 'concretions'. It involves uniting the 'abstract' and the 'concrete'. Ironically, the failure to do this in scientific research, and the uncritical use of 'abstract' terms, results in their inappropriate concretization; they become implicitly translated into entities that obscure operational thinking about social and natural processes. For instance, in his book *Ethology of Mammals*, R F Ewer writes, 'Behavior is something which an animal has got in the same way as it may have horns, teeth, claws, or other structural features' (Klopfer, 1969). In a critical review of Ewer's book, Peter Klopfer takes issue with his statement and the way in which lumping various acts together under a too-general word leads to the drawing of inappropriate analogies between the actions of humans and those of animals. Klopfer writes:

The notion that behavior is a 'noun,' a palpable entity, has been responsible for much of the nonsense that ethologists have uttered.

We read of 'aggression' accumulating and needing discharge, as if it were a fluid liable to seep through cracks in the cranium. I believe we 'contain' aggression about as much as a radio 'contains' the music we hear issuing from it (1969, p 887).

Unfortunately, operational definitions are accorded a lower status in the classroom than knowing the right name, and naming is all too often confused with knowing or understanding. In psychological testing, children who give operational definitions instead of names for a series of objects are considered not to be 'abstracting,' and a child's response 'Animal' to a set of animal pictures is ranked higher than a response such as 'They all have four legs.' However, the first response may be simple knowing the proper word to say – one would not know what the child's actual concept of 'animal' was until one asked – whereas 'they all have four legs' *abstracts* a common characteristic on the basis of individual thought. It is closer to the operational type of definition so important in scientific endeavor.

A humorous example of how language can be manipulated in a purely 'abstract' fashion, with no reference to meaning, is quoted by Ogden and Richards in their classic work, *The Meaning of Meaning*:

Suppose someone to assert: *The gostak distims the doshes.* You do not know what this means; nor do I. But, if we assume that it is English, we know that *the doshes are distimmed by the gostak.* We know too that *one distimmer of doshes is a gostak.* If, moreover, the *doshes* are *galloons*, we know that some *galloons are distimmed by the gostak.* And so we may go on, and so we often do go on (1946, p 46).

A great deal of teaching amounts in essence to going 'on and on' in this manner, and while it is comfortable for the child habituated to playing the game, it can lead to total confusion for the child who is ill at ease with Standard English and who probably suffers more often from the illusion that participation in classroom discussion necessarily involves real *understanding*. I am sometimes saddened as a college teacher when marking a paper that parrots back my words with reasonable accuracy, although I know the student has barely scraped the surface of understanding. More regrettable, however, is the student who searches for meaning but lacks skill in the use of language, the student who is clumsy about expression according to the formalities of 'educated' discourse. While I will reward the effort with a good mark, I know such a student is slated for failure in terms of higher education, while the successful 'bull artist' is headed for success.

All of this is not the fault of teachers as such, of course, but relates to requirements for professional roles in a society where such roles are rapidly proliferating in what are essentially parasitic and mediating arenas; the enormous expansion of the mass media themselves affords the best example. In addition to the old saw, 'It ain't what you know but who that counts,' must be added, 'It ain't what you say but how you say it.' The behaviorial sciences deserve stringent criticism in this respect. Sigmund Koch, editor of *Psychology: A Study of a Science*, a book that embodies the results of a survey conducted for the American Psychological Association, discusses the shortcomings of the social sciences in terms relevant to the present discussion. He speaks of the extent to which an emphasis on formal rules for discovery has resulted in 'ameaningful thought or inquiry' and a 'fictionalistic, conventionalistic' conception of knowledge, so that thousands of studies, such as on the process of learning, for example, can be conducted without improving our actual insight into the learning process. Koch describes 'meaningful thinking' as necessarily wedded to its object. His view brings us full circle – some of what Lévy-Bruhl saw as 'primitive' and deficient he sees, also using the word 'primitive', as wholly desirable:

> *Meaningful thinking* involves a *direct perception* of unveiled relations that seem to spring from the quiddities, particularities of the objects of thought, the problem situations that form the occasions for thought. There is an organic determination of the form and substance of thought by the properties of the object, the terms of the problem. And these are real in the fullest, most vivid, electric, undeniable way. The mind caresses, flows joyously into, over, around, the relational matrix defined by the problem, the object. There is a merging of person and object or problem. It is a fair descriptive generalization to say that meaningful thinking is ontological in some primitive, accepting, artless, unselfconscious sense (1969, pp 14, 64).

Before proceeding further, it would be helpful to sum up the above points in relation to the three assumptions stated to be false at the outset of this article:

First, all meaningful speech (that is, true speech, not the experimental babbling of the infant or confused utterances of the mentally ill) involves a high and specifically human order of abstraction. Strictly speaking, there is no such thing as 'concrete' speech or language.

Second, like language, thought cannot be separated into the 'abstract' and the 'concrete'. Speculative thought is little understood, but almost by definition it involves moving back and forth between the level of specific phenomena – whether events, objects, or situations – and the level of generalization about properties they may have in common. Even formal logic, the most abstract of all fields, is not devoid of 'concrete' loci of reference.

Third, one can say, however, that some people think more than others, or some more profoundly than others. Having said this, one can then argue that group differences in levels of thought would follow from the fact that 'thinking' behavior is professionalized as a major activity for a sizeable group in technologically advanced societies. The difficulty with this position is, according to the viewpoint represented by Koch, that the professionalization of thought (and, we would add, speech) can as readily lead to its stultification as to its enrichment. As an example, Koch writes:

> Consider the problem of 'learning' . . . . Consider the hundreds of theoretical formulations, rational equations, mathematical models of the learning process that have accrued; the thousands of research studies. . . . Consider also that after all this scientistic effort our actual *insight* into the learning process – reflected in every humanly important context in which learning is relevant – has not improved one jot (1969, p 66).

Our enormous advances in the physical sciences are a product of a vast technological machine, coupled with the creative thinking of a very few. And now, when faced with the need for an understanding of the complex interrelations of phenomena, in the face of the threat to man's existence on this earth we have created, we are stymied.

Group differences in styles of speech (and thought), as we presently know them in our society, involve not more or less 'abstracting' behavior, but differences in the areas wherein conceptualization is more consciously developed, and in the ways in which concepts are expressed or elaborated upon. It is to this point that I now turn, in a consideration of metaphorical usage, since it is conceded to be common in the idiom of the black community.

Metaphor, Abstraction, and the Social Contexts of Speech

The elaboration of the metaphor is only one of the characteristics that have been noted for black speech style. Others are the constant innovation of new terms for 'in-group' interchange; the refinement of terminologies for dealing with social situations and social-psychological types; and the marked concern with linguistic strategies for manipulation, competition, or sheer entertainment; all of which evidence a degree of interest in language that stands in marked contrast to the muted behavior of black children and youth when in formal and threatening situations with teachers, testers, and other such authority figures (cf Kochman, 1969; Abrahams, 1970). However, such linguistic concerns, when noted at all in educational circles, are characteristically considered more a matter of 'expressiveness' than of intellectual ability. 'Playing' with language is not often credited as involving conscious and creative thought, or as evidence of intellectual abilities that can be put to use in the arena of traditional education. It also goes unnoted that metaphorical usages may involve a high level of abstraction.

A metaphor is, according to Webster, the 'use of a word or phrase literally denoting one kind of object or idea in place of another by way of suggesting a likeness or analogy between them.' As examples Webster gives 'the ship *plows* the sea,' and 'a *volley* of oaths.' Metaphors are usually seen as belonging to the world of literature and poetry – as vivid ways of bringing to mind visual images or emotional states. Consider, however, the strictly *intellectual* content of the metaphor. At a symposium on metaphor and symbol, D G James stated that a metaphor is one form of symbol. The metaphor 'is the imagination of one thing in the form of another; it is the mode in which the nature, the *being*, the imagined extra-sensual essence of a thing, is represented by the identification with the apparently different . . .' (1960, p 100). Metaphor depends on the abstraction of qualities perceived as similar from dissimilar phenomena. Howard Nemerov writes in an article on the metaphor, 'Metaphor works on a relation of resemblances; one resemblance draws another, or others, after it' (1969, p 628).

A classroom teacher asks for the difference between two pieces on the same subject that she has read aloud, one a prose selection, the other a poem; the first one, a black eight year old proffers, 'thumped out', the second, the poem, 'silked out'. All too often such a response, if noted at all, would be considered a nice example of the 'expressiveness' somehow 'natural' to black children. In fact, however, it is the result of an intellectual process whereby the child has searched his vocabulary to find the words whose qualities most succinctly express his perception. To give another instance from the same classroom, the teacher urges a group of boys not to exclude another child from their activities. The boys argue that the child is not actively isolated by them, but in parts isolates himself. To clinch the point, a metaphor is employed: the child is forgotten as a marble that has rolled away from the center of the game is forgotten. Through metaphorical usage, the salient points of the situation are abstracted and presented as sharply as possible for the teacher's consideration.

Some further examples of metaphorical perspective are taken from the discussion of black workers on the effects of discrimination in employment and how to organize to combat it. There are the enormous odds against which black people must work: 'They clip your wings and tell you to fly'; 'You take the starch out of a shirt and it doesn't iron too good'; indeed, 'You have to learn to step between the raindrops'. There is the need for leaders, but they must have a following, a 'base': 'An airplane can't get along without an airfield'. There is the behavior of union leaders, 'wheels': 'Wheels run over you'. And the black worker who has been given the security of a staff job with his union: 'He's found his hook, and he's put his coat on it'. Mistaken tactics in relation to two union leaders are evaluated: 'We didn't appraise this situation. There were two dogs at each other's throats bleeding each other to death. We should have played it cool and let them fight with each other.' One was defeated: 'His fangs are pulled. . . .' As for a particularly lurid bit of demagogy from a union official: 'It's not even good rubber for a balloon'.

Through the metaphor, the relevant characteristics of a situation are abstracted and stated in the form of an analogy that clearly divests it of extraneous features. Metaphors employ great linguistic economy; there is no need for the overload of explanatory and qualifying terms that are typically employed in exposition. Unfortunately, however, such terms are themselves often considered the hallmark of scientific thought, so the cognitive aspects of metaphorical usages are generally overlooked. Yet, as Kenneth Burke pointed out in *Permanence and Change*, scientific inquiry itself proceeds metaphorically, through the processes of oversimplification, abstraction, and analogical extension (1937, pp 97–124). It is only in its expositions or 'proofs' that science reverses the process of inquiry and proceeds 'logically'.

Through the use of 'analogical extension', metaphors express, in active form, the process whereby abstract terms commonly arise. Owen Barfield writes that the 'tens of thousands of abstract nouns which daily fill the columns of our newspapers, the debating chambers of our legislatures, the consulting rooms of our psychiatrists' once referred to 'the concrete world of sensuous experience' (1960, pp 52–53). As an amusing example, he offers *scruple*, a word derived from the Latin *scrupulus*, which 'originally meant a small, sharp stone – the kind that gets into your shoe and worries you' (p 50). Thus words for being moved, for going ahead, for drifting, for holding in, for answering, become concepts of motivation, progress, tendency, inhibition, responsibility. For this reason, Burke alludes to abstractions as 'dead metaphors' (1937, p 73), and Barfield speaks of language itself as 'an unconscionable tissue of dead, or petrified, metaphors' (Nemerov, 1969). (Clichés like 'leave no stone unturned' are 'completely *fossilized metaphor(s)*' [Barfield, 1960, p 48; italics in the original].)

Herein lies a problem, however, for as Nemerov indicates, 'these metaphors may be not dead but merely sleeping'; they 'may arise from the grave and walk in our sentences ... something that has troubled everyone who has ever tried to write plain expository prose wherein purely mental relations have to be discussed as though they were physical ones' (1969, p 627). Abstract terminologies, whether scientific or humanistic, are far from the precise and neutral tools they are sometimes considered to be. We are somewhat aware of the semantic load carried by terms such as the various 'isms' that incorporate the weight of far-reaching conflicts in their connotations. We are also somewhat aware of stylistic changes in speech in keeping with different situations (such as when we shift gear in style as well as tone of discourse if a family quarrel is interrupted by a telephone call from, say, a department chairman). We are far from aware, however, of a further social dimension incorporated into our terminologies, the one that arises from the fact that words are the end points (or midpoints) in complex sequences of events; they are 'compressed fables, or histories' (Nemerov, 1969, p 635).

It is largely through the process of 'analogical extension' that scientific terminologies become developed. Burke writes:

Indeed, as the documents of science pile up, are we not coming to see that whole works of scientific research, even entire *schools*, are hardly more than the patient repetition, in all its ramifications, of a fertile metaphor? Thus we have, at different eras in history, considered man as the son of God, as an animal, as a political or economic brick, as a machine, each such metaphor, and a hundred others, serving as the cue for an unending line of data and generalizations (1965, p 95; italics in the original).

And the choice of metaphor, the direction of analogical extension, is governed largely by one's viewpoint, or bias, or, in Burke's terms, one's *interest*. The world is like a pie that can be sliced, terminologically, any number of ways, 'and the course of analogical extension is determined by the particular kind of interest uppermost at the time. . . . The poet may be interested in the sea's anger, the chemist in its iodine . . .' (p 104).

As terminologies become established, they become a mark of common sense, of good taste: 'Good taste is manifested through our adherence to the kinds of relationships already indicated by the terminology of common sense' (BURKE, 1965, p 103). All of which makes it easy for the language – and thought – of those low in status to be misinterpreted, sloughed off. In an extraordinarily candid article, Linda Scheffler, a young counselor working with black and Puerto Rican students in a City College of New York SEEK program, writes of them as at first 'literal-minded, deficient in handling abstract concepts and unable to make appropriate generalizations' (SCHEFFLER,

1969, p 114). After working with them closely and consistently, she finds they grow rapidly in 'functional intellectual capacity', and expresses surprise, since this contradicts accepted psychological theory. Scheffler is clear about the steps whereby her own increased self-awareness and ability to deal honestly and informally with the students' problems have enabled her to find points of identification with them. However, she is not aware of the extent to which her original distance from them was affecting her perception of their intellectual abilities, and of the changes in her that followed a mutual moving toward a common basis for identification and communication. For she herself indicates that language style was more of a problem than intellectual ability for the students. She writes:

> Some students who barely passed introductory courses in the basic skills blossomed and succeeded when they got to regular college courses whose content answered some of the many questions they had about the world around them (p 116).

In conclusion, then, the rapidly growing study of language in its full social context reveals it to be a highly ambiguous and flexible tool for handling strategies of action and interaction, and renders meaningless the stereotyped views about class differences in language style stated at the outset of this article. A final example of linguistic strategy is germane to the significance these conclusions hold for educators. A quatrain of Edwin Markham's, 'Outwitted', illustrates – in metaphor – how a terminological shift in the delineation of the 'we' and the 'they', the 'ingroup' – a different slicing of the social pie – redefines as friendly what are originally hostile expectations for attitudes and actions:

> He drew a circle that shut me out—
> Heretic, rebel, a thing to flout.
> But love and I had the wit to win:
> We drew a circle that took him in!

Bibliography

ROGER D ABRAHAMS, *Positively Black*. Prentice-Hall, Englewood Cliffs, NJ, 1970.

STEPHEN S BARATZ and JOAN C BARATZ, 'Negro Ghetto Children and Urban Education: A Cultural Solution', *Social Education*, **33** (April 1969): 401–405.

OWEN BARFIELD, 'The Meaning of the Word "Literal" '. In L C KNIGHTS and BASIL COTTLE (eds), *Metaphor and Symbol*. Butterworths, London, 1960.

FRANZ BOAS, *The Mind of Primitive Man*. Macmillan, New York, 1938.

KENNETH BURKE, *Attitudes Towards History*. **2.** New Republic, New York, 1937.

——, *A Grammar of Motives*. Prentice-Hall, Englewood Cliffs, NJ, 1945.

——, 'Definition of Man'. *The Hudson Review* **16** (Winter 1963–1964).

——, *Permanence and Change*. Bobbs-Merrill Co, New York, 1965.

——, *Language As Symbolic Action*. University of California Press, Berkeley, 1966.

GEORGE A DORSEY, *The Arapaho Sun Dance*. Columbian Field Museum Publication No 75, *Anthropological Series*, **4** (1903).

ERNEST DRUCKER, 'Cognitive Styles and Class Stereotypes'. In ELEANOR BURKE LEACOCK (ed), *The Culture of Poverty: A Critique*. Simon and Schuster, New York, 1971.

JOSHUA A FISHMAN, Review of VERNON, *Intelligence and Cultural Environment*, and BARATZ and SHUY (eds), *Teaching Black Children to Read*. In *Science* **165** (September 12, 1969): 1108–1109.

EDGAR Z FRIEDENBERG, 'What Are Our Schools Trying to Do?' *The New York Times Book Review* (Special Educational Supplement), September 4, 1969.

GRACE GRAHAM, *The Public School in the American Community*. Harper & Row, New York, 1963.

JOSEPH GLICK, 'Thinking About Thinking, Aspects of Conceptual Organization among the Kpele of Liberia'. Paper given at the meeting of the American Anthropological Association, November 1969.

J P GUILFORD, 'Intelligence Has Three Facets'. *Science* **164** (May 10, 1968): 615–620.

G W F HEGEL, In WALTER KAUFMAN (ed and trans), *Hegel: Texts and Commentary*. Doubleday, Gardan City, NY, 1966.

D G JAMES, 'Metaphor and Symbol'. In L C KNIGHTS and BASIL COTTLE (eds), *Metaphor and Symbol*. Butterworths, London, 1960.

PETER H KLOPFER, Review of EWER, *Ethology of Mammals*. In *Science*, **165** (August 29, 1969), 887.

SIGMUND KOCH, 'Psychology Cannot Be a Coherent Science'. *Psychology Today* **3** (September 1969).

THOMAS KOCHMAN, '"Rapping" in the Black Ghetto'. *Trans-action* **6** (February 1969).

ELEANOR LEACOCK, 'Some Aspects of the Philosophy of the Cheyenne and Arapaho Indians'. Master's Thesis, Columbia University, 1946.

ERIC H LENNEBERG, 'On Explaining Language'. *Science*, **164** (May 9, 1969), 635–643.

LUCIEN LÉVY-BRUHL, *Primitive Mentality*. 1923. Reprint. Beacon, Boston, 1966.

HERBERT MARCUSE, *One-Dimensional Man*. Beacon, Boston, 1964.

HOWARD NEMEROV, 'On Metaphor'. *The Virginia Quaterly Review* **45** (Autumn 1969).

C K OGDEN and I A RICHARDS, *The Meaning of Meaning*. Harcourt, Brace, New York, 1946.

PAUL RADIN, *Primitive Man as Philosopher*. D Appleton and Company, New York, 1927.

——, *The World of Primitive Man*. Henry Schuman, New York, 1953.

LINDA WEINGARTEN SCHEFFLER, 'What SEEK Kids Taught Their Counselor'. *The New York Times Magazine* (November 16, 1969).

PHILIP E VERNON, *Intelligence and Cultural Environment*. Methuen, London, 1969.

HEINZ WERNER, *Comparative Psychology of Mental Development*. Science Editions, New York, 1961.

LESLIE A WHITE, *The Science of Culture*. Farrar, Straus, New York, 1949.

BENJAMIN LEE WHORF, *Language, Thought, and Reality*. MIT Press, Cambridge, Mass, 1956.

29

Cherokee School Society and the Intercultural Classroom *

Robert Dumont and Murray Wax

In this essay we wish to focus on the schools attended by Indian children in the cases where they are the preponderant element of reservations, where the federal government operates a special school system under the administration of the Bureau of Indian Affairs, but also in other regions by virtue of covert systems of segregation. As in the case of Negro/white segregation, the basis is usually ecological. Thus, in northeastern Oklahoma the rural concentrations of Tribal Cherokee along the stream beds in the hill country predispose toward a segregated system at the elementary levels. But the guiding principle is social, so that there is reverse bussing of Tribal Cherokee children living in towns and of middle-class white children living in the countryside. Within the rural elementary schools, the Indian children confront educators who are ethnically and linguistically alien, even when they appear to be neighbours (of Cherokee and non-Cherokee descent) from an adjacent or similar geographic area.

Such classrooms may be denominated as 'cross-cultural', although the ingredients contributed by each party seem to be weighted against the Indian pupils. The nature and layout of the school campus, the structure and spatial divisions of the school buildings, the very chairs and their array, all these are products of the greater society and its culture – indeed, they may at first glance seem so conventional that they fail to register with the academic observer the significance of their presence within a cross-cultural transaction. Equally conventional, and almost more difficult to apprehend as significant, is the temporal structure: the school period; the school day; and the school calendar. The spatial and temporal grid by which the lives of the Indian pupils are organized is foreign to their native traditions, manifesting as it does the symbolic structure of the society which has encompassed them.

* *Human Organization*. **28**, No. 3, Fall, 1969, 219–225.

The observer thus anticipates that the classroom will be the arena for an unequal clash of cultures. Since the parental society is fenced out of the school, whatever distinctive traditions have been transmitted to their children will now be 'taught out' of them; and the wealth, power, and technical supremacy of the greater society will smash and engulf these traditionalized folk. Forced to attend school, the Indian children there must face educators who derive their financial support, their training and ideology, their professional affiliation and bureaucratic status, from a complex of agencies and institutions based far outside the local Indian community. The process is designed to be unidirectional; the children are to be 'educated' and the Indian communities thus to be transformed. Meanwhile, neither the educator nor the agencies for which he is a representative are presumed to be altered – at least by the learning process.

Cherokees in the Classroom

The classrooms where Indian students and a white teacher create a complex and shifting sequence of interactions exhibit as many varieties and reality and illusion as there are possible observers. One such illusion – in the eyes of the white educators – is that the Cherokee are model pupils. Within their homes they have learnt that restraint and caution is the proper mode of relating to others; therefore in the classroom the teacher finds it unnecessary to enforce discipline. As early as the second grade, the children sit with perfect posture, absorbed in their readers, rarely talking – and then only in the softest of tones – and never fidgeting. Even when they are marking time, unable to understand what is occurring within the classroom, or bored by what they are able to understand, they make themselves unobtrusive while keeping one ear attuned to the educational interchange. They respect competence in scholastic work, and their voluntary activities both in and out of school are organized surprisingly often and with great intensity about such skills. Eager to learn, they devote long periods of time to their assignments, while older and more experienced students instruct their siblings in the more advanced arithmetic they will be encountering at higher grade levels.

To the alien observer (whether local teacher or otherwise), the Cherokee children seem to love to 'play school'. The senior author, for example, recalls talking during one recess period with an elderly white woman who had deovted many years to teaching in a one-room school situated in an isolated rural Cherokee community and who now was responsible for the intermediate grades in a more consolidated enterprise that still was predominantly Cherokee. 'You just have to watch these children,' she said. 'If you don't pay no mind,

335

they'll stay in all recess. They like to play school.' And, as if to illustrate her point, she excused herself, went back into the school building, and returned with a straggle of children. 'They told me they had work they wanted to do, but it is too nice for them to stay inside ... You know, I forgot how noisy students were until I went to (the County Seat) for a teachers' meeting. It's time for me to ring the bell now. If I don't, they will come around and remind me pretty soon.'

Given the seeming dedication of her pupils, the naive observer might have judged this woman an exceedingly skilled and effective teacher. Yet in reality, she was rather a poor teacher, and at the time of graduation the pupils of her one-room school knew scarcely any English – a fact so well known that parents said of her, 'She don't teach them anything!'

Like many of her white colleagues, this woman was interpreting Cherokee conduct from within her own culture, as is evident in her description of the intensive involvement of her pupils in learning tasks as '*playing* school'. In kindred fashion, other teachers describe the silence of the students as timidity or shyness, and their control and restraint as docility. Most teachers are unable to perceive more than their own phase of the complex reality which occurs within their classrooms because they are too firmly set within their own traditions, being the products of rural towns and of small state teachers' colleges, and now working within and limited by a tightly-structured institutional context. Certainly, one benefit of teaching Indians in rural schools is that the educators are sheltered from observation and criticism. Except for their own consciences and professional ideologies, no one cares about, guides or supervises their performance, and little pressure is exerted to encourage them to enlarge their awareness of classroom realities.

Even for ourselves – who have had much experience in observing Indian classrooms – many hours of patient and careful watching were required, plus the development of some intimacy with the local community, before we began to appreciate the complexities of interaction within the Cherokee schoolroom. The shape assumed by the clash of cultures was a subtle one. At first, it could be appreciated most easily in the frustration of the teachers; the war within the classrooms was so cold that its daily battles were not evident, except at the close of the day as the teachers assessed their lack of pedagogical accomplishment. Those teachers who defined their mission as a 'teaching out' of native traditions were failing to make any headway; and some of these good people had come to doubt their ability to work with such difficult and retiring children (actually, as we soon discovered, their classes contained a fair share of youngsters who were eager, alert, intelligent,

336

and industrious). A few teachers had resigned themselves to marking time, while surrendering all notions of genuine instruction.

As these phenomena began to impress themselves upon us, we began to discern in these classrooms an active social entity that we came to call 'The Cherokee School Society'. Later still, we were surprised to discover in other classrooms, which we came to call 'Intercultural Classrooms', that this Society remained latent and that instead the teacher and students were constructing intercultural bridges for communication and instruction (these will be discussed in the next section).

In order to comprehend the complexity of classroom interaction, we need to remind ourselves that the children who perform here as pupils have been socialized (or enculturated) within the world of the Tribal Cherokee as fully and extensively as have any children of their age in other communities. In short, we must disregard the material poverty of the Tribal Cherokee families and their lower-class status and avoid any of the cant about 'cultural deprivation' or 'cultural disadvantage'. These children are culturally alien, and for the out- sider (whether educator or social researcher) to enter into their universe is as demanding as the mastering of an utterly foreign tongue. In the compass of a brief article, we can do no more than indicate a few of the more striking evidences of this distinctive cul- tural background.

Even in the first grade, Cherokee children exhibit a remarkable propensity for precision and thoroughness. Asked to arrange a set of colored matchsticks into a pyramidal form, the children became so thoroughly involved in maintaining an impeccable vertical and horiz- tonal alignment that they were oblivious to the number learning they were supposed to acquire via this digital exercise. These six year olds do not resolve the task by leaving it at the level of achievement for which their physical dexterity would suffice, but continue to man- ipulate the sticks in a patient effort to create order beyond the limita- tions of the material and their own skills. As they mature, the Cherokee students continue this patient and determined ordering of the world, but as a congregate activity that is more often directed at social than physical relationships. At times, this orientation is man- ifested in an effort toward a precision in social affairs that is startling to witness in persons so young (here, sixth graders):

The teacher has asked about the kinds of things which early pion- eers would say to each other in the evening around the campfire as they were traveling.
Jane: 'Save your food.'
Teacher: 'That's preaching.'

Jane and Sally (together): 'No.'

Jane: 'That is just to tell you.' (The tone of voice makes her sound just like a teacher.)

The teacher agrees, and his acquiescent tone makes him sound like a student. He continues, 'They would get you in a room . . .'

Jane interrupts: 'Not in a room.'

Teacher: 'In around a campfire then.' He continues by asking if everyone would be given a chance to speak or just representatives.

Dick: 'That would take all night; they might forget.' Jane and Sally agree that representatives would be the right way.

The foregoing is as significant for the form of interaction, as it is revealing of the students' concern for the precise reconstruction of a historical event. The students have wrought a reversal of roles, so that *their* standards of precision and *their* notions of social intercourse emerge as normative for the discussion.

Although this kind of exchange may be rare – actually it is typical only of the Intercultural Classroom – we have cited it here, as reflecting many of the norms of Cherokee students. As healthy children, they are oriented toward the world of their elders, and they see their adult goal as participating in the Cherokee community of their parents. In this sense, the art of relating to other persons so that learning, or other co-operative efforts, may proceed fruitfully and without friction becomes more important to them than the mastery of particular scholastic tasks, whose relevance in any case may be dubious. In the matrix of the classroom they learn to sustain, order, and control the relationships of a Cherokee community; in so doing they are proceeding toward adult maturity and responsibility. According to these norms, the educational exchange is voluntary for both students and teachers and is governed by a mutual respect.

In any educational transaction, the Cherokee School Society is actively judging the competence of the teacher and allowing him a corresponding function as leader. Their collective appraisal does not tolerate the authoritarian stance assumed by some educators. ('You must learn this!') but rather facilitates the emergence of a situation in which the teacher leads because he knows ('I am teaching you this because you are indicating that you wish to learn . . .') A consequence of this configuration (or, in the eyes of an unsympathetic observer, a symptom) is that the Cherokee students may organize themselves to resist certain categories of knowledge that the school administration has formally chosen to require of them.

We must bear in mind that within the Tribal Cherokee community, the reading or writing of English, calculating arithmetically, and even speaking English have minor employment and minimal utility.

338

By the intermediate grades, the students perceive that, with no more than a marginal proficiency in spoken or written English, their elders are nonetheless leading satisfactory lives as *Cherokees*. Attempts to exhort them toward a high standard of English proficiency and a lengthy period of time-serving in school are likely to evoke a sophisticated negative reaction. After one such educational sermon, a ten-year-old boy bluntly pointed out to his teacher that a Cherokee adult, greatly admired within the local community – and senior kin to many of the pupils present – had only a fifth-grade education. When the teacher attempted to evade this rebuttal by suggesting that the students would, as adults, feel inferior because they lacked a lengthy education and could not speak good English, the pupils were again able to rebut. To the teacher's challenge, 'Who would you talk to?' the same boy responded, 'To other Cherokee!'

Orienting themselves toward the community of their elders, the Cherokee students respond to the pressures of the alien educators by organizing themselves as The Cherokee School Society. As the teacher molds the outer forms of class procedure, the children exploit his obtuseness as a white alien to construct the terms on which they will act as students. But, while among the Oglala Sioux this transformation is effected with a wondrous boldness and insouciance, here among the Cherokee it is with an exquisite social sensibility. A gesture, an inflection in voice, a movement of the eye is as meaningful as a large volume of words would be for their white peers. By the upper elementary grades, the result is a multiple reality according to which the adolescent Cherokee appear now as quiet and shy, or again as stoical and calm, or yet again (apparent only after prolonged observation) as engaged in the most intricate web of sociable interaction. Such delicacy of intercourse, so refined a sensibility, reflects and requires a precision of movement, a neat and exact ordering of the universe.

Interestingly, the Cherokee School Society does not reject the curricular tasks formulated by the alien educational administrators. In fact, the pupils proceed with their usual patient intensity to labor at assignments that can have no bearing on their tradition or experience. The fact that they are unable to relate these materials meaningfully to life within the Cherokee community acts as an increasing barrier to their mastery of them. In particular, the fact that most students have acquired no more than rudimentary proficiency in spoken English means that the involved patterns of the printed language in the advanced texts are beyond their most diligent endeavours; neither the language nor the topics can be deciphered.

So far, we have emphasized that the Cherokee students are interested in learning and that, from the viewpoint of the educator, they are docile pupils. Yet the cultural differences noted, and the basic social separateness and lack of communication, ensure that conflicts will develop and become more intensive as the students mature. The school cannot proceed along the trackways established by educational authority, nor can it be switched by the students into becoming an adjunct of the rural Cherokee community. Hence, as the children mature, the tension within the schoolroom becomes more extreme. Since the participants are one adult and many children, and since the latter are imbued with a cultural standard of nonviolence and passive resistance, open confrontations do not occur. Instead, what typically happens is that, by the seventh and eighth grades the students have surrounded themselves with a wall of silence impenetrable by the outsider, while sheltering a rich emotional communion among themselves. The silence is positive, not simply negative or withdrawing, and it shelters them so that, among other things, they can pursue their scholastic interests in their own style and pace. By their silence they exercise control over the teacher and maneuver him toward a mode of participation that meets their standard, as the following instance illustrates:

Teacher: 'Who was Dwight David Eisenhower?'

Silence.

Teacher: 'Have you heard of him, Joan?' She moves her eyes from his stare and smiles briefly.

Very quickly, the teacher jumps to the next person. There is something in his voice that is light and not deadly serious or moralistic in the way that is customary of him. He is just having fun, and this comes through so that the kids have picked it up. They respond to the tone, not to the question, 'Alice?'

Alice leans back in her chair; her blank stare into space has disappeared, and her eyes are averted. She blushes. Now, she grins.

The teacher does not wait, 'Wayne?'

Wayne is sitting straight, and his face wears a cockeyed smile that says he knows something. He says nothing.

Seeing the foxy grin, the teacher shifts again, 'Wayne, you know?' This is a question and that makes all the difference. There is no challenge, no game-playing, and the interrogation mark challenges Wayne's competency. But Wayne maintains his foxy grin and shakes his head, negative.

Quickly, the teacher calls on another. 'Jake?' He bends his head down and grins but says nothing.

Teacher (in an authoritative tone): 'Nancy, tell me.' But she says nothing, keeping her head lowered, although usually she answers

340

when called upon. The teacher switches tones again, so that what he is asking of Nancy has become a command. Perhaps he catches this, for he switches again to the lighter tone, and says; 'Tell me, Debra.'

The only one in the room who doesn't speak Cherokee, Debra answers in a flat voice: 'President.'

As soon as the answer is given, there are many covert smiles, and Alice blushes. They all knew who he was.

To most educators and observers, such an incident is perplexing. Who within that classroom really is exercising authority? Are the students deficient in their comprehension either of English or of the subject matter? Are they, perhaps, flexing their social muscles and mocking the teacher – because they don't like the lesson, they don't like him to act as he is acting, or why? For the Cherokee School Society has created within the formal confines of the institutional classroom another social edifice, their own 'classroom', so that at times there appears to be not simply a clash of cultural traditions but a cold war between rival definitions of the classroom. Such tension is not proper within Cherokee tradition, since the Tribal Cherokee value harmonious social relationships and frown upon social conflict. Moderate disagreement is resolved by prolonged discussion interspersed, wherever possible, by joking and jesting, while severe disagreement leads to withdrawal from the conflict-inducing situation. Given the compulsory nature of school attendance, however, the students cannot withdraw from the classroom, much as they might wish to, and the teacher can withdraw only by losing his job and his income. Thus, an unmanageable tension may develop if the teacher is unable to recognize the Cherokee pupils as his peers who, through open discussion may share with him in the decisions as to the organizing and operating of the school.

The unresolved conflict of cultural differences typifies these classrooms. Within them, there is little pedagogy, much silence, and an atmosphere that is apprehended by Indians (or observers of kindred sensibility) as ominous with tension. The following incident, participated in by Dumont, exhibits all these features in miniature:

The classroom was small and the teacher had begun to relate a joke to Dumont. Not far away were seated four teenage Cherokee, and the teacher decided to include them within the range of his ebullience: 'Boys, I want to tell you a joke . . .' It was one of those that played upon the stoical endurance of the Indians in adapting to the whimsical wishes of whites, and to narrate it in the classroom context was highly ironic. The plot and phrasing were simple, and easily apprehended by the students. But when the teacher had finished, they merely continued looking toward him, with their eyes focussed, not upon him, but fixed at some point above or to the side of his eyes. As he awaited their laughter, their expressions did not alter but they continued to stare at the same fixed point and then gradually lowered their heads to their work.

The Cherokee School Society maintains a rigid law of balance that says, in effect, we will change when the teacher changes. If the teacher becomes involved in appreciating the ways of his students, then they will respond with an interest in his ways. Needless to say, the older the students become, the higher their grade-level, the less is the likelihood that this reciprocity will be initiated by their educators. There is thus a deep tragedy, for it is the students who lose and suffer the most. Yet the School Society is their technique for protecting themselves in order to endure the alien intrusiveness of the teacher and the discourtesy and barbarity of the school. Occasionally, the observer and students experience a happier interlude, for some teachers are able to enter into a real intercultural exchange. Unfortunately, they are as rare as they are remarkable. And they are sometimes unaware of their truly prodigious achievements in establishing what we term the Intercultural Classroom.

The Intercultural Classroom

Within the Intercultural Classroom, Tribal Cherokee students do such remarkable things as engaging in lengthy conversation with the teacher about academic subjects. For this to occur, the teacher must be responsive to the distinctive norms and expectations of the students; but, strikingly, he need not abide by these nor accept norms as long as he is able to persuade the students of his willingness to learn about them and to accommodate to them. This attitude places the teacher on a plane of parity such that he must learn from his students the most rudimentary Cherokee cultural prescriptions. Naturally, both parties experience conflicts in this reshuffling of teacher/learner roles. Certainly, such interaction is not what the teacher has been trained to sustain. Yet there arise structured devices for reducing these conflicts.

For instance, to bridge the social breaches that are always opening, the Cherokee students urge forward one of their members – not always the same person – to mediate and harmonize. Then, if the teacher, by an unconscious presumption, disrupts the harmonious flow of class activity, it is the mediator whose deft maneuver reduces the intensity of the tension and relaxes the participants. In a sense, what the mediator does is to restore parity between teacher and students by removing the nimbus of authority from the teacher, thus allowing the students to work out with the teacher a compromise which redirects class activities and so permits them to regain their proper tempo. The teacher is freed to pursue the subject matter, but as scholastic assistant rather than classroom tyrant. With this in mind, let us examine the sequence of events which ended in a conversational repartee already quoted:

They are reading about important men in history and have just finished with a section about adult educators.

Teacher: (Referring to observers) 'We have two distinguished educators here. Does this make you feel proud?'

It is quiet for the first time in the room. It is likely that the students are all thinking, how could we be proud of educators! As observer, I am uneasy and expectant; I wonder who will break the silence and how he will handle the delicate situation.

John: 'I don't like schools myself.'(!)

Teacher: 'Would you quit school if you could? (He's asking for it!)

John (a firm answer): 'Yes.'

Teacher: 'Suppose that your dad came and said you could quit, but he brought you a shovel and said, "Dig a ditch from here to Brown's house," since you weren't going to school.'

John: 'Okay.'

Another student: 'He might learn something.'

Everyone finds this humorous; the class is in good spirits and is moving along.

John, too, is quick to reply: 'Might strike gold.' The topic has been discussed earlier in class. (The interaction develops and others become involved, including the more reticent students.)

Here it is John who has played, and most successfully, the role in mediator. The teacher had ventured into a delicate area that had the potential of disrupting the classroom atmosphere. The responding silence was a token of the social peril, and John, who so often among his peers had assumed the mediating role, moved forward first, boldly countering with a declaration as strong as the teacher's. As a consequence, he redefined the structure of the interaction and became the initiator of the exchange, while the teacher merely sustained it. A cultural bridge was thereby constructed, accessible alike to students and teacher; and John's 'Okay' is his consent to the conditions of the structure.

The mediating role becomes less necessary as the teacher grows more attuned to the interactional norms of Indian society; it becomes more difficult (if more essential) if the teacher insists on maintaining a tyrannical control over the classroom. Yet, even as the teacher is attuned, some function is reserved for a mediator, for the teacher tends to proceed in terms of work to be done, while the mediator explores how the task can be redefined within the framework of the Cherokee student. His is a work of adaptation, and insofar as he is successful, the classroom becomes *intercultural* – a locus where persons of different cultural traditions can engage in mutually beneficial transactions without affront to either party.

What must the teacher do to foster the emergence of an intercultural classroom within the cross-cultural situation? The answer would require another essay at least as long as the present one, but it may be helpful to quote the remarks of one teacher in the region:

'I can't follow a lesson plan, and I just go along by ear. I've taught Cherokee students for six years in high school, and this is my first (year) in elementary school.' Referring then to his experiences as a high school coach, he continued, 'The thing you have to do, if you get a team, is that you got to get them to co-operate. . . .'

At first glance, this appears at odds with our earlier assertions about the spontaneous emergence of the Cherokee School Society, not to mention contradictory to the conventional notions that Indians will not compete with each other. But what he is explaining is that unless the teacher chooses to recognize the social nature of the classroom and to work toward integrating his teaching with that life, he will not be able to elicit active learning experiences from his pupils. Or, to put it negatively, if the teacher does not work with his Indian students as a social group, their union will be directed toward other goals. Yet the teacher can secure their response only if he 'gets them' to co-operate; he cannot 'make them' do so.

Conclusion

The foregoing report provides the basis for judgments and hypotheses on a variety of levels. On the practical level, it would seem that ethnic integration is not an essential precondition for satisfactory education of groups from a low socio-economic background. The Tribal Cherokee certainly are impoverished and poorly educated. Nevertheless, we would predict that the consolidation of rural schools into larger, better-staffed, and better equipped schools in northeastern Oklahoma may actually lead to deterioration rather than improvement of the educational condition. Given the ethos of the Tribal Cherokee, consolidations may mean the irremedial loss of many opportunities for assisting their children educationally.

On the methodological level, we are reminded of how sociologically valuable it is for researchers to focus on the frontier situation 'where peoples meet'. The resulting accommodations, adaptations, and divisions of labor are an enlightening and fascinating phenomenon,

344

which especially deserve to be studied as a corrective to those theoretical systems which regard the national society as an integrated social system. On the methodological level also, our study illustrates anew the value of ethnographic observations of classroom activities. Basic and simple as it may seem, and unpretentious in the face of modern testing procedures, direct observation still has much to teach us.

Finally, on the substantive level, the research reported here cautions against the erosion of our conceptual armamentarium when researchers allow their research problems to be defined by educational administrators. When that happens, the educational situation of people such as the Indians tends to be conceived in terms of individual pupils and their 'cultural deprivation'. The researcher then is asked to assist the administration in raising these disadvantaged individuals to the point where they can compete in school in the same fashion as do the middle-class children. Our research is a reminder that such styles of conceptualization neglect the social nature of the classrooms and the social ties among the pupils. They also neglect the tension between teacher and pupils as a social group, and the struggles that occur when the teacher presses for individualistic achievement at the expense of group solidarity.

30

On the Job *

Blanche Geer, Jack Hass, Charles V Vona,
Stephen J Miller, Clyde Woods, and Howard S
Becker

Our next example is not a school, but a hospital training program for
nursing assistants. The hospital hires trainees on a probationary basis
when it needs new workers, and a small group (two to five persons)
usually takes the program together. Trainees are carefully selected,
but vary considerably in age, education, background, and experience.
They are required to take the program even though they have had
previous hospital experience.

During the first ten to twelve weeks, trainees have two one-hour
classes daily, taught by a nurse in charge of training. For the rest of
the day, they work as nursing assistants on a training floor of the
hospital – bathing patients, making beds, cleaning rooms, and serving
trays of food. The nurse in charge assigns patients to trainees just as
she does to others on her staff. The trainee is much on his own; in
some cases, he is the only nursing assistant on the floor. Nominally,
the charge nurse supervises his work; the teaching nurse, his learning.

The trainee's problems in learning the ropes of the classroom situation are similar to those students face in ordinary schools. He must
discover what the teacher wants him to learn and how to demonstrate
his learning. The process is one of gradual discrimination. He relies
on what the teacher herself says she wants, and supplements this
information with such other cues as the amount of time devoted to
various types of instruction and the emphasis put upon them by
techniques the teacher uses in class. The instructor's unscheduled
visits to the training floors provide further insight into her wishes.

In class, the teaching nurse presents information on procedures,
diseases, and relationships with patients and other personnel on the
floor. Her instruction in procedures is consistently detailed and thorough:

* I DEUTSCHER and E THOMPSON, *Among the People; Encounters with the Poor*,
Basic Books, 1968, 218–223, 228–230.

Then Miss Thomas [instructor] went to the blackboard and drew the outline of another kind of binder. She drew a 'T' on the board, with a split down the bottom part of the 'T'. 'This,' she explained, 'is known as a "T" binder as is used for patients who have had rectal surgery.' She turned to her desk and while demonstrating the folding of the binder around the patient, she said . . . 'Take the two straps and wrap them around the waist and then take each one of these end pieces and bring them up through the legs, cross them, and pin them on to the middle section. This holds the dressing in place for the patient.' She continued, 'Well, I think we'll be able to put this on Mr Stone [dummy patient]. We have time and it will be good practice.'

Organizing the material into a series of steps, the teacher describes, explains, demonstrates, and offers time for practice. Although it is impossible for her to check each procedure performed on the training floor and trainees know this, they quickly learn that she often uses her visits to check their work closely. Things which trainees do every day – making beds and keeping patients clean – are especially easy to check.

Classroom instruction about disease includes discussion, but does not receive the emphasis of extended and meticulous presentation accorded to procedures:

Miss Thomas started out by asking what kind of infectious diseases they might encounter in the hospital. Mrs Smith [trainee] said, 'TB' Miss Thomas wrote TB on the board and asked for the Latin name. Both Al and Mrs Smith [trainees] had difficulty pronouncing the name, but after several tries Mrs Smith finally blurted out, 'Tubercula bacillus,' which Miss Thomas wrote on the board. Then Miss Thomas asked, 'What is tubercula bacillus?' Al said, 'It's a germ.' Miss Thomas wrote 'germ' after 'Tubercula bacillus' and then asked, 'How's it contracted?' Mrs Smith responded, 'It's passed through the air, it's airborne, you know, like coughing or sneezing, or sputum.'

Trainees learn the names of diseases and how to pronounce them, and a little about their causes and how they are contracted. It is information the trainee seldom uses in his work; failure to use it does not leave evidence of a sort the instructor can easily observe.

The third and least concrete type of instruction the teaching nurse offers – information about relationships with others – receives still less emphasis, as we suspect it does in most training programs and schools. Rarely explicit, the instructor hints at the complexities of the trainee's situation on the floor – a situation in which she herself is involved, since a trainee's performance reflects her teaching:

I [instructor] want you to know how to do these neatly and accurately, so that the nurses will never be able to say, if they do have you do these, that you didn't do them right.

At work on a training floor, the trainee discovers that the order of emphasis in the classroom – procedures come first in importance, medical information second, and interaction with others third – is virtually reversed. Learning the ropes is a matter of interpreting new priorities and defining in action the responsibilities his work entails. The trainee does this in a situation which provides little teaching in the conventional sense, but many subtle clues which guide his developing understanding of what people on the floor, both staff and patients, expect of him.

The priorities of the job are among the first things the trainee learns. He has to decide whether being a trainee makes him primarily a student responsible to the teaching nurse or a worker responsible for getting things done:

Al said, 'What really fouls me up is when Miss Thomas comes and checks my work. She is a very complete and thorough woman and expects you to spend a half an hour with each patient. If I did this, I would never finish my work.' He gave me an example, 'She expects you to do a bed unit in about a half an hour and then she comes in and checks it very carefully. She even goes to the extent of taking a fingernail file and scrapes the frame of the bed to see if there is any dirt. The best I can do is make sure that there is no dust around.'

Although he knows that the teaching nurse makes reports on his progress, the trainee has also learned that the head nurse wants a smoothly running floor with all patients cared for and all tasks somehow done, and he tries to do it.

Since classwork follows its own schedule of topics, trainees must sometimes decide whether to do things they have not yet been taught in class. Aware of this possibility, the instructor warns them to call her for assistance, but the request often goes unheeded:

[In this example, the trainee was turning a patient on a stryker frame, an extremely complicated and dangerous maneuver which requires, by hospital rule, two persons to execute it.]

I asked Al, 'Have you done this in class already?' He said, 'Oh no, we haven't come to this yet.' I asked him how he learned about it, and he said, 'Well, I guess it's OJT [on-the-job training]. I just watch someone and pick it up that way.' He continued, 'You know there is supposed to be two people doing this anyway.'

In this instance, the trainee not only puts getting his work done ahead of obeying a hospital rule, he also defines learning as something he

348

must do on his own when his work demands it.

He learns that his relationship with patients is an important part of his job. In a sense, they are his teachers on the floor: they define the situation and know from experience how things should be done. They tell the trainee what to do:

> Al placed the tray of food on the stand but the patient complained, 'How do you expect me to reach the food? Hand me my meat loaf.' Al gave the patient his meat loaf, the patient ate it out of his hand and then said, 'Gimme my tools [meaning knife and fork] so I can eat the rest of this.'

but make completing his work more difficult by unpredictably undoing it:

> The heavy-set nurse entered and said to Al, 'That Mr Teller made a mess, he spit up all his water. I wonder if when you get a free minute, whether you could give me a hand.' Al fumbled a little, then replied that he would.

Pressed for time and repeatedly interrupted, the trainee learns to bargain with others, even his superiors whom he is trying to satisfy, in order to get his work done:

> [The head nurse and male attendant from physical therapy] both entered the room. The nurse said, 'Tom, Mr Smith [patient] has to go to PT today. Mr Weeks is here to take him down.' Tom said, 'Sorry, but Mr Smith is not finished yet.' The nurse then asked, 'How long will it be?' Tom replied, 'About five minutes more.' The head nurse said to Tom, 'Well, you finish him up and see if you can get a patient to take Mr Smith downstairs.'

The willingness of the nurses to bargain with him provides the trainee with evidence that they share his definition of the situation. Finishing the assigned tasks has first priority.

As in the barber school, the student's problems in the nursing-assistant training program are the interactional ones so seldom classified as things to be taught in school. The trainee learns the ropes – how to solve his initial problems – as he perceives and uses a set of situational rules which govern the interaction of staff and patients on the training floor. He learns that, although there is seldom time enough to complete assigned tasks, getting them done comes first. Once he has defined his situation in this way, the trainee can make decisions about whose orders to follow and even take orders from patients. He knows when to ask for help and who can help him when he needs it.

In the absence of peers in his immediate situation, the trainee shares his definition of his responsibilities with the floor nurses, and puts himself in a position to bargain with them. The divided line of authority over him may well encourage the trainee to interact with other personnel on the floor, nominally his superiors, almost as if they were peers.

Unlike the barber student, who learns relatively little from his brief interaction with his clients, the nursing assistant in training learns from his patients how to do his work. Because they are people to whom trainees do things, and in this sense are temporarily subordinated clients, patients seem to us poorly cast as teachers of the ropes. But many of them are residents of the hospital before the trainee arrives on the scene and, under the hospital's system of rotating employees, may have dealt with several nursing assistants. They know how his job should be done. Teaching him to do it properly can only add to their comfort.

The high standards of performance taught him in class can seldom be reached on the job, but the disjunction presents a less disorienting problem for the trainee than one might expect, since class and work go on at the same time and the demands of the job (if only because they fill most of his day) have priority from the beginning. Classes are brief, and the trainee sees relatively little of his classmates afterward. Since they usually work on separate floors, the fact that their experiences are similar affects trainees less than the exigencies of their immediate situation on the floor. Learning the ropes is a matter of learning to get work done in ways both charge nurse and patients will approve.

* * *

Discussion

At the beginning of this chapter, we asked several questions about situational learning, or learning the ropes. These were: (1) what are the ropes? (2) how are they learned? (3) do they differ from one training situation to another? (4) who teaches them? and (5) what is the relation of the structure of a training program to the process of situational learning in trainees? Perhaps we are now in a position to advance tentative answers to these questions.

It should be clear that ropes are facts about persons, places, and things which the trainee thinks relevant to mastering his situation. To learn the ropes is not only to become aware of these facts; it is also a matter of learning how to deal with them to advantage.

If we think only of the ropes which present problems to the trainee, they differ greatly from one of our training situations to another. As we have seen, it is not always made clear to the trainee who is in charge of him. If it is not, an important part of situational learning may be making a choice between two competing authorities, as in the program for nursing assistants. Similarly, sequences of study or work are not always laid down for him; the barber student has to decide for himself what to do and when. Moreover, the newcomer cannot be guided by the public goals of a program in deciding what courses of action are appropriate. Success, as in the case of the intern, may entail the mastery of managerial skills apparently unrelated to graduate training in medicine.

In another and more abstract sense, the ropes are the same in all four training situations, but one program may be structured in a way that makes the learning of certain ropes difficult where another makes the same thing easy. In each situation, the newcomer takes the same steps. These include identifying persons and groups which affect his progress, learning what they do and what they know which may help him, and, if only by trial and error, how to interact with them properly.

Three of our studies include data which suggest that the trainee learns the ropes by making a social map of his new surroundings and relating the actions of others to his own. Although he is unlikely to formulate his ideas clearly unless action presents problems, he nevertheless defines his situation and acts on the definition. The business-machine student has a definition presented to him by the regular teacher; the barber student painfully achieves one by trial and error and observing his peers. The nursing-assistant trainee, despite his low status, sees that getting his work done has first priority, although he cannot anticipate the interruptions of staff from other parts of the hospital. Better placed in the hierarchy, the intern understands that his position permits him to search out the groups whose work affects his own in order to learn their habits and circumvent delays.

Our data indicate that teachers, books, customers, patients, bosses, subordinates, auxiliary personnel, and machines – in fact, any frequent contact – may become sources of situational learning. Moreover, we may infer that trainees are capable of considerable ingenuity in finding teachers. If their ordinary teacher is not available, they turn to peers; if peers are unavailable, they make use of client-subordinates; supplied with groups of superiors and subordinates, they tactfully exploit them all.

Perhaps we have said enough to suggest that the structure of a training program can facilitate or impede situational learning. The ingenuity of trainees further implies that they know that failure to learn the ropes may preclude learning anything else. If the intern does not learn whom to consult and how to secure his help, he will not learn what the consulting physician can teach him about medicine. If the barber student does not learn to get on with his fellows, they will not teach him to barber and, since they are a major source of substantive knowledge in the school, he may not learn much barbering.

We conclude that the ability to learn the ropes is closely related to successful negotiation of the training period. And, if there is a capacity for situational learning distinct from that of ordinary learning, as there may be, students who fail in training may fail because they have not learned the ropes – a kind of learning seldom included in the ordinary school curriculum.

31

History, Culture, and Subjective Experience *

Howard S Becker

The scientific literature and, even more, the popular press frequently state that recreational drug use produces a psychosis. The nature of 'psychosis' is seldom defined, as though it were intuitively clear. Writers usually seem to mean a mental disturbance of some unspecified kind, involving auditory and visual hallucinations, an inability to control one's stream of thought, and a tendency to engage in socially inappropriate behavior, either because one has lost the sense that it is inappropriate or because one cannot stop oneself. In addition, and perhaps most important, psychosis is thought to be a state that will last long beyond the specific event that provoked it. However it occurred, it is thought to mark a more-or-less permanent change in the psyche and this, after all, is why we think of it as such a bad thing. Over indulgence in alcohol produces many of the symptoms cited but this frightens no one because we understand that they will soon go away.

Verified reports of drug-induced psychoses are scarcer than one might think. Nevertheless, let us assume that these reports have not been fabricated, but represent an interpretation by the reporter of something that really happened. In the light of the findings just cited, what kind of event can we imagine to have occurred that might have been interpreted as a 'psychotic episode'? (I use the word 'imagine' advisedly, for the available case reports usually do not furnish sufficient material to allow us to do more than imagine what might have happened.)

The most likely sequence of events is this. The inexperienced user has certain unusual subjective experiences, which he may or may not attribute to having taken the drug. He may find his perception of space distorted, so that he has difficulty climbing a flight of stairs. He

---

* Howard S Becker (ed), *Institutions and the Person: Essays in Honour of Everett C Hughes*, Aldine Publishing Co, 1968.

may find his train of thought so confused that he is unable to carry on a normal conversation and hears himself making totally inappropriate remarks. He may see or hear things in a way that he suspects is quite different from the way others see and hear them.

Whether or not he attributes what is happening to the drug, the experiences are likely to be upsetting. One of the ways we know that we are normal human beings is that our perceptual world, on the evidence available to use, seems to be pretty much the same as other people's. We see and hear the same things, make the same kind of sense out of them and, where perceptions differ, can explain the difference by a difference in situation or perspective. We may take for granted that the inexperienced drug user, though he wanted to get 'high', did not expect an experience so radical as to call into question that common sense set of assumptions.

In any society whose culture contains notions of sanity and insanity, the person who finds his subjective state altered in the way described may think he has become insane. We learn at a young age that a person who 'acts funny', 'sees things', 'hears things', or has other bizarre and unusual experiences may have become 'crazy', 'nuts', 'loony' or a host of other synonyms. When a drug user identifies some of these untoward events occurring in his own experience, he may decide that he merits one of those titles – that he has lost his grip on reality, his control of himself, and has in fact 'gone crazy'. The interpretation implies the corollary that the change is irreversible or, at least, that things are not going to be changed back very easily. The drug experience, perhaps originally intended as a momentary entertainment, now looms as a momentous event which will disrupt one's life, possibly permanently. Faced with this conclusion, the person develops a full-blown anxiety attack, but it is an anxiety caused by his reaction to the drug experience rather than a direct consequence of drug use itself. (In this connection, it is interesting that, in the published reports of LSD psychoses, acute anxiety attacks appear as the largest category of untoward reaction.)

It is perhaps easier to grasp what this must feel like if we imagine that, having taken several social drinks at a party, we were suddenly to see vari-colored snakes peering out at us from behind the furniture. We would instantly recognize this as a sign of *delirium tremens*, and would no doubt become severely anxious at the prospect of having developed such a serious mental illness. Some such panic is likely to grip the recreational drugs-user who interprets his experience as a sign of insanity.

Though I have put the argument with respect to the inexperienced user, long time users of recreational drugs sometimes have similar experiences. They may experiment with a higher dosage than they are used to and experience effects unlike anything they have known before. This can easily occur when using drugs purchased in the illicit market, where quality may vary greatly, so that the user inadvertently gets more than he can handle.

The scientific literature does not report any verified cases of people acting on their distorted perceptions so as to harm themselves and others, but such cases have been reported in the press. Press reports of drug-related events are very unreliable, but it may be that users, have, for instance, stepped out of a second storey window, deluded by the drug into thinking it only a few feet to the ground. If such cases have occurred, they too may be interpreted as examples of psychosis, but a different mechanism than the one just discussed would be involved. The person, presumably, would have failed to make the necessary correction for the drug-induced distortion, a correction, however, that experienced users assert can be made. Thus, a novice marihuana user will find it difficult to drive while 'high', but experienced users have no difficulty. Similarly, novices find it difficult to manage their relations with people who are not also under the influence of drugs, but experienced users can control their thinking and actions so as to behave appropriately. Although it is commonly assumed that a person under the influence of LSD must avoid ordinary social situations for 12 or more hours, I have been told of at least one user who takes the drug and then goes to work; she explained that once you learn 'how to handle it' (ie make the necessary corrections for distortions caused by the drug) there is no problem.

In short, the most likely interpretation we can make of the drug-induced psychoses reported is that they are either severe anxiety reactions to an event interpreted and experienced as insanity, or failures by the user to correct, in carrying out some ordinary action, for the perceptual distortions caused by the drug. If the interpretation is correct, then untoward mental effects produced by drugs depend in some part on its physiological action, but to a much larger degree find their origin in the definitions and conceptions the user applies to that action. These can vary with the individual's personal make-up, a possibility psychiatrists are most alive to, or with the groups he participates in, the trail I shall pursue here.

The Influence of Drug-Using Cultures
While there are no reliable figures, it is obvious that a very large number of people use recreational drugs, primarily marihuana and LSD. From the previous analysis one might suppose that, therefore, a great many people would have disquieting symptoms and, given the

ubiquity in our society of the concept of insanity, that many would decide they had gone crazy and thus have a drug-induced anxiety attack. But very few such reactions occur. Although there must be more than are reported in the professional literature, it is unlikely that drugs have this effect in any large number of cases. If they did there would necessarily be many more verified accounts than are presently available. Since the psychotic reaction stems from a definition of the drug-induced experience, the explanation of this paradox must lie in the availability of competing definitions of the subjective states produced by drugs.

Competing definitions come to the user from other users who, to his knowledge, have had sufficient experience with the drug to speak with authority. He knows that the drug does not produce permanent disabling damage in all cases, for he can see that these other users do not suffer from it. The question, of course, remains whether it may not produce damage in some cases and whether his is one of them, no matter how rare.

When someone experiences disturbing effects, other users typically assure him that the change in his subjective experience is neither rare nor dangerous. They have seen similar reactions before, and may even have experienced them themselves with no lasting harm. In any event they have some folk knowledge about how to handle the problem.

They may, for instance, know of an antidote for the frightening effects; thus, marihuana users, confronted with someone who has gotten 'too high', encourage him to eat, an apparently effective countermeasure. They talk reassuringly about their own experiences, 'normalizing' the frightening symptom by treating it, matter-of-factly, as temporary. They maintain surveillance over the affected person, preventing any physically or socially dangerous activity. They may, for instance, keep him from driving or from making a public display that will bring him to the attention of the police or others who would disapprove of his drug use. They show him how to allow for the perceptual distortion the drug causes and teach him how to manage interaction with nonusers.

They redefine the experience he is having as desirable rather than frightening, as the end for which the drug is taken. What they tell him carries conviction because he can see that it is not some idiosyncratic belief but is instead culturally shared. It is what 'everyone' who uses the drug knows. In all these ways, experienced users prevent the episode from having lasting effects and reassure the novice that whatever he feels will come to a timely and harmless end.

The anxious novice thus has an alternative to defining his experience as 'going crazy'. He may redefine the event immediately or, having been watched over by others throughout the anxiety attack, decide that it was not so bad after all and not fear its reoccurrence. He 'learns' that his original definition was 'incorrect' and that the alternative offered by other users more nearly describes what he has experienced.

Available knowledge does not tell us how often this mechanism comes into play or how effective it is in preventing untoward psychological reactions; no research has been addressed to this point. In the case of marihuana, at least, the paucity of reported cases of permanent damage coupled with the undoubted increase in use suggests that it may be an effective mechanism.

For such a mechanism to operate, a number of conditions must be met. First, the drug must not produce, quite apart from the user's interpretations, permanent damage to the mind. No amount of social redefinition can undo the damage done by toxic alcohols, or the effects of a lethal dose of an opiate or barbiturate. This analysis, therefore, does not apply to drugs known to have such effects.

Second, users of the drug must share a set of understandings – a culture – which includes, in addition to material on how to obtain and ingest the drug, definitions of the typical effects, the typical course of the experience, the permanence of the effects, and a description of methods for dealing with someone who suffers an anxiety attack because of drug use or attempts to act on the basis of distorted perceptions. Users should have available to them, largely through face-to-face participation with other users but possibly in such other ways as reading as well, the definitions contained in that culture, which they can apply in place of the common-sense definitions available to the inexperienced man in the street.

Third, the drug should ordinarily be used in the group settings, where other users can present the definitions of the drug-using culture to the person whose inner experience is so unusual as to provoke use of the common-sense category of insanity. Drugs for which technology and custom promote group use should produce a lower incidence of 'psychotic episodes.'

The last two conditions suggest, as is the case, that marihuana, surrounded by an elaborate culture and ordinarily used in group settings, should produce few 'psychotic' episodes. At the same time, they suggest the prediction that drugs which have not spawned a culture and are ordinarily used in private, such as barbiturates, will produce more such episodes. I suggest possible research along these lines below.

Non-User Interpretations

A user suffering from drug-induced anxiety may also come into contact with non-users who will offer him definitions, depending on their own perspectives and experiences, that may validate the diagnosis of 'going crazy' and thus prolong the episode, possibly producing relatively permanent disability. These non-users include family members and police, but most important among them are psychiatrists and psychiatrically oriented physicians. (Remember that when we speak of reported cases of psychosis, the report is ordinarily made by a physician, though police may also use the term in reporting a case to the press.)

Medical knowledge about the recreational use of drugs is spotty. Little research has been done, and its results are not at the fingertips of physicians who do not specialize in the area. (In the case of LSD, of course, there has been a good deal of research, but its conclusions are not clear and, in any case, have not yet been spread throughout the profession.) Psychiatrists are not anxious to treat drug users, so few of them have accumulated any clinical experience with the phenomenon. Nevertheless, a user who develops severe and uncontrollable anxiety will probably be brought, if he is brought anywhere, to a physician for treatment. Most probably, he will be brought to a psychiatric hospital, if one is available; if not, to a hospital emergency room, where a psychiatric resident will be called once the connection with drugs is established, or to a private psychiatrist.

Physicians, confronted with a case of drug-induced anxiety and lacking specific knowledge of its character or proper treatment, rely on a kind of generalized diagnosis. They reason that people probably do not use drugs unless they are suffering from a severe underlying personality disturbance; that use of the drug may allow repressed conflicts to come into the open where they will prove unmanageable; that the drug in this way provokes a true psychosis; and, therefore, that the patient confronting them is psychotic. Furthermore, even though the effects of the drug wear off, the psychosis may not, for the repressed psychological problems it has brought to the surface may not recede as it is metabolized and excreted from the body.

Given such a diagnosis, the physician knows what to do. He hospitalizes the patient for observation and prepares, where possible, for long-term therapy designed to repair the damage done to the psychic defenses or to deal with the conflict unmasked by the drug. Both hospitalization and therapy are likely to reinforce the definition of the drug experience as insanity, for in both the patient will be required to 'understand' that he is mentally ill as a precondition for return to the world.

358

The physician then, does *not* treat the anxiety attack as a localized phenomenon, to be treated in a symptomatic way, but as an outbreak of a serious disease heretofore hidden. He may thus prolong the serious effects beyond the time they might have lasted had the user instead come into contact with other users. This analysis, of course, is frankly speculative; what is required is study of the way physicians treat cases of the kind described and, especially, comparative study of the effects of treatment of drug-induced anxiety attacks by physicians and by drug users.

Another category of non-users deserves mention. Literary men and journalists publicize definitions of drug experiences, either of their own invention or those borrowed from users, psychiatrists or police. (Some members of this category use drugs themselves, so it may be a little confusing to classify them as non-users; in any case, the definitions are provided outside the ordinary channels of communication in the drug-using world.) The definitions of literary men – novelists, essayists and poets – grow out of a long professional tradition, beginning with De Quincey's *Confessions*, and are likely to be colored by that tradition. Literary descriptions dwell on the fantasy component of the experience, on its cosmic and ineffable character, and on the threat of madness. Such widely available definitions furnish some of the substance out of which a user may develop his own definition, in the absence of definitions from the drug-using culture.

Journalists use any of a number of approaches conventional in their craft; what they write is greatly influenced by their own professional needs. They must write about 'news', about events which have occurred recently and require reporting and interpretation. Furthermore, they need 'sources', persons to whom authoritative statements can be attributed. Both needs dispose them to reproduce the line taken by law enforcement officials and physicians, for news is often made by the passage of a law or by a public statement which follows an alarming event, such as a bizarre murder or a suicide. So journalistic reports frequently dwell on the theme of madness or suicide, a tendency intensified by the newsman's desire to tell a dramatic story. Some journalists, of course, will take the other side in the argument, but even then, because they argue against the theme of madness, the emphasis on that theme is maintained. Public discussion of drug use thus tends to strengthen those stereotypes that would lead the users who suffer disturbing effects to interpret their experience as 'going crazy'.

An Historical Dimension

A number of variables, then, affect the character of drug-induced experiences. It remains to show that the experiences themselves are likely to vary according to when they occur in the history of use of a given drug in a society. In particular, it seems likely that the experience of acute anxiety caused by drug use will so vary.

Consider the following sequence of possible events, which may be regarded as a natural history of the assimilation of an intoxicating drug by a society. Someone in the society discovers, rediscovers or invents a drug which has the properties described earlier. The ability of the drug to alter subjective experience in desireable ways becomes known to increasing numbers of people, and the drug itself simultaneously becomes available, along with the information needed to make its use effective. Use increases, but users do not have a sufficient amount of experience with the drug to form a stable conception of it as an object. They do not know what it can do to the mind, have no firm idea of the variety of effects it can produce, and are not sure how permanent or dangerous the effects are. They do not know if the effects can be controlled or how. No drug-using culture exists, and there is thus no authoritative alternative with which to counter the possible definition, when and if it comes to mind, of the drug experience as madness. 'Psychotic episodes' occur frequently.

But individuals accumulate experience with the drug and communicate their experiences to one another. Consensus develops about the drug's subjective effects, their duration, proper dosages, predictable dangers and how they may be avoided; all these points become matters of common knowledge, validated by their acceptance in a world of users. A culture exists. When a user experiences bewildering or frightening effects, he has available to him an authoritative alternative to the lay notion that he has gone mad. Every time he uses cultural conceptions to interpret drug experiences and control his response to them, he strengthens his belief that the culture is indeed a reliable source of knowledge. 'Psychotic episodes' occur less frequently in proportion to the growth of the culture to cover the range of possible effects and its spread to a greater proportion of users. Novice users, to whom the effects are most unfamiliar and who therefore might be expected to suffer most from drug-induced anxiety, learn the culture from older users in casual conversation and in more serious teaching sessions and are thus protected from the dangers of 'panicking' or 'flipping out'.

The incidence of 'psychoses', then, is a function of the stage of development of a drug-using culture. Individual experience varies with historical stages and the kinds of cultural and social organization associated with them.

Is this model a useful guide to reality? The only drug for which there is sufficient evidence to attempt an evaluation is marihuana;

even there the evidence is equivocal, but it is consistent with the model. On this interpretation, the early history of marihuana use in the United States should be marked by reports of marihuana-induced psychoses. In the absence of a fully formed drug-using culture, some users would experience disquieting symptoms and have no alternative to the idea that they were losing their minds. They would turn up at psychiatric facilities in acute states of anxiety and doctors, eliciting a history of marihuana use, would interpret the episode as a psychotic breakdown. When, however, the culture reached full flower and spread throughout the user population, the number of psychoses should have dropped even though (as a variety of evidence suggests) the number of users increased greatly. Using the definitions made available by the culture, users who had unexpectedly severe symptoms could interpret them in such a way as to reduce or control anxiety and would thus no longer come to the attention of those likely to report them as cases of psychosis.

*   *   *

LSD

We cannot predict the history of LSD by direct analogy to the history of marihuana, for a number of important conditions may vary. We must first ask whether the drug has, apart from the definitions users impose on their experience, any demonstrated causal relation to psychoses. There is a great deal of controversy on this point, and any reading of the evidence must be tentative. My own opinion is that LSD has essentially the same characteristics as those described in the first part of this paper; its effects may be more powerful than those of other drugs that have been studied, but they too are subject to differing interpretations by users, so that the mechanisms I have described come into play.

The cases reported in the literature are, like those reported for marihuana, mostly panic reactions to the drug experience, occasioned by the user's interpretation that he has lost his mind, or further disturbance among people already disturbed. There are no cases of permanent derangement directly traceable to the drug, with one puzzling exception (puzzling to those who report it as well as to me). In a few cases the visual and auditory distortions produced by the drug recur weeks or months after it was last ingested; this sometimes produces severe upset among those who experience it. Observers are at a loss to explain the phenomenon, except for Rosenthal, who proposes that the drug may have a specific effect on the nerve pathways involved in vision; but this theory, should it prove correct, is a long way from dealing with questions of possible psychosis.

The whole question is confused by the extraordinary assertions about the effects of LSD made by both proponents and opponents of its use. Both sides agree that it has a very strong effect on the mind, disagreeing only as to whether this powerful effect is benign or malignant. Leary, for example, argues that we must 'go out of our minds in order to use our heads', and that this can be accomplished by using LSD. Opponents agree that it can drive you out of your mind, but do not share Leary's view that this is a desireable goal. In any case, we need not accept the premise simply because both parties to the controversy do.

Let us not assume then, in the absence of more definitive evidence, that the drug does not in itself produce lasting derangement, that such psychotic episodes as are now reported are largely a result of panic at the possible meaning of the experience, that users who 'freak out' do so because they fear they have permanently damaged their minds. Is there an LSD-using culture? In what stage of development is it? Are the reported episodes of psychosis congruent with what our model would predict, given that stage of development?

Here again my discussion must be speculative, for no serious study of this culture is yet available. It appears likely, however, that such a culture is in an early stage of development. Several conceptions of the drug and its possible effects exist, but no stable consensus has arisen. Radio, television and the popular press present a variety of interpretations, many of them contradictory. There is widespread disagreement, even among users, about possible dangers. Some certainly believe that use (or injudicious use) can lead to severe mental difficulty.

At the same time, my preliminary inquiries and observations hinted at the development (or at least the beginnings) of a culture similar to that surrounding marihuana use. Users with some experience discuss their symptoms and translate from one idiosyncratic description into another, developing a common conception of effects as they talk. The notion that a 'bad trip' can be brought to a speedy conclusion by taking thorazine by mouth (or, when immediate action is required, intravenously) has spread. Users are also beginning to develop a set of safeguards against committing irrational acts while under the drug's influence. Many feel, for instance, that one should take one's 'trip' in the company of experienced users who are not under the drug's influence at the time; they will be able to see you through bad times and restrain you when necessary. A conception of the appropriate dose is rapidly becoming common knowledge. Users understand that they may have to 'sit up with' people who have panicked as a result of the drug's effects, and they talk of techniques that have proved useful in this enterprise. All this suggests that a common conception of the drug is developing which will eventually see it defined as pleasurable and desirable, with possible untoward effects that can however be controlled.

32

Navajo Film Makers *

Sol Worth and John Adair

In the initial planning we were not certain that our subjects would have the motivation essential to learning enough about the camera and editing to give us significant results, even though we planned to pay them a modest wage. Unlike being a subject in the Rorschach, Thematic Apperception, or Draw-a-Man tests, participation in this would necessitate sustaining motivation over several months. It had been noted that polaroid photographs had become attractive to the Navajo, and this suggested to us that their motivation would be strengthened by quick feedback of the footage they would shoot. We therefore arranged to have the film exposed on one day, developed, printed and returned within the following two days.

We had originally explained that Worth was a teacher of film in an Eastern university and that he wanted to teach some Navajo people to make movies. For the first week the students had us repeat this explanation quite often, and also asked why we wanted to do this. Worth explained that he only taught college students and 'wanted to learn more about how to teach all kinds of students'. He said that he would teach them and ask them questions, emphasizing each time that they could make a film about *anything they liked*, in any way they wanted.

We had previously made arrangement with the teacher in the Bureau of Indian Affairs school at Pine Springs (a boarding school for grades 1 and 2) for us to use the boys' dormitory wing as classroom, editing room, and living space for our research team and for Al Clah. This wing was roughly fifty feet long and twenty feet wide, having a four-foot aisle down the center, with four compartments for sleeping, two compartments for editing, one as a classroom, one for storing equipment, and the aisle for projection. We did most of our teaching either in the dormitory or sitting just outside it under the piñon trees.

We brought with us, in four portable cases easily carried by two people, all the equipment we needed: four Bell and Howell 70 DH 3-lens turret, 16 mm cameras; four Zeiss Movieskop viewers; four sets of

* *American Anthropologist*, **72**, 1970

rewinds and related equipment; and about 10 000 feet of 16 mm negative film. We also had four exposure meters and two tripods.

The first day was spent moving bunk beds and improvising editing tables, giving us all a chance to get to know one another, and giving the Navajos a chance to see and to touch everything. Worth named every piece of equipment and had the students suggest places for storage.

The same day, *before* Worth said anything about movies, we interviewed each of the six Navajo in a small office we had set up in back of the trading post. We introduced the tape recorder to them, explaining that we would operate it to begin with, but that later we would teach them to use it and they could, if they wished, work it for our interviews or for any purpose of their choosing. There was no objection to being interviewed, both the boys and the girls watching avidly as Worth loaded tape and tested the machine.

In the initial interviews (so arranged that the students could not talk with one another before Worth spoke with them) we asked each of them individually what they expected of the summer's activity. We constantly used such phrases as 'You can make any kind of movie you want to'; 'You can make it about anything you want'; and 'I won't tell you what to do.'

We had decided that when Worth began instruction he would stick as closely as possible to the technology, trying to avoid any conceptualizing about what a film is or how one edits. On the second day he started talking to the students about making pictures, touching on the fact that peoples across time and cultures had all made pictures, and that movies were just another kind of picture. He mentioned Greeks, Egyptians, Europeans, Americans, Indian sand painting, drawing, sculpture, and weaving, generally trying to make the point that people always had special and *different* reasons for making pictures and that the students could decide what *they* wanted to show in this new way.

After an hour Worth asked for questions. Mike was the only one who had a question. He wanted to know if 'there was any people who didn't like to have their pictures taken'. Neither artist nor craftsman nor politician, Mike was worried about the sanctions that *might* be applied against him if he took pictures of people 'who didn't want you to' or 'who might not like it afterwards'. Although he made a film, he was the only one who showed discomfort about the process all the way through. He was also the only one who later questioned whether we should show the finished films to the community. When Mike asked his question about people who didn't want their picture taken, Worth replied that he knew of several such cases. He told of trying to take pictures in a synagogue and having the Rabbi ask him to stop because his religion didn't allow picture taking. Worth explained that in that situation he immediately withdrew. Adair mentioned that when we had come to Pine Springs two months before we had been invited to a Sing, and Worth, who carried a still camera hanging from a strap around his neck, had been asked not to take pictures. Mike seemed satisfied that he would not have to take pictures when people didn't want him to.

Not all our students, however, felt this way. Johnny created an incident that almost caused the community to ask us to leave, by taking movies during an Enemy Way (Squaw Dance) ceremony. The ceremony didn't go well – some of the ritual behavior was not carried out correctly (the drum stick broke) – and the ceremony had to be repeated, at great cost to the community. This was a traumatic, expensive, and unhealthy situation for the community, and Johnny's movie-making was used as an excuse for things having gone badly. Eventually, a delegation arrived at the schoolhouse and asked Johnny either to give up the film footage taken during the ceremony or pay $100 and six sheep. Johnny decided to give up the footage, but this did not make him fearful about continuing; as a matter of fact, he was so enthusiastic that he subsequently made two films.

At about eleven o'clock of the second day, Worth began to explain the actual workings of a movie camera. He did this in much the same way that he had taught his graduate students at the University of Pennsylvania – that is, by explaining the principles of photography, touching upon how lenses worked, how silver salts on film reacted to light in much the same way that the silver which the Navajo knew and worked with tarnished when exposed to light, and how an image was fixed by hypo salts so it wouldn't continue reacting to light. Then, by using drawings and diagrams on an improvised blackboard as much as possible, he explained how a movie camera worked. He described briefly the notion that a movie was a series of still photographs made in rapid sequence and projected back at the same rate of speed. This led to a discussion of the mechanisms by which the film was transported from one roll to another, passing behind the lens, stopping for the correct exposure, and then moving on so that the next still picture could be made. He pointed out the camera gate, shutter, and claw for advancing the film, and the necessity for film loops so as to allow smooth and even passage of film across the lens. He explained briefly about the ways in which exposure was controlled (F-stop and shutter) but told the students that the exposure meter would be described the next day.

This preliminary talk took about an hour. We noticed then that

366

there seemed very little tension on the part of the Navajo in this strange learning situation. They were quite relaxed, very attentive, and seemed to be absorbing all that Worth was saying, although some of the words must have been quite strange to them. Although Worth tried not to use technical or jargon words, a check of the tapes of this session showed that a great many such words ('gamma', 'diaphragm', 'variable', and so on) did creep in. It became evident in later sessions that learning the use of and acquiring the ability to manipulate the materials was not dependent on knowing the names of specific parts but rather on understanding their function. It took most of the students all summer to learn the names of the parts of the cameras, projectors, and editing equipment, but they constantly referred to them by paraphrases describing their function. The diaphragm ring on a lens, for example, which set the correct exposure, was commonly called 'the thing you turn for exposure' or, shorter, 'the exposure turner', much as we frequently refer to a thing as 'the gizmo that. . . .'

After lunch Worth demonstrated, rather than explained, the workings of a 16 mm Bell and Howell triple-lens turret camera, pointing out how exposure settings and focus settings were made on the lens, how the viewing system worked, and how the camera was loaded. It had been his experience with graduate students that four or five hours of both explanation and practice were needed before the camera could be loaded and used properly.

As soon as Worth finished his first loading run-through, he passed the camera around so that each of the students could examine it. He thought they would then require individual instruction before they themselves could load and be ready to use it. To his surprise, Johnny asked if he could load the camera. Worth gave him a scrap piece of film and said 'Sure'. Johnny showed no fear of the new experience and in two tries was able to load the camera perfectly.

Within an hour all students had shown they could load the camera. This requires a fair amount of finger dexterity in order to get into tiny spaces, an ability to manipulate several parts of small size in a definite sequence, and the ability to understand the notion of film loop size, claw engagement, and accurate windup procedures. Although the Navajo are known for their willingness to participate in innovative situations, we were still somewhat surprised at the rapidity and ease with which they mastered this and most other mechanical and conceptual tasks related to film-making.

After the students had practised loading for about half an hour we went outside where Worth showed them how to look through the viewfinder and hold the camera. He explained that he wanted to shoot one hundred feet of film so that the roll could be sent to the laboratory for developing that day. He took about ten shots of the students standing around. He said nothing to explain what he was doing or why he was shooting with any particular lens. What they certainly observed was taking an exposure reading, winding the camera spring, focussing, and changing lenses.

He then asked each student to take some pictures of 'anything you want'. Most spent some time exploring the different images available through the various focal length viewfinders and practised holding the camera up to their eyes. Some made shots of children in the school playground, others of the buildings, and some chose natural objects (rocks, trees, and so on).

We finished shooting at about five o'clock, and Richard Chalfen (our graduate assistant) drove off to Gallup to put the film on the plane to the processing lab. By this time, the second day of the project but actually the first day of instruction, we had been able to teach our students enough to load and use a motion picture camera and actually to shoot their first footage.

As a guide to how and what we would teach we had begun, among ourselves, to use a speculative analogy. Suppose we could find a group of humans who were very much like us in most ways, except that they didn't have the little machine in their throats that enabled them to make the sounds that would eventually become verbal communication in the form of language. Suppose we brought them a 'box' that could make for them all the varieties of sound that the human voice can. Suppose further that we merely taught them how the box worked and observed (1) whether they used it, (2) whether they used all the sounds, and (3) whether they organized their selected units of sound in such a way that we could observe a 'pattern'.

Our rule of thumb was to teach our Navajo students the 'machine' (film and camera) and its mechanical works only, and to observe what set of images they produced and what system they imposed upon them, when and if they organized the images then produced. By the end of the first week, they had been taught to use the exposure meter, the camera, the viewer, rewinds, splicer, and Bell and Howell projector. It was the introduction of editing that posed the greatest problem for us. We decided that we would introduce a splicer and show them how it worked, hoping that they would discover or develop principles of film organization by themselves. Worth explained that a splicer was a machine for pasting pieces of film together. It could be used to repair film that tore or to put together lengths of film for any other purpose. We were aware that the very notion of putting lengths of film together was a basic step in the development of any structure. . . .

368

It might be useful to describe some of the first one-minute films made by the Navajo students. Mike said he wanted to make a movie of a piñon tree. He wanted to show 'how it grow'. He set about finding a piñon seedling and making a shot of it. Then he photographed a little taller tree and so on, until he had photographed a series of seven cademes ending with a full-grown tree. Worth thought he was finished, but he continued with a dead piñon tree, that still had some growth on it, then a tree that had fallen to the ground, then some dead branches, then a piñon nut, ending with a shot of the same piñon bush he started with.

When the film was returned from the laboratory and shown to the group, we detected some puzzled looks. The film consisted of twelve cademes, as described above. Although Mike and the others couldn't then make clear the reasons for their surprise at the result of their first shooting experience, Mike later was able to articulate his difficulty. He had photographed a sequence of trees in a particular order, a cademe sequence. Its sequence and semantic content, he felt, should imply the meaning 'how a piñon tree grows'. Instead, all the images had the same spatial relation to the size of the screen; that is, because he shot all the trees, both small and large, as close-ups (filling the full frame), he failed to communicate the process of growth which can be shown when something little becomes big. Because all the images – those that represented 'in reality' big things and those that represented small ones – were made to appear the same size in relation to the size of the screen, their representative or iconic qualities of 'bigness' and 'littleness', which were the relevant semantic dimensions of the cademes, were lost.

In another case, that of Johnny, we have evidence of the independent discovery of what might be called the modifier-object relationship. Johnny said he wanted to make a movie about a horse. After getting permission from its owner to use a horse that was tethered near the trading post, Johnny started shooting. First he proceeded to examine the horse through the various focal-length viewfinders on the camera. He remained in the same spatial relation to the horse but tried 'seeing' the horse from the different 'distances' that various focal-length lenses allow. He finally told Worth that he was going to make pictures of 'pieces of the horse' so that you (meaning Worth) would get to know a Navajo horse when 'you see my film'.

He shot about ten close-ups, of the head, the eyes, the tail, the penis, the legs, and so on. He took perhaps two minutes of thought to determine each shot. He worked quietly, asking few questions, setting exposure and distance with care. After about twenty minutes, he started looking at Worth frequently, not turning his head all the way, but with that quick sideways movement of the pupil characteristic of the Navajo. Then he said 'Mr Worth, if I show pieces of this horse, then tomorrow take a picture of a complete horse at the Squaw Dance – or lots of horses, can I paste them together and will people think that I'm showing pieces of all the horses?'

Worth managed to restrain himself and said merely, 'What do you think?' Johnny thought a bit and said, 'I'd have to think about it more but I think this is so with movies.' Worth asked, 'What is so?' And Johnny replied, 'That when you paste pieces of a horse in between pictures of a whole horse people will think it's part of the same horse.'

During the rest of that week the students worked on their 100-foot films, and we interviewed them about the 'real' (as they called them) films that they were to start the following week. All the students now knew very clearly just what they wanted to do. This is in contrast to Worth's graduate students, who frequently are not certain of their subject matter for several months and often for as long as six months. Susie wanted to make a film about her mother weaving a rug. She wanted to 'show how hard it is, how good my mother is, and why Navajo rugs must be so expensive'. Johnny was going to make a film about a silversmith. It also 'should show how good Navajos are with silver', and 'how hard it is to make good jewelry'. Mike wanted to make a film about a lake, 'just to show all things there are there'. Al kept talking about a film that would have 'lots of symbols', that would be about 'the world', and that we would understand 'later'. Mary Jane and Maxine decided that they wanted to work together and that they wanted to make a film about the old ways, 'about our grandfather, who is a very important medicine man'.

By the second week, when they started working on their 'real' films, we stopped any formal instruction. We would answer questions, and we drove them to whatever sites they wanted to go to for their photographing. This, of course, gave us a natural excuse to hang around as observers. Our observations were quite extensive and on many levels. Adair obtained life histories on each student and his place and position in the community, and on his relations with Worth and Chalfen as teachers. He kept a running record of the community's reactions to the film-making project. We all kept extensive notes and tapes of how the students conceived, photographed, and edited their films.

On their conceptualizations of their films in progress we obtained frequent taped interviews, asking such questions as 'What do you want to make your film about?' 'Why?' 'Who is it for?' 'What will happen when people see it?' and so on. As work continued we asked what they wanted to shoot *tomorrow*: 'Where does it fit into the film?'

370

'Why do you need that?' 'How will you do it?' As the film came back from the lab we viewed it and asked our students how they liked what they had done. As the editing progressed we asked 'Why does this shot go with that one?' 'Why did you leave that out?' 'What's the purpose of that?' 'Why did you splice here instead of here?' When the films were finished we asked each one in an extended interview why he had chosen each shot and what it meant in the film. These tapes are all transcribed now and are part of the material we are analyzing.

Other kinds of data were provided by our observations of how the students were photographing and editing. Our daily field notes are full of remarks such as 'They are doing it all wrong,' 'They don't start at the beginning,' 'They have no idea of how an event is structured,' and 'They don't know how to spot the important things.'

While Susie Bennally was working on her film, we observed how smoothly the film-making procedure became integrated into the daily life of Susie and her mother and father. People wandering by would stop and look through the viewfinder. Susie's mother, Alta Kahn, was quietly curious and asked several times if she could look through the camera, which Susie let her do. The evident satisfaction that her mother showed provided us with the opportunity to see if it would be possible to pass on to a non-English speaker the same technology we had taught the bilingual. We asked Susie if she would be willing to teach her mother to make movies. Although Susie was extremely shy, she responded to this in a more overtly positive way than to almost anything else we had asked her to do. In agreeing to teach her mother, however, Susie laid down the rules of the game. She must be alone with her mother at first, and then Worth might observe her and record on tape what was said. (Worth was not allowed to come between mother and daughter.) Also, the mother must be able to see the film as it was returned from the laboratory, in privacy, and no other Navajo was to be around during the editing.

That the mother was readily able to learn to shoot and edit is an indication of the ability of a monolingual Navajo to learn new technology quickly, but, more importantly, it is corroboration of the method of letting the participants in the transfer of the technology structure situations that are compatible with traditional role enactment.

Johnny Nelson, in an interview, brought out his feeling that Worth could teach a Navajo medicine man to make film depicting ritual performances, providing he worked with an intermediary, like himself, in the role of interpreter. He was also of the opinion that the medicine men would be interested in this means of preserving ceremonies for future generations.

The fieldwork was completed in two months, during June and July of 1966. The Navajo students made seven twenty-minute films and five smaller one- and two-minute films.

By July 24 all the films were finished in rough cut except the one being made by Susie's mother. On the afternoon of the 25th, we showed the films to the community. At the suggestion of the Tsosie sisters, notices had been placed in the trading post and elsewhere with the wording 'World Premiere Navajo Films'. Approximately 60 Navajo showed up, including children. After the showing Adair interviewed nine of the adults, five of whom were women and four men. We were especially interested in what the films 'said' to the interviewees and how they evaluated them.

Generally speaking, the films were liked because they conveyed information. Some typical responses were: 'Yes, that certainly teaches a lot of good things about weaving', 'I think they all bring out good points as far as learning is concerned', and 'there is a lot of teaching behind this work'. The films concerned with crafts were highly valued because they were related to the economic welfare of the community. One of the respondents said she liked the films because they taught

> how to do these things. I think that is what the film is intended for. The same is true of the silversmithing. This should also be taught to the children.

Others responded:

> This is the type of work that some of the people are supporting their families . . . so it is good and a good thing to know.
>
> Perhaps the Navajo rugs would bring a little more money from now on . . . White people never give much money for anything. Maybe this is why they want to show them and how the rugs are made.
>
> It was showing how to make silver crafts which will bring more money and will be on demand.

Johnny's film showing how a shallow well is made was liked because it 'teaches how to fix water so you can always have clean water to use', and the Tsosie sisters' *The Spirit of the Navajo* was liked because 'He (the medicine man) did not make any mistake. He performed the ceremony like he should.'

In these nine interviews we had two instances in which the Navajos made some rather interesting remarks about their reasons for not understanding certain films (*Intrepid Shadows* and *Shallow Well*). Both these films were somewhat outside the framework of Navajo cognition; *Intrepid Shadows* because of its complex form, and *Shallow Well* because of its nontraditional subject matter.

When asked, 'Does that film tell you anything?' one respondent, a woman aged 44, with one year of schooling, who stated in the same interview 'I never been to a movie before' replied,

'I cannot understand English. It was telling all about it in English which I couldn't understand.

Another response was,

That picture was also being explained in English. The reason I didn't get the meaning is because I can't understand English.

None of the films, of course, had any sound at all. Since these interviews were conducted in Navajo, we didn't see the translated tapes until we left the reservation, and have not been able to question our informants further along these lines. We can only speculate that when someone in a situation such as we are describing sees a film they don't understand, it seems reasonable (not only to the subject in this case but also to the Navajo interpreter) to assume it is in a language different from theirs. In this case, since we spoke English and she didn't, and she couldn't understand the film, she assumed that the film, in effect, spoke in English even though the film was silent.

33

Pedagogy of the Oppressed *

Paulo Freire

A careful analysis of the teacher-student relationship at any level, inside or outside the school, reveals its fundamentally *narrative* character. This relationship involves a narrating subject (the teacher) and patient, listening objects (the students). The contents, whether values or empirical dimensions of reality, tend in the process of being narrated to become lifeless and petrified. Education is suffering from narration sickness.

The teacher talks about reality as if it were motionless, static, compartmentalized, and predictable. Or else he expounds on a topic completely alien to the existential experience of the students. His task is to 'fill' the students with the contents of his narration – contents which are detached from reality, disconnected from the totality that engendered them and could give them significance. Words are emptied of their concreteness and become a hollow, alienated, and alienating verbosity.

The outstanding characteristic of this narrative education, then, is the sonority of words, not their transforming power. 'Four times four is sixteen; the capital of Pará is Belém.' The student records, memorizes, and repeats these phrases without perceiving what four times four really means, or realizing the true significance of 'capital' in the affirmation 'the capital of Pará is Belém', that is, what Belém means for Pará and what Pará means for Brazil.

Narration (with the teacher as narrator) leads the students to memorize mechanically the narrated content. Worse yet, it turns them into 'containers', into 'receptacles' to be 'filled' by the teacher. The more completely he fills the receptacles, the better a teacher he is. The more meekly the receptacles permit themselves to be filled, the better students they are.

Education thus becomes an act of depositing, in which the students are the depositories and the teacher is the depositor. Instead of com-

* * *

* *Pedagogy of the Oppressed*, Herder and Herder, New York, 1970. Penguin 1972.

municating, the teacher issues communiqués and makes deposits which the students patiently receive, memorize, and repeat. This is the 'banking' concept of education, in which the scope of action allowed to the students extends only as far as receiving, filing, and storing the deposits. They do, it is true, have the opportunity to become collectors or cataloguers of the things they store. But in the last analysis, it is men themselves who are filed away through the lack of creativity, transformation, and knowledge in this (at best) misguided system. For apart from inquiry, apart from the praxis, men cannot be truly human. Knowledge emerges only through invention and re-invention, through the restless, impatient, continuing, hopeful inquiry men pursue in the world, with the world, and with each other.

In the banking concept of education, knowledge is a gift bestowed by those who consider themselves knowledeable upon those whom they consider to know nothing. Projecting an absolute ignorance on to others, a characteristic of the ideology of oppression, negates education and knowledge as processes of inquiry. The teacher presents himself to his students as their necessary opposite; by considering their ignorance absolute, he justifies his own existence. The students, alienated like the slave in the Hegelian dialectic, accept their ignorance as justifying the teacher's existence – but, unlike the slave, they never discover that they educate the teacher.

The *raison d'être* of libertarian education, on the other hand, lies in its drive towards reconciliation. Education must begin with the solution of the teacher-student contradiction, by reconciling the poles of the contradiction so that both are simultaneously teachers *and* students.

This solution is not (nor can it be) found in the banking concept. On the contrary, banking education maintains and even stimulates the contradiction through the following attitudes and practices, which mirror oppressive society as a whole:

(a) the teacher teaches and the students are taught;

(b) the teacher knows everything and the students know nothing;

(c) the teacher thinks and the students are thought about;

(d) the teacher talks and the students listen – meekly;

(e) the teacher disciplines and the students are disciplined;

(f) the teacher chooses and enforces his choice, and the students comply;

(g) the teacher acts and the students have the illusion of acting through the action of the teacher;

(h) the teacher chooses the program content, and the students (who were not consulted) adapt to it;

(*i*) the teacher confuses the authority of knowledge with his own professional authority, which he sets in opposition to the freedom of the students;

(*j*) the teacher is the subject of the learning process, while the pupils are mere objects.

It is not surprising that the banking concept of education regards men as adaptable, manageable beings. The more students work at storing the deposits entrusted to them, the less they develop the critical consciousness which would result from their intervention in the world as transformers of that world. The more completely they accept the passive role imposed on them, the more they tend simply to adapt to the world as it is and to the fragmented view of reality deposited in them.

The capability of banking education to minimize or annul the students' creative power and to stimulate their credulity serves the interests of the oppressors, who care neither to have the world revealed nor to see it transformed. The oppressors use their 'humanitarianism' to preserve a profitable situation. Thus they react almost instinctively against any experiment in education which stimulates the critical faculties and is not content with a partial view of reality but always seeks out the ties which link one point to another and one problem to another.

Indeed, the interests of the oppressors lie in 'changing the consciousness of the oppressed, not the situation which oppresses them'; for the more the oppressed can be led to adapt to that situation, the more easily they can be dominated. To achieve this end, the oppressors use the banking concept of education in conjunction with a paternalistic social action apparatus, within which the oppressed receive the euphemistic title of 'welfare recipients'. They are treated as individual cases, as marginal men who deviate from the general configuration of a 'good, organized, and just' society. The oppressed are regarded as the pathology of the healthy society, which must therefore adjust these 'incompetent and lazy' folk to its own patterns by changing their mentality. These marginals need to be 'integrated', 'incorporated' into the healthy society that they have 'forsaken'.

The truth is, however, that the oppressed are not 'marginals', are not men living 'outside' society. They have always been 'inside' – inside the structure which made them 'beings for others'. The solution is not to 'integrate' them into the structure of oppression, but to transform that structure so that they can become 'beings for themselves'. Such transformation, of course, would undermine the oppressors' purposes; hence their utilization of the banking concept of education to avoid the threat of student *conscientização*.

The banking approach to adult education, for example, will never propose to students that they critically consider reality. It will deal instead with such vital questions as whether Roger gave green grass to the goat, and insist upon the importance of learning that, on the contrary, Roger gave green grass to the rabbit. The 'humanism' of the banking approach masks the effort to turn men into automatons – the very negation of their ontological vocation to be more fully human.

Those who use the banking approach, knowingly or unknowingly (for there are innumerable well-intentioned bank-clerk teachers who do not realize that they are serving only to dehumanize), fail to perceive that the deposits themselves contain contradictions about reality. But, sooner or later, these contradictions may lead formerly passive students to turn against their domestication and the attempt to domesticate reality. They may discover through existential experience that their present way of life is irreconcilable with their vocation to become fully human. They may perceive through their relations with reality that reality is really a *process*, undergoing constant transformation. If men are searchers and their ontological vocation is humanization, sooner or later they may perceive the contradiction in which banking education seeks to maintain them, and then engage themselves in the struggle for their liberation.

But the humanist, revolutionary educator cannot wait for this possibility to materialize. From the outset, his efforts must coincide with those of the students to engage in critical thinking and the quest for mutual humanization. His efforts must be imbued with a profound trust in men and their creative power. To achieve this, he must be a partner of the students in his relations with them.

The banking concept does not admit to such partnership – and necessarily so. To resolve the teacher-student contradiction, to exchange the role of depositor, prescriber, domesticator, for the role of student among students would be to undermine the power of oppression and serve the cause of liberation.

Implicit in the banking concept is the assumption of a dichotomy between man and the world: man is merely *in* the world, not *with* the world or with others; man is spectator, not re-creator. In this view, man is not a conscious being *(corpo consciente)*; he is rather the possessor of *a* consciousness: an empty 'mind' passively open to the reception of deposits of reality from the world outside. For example, my desk, my books, my coffee cup, all the objects before me – as bits of the world which surrounds me – would be 'inside' me, exactly as I am inside my study right now. This view makes no distinction between being accessible to consciousness and entering consciousness. The distinction, however, is essential: the objects which surround me are simply accessible to my consciousness, not located within it. I am aware of them, but they are not inside me.

It follows logically from the banking notion of consciousness that the educator's role is to regulate the way the world 'enters into' the students. His task is to organize a process which already occurs spontaneously, to 'fill' the students by making deposits of information which he considers to constitute true knowledge.[1] And since men 'receive' the world as passive entities, education should make them more passive still, and adapt them to the world. The educated man is the adapted man, because he is better 'fit' for the world. Translated into practice, this concept is well suited to the purposes of the oppressors, whose tranquility rests on how well men fit the world the oppressors have created, and how little they question it.

The more completely the majority adapt to the purposes which the dominant minority prescribe for them (thereby depriving them of the right to their own purposes), the more easily the minority can continue to prescribe. The theory and practice of banking education serve this end quite efficiently. Verbalistic lessons, reading requirements, the methods for evaluating 'knowledge', the distance between the teacher and the taught, the criteria for promotion: everything in this ready-to-wear approach serves to obviate thinking.

The bank-clerk educator does not realize that there is no true security in his hypertrophied role, that one must seek to live *with* others in solidarity. One cannot impose oneself, nor even merely co-exist with one's students. Solidarity requires true communication, and the concept by which such an educator is guided fears and proscribes communication.

Yet only through communication can human life hold meaning. The teacher's thinking is authenticated only by the authenticity of the students' thinking. The teacher cannot think for his students, nor can he impose his thought on them. Authentic thinking, thinking that is concerned about *reality*, does not take place in ivory tower isolation, but only in communication. If it is true that thought has meaning only when generated by action upon the world, the subordination of students to teachers becomes impossible.

Because banking education begins with a false understanding of men as objects, it cannot promote the development of what Fromm calls 'biophily', but instead produces its opposite: 'necrophily'.

While life is characterized by growth in a structured, functional manner, the necrophilous person loves all that does not grow, all that is mechanical. The necrophilous person is driven by the desire to transform the organic into the inorganic, to approach life

378

mechanically, as if all living persons were things. ... Memory, rather than experience; having, rather than being is what counts. The necrophilous person can relate to an object – a flower or a person – only if he possesses it; hence a threat to his possession is a threat to himself; if he loses possession he loses contact with the world. ... He loves control, and in the act of controlling he kills life.

Oppression – overwhelming control – is necrophilic; it is nourished by love of death, not life. The banking concept of education, which serves the interests of oppression, is also necrophilic. Based on a mechanistic, static, naturalistic, spatialized view of consciousness, it transforms students into receiving objects. It attempts to control thinking and action, leads men to adjust to the world, and inhibits their creative power.

When their efforts to act responsibly are frustrated, when they find themselves unable to use their faculties, men suffer. 'This suffering due to impotence is rooted in the very fact that the human equili-brium has been disturbed.' But the inability to act which causes men's anguish also causes them to reject their impotence, by attempting

... to restore [their] capacity to act. But can [they], and how? One way is to submit to and identify with a person or group having power. By this symbolic participation in another person's life, [men have] the illusion of acting, when in reality [they] only submit to and become a part of those who act.[2]

Populist manifestations perhaps best exemplify this type of behavior by the oppressed, who, by identifying with charismatic leaders, come to feel that they themselves are active and effective. The rebellion they express as they emerge in the historical process is motivated by that desire to act effectively. The dominant elites consider the remedy to be more domination and repression, carried out in the name of freedom, order, and social peace (that is, the peace of the elites). Thus they can condemn – logically, from their point of view – 'the violence of a strike by workers and [can] call upon the state in the same breath to use violence in putting down the strike'.

Education as the exercise of domination stimulates the credulity of students, with the ideological intent (often not perceived by educators) of indoctrinating them to adapt to the world of oppression. This accusation is not made in the naïve hope that the dominant elites will thereby simply abandon the practice. Its objective is to call the attention of true humanists to the fact that they cannot use banking educational methods in the pursuit of liberation, for they would only negate that very pursuit. Nor may a revolutionary society inherit these methods from an oppressor society. The revolutionary society which practices banking education is either misguided or mistrusting or men. In either event, it is threatened by the specter of reaction.

Unfortunately, those who espouse the cause of liberation are themselves surrounded and influenced by the climate which generates the banking concept, and often do not perceive its true significance or its dehumanizing power. Paradoxically, then, they utilize this same instrument of alienation in what they consider an effort to liberate. Indeed, some 'revolutionaries' brand as 'innocents', 'dreamers', or even 'reactionaries' those who would challenge this educational practice. But one does not liberate men by alienating them. Authentic liberation – the process of humanization – is not another deposit to be made in men. Liberation is a praxis: the action and reflection of men upon their world in order to transform it. Those truly committed to the cause of liberation can accept neither the mechanistic concept of consciousness as an empty vessel to be filled, nor the use of banking methods of domination (propaganda, slogans – deposits) in the name of liberation.

Those truly committed to liberation must reject the banking concept in its entirety, adopting instead a concept of men as conscious beings, and consciousness as consciousness intent upon the world. They must abandon the educational goal of deposit-making and replace it with the posing of the problems of men in their relations with the world. 'Problem-posing' education, responding to the essence of consciousness – *intentionality* – rejects communiqués and embodies communication. It epitomizes the special characteristic of consciousness: being *conscious of*, not only as intent on objects but as turned in upon itself in a Jasperian 'split' – consciousness as consciousness *of* consciousness.

Liberating education consists in acts of cognition, not transferrals of information. It is a learning situation in which the cognizable object (far from being the end of the cognitive act) intermediates the cognitive actors – teacher on the one hand and students on the other. Accordingly, the practice of problem-posing education entails at the outset that the teacher-student contradiction be resolved. Diagonal relations – indispensable to the capacity of cognitive actors to co-operate in perceiving the same cognizable object – are otherwise impossible.

Indeed, problem-posing education, which breaks with the vertical patterns characteristic of banking education, can fulfill its function as the practice of freedom only if it can overcome the above contradiction. Through dialogue, the teacher-of-the-students and the students-of-the-teacher cease to exist and a new term emerges: teacher-student with students-teachers. The teacher is no longer merely the-one-who-teaches, but one who is himself taught in dialogue with the students, who in turn while being taught also teach. They become jointly responsible for a process in which all grow. In this process, arguments based on 'authority' are no longer valid; in order to function, authority must be *on the side of* freedom, not *against* it. Here, no one teaches another, nor is anyone self-taught. Men teach each other, mediated by the world, by the cognizable objects which in banking education are 'owned' by the teacher.

The banking concept (with its tendency to dichotomize everything) distinguishes two stages in the action of the educator. During the first, he cognizes a cognizable object while he prepares his lessons in his study or his laboratory; during the second, he expounds to his students about that object. The students are not called upon to know, but to memorize the contents narrated by the teacher. Nor do the students practice any act of cognition, since the object towards which that act should be directed is the property of the teacher rather than a medium evoking the critical reflection of both teacher and students. Hence in the name of the 'preservation of culture and knowledge' we have a system which achieves neither true knowledge nor true culture.

The problem-posing method does not dichotomize the activity of the teacher-student: he is not 'cognitive' at one point and 'narrative' at another. He is always 'cognitive', whether preparing a project or engaging in dialogue with the students. He does not regard cognizable objects as his private property, but as the object of reflection by himself and the students. In this way, the problem-posing educator constantly re-forms his reflections in the reflection of the students. The students – no longer docile listeners – are now critical co-investigators in dialogue with the teacher. The teacher presents the material to the students for their consideration, and re-considers his earlier considerations as the students express their own. The role of the problem-posing educator is to create, together with the students, the conditions under which knowledge at the level of the *doxa* is superseded by true knowledge, at the level of the *logos*.

Whereas banking education anesthetizes and inhibits creative power, problem-posing education involves a constant unveiling of reality. The former attempts to maintain the *submersion* of consciousness; the latter strives for the *emergence* of consciousness and *critical intervention* in reality.

Students, as they are increasingly posed with problems relating to themselves in the world and with the world, will feel increasingly challenged and obliged to respond to that challenge. Because they apprehend the challenge as interrelated to other problems within a total context, not as a theoretical question, the resulting comprehension tends to be increasingly critical and thus constantly less alienated. Their response to the challenge evokes new challenges, followed by new understandings; and gradually the students come to regard themselves as committed.

Education as the practice of freedom – as opposed to education as the practice of domination – denies that man is abstract, isolated, independent, and unattached to the world; it also denies that the world exists as a reality apart from men. Authentic reflection considers neither abstract man nor the world without men, but men in their relations with the world. In these relations consciousness and world are simultaneous: consciousness neither precedes the world nor follows it.

* * *

In one of our culture circles in Chile, the group was discussing the anthropological concept of culture. In the midst of the discussion, a peasant who by banking standards was completely ignorant said: 'Now I see that without man there is no world'. When the educator responded: 'Let's say, for the sake of argument, that all the men on earth were to die, but that the earth itself remained, together with trees, birds, animals, rivers, seas, the stars . . . wouldn't all this be a world?' 'Oh no,' the peasant replied emphatically. 'There would be no one to say: "This is a world".'

The peasant wished to express the idea that there would be lacking the consciousness of the world which necessarily implies the world of consciousness. *I* cannot exist without a *not-I*. In turn, the *not-I* depends on that existence. The world which brings consciousness into existence becomes the world *of* that consciousness. Hence, the previously cited affirmation of Sartre: '*La conscience et le monde sont dormés d'un même coup.*'

As men, simultaneously reflecting on themselves and on the world, increase the scope of their perception, they begin to direct their observations towards previously inconspicuous phenomena:

> In perception properly so-called, as an explicit awareness [*Gewahren*], I am turned towards the object, to the paper, for instance. I apprehend it as being this here and now. The apprehension is a singling out, every object having a background in experience. Around and about the paper lie books, pencils, ink-well, and so forth, and these in a certain sense are also 'perceived', perceptually there, in the 'field of intuition'; but whilst I was turned towards the paper there was no turning in their direction, nor any apprehending of them, not even in a secondary sense. They ap-

382

peared and yet were not singled out, were not posited on their own account. Every perception of a thing has such a zone of background intuitions or background awareness, if 'intuiting' already includes the state of being turned towards, and this also is a 'conscious experience', or more briefly a 'consciousness of' all indeed that in point of fact lies in the co-perceived objective background.[3] That which had existed objectively but had not been perceived in its deeper implications (if indeed it was perceived at all) begins to 'stand out', assuming the character of a problem and therefore of challenge. Thus, men begin to single out elements from their 'background awareness' and to reflect upon them. These elements are now objects of men's consideration, and, as such, objects of their action and cognition.

In problem-posing education, men develop their power to perceive critically *the way they exist* in the world *with which* and *in which* they find themselves; they come to see the world not as a static reality, but as a reality in process, in transformation. Although the dialectical relations of men with the world exist independently of how these relations are perceived (or whether or not they are perceived at all), it is also true that the form of action men adopt is to a large extent a function of how they perceive themselves in the world. Hence, the teacher-student and the students-teachers reflect simultaneously on themselves and the world without dichotomizing this reflection from action, and thus establish an authentic form of thought and action.

Once again, the two educational concepts and practices under analysis come into conflict. Banking education (for obvious reasons) attempts, by mythicizing reality, to conceal certain facts which explain the way men exist in the world; problem-posing education sets itself the task of demythologizing. Banking education resists dialogue; problem-posing education regards dialogue as indispensable to the act of cognition which unveils reality. Banking education treats students as objects of assistance; problem-posing education makes them critical thinkers. Banking education inhibits creativity and domesticates (although it cannot completely destroy) the *intentionality* of consciousness by isolating consciousness from the world, thereby denying men their ontological and historical vocation of becoming more fully human. Problem-posing education bases itself on creativity and stimulates true reflection and action upon reality, thereby responding to the vocation of men as beings who are authentic only when engaged in inquiry and creative transformation. In sum: banking theory and practice, as immobilizing and fixating forces, fail to acknowledge men as historical beings; problem-posing theory and practice take man's historicity as their starting point.

Problem-posing education affirms men as beings in the process of *becoming* – as unfinished, uncompleted beings in and with a likewise unfinished reality. Indeed, in contrast to other animals who are unfinished, but not historical, men know themselves to be unfinished; they are aware of their incompletion. In this incompletion and this awareness lie the very roots of education as an exclusively human manifestation. The unfinished character of men and the transformational character of reality necessitate that education be an ongoing activity.

Education is thus constantly remade in the praxis. In order to *be*, it must *become*. Its 'duration' (in the Bergsonian meaning of the word) is found in the interplay of the opposites *permanence* and *change*. The banking method emphasizes permanence and becomes reactionary; problem-posing education – which accepts neither a 'well-behaved' present nor a predetermined future – roots itself in the dynamic present and becomes revolutionary.

Problem-posing education is revolutionary futurity. Hence it is prophetic (and, as such, hopeful). Hence, it corresponds to the historical nature of man. Hence, it affirms men as beings who transcend themselves, who move forward and look ahead, for whom immobility represents a fatal threat, for whom looking at the past must only be a means of understanding more clearly what and who they are so that they can more wisely build the future. Hence, it identifies with the movement which engages men as beings aware of their incompletion – an historical movement which has its point of departure, its subjects and its objective.

The point of departure of the movement lies in men themselves. But since men do not exist apart from the world, apart from reality, the movement must begin with the men-world relationship. Accordingly, the point of departure must always be with men in the 'here and now', which constitutes the situation within which they are submerged, from which they emerge, and in which they intervene. Only by starting from this situation – which determines their perception of it – can they begin to move. To do this authentically they must perceive their state not as fated and unalterable, but merely as limiting – and therefore challenging.

Whereas the banking method directly or indirectly reinforces men's fatalistic perception of their situation, the problem-posing method presents this very situation to them as a problem. As the situation becomes the object of their cognition, the naïve or magical perception which produced their fatalism gives way to perception which is able to perceive itself even as it perceives reality, and can thus be critically objective about that reality.

A deepened consciousness of their situation leads men to apprehend that situation as an historical reality susceptible of transformation. Resignation gives way to the drive for transformation and inquiry, over which men feel themselves to be in control. If men, as historical beings necessarily engaged with other men in a movement of inquiry, did not control that movement, it would be (and is) a violation of men's humanity. Any situation in which some men prevent others from engaging in the process of inquiry is one of violence. The means used are not important; to alienate men from their own decision-making is to change them into objects.

This movement of inquiry must be directed towards humanization – man's historical vocation. The pursuit of full humanity, however, cannot be carried out in isolation or individualism, but only in fellowship and solidarity; therefore it cannot unfold in the antagonistic relations between oppressors and oppressed. No one can be authentically human while he prevents others from being so. Attempting *to be more* human, individualistically, leads to *having more*, egotistically: a form of dehumanization. Not that it is not fundamental *to have* in order *to be* human. Precisely because it *is* necessary, some men's *having* must not be allowed to constitute an obstacle to others' *having*, must not consolidate the power of the former to crush the latter.

Problem-posing education, as a humanist and liberating praxis, posits as fundamental that men subjected to domination must fight for their emancipation. To that end, it enables teachers and students to become Subjects of the educational process by overcoming authoritarianism and an alienating intellectualism; it also enables men to overcome their false perception of reality. The world – no longer something to be described with deceptive words – becomes the object of that transforming action by men which results in their humanization.

Problem-posing education does not and cannot serve the interests of the oppressor. No oppressive order could permit the oppressed to begin to question: Why? While only a revolutionary society can carry out this education in systematic terms, the revolutionary leaders need not take full power before they can employ the method. In the revolutionary process, the leaders cannot utilize the banking method as an interim measure, justified on grounds of expediency, with the intention of *later* behaving in a genuinely revolutionary fashion. They must be revolutionary – that is to say, dialogical – from the outset.

References

¹ This concept corresponds to what Sartre calls the 'digestive' or 'nutritive' concept of education, in which knowledge is 'fed' by the teacher to the students to 'fill them out'. See JEAN-PAUL SARTRE, 'Une idée fundamentale de la phénomenologie de Husserl: L'intentionalité,' *Situations I* (Paris, 1947).

² FROMM, *op cit* p 31.

³ EDMUND HUSSERL, *Ideas – General Introduction to Pure Phenomenology* (London, 1969), 105–106.

Part Six

Knowledge as a Corpus

There has been a recent renewal of interest in what Blum (1971) has aptly called 'a sociological description of intellectual activity as the organization of social action'. As suggested elsewhere (YOUNG 1973) and as exemplified in Brown's (1973) recent collection, this has had unfortunate consequences for sociological enquiry in education; a new category 'the sociology of the curriculum' has taken on a kind of life of its own. In this collection we have set out to offer an explicit alternative. To recognize the socially constructed character of education is to realize as Williams and Hoare do in the first extracts in this section that this is not a call for a separate sociology of the curriculum (what ever that may refer to), but for a radical reformulation of questions of selection, equality, school organization and the wider issues of mobility and social change. To put it another way, these extracts are arguing that knowledge or 'curriculum' cannot be viewed as somehow independent of the social relations in which it is embedded.

The extract from Kuhn, which points to the way scientists, through the activities of text-book writers, display and make available an authoritative view of the world as *the* world for practitioners to master, addresses wider possibilities of examining how versions of the world are *made* real to students and pupils, not only through textbook writers but also through the everyday practices of question and answer by teachers in school.

The extracts from Dickens and Ellis, and the papers by Frake, Conklin and Radin can be viewed as critically addressing the contextual or situational character of knowledge. Through the unashamedly humourous dialogues between Mr Gradgrind and Cecilia and Mr Wentworth and Mason, the ways in which conceptions of knowledge and 'subjects' close off the world and arbitrarily attribute status to some knowings and not to others is well illustrated. The point is evocatively made in Radin's paper through examples of poetry and prose of non-literate societies, which also raises questions about the goodness-to-fit models of literacy and forms of thinking in, for example, the work of Goody and Watt (1963). Important areas of enquiry into the widely assumed necessity of writing as a prerequisite of many so-called 'higher-order' intellectual activities are also suggested. The more specific accounts by Frake and Conklin illustrate that talk of knowledge, whether it is of colour or 'asking for a drink', or whether it is the claims of educators to be able to postulate certain 'universalistic' meanings as explanations, is to fail to recognize the socially contexted nature of all knowledge. Just as Frake, in learning how to ask for a drink, also learnt how to be accepted as a member of a community, so the pupil, if he picks up the grounds of the teacher's questions, not only learns how, when and what to answer, but how to be identified as an acceptable pupil. Conklin's paper suggests that if one 'knows' the contexts and meanings of everyday life among the Hanunóo, their colour categories are as much a coherent 'body of knowledge' as Western botanical systems. Such accounts suggest the constructed nature of what we have come to call 'formal' bodies of knowledge or 'disciplines', and enable us to see them like the 'knowledge' reported by ethnographers, as the ongoing accomplishment of members.

The extract by Schutz and the paper by Greene can be viewed as drawing together some of the themes raised in this section. In contradiction to the traditional wisdom of 'curriculum theorists' such as Bloom and Hirst with their socially prescribed disciplines, hierarchies of knowing etc, Greene argues that reason, order and rationality can be envisaged, not as the property of some, but 'the culmination of his [the learner's] constitution of the world', a point developed at some length by Jenks (1973).

References

A BLUM, *The Corpus of Knowledge as a Normative Order*, in YOUNG (1971).

R BROWN (ed), *Knowledge, Education and Cultural Change*, Tavistock, 1973.

J GOODY and I WATT (1963), 'The consequences of literacy', *Comparative Studies in History*

C JENKS (1973), 'Forms of knowledge and powers of the mind', in C JENKS (1976), *Education, Rationality and the Social Organization of Knowledge*, Routledge and Kegan Paul.

M F D YOUNG (1973), 'Taking sides against the probable', in C JENKS (1976), *Education, Rationality and the Social Organization of Knowledge*.

34

Rules for all ranks and food for every mind? *

Raymond Williams

There are clear and obvious connections between the quality of a culture and the quality of its system of education. In our own time we have settled to saying that the improvement of our culture is a matter of improving and extending our national education, and in one sense this is obviously true. Yet we speak sometimes as if education were a fixed abstraction, a settled body of teaching and learning, and as if the only problem it presents to us is that of distribution: this amount, for this period of time, to this or that group. The business of organizing education – creating types of institution, deciding lengths of courses, agreeing conditions of entry and duration – is certainly important. Yet to conduct this business as if it were the distribution of a simple product is wholly misleading. It is not only that the way in which education is organized can be seen to express, consciously and unconsciously, the wider organization of a culture and a society, so that what has been thought of as simple distribution is in fact an active shaping to particular social ends. It is also that the content of education, which is subject to great historical variation, again expresses, again both consciously and unconsciously, certain basic elements in the culture, what is thought of as 'an education' being in fact a particular selection, a particular set of emphases and omissions. Further, when this selection of content is examined more closely, it will be seen to be one of the decisive factors affecting its distribution: the cultural choices involved in the selection of content have an organic relation to the social choices involved in the practical organization. If we are to discuss education adequately, we must examine, in historical and analytic terms, this organic relation, for to be conscious of a choice made is to be conscious of further and alternative choices available, and at a time when changes, under a multitude of pressures, will in any case occur, this degree of consciousness is vital.

* From *The Long Revolution*, Chatto and Windus, 1961, 125–144.

389

We cannot begin with the aims of education as abstract definitions. If we look at actual educational systems, we can distinguish three general purposes, but their character is such that we can by no means separate them. We can, for example, distinguish a major general purpose: that of training the members of a group to the 'social character' or 'pattern of culture' which is dominant in the group or by which the group lives. To the extent that this 'social character' is generally accepted, education towards it will not normally be thought of as one possible training among many, but as a natural training which everyone in the society must acquire. Yet when, as often happens, the 'social character' is changing, or when, again, there are alternative 'social characters' within a given society, this 'natural training' can be something very different, and can be seen, by others, as 'indoctrination'. Some writers distinguish this social training from the teaching of particular skills, the former being general atmosphere or background, the latter being specialized instruction. Yet the 'social character' is always and everywhere much more than particular habits of civility and behaviour; it is also the transmission of a particular system of values, in the field of group loyalty, authority, justice, and living purposes. I know of no educational system which fails to contain this kind of training, and the important point is that it is impossible ultimately to separate this training from the specialized training. The teaching of skills prepares a rising generation for its varieties of adult work, but this work, and all the relations governing it, will be found to exist within the given 'social character'; indeed one function of the 'social character' is to make the available kinds of work, and the valuations and relations which arise from them, acceptable. And if we cannot separate general social training from specialized training, since one is given, consciously or unconsciously, in terms of the other, neither can we separate the third distinguishable purpose: what we call a 'general education', or, in Sir Fred Clarke's term, 'education for culture'. Schematically one can say that a child must be taught, first, the accepted behaviour and values of his society; second, the general knowledge and attitudes appropriate to an educated man, and third, a particular skill by which he will earn his living and contribute to the welfare of his society. In fact, just as the particular skill and the accepted behaviour and values are necessarily related, so, we shall find, both are related to, and help to determine, the kind of general knowledge and attitudes appropriate to an educated man. It is never a purely arbitrary selection, nor a simple process of 'indoctrination', for if the governing social character is accepted, even if only by a ruling minority, it is accepted in terms of its value: the general training necessary to a man is bound to be seen in the context of the values which the 'social character' embodies and transmits. If we believe in a particular 'social character', a particular set of attitudes and values, we naturally believe that the general education which follows from these is the best that can be offered to anyone: it does not feel like 'indoctrination', or even 'training'; it feels like offering to this man the best that can be given.

If we turn to historical analysis, the importance of these points becomes clear, for we shall see not only the variations of 'the best that can be given', but the actual and complex relations between the three aims cited: see the training of social character shading into specialized training for particular kinds of work, and the definitions of general education taking their colour from both. I propose to examine the history of English education from this particular point of view: to see the changing complex of actual relations, in social training, subjects taught, definitions of general education, in the context of a developing society. And since we ourselves are not at the end of history, but at a point in this complex development, the historical account will necessarily lead to an analysis of our own educational values and methods.

I

The beginnings of English education show very clearly the close relationships between training for a vocation, training to a social character, and training a particular civilization. The first English schools, from the late sixth century, had a primarily vocational intention, but this was such that it implied a particular social training and a particular definition of a proper general knowledge. The conscious object of these early schools, attached to cathedrals and to monasteries, was to train intending priests and monks to conduct and understand the services of the Church, and to read the Bible and the writings of the Christian Fathers. The break since the withdrawal of Roman power, and the new settlements by peoples of a different language, left a people largely without Latin at a time when the dominant religion, and a large part of all available learning, were in the unknown language. Augustine has been well described as coming to convert England 'with the Latin-service book in one hand, and the Latin grammar in the other' (LEACH). Two kinds of school, often in practice connected, were instituted: the grammar school, to teach Latin, and the song school, to teach church singing. Necessarily, in view of their objects, the specialized training of both these schools was part of a general training to Christianity and the particular social character it then carried. Yet the grammar school, especially, could not be confined to this limited aim. Over eight centuries, from before the coming of these schools to England (based, as they were, on Greek and Roman models) until the centuries before the Renaissance, a crucial argument about the content of their education is most interestingly in evidence. Latin must be taught, or the Church could not continue, but ability in it led not only to the Bible and the Fathers, but also to the whole range of Latin literature and 'pagan' philosophy. The problems this raised are well illustrated in a letter from Pope Gregory to Bishop Desiderius in Gaul:

> ... A circumstance came to our notice, which cannot be mentioned without shame, namely that you, our brother, give lessons in grammar. This news caused us such annoyance and disgust that all our joy at the good we had heard earlier was turned to sorrow and distress, since the same lips cannot sing the praises of Jove and the praises of Christ. Consider yourself how serious and shocking it is that a bishop should pursue an activity unsuitable even for a pious layman. We have already in hand the granting of your request, easy in mind and untroubled by doubts, provided that this information which has come to us shall have been proved manifestly untrue, and you will not be shown to spend your time on the follies of secular literature.

Yet 'grammar', the basis of the new schools, was not understood at this time as merely the bones of a language (that is only a late medieval meaning): it was a preparation for reading, especially reading aloud, and was taken to involve comprehension and commentary, so that content was inseparable. On both educational and religious grounds, the 'grammar-book' was the expedient resorted to: first, the anthology, which not only made a variety of texts available but could select them on grounds of suitability of content; later the systematic grammars and the teaching dialogues. The inquiring student could and did read further, especially into Vergil and Ovid, but the nature of the selective tradition was such that a large part of classical thought, particularly in philosophy and science, remained neglected. Several actual curricula have come down to us from this early period. Bede speaks of Theodore and Hadrian, at Canterbury, teaching 'the rules of metric, astronomy and the computus as well as the works of the saints', and Alcuin's account of the teaching at York refers to grammar, rhetoric, law, poetry, astronomy, natural history, arithmetic, geometry, music, and the Scriptures. Yet, when we look at actual textbooks, we see how these subjects were organized by the dominant principles of Latin and the Church. Scripture was the central subject, and rhetoric teaching was mainly a study of verbal forms in the Bible. Grammar was the teaching of Latin, and versification was in the same context, though at times it extended to relate to poetry in the vernacular. Mathematics, including astronomy, was centred on the intricacies of the Church calendar, simple general exercises being an introduction to the all-important 'computus' centred on the controversy about the date of Easter. Music and law were vocational studies for the services and administration of the Church, and the natural history, by contrast with the Aristotelians, was literary and anecdotal. Geography, history, and the natural sciences found little place in such a scheme, though it must be remembered that Bede, with this teaching, wrote a substantial history of England.

It is difficult to be certain how far, if at all, this kind of education was made available to others than intending priests and monks. There was probably an occasional extension, and there are certainly some recorded cases of the education of young members of royal and noble families. In England, in any case, the development of the schools was interrupted by the Danish invasions, to such an extent that the system had to be reconstructed under the influence of Alfred, and we have little positive evidence again until the tenth and eleventh centuries. The new pattern is very similar to the old, even after the Norman invasion when French replaced English as the vernacular medium for teaching Latin. There are grammar schools and song schools, attached to cathedrals, monasteries and collegiate churches, and the vocational curriculum is still evident. Then, in the twelfth century, there is an important expansion, both in institutions and in teaching. The cathedral schools multiplied, and in the following century, in Oxford, the first colleges and the idea of a university appeared. The movement was closely related to extensions of the curriculum, in that rhetoric, at the primary stage, grew to rank equally with grammar, while in the secondary stages, and certainly in the universities, there was a major growth in logic, related to the increasing availability of some of the major writings of Aristotle, and an extension and specialization in the advanced faculties of law, medicine, and theology. Although education remained within a firm Christian framework, the concept of a liberal education, as a preparation for the specialized study of law, medicine, or theology, can be seen shaping itself. The concept of the Seven Liberal Arts (the *trivium* of grammar, rhetoric, and dialectic, the *quadrivium* of music, arithmetic, geometry, and astronomy) goes back to at least the fifth century, but it was only now that it began to be realized with any adequacy, as new material from classical learning, and new attitudes towards it, flowed in. Teachers, instead of being appointed, were now more formally licensed (university degrees were licences to teach). Some extension of studies to practical secular needs is also evident, as for example in the teaching of letter-writing, a growing need as administration became more complex. There is some evidence of writing-schools, as distinct from grammar and song schools, at which letter-writing and practical accounting were taught, for a new class. Some schools again, though needing to be licensed by the Church, were otherwise independent.

A very large part of medieval education remained vocational, but the development of philosophy, medicine, and law had the effect of removing parts of the educational system from the direct supervision of the Church, and the universities' fight for their independence, as corporate learned bodies deciding their own conditions for granting degrees and hence licences to teach, was to an important extent successful. Between the thirteenth and the end of the fifteenth centuries the network of grammar and song schools, attached to cathedrals, monasteries, collegiate churches and chantries, was added to by the creation of virtually independent schools, such as Winchester and Eton, in close relation with new colleges at Oxford and Cambridge. Figures are quite uncertain, but it has been estimated by the best authority, Leach, that for a population, on the eve of the Reformation, of some $2\frac{1}{4}$ millions, there may have been as many as 400 schools, or one school to 5625 people. (In 1864 there was one grammar school to every 23 750 people.) Yet two other aspects of medieval education must be noted: the apprenticeship system, in the crafts and trades, and the chivalry system, by which young boys of noble family were sent as pages to great houses and lived through a graduated course of training to knighthood. The existence of these two systems, alongside the academic system, reminds us of the determining effect on education of the actual social structure. The labouring poor were largely left out of account, although there are notable cases of individual boys getting a complete education, through school and university, by outstanding promise and merit. For the rest, education was organized in general relation to a firm structure of inherited and destined status and condition: the craft apprentices, the future knights, the future clerisy. The system, while clear, is not perfect, for academic education seems on the whole to have outrun demand. Even with something like one ordained clerk to forty of the population, there was not room for all with an academic education to live by it, and the lower ranks of the clergy were in any case very poor. Further, the clerisy was perhaps recruited from a more varied social background than in the directly class-based apprenticeship and chivalry systems. Provision, in almost all early foundations, for 'poor scholars', can be variously interpreted, but at least the system was reasonably open. In this connection, the nature of the new indepen-

394

dent schools, such as Winchester and Eton, is particularly important. At Winchester, apart from founder's kin, there were to be commoners paying their own cost, who would be ruling-class boys, and 'poor and needy scholars' of good character and well-conditioned, of gentlemanly habits, able for school, completely learned in reading, plainsong and old Donatus' (Latin Grammar). Because of their independent status, such schools were not tied to one locality, and admission on a national basis was begun. It has been suggested, perhaps with reason, that such an institution was bound to develop into the public-school as we know it, drawing increasingly on a single class, and combining in its way of life the educational methods of the grammar schools and the social training, by 'boarding-out', of the chivalric system. In view of the close connection between these schools and colleges of the universities, any such development was bound to affect the educational system as a whole.

II

Matthew Arnold once argued that much had been lost in English education because while the schools were reorganized by the Reformation their teaching was not redirected by the Renaissance. In the matter of actual schools, the Reformation of course made many changes, closing or reducing in status a number of old foundations, instituting perhaps an equal number of new. The central institution remained the Grammar School, but there is an important change in sponsorship, of the kind first evident in the fifteenth century. Where the typical medieval grammar school had been a Church foundation, the typical new grammar school was a private foundation, supervised in variable degree by Church and State. Yet the educational tradition of the grammar schools survived, with little change, and we can agree with Milton and Arnold that this was damaging. Greek and sometimes Hebrew were added to the main Latin curriculum, and the main gain was an expansion in the study of literature. But the grammar school's kind of teaching, and even more that of the universities, remained rigid and narrow, and forms such as the theme and the disputation, which had once been creative, were isolated and mechanical. The major achievements of the Renaissance, in the vernacular literatures, in geographical discovery, in new painting and music, in the new spirit in philosophy and physical inquiry, in changing attitudes to the individual, had little effect on the standard forms of general education. Yet, outside these traditional institutions, primary schools in English seem to have increased, in a bewildering variety of forms, ranging from instruction by priests to private adventure schools, often as a sideline to shopkeeping and trade. In many

395

cases, the 'petties' or 'ABCs' were proper schools, sometimes linked to the grammar schools, sometimes, where old endowments had shrunk, virtually taking over grammar schools. In addition, there was some development of 'writing schools', teaching scrivener's English and the casting of accounts – an obvious need in the considerable expansion of trade – and in some cases such teaching became incorporated in grammar schools. It is a complex pattern, yet three trends are clear: the increase in vernacular teaching, the failure of the traditional institutions to adapt either to a changing economy or to an expanding culture, and the passing of most of the leading schools from sponsorship by a national institution to private benefaction.

In the seventeenth century, there were important developments in educational theory, some of which had practical effect. The main educational theories of the Renaissance, in particular the ideal of the scholar-courtier, had had little effect on English institutions, and indeed had the paradoxical effect of reducing the status of schools as such, and setting the alternative pattern, drawing in part on the chivalric tradition, of education at home through a private tutor: a preference, in many families, which lasted well into the nineteenth century. Specific professional institutions, particularly in law, gained in importance, but meanwhile, to serve a different class, new general institutions, the Dissenting Academies, were beginning to appear. Nonconformists, after the Restoration, were seriously discriminated against by the traditional institutions, and replied by setting up their own academies, at a higher secondary or university level of teaching. These varied considerably in quality, but it can fairly be claimed that in the best of them, in the eighteenth century, a new definition of the content of a general education was worked out and put into practice. Here, for the first time, the curriculum begins to take its modern shape, with the addition of mathematics, geography, modern languages, and, crucially, the physical sciences. The older grammar schools, in the same period, changed in differing ways. The nine leading schools, seven of them boarding institutions, kept mainly to the traditional curriculum of the classics, and, while less socially exclusive than they were to become, tended on the whole to serve the aristocracy and the squirearchy, on a national basis. The majority of the endowed grammar schools served their immediate localities, with a reasonably broad social base, but still mainly with the old curriculum. But those older schools situated in the larger cities, greatly influenced by the many merchants and tradesmen whom they served, combined, in the eighteenth century, a quiet varied social composition with some broadening of the curriculum, particularly in mathematics and natural sciences. The universities reflected this complex picture, for while there was substantial adherence to the old curriculum, and what seems to have been a decline in teaching standards, there was some serious development in mathematics and the sciences, and the percentage of 'poor' students – sons of farmers, craftsmen, small tradesmen – though falling during the century, was still quite substantial. Of the three old professions, the clergy was still mainly served by the universities, while law and medicine were mainly now outside them. Of the new professions, particularly in science, engineering, and arts, a majority of entrants were trained outside the universities, as were also most of the new merchants and manufacturers. The eighteenth century is remarkable for the growth of a number of new vocational academies, serving commerce, engineering, the arts, and the armed services.

As for primary education, the haphazard system of parish and private adventure schools still survived, and there was some growth in preparatory schools serving the various academies and older foundations. But increasing urbanization was raising new problems, to which solutions were very slow in coming. The Charity School movement, from the end of the seventeenth century, represents the main effort, and its combination of a new kind of intention – the moral rescue as opposed to the moral instruction of the poor – with a more formal definition of elementary education as that appropriate to a particular social class, casts its shadow ahead. By the last quarter of the eighteenth century, with the quickening of pace of the Industrial Revolution, the whole educational system was under new pressures which would eventually transform it.

III

In the seventy years between 1751 and 1821, the population of the British mainland doubled from seven to fourteen millions, and by 1871, at twenty-six millions, it had nearly doubled again. In addition to this remarkable expansion, the proportion of the population living in towns, including the new industrial towns, and also the proportion of children in the population as a whole, again remarkably increased. These changes would have been enough to disorganize a much better system of education than the eighteenth century actually had, and the first half of the nineteenth century is full of reports showing the utter inadequacy, in part revealed, in part created, by the social and economic transformation. The desire to reorganize education, on a fuller basis than hitherto, was the motive of many of these reports, but at the same time the forces opposed to any general reform were very strong. In 1816, of 12 000 parishes examined, 3500 had no school, 3000 had endowed schools of varying quality, and 5500 had unendowed schools, of a quality even more variable. But to do anything about this the reformers had to get past the representative opinion of a Justice of the Peace in 1807:

> It is doubtless desirable that the poor should be generally instructed in *reading*, if it were only for the best of purposes – that they may read the Scriptures. As to *writing* and *arithmetic*, it may be apprehended that such a degree of knowledge would produce in them a disrelish for the laborious occupations of life.

It is true that at no previous period had the poor, as a whole, been educated, although in exceptional parishes the attempt was made. But there had been provision, again and again, for the exceptional poor boy to get to the university. Under the new dispensation, education was organized on a more rigid class basis.

> To every class we have a school assign'd
> Rules for all ranks and food for every mind.
> (Crabbe.)

Only the last clause was untrue.

But the process of change from a system of social orders, based on localities, to a national system of social classes – a change extending from the fifteenth to the late eighteenth centuries – was now virtually complete, and its result was a new kind of class-determined education. Higher education became a virtual monopoly, excluding the new working class, and the idea of universal education, except within the narrow limits of 'moral rescue', was widely opposed as a matter of principle.

* * *

The first new educational institutions of the Industrial Revolution were the industrial schools, providing manual training and elementary instruction, and, much more important, the Sunday schools, available to adults as well as children, and, while varying in methods, mainly organized on the principle noted: that for moral reasons the poor must learn to read the Bible, but that writing and arithmetic, to say nothing of more dangerous subjects, were less necessary or even harmful. In the new kinds of day school, under the rival systems of Lancaster and Bell, teaching was similarly based on the Bible, but by a new method – what Bell called 'the STEAM ENGINE of the MORAL WORLD' – which by the use of monitors and standard repetitive exercises allowed one master to teach many hundreds of children simultaneously in one room. It has been estimated that with the development of Sunday schools and the new day schools, and with the surviving parish and adventure schools, some 875 000 children, out of a possible 1 500 000, attended a school of some kind for some period in

1816, and that in 1835 the figure was 1 450 000 out of 1 750 000. To assess these figures adequately, we must remember that the same inquiries showed an average duration of school attendance, in 1835, of one year. From the eighteenth century some assistance to schools from the rates had been empowered in a few places, and from the 1830's there was a beginning of national assistance in school building. By 1851, the average duration of school attendance had been raised to two years, and by 1861 an estimated 2 500 000 children, out of a possible 2 750 000 may have been in some form of school attendance, though still of very mixed quality and with the majority leaving before they were eleven. The curriculum was broadening a little, usually now including writing and arithmetic, and in some schools other general subjects. The Revised Code of 1862 instituted a system of payment by results in relation to definite standards in reading, writing, and arithmetic (reading a short paragraph in a newspaper; writing similar matter from dictation; working sums in practice and fractions). Increasing public aid to the schools was thus tied to the old criterion of a minimum standard. In 1870, school boards were established, to complete the network of schools and bring them under a clearer kind of supervision, and in 1876 and 1880 this extension was confirmed by making universal elementary schooling compulsory. In 1893, the leaving age was raised to 11, in 1899 to 12, and in 1900 to a permissive 14. Thus by the end of the century a national system of elementary schooling, still largely confined to the provision of a minimum standard, had been set going.

Meanwhile, the old grammar schools had been widely developed, as the institutions of a largely separate class, served mainly, at the primary stage, by an extended network of preparatory schools. Attendances at the old schools, particularly at the leading nine, had begun to revive in the period 1790–1830, and in their different ways Butler at Shrewsbury, from 1798, and Arnold at Rugby, from 1824, had begun to change their character. Arnold's influence was not mainly on the curriculum, but on the re-establishment of social purpose, the education of Christian gentlemen. Butler's influence is perhaps even more significant, for his emphasis on examination-passing marks the beginning of a major trend. By the 1830's, the examination system between these schools and the universities was firmly established, and this, while raising educational standards within the institutions, had the effect of reinforcing the now marked limitation of the universities to entrants from a narrow social class. In the curriculum, classics were 'business' and other subjects were extras, but the establishment of the Civil Service Commission and the Board of Military Education, from mid-century, had the effect of promoting mathematics and modern languages, and of further organizing the schools in terms of examinations. In the 1840's, there were altogether some 700 grammar schools, and more than 2000 non-classical endowed schools, but an inquiry showed in 1868 that in two-thirds of the towns of England there were no secondary schools of any kind, and in the remaining third there were marked differences of quality. In the late 1860's, through two commissions and the Public Schools Act of 1868, the reorganization of secondary education, still on a narrow class basis, was conceived and in part carried through. The Act of 1868 broke many of the old foundation statutes, and instituted new governing bodies. From this date, the new curriculum (classics, mathematics, one modern language, two natural sciences, history, geography, drawing, and music) and the confirmation of a separate class of 'public schools', were established. The Headmasters' Conference, embracing the many new nineteenth-century schools of this type, and some of the old foundations, was begun in 1869. The Taunton Commission of 1867 envisaged three grades of secondary school: those for the upper and upper-middle classes, keeping their boys till 18 and giving a 'liberal education' in preparation for the universities and the old professions; those for the middle classes, keeping their boys till 16 and preparing them for the Army, the newer professions, and many departments of the Civil Service; and those for the lower middle classes, keeping their boys until 14, and fitting them for living as 'small tenant farmers, small tradesmen, and superior artisans'. Where possible, minorities should be enabled to pass to a higher grade, and in particular there might be a connection between third-grade secondary schools and the elementary schools, enabling some sons of labourers to go on to secondary education. Secondary education, in these three grades, should be made available to 10 children for every 1000 of the population, and of these 8 would be in the third grade. In practice this would mean a national total of 64 000 children in the first and second grades, and 256 000 in the third grade, out of some 4 000 000 children. 'It is obvious', the Commission commented, in relation to its tripartite grading, 'that these distinctions correspond roughly, but by no means exactly, to the gradations of society'.

In practice, while secondary education was not yet a public responsibility, the effect of this suggested organization was uneven. From the 1850s, a system of University Local Examinations, first called 'Middle-Class Examinations', had enabled endowed and proprietary schools of the first and second grades to aim at some recognized national standard of secondary education, and the extension of the examination system by official and professional bodies had the same rationalizing effect. The campaign for the secondary education of girls was beginning to show results, and then in 1889 Wales took the lead, with an Intermediate Education Act which succeeded in establishing an organized secondary system linking the board and voluntary elementary schools with the universities, and providing for both boys and girls. In 1902 the creation of Local Education Authorities, with responsibility for the full educational needs of their areas, laid the basis for a national system of secondary education. The third-grade school had been overtaken by the raising of the elementary school-leaving age, and it was to the creation of first- and second-grade secondary schools that the new authorities, with varying energy, applied themselves. The Board of Education had come into existence in 1899, and in 1904 it defined a four-year secondary course, leading to a certificate, in English language and literature, geography, history, a language other than English, mathematics, science, drawing, manual work, physical training, and household crafts for girls. If we look back from this to the eighteenth-century curriculum of the Dissenting Academies, we shall see where the main line of the tradition lies.

Meanwhile, in the course of the century, university education had been radically changed. The institution of public examinations, in Cambridge from the eighteenth century, in Oxford from the early years of the nineteenth, had an important effect on teaching, which did not pass without protest that the examination system was making education mechanical. At the same time, the religious exclusiveness of the ancient universities, and the effective restriction of the curriculum to classics and mathematics, led to the foundation of London University (1828–1836), while the new University of Durham (1832), though governed by the Church had a notably broader curriculum. Reforming movements at Oxford and Cambridge led to substantial statutory changes in the 1850's, with the dual aim of broadening the range of subjects offered, and ensuring a social representation wider than that of 'prospective parsons, prospective lawyers, (and) young men of rank and fortune'. Further legislative changes in the 1870's and 1880's, and the reorganization and extension of faculties, led to the achievement of modern university status. Meanwhile, university colleges were springing up, and the foundations of Manchester, Nottingham, Reading, Southampton, Leeds, Liverpool, Sheffield, and Birmingham, together with the three Welsh colleges, were being laid.

The nineteenth-century achievement is evidently a major reorganization of elementary, secondary, and university education, along lines which in general we still follow. Both in kinds of institution, and in the matter and manner of education, it shows the reorganization of

401

learning by a radically changed society, in which the growth of industry and of democracy were the leading elements, and in terms of change both in the dominant social character and in types of adult work. At no time in England have the effects of these influences on the very concept of education been clearer, but, precisely because this was so, a fundamental argument about the purposes of education was the century's most interesting contribution. Two strands of this argument can be separated: the idea of education for all, and the definition of a liberal education. The former, as we have seen, was fiercely argued, and the history of the century represents the victory of those who, in the early decades, had been a minority. Two major factors can be distinguished: the rise of an organized working class, which demanded education, and the needs of an expanding and changing economy. In practice, these were closely interwoven, in the long debate, and the victory of the reformers rested on three elements: genuine response to the growth of democracy, as in men like Mill, Carlyle, Ruskin, and Arnold; protective response, the new version of 'moral rescue', very evident in the arguments for the 1870 Education Act in relation to the franchise extensions of 1867 – 'our future masters . . . should at least learn their letters'; and the practical response, perhaps decisive, which led Forster in 1870 to use as his principal argument: 'upon the speedy provision of elementary education depends our industrial prosperity'. In the growth of secondary education this economic argument was even more central.

The democratic and the industrial arguments are both sound, but the great persuasiveness of the latter led to the definition of education in terms of future adult work, with the parallel clause of teaching the required social character – habits of regularity, 'self-discipline', obedience, and trained effort. Such a definition was challenged from two sides, by those with wider sympathies with the general growth of democracy, and by those with an older conception of liberal education, in relation to man's health as a spiritual being. This interesting alliance is broadly that which I traced as a tradition in *Culture and Society*, and the educational argument was always near the centre of this continuing tradition. On the one hand it was argued, by men with widely differing attitudes to the rise of democracy and of working-class organization, that men had a natural human right to be educated, and that any good society depended on governments accepting this principle as their duty. On the other hand, often by men deeply opposed to democracy, it was argued that man's spiritual health depended on a kind of education which was more than a training for some specialized work, a kind variously described as 'liberal', 'humane', or 'cultural'. The great complexity of the general

402

argument, which is still unfinished, can be seen from the fact that the public educators, as we may call the first group, were frequently in alliance with the powerful group which promoted education in terms of training and disciplining the poor, as workers and citizens, while the defenders of 'liberal education' were commonly against both: against the former because liberal education would be vulgarized by extension to the 'masses'; against the latter because liberal education would be destroyed by being turned into a system of specialized and technical training. Yet the public educators inevitably drew on the arguments of the defenders of the old 'liberal' education, as a way of preventing universal education being narrowed to a system of pre-industrial instruction. These three groups – the public educators, the industrial trainers, and the old humanists – are still to be distinguished in our own time, and we shall see, later, their influence in twentieth-century developments. In general, the curriculum which the nineteenth century evolved can be seen as a compromise between all three groups, but with the industrial trainers predominant. The significant case is the long controversy over science and technical education. If we look at the range of scientific discovery between the seventeenth and the end of the nineteenth centuries, it is clear that its importance lies only in part in its transformation of the techniques of production and communication; indeed lies equally in its transformation of man's view of himself and of his world. Yet the decisive educational interpretation of this new knowledge was not in terms of its essential contribution to liberal studies, but in terms of technical training for a particular class of men. The old humanists muddled the issue by claiming a fundamental distinction between their traditional learning and that of the new disciplines, and it was from this kind of thinking that there developed the absurd defensive reaction that all real learning was undertaken without thought of practical advantage. In fact, as the educational history shows, the classical linguistic disciplines were primarily vocational, but these particular vocations had acquired a separate traditional dignity, which was refused to vocations now of equal human relevance. Thus, instead of the new learning broadening a general curriculum, it was neglected, and in the end reluctantly admitted on the grounds that it was of a purely technical kind. The pressure of the industrial trainers eventually prevailed, though not with any general adequacy until the Technical Instruction Act of 1889, and even here, significantly, it was 'instruction' rather than 'education'. This history was damaging both to general education and to the new kinds of vocational training, and yet it was only an exceptional man, such as Huxley, who could see this at the time and consequently argue in the only adequate way:

that science must become a part of general education and of liberal culture, and that, as a further provision, there must be an adequate system of specific professional training, in all kinds of scientific and technical work, on the same principle as the further professional training of doctors, lawyers, teachers, artists, and clergy. We can take only a limited satisfaction in the knowledge that the industrial trainers won, inert and stupid as the old humanists were and have continued to be. Huxley was a public educator, in the full sense, and it was only in this tradition that the problem might have been solved.

The shadow of class thinking lies over this as over so much other nineteenth-century educational thinking. The continued relegation of trade and industry to lower social classes, and the desire of successful industrialists that their sons should move into the now largely irrelevant class of gentry, were alike extremely damaging to English education and English life. As at the Reformation, a period of major reconstruction of institutions was undertaken largely without reference to the best learning of the age, and without any successful redefinition of the purposes of education and of the content of a contemporary liberal culture. The beginnings of technical instruction in the Mechanics' Institutes might have developed into a successful redefinition, but again it was the training of a specific class, whereas in fact the new sciences were radical elements in the society as a whole: a society which had changed its economy, which under pressure was changing its institutions, but which, at the centres of power, was refusing to change its ways of thinking. And then to the new working class, the offered isolation of science and technical instruction was largely unacceptable, for it was precisely in the interaction between techniques and their general living that this class was coming to its new consciousness. Politics, in the wide sense of discussing the quality and direction of their living, was excluded from these Institutes, as it was to remain largely excluded from the whole of nineteenth-century education. It was only very slowly, and then only in the sphere of adult education, that the working class, drawing indeed on very old intellectual traditions and on important dissenting elements in the English educational tradition, made its contribution to the modern educational debate. This contribution – the students' choice of subject, the relation of disciplines to actual contemporary living, and the parity of general discussion with expert instruction – remains important, but made little headway in the general educational organization. Like the individual public educators, their time was not yet.

35

Education: Programmes or Men *

Quintin Hoare

It is, however, possible to isolate four main schools of educational thought, each of which contains a partial validity; it is only by criticizing them that a socialist alternative can be concretely posed. They can be characterized as, respectively, the conservatives, the rationalizers, the romantics and the democrats.

The Conservative Position

The conservative position – extremely strong among university and grammar school teachers – represents the rearguard action of elite education, of the classical curriculum, and of the intellectuals who are subordinate to change, as in Amis' *More will be worse*. Sometimes it rests on a more conscious and elaborated conservative ideology such as that of Eliot, Oakeshott, Leavis or Bantock, or on an articulated pseudo-scientific view of human intelligence such as that of Burt. Its concern for 'high culture' might be seen as partially defensible for all its undemocratic implications, were its programme not so manifestly and pathetically a defence of the *status quo*, as a few quotations from Bantock will show: 'My "plan", then, has none of the heroic proportions of the others. It involves achievement by means of "small adjustments and re-adjustments which can continually be improved upon" ... Existing good schools would remain untouched ... The most that can be expected is a reasonable degree of mobility – and this, at least, has been achieved.' When it comes down to actual prescriptions, and above all to the curriculum, 'concern for high culture' is revealed as Oakeshottian defence of the existing system, with a dash of Popperian piecemeal tinkering and more domestic education for those girls and more manual education for those boys who are 'less able'.

The survival of this school of thought, although it is making its stand in defence of the grammar school and against university expansion, is in fact made possible principally by the survival of the private sector of education and of a similarly aristocratic conception of educa-

* *New Left Review*, **32**, 1967.

tion in Oxford and Cambridge, and their deeply hierarchical influence on the whole educational system. The extent to which provincial universities are subordinate to the models and values of Oxford and Cambridge hardly needs stressing, nor the degree to which grammar schools and even comprehensives imitate public school mores. The aristocratic ideal yields, in practice, to a simple defence of privileged roads to the top against the floodtide of meritocracy. Yet on the theoretical plane, a concern for cultural excellence, and resistance to the encroachments of vocational education and its ideologues, which form much of the philosophical substratum of the conservative tradition, need to be integrated, in a new form, into any socialist educational programme.

The Rationalizers of the System

The second, and currently most influential, school of educational thought is a product of the expansions of education over the last 90 years. It could be said to express the aspirations of the fast-growing new middle-classes, above all the technicians and white-collar workers, who chafe at the closed, aristocratic hierarchies of British society, but whose horizon is one of an open merit-determined escalator – who in Britain, without a mass socialist party, have never been offered the possibility of a classless society. This outlook is represented at one end of an ideological spectrum by the official reports – Newsom, Robbins – and by Vaizey; at the other by Floud and Halsey. It is, above all, concerned with the organizational modalities of the school system. It denounced its inadequacies and inflexibility, the 'wastage' of its selection system and its excessive restriction of channels of mobility, its denial of equality of opportunity. Clearly the attack mounted by the most radical thinkers of this school on the inherent deficiencies of the present system, and their consequent powerful support for the reorganization of secondary education along comprehensive lines, does contribute greatly to the unlocking of the present situation, and has a significant overlap with socialist demands as such. But this approach does not intrinsically transcend the limits of a modernizing, propulsive neo-capitalism. It offers no serious challenge to the present content and values of British education. When Halsey, for example, does try to come to grips with the content of education, in his essay 'British universities and intellectual life' his radicalism collapses ignominiously before the most vulgar myths of the ruling class ideology: 'Educationally they (Oxford and Cambridge) have stood for a broad humanism against a narrow professionalism, for "education" as opposed to "training".' and again: 'The success of Britain as an imperial power in the 19th century and especially the quiet and incorruptible efficiency of its high ranking civil servants and colonial administrators commanded universal (*sic*) esteem and was at the same time a powerful validation of its educational institutions and high values placed within them on classical studies and liberal arts.'

Comprehensive education, if it remains streamed, is only a rationalized form of the present tripartite system. But once it is realized that the same arguments which have been marshalled against the tripartite system on the grounds of built-in class bias and the self-fulfilling character of 'intelligence tests' apply equally well to streaming, then the whole concept of education comes into question, since unstreaming classes involves profound changes in teaching methods, changes in teachers' training, and above all changes in curriculum.

At the same time, those thinkers who have been most concerned with the rationalization of the educational system have also been the strongest advocates of educational expansion. A socialist education should be designed to meet and develop human *needs*, and as Raymond Williams says, to 'keep the learning process going, for as long as possible, in every life'. Expansion divorced from such an aim can only too easily consist simply in a more highly developed system of vocational training, which relieves industry of a still greater part of the costs of training its new recruits, transferring this charge to the community.

Romantic Education

The third tradition springs from Rousseau, Pestalozzi, Froebel, and Montessori, and from Freudian psychology. Romantic, reacting against orthodox curricula and methods, showing great concern for the *individual's* self-realization, enriched in this century by the advances of modern child-psychology with its emphasis on play and free expression, it could be said to represent the liberal wing of the bourgeoisie – its conscience. Whereas the readers of the *New Scientist* and of *New Society* might be expected to be overwhelmingly among the 'rationalizers', the readers of the *New Statesman* would probably be divided between rationalizers and romantics. In Britain this tradition has produced no major educational thinker, but it gave rise at the beginning of the century to a number of 'progressive' private schools such as Bedales, Summerhill, and Dartington. It has had its most important influence since the Second World War in the area of primary education, and in the 'failure' streams of secondary moderns and comprehensives. In so far as it has been responsible for the introduction of new teaching methods and for some kind of assimilation of modern child-psychology *anywhere*, it is of obvious human significance. It has also expressed an admirable resistance on the part of teachers to the 'rat-race' character of existing education and an affirmation of humane values against the inhuman priorities imposed by the economy. However, throughout its long history this tradition has failed to transcend its oppositional, escapist character, and has failed to do more than salvage a minority from being broken by the system. It has been burdened by its acceptance of romantic conceptions of the individual personality which have reinforced rather than challenged the prevalent British orthodoxy stemming from Locke, which sees each child as possessing *given* faculties which must be brought out by education. Above all, it has grasped only one aspect of the educational process – the provision of an environment in which children can grow as freely and creatively as possible. But it has conceived of this environment as an island within the englobing system, renouncing implicitly any aspiration to fight or even comprehend the system itself. Its curricular innovations have been limited to an adulteration of the old syllabus, with the introduction of some manual skills and a higher proportion of creative work. David Holbrook, who is representative of a vulgarized but typical and influential version of this school of thought, has encapsulated its inadequacy in the inimitable dictum: 'We need to restore to secondary education the poetic function – that poetic function which is the basis of all human activity'. That 'the poetic function is the basis of all human activity' is clearly nonsense. What is true is that there is a real risk of its being made the opium of the lower stream children. It comes as no surprise to find the educational establishment unanimous in its praise for Holbrook and his brave work, as the Victorian bourgeoisie was for the work of the Salvation Army. The ever-present danger for this whole school of thought is that it can so easily be absorbed and used as a palliative where the system breaks down, thus becoming complicit with the very education it purports to challenge. However, it has given birth to most of the really original reflection on teaching methods. Its stress on play, on group learning, on flexible classroom organization, and its rejection of the traditional teacher-pupil relationship, are permanent contributions. Above all, it alone among the major traditions of educational thinking in Britain, has accepted Freud. The great achievement of Freud and his successors in exploring the formation of the individual personality in childhood represents a fundamental acquisition, which must be pivotal to any contemporary socialist discussion. One of the most crippling failures of the socialist intellectual tradition in this century has been its failure to integrate either the romantic and anarchist 'movement' – except perhaps in the early years of the Russian revolution – or the Freudian oeuvre – except in the work of individual thinkers such as Sartre and Marcuse.

408

The Democratic Tradition

The last major tradition is that of those thinkers who, in Raymond Williams' words 'made a generous response to the growth of democracy' – the tradition of Mill, Carlyle, Ruskin and Arnold in the last century, and of Williams himself in the twentieth century. It provided the philosophical expression of the pressure towards universal education, as it now provides the overt ideology of the campaign for comprehensive education. But although the supporters of comprehensive education explicitly situate themselves in this tradition, there is often something rhetorical about their use of democratic arguments. The logic of Vaizey's arguments in favour of education expansion as a good capital investment reinforces the vocational conception of education which is precisely the opposite of a democratic conception. Similarly Floud and Halsey argue against selective education on the grounds that it is not 'fair', thereby implying an acceptance of vocational purpose as the main purpose of the schools. In both cases, the 'democratic' formulations appear subordinate to, and in fact implicitly contradicted by, the principal argument in terms of life-chances.

Thus much of the educational thinking that purports to be within this tradition, in fact, tends in precisely the opposite direction. However, a democratic conception of public education holds out in the primary school syllabus, despite the prevalence of streaming the downward pressure – ideological as well as practical of selective secondary education. It is also the rationale of adult education. Its theoretical weakness is potentially compensated by the untapped reserves of response to it among teachers, among parents, and among children. It is the tradition which underpins the comprehensive school despite the ideologies of the present campaign. In recent years it has received one major reformulation in the work of Raymond Williams. Since this represents the most ambitious and radical attempt by a British socialist to challenge the existing system, and to present an alternative to its curriculum, it deserves the most careful attention.

Williams, after a historical account of the development of educational theory and reality in Britain, presents a draft curriculum – which he suggests as a minimum standard for every educationally normal child:

(*a*) Extensive practice in the fundamental languages of English and mathematics.

(*b*) General knowledge of ourselves and our environment, taught at the secondary stage not as separate academic disciplines but as general knowledge drawn from the disciplines which clarify at a higher stage, ie (i) biology, psychology; (ii) social history, law and political institutions, sociology, descriptive economics, geography including actual industry and trade; (iii) physics and chemistry.

(c) History and criticism of literature, the visual arts, music, dramatic performance, landscape and architecture.

(d) Extensive practice in democratic procedures, including meetings, negotiations, and the selection and conduct of leaders in democratic organizations. Extensive practice in the use of libraries, newspapers and magazines, radio and television programmes, and other sources of information, opinion and influence.

(e) Introduction to at least one culture, including its language, history, geography, institutions and arts, to be given in part by visiting and exchange. He proposes that this could form a common education to the age of 16, when compulsory schooling would cease. Further education would take place in a variety of institutions, in which vocational training and general education could take place side by side, and in which students would participate in organization and control.

Certain of the stresses of Williams' draft are clearly of the greatest importance (it is not the intention here to discuss details of the suggestions). The stress on an integral and rational curriculum is a genuine attack on instrumental or vocational education. Science would be taught as it should be and never has been in Britain as an essential element of contemporary man's view of himself and his world. The whole of contemporary culture and all the arts would be part of the curriculum. It must also be clear that this programme implies the liquidation of the private sector, the end of tripartism and of streaming, of sex segregation and differentiation. It would involve a massive expansion and retraining of the teaching staff, an extension of the school career, and a reorganization of the universities, in short, it is a deliberately maximalist programme, and a good one. The immense merit and importance of Williams' proposals are evident. They represent the *only* authentic socialist programme for our educational system in Britain today.

But at the same time, this programme suffers from a fundamental weakness. Williams' present his draft as a reform which could be accepted by an enlightened society. There is no discussion of who could impose it and who would oppose it, and no reference to the concrete politico-cultural structure of Britain or the existing social composition and outlook of the teachers. Williams' fundamental mode of presentation is the rational appeal to men of good will. 'We

410

can see a certain way ahead . . . the only sensible answer . . . We shall have to think in terms of . . .' This 'we' is revealing, for it clearly does not in the context mean socialists: ('We still think of required levels of general culture, according to certain classes of work'). It is based on some unspecified consensus in an extra-historical sphere. 'In terms of such a definition (referring to his draft curriculum) we could revise our institutions.' With any other writer one would see this as a singular mystification. *Whose* institutions? *Who* could 'revise' them?

Williams' whole scheme in effect hangs in the air, suspended in a kind of atemporal void. There is a basic failure to ground the proposed programme in any actual historical situation. Above all he completely overlooks the fundamental fact that a reform of the educational system involves a reform of the educators as well, and that this is a *political* task, which immediately ricochets back to the question of transforming consciousness and ideology throughout society. As they stand, Williams' proposals remain purely 'institutional', exhibiting a detachment from actual political reality, which can lead him in another field to suggest that the socialist solution for the capitalist press should be to transfer the papers to the journalists who work for them. The idea that the *Daily Express* – or for that matter *The Times* – journalists, if they controlled the paper democratically, would produce a 'democratic' newspaper ignores the obvious fact that social institutions of this kind – schools or press – produce the men to fit them.

The corruption of the *human material* in each sector cannot be put in parentheses in proposing their transformation. It must enter into the initial determination of what the programme should be.

The Revolutionary Alternative

In other words, a socialist programme cannot consist of a purely *conceptual* alternative. It implies precisely the fusion of theory and praxis, and a rejection of the idea that socialism can be brought about by the simple advocacy of ethnically superior policies, without a revolutionary movement capable of contesting capitalist society as a whole and prefiguring a new cultural order. Such an alternative would represent a junction of programme and strategy, of theory of man and of political action. Of course, to speak of such an alternative in Britain today is 'unreal', but it is only by starting to think in these terms that established reality can be challenged.

A socialist theory of education would resume at a higher level the valid elements in all the theories discussed above, combating and integrating them at the same time. It would be distinguished from each in precise, inter-related ways:

1 As opposed to the conservative tradition, it would stress education as the development of *critical* reason (in Marcuse's sense of the word) in the child – a questioning attitude towards all existing reality.

2 As opposed to the romantic school it would embody a full acceptance of the *social* character of man, rejecting for ever the notion of a pre-social dimension of human existence – the image of Emile.

3 As opposed to rationalizers it would insist on the *active* nature of the child's participation in the learning process, and contest the mechanist conception of education as the transmission of fixed skills.

4 As opposed to the democratic tradition, it would be *dialectical*, treating all human reality as radically historical, refusing to consider programmes outside of men to execute, emasculate or refuse them.

36

Text Book Knowledge *

T S Kuhn

We must still ask how scientific revolutions close. Before doing so, however, a last attempt to reinforce conviction about their existence and nature seems called for. I have so far tried to display revolutions by illustration, and the examples could be multiplied *ad nauseam*. But clearly, most of them, which were deliberately selected for their familiarity, have customarily been viewed not as revolutions but as additions to scientific knowledge. That same view could equally well be taken of any additional illustrations, and these would probably be ineffective. I suggest that there are excellent reasons why revolutions have proved to be so nearly invisible. Both scientists and laymen take much of their image of creative scientific activity from an author-itative source that systematically disguises – partly for important functional reasons – the existence and significance of scientific revolu-tions. Only when the nature of that authority is recognized and analyzed can one hope to make historical example fully effective. Furthermore, though the point can be fully developed only in my concluding section, the analysis now required will begin to indicate one of the aspects of scientific work that most clearly distinguishes it from every other creative pursuit except perhaps theology.

As the source of authority, I have in mind principally textbooks of science together with both the popularizations and the philosophical works modeled on them. All three of these categories – until recently no other significant sources of information about science have been available except through the practice of research – have one thing in common. They address themselves to an already articulated body of problems, data, and theory, most often to the particular set of par-adigms to which the scientific community is committed at the time they are written. Textbooks themselves aim to communicate the vocabulary and syntax of a contemporary scientific language. Popularizations attempt to describe these same applications in a lan-

* *The Structure of Scientific Revolutions*, Chicago University Press, 1962, ch 11.

guage closer to that of everyday life. And philosophy of science, particularly that of the English-speaking world, analyzes the logical structure of the same completed body of scientific knowledge. Though a fuller treatment would necessarily deal with the very real distinctions between these three genres, it is their similarities that most concern us here. All three record the stable *outcome* of past revolutions and thus display the bases of the current normal-scientific tradition. To fulfill their function they need not provide authentic information about the way in which those bases were first recognized and then embraced by the profession. In the case of textbooks, at least, there are even good reasons why, in these matters, they should be systematically misleading.

We noticed in Section II that an increasing reliance on textbooks or their equivalent was an invariable concomitant of the emergence of a first paradigm in any field of science. The concluding section of this essay will argue that the domination of a mature science by such texts significantly differentiates its developmental pattern from that of other fields. For the moment let us simply take it for granted that, to an extent unprecedented in other fields, both the layman's and the practitioner's knowledge of science is based on textbooks and a few other types of literature derived from them. Textbooks, however, being pedagogic vehicles for the perpetuation of normal science, have to be rewritten in whole or in part whenever the language, problem-structure, or standards of normal science change. In short, they have to be rewritten in the aftermath of each scientific revolution, and, once rewritten, they inevitably disguise not only the role but the very existence of the revolutions that produced them. Unless he has personally experienced a revolution in his own lifetime, the historical sense either of the working scientist or of the lay reader of textbook literature extends only to the outcome of the most recent revolutions in the field.

Textbooks thus begin by truncating the scientist's sense of his discipline's history and then proceed to supply a substitute for what they have eliminated. Characteristically, textbooks of science contain just a bit of history, either in an introductory chapter or, more often, in scattered references to the great heroes of an earlier age. From such references both students and professionals come to feel like participants in a long-standing historical tradition. Yet the textbook-derived tradition in which scientists come to sense their participation is one that, in fact, never existed. For reasons that are both obvious and highly functional, science textbooks (and too many of the older histories of science) refer only to that part of the work of past scientists that can easily be viewed as contributions to the statement and solution of the texts' paradigm problems. Partly by selection and partly by distortion, the scientists of earlier ages are implicitly represented as having worked upon the same set of fixed problems and in accordance with the same set of fixed canons that the most recent revolution in scientific theory and method has made seem scientific. No wonder that textbooks and the historical tradition they imply have to be rewritten after each scientific revolution. And no wonder that, as they are rewritten, science once again comes to seem largely cumulative.

Scientists are not, of course, the only group that tends to see its discipline's past developing linearly towards its present vantage. The temptation to write history backward is both omnipresent and perennial. But scientists are more affected by the temptation to rewrite history, partly because the results of scientific research show no obvious dependence upon the historical context of the inquiry, and partly because, except during crisis and revolution, the scientist's contemporary position seems so secure. More historical detail, whether of science's present or of its past, or more responsibility to the historical details that are presented, could only give artificial status to human idiosyncrasy, error, and confusion. Why dignify what science's best and most persistent efforts have made it possible to discard? The depreciation of historical fact is deeply, and probably functionally, ingrained in the ideology of the scientific profession, the same profession that places the highest of all values upon factual details of other sorts. Whitehead caught the unhistorical spirit of the scientific community when he wrote, 'A science that hesitates to forget its founders is lost.' Yet he was not quite right, for the sciences, like other professional enterprises, do need their heroes and do preserve their names. Fortunately, instead of forgetting these heroes, scientists have been able to forget or revise their works.

The result is a persistent tendency to make the history of science look linear or cumulative, a tendency that even affects scientists looking back at their own research. For example, all three of Dalton's incompatible accounts of the development of his chemical atomism make it appear that he was interested from an early date in just those chemical problems of combining proportions that he was later famous for having solved. Actually those problems seem only to have occurred to him with their solutions, and then not until his own creative work was very nearly complete. What all of Dalton's accounts omit are the revolutionary effects of applying to chemistry a set of questions and concepts previously restricted to physics and meteorology. That is what Dalton did, and the result was a reorientation toward the field, a reorientation that taught chemists to ask new questions about and to draw new conclusions from old data.

Or again, Newton wrote that Galileo had discovered that the constant force of gravity produces a motion proportional to the square of the time. In fact, Galileo's kinematic theorem does take that form when embedded in the matrix of Newton's own dynamical concepts. But Galileo said nothing of the sort. His discussion of falling bodies rarely alludes to forces, much less to a uniform gravitational force that causes bodies to fall. By crediting to Galileo the answer to a question that Galileo's paradigms did not permit to be asked, Newton's account hides the effect of a small but revolutionary reformulation in the questions that scientists asked about motion as well as in the answers they felt able to accept. But it is just this sort of change in the formulation of questions and answers that accounts, far more than novel empirical discoveries, for the transition from Aristotelian to Galilean and from Galilean to Newtonian dynamics. By disguising such changes, the textbook tendency to make the development of science linear hides a process that lies at the heart of the most significant episodes of scientific development.

The preceding examples display, each within the context of a single revolution, the beginnings of a reconstruction of history that is regularly completed by postrevolutionary science texts. But in that completion more is involved than a multiplication of the historical misconstructions illustrated above. Those misconstructions render revolutions invisible; the arrangement of the still visible material in science texts implies a process that, if it existed, would deny revolutions a function. Because they aim quickly to acquaint the student with what the contemporary scientific community thinks it knows, textbooks treat the various experiments, concepts, laws, and theories of the current normal science as separately and as nearly seriatim as possible. As pedagogy this technique of presentation in unexceptionable. But when combined with the generally unhistorical air of science writing and with the occasional systematic misconstructions discussed above, one strong impression is overwhelmingly likely to follow: science has reached its present state by a series of individual discoveries and inventions that, when gathered together, constitute the modern body of technical knowledge. From the beginning of the scientific enterprise, a textbook presentation implies, scientists have striven for the particular objectives that are embodied in today's paradigms. One by one, in a process often compared to the addition of bricks to a building, scientists have added another fact, concept, law, or theory to the body of information supplied in the contemporary science text.

But that is not the way a science develops. Many of the puzzles of contemporary normal science did not exist until after the most recent scientific revolution. Very few of them can be traced back to the historic beginning of the science within which they now occur. Earlier generations pursued their own problems with their own instruments and their own canons of solution. Nor is it just the problems that have changed. Rather the whole network of fact and theory that the textbook paradigm fits to nature has shifted. Is the constancy of chemical composition, for example, a mere fact of experience that chemists could have discovered by experiment within any one of the worlds within which chemists have practiced? Or is it rather one element – and an indubitable one, at that – in a new fabric of associated fact and theory that Dalton fitted to the earlier chemical experience as a whole, changing that experience in the process? Or by the same token, is the constant acceleration produced by a constant force a mere fact that students of dynamics have always sought, or is it rather the answer to a question that first arose only within Newtonian theory and that that theory could answer from the body of information available before the question was asked?

These questions are here asked about what appear as the piecemeal-discovered facts of a textbook presentation. But obviously, they have implications as well for what the text presents as theories. Those theories, of course, do 'fit the facts', but only by transforming previously accessible information into facts that, for the preceding paradigm, had not existed at all. And that means that theories too do not evolve piecemeal to fit facts that were there all the time. Rather, they emerge together with the facts they fit from a revolutionary reformulation of the preceding scientific tradition, a tradition within which the knowledge-mediated relationship between the scientist and nature was not quite the same.

One last example may clarify this account of the impact of textbook presentation upon our image of scientific development. Every elementary chemistry text must discuss the concept of a chemical element. Almost always, when that notion is introduced, its origin is attributed to the seventeenth-century chemist, Robert Boyle, in whose *Sceptical Chymist* the attentive reader will find a definition of 'element' quite close to that in use today. Reference to Boyle's contribution helps to make the neophyte aware that chemistry did not begin with the sulfa drugs; in addition, it tells him that one of the scientist's traditional tasks is to invent concepts of this sort. As a part of the pedagogic arsenal that makes a man a scientist, the attribution is immensely successful. Nevertheless, it illustrates once more the pattern of historical mistakes that misleads both students and laymen about the nature of the scientific enterprise.

According to Boyle, who was quite right, his 'definition' of an element was no more than a paraphrase of a traditional chemical concept; Boyle offered it only in order to argue that no such thing as a chemical element exists; as history, the textbook version of Boyle's contribution is quite mistaken. That mistake, of course, is trivial, though no more so than any other misrepresentation of data. What is not trivial, however, is the impression of science fostered when this sort of mistake is first compounded and then built into the technical structure of the text. Like 'time', 'energy', 'force', or 'particle', the concept of an element is the sort of textbook ingredient that is often not invented or discovered at all. Boyle's definition, in particular, can be traced back at least to Aristotle and forward through Lavoisier into modern texts. Yet that is not to say that science has possessed the modern concept of an element since antiquity. Verbal definitions like Boyle's have little scientific content when considered by themselves. They are not full logical specifications of meaning (if there are such), but more nearly pedagogic aids. The scientific concepts to which they point gain full significance only when related, within a text or other systematic presentation, to other scientific concepts, to manipulative procedures, and to paradigm applications. It follows that concepts like that of an element can scarcely be invented independent of context. Furthermore, given the context, they rarely require invention because they are already at hand. Both Boyle and Lavoisier changed the chemical significance of 'element' in important ways. But they did not invent the notion or even change the verbal formula that serves as its definition. Nor, as we have seen, did Einstein have to invent or even explicitly redefine 'space' and 'time' in order to give them new meaning within the context of his work.

What then was Boyle's historical function in that part of his work that includes the famous 'definition'? He was a leader of a scientific revolution that, by changing the relation of 'element' to chemical manipulation and chemical theory, transformed the notion into a tool quite different from what it had been before and transformed both chemistry and the chemist's world in the process. Other revolutions, including the one that centers around Lavoisier, were required to give the concept its modern form and function. But Boyle provides a typical example both of the process involved at each of these stages and of what happens to that process when existing knowledge is embodied in a textbook. More than any other single aspect of science, that pedagogic form has determined our image of the nature of science and of the role of discovery and invention in its advance.

37

The One Thing Needful

Charles Dickens *

'Now, what I want is, Facts. Teach these boys and girls nothing but Facts. Facts alone are wanted in life. Plants nothing else, and root out everything else. You can only form the minds of reasoning animals upon Facts: nothing else will ever be of any service to them. This is the principle on which I bring up my own children, and this is the principle on which I bring up these children. Stick to Facts, sir!'

The scene was a plain, bare, monotonous vault of a schoolroom, and the speaker's square forefinger emphasized his observations by underscoring every sentence with a line of the schoolmaster's sleeve. The emphasis was helped by the speaker's square wall of a forehead, which had his eyebrows for its base, while his eyes found commodious cellarage in two dark caves, overshadowed by the wall. The emphasis was helped by the speaker's mouth, which was wide, thin, and hard set. The emphasis was helped by the speaker's voice, which was inflexible, dry, and dictatorial. The emphasis was helped by the speaker's hair, which bristled on the skirts of his bald head, a plantation of firs to keep the wind from its shining surface, all covered with knobs, like the crust of a plum pie, as if the head had scarcely warehouse-room for the hard facts stored inside. The speaker's obstinate carriage, square coat, square legs, square shoulders – nay, his very neckcloth, trained to take him by the throat with an unaccommodating grasp, like a stubborn fact, as it was, – all helped the emphasis.

'In this life, we want nothing but Facts, sir; nothing but Facts!'

The speaker, and the schoolmaster, and the third grown person present, all backed a little, and swept with their eyes the inclined plane of little vessels then and there arranged in order, ready to have imperial gallons of facts poured into them until they were full to the brim.

* *Christmas Books and Hard Times*, Chapman and Hall Edition – London, 1891, 353–8.

Murdering the Innocents

Thomas Gradgrind, sir. A man of realities. A man of facts and calculations. A man who proceeds upon the principle that two and two are four, and nothing over, and who is not to be talked into allowing for anything over. Thomas Gradgrind, sir – peremptorily Thomas – Thomas Gradgrind. With a rule and a pair of scales, and the multiplication table always in his pocket, sir, ready to weigh and measure any parcel of human nature, and tell you exactly what it comes to. It is a mere question of figures, a case of simple arithmetic. You might hope to get some other nonsensical belief into the head of George Gradgrind, or Augustus Gradgrind, or John Gradgrind, or Joseph Gradgrind (all suppositions, non-existent persons), but into the head of Thomas Gradgrind – no, sir!

In such terms Mr Gradgrind always mentally introduced himself, whether to his private circle of acquaintance, or to the public in general. In such terms, no doubt, substituting the words 'boys and girls', for 'sir', Thomas Gradgrind now presented Thomas Gradgrind to the little pitchers before him, who were to be filled so full of facts.

Indeed, as he eagerly sparkled at them from the cellarage before mentioned, he seemed a kind of cannon loaded to the muzzle with facts, and prepared to blow them clean out of the regions of childhood at one discharge. He seemed a galvanizing apparatus, too, charged with a grim mechanical substitute for the tender young imaginations that were to be stormed away.

'Girl number twenty,' said Mr Gradgrind, squarely pointing with his square forefinger, 'I don't know that girl. Who is that girl?'

'Sissy Jupe, sir,' explained number twenty, blushing, standing up, and curtseying.

'Sissy is not a name,' said Mr Gradgrind. 'Don't call yourself Sissy. Call yourself Cecilia.'

'It's father as calls me Sissy, sir,' returned the young girl in a trembling voice, and with another curtsey.

'Then he has no business to do it,' said Mr Gradgrind. 'Tell him he mustn't. Cecilia Jupe. Let me see. What is your father?'

'He belongs to the horse-riding, if you please, sir.'

Mr Gradgrind frowned, and waved off the objectionable calling with his hand.

'We don't want to know anything about that, here. You mustn't tell us about that, here. Your father breaks horses, don't he?'

'If you please, sir, when they can get any to break, they do break horses in the ring, sir.'

'You mustn't tell us about the ring, here. Very well, then. Describe your father as a horsebreaker. He doctors sick horses, I dare say?'

'Oh yes, sir.'

'Very well then. He is a veterinary surgeon, a farrier, and horse-breaker. Give me your definition of a horse.'

(Sissy Jupe thrown into the greatest alarm by this demand.)

'Girl number twenty unable to define a horse!' said Mr Gradgrind, for the general behoof of all the little pitchers. 'Girl number twenty possessed of no facts, in reference to one of the commonest of animals! Some boy's definition of a horse. Bitzer, yours.'

The square finger, moving here and there, lighted suddenly on Bitzer, perhaps because he chanced to sit in the same ray of sunlight which, darting in at one of the bare windows of the intensely white-washed room, irradiated Sissy. For, the boys and girls sat on the face of the inclined plane in two compact bodies, divided up the centre by a narrow interval; and Sissy, being at the corner of a row on the sunny side, came in for the beginning of a sunbeam, of which Bitzer, being at the corner of a row on the other side, a few rows in advance, caught the end. But, whereas the girl was so dark-eyed and dark-haired, that she seemed to receive a deeper and more lustrous colour from the sun, when it shone upon her, the boy was so light-eyed and light-haired that the self-same rays appeared to draw out of him what little colour he ever possessed. His cold eyes would hardly have been eyes, but for the short ends of lashes which, by bringing them into immediate contrast with something paler than themselves, expressed their form. His short-cropped hair might have been a mere continuation of the sandy freckles on his forehead and face. His skin was so unwholesomely deficient in the natural tinge, that he looked as though, if he were cut, he would bleed white.

'Bitzer,' said Thomas Gradgrind. 'Your definition of a horse.'

'Quadruped. Graminivorous. Forty teeth, namely twenty-four grinders, four eye-teeth, and twelve incisive. Sheds coat in the spring; in marshy countries, sheds hoofs, too. Hoofs hard, but requiring to be shod with iron. Age known by marks in mouth.' Thus (and much more) Bitzer.

'Now girl number twenty,' said Mr Gradgrind. 'You know what a horse is.'

She curtseyed again, and would have blushed deeper, if she could have blushed deeper than she had blushed all this time. Bitzer, after rapidly blinking at Thomas Gradgrind with both eyes at once, and so catching the light upon his quivering ends of lashes that they looked like the antennæ of busy insects, put his knuckles to his freckled forehead, and sat down again.

The third gentleman now stepped forth. A mighty man at cutting and drying, he was; a government officer; in his way (and in most other people's too), a professed pugilist; always in training, always with a system to force down the general throat like a bolus, always to be heard of at the bar of his little Public-office, ready to fight all England. To continue in fistic phraseology, he had a genius for coming up to the scratch, wherever and whatever it was, and proving himself an ugly customer. He would go in and damage any subject whatever with his right, follow up with his left, stop, exchange, counter, bore his opponent (he always fought All England) to the ropes, and fall upon him neatly. He was certain to knock the wind out of common sense, and render that unlucky adversary deaf to the call of time. And he had it in charge from high authority to bring about the great public-office Millennium, when Commissioners should reign on earth.

'Very well,' said this gentleman, briskly smiling, and folding his arms. 'That's a horse. Now, let me ask you girls and boys, Would you paper a room with representations of horses?'

After a pause, one half of the children cried in chorus, 'Yes, sir!' Upon which the other half, seeing in the gentleman's face that Yes was wrong, cried out in chorus, 'No, sir!' – as the custom is, in these examinations.

'Of course, No. Why wouldn't you?'

A pause. One corpulent slow boy, with a wheezy manner of breathing, ventured the answer, Because he wouldn't paper a room at all, but would paint it.

'You *must* paper it,' said the gentleman, rather warmly.

'You must paper it,' said Thomas Gradgrind, 'whether you like it or not. Don't tell *us* you wouldn't paper it. What do you mean, boy?'

'I'll explain to you, then,' said the gentleman, after another and a dismal pause, 'why you wouldn't paper a room with representations of horses. Do you ever see horses walking up and down the sides of rooms in reality – in fact? Do you?'

'Yes, sir!' from one half. 'No, sir!' from the other.

'Of course no,' said the gentleman, with an indignant look at the wrong half. 'Why, then, you are not to see anywhere, what you don't see in fact; you are not to have anywhere, what you don't have in fact. What is called Taste, is only another name for Fact.'

Thomas Gradgrind nodded his approbation.

'This is a new principle, a discovery, a great discovery,' said the gentleman. 'Now, I'll try you again. Suppose you were going to carpet a room. Would you use a carpet having a representation of flowers upon it!'

There being a general conviction by this time that 'No, sir!' was always the right answer to this gentleman, the chorus of No was very strong. Only a few feeble stragglers said Yes; among them Sissy Jupe.

'Girl number twenty,' said the gentleman, smiling in the calm strength of knowledge.

Sissy blushed, and stood up.

'So you would carpet your room – or your husband's room, if you were a grown woman, and had a husband – with representations of flowers, would you?' said the gentleman. 'Why would you?'

'If you please, sir, I am very fond of flowers,' returned the girl.

'And is that why you would put tables and chairs upon them, and have people walking over them with heavy boots?'

'It wouldn't hurt them, sir. They wouldn't crush and wither, if you please, sir. They would be the pictures of what was very pretty and pleasant, and I would fancy – –'

'Ay, ay, ay! But you mustn't fancy,' cried the gentleman, quite elated by coming so happily to his point. 'That's it! You are never to fancy.'

'You are not, Cecilia Jupe,' Thomas Gradgrind solemnly repeated, 'to do anything of that kind.'

'Fact, fact, fact!' said the gentleman. And 'Fact, fact, fact!' repeated Thomas Gradgrind.

'You are to be in all things regulated and governed,' said the gentleman, 'by fact. We hope to have, before long, a board of fact, composed of commissioners of fact, who will force the people to be a people of fact, and of nothing but fact. You must discard the word Fancy altogether. You have nothing to do with it. You are not to have, in any object of use or ornament, what would be a contradiction in fact. You don't walk upon flowers in fact; you cannot be allowed to walk upon flowers in carpets. You don't find that foreign birds and butterflies come and perch upon your crockery; you cannot be permitted to paint foreign birds and butterflies upon your crockery. You never meet with quadrupeds going up and down walls; you must not have quadrupeds represented upon walls. You must use,' said the gentleman, 'for all those purposes, combinations and modifications (in primary colours) of mathematical figures which are susceptible of proof and demonstration. This is the new discovery. This is fact. This is taste.'

The girl curtseyed, and sat down. She was very young, and she looked as if she were frightened by the matter of fact prospect the world afforded.

'Now, if Mr M'Choakumchild,' said the gentleman, 'will proceed to give his first lesson here. Mr Gradgrind, I shall be happy, at your request, to observe his mode of procedure.'

Mr Gradgrind was much obliged. 'Mr M'Choakumchild, we only wait for you.'

So, Mr M'Choakumchild began in his best manner. He and some one hundred and forty other schoolmasters, had been lately turned at the same time, in the same factory, on the same principles, like so many pianoforte legs. He had been put through an immense variety of paces, and had answered volumes of head-breaking questions. Orthography, etymology, syntax, and prosody, biography, astronomy, geography, and general cosmography, the sciences of compound proportion, algebra, land-surveying and levelling, vocal music, and drawing from models, were all at the ends of his ten chilled fingers. He had worked his stony way into Her Majesty's most Honourable Privy Council's Schedule B, and had taken the bloom off the higher branches of mathematics and physical science, French, German, Latin, and Greek. He knew all about all the Water Sheds of all the world (whatever they are), and all the histories of all the peoples, and all the names of all the rivers and mountains, and all the productions, manners, and customs of all the countries, and all their boundaries and bearings on the two and thirty points of the compass. Ah, rather overdone, M'Choakumchild. If he had only learnt a little less, how infinitely better he might have taught much more!

He went to work in this preparatory lesson, not unlike Morgiana in the Forty Thieves: looking into all the vessels ranged before him, one after another, to see what they contained. Say, good M'Choakumchild. When from thy boiling store, thou shalt fill each jar brimful by-and-by, dost thou think that thou wilt always kill outright the robber Fancy lurking within – or sometimes only maim him and distort him!

38

Getting rid of the hypotenuse *
H F Ellis

Every mathematics master dreads the day when he will have to explain the Theorem of Pythagoras to boys who have never met it before. Term after term I get this same feeling of helplessness. The whole thing is ridiculous. With co-operation and proper attention even a dull form should be able to grasp the principles involved and the main lines of the proof in an hour's good hard work; knowledge of the construction will come with practice. But IIIA do *not* co-operate. They are too prone to let their minds wander, to be led astray by what are from the point of view of geometry only side issues, to *make*, as I am always telling them, difficulties instead of going straight at the task and getting it done. It is not that they are lazy. That I could deal with, for I come down like a ton of bricks on idleness in any shape or form. It is rather, I think, a failure to understand the *importance* of what it is we are trying to do.

'This morning,' I said to them, 'we are going to prove that the square on the hypotenuse of a right-angled triangle is equal to the sum of the squares on the other two sides.'

'Is that a likely thing to happen?' Mason asked.

I told the others to be quiet and asked Mason what he meant.

'I mean is a right-angled triangle likely to have a square on its hypotenuse?'

'I'm afraid I don't quite follow you, Mason,' I said. 'If I draw a right-angled triangle on the board and then draw a square on the side opposite the right angle, it has got a square on its hypotenuse. The question whether it is *likely* to have such a square does not arise.'

'Not on the board, sir, no. But I mean in real life. I mean if real-life triangles don't have squares on their hypotenuses there wouldn't be much point in proving that they are equal to whatever it is they are equal to, would it, sir?'

'You mean "would *there*," you chump.'

* *The Vexations of A J Wentworth BA*, origin unknown, author sometime literary editor of *Punch*.

'Be quiet, Etheridge,' I said.

'I see what Mason means, sir,' said Hillman. 'I mean it would be a pretty fluke if a triangle had squares on all its three sides at once, wouldn't it, sir?'

'There is no question of a fluke about it,' I said, beginning to lose patience. 'Now attend to me, all of you.' I then drew on the board a right-angled triangle ABC, and on the sides AB, AC and BC proceeded to construct squares ABDE, ACFG and BCHJ respectively.

'What is there funny about that, Atkins?' I asked when I had finished.

'Nothing,' he said.

'Then why laugh?'

It is constant vexation to me that these boys seem to be amused at nothing at all. I do not want them to be glum and dispirited, of course; there are times when we all have a good laugh together and no harm is done. But this inane giggling at nothing simply holds up the work of the set. I gave Atkins a sharp warning and turned to Mason.

'Now, Mason,' I said, 'that wasn't very difficult, was it? My triangle's got squares on each of its sides.'

'My canary's got circles under its eyes,' sang a voice, and there was an immediate outburst of laughter at this piece of downright impertinence.

'Was that you, Williamson?' I demanded sternly.

'No, sir.'

'Then who was it?'

There was no reply.

'Filthy Dick passed the window just then, sir,' suggested Clarke, who sits by it. 'It must have been him.'

'He,' said Etheridge.

'You shut up, Etheridge. You don't know everything.'

'Clarke,' I cried, 'you will come and see me at the end of the period. And you too, Etheridge. I will not have these interruptions.'

'He meant the gardener's boy,' explained Mason. 'We call him Filthy Dick because he never washes. You should see his neck.'

'Never mind that now, Mason. The point is, are you prepared to admit that this figure on the board is a triangle with squares on each of its sides?'

'I suppose so, sir. Only it looks more like three squares joined together now, with a space in the middle.'

'Very well, Mason,' I said wearily. 'Let us put it that when three squares have their corners touching in such a way that the space enclosed between them is a right-angled triangle, the largest square is equal to the sum of the two smaller squares. Will that satisfy you?'

'All right by me, sir,' said Mason.

'Anything to get rid of the hypotenuse,' said Anderson.

39

The Literature of Primitive Peoples *
Paul Radin

To speak of oral narratives or song-poems, particularly those of primitive peoples, as constituting true literature has until recently met with the greatest suspicion not only from the general public but from students of literature and, indeed, from most ethnologists as well. Their objections are basically of two kinds. No literature is possible, they contend, without writing, and the languages spoken by primitive peoples are inadequate both in vocabulary and the ranges of ideas which can be expressed in them to permit the development of what we call true literature. Both of these contentions are, I feel, quite incorrect. One has only to read such studies as those of F Boas[1] and Edward Sapir[2] to realize on how slight a basis of fact such statements rest. There is no need, consequently, to spend any time refuting the theories of philosophers like Lévy-Bruhl[3] or E Cassirer[4] concerning the structure of primitive languages. The only thing that can be said in defense of their generalizations is that, given the manner in which many of the recorders of these languages presented their data and the many loose statements they made, it is easy to see how Lévy-Bruhl and Cassirer and those who were influenced by them arrived at their unsound generalizations. The first objection, particularly, that without writing no substantial literature can possibly develop, will, I am certain, be adequately disproved by the examples of prose and poetry which I am presenting in this essay.

The absence of writing does, however, entail a number of consequences for the forms which certain types of compositions assume and upon one of these I would like to comment. I am referring particularly to traditional prose narratives. These can best be understood if we regard them as dramas in which the reciter, the raconteur, impersonates the various characters of the tale or novelette he is narrating. His role as an actor is here more important than his role as transmitter of a specific traditional text, for it is by his skill and excellence as an actor that his audience judges him. His personality,

* *Diogenes*, Winter 1958, © 1955 Mario Casalini Ltd, Montreal.

his temperamental make-up, his style, in consequence play a determining role. He may interpolate or omit, amplify or shorten, reorganize or reinterpret to an amazing degree without encountering any serious criticism as long as what is regarded as the basic core of the plot is not affected. These interpolations are rarely creations of his own, but consist of traditionally fixed episodes, themes, motifs, imagery, epithets. Interpolations of one kind or another, let me point out, have always been the privilege of actors. We find them in the classical drama of ancient Greece, in that of the Golden Age in Spain and in that of the Elizabethan Age. They are found even today, especially in comedy. An oral dramatic text is never as fixed as one which is primarily to be read.

We thus come to one of the essential problems of all traditional oral narratives. Does a fixed text in our sense of the term exist? The answer must be in the negative. The reasons for this are many, the two most important being that, first, the community demands of the author-raconteur fixity only for the basic plot and secondly that the actions and behavior of the figures in the plot are always supposed to be intelligible to a contemporary audience. This means that a text is being continually re-edited. Under such circumstances one would expect considerable confusion in the structure of these narratives, which is indeed frequently true. However, accomplished narrators succeed in integrating their material with amazing skill although rarely is this integration perfect.

Where the raconteur-actor-editor plays so all-dominating a role one might very well ask what is left for the audience. Does it, like the audience at our theatre, simply listen and pass judgment on the skill of the raconteur-actor? It does all this and more. Strange as it may seem to us, an audience in an aboriginal tribe is far better prepared to understand the implications of their literature than we often are of our own. Every person there – parts of Africa and Polynesia-Micronesia perhaps excepted – has an all-embracing knowledge of his culture and participates in every aspect of it: every person has a complete knowledge of his language. There are no 'illiterate' nor ignorant individuals. An audience thus comes prepared esthetically, culturally, and critically, to listen to a narrative in a manner that can only be compared to an Athenian audience of the fifth century BC – on a different level, of course.

I have so far spoken primarily of the imaginative traditional prose narratives where, strictly speaking, there are no authors but only rearrangers, reinterpreters and editors. But there exist in each tribe, in addition to these traditional narratives which can be said to constitute the classical literature, other narratives constituting the contemporary literature, which have true authors and where the themes are taken from the life of the community and from personal events in the life of an individual. These two types of narrative differ fundamentally in subject-matter, in diction, and, at times, in vocabulary. In many tribes, especially in North America, they have special designations. Unfortunately ethnologists have neglected the contemporary because they have so largely concentrated their attention upon the classical and sacred literatures. However there is also a marked tendency for native priests, medicinemen, and tribal dignitaries, from whom, after all, most of our material is obtained, to place the contemporary literature in a lower category.

In these contemporary narratives, of course, much depends upon the skill and artistry of the author. Although he generally follows the style or styles laid down by older literary traditions he can also embark on experiments and attempt to create new styles. Such new styles are often due to contacts with other tribes. Here we have some controls. The recent contact with white investigators, for instance, has led to the emergence of a number of new literary categories. I am thinking particularly of autobiographies and the descriptions of the various aspects of culture, especially of religion and ritual. These never existed before the coming of the ethnologists. It is therefore of great significance for the history of primitive literatures to determine the degree to which the new categories and styles resemble the older ones. It is also of unusual interest for the student of comparative literature to realize that within less than two generations American Indians have developed the technique for composing well-rounded autobiographies which compare more than favourably with those of the ancient Greeks and Romans and can, indeed, stand comparison with some of the best in our own cultures. The *Autobiography of a Winnebago Indian*[5] which I collected some years ago can very well take its place by the side of that of so consummate a master as Benvenuto Cellini.

In poetry the text, likewise, is not fixed, except for the larger epics of the Polynesians and some of the Malayan tribes and, generally, for religious chants as a whole. Naturally poems are composed in traditional forms, but within these forms the composer is permitted absolute freedom to a far greater extent, in fact, than even in the contemporary prose narratives. He can use any image he wishes and he can be as personal in his allusions as he desires to be. One of the difficulties of understanding many short poems, particularly those of the American Indians, is that they are often so personal as to be unintelligible without a commentary.

There are thus both varying texts and unalterably fixed texts among primitive peoples, although unquestionably fixity of text is not regarded as a virtue, as it has come to be in Western European civilizations, particularly during the last two centuries. We cannot emphasize too strongly the fact that the excellence of a literature has nothing to do with the number of fixed texts found in it. If I seem to overstress this point, that is because it has at times been contended that where there is so great a variability for a given narrative no possibility for the development of a significant literature exists.

We come now to the last of the basic questions to be clarified before we can turn to our specific task, the characterization of some of the main aboriginal literatures. How is an author-raconteur trained? How does he learn his art? And how does one compose a poem in the absence of writing, and, what is far more important, in the absence of privacy? Be it remembered that privacy can hardly be said to exist in aboriginal communities.

The first question is easily answered. A raconteur learns his art directly from an elder, generally a relative. Such training may take a long time and it is always expensive. As a result only those individuals who have real talent and ambition persevere. However, the recital of narratives is not confined to specially trained individuals. Many persons know a few traditional narratives, own them, in fact, and can often tell these few as well as the 'professional' raconteur. No training certainly is required for the recital of the contemporary narratives. In the Americas, in fact, and in most areas where no caste systems or markedly developed class organisations exist, there actually are no special groups of guilds of professional raconteurs, ie, individuals who spend a considerable part of their time at such a task. This is quite different in many portions of Africa, Polynesia, and certain parts of the Southwest Pacific. There we find well-organized guilds of professional raconteurs who alone know the narratives and have the right to tell them.

The second of our questions is more difficult to answer, not only because of the nature of the subject but because we have little information to fall back upon. Moreover it is complicated by the additional fact that most poems are enclosed in a musical framework. We know enough about the interrelationship of this musical framework to the words to state that sometimes the music is primary, sometimes the words, the exact nature of the relationship often being dependent upon the poet and his inspiration. I see no reason for believing, however, that, by and large, the situation encountered here with regard to the interrelationship between words and music is very much different from what existed in the case of the Greek lyric poets or what held for the choruses of the Greek dramas of antiquity. We are possibly also dealing here with meters, although this is still problematical.

There is often a native theory of inspiration. Among most American Indian tribes poems are supposed to come to individuals in dreams, dreams here meaning that they have come more or less unsought. An Eskimo named Orpingalik, known for his poetical gifts, gave the great Danish ethnologist, Knud Rasmussen, a well-thought-out theory of inspiration that leaves little unsaid on the subject. 'Songs (poems) are thoughts,' he told Rasmussen, 'sung out with the breath when people are moved by great forces and ordinary speech no longer suffices. Man is moved just like the ice floe sailing here and there out in the current. His thoughts are driven by a flowing force when he feels joy, when he feels fear, when he feels sorrow. Thoughts can wash over him like a flood, making his breath come in gasps and his heart throb. Something like an abatement in the weather will keep him thawed up. And then it will happen that we, who always think we are small, will feel still smaller. And we will fear to use words. But it will happen that the words we need will come of themselves. When the words we want to use shoot up of themselves – we get a new song.'

Similar in strain is the explanation of how songs are composed which was given Rasmussen by the Greenland Eskimo Kilimé. 'All songs come to man when he is alone in the great solitude. They come to him in the wake of tears, of tears that spring from the deep recesses of the heart or they come to him suddenly accompanied by joy and laughter which wells up within us, we know not how, as we ponder upon life and look out upon the wonders of the world around us.

'Then, without our volition, without our knowledge, words come to us in song that do not belong to everyday speech. They come to us with every breath we take and become the property of those who possess the skill to weave them together for others.'[7]

This is, of course, pure theory and tells only half of the story. The other part consists of the arduous labor required for fitting the words into their proper frame, and knowledge of the traditional rules, of the stereotyped images, and formulae. All this our Eskimos Orpingalik and Kilimé must have known, for their poems conform strictly to the rules, but this they forgot to tell us. Other less philosophically inclined poets fortunately give us a better clue as to how they go about the task of composing a poem. On the island of Buin in the Solomon Islands, for instance, there are professional poets who, according to Thurnwald[8], all compose in the same way. A man goes into the forest to be undisturbed, selects a melody and then attempts to fit words to it. He will test these words repeatedly until he is satisfied that they conform to the rhythms of the melody. But to judge from the numerous song-poems Thurnwald has published this again is only half of the explanation and represents the portion that our Eskimo poets omitted. Poetic inspiration plays as great a role here as everywhere else. The professional poets of Buin are, after all, selected for their special gifts. That they often are commissioned to compose a poem for a particular occasion and are even told to include certain details, is of secondary importance. So was Pindar commissioned. As poets they wish to appeal to the listener's emotions and this they will do by striking imagery, by mythical allusions, by a special language and a special phrasing. The rhythmical units of the melody which Thurnwald emphasizes so strongly are pushed into the background. In short, our Buin poet's description of how he composes possesses no more validity than did that of the Eskimos Orpingalik and Kilimé.

In parts of Africa we find a description of the technique for composing song-poems strictly analogous to that given by the Buin. For example, among the Ila and Thonga of southeastern Africa there exists a class of song called *Impango*, sung only by women on any occasion when people gather together, at work, at a so-called beerdrink, in preparation for a journey, etc. There are in each village a number of women who are well-reputed composers of the music for such songs. Should a woman want such a song composed she first selects a subject for it and then the words. The words may be in praise of her husband, of her lover or of herself and will be connected with certain specific events such, for instance, as her husband's prowess in killing some fierce animal. She will then have some provisional melody accompany her words. With these she goes to the musiccomposer and sings the first half dozen words. The music expert, having ascertained whether, for instance, she wishes her song to start on a low or a high tone, then composes a few phrases of music which will conform to the first phrase as sung to her by the composer of the words. Then the music expert sets to work and composes the music for the whole song.

Yet here again the poems belie the theory. No fitting of words simply for the purpose of having them conform to the rhythm of a melody could possibly produce poems like the two following from the *Fan of the Congo*.

DIRGE ON THE DEATH OF A FATHER [9]

Father, my father, why have you left your hearth?
O father, did someone strike you down?
Someone whom vengeance demand that you slay?
And now your ghost has wandered to the other shore.

433

Father, my father, why have you left your hearth?
Though the skies have cleared, our vision is obscured.
From the trees the water falls in measured drops;
The rat has left his hole.

Behold our father's home!
Gather the grass for his grave
And spread it now here, now there.
Things once invisible he now can see.

SONG TO THE FIRE-GOBLIN [10]

I

Fire seen only at night,
The deep night;
Fire which burns without heat
And shines without burning;
Friendless, knowing no home and no hearth,
Bodiless, yet you fly.
Transparent fire of the palms,
Fearless, I ask for your aid.

II

Sorcerer's fire! Tell me
Who was your father, who was your mother?
Where do they dwell?
But, indeed, you are your father, you your mother!
You go your way and we see no mark.
Dry woods have not given you birth.
No ashes did you give to mankind.
Though you die yet you know not death!
Tell me, are you some wandering soul
That has taken your form unaware?

III

Sorcerer's fire!
O spirit of waters below, of the air overhead!
Light that shines from afar
Fly that illumines the marsh
Bird without wings, form without body,
Essence of fire, hear!
Fearless I ask for your aid.

Despite the fact that professional poets functioning very much as described for the Buin are to be found in many portions of the aboriginal world, the composing of poems is definitely not an art confined to them alone. In all primitive civilizations there are occasions when every person will attempt to compose a poem. We find accordingly, many individuals in every tribe who have composed at least one or two. To do so some special skill and certainly special knowledge were required. Naturally when thousands of poems are composed in one generation few will have great merit, either from our point of view or from that of primitive peoples. Yet it is quite surprising how good some of these are from any point of view. Let me give a few examples from North America, composed by individuals who were not professional poets, to show the nature of their subject-matter, the technical knowledge which was required of the composer, and what a listener had to know in order to understand the allusions contained in them and to appreciate the meaning of the imagery, free and stereotyped.

I

ESKIMO[11]

The white hounds of dawn I see approaching.
Away, away, or I will yoke you to my sleigh!

This is a poem composed by an Eskimo woman as she lay dying and fighting death. Both these lines are well known stereotyped images, one for death, the other for life.

II

TLINGIT[12]

Drifting along toward the shore runs the nation's canoe,
With it my uncle. He is destroyed.
Never again can I expect to see him here.
To him it has happened just as to Kashkatkl and his brothers.
They waded out across the Stikine.
Their sister, disobeying, looked at them
And they became stone.

To understand this poem one has to know an episode in a well known myth. *Nation's canoe* means an important chief; *to become stone* signifies being drowned.

III

TLINGIT[13]

Would that I were like her who was helped by Taxgwas!
If I were like the one he helped, that woman,
Indeed I could build my brother's house anew!
But he, my brother, I fear, has gone into the trial of the sun.
And that never again I will see him.

This song was composed by a woman about her drowned brother, Taxgwas. The first two lines refer to some incident in his life; the last three are stereotyped poetical formulae.

IV

WINNEBAGO [14]

I, even I, shall die some day.
Of what value is it then to be alive?

This is a poem composed by an Indian after a day of drinking and debauchery. It subsequently became a favorite drinking song.

V

OJIBWA [15]

1

A loon I thought it was,
Yet it was my love's splashing oar.

2

To Saulte Ste Marie he has departed.
My love, he has gone before me
And never again will I see him

VI

OJIBWA [16]

As my eyes search the prairie
I feel the summer in the spring.

VII

OJIBWA [17]

The odor of death, the odor of death,
I smell the odor of death
In front of my body.

VIII

TLINGIT [18]

If one had control of death,
Very easy it would be
To die with a Wolf Woman.
It would be very pleasant.

Let me compare a poem by an extremely gifted Eskimo with these poems by amateurs.

1

A wonderful occupation [19]
Making songs!
But all too often they
Are failures.

2

A wonderful fate
Getting wishes fulfilled!
But all too often they
Slip past.

3

A wonderful occupation
Hunting caribou!
But all too rarely we
Excel at it
So that we stand
Like a bright flame
Over the plain.

From this brief discussion one fact assuredly emerges clearly: that the conditions for the development of true literatures among primitive peoples exist in abundance. There are creative artists; there exist highly developed literary forms for both prose and poetry, and there exists a mature and educated audience. How varied these literatures can be, how in each area special literary styles and literary forms have arisen so that we can legitimately speak of an African literature, for instance, as set off against a Polynesian, Melanesian, North American Indian or Eskimo literature, how within each area, indeed, within each tribe, multiple styles exist, I shall now attempt to demonstrate, although I shall limit myself primarily to the African and Eskimo literatures.

I

Most of the older students of primitive cultures and, unfortunately, not a few of the more recent ones, have always tacitly assumed that aboriginal societies had no history or at least that they possessed no significant historical sequences. As these were a thousand or more years ago, so, essentially, they are today, or were until the appearance of the white man. Nothing could be more erroneous. The civilizations of few sections of the aboriginal world can be understood unless we realize that contacts with other tribes and other cultures took place long before the influence of the great European and African-Asiatic civilizations was ever felt. With these contacts must have come about numerous changes. In fact, indications of such cultural transformations, sometimes slight, sometimes profound, are clearly discernible. With the recognition of this fact – that all aboriginal civilizations have had a long history with periods of stability alternating with periods of crisis and change, and with periods of isolation followed by periods of contact – we must begin. Otherwise it will be impossible to understand why one area or one tribe has developed one type of literature, and another a second type, and what has brought about the special physiognomies of the various literatures. I do not, of course, mean that the specific traits of a given culture are to be regarded simply as a function of such changes. Other factors of equal and, at times, far greater importance must also be taken into consideration, such as the physical environment, the degree of culture integration achieved, and specific events occurring within each tribe. Bearing this in mind, let us now attempt our characterization of primitive literatures. I shall confine myself to just two such literatures, referring to the others only incidentally. I am selecting for comment those of Negro Africa and of the Eskimo because of the contrast they offer.

By Negro Africa I mean, roughly speaking, Africa south of the Sahara, always excepting the Bushmen. Its traditional imaginative prose literature is set off sharply in form and content from that of all other areas. Nowhere else, for example, do we find anything remotely approaching the sophistication which we encounter here. Nowhere else do we find man and human relations depicted with such stark realism. How are we to account for it? Explanations in terms of race or climate are out of the question. It must be the reflection of a particular social milieu, and here an understanding of the history of Negro Africa is vital. Rarely, in any area, have there been such frequent impingements of cultures upon one another, cultures often differing fundamentally in type and complexity. Moreover, nowhere in the aboriginal world were there so many crises, so much shifting of population, so much chaos and confusion. It is during the breakdown of a culture, in periods of transition, that man tends to be sophisticated, realistic, cynical, and sceptical and that certain aspects of the creative imagination find no expression. In Africa, for instance, it would seem that the mythopoeic imagination, using this term here in its broadest sense, is apparently no longer permitted to function freely, at least in the traditional narratives, and that where it does persist it has been given a new, essentially rationalistic, dress. To indicate what I mean by this statement let me compare the following short narratives, one from the Ojibwa of Ontario,[20] Canada, and the other from the West African Ekoi:[21]

I

Once an old man said to his children, 'In two days he is going to pass, the white animal.' The children were very glad that they were going to see this animal and one of them asked his father, 'Father, is this the animal who brings the morning?' And the father answered, 'Yes. After a while you will hear him coming along and singing.'

So within two days' time he told his children, 'Remember, today you will hear him just before dawn. Look! Look! He is coming now.'

'*Awihihi, awihihi.*' Thus he passed along toward the west singing and it was morning.

II

Mouse goes everywhere. Through rich men's houses she creeps and she visits even the poorest. At night, with her bright little eyes, she watches the doing of secret things, and no treasure chamber is so safe but she can tunnel through and see what is hidden.

In olden days she wove a story child from all that she saw and to each of these she gave a gown of different color – white, red, blue or black. The stories became her children and lived in her house and served her because she had no children of her own.

Comment here is just as unnecessary as it is when we contrast the conventional opening of many Ojibwa narratives, 'Once my story lived,' with the conventional beginning of those of the Ashanti, 'We really do not mean, we really do not mean that what we are going to say is true.'

Two utterly distinct and different cultural and literary traditions are involved here. To say that in the first case we are dealing with a simple, undifferentiated culture where man is still completely under the sway of his dream life and his fantasies, as quite a number of scholars, notably psychoanalysts, would contend, is belied by the facts. No such people exist. Be it also remembered that in civilizations far more complex than the Ojibwa, in most of North and South America and Polynesia, for instance, the mythopoeic imagination is still functioning in full vigor. Nor should we forget that it is found in Aeschylus and in all the great sophisticated oriental civilizations.

What has happened in Negro African cultures then, and finds its expression in their traditional prose literature, is thus only to be explained by their history and the influence of historical conditions upon their attitude towards animals, man, society, nature, and God. In my *African Folktales* narrative upon narrative brings this out clearly. Animals, nature, God, they have all been thoroughly humanized and, having been humanized, can then be assessed as man is assessed. Perhaps that is why there is no special genre devoted to satire in African literature, neither in prose nor in poetry. Man is depicted as he is. That is a sufficient satire. So likewise are animals, God, and nature depicted. They cast no shadows; they have no

439

protecting *personae*. However only destruction and tragedy can result when man meets his fellowman, nature, and God in such fashion.

Let us examine the plots of four narratives given in *African Folktales* [22], The Bantu Bena Mukuni tale entitled *Let the Big Drum Roll* [23], the Bena Mukuni *How an Unborn Child Avenged his Mother's Death* [24], the Bantu Baronga *The Wonder Worker of the Plains* [25] and the Bantu Baila tale of *The Woman Who Went in Search of God* [26]. Basically there is no reason why, in the first, the king should be murdered, that in the second the husband should murder his pregnant wife, that in the third the whole tribe should be destroyed, and that in the fourth the old woman should not die. But if man insists upon approaching his fellowman, nature, and God naked, without protecting illusions or fictions, only violence can be the outcome and he is consumed and destroyed. Nor is it without significance that nowhere in any of these tales are the actors represented as penitent or aware of their crimes. Indeed it is wrong to call their actions crimes. Given the viewpoint that is reflected in these narratives, the actors are simply morally unaware.

Although themes reflecting this attitude toward man and the world are the dominant ones today, this does not mean that they always have been so. It is best, in fact, to regard the prevalence of these themes as part of a style, originally reflecting certain social conditions developed many generations ago, which has persisted in the traditional prose narratives and driven out other styles. Yet other themes and styles are still found today although they are not common. Take, for example, the Bantu Ambundu tale of *The Son of Kimanaueze* and *The Daughter of the Sun and Moon* [27]. That themes of this type were at one time much commoner we may safely assume. We can, in fact, still find them in many tales that have been today completely revised and reorganized in terms of the newer realistic style. This older viewpoint is also evident in many of the animal tales, particularly among the Southern Bantu.

The only respect in which the non-traditional narratives differ from those of other areas is in the development of formal semi-religious, semi-philosophical discourses such as those found in West Africa among the Ewe [28]. In the latter we find the same realistic appraisal of the world so characteristic of the traditional narratives. One example will have to suffice:

God made everything in the world. He alone has been great from the beginning of time. God made all men. ... God is wise for he has created everything on the earth and accompanies men and animals everywhere. ... No person can understand his wisdom. ...

440

He himself made the good and the bad people. He is compassionate. But he does not always know how to act justly for he gave us death.

God acts unjustly for he made some people good and others bad. I and my companions work together in the fields; the crops of one prosper and those of others fail. This proves that God is unjust and treats men unequally. God treats us, our children and our wives who perish, unkindly. If men behave like that we say nothing, but when God acts thus it hurts us. From this we are right in inferring that God is unjust.

In the other main branches of prose literature which have attained significant development, in aboriginal Africa, the riddles and the proverbs, sophistication and realism are also dominant. The realism of the proverbs is accompanied by a profound and detached philosophic insight and understanding in which love and compassion are given their due place, something which is strikingly absent from the traditional prose narratives. Perhaps nowhere in the world has the proverb attained a more artistic expression than here in Africa. Rarely has so much been said in so concise, pithy, and artistic a form. We have today a tendency to dismiss such a literary genre with a shrug of the shoulders. That, of course, is a Western European prejudice. The proverb is still a legitimate literary form in the Orient and it was not despised in ancient Greece.

In contrast to the prose, no generalizations can be made for the poetry that would hold for the whole continent. There exist a few stylistic forms that are found everywhere, such as the poems consisting of solo and chorus or those that serve as a text for a prose expansion, or the dirges for the dead. But apart from these each area and tribe has developed its own forms and stresses themes referring to its own interests and connected with its own special history. Where monarchies exist or where societies are complexly organized the poets often constitute a professional and privileged order. They play the role of poet-laureates whose duty it is to glorify the rulers and the particular interests and ideals of their nation. Let me select the Bantu Ruanda to illustrate what these poets take as their subject matter.

Among the Ruanda there are three main genres of poetry, all of them taking the form of odes or small epics, those in praise of the king, those in praise of the warrior and his deeds, and those in praise of their most prized possession, the cow. These odes are one of the distinctive achievements of Africa. Those in praise of the king consist of a long series of stereotyped complements, stereotyped images and allusions which only a member of the tribe could possibly understand

and appreciate. As an example, let me quote part of an ode composed to celebrate the accession to the throne of the king Mutara in 1810: [29]

You are a vessel forged without defect,
Fashioned by hammers, chosen and select;
Born of Ruaniko's most sacred trees,
Your brethren, scions of Cyillima.
Indolence never touched you nor did sloth.
Your arms, unfailing, brought us victory
Just as it did your kin, Ruanda's ancient kings.

You are the happy searcher after game.
You nourish us and grant us your protection.
O king of great renown and without blame,
Have we not seen the deeds where you excelled?
A king of many virtues, hero you.
A jewel precious are you and so large
That from Buriza down to Buremera you stretch.

Ruler of Tanda, you, all-powerful,
From days of old your fief it was Rutanga,
Your ancient home Gasabo,
There where the heifers play.
Hero without fault and without blame,
Giver of laws, unalterable words,
Owner of lands that overflow with wealth,
Master and king, your subjects here we stand
And in Ruanda may you always rule. . . .

Equal you are to those that I have praised,
In no way second,
O clothed in joy and happiness!
These drums attest your gentleness and worth.
Young though you be, in valor you are clothed.
Your horns already stand erect and straight
Despite your youth, most precious calf!
Mighty will you become I know,
When you have come to man's estate,
Mighty and strong and proud, a bull.
Great conqueror of hungers.
Where will the nations flee,
Those who were slow to serve you?
Protector of our flock, lengthen this day,
Give me your ear that I may pay respect. . . .
I am not one who falters, whom slander finds:
Others may hesitate, this well I know, not I.

Pleasure and happiness reside within my breast
Since that rare day when to your home I came.
Giver of joy, our refuge,
Turn upon us the fulness of your power.
And now a happy message do I bring,
I who did find the chambers of our lord,

That gracious home, radiant and full of smiles,
Immaculate and clean as kaoline.
There did I see and come upon the king,
In semblance like a newly risen moon,
His features like a diamond without flaw.
Resplendent did his beauty flash on me
And there came a new afflatus added to the old.
Upon my head a garland there was placed.
And thus I danced crowned with the sacred badge,
Nor can the best of bards find me at fault.

Here we are in a world comparable to that of Pindar, a world in which heroic lays and odes are born, as the well-known French scholar, Père Laydevant, has justly pointed out.[30] The poetic inspiration found in these odes is not generally of the highest kind. Negro African poetry at its best is to be found elsewhere, in the elegies for the dead, in the religious 'hymns', and in the short philosophic lyrics. Take, for example, the following 'hymns' from the upper Guinea coast[31].

I

1

The sun shines brightly, it burns down upon us.
In glory rises the moon, rises into the skies.
Rain falls on earth and, changing, the sun shines upon us.
Sun, moon and rain may change, but over them all there towers
God, from whose eye nothing escapes and is hidden.
Though you may stay at home, or though you may live on the waters,
Though under darkest shade of the trees you recline
Over it all dwells God.

2

Did you think in your pride or believe an orphan was ever below you,
You could covet his wealth and secretly then betray him,
There would be none to behold and none to detect you?
Call but to mind the fact that God is there, ever above you
And in the days to come he will find and he will repay you,
Though not today, today, though not today it may be.
Yes, in the days to come God will find and he will repay you.
Was in your mind the thought, was in your heart the feeling
It is a slave I have robbed, only, indeed, an orphan?
But in the days to come God will find and he will repay you,
Though not today, today, though not today it may be.

II

O Sango, you, you are the master.
You punish in wrath, evil and guilty alike,
And you take in your hands the stones, the fiery weapons,

To crush those below; all these are broken.
Fires break out, the woods burn and all is consumed.
Trees fall, are destroyed, death threatens the living.

Or take again the following from the Ewe of West Africa: [32]

I

Death has been with us from all time;
The heavy burden long ago began.
Not I can loose the bonds.
Water does not refuse to dissolve
Even a large crystal of salt.
And so to the world of the dead
The good too must descend.

II

Large is the city of the nether world
Whither kings too must go
Nevermore to return.
Cease then your plaint, O mother of an only child!
Your plaint O cease, mother of an only child!
For when did an only child
Receive the gift of immortality?
So be it, mother of an only child,
And cease your wail, and cease your wail!

III

(The singers approach)
A great thing we desire to do,
A *kposu* song, an *adzoli* song,
To sing we shall begin:
Awute here lies dead,
He now lies on his bier.
Death did announce himself to him.
O dead friend lying on your bier
Return once more, your bonds to loose!

(The deceased appears and speaks)
You all now know
Within my body the word has perished,
Within Awute speech has died.

Who was it destroyed my body?
'Twas death dragged it away;
A warrior snatched it from my body.

(Death appears and speaks)
Now my turn it is to sing!
I came and thundered,
I had my lightning flash upon the tree
And threw him down!

444

Come let us go!
Footsteps, I hear, people are approaching.
An evil brother does announce himself;
Inopportune he comes.

With these poems I shall leave African literature and turn to one which could not possibly be more different, that of the Eskimo. Here too a stark realism pervades both prose and poetry, but there is no oversophistication and, above all, no cynicism. Nowhere is death and starvation so omnipresent, nowhere is nature so cruel and nowhere is man, possibly, so violent. What then has made for the amazing contrast between the two types of realism? The answer, I feel, is simple. Cruelty, bloodshed, destruction among the Eskimo are not palpably man-made as in Africa. No conquests, with all their attendant horrors and with the demoralization which comes in their wake, have swept over this land. No aboriginal civilization is more completely integrated. It is this integration which has protected the Eskimo against inherently false emphases and evaluations and which has permitted him to retain one virtue which is seemingly absent in the civilizations of Negro Africa and many parts of Indonesia, Malaysia and Melanesia: humility. This humility brings with it a philosophic detachment which can critically evaluate man, yet still sympathize with him even in misfortunes he has brought upon himself. The Eskimos can do this because they see man in his proper proportions as a mote in an enormous universe and as a being forced by nature and life itself to do violence to other living creatures which have as much right to life as has man.

In no area in the world, civilized or aboriginal, is there more respect for life, for all life, human and non-human, and so much unadulterated enjoyment of life. The will to live under the conditions existing in Arctic North America is an achievement and as such the Eskimos celebrate it. Only because it is something that has to be achieved can they face life, acquiesce in what it offers of good and evil, of misfortune and happiness, and only because it has to be achieved does it mean so much to them. An informant of Rasmussen tells how she came upon a woman who, when she and her family were isolated during a terrible winter, saved herself from death by consuming the dead body of her husband. When discovered, half crazed, she shrieked at her rescuers not to approach her, that she was defiled and unfit for human companionship. The answer of the rescuers was simple and direct: 'You had the will to live.'

But life to the Eskimo means life at its best moments: youth and maturity, not old age. Old age is a time for recalling the past when one was happy and active. Such reminiscences form the theme of innumerable poems. Some of them have a touch of the sentimental which a delightful sense of humor generally corrects, for on truthfulness in such matters the Eskimo lays great stress. 'Our narratives,' an old Eskimo told Rasmussen, 'deal with the experiences of man and these experiences are not always pleasant or pretty. But it is not proper to change our stories to make them more acceptable to our ears, that is if we wish to tell the truth. Words must be the echo of what has happened and cannot be made to conform to the mood and the taste of the listener.'

Let me quote one of the best of such poems: [33]

1

Often I return
To my little song.
And patiently I hum it
Above the fishing hole
In the ice.
This simple little song
I can keep on humming,
I, who else too quickly
Tire when fishing –
Up the stream.

2

Cold blows the wind
Where I stand on the ice,
I am not long in giving up!
When I get home
With a catch that does not suffice,
I usually say
It was the fish
That failed –
Up the stream.

3

And yet, glorious is it
To roam
The river's snow-soft ice
As long as my legs care.
Alas, My life has now glided
Far from the wide views of the peaks
Deep down into the vale of age –
Up the stream.

4

If I go hunting the land beasts,
Or if I try to fish,
Quickly I fall to my knees,
Stricken with faintness.

Never again shall I feel
The wildness of strength,
When on an errand I go over the land
From my house and those I provide for –
Up the stream.

5

A worn-out man, that's all,
A fisher, who ever without luck
Makes holes in river or lake ice
Where no trout will bite.

6

But life itself is still
So full of goading excitement!
I alone,
I have only my song,
Though it too is slipping from me.

7

For I am merely
Quite an ordinary hunter,
Who never inherited song
From the twittering birds of the sky.

In the traditional prose narratives purely human themes greatly predominate. These are really novelettes and are probably not very old. But the Eskimo places them in the category of narratives referring to events of the ancient past, to which also the comparatively few animal tales belong. They are often difficult to distinguish from narratives that belong to the second category, that of contemporary literature. However, the most characteristic compositions in their contemporary literature belong to the domain of their shamanistic experiences. They are really snatches of autobiography.

Yet, excellent as is their prose, the real achievement of the Eskimo lies in the realm of poetry. Here they have not been equalled by any other aboriginal people, with the possible exception of the Polynesians. That they should have as their subject matter the joy of living and the beauties of the world is not strange considering the nature of Eskimo philosophy.

All primitive peoples celebrate the happenings of their life, important or unimportant, in song, but such technical perfection as that of the Eskimo has been achieved by few others. This is manifest in every composition. Take, for example, the following poems:

I [34]

I arise from rest with movements swift
As the beat of a raven's wings,
Thus I arise
To meet the day.
My face is turned from the dark of night
To gaze at the dawn of day
Now whitening in the sky.

II [35]

The hands around my dwelling
Are more beautiful
From the day
When it is given to me to see
Faces I have never seen before.
All is more beautiful,
All is more beautiful,
And life is thankfulness.
These guests of mine
Make my house grand.

III [36]

Ajaha, ajaha!
I journeyed in my kayak
To search for some land.
Ajaha, ajaha!
And I came upon a snowdrift
As it began to melt,
Ajahaija, ajaha!
Spring now I knew was near,
Winter was past.
Ajahaija, ajaihaija!
And I was afraid
That my eyes would become
Weak, far too weak
To behold all that glory.
Ajahaija,
Ajahaija,
Ajaha.

IV [37]

I

Fear seizes me
When I think of being alone.
What a wish, to be far from men
As happy one sits among friends!

2

What a joy it is to sense,
To witness summer's approach
As it comes to this world of ours;
To behold the sun,
The day-sun, the night-sun,
Going its ancient way!

3

Fear seizes me
When I mark the winter's approach
As it comes to this world of ours;
To behold the moon,
The half moon, the full moon,
Going its ancient way!

4

Whither does all this tend?
Would that my steps went eastward!
Yes, never again, well I know,
Will I see him, my father's kin.

The Eskimos have a large number of special genres of poetry, the most famous being the versified lampoon. On specified occasions men and women assemble to hear individuals, generally gifted poets, hurl insults at one another. These versified lampoons are highly stylized and very difficult to understand because they deal with incidents in the personal lives of the combatants. Such poetic duels can be quite long, lasting at times an hour. They consist of attacks and answers. In many of these poems it is regarded as artistic to compose in riddles, or only to give hints without stating clearly what is meant. The audience is thus kept in a continuous state of tension, although rarely for long, since among the Eskimo everyone's affairs are matters of community knowledge.

Let me quote snatches from one such poetic duel[38] where the meaning is clear. The contest is between a man named Marratse and one named Equerqo, who had stolen Marratse's wife.

MARRATSE'S ATTACK

Words let me split,
Small words, sharp words,
Like the splinters
Which, with my axe, I cut up.
A song I shall sing of old days,
A breath from the distant past,
A sad and a plaintive song,
Forgetfulness to bring to my wife,

She who was snatched from me
By a prattler, a liar.
Bitterly has she suffered from him,
That lover of human flesh,
Cannibal, miscreant,
Spewed up from starvation days!

EQUERQO'S ANSWER

Only amazement I feel
At your preposterous words.
Only anger they cause
And the urge to laugh,
You with your mocking song,
Placing on me that guilt.
Did you think you could frighten me,
I who many a time challenged death?
Hei, hei! So you sing to my wife
Who once was yours in the days
When kindness you forgot.
Alone she was in those days.
Yet never in combats of song
Did you challenge your foes for her.
Ah, but now she is mine,
Never again shall False lovers like you,
Deceivers, come singing into our tent.

Eskimo poetry is exclusively lyrical, but within that genre what has been achieved is amazing. Equally amazing is the Eskimo's awareness of their technique. As one of them once said, 'The most festive of all things is joy in beautiful, smooth words and one's ability to express them.' [39] It is not by chance, then, but because they have occupied themselves with the problem, that they attempt to explain what poetic inspiration is. I have already given one such explanation; let me now add another. 'All songs,' so an old Eskimo claimed, 'come to us in the great solitary open places. Sometimes they come to us in the form of tears, at other times from the depths of our hearts or, again, they may come in the form of joyous laughter springing from the happiness which wells up within us as we behold the grandeur of the world and ponder over the meaning of life. Without our knowing how, words and melodies come into being, words we do not use in common speech.' [40]

How are we to account for this amazing literary achievement? It is an important question to answer. A highly developed literary tradition must lie behind it, and we have difficulty, at first, in believing it was achieved in the inhospitable and frightful environment in which the Eskimo now lives. Is it conceivable, as they themselves claim, that song and laughter was the answer they gave to the challenge of nature? Possibly. But this is only part of the answer. To explain the Eskimo literary achievement, to completely explain the literary achievement of any aboriginal civilization, we must assume that all peoples, at all times, carry within them the possibilities of developing significant and mature literatures if social and economic conditions are not too destructive. Only on such an assumption can we explain the song cycles of the Australian aborigines of Northeastern Arnhem Land, cycles that are true epics – this song, for instance, that a 'lowly' Australian poet sings:[41]

Tidal waters flowing,
White foam on the waves,
Fresh water flowing,
From rains into the stream.
Into the waters falling,
Soft bark of the papertrees,
Rain from the clouds falling,
The stream's waters swirling –
Thus she emerged
And walked upon the land.

References

[1] *Handbook of American Indian Languages, Bull.* **40**, Bureau of American Ethnology, Wash DC, 1911–1935.

[2] *Language: an introduction to the study of speech*, Harcourt Brace, New York, 1921.

[3] *Les fonctions mentales dans les sociétiés inférieures*, 5th ed Paris, 1922, 151–257, Eng ed, *How natives think*, Allen & Unwin, London, 1926.

[4] Philosophie der symbolischen Formen, **I**, *Die Sprache* (Berlin 1923), Eng ed, *The Philosophy of Symbolic Forms* Yale University Press, New Haven, 1953.

[5] P RADIN, University of California Publications in American Archeology & Ethnology, 1920, **16**, 381–473.

[6] *The Netsilik Eskimos*, Report on Fifth Thule Expedition, **VIII**, Copenhagen, 1931, 321.

[7] *Grönlandsagen*, Berlin, 1922, 229, translated from the German, cf his *The Eagle's Gift*, New York, 1932, 8 ff.

[8] R C THURNWALD, *Profane Literature of Buin*, Yale University Publications in Anthropology, 1936, 3–15.

[10] P H TRILLES, 'Les légendes des Bena Kanioka et le Folklore Bantou' in *Anthropos*, **IV**, Vienna, 1909, 965, translated from the French.

[11] Unpublished.

[12] J R SWANTON, *Tlingit Myths and Texts*, Bureau of American Ethnology, Wash, DC, 410.

[13] *Ibid*, 411.

[14] P RADIN, *op cit*, 423.

[15] F DENSMORE, *Chippewa Music II, Bull.* **53**, Bureau of American Ethnology, Wash, DC, 129.

[16] *Ibid*, 254.

[17] *Ibid*, 83.

[18] J R SWANTON, *op cit*, 415.

[19] K RASMUSSEN, *op cit*, in no 6, 511.

[20] P RADIN, manuscript.

[21] P A TALBOT, *In the Shadow of the Bush*, London, 1912.

[22] *African Folk Tales*, New York, 1953.

[23] J TORREND, *Specimens of Bantu Folklore from Northern Rhodesia*, London, 1921, 24–26.

[24] *African Folktales and Sculpture*, 186 ff.

[25] *Ibid*, 229 ff.

[26] *Ibid*, 305.

[27] *Ibid*, 73 ff.

[28] J SPIETH, *Die Ewe-Staemme*, Leipzig, 1906, 834–836.

[29] Translated from the French of the unpublished essay by A KAGAME, *La Poésie au Ruanda*, kindly placed at my disposal.

[30] '*La Poesie chez les Basuto*', Africa, **III**, London, 1930, 523–535.

[31] D WESTERMANN, 'Gottesvorstellungen in Oberguinea', *Africa*, **I**, 195, 204, translated from the German.

[32] J SPIETH, *Die Religion der Eweer*, 236 ff, Göttingen, Vanderhoeck & Rupprecht, 1911, translated from the German.

[33] K RASMUSSEN, *op cit*, 6, 509.

[34] K RASMUSSEN, *Intellectual Culture of the Inglulik Eskimos*, Report on Fifth Thule Expedition, **VII**, Copenhagen, 1929, 27.

[35] *Ibid*, 47.

[36] K RASMUSSEN, *Grönlandsagen*, text translated into German by J. Koppel, 238, translated from the German.

[37] K RASMUSSEN, *Rasmussen's Thulefahn*, translated into German by F SIEBURG, 430, Berlin, 1922, translated from the German.

[38] *Ibid*, 235–236, translated from the German.

[39] K RASMUSSEN, *The Eagle's Gift*.

[40] K RASMUSSEN, *Grönlandsagen*, 230, translated from the German.

[41] R M BERNDT, *Kunapipi*, **vii**, Melbourne, Cheshire, 1951.

40

How to ask for a drink in Subanun *
C O Frake †

Ward Goodenough (1957) has proposed that a description of a culture – an ethnography – should properly specify what it is that a
stranger to a society would have to know in order appropriately to
perform any role in any scene staged by the society. If an ethnographer of Subanun culture were to take this notion seriously, one of the
most crucial sets of instructions to provide would be that specifying
how to ask for a drink. Anyone who cannot perform this operation
successfully will be automatically excluded from the stage upon which
some of the most dramatic scenes of Subanun life are performed.

To ask appropriately for a drink among the Subanun it is not
enough to know how to construct a grammatical utterance in
Subanun translatable in English as a request for a drink. Rendering
such an utterance might elicit praise for one's fluency in Subanun,
but it probably would not get one a drink. To speak appropriately it
is not enough to speak grammatically or even sensibly (in fact some
speech settings may require the uttering of nonsense as is the case with
the semantic-reversal type of speech play common in the Philippines.
See CONKLIN, 1959). Our stranger requires more than a grammar and
a lexicon; he needs what Hymes (1962) has called an ethnography of
speaking: a specification of what kinds of things to say in what message forms to what kinds of people in what kinds of situations. Of
course an ethnography of speaking cannot provide rules specifying

---

* The Subanun are pagan swidden agriculturists occupying the moun-
tainous interior of Zamboanga Peninsula on the island of Mindanao in the
Philippines. This paper refers to the Eastern Subanun of Zamboanga del
Norte Province. Descriptions of Subanun social structure, festive activities,
and some aspects of *gasi* manufacture are given in Frake 1960, 1963, 1964a,
and 1964b. The ethnographic methodology of this paper is that described in
Frake 1964b. Single quotation marks enclose English substitutes for (but not
translations of) Subanun expressions.

† C O FRAKE, 'How to ask for a drink in Subanun', *American Anthropologist*,
66, 1964, no. 6, part 2, pp. 127–132.

exactly what message to select in a given situation. If messages were perfectly predictable from a knowledge of the culture, there would be little point in saying anything. But when a person selects a message, he does so from a set of appropriate alternatives. The task of an ethnographer of speaking is to specify what the appropriate alternatives are in a given situation and what the consequences are of selecting one alternative over another.

Drinking defined. Of the various substances which the Subanun consider 'drinkable', we are here here concerned only with a subset called *gasi*, a rice-yeast fermented beverage made of a rice, manioc, maize, and/or Job's tears mash. *Gasi*, glossed in this paper as 'beer', contrasts in linguistic labelling, drinking technique, and social context with all other Subanun beverages (*tebaq* 'toddy', *sebug* 'wine', *binu*, 'liquor', *sabaw* 'juice-broth', *tubig* 'water').

The context of drinking. Focussed social gatherings (GOFFMAN, 1961) among the Subanun fall into two sharply contrasted sets: festive gatherings of 'festivities' and nonfestive or informal gatherings (FRAKE, 1964b). The diagnostic feature of a festivity is the consumption of a festive meal as a necessary incident in the encounter. A 'meal' among the Subanun necessarily comprises a serving of a cooked starchy-staple food, the 'main dish', and ordinarily also includes a 'side dish' of vegetables, fish, or meat. A festive meal, or 'feast', is a meal with a meat side dish. A 'festivity' comprises all socially relevant events occurring between the arrival and dispersal of participants in a feast. Apart from a feast, the necessary features of a festivity are (1) an occasioning event, (2) multi-family participation, and (3) beer. The drinking of beer, unlike the consumption of any other beverage, occurs only during a festivity and must occur as part of any festivity. It occupies a crucial position as a focus of formal social gatherings.

Drinking technique. 'Beer', uniquely among Subanun drinks, is drunk with bamboo straws inserted to the bottom of a Chinese jar containing the fermented mash. Just prior to drinking, the jar is filled to the rim with water. Except in certain types of game drinking, one person drinks at a time, after which another person replenishes the water from an agreed-upon 'measure'. As one sucks on the straw, the water disappears down through the mash where it picks up a surprising amount of alcohol and an indescribable taste. After initial rounds of tasting, drinking etiquette requires one to gauge his consumption so that when a full measure of water is added, the water level rises exactly even with the jar rim.

The drinking encounter. Each beer jar provided for a festivity becomes

454

the focus of a gathering of persons who take turns drinking. A *turn* is a single period of continuous drinking by one person. Each change of drinkers marks a new turn. A circuit of turns through the gathering is a *round*. As drinking progresses, rounds change in character with regard to the number and length of constituent turns and to variations in drinking techniques. Differences in these features among successive sets of rounds mark three distinct stages of the drinking encounter: tasting, competitive drinking and game drinking (table 1).

Table 1 SUBANUN DRINKING TALK

Encounter stages	Discourse stages	Focus of speech acts	Function
1 Tasting	1 Invitation – permission	Role expression	Assignment of role distances and authority relations to participants
2 Competitive drinking	2 Jar talk	Role expression and context definition	Allocation of encounter resources (turns at drinking and talking)
	3 Discussion 3 1 Gossip 3 2 Deliberation	Topic	Exchange of information; disputation, arbitration; deciding issues on basis of cogent argument
3 Game drinking	4 Display of verbal art	Stylistic	Establishment of euphoria. Deciding issues on basis of skills in use of special styles of discourse (singing, verse)

Segments of a drinking encounter:
1 A turn (continuous drinking by one person)
2 A round (a set of related turns)
3 Encounter stage (a set of related rounds)

Segments of drinking talk:
1 An utterance (continuous speech by one person)
2 An exchange (a set of related utterances)
3 Discourse stage (a set of related exchanges)

The first round is devoted to *tasting*, each person taking a brief turn with little regard to formal measurement of consumption. Successive turns become longer and the number of turns per round fewer, thus cutting out some of the participants in the encounter. These individuals go to other jars if available or withdraw from drinking during this stage of *competitive drinking*. Measurement is an important aspect of competitive rounds, participants keeping a mental record of

455

each other's consumption. Within a round, successive drinkers must equal the consumption of the drinker who initiated the round. In later rounds, as the brew becomes weaker, the measure tends to be raised. Continued competitive drinking may assume an altered character signaled by accompanying music, dancing, and singing. The scope of the gathering may enlarge and turns become shorter. Special types of drinking games occur: 'chugalug' (*sangayuq*) and dual-drinking by opposite-sexed partners under the cover of a blanket. These rounds form a stage of *game drinking*.

Drinking talk. The Subanun expression for drinking talk, *taluq bwat dig beksuk* 'talk from the straw', suggests an image of the drinking straw as a channel not only of the drink but also of drinking talk. The two activities, drinking and talking, are closely interrelated in that how one talks bears on how much one drinks and the converse is, quite obviously, also true. Except for 'religious offerings', which must precede drinking, whatever business is to be transacted during a festivity occurs during drinking encounters. Consequently drinking talk is a major medium of interfamily communication. Especially for an adult male, one's role in the society at large, insofar as it is subject to manipulation, depends to a considerable extent on one's verbal performance during drinking encounters.

Subanun society contains no absolute, society-wide status positions or offices which automatically entitle their holder to deference from and authority over others. The closest approximation to such a formal office is the status of religious specialist or 'medium' who is deferred to in religious matters but who has no special voice in affairs outside his domain (FRAKE, 1964b). Assumption of decision-making roles in legal, economic, and ecological domains depends not on acquisition of an office but on continuing demonstration of one's ability to make decisions within the context of social encounters. This ability in turn depends on the amount of deference one can evoke from other participants in the encounter. Although relevant, no external status attributes of sex, age or wealth are sufficient to guarantee such deference; it must be elicited through one's skill in the use of speech. Apart from age, sex and reputation from performances in previous encounters, the most salient external attributes brought to an encounter by a participant are his relational roles based on kinship, neighborhood and friendship with specific other participants. Because of consanguineal endogamy and residential mobility, the relationship ties between an ego and any given alter are likely to be multiple and complex, giving wide latitude for manipulation of roles within particular encounters. Moreover, most kinship roles permit a range of interpretation depending upon other features of the relationship such as friendship and residential proximity.

The strategy of drinking talk is to manipulate the assignment of role relations among participants so that, within the limits of one's external status attributes, one can maximize his share of encounter resources (drink and talk), thereby having an opportunity to assume an esteem-attracting and authority-wielding role. Variations in the kinds of messages sent during periods devoted to different aspects of this strategic plan mark four distinct *discourse stages* within the drinking talk of the encounter: invitation-permission, jar talk, discussion, and display of verbal art (table 1). The constituents of a discourse stage are *exchanges*: sets of utterances with a common topic focus. (Boundaries of exchanges in American speech are often marked by such expressions as 'Not to change the subject, but . . .' or 'By the way, that reminds me . . .'.) The constituents of exchanges are *utterances*: stretches of continuous speech by one person.

1 Invitation-Permission. The Subanun designate the discourse of the initial tasting round as 'asking permission'. The provider of the jar initiates the tasting round by inviting someone to drink, thereby signaling that this person is the one to whom he and those closest to him in the encounter owe the greatest initial deference on the basis of external status attributes. The invited drinker squats before the jar and asks permission to drink of the other participants. He has two variables to manipulate: the order in which he addresses the other participants and the terms of address he employs. Apart from the latter variable, message form remains relatively constant: *naa, A, sep pa u* 'Well, *A*, I will be drinking.' (*A* represents a term of address.) Role relations with persons who are not lineal consanguineal or lineal affinal kin (Mo, F, Ch, Sp, SpPr, ChSP, ChSpPr) permit a variety of forms of address each with different implications for social distance with respect to ego (Frake, 1960). The drinker's final opportunity to express role relations comes when he finishes tasting and invites another (ordinarily the person who invited him) to drink.

2 Jar talk. As competitive drinking begins, asking permission is reduced in scope and importance, and there is an increase in messages sent during drinking itself. The topic focus of these exchanges is the drink being consumed. The drinker responds to queries about the taste and strength of the beer, explanations are advanced for its virtues and defects, and the performance of drinkers is evaluated. During this stage the topic of messages is predictable. The informative aspect of the messages is the quantity and quality of verbal responses a drinker can elicit. This information signals the amount of drinking

457

and talking time the gathering will allot him. Those who receive little encouragement drop out, and the encounter is reduced generally to less than half-a-dozen persons, who can thereby intensify their interaction with each other and with the beer straw.

3 Discussion. As the size and role-structure of the gathering becomes defined, discourse changes in topic to removed referents, usually beginning with relatively trivial gossip, proceeding to more important subjects of current interest, and, finally, in many cases arriving at litigation. Since there are no juro-political offices in Subanun society, a legal case is not only a contest between litigants but also one between persons attempting to assume a role of legal authority by settling the case. Success in effecting legal decisions depends on achieving a commanding role in the encounter and on debating effectively from that position. Since there are no sanctions of force legally applicable to back up a decision, the payment of a fine in compliance with a decision is final testimony to the prowess in verbal combat of the person who made the decision.

4 Display of verbal art. If drinking continues long enough, the focus of messages shifts from their topics to play with message forms themselves, following stylized patterns of song and verse composition. Songs and verses are composed on the spot to carry on discussions in an operetta-like setting. Even unsettled litigation may be continued in this manner, the basis for decision being shifted from cogent argument to verbal artistry. The most prestigious kinds of drinking songs require the mastery of an esoteric vocabulary by means of which each line is repeated with a semantically equivalent but formally different line. Game drinking is a frequent accompaniment to these displays of verbal art. Together they help assure that the festivity will end with good feelings among all participants, a goal which is explicitly stated by the Subanun. Participants who have displayed marked hostility toward each other during the course of drinking talk may be singled out for special ritual treatment designed to restore good feelings.

The Subanun drinking encounter thus provides a structured setting within which one's social relationships beyond his everyday associates can be extended, defined, and manipulated through the use of speech. The cultural patterning of drinking talk lays out an ordered scheme of role play through the use of terms of address, through discussion and argument, and through display of verbal art. The most skilled in 'talking from the straw' are the *de facto* leaders of the society. In instructing our stranger to Subanun society how to ask for a drink, we have at the same time instructed him how to get ahead socially.

458

References

H C CONKLIN, 'Linguistic play in its cultural setting', *Language*, **35**, 631–36, 1959.

C O FRAKE, 'The Eastern Subanun of Mindanao', in G P MURDOCK (ed), *Social Structure in Southeast Asia*, Viking Publications in Anthropology, **29**, 51–64, 1960.

C O FRAKE, 'Litigation in Lipay: a study in Subanun law', *The Proceedings of the Ninth Pacific Science Congress*, 1957, **3**, Bangkok, 1963.

C O FRAKE (1964a), 'Notes on queries in ethnography', *Amer Anthrop*, **66**, no 3, part 2, 132–45.

C O FRAKE (1964b), 'A structural description of Subanun "religious behavior" ', in W G GOODENOUGH (ed), *Explorations in Cultural Anthropology: Essays in Honor of George Peter Murdock*, McGraw-Hill.

E GOFFMAN (1961), *Encounters: Two Studies in the Sociology of Interaction*, Bobbs-Merrill.

W G GOODENOUGH (1957), 'Cultural anthropology and linguistics', in P I GARVIN (ed), *Report of the Seventh Annual Round Table Meeting on Linguistics and Language Study*, Georgetown University Monograph Series on Language and Linguistics, **9**, 167–73.

D H HYMES (1962), 'The ethnography of speaking', in T GLADWIN and W C STURTEVANT (eds), *Anthropology and Human Behaviour*, Anthropological Society of Washington, 15–53.

41

Hanunóo Color Categories *

Harold C Conklin

In following brief analysis of a specific Philippine color system I shall attempt to show how various ethnographic field techniques may be combined profitably in the study of lexical sets relating to perceptual categorization.

Recently, I completed more than a year's field research on Hanunóo folkbotany.[1] In this type of work one soon becomes acutely aware of problems connected with understanding the local system of color categorization[2] because plant determinations so often depend on chromatic differences in the appearance of flowers or vegetative structures – both in taxoniomic botany and in popular systems of classification. It is no accident that one of the most detailed accounts of native color terminology in the Malayo-Polynesian area was written by a botanist[3]. I was, therefore, greatly concerned with Hanunóo color categories during the entire period of my ethnobotanical research. Before summarizing the specific results of my analysis of the Hanunóo material, however, I should like to draw attention to several general considerations.

1 Color, in a western technical sense, is not a universal concept and in many languages such as Hanunóo there is no unitary terminological equivalent. In our technical literature definitions state that color is the evaluation of the visual sense of that quality of light (reflected or transmitted by some substance) which is basically determined by its spectral composition. The spectrum is the range of visible color in light measured in wave lengths (400 [deep red] to 700 [blue-violet] millimicrons)[4]. The total color sphere – holding any set of external and surface conditions constant – includes two other dimensions, in addition to that of spectral position or hue. One is saturation or intensity (chroma), the other brightness or brilliance (value). These three perceptual dimensions are usually combined into a co-ordination

* Reprinted from *Southwestern Journal of Anthropology*, **11**, Winter, 1955, Copyright, 1955, University of New Mexico. All rights reserved.

system as a cylindrical continuum known as the color solid. Saturation diminishes toward the central axis which forms the achromatic core of neutral grays from the white at the end of greatest brightness to black at the opposite extremity. Hue varies with circumferential position. Although technically speaking *black* is the absence of any 'color', *white*, in the presence of all visible color wave lengths, and neutral *grays* lack spectral distinction, these achromatic positions within the color solid are often included with spectrally-defined positions in the categories distinguished in popular color systems.

2 Under laboratory conditions, color *discrimination* is probably the same for all human populations, irrespective of language; but the manner in which different languages classify the millions[5] of 'colors' which every normal individual can discriminate *differ*. Many stimuli are classified as equivalent, as extensive, cognitive – or perceptual – screening takes place[6]. Requirements of specification may differ considerably from one culturally-defined situation to another. The largest collection[7] of English color names runs to over 3000 entries, yet only eight of these occur very commonly[8]. Recent testing by Lenneberg and others[9] demonstrates a high correlation in English and in Zuñi between ready color vocabulary and *ease in recognition of colors*. Although this is only a beginning it does show how the structure of a lexical set may affect color perception. It may also be possible to determine certain nonlinguistic correlates for color terminology. Color terms are a part of the vocabulary of particular languages and only the intracultural analysis of such lexical sets and their correlates can provide the key to their understanding and range of applicability. The study of isolated and assumed translations in other languages can lead only to confusion[10].

In the field I began to investigate Hanunóo color classification in a number of ways, including the eliciting of linguistic responses from a large nuumber of informants to painted cards, dyed fabrics, other previously prepared materials[11], and the recording of visual-quality attributes taken from descriptions of specific items of the natural and artificial surroundings. This resulted in the collection of a profusion of attributive words of the nonformal – and therefore in a sense 'color' type. There were at first many inconsistencies and a high degree of overlap for which the controls used did not seem to account. However, as the work with plant specimens and minute floristic differentiation progressed, I noted that in *contrastive* situations this initial confusion and incongruity of informants' responses did not usually occur. In such situations, where the 'nonformal (ie, not spatially organized) visible quality'[12] of one substance (plant part, dyed thread, or color card) was to be related to and contrasted with that of another, both of which were either at hand or well known terminological agreement was reached with relative ease. Such a defined situation seemed to provide the frame necessary for establishing a known level of specification. Where needed, a greater degree of specification (often employing different root morphemes) could be and was made. Otherwise, such finer distinctions were ignored. This hint of terminologically significant levels led to a reexamination of all color data and the following analysis emerged.

Color distinctions in Hanunóo are made at two levels of contrast. The first, higher, more general level consists of an all-inclusive, coordinate, four-way classification which lies at the core of the color system. The four categories are mutually exclusive in contrastive contexts, but may overlap slightly in absolute (ie, spectrally, or in other measurable) terms. The second level, including several sublevels, consists of hundreds of specific color categories, many of which overlap and interdigitate. Terminologically, there is 'unanimous agreement'[13] on the designations for the four Level L categories, but considerable lack of unanimity – with a few explainable exceptions – in the use of terms at Level II.

The four Level I terms are:

1 (*ma*) *bīru*[14] 'relative darkness (of shade of color); blackness' (black)

2 (*ma*) *lagti* 'relative lightness (or tint of color); whiteness' (white)

3 (*ma*) *rara* 'relative presence of red; redness' (red)

4 (*ma*) *latuy* 'relative presence of light greenness; greenness' (green)

The three-dimensional color solid is divided by this Level I categorization into four unequal parts; the largest is *mabīru*, the smallest *malatuy*. While boundaries separating these categories cannot be set in absolute terms, the focal points (differing slightly in size, themselves) within the four sections, can be limited more or less to black, white, orange-red, and leaf-green respectively. In general terms, *mabīru* includes the range usually covered in English by black, violet, indigo, blue, dark green, dark gray, and deep shades of other colors and mixtures; *marara*, maroon, red, orange, yellow, and mixtures in which these qualities are seen to predominate; *malatuy*, light green, and mixtures of green, yellow, and light brown. All color terms can be reduced to one of these four but none of the four is reducible. This does not mean that other color terms are synonyms, but that they designate color categories of greater specification within four recognized color realms.

The basis of this Level I classification appears to have certain correlates beyond what is usually considered the range of chromatic differentiation, and which are associated with nonlinguistic pheno-

462

mena in the external environment. First, there is the opposition between light and dark, obvious in the contrasted ranges of meaning of *lagti'* and *bīru*. Second, there is an opposition between dryness or desiccation and wetness or freshness (succulence) in visible components of the natural environment which are reflected in the terms *rara'* and *latuy* respectively. This distinction is of particular significance in terms of plant life. Almost all living plant types possess some fresh, succulent, and often 'greenish' parts. To eat any kind of raw, uncooked food, particularly fresh fruits or vegetables, is known as *paglat-un* (∠ *latuy*). A shiny, wet, brown-coloured section of newly-cut bamboo is *malatuy* (not *marara'*). Dried-out or matured plant material such as certain kinds of yellowed bamboo or hardened kernels of mature or parched corn are *marara'*. To become desiccated, to lose all moisture, is known as *mamara'* (∠ *para'*) 'desiccation'; and parenthetically, I might add that there are morphological and historical reasons – aside from Hanunóo folk etymologizing – to believe that at least the final syllables of these two forms are derived from a common root). A third opposition, dividing the two already suggested, is that of deep, unfading, indelible, and hence often more desired material as against pale, weak, faded, bleached, or 'colorless' substance, a distinction contrasting *mabīru* and *marara* with *malagti* and *malatuy*. This opposition holds for manufactured items and trade goods as well as for some natural products (eg, red and white trade beads, red being more valuable by Hanunóo standards; indigo-dyed cotton sarongs, the most prized being those dyed most often and hence of the deepest indigo color – sometimes obscuring completely the designs formed originally by *white* wrap yarns; etc). Within each of these Level I categories, increased aesthetic value attaches as the focal points mentioned above are approached. There is only one exception: the color which is most tangibly visible in their jungle surroundings, the green (even the focal point near light- or yellow-green) of the natural vegetation, is *not* valued decoratively. Green beads, for example, are 'unattractive', worthless. Clothing and ornament are valued in proportion to the sharpness of contract between, and the intensity (lack of mixture, deep quality) of 'black', 'red', and 'white'.

Level II terminology is normally employed only when greater specification than is possible at Level I is required, or when the name of an object referred to happens also to be a 'color' term (eg *bulawan* 'gold'; golden [color]'). Level II terms are of two kinds: relatively specific color words like (*ma*) *dapug* 'gray' (∠ *dapug* 'hearth'; 'ashes'), (*ma*) *arum* 'violet', (*ma*) *dilaw* 'yellow' (∠ *dilaw* 'tumeric'); and constructions, based on such specific terms – or on Level I names – but involving further derivations, such as *mabirubiru* 'somewhat *mabīru*' (more specific than *mabīru* alone only in that a color which is *not* a solid, deep black is implied, ie, a color classed within the *mabīru* category at Level I, but not at or near the focal point), *mabīru* (*gid*) 'very *mabīru*' (here something close to the focal center of jet black is designated), and *madilawdilaw* 'weak yellow'. Much attention is paid to the texture of the surface referred to, the resulting degree and type of reflection (iridescent, sparkling, dull), and to admixture of other nonformal qualities. Frequently these noncolormetric aspects are considered of primary importance, the more spectrally-definable qualities serving only as secondary attributes. In either case polymorphemic descriptions are common.

At Level II there is a noticeable difference in the ready color vocabulary of men as compared to women. The former excel (in the degree of specification to which they carry such classification terminologically) in the ranges of 'reds' and 'grays' (animals, hair, feather, etc); the latter, in 'blues' (shades of indigo-dyed fabrics). No discernible similar difference holds for the 'greens' or 'whites'.

In short, we have seen that the apparent complexity of the Hanunóo color system can be reduced at the most generalized level to four basic terms which are associated with lightness, darkness, wetness, and dryness. This intracultural analysis demonstrates that what appears to be color 'confusion' at first may result from an inadequate knowledge of the internal structure of a color system and from a failure to distinguish sharply between sensory reception on the one hand and perceptual categorization on the other.

References

[1] Field work among the Hanunóo on Mindoro Island (1952–1954) was supported by grants from the Social Science Research Council, the Ford Foundation, and the Guggenheim Foundation.

[2] CONKLIN, 1954a, 1954b.

[3] BARTLETT, 1929.

[4] OSGOOD, 1953, 137.

[5] Estimates range from 7 500 000 to more than 10 000 000 (Optical Society of America, 1953; EVANS, 1948, 230).

[6] LOUNSBURY, 1953.

[7] MAERZ and PAUL, 1950.

[8] THORNDIKE and LORGE, 1944.

[9] LENNEBERG 1953 468–471; LENNEBERG and ROBERTS, 1954; BROWN and LENNEBERG, 1954.

[10] LENNEBERG, 1953, 464–466; HJELMSLEV, 1953, 33.

[11] Cf RAY, 1952, 1953.

[12] The lack of a term similar in semantic range to our word 'color' makes abstract interrogation in Hanunóo about such matters complicated. Except for leading questions (naming some visual-quality attribute as a possibility),

only circumlocutions such as *kabitay fida nu pagbantayun?* 'How is it to look at?' are possible. If this results in description of spatial organization or form, the inquiry may be narrowed by the specification *bukun kay anyu* 'not its shape (or form)'.

[13] LENNEBERG, 1953, 469

[14] These forms occur as attributes with the prefix *ma-* 'exhibiting, having' as indicated above in parentheses, or as free words (abstracts).

Bibliography

HARLEY HARRIS BARTLETT, *Color Nomenclature in Batak and Malay*, Papers, Michigan Academy of Science, Arts and Letters, **10**, 1–52, Ann Arbor, 1929.

ROGER W BROWN and ERIC H LENNEBERG, 'A Study in Language and Cognition', *Journal of Abnormal and Social Psychology*, **49**, 454–462, 1954.

HAROLD C CONKLIN, *The Relation of Hanunóo to the Plant World*, Doctoral dissertation, Yale University, New Haven, 1954a; 'An Ethnoecological Approach to Shifting Agriculture', *Transactions*, New York Academy of Sciences, ser II, **17**, 133–142, New York, 1954b.

RALPH M EVANS, *An Introduction to Color*, Wiley, New York, 1948.

LOUIS HJELMSLEY, 'Prolegomena to a Theory of Language', Indiana University Publications in Anthropology and Linguistics, Memoir 7 of the *International Journal of American Linguistics* [translated by FRANCIS J WHIT-FIELD], Bloomington, 1953.

ERIC H LENNEBERG, 'Cognition in Ethnolinguistics' (*Language*, **29**, 463–471, Baltimore, 1953.

ERIC H LENNEBERG and JOHN M ROBERTS, *The Language of Experience, a Case Study*, Communications Program, Center of International Studies, Massachusetts Institute of Technology, Cambridge: hectographed, 45 pp. and 9 figs., 1954.

FLOYD G LOUNSBURY, 'Introduction' [section on Linguistics and Psychology] (in *Results of the Conference of Anthropologists and Linguists*, 47–49, Memoir 8, *International Journal of American Linguistics*, Baltimore), 1963.

A MAERZ and M R PAUL, *A Dictionary of Color*, McGraw-Hill, New York, 1930.

OPTICAL SOCIETY OF AMERICA, COMMITTEE ON COLORIMETRY, *The Science of Color*, Crowell, New York, 1953.

CHARLES E OSGOOD, *Method and Theory in Experimental Psychology*, Oxford University Press, New York, 1953.

VERNE F RAY, 'Techniques and Problems in the Study of Human Color Perception', *Southwestern Journal of Anthropology*, **8**, 251–259, 1952; 'Human Color Perception and Behavioral Response', *Transactions*, New York, Academy of Sciences, ser II, **16**, 98–104, New York.

E L THORNDIKE and I LORGE, *The Teacher's Word Book of 30,000 Words* (Teachers' College, Columbia University, New York), 1944.

42

Recipe Knowledge *

Alfred Schutz

We are now prepared to answer at least two of the questions with which we started: To what extent are significative and symbolic appresentations dependent upon the sociocultural environment? How is intersubjectivity as such and how are social groups experienced by significative and symbolic appresentations?

The first question deals with the main problem of any sociology of knowledge that does not misunderstand its task. To answer it we start again from our experience of the reality of everyday life which, as a sociocultural world, is permeated by appresentational reference. When in section III we developed the concepts of marks and indications, we assumed for the sake of clearer presentation that a supposedly insulated individual has to 'map out' the world within his reach. In truth, man finds himself from the outset in surroundings already 'mapped out' for him by Others, ie, 'premarked', 'preindicated', 'presignified', and even 'presymbolized'. Thus, his biographical situation in everyday life is always an historical one because it is constituted by the sociocultural process which had led to the actual configuration of this environment. Hence, only a small fraction of man's stock of knowledge at hand originates in his own individual experience. The greater portion of his knowledge is *socially derived*, handed down to him by his parents and teachers as his social heritage. It consists of a set of systems of relevant typifications, of typical solutions for typical practical and theoretical problems, of typical precepts for typical behavior, including the pertinent system of appresentational references. All this knowledge is taken for granted beyond question by the respective social group and is thus '*socially approved* knowledge'. This concept comes very near to what Max Scheler called the '*relativ natuerliche Weltanschauung*' (relative natural conception of the world) prevailing in a social group and also Sumner's

---

* ALFRED SCHUTZ, *Collected Papers*, **1**, Martinus Nijhoff, The Hague, 347–352.

classical theory of the folkways of the in-group which are taken by its members as the only right, good, and efficient way of life.

Socially approved knowledge consists, thus, of a set of recipes designed to help each member of the group to define his situation in the reality of everyday life in a typical way. It is entirely irrelevant for a description of a world taken for granted by a particular society whether the socially approved and derived knowledge is indeed true knowledge. All elements of such knowledge, including appresentational references of any kind, if *believed* to be true are real components of the 'definition of the situation' by the members of the group. The 'definition of the situation' refers to the so-called 'Thomas theorem' well known to sociologists: 'If men define situations as real, they are real in their consequences.' Applied to our problem and translated into our terminology this means: if an appresentational relationship is socially approved, then the appresented object, fact, or event is believed beyond question to be in its typicality an element of the world taken for granted.

In the process of transmitting socially approved knowledge the learning of the vernacular of the mother tongue has a particularly important function. The native language can be taken as a set of references which, in accordance with the relative natural conception of the world as approved by the linguistic community, have predetermined what features of the world are worthy of being expressed, and therewith what qualities of these features and what relations among them deserve attention, and what typifications, conceptualizations, abstractions, generalizations, and idealizations are relevant for achieving typical results by typical means. Not only the vocabulary but also the morphology and the syntax of any vernacular reflects the socially approved relevance system of the linguistic group. If, for example, the Arabian language has several hundred nouns for denoting various kinds of camels but none for the general concept 'camel'; if in certain North American Indian languages the simple notion, 'I see a man,' cannot be expressed without indicating by prefixes, suffixes, and interfixes whether this man stands or sits or walks, whether he is visible to the speaker or to the auditors; if the Greek language has developed morphological particularities such as the dual number, the optative mood, the aorist tense, and the medium voice of the verb; if the French language, so eminently suited to express philosophical thoughts, has for both 'consciousness' and 'conscience' a single term, namely, *'conscience'* – then all these facts reveal the relative natural conception of the world approved by the respective linguistic groups.

On the other hand, the determination of what is worthwhile and

467

what is necessary to communicate depends on the typical, practical, and theoretical problems which have to be solved, and these will be different for men and women, for the young and for the old, for the hunter and for the fisherman, and in general, for the various social roles assumed by the members of the group. Each kind of activity has its particular relevance aspects for the performer and requires a set of particular technical terms. This is because our knowledge is *socially distributed*; each of us has precise and distinct knowledge only about that particular field in which he is an expert. Among experts a certain technical knowledge is taken for granted, but exactly this technical knowledge is inaccessible to the layman. Some things can be supposed as well known and self-explanatory and others as needing an explanation, depending upon whether I talk to a person of my sex, age, and occupation, or to somebody not sharing with me this common situation within society, or whether I talk to a member of my family, a neighbor, or to a stranger, to a partner or a nonparticipant in a particular venture, etc.

William James has already observed that a language does not merely consist in the content of an ideally complete dictionary and an ideally complete and arranged grammar. The dictionary gives us only the kernal of meaning of the words which are surrounded by 'fringes'. We may add that these fringes are of various kinds: those originating in a particular personal use by the speaker, others originating in the context of the speech in which the term is used, still others depending upon the addressee of my speech, or the situation in which the speech occurs, or the purpose of the communication, and, finally, upon the problem at hand to be solved. What has been stated about language holds good in general for appresentational references of all kinds. In communication or in social intercourse each appresentational reference, if socially approved, constitutes merely the kernel around which fringes of the kind described are attached.

But all this already presupposes an existing typification of social relations, of social forms of intercommunication, of social stratification taken for granted by the group, and therefore socially approved by it. This whole system of types under which any social group experiences itself has to be learned by a process of acculturation. The same holds for the various marks and indications for the position, status, role, and prestige each individual occupies or has within the stratification of the group. In order to find my bearings within the social group, I have to know the different ways of dressing and behaving, the manifold insignia, emblems, tools, etc, which are considered by the group as indicating social status and are therefore socially approved as relevant. They indicate also the typical behavior, actions, and

468

motives which I may expect from a chief, a medicine man, a priest, a hunter, a married woman, a young girl, etc. In a word, I have to learn the typical social roles and the typical expectations of the behavior of the incumbents of such roles, in order to assume the appropriate corresponding role and the appropriate corresponding behavior expected to be approved by the social group. At the same time, I have to learn the typical distribution of knowledge prevailing in this group, and this involves knowledge of the appresentational, referential, and interpretive schemes which each of the subgroups takes for granted and applies to its respective appresentational reference. All this knowledge is in turn, of course, socially derived.

Let us focus and summarize our findings. We may say that in terms of the relevance system the following are all socially determined: first, the unquestioned matrix within which any inquiry starts; second, the elements of knowledge which have to be considered as socially approved and which might, therefore, be taken for granted (here we would add that those elements which might become problematic are traced out by the social situation); third, which procedures (with respect to signs and symbols) – practical, magical, political, religious, poetical, scientific, etc – are appropriate for dealing with the problem involved; fourth, the typical conditions under which a problem can be considered as solved and the conditions under which an inquiry may be broken off and the results incorporated into the stock of knowledge taken for granted. This is of particular importance for symbolic references to myths and to rituals. If the successful connecting of a problem at hand with a socially approved symbol is considered as its typical solution, then the appresentational relationship thus established may continue to function as an appresenting element of other and higher symbolizations which might be founded on the problem deemed typically solved.

43

Curriculum and Consciousness *

Maxine Greene

Curriculum, from the learner's standpoint, ordinarily represents little more than an arrangement of subjects, a structure of socially prescribed knowledge or a complex system of meaning which may or may not fall within his grasp.[1] Rarely does it signify possibility for him as an existing person, mainly concerned with making sense of his own life-world. Rarely does it promise occasions for ordering the materials of that world, for imposing 'configurations' by means of experiences and perspectives made available for a personally conducted cognitive action. Sartre says that 'knowing is a moment of *praxis*', opening into 'what has not yet been'.[2] Preoccupied with priorities, purposes, programs of 'intended learning' and intended (or unintended) manipulation, we pay too little attention to the individual in quest of his own future, bent on surpassing what is merely 'given', on breaking through the everyday. We are still too prone to dichotomize: to think of 'disciplines' or 'public traditions' or 'accumulated wisdom' or 'common culture' (individualization despite) as objectively existent, external to the knower – there to be discovered, mastered, learned.[3]

Quite aware that this may evoke Dewey's argument in *The Child and the Curriculum*, aware of how times have changed since 1902, I have gone in search of contemporary analogies to shed light on what I mean. ('Solution comes,' Dewey wrote, 'only by getting away from the meaning of terms that is already fixed upon and coming to see the conditions from another point of view, and hence in a fresh light.'[4]) My other point of view is that of literary criticism, or more properly philosophy of criticism, which attempts to explicate the modes of explanation, description, interpretation, and evaluation involved in particular critical approaches. There is presently an emerging philosophic controversy between two such approaches, one associated with England and the United States, the other with the Continent, primarily France and Switzerland; and it is in the differences in orientation that I have found some clues.

* *Teachers' College Record,* **73**, no 2, 1971, 253–269.

These differences are, it will be evident, closely connected to those separating what is known as analytic or language philosophy from existentialism and, phenomenology. The dominant tendency in British and American literary criticism has been to conceive literary works as objects or artifacts, best understood in relative isolation from the writer's personal biography and undistorted by associations brought to the work from the reader's own daily life. The new critics on the Continent have been called 'critics of consciousness'.[5] They are breaking with the notion that a literary work can be dealt with objectively, divorced from experience. In fact, they treat each work as a manifestation of an individual writer's experience, a gradual growth of consciousness into expression. This is in sharp contrast to such a view as T S Eliot's emphasizing the autonomy and the 'impersonality' of literary art. 'We can only say,' he wrote in an introduction to *The Sacred Wood*, 'that a poem, in some sense, has its own life; that its parts form something quite different from a body of neatly ordered biographical data; that the feeling, or emotion, or vision resulting from the poem is something different from the feeling or emotion or vision in the mind of the poet.'[6] Those who take this approach or an approach to a work of art as 'a self-enclosed isolated structure'[7] are likely to prescribe that purely aesthetic values are to be found in literature, the values associated with 'significant form'[8] or, at most, with the contemplation of an 'intrinsically interesting possible'.[9] M H Abrams has called this an 'austere dedication to the poem *per se*',[10] for all the enlightening analysis and explication it has produced. 'But it threatens also to commit us,' he wrote, 'to the concept of a poem as a language game, or as a floating Laputa, insulated from life and essential human concerns in a way that accords poorly with our experience in reading a great work of literature.'

For the critic of consciousness, literature is viewed as a genesis, a conscious effort on the part of an individual artist to understand his own experience by framing it in language. The reader who encounters the work must recreate it in terms of *his* consciousness. In order to penetrate it, to experience it existentially and empathetically, he must try to place himself within the 'interior space'[11] of the writer's mind as it is slowly revealed in the course of his work. Clearly, the reader requires a variety of cues if he is to situate himself in this way; and these are ostensibly provided by the expressions and attitudes he finds in the book, devices which he must accept as orientations and indications – 'norms', perhaps, to govern his recreation. *His* subjectivity is the substance of the literary object; but, if he is to perceive the identity emerging through the enactments of the book, he must subordinate his own personality as he brackets out his everyday, 'natural' world[12]. His objective in doing so, however, is not to analyze or explicate or evaluate; it is to extract the experience made manifest by means of the work. Sartre says this more concretely:

> Reading seems, in fact, to be the synthesis of perception and creation. . . . The object is essential because it is strictly transcendent, because it imposes its own structures, and because one must wait for it and observe it; but the subject is also essential because it is required not only to disclose the object (that is, to make *there be* an object) but also that this object might *be* (that is, to produce it). In a word, the reader is conscious of disclosing in creating, of creating by disclosing. . . . If he is inattentive, tired, stupid, or thoughtless most of the relations will escape him. He will never manage to 'catch on' to the object (in the sense in which we see that fire 'catches' or 'doesn't catch'). He will draw some phrases out of the shadow, but they will appear as random strokes. If he is at his best, he will project beyond the words a synthetic form, each phrase of which will be no more than a partial function: the 'theme', the 'subject', or the 'meaning'.[13]

There must be, he is suggesting, continual reconstructions if a work of literature is to become meaningful. The structures involved are generated over a period of time, depending upon the perceptiveness and attentiveness of the reader. The reader, however, does not simply regenerate what the artist intended. His imagination can move him beyond the artist's traces, 'to project beyond the *words* a synthetic form', to constitute a new totality. The autonomy of the art object is sacrificed in this orientation; the reader, conscious of lending his own life to the book, discovers deeper and more complex levels than the level of 'significant form'. (Sartre says, for instance, that 'Raskolnikov's waiting is *my* waiting, which I lend him. Without this impatience of the reader he would remain only a collection of signs. His hatred of the police magistrate who questions him is my hatred which has been solicited and wheedled out of me by signs, and the police magistrate himself would not exist without the hatred I have for him via Raskolnikov.'[14])

Disclosure, Reconstruction, Generation

The reader, using his imagination, must move within his own subjectivity and break with the common sense world he normally takes for granted. If he could not suspend his ordinary ways of perceiving, if he could not allow for the possibility that the horizons of daily life are not inalterable, he would not be able to engage with literature at all. As Dewey put it: 'There is work done on the part of the percipient as there is on the part of the artist. The one who is too lazy, idle, or indurated in convention to perform this work will not see or hear. His "appreciation" will be a mixture of scraps of learning with conformity to norms of conventional admiration and with a confused, even if genuine, emotional excitation.'[15] The 'work' with which we are here concerned is one of disclosure, reconstruction, generation. It is a work which culminates in a bringing something into being by the reader – in a 'going beyond' what he has been[16].

Although I am going to claim that learning, to be meaningful, must involve such a 'going beyond'. I am not going to claim that it must also be in the imaginative mode. Nor am I going to assert that, in order to surpass the 'given', the individual is required to move into and remain within a sealed subjectivity. What I find suggestive in the criticism of consciousness is the stress on the gradual disclosure of structures by the reader. The process is, as I have said, governed by certain cues or norms perceived in the course of reading. These demand, if they are to be perceived, what Jean Piaget has called a 'continual "decentering" without which [the individual subject] cannot become free from his intellectual egocentricity'[17].

The difference between Piaget and those interested in consciousness is, of course, considerable. For one thing, he counts himself among those who prefer not to characterize the subject in terms of its 'lived experience'. For another thing, he says categorically that 'the "lived" can only have a very minor role in the construction of cognitive structures, for these do not belong to the subject's *consciousness* but to his operational *behavior*, which is something quite different'[18]. I am not convinced that they are as different as he conceives them to be. Moreover, I think his differentiation between the 'individual subject' and what he calls 'the epistemic subject, that cognitive nucleus which is common to all subjects at the same level'[19], is useful and may well shed light on the problem of curriculum, viewed from the vantage point of consciousness. Piaget is aware that his stress on the 'epistemic subject' looks as if he were subsuming the individual under some impersonal abstraction[20], but his discussion is not far removed from those of Sartre and the critics of consciousness, particularly when they talk of the subject entering into a process of generating structures whose being (like the structures Piaget has in mind) consists in their 'coming to be'.

Merleau-Ponty, as concerned as Piaget with the achievement of rationality, believes that there is a primary reality which must be taken into account if the growth of 'intellectual consciousness' is to be understood. This primary reality is a perceived life-world; and the structures of the 'perceptual consciousness'[21] through which the child first comes in contact with his environment underlie all the higher level structures which develop later in his life. In the prereflective, infantile stage of life he is obviously incapable of generating cognitive structures. The stage is characterized by what Merleau-Ponty calls 'egocentrism' because the 'me' is part of an anonymous collectivity, unaware of itself, capable of living 'as easily in others as it does in itself'[22]. Nevertheless, even then, before meanings and configurations are imposed, there is an original world, a natural and social world in which the child is involved corporeally and affectively. Perceiving that world, he effects certain relations within his experience. He organizes and 'informs' it before he is capable of logical and predicative thought. This means for Merleau-Ponty that consciousness exists primordially – the ground of all knowledge and rationality.

The growing child assimilates a language system and becomes habituated to using language as 'an open system of expression' which is capable of expressing 'an indeterminate number of cognitions or ideas to come'[23]. His acts of naming and expression take place, however, around a core of primary meaning found in 'the silence of primary consciousness'. This silence may be understood as the fundamental awareness of being present in the world. It resembles what Paulo Freire calls 'background awareness'[24] of an existential situation, a situation actually lived before the codifications which make new perceptions possible. Talking about the effort to help peasants perceive their own reality differently (to enable them, in other words, to learn), Freire says they must somehow make explicit their 'real consciousness' of their worlds, or what they experienced while living through situations they later learn to codify.

The point is that the world is constituted for the child (by means of the behavior called perception) prior to the 'construction of cognitive structures'. This does not imply that he lives his life primarily in that world. He moves outward into diverse realms of experience in his search for meaning. When he confronts and engages with the apparently independent structures associated with rationality, the so-called cognitive structures, it is likely that he does so as an 'epistemic subject', bracketing out for the time his subjectivity, even his presence to himself[25]. But the awareness remains in the background; the original perceptual reality continues as the ground of rationality, the base from which the leap to the theoretical is taken.

Merleau-Ponty, recognizing that psychologists treat consciousness as 'an object to be studied', writes that it is simply not accessible to mere factual observation:

The psychologist always tends to make consciousness into just such an object of observation. But all the factual truths to which psy-

474

chology has access can be applied to the concrete subject only after a philosophical correction. Psychology, like physics and the other sciences of nature, uses the method of induction, which starts from facts and then assembles them. But it is very evident that this induction will remain blind if we do not know in some other way, and indeed from the inside of consciousness itself, what this induction is dealing with[26].

Induction must be combined 'with the reflective knowledge that we can obtain from ourselves as conscious objects'. This is not a recommendation that the individual engage in introspection. Consciousness, being intentional, throws itself outward *towards* the world. Reflecting upon himself as a conscious object, the individual – the learner, perhaps – reflects upon his relation to the world, his manner of comporting himself with respect to it, the changing perspectives through which the world presents itself to him. Merleau-Ponty talks about the need continually to rediscover 'my actual presence to myself, the fact of my consciousness which is in the last resort what the world and the concept of consciousness mean.'[27] This means remaining in contact with one's own perceptions, one's own experiences, and striving to constitute their meanings. It means achieving a state of what Schutz calls 'wide-awakeness ... a plane of consciousness of highest tension originating in an attitude of full attention to life and its requirements'[28]. Like Sartre, Schutz emphasizes the importance of attentiveness for arriving at new perceptions, for carrying out cognitive projects. All this seems to me to be highly suggestive for a conception of a learner who is 'open to the world'[29], eager, indeed *condemned* to give meaning to it – and, in the process of doing so, recreating or generating the materials of a curriculum in terms of his own consciousness.

Some Alternative Views

There are, of course, alternative views of consequence for education today. R S Peters, agreeing with his philosophic precursors that consciousness is the hallmark of mind and always 'related in its different modes to objects', asserts that the 'objects of consciousness are first and foremost objects in a public world that are marked out and differentiated by a public language into which the individual is initiated'[30]. (It should be said that Peters is, *par excellence*, the exponent of an 'objective' or 'analytic' approach to curriculum, closely related to the objective approach to literary criticism.) He grants that the individual 'represents a unique and unrepeatable viewpoint on this public world'; but his primary stress is placed upon the way in which the learning of language is linked to the discovery of that separately existing world of 'objects in space and time'. Consciousness, for Peters, cannot be explained except in connection with the demarcations of the public world which meaning makes possible. It becomes contingent upon initiation into public traditions, into (it turns out) the academic disciplines. Since such an initiation is required if modes of consciousness are to be effectively differentiated, the mind must finally be understood as a 'product' of such initiation. The individual must be enabled to achieve a state of mind characterized by 'a mastery of and care for the worthwhile things that have been transmitted, which are viewed in some kind of cognitive perspective'[31].

Philip H Phenix argues similarly that 'the curriculum should consist entirely of knowledge which comes from the disciplines, for the reason that the disciplines reveal knowledge in its teachable forms'[32]. He, however, pays more heed to what he calls 'the experience of reflective self-consciousness'[33], which he associates specifically with 'concrete existence in direct personal encounter'[34]. The meanings arising out of such encounter are expressed, for him, in existential philosophy, religion, psychology, and certain dimensions of imaginative literature. They are, thus, to be considered as one of the six 'realms of meaning' through mastery of which man is enabled to achieve self-transcendence. Self-transcendence, for Phenix, involves a duality which enables the learner to feel himself to be agent and knower, and at once to identify with what he comes to know. Self-transcendence is the ground of meaning; but it culminates in the engendering of a range of 'essential meanings', the achievement of a hierarchy in which all fundamental patterns of meaning are related and through which human existence can be fulfilled. The inner life of generic man is clearly encompassed by this scheme; but what is excluded, I believe, is what has been called the 'subjectivity of the actor', the *individual* actor ineluctably present to himself. What is excluded is the feeling of separateness, of strangeness when such a person is confronted with the articulated curriculum intended to counteract meaninglessness.

Schutz writes:

When a stranger comes to the town, he has to learn to orientate in it and to know it. Nothing is self-explanatory for him and he has to ask an expert . . . to learn how to get from one point to another. He may, of course, refer to a map of the town, but even to use the map successfully he must know the meaning of the signs on the map, the exact point within the town where he stands and its correlative on the map, and at least one more point in order correctly to relate the signs on the map to the real objects in the city[35].

The prestructured curriculum resembles such a map; the learner, the stranger just arrived in town. For the cartographer, the town is an 'object of his science', a science which has developed standards of operation and rules for the correct drawing of maps. In the case of the curriculum-maker, the public tradition or the natural order of things is 'the object' of his design activities. Here too there are standards of operation: the subject matter organized into disciplines must be communicable; it must be appropriate to whatever are conceived as educational aims. Phenix has written that education should be understood as 'a guided recapitulation of the processes of inquiry which gave rise to the fruitful bodies of organized knowledge comprising the disciplines'[36]. Using the metaphor of the map, we might say that this is like asking a newcomer in search of direction to recapitulate the complex processes by which the cartographer made his map. The map may represent a fairly complete charting of the town; and it may ultimately be extremely useful for the individual to be able to take a cartographer's perspective. When that individual first arrives, however, his peculiar plight ought not to be overlooked: his 'background awareness' of being alive in an unstable world; his reasons for consulting the map; the interests he is pursuing as he attempts to orient himself when he can no longer proceed by rule of thumb. He himself may recognize that he will have to come to understand the signs on the map if he is to make use of it. Certainly he will have to decipher the relationship between those signs and 'real objects in the city'. But his initial concern will be conditioned by the 'objects' he wants to bring into visibility, by the landmarks he needs to identify if he is to proceed on his way.

Learning – A Mode of Orientation

Turning from newcomer to learner (contemporary learner, in our particular world), I am suggesting that his focal concern is with ordering the materials of his own life-world when dislocations occur, when what was once familiar abruptly appears strange. This may come about on an occasion when 'future shock' is experienced, as it so frequently is today. Anyone who has lived through a campus disruption, a teacher's strike, a guerilla theatre production, a sit-in (or a be-in, or a feel-in) knows full well what Alvin Toffler means when he writes about the acceleration of change. 'We no longer "feel" life as men did in the past,' he says. 'And this is the ultimate difference, the distinction that separates the truly contemporary man from all others. For this acceleration lies behind the impermanence – the transience – that penetrates and tinctures our consciousness, radically affecting the way we relate to other people, to things, to the entire universe of ideas, art and values'[37]. Obviously, this does not happen in everyone's life; but it is far more likely to occur than ever before in history, if it is indeed the case that change has speeded up and that forces are being released which we have not yet learned to control. My point is that the contemporary learner is more likely than his predecessors to experience moments of strangeness, moments when the recipes he has inherited for the solution of typical problems no longer seem to work. If Merleau-Ponty is right and the search for rationality is indeed grounded in a primary or perceptual consciousness, the individual may be fundamentally aware that the structures of 'reality' are contingent upon the perspective taken and that most achieved orders are therefore precarious.

The stage sets are always likely to collapse[38]. Someone is always likely to ask unexpectedly, as in Pinter's *The Dumb Waiter*, 'Who cleans up after we're gone?'[39] Someone is equally likely to cry out, 'You seem to have no conception of where we stand! You won't find the answer written down for you in the bowl of a compass – I can tell you that'[40]. Disorder, in other words, is continually breaking in; meaninglessness is recurrently overcoming landscapes which once were demarcated, meaningful. It is at moments like these that the individual reaches out to reconstitute meaning, to close the gaps, to make sense once again. It is at moments like these that he will be moved to pore over maps, to disclose or generate structures of knowledge which may provide him unifying perspectives and thus enable him to restore order once again. His learning, I am saying, is a mode of orientation – or reorientation – in a place suddenly become unfamiliar. And 'place' is a metaphor, in this context, for a domain of consciousness, intending, forever thrusting outward, 'open to the world'. The curriculum, the structures of knowledge, must be presented to such a consciousness as possibility. Like the work of literature in Sartre's viewing, it requires a subject if it is to be disclosed; it can only *be* disclosed if the learner, himself engaged in generating the structures, lends the curriculum his life. If the curriculum, on the other hand, is seen as external to the search for meaning, it becomes an alien and an alienating edifice, a kind of 'Crystal Palace' of ideas[41].

There is, then, a kind of resemblance between the ways in which a learner confronts socially prescribed knowledge and the ways in which a stranger looks at a map when he is trying to determine where he is in relation to where he wants to go. In Kafka's novel, *Amerika*, I find a peculiarly suggestive description of the predicament of someone who is at once a stranger and a potential learner (although, it eventually turns out, he never succeeds in being taught). He is Karl

Rossmann, who has been 'packed off to America' by his parents and who likes to stand on a balcony at his Uncle Jacob's house in New York and look down on the busy street:

> From morning to evening and far into the dreaming night that street was a channel for the constant stream of traffic which, seen from above, looked like an inextricable confusion, forever newly improvised, of foreshortened human figures and the roofs of all kinds of vehicles, sending into the upper air another confusion, more riotous and complicated, of noises, dusts and smells, all of it enveloped and penetrated by a flood of light which the multitudinous objects in the street scattered, carried off and again busily brought back, with an effect as palpable to the dazzled eye as if a glass roof stretched over the street were being violently smashed into fragments at every moment[42].

Karl's uncle tells him that the indulgence of idly gazing at the busy life of the city might be permissible if Karl were traveling for pleasure; 'but for one who intended to remain in the States it was sheer ruination'. He is going to have to make judgments which will shape his future life; he will have, in effect, to be reborn. This being so, it is not enough for him to treat the unfamiliar landscape as something to admire and wonder at (as if it were a cubist construction or a kaleidoscope). Karl's habitual interpretations (learned far away in Prague) do not suffice to clarify what he sees. If he is to learn, he must identify what is questionable, try to break through what is obscure. Action is required of him, not mere gazing; *praxis*, not mere reverie.

If he is to undertake action, however, he must do so against the background of his original perceptions, with a clear sense of being present to himself. He must do so, too, against the background of his European experience, of the experience of rejection, of being 'packed off' for reasons never quite understood. Only with that sort of awareness will he be capable of the attentiveness and commitment needed to engage with the world and make it meaningful. Only with the ability to be reflective about what he is doing will he be brave enough to incorporate his past into the present, to link the present to a future. All this will demand a conscious appropriation of new perspectives on his experience and a continual reordering of that experience as new horizons of the 'Amerika' become visible, as new problems arise. The point is that Karl Rossmann, an immigrant in an already structured and charted world, must be conscious enough of himself to strive towards rationality; only if he achieves rationality will he avoid humiliations and survive.

As Kafka tells it, he never does attain that rationality; and so he is continually manipulated by forces without and within. He never learns, for example, that there can be no justice if there is no good will, even though he repeatedly and sometimes eloquently asks for justice from the authorities – always to no avail. The ship captains and pursers, the business men, the head waiters and porters all function according to official codes of discipline which are beyond his comprehension. He has been plunged into a public world with its own intricate prescriptions, idiosyncratic structures, and hierarchies; but he has no way of appropriating it or of constituting meanings. Throughout most of the novel, he clings to his symbolic box (with the photograph of his parents, the memorabilia of childhood and home). The box may be egocentrism; it may signify his incapacity to embark upon the 'decentering' required if he is to begin generating for himself the structures of what surrounds.

In his case (and, I would say, in the case of many other people) the 'decentering' that is necessary is not solely a cognitive affair, as Piaget insists it is. Merleau-Ponty speaks of a 'lived decentering'[43], exemplified by a child's learning 'to relativize the notions of the youngest and the eldest' (to learn, eg to become the eldest in relation to the newborn child) or by his learning to think in terms of reciprocity. This happens, as it would have to happen to Karl, through actions undertaken within the 'vital order', not merely through intellectual categorization. It does not exclude the possibility that a phenomenon analogous to Piaget's 'epistemic subject' emerges, although there appears to be no reason (except, perhaps, from the viewpoint of empirical psychology) for separating it off from the 'individual subject': (In fact, the apparent difference between Piaget and those who talk of 'lived experience' may turn upon a definition of 'consciousness'. Piaget, as has been noted[44], distinguishes between 'consciousness' and 'operational behavior', as if consciousness did *not* involve a turning outward to things, a continuing reflection upon situationality, a generation of cognitive structures.) In any case, every individual who consciously seeks out meaning is involved in asking questions which demand essentially epistemic responses[45]. These responses, even if incomplete, are knowledge claims; and, as more and more questions are asked, there is an increasing 'sedimentation' of meanings which result from the interpretation of past experiences looked at from the vantage point of the present. Meanings do not inhere in the experiences that emerge; they have to be constituted, and they can only be constituted through cognitive action.

Returning to Karl Rossmann and his inability to take such action, I have been suggesting that he *cannot* make his own 'primary consciousness' background so long as he clings to his box; nor can he actively interpret his past experience. He cannot (to stretch Piaget's point somewhat) become or will himself to be an 'epistemic subject'. He is, as Freire puts it, submerged in a 'dense, enveloping reality or a tormenting blind alley' and will be unless he can 'perceive it as an objective-problematic situation'[46]. Only then will he be able to intervene in his own reality with attentiveness, with awareness – to act upon his situation and make sense.

It would help if the looming structures which are so incomprehensible to Karl were somehow rendered cognitively available to him. Karl might then' (with the help of a teacher willing to engage in dialogue with him, to help him pose his problems) reach out to question in terms of what he feels is thematically relevant or 'worth questioning'[47]. Because the stock of knowledge he carries with him does not suffice for a definition of situations in which porters manhandle him and women degrade him, in which he is penalized for every spontaneous action, he cannot easily refer to previous situations for clues. In order to cope with this, he needs to single out a single relevant element at first (from all the elements in what is happening) to transmute into a theme for his 'knowing consciousness'. There is the cruel treatment meted out to him, for example, by the Head Porter who feels it his duty 'to attend to things that other people neglect'. (He adds that, since he is in charge of all the doors of the hotel [including the 'doorless exits'], he is 'in a sense placed over everyone', and everyone has to obey him absolutely. If it were not for his repairing the omissions of the Head Waiter in the name of the hotel management, he believes, 'such a great organization would be unthinkable'[48].) The porter's violence against Karl might well become the relevant element, the origin of a theme.

Making Connections

'What makes the theme to be a theme,' Schutz writes, 'is determined by motivationally relevant interest-situations and spheres of problems. The theme which thus has become relevant has now, however, become a problem to which a solution, practical, theoretical, or emotional, must be given.'[49] The problem for Karl, like relevant problems facing any individual, is connected with and a consequence of a great number of other perplexities, other dislocations in his life. If he had not been so badly exploited by authority figures in time past, if he were not so childishly given to blind trust in adults, if he were not so likely to follow impulse at inappropriate moments, he would never have been assaulted by the Head Porter. At this point, however, once the specific problem (the assault) has been determined to be thematically relevant for him, it can be detached from the motivational context out of which it derived. The meshwork of related perplexities remains, however, as an outer horizon, waiting to be explored or questioned when necessary. The thematically relevant element can then be made interesting in its own right and worth questioning. In the foreground, as it were, the focus of concern, it can be defined against the background of the total situation. The situation is not in any sense obliterated or forgotten. It is *there*, at the fringe of Karl's attention while the focal problem is being solved; but it is, to an extent, 'bracketed out'. With this bracketing out and this foreground focussing, Karl may be for the first time in a condition of wide-awakeness, ready to pay active attention to what has become so questionable and so troubling, ready to take the kind of action which will move him ahead into a future as it gives him perspective on his past.

The action he might take involves more than what is understood as problem-solving. He has, after all, had some rudimentary knowledge of the Head Porter's role, a knowledge conditioned by certain typifications effected in the prepredicative days of early childhood. At that point in time, he did not articulate his experience in terms of sense data or even in terms of individual figures standing out against a background. He saw typical structures according to particular zones of relevancy. This means that he probably saw his father, or the man who was father, not only as bearded face next to his mother, not only as large figure in the doorway, but as over-bearing, threatening, incomprehensible Authority who was 'placed over everyone' and had the right to inflict pain. Enabled, years later, to confront something thematically relevant, the boy may be solicited to recognize his present knowledge of the porter as the sediment of previous mental processes[50]. The knowledge of the porter, therefore, has a history beginning in primordial perceptions; and the boy may succeed in moving back from what is seemingly 'given' through the diverse mental processes which constituted the porter over time. Doing so, he will be exploring both the inner and outer horizons of the problem, making connections within the field of his consciousness, interpreting his own past as it bears on his present, reflecting upon his own knowing.

And that is not all. Having made such connections between the relevant theme and other dimensions of his experience, he may be ready to solve his problem; he may even feel that the problem is solved. This, however, puts him into position to move out of his own inner time (in which all acts are somehow continuous and bound together) into the intersubjective world where he can function as an epistemic subject. Having engaged in a reflexive consideration of the activity of his own consciousness, he can now shift his attention back to the life-world which had been rendered so unrecognizable by the

Head Porter's assault. Here too, meanings must be constituted; the 'great organization' must be understood, so that Karl can orient himself once again in the everyday. Bracketing out his subjectivity for the time, he may find many ways of engaging as a theoretical inquirer with the problem of authority in hotels and the multiple socioeconomic problems connected with that. He will voluntarily become, when inquiring in this way, a partial self, an inquirer deliberately acting a role in a community of inquirers. I am suggesting that he could not do so as effectively or as authentically if he had not first synthesized the materials within his inner time, constituted meaning in his world.

The analogy to the curriculum question, I hope, is clear. Treating Karl as a potential learner, I have considered the hotels and the other structured organizations in his world as analogous to the structures of prescribed knowledge – or to the curriculum. I have suggested that the individual, in our case the student, will only be in a position to learn when he is committed to act upon his world. If he is content to admire it or simply accept it as given, if he is incapable of breaking with egocentrism, he will remain alienated from himself and his own possibilities; he will wander lost and victimized upon the road; he will be unable to learn. He may be conditioned; he may be trained. He may even have some rote memory of certain elements of the curriculum; but no matter how well devised is that curriculum, no matter how well adapted to the stages of his growth, learning (as disclosure, as generating structures, as engendering meanings, as achieving mastery) will not occur.

At once, I have tried to say that unease and disorder are increasingly endemic in contemporary life, and that more and more persons are finding the recipes they habitually use inadequate for sense-making in a changing world. This puts them, more and more frequently in the position of strangers or immigrants trying to orient themselves in an unfamiliar town. The desire, indeed the *need*, for orientation is equivalent to the desire to constitute meanings, all sorts of meanings, in the many dimensions of existence. But this desire, I have suggested, is not satisfied by the authoritative confrontation of student with knowledge structures (no matter how 'teachable' the forms in which the knowledge is revealed). It is surely not satisfied when the instructional situation is conceived to be, as G K Plochmann has written, one in which the teacher is endeavoring 'with respect to his subject matter, to bring the understanding of the learner in equality with his own understanding'[51]. Described in that fashion, with 'learner' conceived generically and the 'system' to be taught conceived as pre-existent and objectively real, the instructional situation seems to me to be one that alienates because of the way it ignores both existential predicament and primordial consciousness. Like the approach to literary criticism Abrams describes, the view appears to commit us to a concept of curriculum 'as a floating Laputa, insulated from life and essential human concerns. . . .'[52]

The cries of 'irrelevance' are still too audible for us to content ourselves with this. So are the complaints about depersonalization, processing, and compulsory socialization into a corporate, inhuman world. Michael Novak, expressing some of this, writes that what our institutions 'decide is real is enforced as real'. He calls parents, teachers, and psychiatrists (like policemen and soldiers) 'the enforcers of reality'; then he goes on to say:

> When a young person is being initiated into society, existing norms determine what is to be considered real and what is to be annihilated by silence and disregard. The good, docile student accepts the norms; the recalcitrant student may lack the intelligence – or have too much; may lack maturity – or insist upon being his own man.[53]

I have responses like this in mind when I consult the phenomenologists for an approach to curriculum in the present day. For one thing, they remind us of what it means for an individual to be present to himself; for another, they suggest to us the origins of significant quests for meaning, origins which ought to be held in mind by those willing to enable students to be themselves.

If the existence of a primordial consciousness is taken seriously, it will be recognized that awareness begins perspectively, that our experience is always incomplete. It is true that we have what Merleau-Ponty calls a 'prejudice' in favor of a world of solid, determinate objects, quite independent of our perceptions. Consciousness does, however, have the capacity to return to the precognitive, the primordial, by 'bracketing out' objects as customarily seen. The individual can release himself into his own inner time and rediscover the ways in which objects arise, the ways in which experience develops. In discussing the possibility of Karl Rossmann exploring his own past, I have tried to show what this sort of interior journey can mean. Not only may it result in the effecting of new syntheses within experience; it may result in an awareness of the process of knowing, of believing, of perceiving. It may even result in an understanding of the ways in which meanings have been sedimented in an individual's own personal history. I can think of no more potent mode of combatting those conceived to be 'enforcers of the real', including the curriculum designers.

But then there opens up the possibility of presenting curriculum in such a way that it does not impose or enforce. If the student is enabled to recognize that reason and order may represent the culminating step in his constitution of a world, if he can be enabled to see that what Schutz calls the attainment of a 'reciprocity of perspectives'[54] signifies the achievement of rationality, he may realize what it is to generate the structures of the disciplines on his own initiative, against his own 'background awareness'. Moreover, he may realize that he is projecting beyond his present horizons each time he shifts his attention and takes another perspective on his world. 'To say there exists rationality,' writes Merleau-Ponty, 'is to say that perspectives blend, perceptions confirm each other, a meaning emerges.'[55] He points out that we witness at every moment 'the miracles of related experiences, and yet nobody knows better than we do how this miracle is worked, for we are ourselves this network of relationships.' Curriculum can offer the possibility for students to be the makers of such networks. The problem for their teachers is to stimulate an awareness of the questionable, to aid in the identification of the thematically relevant to beckon beyond the everyday.

I am a psychological and historical structure, and have received, with existence, a manner of existence, a style. All my actions and thoughts stand in a relationship to this structure, and even a philosopher's thought is merely a way of making explicit his hold on the world, and what he is. The fact remains that I am free, not in spite of, or on the hither side of these motivations, but by means of them. For this significant life, this certain significance of nature and history which I am, does not limit my access to the world, but on the contrary is my means of entering into communication with it. It is by being unrestrictedly and unreservedly what I am at present that I have a chance of moving forward; it is by living my time that I am able to understand other times, by plunging into the present and the world by taking on deliberately what I am fortuitously, by willing what I will and doing what I do, that I can go further.[56]

To plunge in; to choose; to disclose; to move: this is the road, it seems to me, to mastery.

References

[1] MAURICE MERLEAU-PONTY, *The Primacy of Perception*, JAMES M EDIE (ed), North-Western University Press, Evanston, 1964, 59.

[2] JEAN-PAUL SARTRE, *Search for a Method*, Alfred A Knopf, New York, 1963, 92.

[3] RYLAND W CRARY, *Humanizing the School: Curriculum Development and Theory*, Alfred A Knopf, New York, 1969, 13.

[4] JOHN DEWEY, 'The Child and the Curriculum', MARTIN S DWORKIN (ed) *Dewey on Education*, New York Teachers College Bureau of Publications, 1959, 91.

[5] SARAH LAWALL, *Critics of Consciousness*, Harvard University Press, Cambridge, Mass, 1968.

[6] T S ELIOT, *The Sacred Wood*, Barnes & Noble University Paperbacks, New York, 1960, x.

[7] DOROTHY WALSH, 'The Cognitive Content of Art', FRANCIS J COLEMAN (ed) *Aesthetics*, McGraw-Hill, New York, 1968, 297.

[8] CLIVE BELL, *Art*, Chatto & Windus, London, 1964.

[9] WALSH, *op cit*.

[10] M H ABRAMS, 'Belief and the Suspension of Belief', M H ABRAMS (ed) *Literature and Belief*, Columbia University Press, New York, 1957, 9.

[11] MAURICE BLANCHOT, *L'Espace littéraire*, Gallimard, Paris, 1965.

[12] See, eg ALFRED SCHUTZ, 'Some Leading Concepts of Phenomenology', MAURICE NATANSON (ed), *Collected Papers* **1**, Martinus Nijhoff, The Hague, 1967, 104–105.

[13] JEAN-PAUL SARTRE, *Literature and Existentialism*, 3rd ed. The Citadel Press, New York, 1965, 43.

[14] *Ibid*, 45.

[15] JOHN DEWEY, *Art as Experience*, Minton, Balch & Company, New York, 1934, 54.

[16] SARTRE, *Search for a Method, op cit*, 91.

[17] JEAN PAGET, *Structuralism*, Basic Books, New York, 1970, 139.

[18] *Ibid*, 68.

[19] *Ibid*, 139.

[20] *Ibid*.

[21] MAURICE MERLEAU-PONTY, *Phenomenology of Perception*, Routledge Kegan Paul Ltd, London, 1962.

[22] MERLEAU-PONTY, *The Primacy of Perception, op cit*, 119.

[23] *Ibid*, 99.

[24] PAULO FREIRE, *Pedagogy of the Oppressed*, Herder and Herder, New York, 1970, 108.

[25] SCHUTZ, 'On Multiple Realities', *op cit*, 248.

[26] MERLEAU-PONTY, *The Primacy of Perception, op cit*, 58.

[27] MERLEAU-PONTY, *Phenomenology of Perception, op cit*, xvii.

[28] SCHUTZ, 'On Multiple Realities', *op cit*.

[29] MERLEAU-PONTY, *op cit*.

[30] R S PETERS, *Ethics and Education*, George Allen and Unwin, London, 1966, 50.

[31] R S PETERS, *Ethics and Education*, Scott Foresman and Co, Glenview, III, 1967, 12.

[32] PHILIP H PHENIX, 'The Uses of the Disciplines as Curriculum Content', DONALD VANDENBERG (ed) *Theory of Knowledge and Problems of Education*, University of Illinois Press, Urbana, Ill, 1969, 195.

[33] PHILIP H PHENIX, *Realms of Meaning*, McGraw-Hill, New York, 1964, 195.

[34] *Ibid*.

[35] SCHUTZ, 'Problem of Rationality in the Social World', MATANSON (ed) *Collected Papers* **II**, Martinus Nijhoff, The Hague, 1967, 66.

[36] PHENIX, 'The Uses of the Disciplines as Curriculum Content', *op cit*, 195.

[37] ALVIN TOFFLER, *Future Shock*, Random House, New York, 1970, 18.

486

[38] ALBERT CAMUS, *The Myth of Sisyphus*, Alfred A Knopf, New York, 1955, 72.

[39] HAROLD PINTER, *The Dumb Waiter*, Grove Press, New York, 1961, 103.

[40] TOM STOPPARD, *Rosencrantz and Guildenstern are Dead*, Grove Press, New York, 1967, 58–59.

[41] *Cf*, FYODOR DOSTEOVSKY, 'Notes from Underground' in *The Short Novels of Dosteovsky*. Dial Press, New York, 1945. 'You believe in a palace of crystal that can never be destroyed . . . a palace at which one will not be able to put out one's tongue or make a long nose on the sly.' 152.

[42] FRANZ KAFKA, *Amerika*, Doubleday Anchor Books, Garden City, N.Y. 1946, 38.

[43] MERLEAU-PONTY, *The Primacy of Perception*, *op cit*, 110.

[44] PIAGET, *op cit*.

[45] RICHARD M ZANER, *The Way of Phenomenology*, Pegasus Books, New York, 1970, 27.

[46] FREIRE, *op cit*, 100.

[47] SCHUTZ, 'The Life-World', NATANSON (ed) *Collected Papers*, **III**, Martinus Nijhoff, The Hague, 1967, 125.

[48] KAFKA, *op cit*, 201.

[49] SCHUTZ, 'The Life-World', *op cit*, 124.

[50] SCHUTZ, 'Some Leading Concepts', *op cit*, 111.

[51] G K PLOCHMANN, 'On the Organic Logic of Teaching and Learning', Vandenberg, *op cit*, 244.

[52] *Cf* footnote 10.

[53] MICHAEL NOVAK, *The Experience of Nothingness*, Harper & Row, New York, 1970, 94.

[54] SCHUTZ, 'Symbols, Reality, and Society', *Collected Papers* **I**, *op cit*, 315.

[55] MERLEAU-PONTY, *Phenomenology of Perception*, *op cit*, xix.

[56] *Ibid*, xix.

Part Seven

Education and Rationality

In many ways this section reflects the major sociological theme of this whole collection of readings. While all sociology is concerned with addressing the problem of rationality, either explicitly or implicitly, it has tended to do so with specific reference to the rationality of the actors being studied. It has largely rested on more or less formalistic ascription of rational schemas assuming a generative status with reference to certain forms of action. This tradition of positivism has produced rationality as something other than an ongoing feature of interpersonal relations; in other words rationality (as a form of understanding) and therefore by necessity sociology, has taken on a normative character.

Our ways of understanding have been obscured by an adoption of highly problematic notions such as 'rational act', 'rational persons' or the 'rational mind of man', which are nevertheless treated in some way as absolute. All these formulations are nothing more than attempts to encapsulate the range of possible meanings that are conveyed among members in social discourse; in this sense they represent mammoth glosses of the everyday practices of members in the production of their sense of society.

Ethnomethodological studies have gone some way towards remedying these tendencies in sociology, by treating rationality as a members' category and by attempting to explicate the members' rules for the construction of 'rational social situations'. However as Blum and McHugh indicate in the first paper of this section, ethnomethodology has not gone far enough – rationality treated as a members' category becomes no less problematic for a theorist seeking to understand a situation than is a conception of rationality imported from outside. We are led back to the ultimate problem that it is the theorist's own conception of rationality that grounds all his talk about social phenomena – whether as education or whatever.

All extracts in this section point our attention to a critical review of our own imposition of essentially ethnocentric ways of understanding and interpreting the actions of others.

44

The Social Ascription of Motives *
Alan F Blum and Peter McHugh

I Introduction

Our intention is to explicate the sociological status of motives. We shall address this issue by describing how ordinary actors employ 'motive' as a practical method for organizing their everyday environments. Since motive is used by ordinary societal members to manage their orderly routines, our explication will be a formulation of the ways in which members' practices are grounded in their knowledge. We shall suggest, that all sociological conceptions require some version of the common sense member (of his practical knowledge); and we shall depict motive as one common sense device for ascribing social membership, since motives are used by members to link particular concrete activities to generally available social rules. Motive, then, is one collective procedure for accomplishing social interaction, and for sorting out the various possibilities for social treatment by linking specific act and social rules in such a way as to generate the constellation of social actions that observers call 'persons', 'members' and 'membership'[1].

II The Sociological Possibility of Motive

Social scientists tend to conceive of motives as private and internal characteristics of persons which impinge upon and coerce these persons into various behaviors. In this view, motives are seen simultaneously (1) as 'causal' antecedent variables (antecedent to the event of interest), and (2) as characteristic 'states' of persons engaging in the behavior. We maintain that these senses of motive are inadequate because they issue from a common misconception of motive, namely that motives are concrete, private and interior 'mainsprings' that reside in people, rather than public and observable courses of action[2].

If sociologists have sought to understand and formulate descriptions of social action, and if the analytic status of social action resides

* *American Sociological Review* **36** (February) 1971, 98–109.

in its character as behavior which is normatively oriented to the very same environment it constitutes, then motive can function as an observer's rule for deciding the normatively ordered character of behavior. That is, motive is a public method for deciding upon the (sociological) existence of action. In this usage, motive is an observer's rule of relevance in that it represents a sociologist's decision (his election) as to how items of concrete behavior are to be reformulated as instance of social action [3].

The classic roster of terms used by sociologists – social class, community, religion, suicide, bureaucracy, conflict, and the like – all require in their various ways this sort of conception. Motive then, serves as a theorist's election that some rule is relevant for explicating the character of some event as an instance of action. Motive is not in this regard a thing in the world but a way of conceiving social action.

In a more precisely sociological sense, it is observers who introduce a topic into behavior, whether motives or any other. Thus, to say that 'social class exists', or that some group is high on need achievement, is for an observer to decide that some collection of persons is oriented to their status as a collective actor and is to be conceived as acting under the auspices of such an orientation. When an observer asserts that the American workers constitute a social class, he is deciding that the collection conceivable as American workers presently show in their behavior their status as a collective actor, the identity of which the observer provides on the basis of their relation to the instruments of production [4].

The upshot of all this – that motives function as observers' rules of relevance – is that though motives might be described as personal properties or characteristics of persons, they acquire their analytic force as observers' rules for depicting grounds of conduct [5]. Motives are a way for an observer to assign relevance to behavior in order that it may be recognized as another instance of normatively ordered action.

It should now be clear why motives cannot be private and internal; if motives are sociologically depicted in the ascription of rules, the ascription of rules itself requires (presupposes) the use of a language that is public and observable. Even when we speak of 'hidden' motives, we are of course engaged in fully intelligible and observable courses of treatment – some public criterion enables us to grasp the topic. The so-called hidden motives, slips, and the like are observable states of affairs which can be discussed in sensible and concerted ways. To treat motives as private is to confuse the state of affairs which motives report with the analytic status of the term, which status is supplied by the public and by generally available rules that make motive reports socially possible and observable modes of social action[6].

III The Grammatical and Factual Perspectives in the Formulation of Motive

We have said that motive is a term regularly employed by actors to accomplish their routine affairs. When practical actors are 'doing motives', they are engaged in formulating themselves and their environments, in constructing and treating with their common sense courses of action. To say 'He had the jealous motive to murder her' is to do no more or less than lay out and characterize an environment in such a way as to report on a social state of affairs, to make some behavior possible, to limit the use of other behavioral possibilities, and so forth. The sociological status of the idea rests on whatever must be known in order to produce motive-talk as a recognizable or observable course of action. To provide a motive, then, is to formulate a situation in such a way as to ascribe a motive to an actor as part of his common sense knowledge, a motive to which he was oriented in producing the action. Thus to give a motive is not to locate a cause of the action, but is for some observer to assert how a behavior is socially intelligible by ascribing a socially available actor's orientation[7]. Questions of orientation do not require factual solutions (they are not either true or false), but rather, grammatical solutions. To talk motives is to talk grammar.

At the same time, however, social psychologists have used motive as a technical term designed to unravel the causal patterning of a sequence of actions (Atkinson, 1958; Cattell, 1957; Lindzey, 1958; Smelser and Smelser, 1963; White, 1963), eg need achievement as an antecedent of economic development (McClelland, et al, 1953). One problem with such technical usage is that it does not reformulate motive from the perspective of a practical member; ie, it ignores motive as a social course of action, and so it fails to provide for the relevance of motive as an activity engaged in by practical members[8].

To treat motive as a cause, as in 'What was his motive for suicide?' is to commit one version of the fallacy which Austin (1965) and others have discussed in detail: the fallacy of presuming that suicide is an act which somehow describes some antecedent state of mind which preceded or caused it. On the contrary, to recognize the act of suicide as an intelligible event-of-conduct is to assign to that behavior its identity as social action, in this case by formulating a motive. Thus, motive is a rule which depicts the social character of the act itself. It is not that his suicide reports some antecedent depression, or that murdering his wife reports his jealousy, or that leaving the party reports upon his boredom. Rather, the character of the suicide, the murder, the departure are identified through the clarification of unstated circumstances which make these actions socially recognizable as suicide, murder and departure. To say 'I want a motive for the murdered wife' is not to say that I want merely his antecedent state of mind which the wife's murder follows, but is instead to explicate the situation (the context, knowledge, conditions) which makes the event socially possible (a recognizable murder).

The best criticism of the causal account of motive is to be found in Melden's *Free Action* (1961) in which he demonstrates that since any conception of a cause presupposes a description of the very action for which the cause is identified, these accounts violate the necessary assumption of the analytic independence of cause and effect in the Humean model of causality. That is, some thing cannot be cited as a cause of an event if this 'something' is involved (presupposed) in the very description of the event; analyses of motive accounts show that whatever is cited as a motive serves to more fully and completely characterize the event for which it is formulated, and cannot then be treated as independent of the event. Melden says: 'this explanation does not refer to a present moment, sliced off from what has gone before and what will follow, but to the present action as an incident in the total proceedings'[9] (1961, 98–99).

This is why it is elliptical to assert that motive describes only and simply a state of mind, when instead it serves to demand an explication of the circumstances which confer upon this putative state of mind its reasonableness as an account. Because such an explication amounts to a theory or formulation, it would be more correct to say that the quest for a motive (why did he kill her?) is a request for a theory.

IV Motive as Surface Structure

We have sought to show that motive acquires its analytic character as a public (methodic) product rather than as a private 'state', and that it is to be understood grammatically (as part of the meaning of an action) rather than as a factual report on some contingent, antecedent event. Now, however, we want to show how the analytic sense of motive is not located through a report of usage, but rather by formulating the conditions of knowledge which make such usage possible.

One option to the technical causal idea is thought to be a conception of motives as member's purposes, reasons, justifications and accounts (Gerth and Mills, 1953; Schutz, 1962; Scott and Lyman, 1968; Shwayder, 1966). In this tradition, the actor is used by the observer as a research informant, whose report acquires analytic status because the actor is thought to be a privileged and exclusive source on questions of his motive.

The paradigmatic procedure here is to ask the actor, 'Why . . . ?' and expect him to cite a reason, goal, or intention, eg, 'Why did you leave the party?'; 'Because I was bored'; 'In order to make my appointment'; etc. In some cases we take these reasons and call them symbols and meanings, but that sort of substitution does not really tell us much about the methodical ways in which such statements are generated to begin with – how, for example, the actor is constrained to cite a reason at all; how it takes the form it does (giving a reason instead of, say, telling a joke); how it comes to be acceptable to the hearer that it *is* an answer. In other words, its status as a common sense practical device, as opposed to mere idiosyncratic noise or gesture or cue, remains unstated[10]. The methodic social and hence sociological feature of motive lies not in the concrete, substantive reason an actor would give for his behavior, but in the organized and sanctionable conditions that would regularly produce the giving of a reason by a competent member in the first place. The reason given is no more than the surface expression of some underlying rule(s) that the former requires in order to be understood (Chomsky, 1965).

The surface performance which is displayed in the use of motive might be that of offering a reason, goal, or intention, but to provide an account of motive in these terms is to ignore the deep structure which makes the surface display possible at all. As we shall investigate below, motive acquires its analytic status by virtue of the fact that it requires for its use certain deep structures for conceiving of 'person', 'member', 'responsibility', 'biography', and the like; these deep structures are absolutely necessary for an ordinary member's competent and sensible employ of motive as a device, because they generate the variety of surface reasons he may cite in any particular case. It is through these deep conditions that an analytic conception of the ordinary sociological use of motive is provided.

It should be clear then, that the similarity which typical symbolic interaction accounts appear to achieve with our present formulation – through such phrases as 'vocabularies of motives' and the like – is misleading, for they treat concrete speech acts – such as giving reasons or justifications, or citing intentions – as providing an analytic explication of motive, whereas we treat such usage as surface phenomena which are made possible by deeper conditions of knowledge. The concrete character of such versions of motive is conveyed in their practice of treating motive as the practical actor's expression of his knowledge, in contrast to the present suggestion that analytic status is supplied through some conception of an observer's method of constructing a practical actor (no matter what he is concretely taken to perform or say).

For example, Gerth and Mills (1953:116) cite Weber as we do but interpret him as using motive as equivalent to 'an adequate reason for conduct'. On the other hand, we are saying that this usage fails to capture the analytic character of motive as an *observer's decision to treat or reformulate* some behavior as a reason, and that this is an entirely different manner. So too, they see motive as 'ascribed through talk' (1953:114) and as a 'term' of the talk itself, whereas, in our view, speech is just a medium for the concrete expression of motive, but it is a set of prior and deeper conditions of knowledge which permit an observer to treat talk as intelligibly predicating motive. The symbolic interactionist finds it impossible to formulate a version of motive that is analytically distinct from conventional versions, because he still conceives of motive as a practical actor's concrete report of his state of mind: he only shifts his focus from the state-of-mind to the talk, by treating the talk as some sort of public indicator of the mind. Gerth and Mills show this quite explicitly when they eventually surrender to a concern for questions such as what the differences are between professed motives and 'real motives' (1953:119); and with the actor's degree of 'awareness' of his motives (1953:125). These are not the questions of those who have grasped the analytic character of motive [11].

We can now locate the major difficulty which unifies the various conventional accounts of motives, ie, the conception which appears to unify the various sorts of troubles we have been discussing; these accounts pose the problem of motives as a factual rather than a grammatical one, which leads easily to the trap of treating motives as causes, as states-of-persons, and as concrete speech-acts such as reasons, accounts, and justifications. And these accounts treat motives as raising a concrete, factual question of 'why?' rather than as attempts to formulate the socially organized conditions under which such a question is sensible to those who raise them. Any strategy which equates the factual surface structure of motive talk with an analytic conception of motive cannot provide any more than a concrete and irrelevant record [12].

In sum, when we speak of motive, we have in mind neither the technical observer's notion of the causes of an action, nor the actor's report of why an action was done. We do not require either an explanation or reason for the action, but rather some description of the socially organized conditions which produce the practical and ordinary use of motive in the mundane affairs of societal members. To locate motive is thus not to 'find' anything but to describe the necessary and analytically prior understandings and conventions which *must* be employed in order for a member even to invoke motive as a method for making a social environment orderly and sensible.

V The Deep Structure of Motives

A Motives Are Observers' Rules

Motives acquire their analytic status as observers' rules. They are not forces or events in the world extraneous to an observer. Motives are sociologically possible only because some practical observer has methods and procedures – ie, rules – for locating them as events in the world, not because that is where they really are. Because events cannot 'exist' sociologically except as courses of treatment, and because courses of treatment are not intelligible except through available social rules, motives cannot be located except by rule. Consequently, motives are accomplished exclusively through the use of such methods and procedures.

When a member says 'He had the jealous motive to . . . ,' we expect that the statement can be understood as a description of possible behavior. Of course, there can be disagreement with the surface content of the statement – perhaps he did not have the jealous motive – but it nevertheless remains an intelligible remark because it describes an understandable or socially possible motivated action. Others do not think every such statement literal nonsense. This is again to distinguish between concrete surface phenomena or causal properties (whether the object does or does not have the jealous motive) and the analytic deep structure that makes such phenomena possible (that an observer can talk intelligibly about jealous motive, whatever the factual status of his talk).

The point here is that there must be some rule – of language, interpretation, or culture – by which motive-talk takes life as a description.

Now to say that some rule is available is to remove the sociological habitat of motive from object (the person who had the jealous motive) to discourse about the object (how it is understood that a motive ascription has been made). This is to say, again, that the sociological import of motive resides in its procedural implications for the *treatment* of objects and not in the states of the objects themselves. Motive is a procedure.

This first feature brings motive into the full corpus of sociological ideas: rules must exist for such a procedure as motive to exist. They are socially organized treatments. Motive is not something an actor has – it is not a property of an actor. It is not something the sociologist decides that some person owns, in the sense that it is the 'thing' which he owns. Rather, motive is a member's method for deciding what alter owns. Thus, the sociologist does not search for motives in objects of talk and treatment, but in the talk and treatment itself[13].

One socially organized condition for addressing the topic of motive, therefore, is the assumption of the availability or relevance of a motive ascription rule. The necessary availability of such a rule, or rules, can be seen by noting that motives are a common sense class of events, in that to do (observe) motives is not to be exclusively doing (observing) something else (writing a play, sleeping). That motives are the topic in any case, as opposed to some other topic or no topic, requires that others understand they are the topic, which in turn requires that the socially available rule for introducing the class 'doing motives' be displayed in the behavior of the introducer. As with any form of social behavior, the members themselves conceive the doing of motives to be rule-guided. Thus, one kind of common-sense-sociological rule is the motive ascription rule, and the most elemental necessary feature of this deep rule is: there are rules for the ascription of motives.

B Motivated Objects Are Theorizers

One rule for the ascription of motives therefore is that the observer-user knows there are motive-ascribing rules. A concomitant of this first rule is that the ascriber know (assume, presume) that the *object* knows there are motive-ascribing rules.

In order to be called motivated, the object of an ascription cannot be treated as if he were doing the behavior haphazardly or coincidentally. He is, in other words, treated as if he has the capacity to 'know what he's doing'. Any object thought to be unable to know what it is doing cannot be treated as motivated, even though that object resembles a human organism, eg, a brute or an infant. That ascribers know there are rules requires that they impute knowledge to the object that there are rules[14]. Otherwise, the ascriber's knowledge could not be conceived by him to be a practical guide to the object's behavior, since the latter could not be deemed to be oriented.

Alter, as rule-guided, incorporates the fundamental sociological principle that generally available rules are the analytic equivalent of membership (community, group, pair, etc). Rules make actors' methodicity and concert possible by transforming what would otherwise be nonsense into intelligible social behavior. That alter can be conceived (by observing ego and sociologist) to be rule-guided

498

encompasses the status of motives within general sociology: motive, as with any other sociological classification, refers to certain actions by rule-guided ascribers and objects. The ascriber is rule-guided in his characterization of an object, while the object is (assumed to be) rule-guided in his behavior, and thus assumed to 'know what he's doing'. Both ego and alter assume of one another that they are, or could be, doing motives. Each is a theorizer, in the sense that both must be looking to rules in order to carry off their activity as doing motives. For motive treatment to occur, as for any kind of membership treatment to occur, ego and alter must necessarily generate for one another their status as members oriented to rules. Here a set of concrete activities is so formulated that those activities become members through the application of a corpus of rules. This is a detailed way of saying they are members of a social relation[15].

By 'rule-guided' we do not mean that actors are automata governed by abstract rules, that rules are clear and unchanging and automatically applied, or that it cannot be difficult, confusing, and vague for members to act like members. We do not mean that actors are rule-governed (Bennet, 1964). On the contrary, it is those who can behave but not act whom we conceive to be rule-governed automata, for they seem only to play out as mechanisms the untransformed universal needs and drives of every man[16]. The distinction between rule-governed and rule-guided is comparable to the one between behavior and action, and it is surely correct that the use of rules by members is an accomplishment in the hardiest sense of the term. We are only asserting that ego and alter must assume, however difficult the application of substantive ascriptions, that *some* corpus of membership rules is being used in behavioral displays before they can be characterized by substantive motive schema. It is necessary that ascriber and object are assumed to be of a certain kind, namely theorizers.

We are not suggesting either that members always neatly agree on what is happening around them, or that the substance of rules is common to all interactants. Whether behavior goes well or badly, whether it 'deviates' or 'conforms', is not an issue. We do not equate the deep notion of theoreticity with the substance of interaction. Theoreticity is the observed, rule-guided identification of the doing of anything at all, whether well or badly, whether deviant or conforming. (Even to be considered one or the other requires that some imputation of rule be used.)

Take the case of mental illness. If the person is conceived by members to be doing nothing in particular, to be merely a set of either random or universal behaviors, then no question of motive will ever arise (or will arise only once, to be dismissed by the finding of non-membership). Only when being crazy can be seen as organized or rule-guided – again, as being a display of some membership – does the possibility of motivated mental patients occur.

To be theoretic is thus to be conceivable by some observer as methodically rule-guided, rather than haphazard in behavior. To ascribe a motive, among other ascriptions, is of course to formulate the intelligible character of some behavior. The warrant for motive ascription is that the object be theoretic, that his behavior is capable of being formulated as action, just as it is the warrant for any common-sense facet of membership.

C Motives Have a Grammar

A third organized condition of motive ascription is a grammar that locates for a potential or would-be ascriber those conditions in the world which give notice that an ascription is to be done. The grammar moves a motive rule into behavior, from availability to ascription. It is a (collection of) rule(s) of use for the doing of an ascription. It depicts for the observer a procedure for actually ascribing available designations to a world populated by members. The grammar links a phenomenon in the world to the available corpus of designations.

This grammar of motives is used whenever an event is to be collected within a biography. We may think of the biography as a collection of 'owned experiences,' in that actors conceive themselves as having particular pasts which routinely inform an ovserver about the possibilities for their behavior; and we may think of events as some observer's definition of a situated environment of objects, specific to time and place. Motives are the social characterizations, generally available, the grammar which is used when biography and event are to be linked. The grammar produces for the ascriber a relation between some practical phenomenon and the common sense biography with which that event now comes to be associated through the process of ascription. A common sense biography is the observer's version of a set of owned experiences (husband), a set which comes into contact with, or is juxtaposed against, particular concrete (and hence socially problematic) phenomena in the world (dead wife). The grammar is the rule (connect the experience – husband – with the event – dead wife) that conjoins the two as an accomplishment of organized and concerted treatment (a jealous motive).

Imagine a hypothetical community where a murder is committed, and the husband of the victim is eventually identified as the killer. Initially, everyone could be suspect, and to 'look for the motive' is to address the links between the murder and various collections of owned experience in the community. The ways these experiences are joined with murdered wife methodically generate the motivated (or not) character of any link.

The idea of motive thus serves to formulate for members their interactions, insofar as they conceive interaction as experiences framed in events. Actors are thought by observers to have biographies and to engage the world with them. The grammar produces the link between the two. Motives are resources for connecting an event with a biography, and they generate the event as a member of the class of experiences owned by a body (as depicted in common sense).

Similarly, motives depict for us how the event shows or displays a biography. Insofar as the biography and the event can be seen to be membership, this is done through the ascription of motive. Otherwise – in the absence of such a grammar – observers would be unable to organize the current and flow of socially intelligible events, nor could they observe the products of biography; ie, they could not see interaction as a course of history. They would be without a temporal method. Events could only be seen to be performed and disembodied, not enacted by some theoretic-nontheoretic incumbent of a situated social world. Motives thus characterize biographies enacting events are specific to events and distinctive of biographies. They are a grammar in that they methodically collect these disparate phenomena. And they are social in that they transform what would otherwise be fragmentary series of unconnected immediate events into generally intelligible social courses of behavior. It is through motive as a culturally available designation that the observer recovers alter's membership out of observed temporal phenomena, because motives delineate the biographical auspices of acts in situations.

D Motives Formulate a Type of Person

The grammar, then, includes some collection of owned experiences which can be allocated to the agent of the act, and some rule(s) for showing the related character of the event and the collection of experiences. Because there are alternative collections (of experience) available, the use of the grammar poses a selectional problem for its user in this sense: it has to include a search procedure for deciding the relevance of one biography (one collection) as compared to other possibilities. The search procedure is essentially the rule for showing the *possible* relevance of the biography for the event. Such a rule amounts to the formulation of a type-of-person.

Thus, when users formulate the biography called 'husband', the relevance of which to the event 'murdered wife' is decided through a formulation of circumstances and characteristics such as jealousy, they are formulating the biography (husband) as the type of person whose jealousy could produce the event of murdered wife. In this way the grammar is a provision for explicating the link between the biography and the event and this explication is supplied by the formulation of a type of person.

The grammar of motives enables members regularly to address the fact that the relevance of biography to event is formulable through a rule which locates the owner of the biography as the type of person who would do the event[17]. Type of person, then, explicates the circumstances and understandings required to assert the relevance of any biography for the event. The heart of the grammar is thus its rule for formulating a type of person. It is in this sense that any observer's ascription of a motive serves to formulate for some activity, a person.

E Motives Formulate Actors' Methods

If the application of the grammar is equivalent to the formulation of a type of person, what is required of such a formulation? Note that type of person is an identification of certain characteristics, traits, dispositions, and behaviors which make ownership of the biography relevant to the event. While the items on such a list (characteristics, traits, dispositions, behaviors) all tend to itemize concrete features of the person, they only acquire their analytic sociological interest as descriptions of possible ways of relating to the event, ie, as potential courses of action. To formulate a type of person is to formulate a course of action on the grounds that no matter what one predicates substantively of persons to make their biographies relevant to the event, such relevance is only assigned on the assumption that the predicates depict a typical, possible course of action. Person, then, depicts a typical possible actor.

To say his motive in murdering his wife was his jealousy is to explicate the circumstances which make him the type of jealous person who would (could) murder his wife – that murdering his wife is one possible method available to him for doing jealousy. In this way, the event is formulated as the agent's possible method for doing whatever the formulation of the motive requires as a course of action.

He killed himself because he was depressed, or he left the party because he was bored – both are observers' ways of saying that killing oneself is a method of doing depression, or that prematurely leaving the party is a way of doing boredom. This understanding is important because members regularly raise the question of motive and address it as a sensible topic only of those classes of events which are recognizable as possible products of actors' methods. Questions such as 'What was your motive in spilling the ink?' (Austin, 1966), or 'what was

502

your motive in speaking so softly?' come up in ordinary usage when something is fishy, *and* when it is sensible to ascribe to an actor some methodic display of intention or purpose. To assign a motive is then necessarily to assume that the event exhibits possible methodicity.

As we have stated, at the deepest level such methodicity is addressed in the observer's conception of the event as showing the agent's character as a type of person – by the agent's being formulable as a possible method, as it were, to 'do' whatever type of person which he is formulated as[18]. The observer assumes, then, that the agent shows in the event (uses the event as) one possible method of identifying himself through his action as a particular type of person: that the murder of his wife identifies him as a jealous type of person, leaving the party as a bored person, and so forth.

When an observer formulates a member in this sense, he is stipulating that whosoever he is formulating has knowledge to act under the auspices of his (the observer's) formulation of a type of person. The formulation of a type of person (of one who has a motive) thus requires the observer to assume that the one so formulated is capable of 'showing' the type of person for which the observer's formulation provides. Therefore, when the observer formulates a motive, he is formulating a type of person and is required to assume that the one so formulated is a member in the deep sense of the term, ie, as one who can generally be expected to know what he's doing in the possible circumstances where he might or could be doing it, circumstances which include those of motive ascription.

No matter what members conceive themselves to be doing when they ascribe motives, we say they are engaged in conceiving others (or self) to be doing whatever activities they do because they 'own' a particular collection of experiences which can be used as a normative order for creating sensible events. Those to whom motives are ascribed are thus formulated under the auspices of the following requirements: (1) That they treat such a collection of experiences as possible grounds of action in situations, (2) that other collections of experiences are possible alternative grounds of action, (3) that the activity which is done is the actor's way of showing, to the one who ascribes, the relevance of his own collection of experiences (of showing himself as a type of person), and (4) since every kind of showing as type of person is a method of excluding other possible persons, that the actor as *this* type of person is selectively doing whatever he comes to (since according to his theoretic status in common, he could have come to something else.) It is in these ways that regular motive ascriptions are regularly introduced in regular social intercourse; it is in these ways that motives formulate actors' methods.

VI Summary

In summary, we have attempted to depict the socially organized conditions which members tacitly accredit in their accomplishment of motive as a sensible and observable event. We have tried to demonstrate that motive can be sociological by showing that motive shares with all matters of sociological interest (class, bureaucracy, suicide, etc) a status as a common sense formulation. Motive depicts for any observer a course of social action.

Motive is a sociological procedure for describing how organisms show themselves as persons. To gain an identity as a person requires that disparate activities and experience can be collected by actors under some typification, a process which makes the activities graspable for them through the formulation of alter's motivated identity. The condition of membership in common makes it possible for an observer to expect that alter, because he knows what he's doing and hence is responsible, will use common rules as a standard of orientation when he displays his biography in situations, thus knowledgably revealing his type of person.

Given (the observer's imputation of) alter's capacity for knowing what he is revealing, together with his being a differentiable type of person, the observer can also warrantably conceive alter's future, and thus organize not just the current biography and event but future links between the two as well. Motives are a procedure for organizing an historic and regular interactional future.

Most fundamentally, then, whatever a motivated actor does will show his methods for affirming himself as a person. Being responsible and capable of displaying some other collection of owned experiences, the observer is permitted to note that he nevertheless did display the collection he displayed. For any member to ascribe a motive is thus to do no less than to generate a person. It is to formulate from situated performances a responsibly displayed and differentiated collection of experience.

While each of these public and rule-guided conditions must exist for motive ascription to occur sensibly, they can of course be accomplished in a variety of substantive ways which we have not discussed here. For example, that there is a grammar under which a motive ascription rule is invoked suggests that members regularly differentiate between activities which do and do not require the use of that grammar; ie, there are some activities which needn't be organized according to motive criteria. In the same vein, there are undoubtedly a variety of methods in use by which members identify organisms as possible theoretic actors, eg, the various ways it is decided that a child is enough of a member to be called a theoretical actor and so a potential object of motive ascription.

More centrally, one pervasive feature of social organization concerns members' methods for tracking and formulating biographies from a universe of possibilities, and the various rules for deciding the relevance of particular biographies as particular types of persons. The bureaucratic method, for instance, is probably very different from the familial one. All these are categorization problems which members regularly resolve, methodically producing the organization of their every day environment. To describe such particular solutions requires other papers, the possibility of which we can now begin to grasp. Being interactional and rule-guided – being a social method (just as bureacracy, social class, or institutionalization are methods) – confirms that the status of the deep structure of motive is sociological.

Notes

¹ Readers of an earlier draft commented upon the absence of any mention of ethnomethodology as strange. Limitations of space prohibit us from the sort of detailed comparisons which such a topic requires, and there is unfortunately no adequate description of ethnomethodology in the literature; so, for example, Denzin's paper (1969) is hopeless not merely for his misunderstandings, but for his inadequately concrete conception of analysis; eg, in superficially focusing upon the surface features of the approach – the concern with 'meaning', with the 'actor's point of view', etc – he loses sight of the analytic character of ethnomethodology and of analysis in general. Wilson (1970), on the other hand, may understand ethnomethodology but not what to do about it. If ethnomethodology obviates literal description, then suggesting that we be 'more explicit and self-conscious' (1970:706) is regressive if not vacuous – it is only to ask that we improve on the same literal procedures. As to the contrast between this paper and ethnomethodology, we must first record the great influence of the writings of Garfinkel (1957), though this influence has not worked itself out in our thinking in the ways it has in his students. Ethnomethodology, as it is practised by these students, not only fails to supply our program with its rationale but denies this rationale at critical analytic points. Ethnomethodology seeks to 'rigorously describe' ordinary usage, and despite its significant transformation of standards for conceiving of and describing such usage, it still conducts its inquiries under the auspices of a concrete, positivistic conception of adequacy. Ethnomethodology conceives of such descriptions of usage as analytic 'solutions' to their tasks, whereas our interest is in the production of the idea which makes any conception of relevant usage itself possible. Whereas ethnomethodology uses the ordinary world 'seriously' (they hope to solve analytic problems by doing naturalistic science on this world), we treat the everyday world as a proximate occasion for initiating inquiry and not as a 'fact' to be reproduced. In our respective attitudes toward ordinary language and the everyday world, we have about as much in common with ethnomethodology as Heidegger shares with Austin. Finally, ethnomethodologists would regard our task in this paper as a stimulative exercise in legislating the use of a 'concept', while we would treat such an objection as a failure of analytic nerve, as the

typical positivist gambit (which goes back at least as far as Protagoras) of refusing to exercise analytic authority, despite the fact that such authority grounds their entire enterprise with its intelligibility. Some of these issues are taken up in detail in work now under way.

² This misconception leads to the contention that motives are only peripheral to the classic tradition of, say, Marx or Durkheim – that human motivation plays the role of unstated premises and is properly disregarded for analytic purposes (the ecological argument), or requires explication only in order to account for more of the variance (the social psychological argument of Homans, 1964; Inkeles, 1959). We contend instead that motive plays a central role in such traditions, a role we can recognize if we grasp the analytic status of motive rather than its concrete character.

³ For example, the sociological import of economic determinism in Marx is not the impersonal effects of brute facts upon an organism, but rather his formulation of a meaningful environment constructed by and seeen from the perspective of a typical actor. To say 'economic determinism exists' is to decide to formulate actors as oriented to selected particular features of their socially organized environments in such a way as to enable this orientation (now called 'the economy') to produce their routine actions. To describe economic determinism is then to assign a rule of relevance to actors which serves the purpose of explicating social structure by reference to their grounds of action (the economy) as a set of sociologically intelligible events of social structure (economic determinism).

⁴ This is also the sense in which Weber's *Theory of Social and Economic Organization* (1947) – particularly the sections in which he depicts types of social relationships – can be read in a fundamental way as a set of methods for conceiving of motives. Each relationship is a different method for formulating actors as acting under the auspices of relevances to which they are methodically and selectively oriented.

⁵ Thus, conventional notions of motives as concealed premises or as peripherals that increase variance are incorrect in the fundamental sense that it is in the *observer's* ascription of such rules, and not in the state-of-affairs the ascriptions recommend, that the analytic status of motives resides.

⁶ There may be a concrete psychological state-of-affairs that corresponds to a motive report. We do not address this and so are not trying to run psychologists out of business. Our purpose, again, is to analytically describe the social organization of motive ascriptions as courses of social action.

⁷ This is perhaps what some sociologists intend when they invoke phrases like 'actor's point of view', 'what it means to the actor', and 'significant symbol'.

⁸ Technical versions, which causally locate motives in neural circuits, libidinal arrests and the like, reformulate what is essentially a member's device without respect for those relevances and interests of the member which generate the behaviors of interest to the technician. Whatever the efficacy of neural paths, they have no social relevance except as they can be understood to be employed by the members.

This is not a new criticism and has been stated most articulately by the British ordinary language philosophers (Peters, 1958; Austin, 1965).

⁹ We have not seen successful demonstrations of objections to this position in the philosophical literature, for those who claim that motives *can* be causes, or that motives *do* explain, usually accomplish this by changing the sense of 'cause' and by treating 'explanation' concretely rather than analytically. Of

course, motives *can* be causes if one uses cause in a different sense; our notion is that any different sense makes 'cause' a constituent feature of the action (ie, a presupposed element of the action), and hence, not a 'cause' in the ordinary sense at all. But, one is free to do this. Secondly, motives do explain, but by providing a way to see 'cause' as an intelligible link, not by citing a cause.

[10] We are not making a sampling argument here. Even when an unanalyzed event occurs repeatedly, it remains only a regularity. Lacking analysis, we would still be without an understanding or description of it, regardless of the times and places it had been counted.

[11] Though more ingenious than most, Kenneth Burke (1945) is not exempt from these charges, for in his effort to locate the analytic parameters of motive, he confuses analytic and concrete conditions (ie, the parameters of act, agent, agency, scene, and purpose). However, despite Burke's failure to explicate the grammar of motive, in more than a metaphoric sense, he performs a service by continually keeping before us the notion that the way in which priorities are allocated to these parameters is a function of a theoretic election (that it is observers who formulate motives), though we do not get a description of how such formulations are accomplished.

[12] We are not prescribing how motive-talk should be accomplished; rather, we are stating that under any and all occasions of motive-talk in our society, to which we have reference, such talk requires members to make certain assumptions about their environments. Furthermore, their talk shows that they make these assumptions. Again, whether members know these conditions or can report them to us is analytically irrelevant in the same sense that Chomsky's native speakers cannot concretely reproduce his theory even though they do show its correctness and provide for its formulability through their behavior.

[13] Note, though, that the concrete talk – the speech act(s), the usage – does not provide the observer with the motive (as some versions of sociology might have one believe), but such analytic status is located in terms of the observer's decision as to what must be known in order to recognize in the talk, the analytic 'presence' of motive.

[14] We should perhaps remind the reader here that the phrase 'knows there are rules' does not imply 'knows *the* rules'. All kinds of substantive mistakes and arguments over content and application may occur in the course of motive ascription without ever denying that there are rules. What the rules are, and that rules exist, are two quite different ideas, and correspond to our previous distinction between surface and deep structure, respectively. This same distinction carries through to 'knowing what he's doing'. We can be quite mistaken about what it is we are doing without being treated as if we *couldn't* know, eg, as in therapy.

[15] Take, for example, the brute. There are things which can be said of such an organism, eg, it is enraged, it is contented, it is sleeping, and so forth. These are characterizations, in that they depict some state of affairs, and rule-guided ascriptions at that. But they are not, and could not be, common-sense ascriptions of motives because the brute's behaviors are not thought to be displays by a rule-guided actor – the brute is thought not to be socially 'responsible'. He is thought not be responsible insofar as his activity is, in Weber's terms, behavior rather than action. Nor is the brute thought to be a bona fide member, and for the same reason: he cannot be a member because he cannot be said to know what he's doing through an orientation to

member rules.

[16] Universals remain constants for the brute, and they govern him in the sense that they are not given the differentiated and variable expression that we think of as motivated social action. Jealousy can be a motive precisely because it is not universal in husbands. Think of thirst as a motive here – what would it be like to enact the thirst drive in such a way as to have it said that 'he killed her because he was thirsty?'

[17] While we separate these features of the grammar for analytic purposes, they are concretely indistinct. As one formulates a biography of owned experiences presumed to be relevant to the event, this presumption can already be informed by an unstated rule which has decided that relevance as the kind of person who would do the event.

[18] Perhaps, this is what Aristotle intended in the following: '. . . acts are called just and self-controlled when they are the kinds of acts which a just or self-controlled man would perform, but the just and self-controlled man is not he who performs these acts, but he who also performs them in the way just and self-controlled men do' (1105b 5–9, p 39).

References

ARISTOTLE, *Nicomachean Ethics*, The Bobbs-Merrill Co, Indianapolis, 1962.

J W ATKINSON, (ed) *Motives in Fantasy, Action and Society*. D Van Nostrand, Princeton, 1958.

J L AUSTIN, *How To Do Things with Words*, Oxford University Press, New York; 1965. 'Three ways of spilling ink'. 64–80, 1966; reprinted in J H Gill (ed), *Philosophy Today*, No **1**, Macmillan, New York, 1968.

JONATHAN BENNET, *Rationality: An Essay Towards Analysis*, Humanities Press, New York, 1964.

K BURKE, *The Grammar of Motives*. Prentice-Hall, New York, 1945.

R B CATTELL, *Personality and Motivation Structure and Measurement*, World Book Co, New York, 1957.

NOAM CHOMSKY, *Aspects of the Theory of Syntax*, MIT Press, Cambridge, Mass, 1965.

NORMAN DENZIN, 'Symbolic interactionism and ethnomethodology: A proposed synthesis'. *American Sociological Review* **34** (December):922–934, 1969.

HAROLD GARFINKEL, *Studies in Ethnomethodology*, Prentice-Hall, New York, 1967.

H GERTH and C W MILLS, *Character and Social Structure*, Harcourt Brace and Co, New York, 1953.

CALVIN S HALL and GARDNER LINDZEY, *Theories of Personality*, Wiley, New York, 1957.

GEORGE C HOMANS, 'Bringing men back in'. *American Sociological Review*, **29** (December) 1964 : 809–818.

ALEX INKELES, 'Personality and social structure', in R MERTON, L BROOM, and L COTTRELL (eds), *Sociology Today*. Basic Books, New York, 1959, 249–276.

GARDNER LINDZEY, *The Assessment of Human Motives*, Rinehart, New York, 3–33, 1958.

D C MCCLELLAND, J W ATKINSON, and R A CLARK, *The Achievement Motive*, Appleton-Century-Crofts, New York, 1953.

A I MOLDEN, *Free Action*, Routledge and Kegan Paul, London, 1961.

R S PETERS, *The Concept of Motivation*, Routledge and Kegan Paul, London, 1958.

J PIAGET, *The Language and Thought of the Child*, Harcourt Brace, New York, 1926.

ALFRED SCHUTZ, *Collected Papers*, **Vol. I**. Martinus Nijhoff, The Hague, 1962.

MARVIN B SCOTT and STANFORD LYMAN, 'Accounts.' *American Sociological Review*, **33** (February) : 46–62, 1968.

D S SHWAYDER, *The Stratification of Behavior*. Humanities Press, New York, 1966.

NEIL SMELSER and WILLIAM T SMELSER, 'Introduction'. in SMELSER and SMELSER (eds) *Personality and Social Systems*, Wiley, New York, 1–18, 1963.

MAX WEBER, *The Theory of Social and Economic Organization*. Trans. Talcott Parsons. The Free Press, Glencoe, Illinois, 1947.

ROBERT W WHITE, 'Ego and reality in psychoanalytic theory'. *Psychological Issues* **3** : 71–141, 1963.

T P WILSON, 'Conceptions of interaction and forms of sociological explanation'. *American Sociological Review* **35** (August) : 697–710, 1970.

45

Finding Your Spot*

Carlos Castenada

Sunday 25 June 1961

I stayed with don Juan all afternoon on Friday. I was going to leave
about 7 pm. We were sitting on the porch in front of his house and I
decided to ask him once more about the teaching. It was almost a
routine question and I expected him to refuse again. I asked him if
there was a way in which he could accept just my desire to learn, as if
I were an Indian. He took a long time to answer. I was compelled to
stay because he seemed to be trying to decide something.

Finally he told me that there was a way, and proceeded to delineate a problem. He pointed out that I was very tired sitting on the
floor, and that the proper thing to do was to find a 'spot' (*sitio*) on the
floor where I could sit without fatigue. I had been sitting with my
knees up against my chest and my arms locked around my calves.
When he said I was tired, I realized that my back ached and that I
was quite exhausted.

I waited for him to explain what he meant by a 'spot', but he made
no overt attempt to elucidate the point. I thought that perhaps he
meant that I should change positions, so I got up and sat closer to
him. He protested at my movement and clearly emphasized that a
spot meant a place where a man could feel naturally happy and
strong. He patted the place where he sat and said it was his own spot,
adding that he had posed a riddle I had to solve by myself without
any further deliberation.

What he had posed as a problem to be solved was certainly a
riddle. I had no idea how to begin or even what he had in mind.
Several times I asked for a clue, or at least a hint, as to how to
proceed in locating a point where I felt happy and strong. I insisted
and argued that I had no idea what he really meant because I
couldn't conceive the problem. He suggested I walk around the porch
until I found the spot.

* *The Teachings of Don Juan: a Yaqui Way of Knowledge*, Penguin 1968, 30–
35.

I got up and began to pace the floor. I felt silly and sat down in front of him.

He became very annoyed with me and accused me of not listening, saying that perhaps I did not want to learn. After a while he calmed down and explained to me that not every place was good to sit or be on, and that within the confines of the porch there was one spot that was unique, a spot where I could be at my very best. It was my task to distinguish it from all the other places. The general pattern was that I had to 'feel' all the possible spots that were accessible until I could determine without a doubt which was the right one.

I argued that although the porch was not too large (twelve by eight feet), the number of possible spots was overwhelming, and it would take me a very long time to check all of them and that since he had not specified the size of the spot, the possibilities might be infinite. My arguments were futile. He got up and very sternly warned me that it might take me days to figure out, but that if I did not solve the problem, I might as well leave because he would have nothing to say to me. He emphasized that he knew where my spot was, and that therefore I could not lie to him; he said this was the only way he could accept my desire to learn about Mescalito as a valid reason. He added that nothing in his world was a gift, that whatever there was to learn had to be learned the hard way.

He went around the house to the *chaparral* to urinate. He returned directly into his house through the back.

I thought the assignment to find the alleged spot of happiness was his own way of dismissing me, but I got up and started to pace back and forth. The sky was clear. I could see everything on and near the porch. I must have paced for an hour or more, but nothing happened to reveal the location of the spot. I got tired of walking and sat down; after a few minutes I sat somewhere else, and then at another place, until I had covered the whole floor in a semi-systematic fashion. I deliberately tried to 'feel' differences between places, but I lacked the criteria for differentiation. I felt I was wasting my time, but I stayed. My rationalization was that I had come a long way just to see don Juan, and I really had nothing else to do.

I lay down on my back and put my hands under my head like a pillow, then I rolled over and lay on my stomach for a while. I repeated this rolling process over the entire floor. For the first time I thought I had stumbled upon a vague criterion. I felt warmer when I lay on my back.

I rolled again, this time in the opposite direction, and again covered the length of the floor, lying face down on all the places where I had lain face up during my first rolling tour. I experienced the same warm and cold sensations, depending on my position, but there was no difference between spots.

Then an idea occurred to me which I thought to be brilliant: don Juan's spot! I sat there, and then lay, face down at first, and later on my back, but the place was just like all the others. I stood up. I had had enough. I wanted to say good-bye to don Juan, but I was embarrassed to wake him up. I looked at my watch. It was two o'clock in the morning! I had been rolling for six hours.

At that moment don Juan came out and went around the house to the *chaparral*. He came back and stood at the door. I felt utterly dejected, and I wanted to say something nasty to him and leave. But I realized that it was not his fault; that it was my own choice to go through all that nonsense. I told him I had failed; I had been rolling on his floor like an idiot all night and still couldn't make any sense of his riddle.

He laughed and said that it did not surprise him because I had not proceeded correctly. I had not been using my eyes. That was true, yet I was very sure he had said to feel the difference. I brought that point up, but he argued that one can feel with the eyes, when the eyes are not looking right into things. As far as I was concerned, he said, I had no other means to solve this problem but to use all I had – my eyes.

He went inside. I was certain that he had been watching me. I thought there was no other way for him to know that I had not been using my eyes.

I began to roll again, because that was the most comfortable procedure. This time, however, I rested my chin on my hands and looked at every detail.

After an interval the darkness around me changed. When I focused on the point directly in front of me, the whole peripheral area of my field of vision became brilliantly coloured with a homogeneous greenish yellow. The effect was startling. I kept my eyes fixed on the point in front of me and began to crawl sideways on my stomach, one foot at a time.

Suddenly, at a point near the middle of the floor, I became aware of another change in hue. At a place to my right, still in the periphery of my field of vision, the greenish yellow became intensely purple. I concentrated my attention on it. The purple faded into a pale, but still brilliant, colour which remained steady for the time I kept my attention on it.

I marked the place with my jacket, and called don Juan. He came out to the porch. I was truly excited; I had actually seen the change in hues. He seemed unimpressed, but told me to sit on the spot and report to him what kind of feeling I had.

I sat down and then lay on my back. He stood by me and asked me repeatedly how I felt; but I did not feel anything different. For about fifteen minutes I tried to feel or to see a difference, while don Juan stood by me patiently. I felt disgusted. I had a metallic taste in my mouth. Suddenly I had developed a headache. I was about to get sick. The thought of my nonsensical endeavours irritated me to a point of fury. I got up.

Don Juan must have noticed my profound frustration. He did not laugh, but very seriously stated that I had to be inflexible with myself if I wanted to learn. Only two choices were open to me, he said: either to quit and go home, in which case I would never learn, or to solve the riddle.

He went inside again. I wanted to leave immediately, but I was too bored to drive; besides perceiving the hues had been so startling that I was sure it was a criterion of some sort, and perhaps there were other changes to be detected. Anyway, it was too late to leave. So I sat down, stretched my legs back, and began all over again.

During this round I moved rapidly through each place, passing don Juan's spot, to the end of the floor, and then turned around to cover the outer edge. When I reached the centre, I realized that another change in coloration was taking place, again on the edge of my field of vision. The uniform chartreuse I was seeing all over the area turned, at one spot to my right, into a sharp verdigris. It remained for a moment and then abruptly metamorphosed into another steady hue, different from the other one I had detected earlier. I took off one of my shoes and marked the point, and kept on rolling until I had covered the floor in all possible directions. No other change of coloration took place.

I came back to the point marked with my shoe, and examined it. It was located five to six feet away from the spot marked by my jacket, in a south-easterly direction. There was a large rock next to it. I lay down there for quite some time trying to find clues, looking at every detail, but I did not feel anything different.

I decided to try the other spot. I quickly pivoted on my knees and was about to lie down on my jacket when I felt an unusual apprehension. It was more like a physical sensation of something actually pushing on my stomach. I jumped up and retreated in one movement. The hair on my neck pricked up. My legs had arched slightly, my trunk was bent forward, and my arms stuck out in front of me rigidly with my fingers contracted like a claw. I took notice of my strange posture and my fright increased.

I walked back involuntarily and sat down on the rock next to my shoe. From the rock, I slumped to the floor. I tried to figure out what had happened to cause me such a fright. I thought it must have been the fatigue I was experiencing. It was nearly daytime. I felt silly and embarrassed. Yet I had no way to explain what had frightened me, nor had I figured out what don Juan wanted.

I decided to give it one last try. I got up and slowly approached the place marked by my jacket, and again I felt the same apprehension. This time I made a strong effort to control myself. I sat down, and then knelt in order to lie face down, but I could not lie in spite of my will. I put my hands on the floor in front of me. My breathing accelerated, my stomach was upset, I had a clear sensation of panic, and fought not to run away. I thought don Juan was perhaps watching me. Slowly I crawled back to the other spot and propped my back against the rock. I wanted to rest for a while to organize my thoughts, but I fell asleep.

I heard don Juan talking and laughing above my head. I woke up.

'You have found the spot,' he said.

I did not understand him at first, but he assured me again that the place where I had fallen asleep was the spot in question. He again asked me how I felt lying there. I told him I really did not notice any difference.

He asked me to compare my feelings at that moment with what I had felt while lying on the other spot. For the first time it occurred to me that I could not possibly explain my apprehension of the preceding night. He urged me in a kind of challenging way to sit on the other spot. For some inexplicable reason I was actually afraid of the other place, and did not sit on it. He asserted that only a fool could fail to see the difference.

46

Language, Logic and Culture*
C Wright Mills

Problems of a sociology of knowledge arise when certain conceptions and findings of the cultural sciences are confronted by theories of knowing and methodology. Awareness of the social and economic factors operative in the reflective process has arisen within American sociology as peripheral notations on specific researches and as implicit in psychology when sociologically approached[1].

Sociologies of knowledge have found elaborate statement in other contexts[2], but American social scientists have not assimilated or developed theories adequate to carry on historical reconstructions of thought from a cultural standpoint, nor have they attempted systematically to state the implications of such an attempt for methodology and theories of reflection[3]. Despite this lack of postulational framework and empirical hypotheses, assumed and unanalyzed 'answers' to certain theoretical questions are operative in the minds of many sociologists. It is the business of the theorist to articulate such assumptions as precise hypotheses and to examine them critically.

There are two viewpoints from which the social determination of mentality and ideas may be regarded. These are *historical* and *sociopsychological*. Without a formulation of mind which permits social determinants a role in reflection, assertions on the larger historical level carry less intellectual weight. A theory of mind is needed which conceives social factors as intrinsic to mentality. We may view the problems of a sociology of knowledge on a historical level; but we must also view our generic hypothesis on the socio-psychological level.

One chief defect of extant sociologies of knowledge is that they lack understanding and clear-cut formulations of the *terms* with which they would connect mind and other societal factors. This deficiency is, in turn, rooted in a failure to recognize the psychological problems arising from the acceptance of the generic hypothesis.

*   *   *

* *American Sociological Review*, **4** (5), 1939.

It is not difficult to impute historical relations, but what exactly is a historical relation? Although doctrines, like other complexes in culture, have a sort of existence apart from any one or two biological organisms, we must admit that ultimately reflection (a process whereby beliefs come to be doubted, discarded, or reformulated) has its seat in a minded organism and is a symbolic performance by it. Perhaps any one individual does not seriously dent a given system of belief. Perhaps in the long historical trends of belief, the drift of thought is, as Lecky believed[5], determined more by minute changes effected by hundreds of thinkers than by a dozen 'great' ones. Nevertheless, we must ask for the *modus operandi* of these rejections, reformulations, and acceptances. The rounding out of a systematic sociological theory of knowledge involves our handling that question in socio-psychological categories. Granted that changes in culture influence trends in intellectual work and belief we must ask *how* such influences are exerted. That is a question to be answered by a social psychology, a psychology which studies the impact of social structures and objects, of class biases, and technological changes upon the mind of an organism.

*   *   *

Until we build a set of theoretically substantial hypotheses of socio-psychological nature, our research is likely to remain frustrated and our larger theoretical claims feeble. I wish to advance two such hypotheses.

The first is derived from the social statement of mind presented by G H Mead[10]. It is his concept of the 'generalized other' which, with certain modification and extension, we may employ to show how societal processes enter as determinants into reflection[11]. The generalized other is the internalized audience with which the thinker converses: a focalized and abstracted organization of attitudes of those implicated in the social field of behavior and experience. The structure and contents of selected and subsequently selective social experiences imported into mind constitute the generalized other with which the thinker converses and which is socially limited and limiting[12].

Thinking follows the pattern of conversation. It is a give and take. It is an interplay of meanings. The audience conditions the talker; the other conditions the thinker and the outcome of their interaction is a function of both interactants. From the standpoint of the thinker, the socialization of his thought is coincidental with its revision. The social and intellectual habits and character of the audience, as elements in this interaction, condition the statement of the thinker and the fixation of beliefs evolving from that interplay. Thought is not an interaction as between two impenetrable atoms; it is conversational and dynamic; ie, the elements involved interpenetrate and modify the existence and status of one another. Imported into mind, this symbolic interplay constitutes the structure of mentality.

It is conversing with this internalized organization of collective attitudes that ideas are logically, ie, implicitly, 'tested'. Here they meet recalcitrance and rejection, reformulation and acceptance. Reasoning, as C S Peirce has indicated[13], involves deliberate approval of one's reasoning. One operates logically (applies standardized critiques) upon propositions and arguments (his own included) from the standpoint of a generalized other. It is from this socially constituted viewpoint that one approves or disapproves of given arguments as logical or illogical, valid or invalid.

No individual can be logical unless there be agreement among the members of his universe of discourse as to the validity of some general conception of good reasoning. Deliberate logical approval is based upon comparison of the argument approved with some common idea of how good argument should appear. The 'laws of logic' impose a restriction upon assertion and argument. They are the rules we must follow if we would socialize our thought[14]. They are not arrived at intuitively, nor are they *given*, 'innate within the mind'. They are not to be 'taken as formulating generic characters of existences outside of inquiry or the traits of all possible being'. Rather, the principles of logic are 'the rules by means of which the meanings of our terms are explicated ... the principles of logic are ... conventional without being arbitrary ... they are shaped and selected by the instrumental character of discourse, by the goals of inquiry and discourse.'[15]

There is evidence that the so-called laws of proof may be merely the conventional abstract rules governing what are accepted as valid conversational extensions. What we call illogicality is similar to immorality in that both are deviations from norms. We know that such thought-ways change[16]. Arguments which in the discourse of one group or epoch are accepted as valid, in other times and conversations are not so received[17]. That which was long meditated upon is now brushed aside as illogical. Problems set by one logic are, with a change in interests, outgrown, not solved[18]. The rules of the game change with a shift in interests, and we must accept the dominant rules if we would make an impress upon the profile of thought. Our logical apparatus is formulated by the rebuffs and approvals received from the audiences of our thought. When we converse with ourselves in thought, a generalized other as the carrier of a socially derived logical apparatus restricts and governs the directions of that thought. Although not always the ultimate critique, logical rules serve as an ultimatum for most ideas. Often on this basis are selected out those ideas which will not be spoken, but forgotten; those that will not be experimentally applied, but discarded as incipient hypotheses. In general, conformity to current principles of logic is a necessary condition for the acceptance and diffusion of ideas. This is true because principles of logic are the abstracted statements of social rules derived from the dominant diffusion patterns of ideas. In attempting to implement the socialization of our interests and thought, we acquire and utilize a socially derived logical apparatus. Within the inner forum of reflection, the generalized other functions as a socially derived mechanism through which logical evaluation operates.

* * *

The thinker does not often play an immediate active role in large social strata or institutional frames, and hence, does not build through direct action a generic pattern of habit and value which would constitute a selective detector of 'problems', a background of mind. Nevertheless, there are two other modes by which he may come to be influenced by such residues. He may intentionally identify himself with an ethos [21] rooted in a structure of social habits, thus vicariously participating in articulating a particular social segment's interests; or, if his thought is appreciatively diffused, members of his audience will possess mental characteristics built by direct social action. It is often through such audiences that a thinker is culturally claimed, because, when his doctrine and his *further* thought gravitate toward a responsive audience it means that he has responded (whether he is at first aware of it or not) to 'problems' defined by the activities and values of his audience. A reflective response to a social environment, assimilated by its members, is always related to the 'needs' of that particular environment. Defined operationally (externally and behaviorally), that environment is the largely unreflective behavior patterns of a specific set of groups, eg, a class, or a set of institutions. Viewed internally, as a function or field of mind, we have contended for this environment's influence on thought, because such specific fields of social behavior develop and sustain organized sets of attitudes; when internalized, these constitute a thinker's generalized other which functions as that with and against which he carries on his internal conversation. It is by virtue of this essentially social structure of mind that sociological factors influence the fixation not only of the evaluative but also of the intellectual. On the one hand, the generalized other is an element involved in the functioning and conditioning of the outcome of the reflective processes; it is the seat of a logical apparatus; on the other hand, it is constituted by the organized attitudinal implicates of cultural forms, by institutional ethos, and by the behavior of economic classes.

When confronted with a system of thought, or the reasoned assertions of a thinker, our sociological perspective toward knowledge attempts to 'locate' a set of determinants within contemporaneous fields of societal values. We try to locate the thinker with reference to his assimiliated portion of culture, to delineate the cultural influences in his thought and the influences (if any) of his thought upon cultural changes.

In an attempt to outline approaches to this problem, we now take another angle of departure from which we cast a hypothesis and a methodology. We might conceive the following set of remarks as a formulation of another socio-psychological 'mechanism' connecting thinking with societal patterns. We construct it from a conjunction of the social dimensions of language with the fundamental role of language in thought. By approaching the interrelatedness of sociality and reflection, our perspective enables us to view as a 'unit' matters which have traditionally been handled on three levels of theory. Between them are two 'gaps' which we 'fill'. First, we consider the nature of language and meaning in terms of social behavior. Second, we consider the nature of reflection in terms of meaning and language.

From a concept of language as an 'expression of antecedent ideas', the psychologists have gravitated toward a functional conception of language as a mediator of human behavior. From the isolated grammatical and philological field ethnologists have moved to the social-behavioral setting of linguistic materials[22]. Given additional cogency by their convergence, both these movements proceed toward the notion that the meanings of symbols are defined and redefined by socially co-ordinated actions. The function of words is the mediation of social behavior, and their meanings are dependent upon this social and behavioral function. Semantical changes are surrogates and foci of cultural conflicts and group behavior. Because language functions in the organization and control of behavior patterns, these patterns are determinants of the meanings in a language. Words carry meanings by virtue of dominant interpretations placed upon them by social behavior. Interpretations or meanings spring from the habitual modes of behavior which pivot upon symbols. Such social patterns of behavior constitute the meanings of the symbols. Non-linguistic behaviors are guided or manipulated by linguistic materials, and language is the ubiquitous string in the web of patterned human behavior.

We can view language functionally as a system of social control. A symbol, a recurrent language form gains its status as a symbol, an event with meaning, because it produces a similar response from both the utterer and the hearer [23]. Communication must set up common modes of response in order to be communication; the meaning of language is the common social behavior evoked by it. Symbols are the 'directing pivots' of social behaviors. They are also the indispensable condition of human mentality. The meanings of words are formed and sustained by the interactions of human collectivities, and thought is the manipulation of such meanings. Mind is the interplay of the organism with social situations mediated by symbols. The patterns of social behavior with their 'cultural drifts', values, and political orientations extend a control over thought by means of language. It is only by utilizing the symbols common to his group that a thinker can think and communicate. Language, socially built and maintained, embodies implicit exhortations and social evaluations [24]. By acquiring the categories of a language, we acquire the structured 'ways' of a group, and along with the language, the value-implicates of those 'ways'. Our behavior and perception, our logic and thought, come within the control of a system of language. Along with language, we acquire a set of social norms and values. A vocabulary is not merely a string of words; immanent within it are societal textures – institutional and political coordinates. Back of a vocabulary lie sets of collective action.

No thinker utilizes the total vocabulary afforded by his societal context nor is he limited to it. We acquire the systematic vocabularies of intellectual traditions built by other thinkers from diverse cultures. We build an intellectual orientation by gathering for ourselves a dictionary of interrelated terms. As we 'grow' intellectually, we selectively build new linguistic habits. Like other habits, linguistic or conceptual ones are built on previous residues. Prior linguistic and conceptual accomplishments are conditions for the acquisition of new habits of thought, new meanings. Thinking is the selection and manipulation of available symbolic material.

We may 'locate' a thinker among political and social coordinates by ascertaining what words his functioning vocabulary contains and what nuances of meaning and value they embody. In studying vocabularies, we detect implicit evaluations and the collective patterns behind them, – 'cues' for social behavior. A thinker's social and political 'rationale' is exhibited in his choice and use of words. Vocabularies socially canalize thought.

We must recognize the priority of a system of meanings to a thinker. Thinking influences language very little, but thought, as

Malinowski has indicated, 'having to borrow from (social) action its tool, is largely influenced thereby'.[25] No thinker can assign arbitrary meanings to his terms and be understood. Meaning is antecedently *given*; it is a collective 'creation'. In manipulating a set of socially given symbols, thought is itself manipulated. Symbols are impersonal and imperative determinants of thought because they manifest collective purposes and evaluations. New nuances of meaning which a thinker may give to words are, of course, socially significant in themselves[26], but such 'new' meanings must in their definition draw upon the meanings and organization of collectively established words in order that they may be understood, and they are conditioned thereby; and so is the acceptance and/or rejection of them by others.

Here, again, the thinker is 'circumscribed' by his audience, because, in order to communicate, to be understood, he must 'give' symbols such meanings that they call out the same responses in his audience as they do in himself. The process of 'externalizing' his thought in language is thus, by virtue of the commonness essential to meaning, under the control of the audience. Socialization is accompanied by revision of meaning. Seldom do identical interpretations obtain. Writings get reinterpreted as they are diffused across audiences with different nuances of meanings. We call the tendency to telescope (by variations of interpretation) the meaning of concepts into a given set of social habits, ethnocentricism of meaning[27]. Functionally, ie, as far as communication obtains, the reader is a factor determining what the thinker writes.

A symbol has a different meaning when interpreted by persons actualizing different cultures or strata within a culture. In facing problems incident to a translation from Chinese to English, I A Richards got 'the impression that an unwritten and unelucidatable *tradition* accompanies and directs their interpretation', and that 'this tradition is *by no means uniform*'.[28] We hold that this *tradition* which is *by no means uniform* is the linguistic reflex of the socially controlled behaviors from which a scholar is derived, which he 'lives' (behaviorally and/or vicariously), or which constitutes the audience of his thought, or all three. These 'esoteric determinants of meaning' are the logical interpretants[29], residues derived from the meaningful behavior of such constellations.

A block in social actions, eg, a class conflict, carries a reflex back into our communicative medium and hence into our thought. We then talk past one another. We interpret the same symbol differently. Because the coordinated social actions sustaining the meaning of a given symbol have broken down, the symbol does not call out the same response in members of one group that it does in another, and there is no genuine communication.

*　　*　　*

Different traditions of thinking have different distinctions in their vocabularies, and these differences are related to differences in other spheres of their respective cultural setting. The distinctions in Chinese thinking are quite different from those in Western thought. The Chinese, for example, did not set the subject over against the object, and hence had no 'problem of knowledge'. Nor did Chinese thought of this period separate psychology and physics into two separate studies. Richards suggests:

The problems which for any one tradition are obtrusive – especially the more insoluble of them, and thus, it may seem, the more 'important' – may often have arisen as a result of accident – grammatical or social. (*Op cit*, 3–5).

The manner in which 'lack' of distinctions in a language limits thought and the formulation of problems is aptly illustrated by Richards' analysis of the Chinese word for 'aged'. There is no distinction between age in the chronological sense and the sense of an ethical pattern toward those who are old. Consequently, Mencius cannot separate in his thinking a man's age and the reverence that is due him because of it. Here is a direct connection of a *mos*, embodied in language, with a limitation of thinking. Thinkers of Mencius' period do not 'discuss or treat as open to discussion the rightness of paying respect to age as age'[30]. Their language would not allow a definition of the problem. The employment of one word for both chronological age and the honorable pattern of behavior toward old persons reflects and preserves the unquestioned appropriateness of the reverential conduct better than any separate terms could. Agreement with the *mos* or institution was evoked by the very mentioning of the symbol around which it was organized and which defined it in behavior. Chinese thinking on this head is thus seen to operate within an unquestioned limit set by the language itself.

What if this *mos*, reverence to old age, were to change radically? What if shortage of young men for warriors in a long series of wars force the group to shift its respect to 'young warrior' roles? What would then happen to the old concept now carrying dual meaning? It would become ambiguous and eventually, split. Newly sanctioned social habits force new meanings and changes in old meanings. A distinction would be drawn which was not existent in Mencius' thinking. Problems would result from the competing meanings where before an unquestioned belief had reigned. Thus is reflection related in terms of meanings to areas of conflicts and drifts within social orders[31].

It is a necessary consequence of any unaccustomed perspective that matters traditionally viewed disjunctively, be considered conjunctively. I have presented certain coordinates for a sociological approach to reflection and knowledge, viewing conjointly sociality and mind, language and social habit, the noetic and the cultural. Such contexts may be said to operate as determinants in thought in the sense that given social textures there will be present certain various and limited materials for assimilation; or, in the sense that thinkers programmatically identify themselves with an order of interests. I have analyzed the matter more deeply (1) by instituting the socio-psychological problem of the *modus operandi* of such determinations, and (2) by advancing and partially elaborating as hypotheses two connective mechanisms. It should be apparent that these formulations also provide research leads equipping attempts at concrete reconstructions of intellectual patterns from a cultural standpoint.

References

[1] *Cf* L WIRTH's preface to KARL MANNHEIM's *Ideology and Utopia*, New York, 1936, xxi.

[2] The German *Wissenssoziologie* and the French sociological theories of knowledge. For a reasonably adequate bibliography of the German materials, see WIRTH-SHILS' translation of MANNHEIM, *op cit*, 281 ff. For French, see reviews and monographs in *L'Année Sociologique*, **I-XII**.

[3] *Cf* however, H BECKER's brief, substantive presentations scattered through his and H E BARNES' *Social Thought from Lore to Science*, New York, 1938.

[5] *History of the Rise and Influence of Rationalism in Europe* (1919 edition), **I**, 15–16; **II**, 100–101.

[10] *Mind, Self, and Society*. Chicago, 1934. Also see bibliography of Mead's articles.

[11] *Op cit*, 155 ff.

[12] My conception of the generalized other differs from Mead's in one respect crucial to its usage in the sociology of knowledge: I do not believe (as Mead does, *op cit*, 154) that the generalized other incorporates 'the whole society', but rather that it stands for selected societal segments. Mead's statements regarding this point are, I believe, functions of an inadequate theory of society and of certain democratic persuasions. These are not, however, logically necessary to the general outline of his social theory of mind.

[13] *Collected Papers of Charles Peirce*, **II**, 108, Cambridge, Mass, 1934.

[14] JEAN PIAGET's experiments on children substantiate such a viewpoint. *Cf Language and Thought of the Child*, New York, 1926; *Judgment and Reasoning in the Child*, New York, 1928. For DURKHEIM's view of the rise of logical categories from social forms, see his and MAUSS' monograph in *L'Année Sociologique*, **VI**, Paris, 1903, 1–72; also M GRANET's Durkheimian analysis of non-Aristotelian Chinese categories, in *La Pensée Chinoise*. Paris, 1934.

[15] ERNEST NAGEL, 'Some Theses in the Philosophy of Logic,' *Phil of Sci*, Jan 1938; 49–50. Nagel notes 'a marked tendency' in pure logic towards the view 'that the subject matter of logic is discourse'. The linguistic view of logic I believe eminently sound, but with a growing recognition of the social and behaviorial character of language, it needs to be set within a social context. From another angle, I should ask of Nagel that some order be found among these 'shifts' in the 'goals of inquiry and discourse' which shape and select the principles of logic. Such an attempt would require a sociological implementation. An attempt to isolate the social determinants of 'goals of inquiry and discourse' would not only be in line with the program of the sociology of knowledge but, if successful, would strengthen Nagel's thesis that the principles of logic are 'conventional without being arbitrary'.

[16] BOGOSLOVSKY in his *Technique of Controversy*, New York, 1928, has shown that, eg, JOHN DEWEY's writings reveal grave logical fallacies if judged by the rules of classical logic. He attempts to delineate a new set of logical principles based on an analysis of Dewey's actual modes of thought. Bogoslovsky is tabulating new rules that have come into being. No logician can 'make up' a system of logic. Like coins, they are genuine by virtue of their dominant currency.

[17] *Cf* LECKY, *op cit*, **II**, 100–101, etc. Also SUMNER's *Folkways*, **33**, 174–175, 193–195, 225.

[18] *Cf* DEWEY's article in *Creative Intelligence*, **3**, New York, 1917.

[21] This 'special pleading' is the most usual 'connection' imputed – often it is considered exhaustive. (Eg, S HOOK: *Marxist Quarterly*, **I**, 454). Undoubtedly many social doctrines are definitively affected by their originator's or publicist's interest in intentionally aiding or hindering the perpetuation of a social movement or institution; but I would not confine the connection between thought and other cultural items to a thinker's conscious 'interest' or the conscious utilization of a doctrine as a 'social forensic' by any professional talker. If this were the only connection to be ascertained, then our generic hypothesis would be seriously weakened. We should have to impute to the thinker the attributes of the 'economic man', ie, knowing what are his social interests and thinking accordingly. Moreover, the connection stated merely in terms of 'interest' begs the major question; it tells us nothing as to exactly *how* such 'social interests' climb into thinking, and this is what we must explain. Without such an explanation, the imputation of interest connotes that the relationship occurs 'rationally', within the mind of the thinker, within his conscious intellectual and social intentions. If the sociology of knowledge is to be psychologically limited to this economic man theory of the thinker, we had all better reduce our expectations of it, both as theory and as an integrating viewpoint for cultural reconstruction of intellectual history.

[22] For an excellent summary of these movements' literature, see E ESPER's article 'Language' in *Handbook for Social Psychology*, ed CARL MURCHISON, Worcester, Mass 1934. See his comments on Grace DeLaguna and B Malinowski.

[23] *Cf* MEAD, *op cit*, sec II.

[24] K BURKE puts it thus: 'Speech takes its shape from the fact that it is used by people acting together. It is an adjunct of action – and thus naturally contains the elements of exhortation and threat which stimulate action and give it direction. It thus tends naturally towards the use of implicit moral

weightings: the names for things and operations smuggle in connotations of good and bad – a noun tends to carry with it a kind of invisible adjective, and a verb an invisible adverb.' *Permanence and Change*, 243–244. *Cf* also MARCEL GRANET, *op cit*, for discussion of the heavy value-dimension in Chinese vocabularies and syntax.

25 'The Problem of Meaning in Primitive Languages,' *op cit*, 498.

26 *Cf* KARL MANNHEIM, *op cit*, 74.

27 Eg, approached with this 'lead' in mind, the 'diffusion pattern' of the Bible exhibits one reason for its continuance: its language is capable of being 'strained' (reinterpreted) through the purposes and orientations implicitly contained in the languages of a great variety of cultural segments and milieux.

28 *Mencius on the Mind*, **33**, New York, 1932.

29 The incipient theory of meaning found in C S Peirce is compatible with the sociological slant on meaning. I find in his work an added support for a belief in an intrinsic, controlling relation of social habits to reflection through meaning. For Peirce, 'the ultimate meaning (logical interpretant) of a concept is a habit change'. (*Collected Papers*, **V**, paragraph 476.) Habits are, of course, socially acquired and transmitted.

30 I A RICHARDS, *op cit*, 55–56.

31 I am indebted to C E AYRES for indicating the similar instance involved in the rise of the concept 'capital'. Since Aristotle, it was agreed that money is obviously sterile. Hence, for 'money' and 'wealth', the substitution of the equivocal 'capital' *as a factor in production*. The 'capitalist fallacy' may be regarded as a continuation of the 'mercantilist fallacy' which pivoted around the fluid concept 'wealth'. It is significant that 'capital' emerged in the period and milieu in which bookkeeping underwent its great development. The ambivalence of 'capital' represents in a business culture a confusion of bookkeeping entries with things, machines. As in Mencius' period, no one debated the differences between *pecuniary* and *physical* capital. I am not implying that the classicists' dual usage was deliberately cultivated as special pleading.

47

Deschooling Society *

Ivan Illich

Why We Must Disestablish School

Many students, especially those who are poor, intuitively know what the schools do for them. They school them to confuse process and substance. Once these become blurred, a new logic is assumed: the more treatment there is, the bettter are the results; or, escalation leads to success. The pupil is thereby 'schooled' to confuse teaching with learning, grade advancement with education, a diploma with competence, and fluency with the ability to say something new. His imagination is 'schooled' to accept service in place of value. Medical treatment is mistaken for health care, social work for the improvement of community life, police protection for safety, military poise for national security, the rat race for productive work. Health, learning, dignity, independence, and creative endeavor are defined as little more than the performance of the institutions which claim to serve these ends, and their improvement is made to depend on allocating more resources to the management of hospitals, schools, and other agencies in question.

*   *   *

School initiates, too, the Myth of Unending Consumption. This modern myth is grounded in the belief that process inevitably produces something of value and, therefore, production necessarily produces demand. School teaches us that instruction produces learning. The existence of schools produces the demand for schooling. Once we have learned to need school, all our activities tend to take the shape of client relationships to other specialized institutions. Once the self-taught man or woman has been discredited, all nonprofessional activity is rendered suspect. In school we are taught that valuable learning is the result of attendance; that the value of learning

* *Deschooling Society*, Calder and Boyers, 1971, 38–39.

increases with the amount of input; and, finally, that this value can be measured and documented by grades and certificates.

In fact, learning is the human activity which least needs manipulation by others. Most learning is not the result of instruction. It is rather the result of unhampered participation in a meaningful setting. Most people learn best by being 'with it', yet school makes them identify their personal, cognitive growth with elaborate planning and manipulation.

Once a man or woman has accepted the need for school, he or she is easy prey for other institutions. Once young people have allowed their imaginations to be formed by curricular instruction, they are conditioned to institutional planning of every sort. 'Instruction' smothers the horizon of their imaginations. They cannot be betrayed, but only short-changed, because they have been taught to substitute expectations for hope. They will no longer be surprised, for good or ill, by other people, because they have been taught what to expect from every other person who has been taught as they were. This is true in the case of another person or in the case of a machine.

This transfer of responsibility from self to institution guarantees social regression, especially once it has been accepted as an obligation. So rebels against Alma Mater often 'make it' into her faculty instead of growing into the courage to infect others with their personal teaching and to assume responsibility for the results. This suggests the possibility of a new Oedipus story – Oedipus the Teacher, who 'makes' his mother in order to engender children with her. The man addicted to being taught seeks his security in compulsive teaching. The woman who experiences her knowledge as the result of a process wants to reproduce it in others.

48

Mathematics and the Kpelle *

John Gay and Michael Cole

A bowl of uncooked rice is being passed around the room. 'How many measuring cups of rice do you think are in it?' This question was asked of a group of 60 Peace Corps volunteers in training for service as teachers in Liberia. Each volunteer made his own estimate and the results were tabulated. The estimates ranged from 6 to 20 cups and averaged slightly over 12. In fact, there were exactly 9 cups of rice in the bowl, so an average overestimate of about 35 percent was made. This result is in striking contrast to that achieved by a group of 20 illiterate adult members of the Kpelle tribe of central Liberia. When asked the same question the Kpelle adults estimated the number of cups of rice in the bowl to be slightly under 9, an underestimate of only 8 percent.

Then, to the same group of 60 Peace Corps trainees another problem was given that gave them no difficulty. Eight cards were put faceup on the table. Pasted on the cards were 2 or 5 red or green squares or triangles. The task was to sort the cards into two piles; then, after sorting them once, to sort them again in a different way; and finally, to sort them a third way. The Peace Corps volunteers scarcely hesitated in performing this task. Yet a group of 30 illiterate Kpelle adults found great difficulty in sorting the cards even once. One was unable to sort them at all, and the remainder took an average of more than 1 minute for the first sort. Ten were unable to complete a second sort, and 21 failed to make the third sort. These later sorts, if completed, frequently took as long as 2 minutes.

To the casual American observer, the inability of the Kpelle subjects to sort the cards perhaps seems incredible. In fact, it is just this kind of observation that has led men to say 'Africans think like children', or to speak of the 'primitive mentality'. But what about the Peace Corps volunteers' performance when asked to make a simple

---

* *The New Mathematics and an Old Culture*, Holt Rinehart and Winston, 1967, 1, 34–35, 36–40, 75, 89–91.

numerical estimate? Would this not appear an inept performance to any normal Kpelle adult?

Logic and Reasoning

No occasion arises for a child to use his talent for discovery, or his curiosity, in relation to the subject matter of a course. He is forced to repeat aloud collections of words that, from his point of view, make no sense. He knows that he must please the teacher in order to survive, but he finds what is taught incomprehensible. Therefore he tries to find other ways to survive; he uses his wit to anticipate the teacher. If the material being taught has no apparent pattern, at least he can figure out the teacher. Often the teacher has come from the same Kpelle background as the student, and so his words and actions are more or less predictable. The teacher's words and actions do not seem haphazard, disorganized, and irrelevant. This leads the child to guess at the best way to please the teacher, using nonacademic, social clues. Even when the teacher is not of Kpelle origin, he behaves in a way that makes sense to the Kpelle child, because many of the patterns of Westernized Liberian life duplicate the authority structures of Kpelle life.

It is common for children to shout out an answer to the teacher before he has finished stating a problem. They try to outguess each other to show the teacher how smart they are. For example, a teacher gave the problem, 'Six is two times what number?' When the children heard the words 'six', 'two', and 'times', they shouted 'twelve'. Their experience with the teacher showed that he was always asking the times table, and they guessed he was asking it again. They were wrong – and probably were never quite sure why. They were told the answer was 'three', which probably confirmed their idea that school made no sense whatsoever. They had not discovered the pattern, but considered only the isolated words out of context.

The main techniques in their repertoire of 'scientific method' are rote memory and clever guessing based on familiar clues. Clever anticipation is more important than literal understanding, and logical development is ignored in favour of one-shot guesses.

The child makes little use of logical organization and structure, or argumentation in school. For instance, it seems rare for the child to make use of visual regularities. In one class a series of textbook problems were written in a haphazard fashion on the board. Neither teacher nor student thought of arranging the problems in a neat fashion on the blackboard, even though they were written in a definite sequence in the textbook and part of the lesson depended on seeing the pattern formed by the answers. The groupings we perceive immediately were neither perceived nor used in these classes.

Another example of the same kind concerns sets of stones used to illustrate multiplication problems. For many children an organized group of 3 sets of 4 stones has no more significance than a randomly scattered set of 12 stones. To find the number in each set the child counts them; the visual pattern in the structured case seems to provide no help.

The child is rarely challenged to follow a train of reasoning to its conclusion. Geometry proofs at the high school level are given as exercises to be memorized, not occasions for reasoning. The child knows a proof if he can repeat it, but he is never expected to discover a new proof in a similar problem, based on his understanding of the first problem.

Nor is evidence used to reach general conclusions. The child who cannot tell the answer to the problem, 'One-half of what is eight?' is not encouraged to experiment until he finds an answer. He is supposed to have learned the answer to this particular question. The unwillingness in this case to do practical experiments may be caused in part by his using the word 'one-half' as a vague term for any part of a whole. The word has two usages, one as an arbitrary symbol in arithmetic, and the other as a vague term in village life; the two have little or nothing in common.

Since logical argument is not stressed in the classroom, it is understandable that inconsistencies do not upset the students. A striking case concerns the nature of living things. A Kpelle college student accepted *all* the following statements: (1) the Bible is literally true, thus all living things were created in the six days described in Genesis; (2) the Bible is a book like other books, written by relatively primitive peoples over a long period of time, and contains contradiction and error; (3) all living things have gradually evolved over millions of years from primitive matter; (4) a 'spirit' tree in a nearby village had been cut down, had put itself back together, and had grown to full-size again in one day. He had learned these statements from his Fundamentalist pastor, his college Bible course, his college zoology course, and the still-pervasive animist culture. He accepted all, because all were sanctioned by authorities to which he feels he must pay respect.

The net result of this pattern of difficulties in school is that mathematics, indeed almost the entire curriculum, is not useful outside the classroom. The child has no occasion in village life to use mathematics skills learned by rote in school, and has no knowledge of how to use these skills, other than to please the teacher. The subject is isolated and irrelevant, a curious exercise in memory and sly guessing.

It comes as no surprise, then, when numerical statements are not related to physical reality. The students are unable to estimate and approximate in a word problem. If the problem posed was how much the payroll was for a business that employed 97 men for 21 days at 50 cents a day, the student knew how to perform the necessary multiplications. But he had no idea had to figure out approximately what the answer might be. He could make no sense of the answer which concluded that it was almost the same as 100 men for 20 days at 50 cents a day. In short, he could not relate the classroom method to the real world. Only in the most elementary cases does he use arithmetic in the village, cases which are provided for by traditional techniques.

In summary, Kpelle students who encounter mathematics in Western-oriented schools misuse the English language, learn by rote memory and guessing , do not use logical patterns, and have no use for what they learn. School mathematics has largely failed, and the child produced by the system needs radical help to overcome this failure, no matter what the grade level. He rarely gets the help he needs. His teachers know something is wrong, but they do not understand enough to propose a coherent course of action. In this study we attempt to do both – to understand what lies behind the failure, and to recommend proper and effective relief. We turn now to the mathematical behavior of the Kpelle in their tribal setting, in order to find the materials on which understanding and action depend.

Arithmetical behavior among the Kpelle can be discussed under four major headings which correspond closely to those now current in discussions of mathematics in Western culture. The first is the organization and classification of objects into sets, which is basic to our Western understanding of the foundations of arithmetic. The second is the use of counting systems to describe sets of objects. The third concerns the relations of equality, inequality, and comparison between sets, as well as between numbers. And finally, we consider the operations performed on numbers, corresponding to our addition, subtraction, multiplication, and division.

Sets

We must consider the ways in which the Kpelle form and describe sets of objects. This investigation is particularly important, since the modern approach to teaching elementary arithmetic, from the earliest school years, builds upon the use and description of sets of objects. The mathematics curriculum developed by Educational Services Incorporated for use in African schools is no exception to this pattern. For this reason in particular we must know how Africans themselves classify into sets the objects they encounter in their daily lives.

The Kpelle use the terms *kpulu*, 'group', and *seêi*, 'set', to speak of sets of objects. The word *seêi* has the same root meaning as our English term 'set'. It refers to the result of placing things together. The term *seêi* applies to any collection of distinct, countable objects. One can say, for instance, *kom seêi náan ká ti*. 'Those are four sets of stones', where the stones may be in four random piles or in four straight rows. The term *seêi* is more general than, for instance, the term *pere*, 'row'. The sentence *kom pere náan ká tí* must be translated 'Those are four rows of stones.' In this case the term *pere* and the term *seêi* would have the same reference. But if the set were expanded to include objects of more than one kind, the word *seêi* would be applicable while the word *pere* would not, because *pere* refers only to things that are put in rows.

Other terms for set are also more specific than the term *seêi*. The term *kāya* refers to things within one family or type, such as fruits or vegetables. The *kuu* is a set of people gathered together for some particular purpose, whether a feast, a funeral, or a work group. The suffix -b*ela* refers to a collection of persons. Therefore *tii-k*e-b*ela* are workmen and *taa-b*ela* are townspeople. In English, the term 'regiment' is more specific than the term 'group', to give only one example.

Classification

Members of such sets can be individual objects, or they can be general and indefinite. Two general terms used are *nuu*, 'person', and *s*en, 'thing'. The world of objects seems to be divided roughly into the class of persons and the class of things. Within these classes there are subclasses of objects, such as, *wuru*, 'tree' and *sua*, 'animal', both within the class *s*en, and thus in the class of things. A full description of all possible classes of objects and subclasses within those classes, is a worthwhile project, but is beyond the scope of this case study.

Thus far all the terms for sets of objects have referred to countable objects. We do not normally speak of such material as *molon*, 'rice', or *yá*, 'water', in this way. The hypothetical sentence *molon seêi náan ká tí*, patterned after the sentences given above for stones, means nothing. Rice is not spoken of in sets. One of two modifications in that hypothetical sentence is necessary. Either we must refer to grains of rice by adding the suffix -*kau*, 'seed', in which case we can say *molon-kau seêi náan ká tí*, 'Those are four sets of grains of rice', or we must speak of *molon* by using one of an entirely different class of structure-describing words.

532

The latter class includes such terms as *sane*, 'bottle', bo*ro*, 'bag', *legi*, 'pot', and *kôpi*, 'cup'. Words in this class organize a noncountable mass into countable units, yet not in the same way as the suffix -*kau* isolates bits of the material.

The distinction in Kpelle between countable and noncountable nouns is less fundamental than in English. In English we must state a countable noun as singular or plural, and the noncountable noun in singular form. For example, we can speak of 'a horse' or 'horses', but only of 'air' in normal usage. In Kpelle, however, the fundamental use of any noun is generic, showing neither singularity nor plurality. The statement *séle káa à sua kéte* can be translated with equal ease as 'An elephant is a big animal', 'Elephants are big animals', or '(The) elephant is a big animal'. The term *séle*, 'elephant', is in its root form generic, and the singularity or plurality must be supplied by the context. It can be counted, but it need not be counted. The structural distinction between a word such as elephant and a word such as water may, but need not be, expressed.

There is a suffix used with countable free nouns which resembles our English plural, but which is actually an individualizing form. To add the suffix -*ná* is to think of the items as discrete, counted one by one. A countable set of objects would be individualized only to show that the objects were scattered and not in a uniform, homogeneous collection. Thus we can distinguish *nátée saabai*, 'my three chickens', and *nátée-nà saabai*, 'my three (particular, isolated) chickens'. The second expression focuses the attention one by one on the three chickens – perhaps one near the man's house, one in the cassava patch, and one near the blacksmith's shop. The first expression does not call attention to their physical relation to each other, but refers to their presence as a group.

It appears that the Kpelle language has an adequate vocabulary for dealing with sets of objects. The classification system this vocabulary supports is built into the language and the daily life. The Kpelle know and use sets of stones, bottles of water, bags of rice, and work groups of people, although this type of classification is not conscious and explicit.

These general observations led us to set up a simple problem mentioned in the introductory chapter, in forming sets of objects according to different attributes. Before the beginning of this experiment we feared it might prove too simple, but we hoped to at least determine if there was any difference in the order that the sets were formed. The task was so constructed that the objects could be sorted according to three principles (or attributes): color, number, and form.

In the first problem each subject was given 8 cards (5 inches by 4

533

inches) on which were pictured triangles and squares, either red or green; there were 2 or 5 on a card. These 8 cards were put before the subject in a haphazard arrangement and he was asked to sort them into two groups.

The initial results were astonishing. The task was almost impossibly difficult for all three groups – illiterate children, schoolchildren, and adults. Most often the subject would shuffle the cards around for a while and then look up expectantly. When asked what sort of group had been formed, the answer was a shrug of the shoulders or no answer at all. We asked ourselves if the instructions were inadequate or the material on the cards too difficult to grasp.

In order to find out more about these questions, two modifications were made in the experiment. First of all, we tried to make sure that the subjects understood the instructions by preparing a set of sample cards on which figures were drawn in ink. The figures were large or small dots, some were filled, some open, and located in the center or near the edge of the card. The experimenter began by saying that this pack of cards could be sorted into two groups in different ways and then proceeded to form the groups in each of the three possible ways. The subject was then shown the pack of experimental cards and asked to perform the same kind of task.

Another possible factor we sought to evaluate in this revised experiment was the cultural relevance of the figures on the cards. For this purpose we prepared 8 cards identical to those described earlier, but using instead pictures of a woman beating rice, with a baby on her back, and a man carrying a bucket of water on his head, followed by a dog. These pictures were readily understood and accepted as culturally appropriate. There were either 2 or 5 pictures on a card. The cards themselves were either red or green. Thus, the cards could be sorted according to the picture (man-woman), color, and number. As before, the subjects were requested to sort the cards in three different ways.

The overall effect of the demonstration sorting procedure was to increase the number of sorts that the people made. But severe problems remained. There were no significant differences between the ability to sort the triangle-square and the ability to sort the man-woman cards.

The results of these experiments are summarized in Tables 1 and 2, where the experiment using triangles and squares and that using men and women are grouped together.

The most striking aspects of these data are the relatively small proportion of subjects who managed even a second sort of the cards and the great amount of time each sort required. The average

534

Table 1 PROPORTION OF KPELLE SUBJECTS WHO SUCCESSFULLY SORTED CARDS

	1st Sort	2d Sort	3d Sort
Illiterate Children (42) *	0·95	0·48	0·10
Schoolchildren (50)	1·00	0·72	0·36
Illiterate Adults (63)	0·95	0·65	0·16

Table 2 MEAN TIMES IN SECONDS REQUIRED BY KPELLE SUBJECTS TO SORT CARDS SUCCESSFULLY

	1st Sort	2d Sort	3d Sort
Illiterate Children (42)	56	151	82
Schoolchildren (50)	29	88	131
Illiterate Adults (63)	58	115	103

* In all tables and graphs the numbers of subjects are given in parentheses after the title of the group.

American twelve-year-old takes one look at these cards and instantly proceeds to sort them into the three possible sets. The average Kpelle adult could not complete this task and only two-thirds of the Kpelle adults could make a second grouping. Moreover, the amount of time for the sorts, from one or two minutes, is extraordinarily great.

It is also interesting that there was no special preference for any one attribute. In the test using triangles and squares, 14 persons chose form dimension first, 26 chose color, and 27 chose number. In the test using pictures of women and men, 24 chose form, 32 chose color, and 26 chose number. There is a slight preference for either number or color over form, but the differences are not reliable. Some American authors have tried to show that the attribute chosen first depends on the developmental level of the subjects. No such clear relation is shown by our data. This may be due to cultural differences or to the stimuli we used. The question deserves further study.

What is the relevance of this discussion of sets and classification for arithmetic? Arithmetical procedures among the Kpelle, and very likely among any group of people, are built upon manipulations of sets of objects. The sets of objects normally used in this way are those categorized and classified by the language and culture. We have seen that the Kpelle language is capable of such classification, but the results of this card sorting experiment indicate that the typical Kpelle person finds such classification very difficult in strange situations or when using unfamiliar material. Apparently the linguistic potential for classification does not guarantee that the process will occur. We are certain that had we asked a person to sort cotton goods into country cloth or store cloth, sewed into clothes or not, and whether dirty or clean, no such difficulties would have arisen. Because there was great difficulty when 'nonsense' materials were used, we consider this an important fact to be considered when discussing the Kpelle child's activities in school. Clearly, familiar materials are essential in building a proper foundation for the study of arithmetic.

The natural progression in arithmetic (natural in our Western eyes, and, as we shall see, also probably natural to the Kpelle) is from sets to numbers. One reaction to a set of things is to count them. This the Kpelle do in much the same way we do in English. Their numeral system is basically a decimal system, although buried within the decimal system is a subordinate base-five system. There are cultures whose methods of numeration differ greatly from our own, but the Kpelle is not one of them.

Numerals are used in two forms, one preceded by the noun it counts and the other with a pronoun prefix replacing the noun as shown below. The numerals from 1 to 5 are basic, and are added to 5 to form the numerals from 6 to 9. There are independent numerals for 10 and 100 which are the basis for other numerals as shown below. The Kpelle occasionally use a word for 1000 which is borrowed from the Mandingo language. Some of the more Westernized among them use English terms for higher numerals. Some typical numbers are:

*táa*n — 'one of it'
veere — 'two of it'
nóolu — 'five of it'
nóolu mei da — 'six of it'
nóolu mei feere — 'seven of it'
puu — 'ten of it'
buu káu tòno — 'eleven of it'
buu káu feere — 'twelve of it'
buu feere — 'twenty of it'
buu feere káu lóolu mei da — 'twenty-six of it'
nun *tòno pôlu puu lóolu mei feere káu tòno* — 'one hundred seventy-one of it'
wala feere — 'two thousand'

A typical use of a numeral with a noun is the expression *taa lóolu*. 'five towns', which can be compared with *nóolu*, 'five of it'. There is no term for zero as such in the Kpelle language. But it is possible to refer to an empty set in several ways. For instance, in a game played by successively removing stones from piles, a pile with no stone is

536

referred to by the phrase 'fall in the hole'. In a similar game, the player says of the pile without rocks 'Let's enter old-town site', implying that no one lives there any more. It is also possible to speak of *seei-folo*, 'empty set'. Many different things can be called empty, but all are described by containers or sets of words. For example, a bottle, house, box, hole, mortar, chicken coop, bag, farm, pan, or purse, can all be called empty.

There is a rudimentary fraction system where the word *gbôra*, 'middle', and the word *-kpua*, 'part', are used to indicate portions of wholes. The term *gbôra* is used in the same way as *sama*, 'middle', referring to the middle of a road, or the middle of a hill, or the water in a river which is not full. In no case does the word have a precise meaning. Often the hamlet where persons rest when they are on their way from one village to another is said to be at the middle of the trip. Once we were told that we had reached the 'halfway' town on a long, hot walk. Our expectations proved to be sadly mistaken when we found that the term was not used in a precise, mathematical sense!

That part of a banana which one person receives when two people share a banana is called *gwei-kpua*, 'part of a banana'. Where four are required to share a banana each part may be called *gwei-kpua-kpua*, 'part of a part of a banana'. *Kpua* does not denote exactly half, however, since *gwei-kpua* can also refer to that part of a banana which each of three people receives. One pragmatic informant who was asked to consider this situation said he would mash up the banana and give it out in spoonfuls! In this way he avoided having to describe the exact division into equal portions.

The word *hâvu* has been borrowed from English, and is used in such expressions as *molon iooi feere da hâvu*, 'two and a half stacks of rice'. This term has become part of the Kpelle language, and few recognize its English origin. It has the same indefiniteness of references as *kpua*.

Perhaps the most common counting system among the Kpelle is the sequence of terms *da*, 'some', *támaa*, 'many', and *kélee*, 'all'. They are common answers to the question gee*lu* bé. 'How many?' or 'How much?' A person might say he has some rice, much rice, or all the rice; or he might speak of some people making a farm, many people making a farm, or all the people making a farm. These expressions are vague and imprecise, but they have sufficient precision for the Kpelle who knows approximately what constitutes 'many' when applied to familiar objects.

There are special terms for things which come in pairs. They are referred to as *nyowãa*, 'twins'. Human beings, cassava, plantains, and bananas come in such pairs. Triplets are also called *saaba*n, a term derived from *saaba*, 'three'.

There is an ordinal number system, which is related in a regular way to the cardinal numbers described. Only the term for 'first', *màa-nún*, is irregular. Otherwise the ordinals are formed as in *ñuui veere-gélei*, 'the secondman'. The numeral, preceded by the noun which it modifies, is given the suffix -*gélei*, which is derived indirectly from *géle*, 'sky', or 'day'.

Numbers and Kpelle Culture

We must now determine just what the people do and do not count in daily life. Our observations indicate that it is possible to count many things but that some things are not counted. For instance, it is not proper to count chickens or other domestic animals aloud, for it is believed that some harm will befall them. This has also been the case in many other non-Western cultures, including that of the Old Testament, where it was not considered proper to count people aloud, lest some die. The Liberian government requires the Kpelle to count people from time to time, both for census, and for taxes, but it is not a traditional practice. People count houses, poles for building houses, bags or other measures of rice, kola nuts, and other commonly used items. Counting is not so common an activity as it is in more highly commercial or technological cultures.

There are few occasions for counting beyond approximately 30 or 40. A young man, who spoke Kpelle as his native language, had been through three years of school, and was of at least normal intelligence, could not remember the Kpelle terms for such numbers as 73 or 238. He was able to reconstruct them, but his use of them was far from automatic. Many people cannot solve problems involving numbers higher than 30 or 40. Commonly, round numbers such as 100, are used to indicate any large amount.

The word 'number' is not found in the vocabulary of Kpelle adults. It is possible to construct an artificial word *támaa-laa*, 'many-ness,' but this is more the invention of the linguist (using, to be sure, authentic Kpelle word-construction) than a term in actual use.

Number-magic and numerology appear in the culture. Man is considered to have one more degree of power ·than woman. The number representing man is four and the number representing woman is three. A boy-child is presented to the world on the fourth day, and a girl-child on the third. The boys' Bush school is in session for four years, and the girls' Bush school for three. The burial rites for a man are completed on the fourth day, and those for a woman on the third.

There are proverbs and parables which use numbers. For example, *ífeere ká ní*, 'this is your second,' is a warning that a person should not

538

commit a particular offense for the second time. Or a man can say 'they can say one and then two,' which means that someone has done something to him, but that he will wait until the second time before reacting. 'The ten years did not kill me, is it the eleventh that will kill me?' means that a man has merely done the work he plans to do, and will finish soon. In a court case, this same proverb was interpreted to mean that a creditor could afford to wait a little longer for his money. Numbers are also at times used for a person's name, which happens most often when a man is employed by someone knowing no Kpelle. To refer to a man as *náan*, 'four,' is to curse him.

Divination may involve numbers. The *zoo*, or medicine man, takes two kola nuts and splits them in half. He puts medicine or a 'spirit' stone in a particular kind of leaf. He then throws the kola halves to the ground to determine the outcome of a given matter. If all the kola halves face upwards, it is certain the spirits are concerned about the affair at hand. If two face upward and two face downward, the spirits are divided. If all face down, the spirits are unfavorable and not inclined to help the situation. It is the number of halves in each position which determines the outcome. The *zoo* asks a series of questions of the kola nuts. He will suggest various possibilities, until all the halves face upwards for one of his suggestions. This is taken to be the correct answer. He may identify a guilty person in this way, or find the particular crime someone has committed. The guilty party must then confess the ill feeling or the bad action. The kola nuts are thrown once again to determine if the spirits are satisfied with the confession. When they are finally satisfied, a chicken is killed as a sacrifice, and the blood is sprinkled on the 'spirit' stone or the medicine. This procedure is used to predict the success of any activity of concern to the people.

One cannot help notice the rigged nature of this use of numbers. There is apparently no reliance on the laws of chance, as an analogy between throwing kola nuts and tossing coins might suggest. The *zoo* makes the seemingly chance nature of the process work to his own ends. He manipulates the force to verify his solution of the problem, which he determines on the basis of his knowledge of the situation.

The Kpelle do not, of course, use numbers only in this semi-magical way. They count things, and they use stones to help them in the process. Sets of objects are often noted and matched by sets of stones. For instance, once we counted the number of people in a small village. One of the elders of the town went with us, putting one stone in the pocket of his gown for every person we counted. Similarly, for tax purposes, dollars and persons are matched with stones in the hope that enough dollars can be obtained from enough persons to satisfy the government.

Measurement

In summary, there are several important things we have observed about the measurement behavior of the Kpelle. The most important thing is that measurement is used where it is needed. The Kpelle measure the length of cloth, rope, sticks, and other objects in village life. They measure the volume of rice, water, oil, and other agricultural products. They measure money, since Western economic activity is an increasingly important part of their lives. And they measure time, but primarily in a qualitative way.

Second, units of measure are, in general, not parts of an interrelated system but are specific to the objects measured. Certainly days, weeks, months, and years are not interrelated. The various length measures are used only when they are needed, and are not incorporated into a system. It is true that rice measures are interrelated and coordinated – but this exception is a function related to the importance of rice to the people. Other volume measures are not interrelated. Monetary units are related to one another but only because the relation is imposed by Western culture.

Third, most measurements are approximate, unless there is a real need for exactness. The phenomenal ability of Kpelle illiterate adults to estimate numbers of cups of dry rice depends on their need to buy and sell rice. The Kpelle can speak of exact and approximate measurement – but these terms would be relevant only in the case of trade goods.

Fourth, these measures are made quantitative primarily in economic activities. Length, money, and volume are all quantified because there is an economic need. People have farms, produce crops, sell their surplus, buy other goods, and do so quantitatively. Time is rarely quantified, because it is not as important economically. It is true that some economic factors enter in – the week is the market cycle, the month and year are tied to farming. But time is primarily qualitative, reflecting the character of the moment, not its numerical relation to other moments.

Knowledge and Truth

We can attempt to formulate the Kpelle view of knowledge and truth from the foregoing. Knowledge is the ability to demonstrate one's mastery of the Kpelle way of life. Truth is the conformity of one's statements and actions to that way of life. These definitions are, of course, profoundly relativistic. They are without substance outside the boundaries of Kpelle land. And, indeed, the Kpelle man recognizes that each culture has the right to set its own standards, to recognize knowledge for itself, and to submit to its own truth.

Many facts about the Kpelle seem to fall into place if it is recognized that for them there are no ultimate standards, that the culture is its own reason for existence, that truths are self-validating. The absence of ultimate standards, a direct consequence of the Kpelle understanding of truth and knowledge, is evident in the Kpelle man's willingness to recognize another man's way of life in his own land. The Chinese can grow up to ten times as much rice as the Kpelle under comparable conditions – but that is the Chinese way, not the Kpelle way. The Vai do not eat monkeys and the Kpelle do. Americans boil their water, and the Kpelle do not. The Kpelle man seems to be unconcerned about the contradiction because to him there seems to be no contradiction. Each tribe has its own ways, and the fact that they differ is not at all surprising. This complaisant tolerance might be one of the principal reasons why the Kpelle do not feel challenged to accept the proposals for change made by outsiders. Those children who go to school and acquire a new set of values and ideas are simply regarded as tribal emigrants. They have joined a new tribe by their own choice. What they now do and think is, therefore, quite naturally different from what their parents do and think. They are no longer Kpelle, and they certainly have nothing to tell their parents.

That the Kpelle culture is its own reason for existence is a clear corollary of Kpelle concepts of truth and knowledge. There seem to be ultimately no reasons in education and problem-solving except that most fundamental of all reasons – authority. Moreover, authoritative truths are self-validating. Yesterday's statement of a given truth is the justification for today's statement of it and for tomorrow's action based on it. Thus all values are rooted in the past, and change in essential areas is consequently feared. Such change threatens to shatter the self-validating system of authority. It is not so much 'what is, is is right', as 'what has been, is right'.

This explains why knowledge is primarily a possession of the elders. They have been in most intimate contact with the past. They *are* the past, living on in the present. It rends the fabric of Kpelle society for a man to challenge the authority of his elders. The new generation must listen and imitate, must be subservient, until one day they too will be the living embodiment of the tradition.

Secrecy is basic to Kpelle culture. A child cannot understand the past until he joins the secret society, which is the agency of preservation of the past. A child must mature, must be disciplined, must be prepared to enter into full possession of his culture. He must be shaped and molded so that he will have no desire to change what he has inherited. He must wait silently until his turn arrives to be the elder. Important men in the village became angry when asked how they knew certain mathematical facts. They would not answer. This was not information to be given out lightly, even if they knew the answer. For the old people, a fact is a fact. It cannot be called into doubt. It is self-validating, and needs no reason to support it. The child who asks 'why?' is considered 'frisky' and is beaten for his curiosity.

Knowledge for its own sake seems to have no place in Kpelle society. Education fashions the child in the mold of his ancestors. He learns to do what his parents and the village and the tribe and the history of his people force him to do. Knowledge as a preservative of the community, and as a support for the prestige of the elders, has great value. Education perpetuates a way of life, and so produces a reverence for what has been. It stifles individual creativity that the system might survive.

This helps to explain why 'circular' reasoning seems so prevalent in Kpelle thought. Recall the cases we have mentioned. A person who confesses the crime of killing a baby through witchcraft will have two pieces of evidence for his crime: the baby died, and he had a dream about eating meat. The baby died because he ate him in his dream. And it was the baby he ate in his dream because the because the baby died. Or, women are convinced that they have children because the old woman living in the 'spirit' tree on the edge of town has helped them. They know that the old woman helped them because they have children. In Kpelle society, facts are closed to an empirical test and to the influence of the outside world. Each facet of the tradition is justified by the whole of the tradition, and the whole of the tradition is justified by the parts.

A fact, perhaps a gem of wisdom supported by the elders, is not useful because it will lead to new activities, or because it will open up hitherto unknown pathways to knowledge. What is known is known by the elders, and will be known in due course by the new generation. And what is unknown is destined never to be known. So knowledge is largely unproductive, and there seems to be little need to transfer it to new situations. A fact is relevant in its own context but not in another. One tragic instance of this inability and unwillingness to transfer learning is the case of a worker in a local clinic. His job was to explain to his own Kpelle tribal people the importance of proper medical procedure, so that they would obey the doctor's orders. But when his own child was sick, he did not bring him to the clinic, but allowed him to be treated with traditional medicine. The child died of a disease which could easily have been cured. For this man clinic knowledge had its place within the clinic, and not in his home village.

What then is the need of a careful, analytic, isolating use of language? Why should a Kpelle man pay close attention to the denotation of words and the implications of statements? Such behavior is not ordinarily essential to survival within the Kpelle system. The connotation of words is far more important. A person wins an argument by showing the support of Kpelle tradition for the actions which everyone knows are his. He need not indulge in logical deduction or quote evidence; he need only establish a convincing context for his words and deeds.

For scientists, information is productive, open to challenge and modification, and a source of suggestions for new ways of doing things. In Kpelle society, information is definitive, closed, and conservative. Most Kpelle cannot conceive of a culture not bound to authoritative structures and secrets, but dynamic and creative. In short, his way and the scientist's way are in complete opposition.

In addition to the observations and experimental work (already cited in this book) which support this analysis, there are two other lines of evidence which seem pertinent to a discussion of the Kpelle world view.

Terminology

The first line of evidence comes from an analysis of Kpelle words for truth and knowledge. Contrary to any simplistic hypothesis about the relation between a culture's vocabulary for verbalizing about knowledge and their world view, the Kpelle have a well-developed system of knowledge words. They have terms which correspond roughly to our English words know, believe, true, opinion, trust, error, forget, understand, think, lie, clarify, overlook. The sentences in which these terms are used parallel very closely the corresponding sentences in English. The contrast with our Western scientific method is not at all apparent from this account of Kpelle terminology.

However, we think it would be a mistake to reject our findings on the basis of linguistic evidence. In fact, if we look a bit deeper, we find that we should expect the language to operate in this way. The Kpelle have an internally consistent system of life and thought, in which a person learns, thinks, knows, believes, trusts, forgets, lies, is clever or stupid, honest or dishonest. All of these actions or states are as appropriate within a tradition-oriented, radically relativistic society, as they are within a truth-oriented, scientifically inclined society. The important thing is the use of these words in a context wider than the simply linguistic one. We have found this usage among the Kpelle to be radically different from the usage we expect in the Western scientific community.

49

City Lives *

Alfred Schutz

The fact that the same object has a different appearance to various observers has been illustrated by some philosophers by the example of a city, which though always the same, appears different to different persons according to their individual standpoints. I do not wish to overwork this metaphor, but it helps to make clear the difference between our view of the social world in which we naively live and the social world which is the object of scientific observations. The man brought up in a town will find his way in its streets by following the habits he has acquired in his daily occupations. He may not have a consistent conception of the organisation of the city, and, if he uses the underground railway to go to his office, a large part of the city may remain unknown to him. Nevertheless, he will have a proper sense of the distances between different places and of the directions in which the different points are situated relatively to whatever he regards as the centre. This centre will usually be his home, and it may be sufficient for him to know that he will find nearby an underground line or a bus leading to certain other points to bring them all within his reach. He can, therefore, say that he knows his town, and, though this knowledge is of a very incoherent kind, it is sufficient for all his practical needs.

When a stranger comes to the town, he has to learn to orientate himself in it and to know it. Nothing is self-explanatory for him and he has to ask an expert, in this case a native, to learn how to get from one point to another. He may, of course, refer to a map of the town, but even to use the map successfully he must know the meaning of the signs on the map, the exact point within the town where he stands and its correlative on the map, and at least one more point in order correctly to relate the signs on the map to the real objects in the city.

Entirely different means of orientation must be used by the cartographer who has to draw a map of the city. There are several ways

* 'The Problem of Rationality in the Social World', *Economica*, 1943, from *Collected Papers*, **3**, A BRODERSEN, Martinus Nijhoff, The Hague.

open to him. He can start with a photograph taken from an aeroplane; he can place a theodolite at a known point, measure a certain distance and calculate trigonometrical functions, etc. The science of cartography has developed a standard for such operations, elements the cartographer must know before he begins to draw his map, and rules he must observe if he is to draw his map correctly. The town is the same for all three persons we have mentioned – the native, the foreigner and the cartographer – but for the native it has a special meaning: 'my home town'; for the foreigner it is a place within which he has to live and work for some time: for the cartographer it is an object of his science, he is interested in it only for the purposes of drawing a map. We may say that the same object is considered from different levels.

We should certainly be surprised if we found a cartographer in mapping a town restricting himself to collecting information from natives. Nevertheless, social scientists frequently choose this strange method. They forget that their scientific work is done on a level of interpretation and understanding different from the naïve attitudes of orientation and interpretation peculiar to people in daily life. When these social scientists speak of different levels, they frequently consider the difference between the two levels as entirely and simply one of the degree of concreteness or generality. These two terms, however, are no more than chapter headings for much more complicated problems than those which they directly suggest.

In our daily life, as in our scientific world, we, as human beings, all have the tendency to presume, more or less naïvely, that what we have once verified as valid will remain valid throughout the future, and that what appeared to us beyond question yesterday will still be beyond all question tomorrow. This naïve presumption may be made without danger if we deal with propositions of a purely logical character, or with empirical statements of a very high generality, though it can be shown that these kinds of propositions, too, have only a limited realm of applicability. On the other hand, at a so-called concrete level, we are forced to admit very many suppositions and implications as beyond question. We can even consider the level of our actual research as defined by the total of unquestioned pre-suppositions which we make by placing ourselves at the specific standpoint from which we envisage the interrelation of problems and aspects under scrutiny. Accordingly, passing from one level to another would involve that certain pre-suppositions of our research formerly regarded as beyond all question would now be called in question; and what was formerly a datum of our problem would now become problematic itself. But the simple fact that new problems and aspects of facts emerge with the shift in the point of view, while others that were formerly in the centre of our question disappear, is sufficient to initiate a thorough modification of the meaning of all the terms correctly used at the former level. Careful control of such modifications of the meaning is, therefore, indispensable if we are to avoid the risk of naïvely taking over from one level to another terms and propositions whose validity is essentially limited to a certain level, that is, to its implied suppositions.

Philosophical and in particular phenomenological theory has made very important contributions toward the better understanding of this phenomenon. However, we need not concern ourselves here with this very complicated problem from the phenomenological viewpoint. It will be sufficient to refer to an outstanding thinker of the English-speaking world; to William James and his theory of conception. It was he who taught us that each of our concepts has its fringes surrounding a nucleus of its unmodified meaning. 'In all our voluntary thinking,' he says, 'there is some topic or subject about which all the members of the thought revolve. Relation to our topic or interest is constantly felt in the fringe of our concepts. Each word in a sentence is felt, not only as a word, but as having a meaning. The meaning of a word taken thus dynamically in a sentence may be quite different from its meaning if taken statically or without context.'

It is not for us to discuss here James's theory of the nature of such fringes and their genesis in the stream of thought. For our purpose it will be sufficient to say that already the connection in which a concept or a term is used, and its relation to the topic of interest (and this topic of interest is in our case the *problem*), create specific modifications of the fringes surrounding the nucleus, or even of the nucleus itself. It was also William James who explained that we do not apperceive isolated phenomena, but rather a field of several interrelated and interwoven things as it emerges in the stream of our thought. This theory explains sufficiently for our purposes the phenomenon of the meaning of a term being modified as we pass to another level. I think that these superficial references will be sufficient to indicate the nature of the problem we are dealing with.

The term 'rationality', or at least the concept it envisages, has, within the framework of social science, the specific role of a 'key concept'. It is peculiar to key concepts that, once introduced into an apparently uniform system, they constitute the differentiations between the points of view which we call levels. The meaning of such key concepts therefore, does not depend on the level of the actual research, but, on the contrary, the level on which the research may be done depends upon the meaning attributed to the key concept, the introduction of which has for the first time divided what formerly appeared as a homogeneous field of research into several different levels. Anticipating what we shall have to prove later, we shall say that the level made accessible by the introduction of the term 'rational action' as a chief principle of the method of social sciences is nothing else than the level of theoretical observations and interpretation of the social world.

50

Neo-Tylorianism:
Sound Sense or Sinister Prejudice? *

Robin Horton

Over the last year or two a new pejorative, 'neo-Tylorian', has entered the vocabulary of British social anthropologists. What error is it supposed to castigate?

The short answer seems to be that when someone in a pre-literate society answers questions about the cause of an event by making a statement concerning the activities of invisible personal beings, the neo-Tylorian (following his ancestor Sir E B Tylor) takes the statement at its face value. He accepts it as an attempt at explanation, and goes on to ask why members of the culture in question should try to explain things in this unfamiliar way.

To the layman, this intellectualist approach is likely to seem self-evidently sensible. To the orthodox social anthropologist, however, it is misguided in the extreme. For the anthropologist, it is the height of error to take pre-literate religious belief-statements at their face value. Such statements may be many things; but they are not really attempts at explanation, and should not be analysed as such[1].

This is a very odd position. And its oddity stands out all the more clearly when one reflects that nothings of the kind has ever occurred to members of any other discipline concerned with the study of human beliefs. Thus historians of ideas have long been engaged in trying to answer questions as to why Europeans of earlier ages should have sought to explain worldly events in theoretical terms very different from those to which we are now accustomed. But however strange these theoretical terms have seemed, the historians have never stopped to doubt whether they should take the statements containing them at their face value. For the historians, such statements give every appearance of being attempts at explanation, and should therefore be analysed and interpreted as such[2].

Why should the intellectualist approach, which is perfectly satisfactory to the historian of earlier European ideas, appear so unsatisfactory to the social anthropologist dealing with the ideas of pre-literate,

* *Man* (NS) **3**, 1968.

non-European cultures? Certainly results can have very little to do with the matter. For the historian of ideas, operating on the premiss that 'things are what they seem', has been forging ahead most successfully with his interpretation of the European thought-tradition; but the social anthropologist, operating on the premiss that 'things are *not* what they seem', has had little success in explaining why pre-literate peoples have the kind of ideas they do. If the anthropologist is so adamant in refusing to return to the more straightforward and apparently more productive methods favoured by the historian of ideas, he must have some very powerful negative arguments to support him. In this article, I shall try to identify these arguments and examine their worth. There seem, in fact, to be five principal arguments involved; and in what follows, I shall review them one by one. For illustration, I shall draw principally on the African material with which I am most familiar.

1 *In the sort of pre-literate cultures that social anthropologists study, there has been little development of that ideal of objective understanding of the world which is so central to the modern Western ethos. Hence intellectualist interpretations of the ideas of such cultures are out of order*[3].

Now I think it is fair to say that the emergence of the ideal of objectivity is something peculiar to modern Western culture. But anthropologists using this fact to rule out intellectualist interpretation in non-Western cultures seem to have misunderstood what is involved. Thus the emergence of an ideal of objectivity does not mean the growth of an interest in explanation where there was none before. Rather, it means the growth of a conviction that this interest, if it is to be pursued effectively, must be segregated from the influence of political manipulation, aesthetic values, wish-fulfilment, and so on. Pre-objective cultures, then, are not cultures where the desire to make sense of the world is absent. They are cultures where this desire is still intricately interwoven with many others. Hence what is required in studying them is not an abstention from intellectualist analysis, but a delicate balancing of intellectualist with political, aesthetic and other analyses.

Even with such a balanced, many-angled approach, there is good reason for thinking that, so far as beliefs and ideas are concerned, the intellectualist analysis must take precedence over others. The force of this contention is greatest in relation to the question of political manipulation. Modern social anthropologists have been fascinated by the political manipulation of ideas – perhaps because it is one of the most obvious bridges between the Senior Common Room and the Assembly Place Under the Iroko Tree. However, their analysis of such manipulation has a curious unreality; and I think it can be shown that this unreality is a direct outcome of the policy of rushing in with a political analysis before having made an intellectualist analysis.

An extreme illustration of this point is provided by Edmund Leach's *Political systems of highland Burma* (1954). Leach maintains that Kachin ideas about *nats* (spirits) are nothing but counters in the language of political argument; and it is precisely this contention which convinces one that his analysis is unreal. One cannot help protesting that if the *nats* are nothing more than counters in the power game, why do Kachins waste so much time talking about them? Why do they not couch their political arguments more directly? Less extreme but more instructive is John Middleton's *Lugbara religion* (1960). Here is a book which starts with a vivid but rather conventional analysis of the way in which influential members of Lugbara communities manipulate ideas of ancestral power for political purposes, and ends with what is perhaps the most brilliant intellectualist analysis of an African system of religious ideas yet made. Reading this book in the order in which it was written, one gets the same feeling of unreality as one had from Leach. Why do these people not get on with the politics? Rereading it with the intellectualist analysis put in before the political, one immediately regains a sense of reality. Now it becomes obvious why the old men spend such a lot of time talking about ancestral power and witchcraft when they are struggling for political position. It is because these ideas mean so much to Lugbara as intellectual tools for making sense of the world, that they are such powerful instruments in the hands of the politicians. If they meant nothing in intellectual terms, they would be nothing in the hands of the politicians.

It is because he *has* got things in the right order that a novelist of traditional African life like Chinua Achebe gives us a sense of reality missing from the work of the anthropologists. His *Arrow of God* (1964) in particular, deals with the intricate relations between religious beliefs and power struggles. Indeed, its two principal protagonists are priestly politicians. As backcloth to the struggle between the Eze Ulu and the Eze Idemili, Achebe gives us a compelling picture of the key place that their deities, Ulu and Idemili, occupy in the village world view. It is this backcloth that makes us see not only what powerful tools these deities are in the hands of would-be manipulators, but also what strict limits there must be to manipulation when those involved believe in and live by the ideas they are manipulating. Achebe's book, of course, is a novel and not a work of analysis; but a careful reading of it would do much to help anthropologists regain a sense of proportion in these matters.

To conclude, it is clear that social anthropologists have been seriously misled by the glib phrase 'manipulation of ideas'. What politicians manipulate is not ideas, but people's dependence on ideas as means of ordering, explaining, predicting and controlling their world. Only a prior analysis of the nature of this dependence can pave the way for an adequate grasp of the scope and limitations of manipulation.

2 *Members of pre-literate cultures tend to be of a practical rather than of a theoretical bent. Hence analyses that treat the religious ideas of such cultures as explanatory theories are beside the point*[4].

My first comment on this argument is that the truth of the premiss is dubious. West African experience certainly makes one very chary of asserting that preliterate cultures lack people whose interest in theory outruns their practical concern. Nearly all of us who have worked in this area know the occasional old men who, having retired from the hurly-burly of everyday life, spend much of their time thinking it through and trying to make sense of it. And although there may be few such people in any particular community, they often play a disproportionate part in transmitting ideas to the next generation.

My second comment is that the argument appears to be based on the misleading colloquial opposition of 'theory' and 'practice'. As I have pointed out in a recent article, one of the principal intellectual functions of traditional African religious theory is that of placing everyday events in a wider causal context than common sense provides (HORTON 1967a: 53–8). Traditional religious theory, indeed, complements common sense in its concern for the diagnosis, prediction and control of events. It is thus as intimately linked as is common sense with the practical concerns of its users. Conversely, it is reasonable to suppose that these practical concerns have played as great a part in stimulating the development of theory as they have in stimulating the development of common sense. So even if there were such a thing as a culture carried entirely by hard-headed pragmatists, one would still expect to find plenty of theory in it. Even in such a culture, then, there would be room for an intellectualist analysis.

3 *The ideas of pre-literate cultures seldom form logically consistent systems. Hence in such cultures an intellectualist analysis, which assumes a search for logical consistency, is inappropriate*[5].

A short answer to this argument is that the modern Western world-view is far from forming a logically consistent whole – especially where ideas about the nature of man are concerned! But this in no way stops us from interpreting the history of Western thought in terms of a striving for consistency. The achievement of consistency is one thing; the striving for it quite another.

Some social anthropologists go so far as to admit the reality of this striving in pre-literate cultures, but suggest that those involved are few in number and highly atypical[6]. Here, in fact, we are back with our old men whose interest in theory outruns their practical concern; and the answer is much the same as that given to argument 2. These people may be few and atypical, but they characteristically play a crucial part in the transmission of ideas to the next generation. Hence the ideas of the general population bear the stamp of their interests.

In traditional Africa, the most significant index of the striving for consistency is the well-nigh ubiquitous presence of the idea of a supreme being who is the sustainer of all the lesser spiritual agencies, and who is indeed the ultimate prime mover of everything. If it is nothing else, this concept is surely an assertion that beneath the diversity and apparent haphazardness of the world of appearance, there is an ultimate unity and an ultimate consistency. The ways of the supreme being are often said to be somewhat inscrutable as compared with the ways of the lesser spirits – an admission that the details of this ultimate unity and consistency are perhaps beyond the power of men to work out. But the very existence of the concept is a profession of faith that it is there.

4 *The ideas which neo-Tylorians treat as explanatory are religious ideas, and we know from our experience in modern Western culture that religious ideas do not 'really' attempt to explain the events in the space-time world. They are concerned with other things.*[7]

Here we have the fallacy of regarding belief in spiritual beings as something which serves the same basic human aspiration wherever it occurs. A little thought should remind us that over the last fifteen hundred years of European history, religion has slowly abdicated a very considerable interest in the explanation, prediction and control of worldly events to the emerging sciences (FIRTH 1950). Hence modern western Christianity's lack of interest in these things is a very poor index by which to judge early Christianity. It is an even poorer index by which to judge traditional religions in pre-literate cultures.

All this was brought home to me very vividly by an aspect of my own fieldwork experience among the Kalabari people of the Niger delta. In Kalabari communities, traditional religious practitioners, orthodox Christian churches and breakaway spiritualist sects form a most interesting triangle. In this triangle, traditional practitioners and spiritualist sects are sworn enemies, whilst both compete for the friendship of the orthodox churches. Why should this be so? In the first place, the traditional practitioners and the spiritualists are direct competitors. Both diagnose and attempt to cure a variety of misfortunes and diseases, and their claims to significance are based on these activities. The diagnostic and curative techniques of the spiritualists are in fact so similar to those of the traditionalists that the latter often accuse them of stealing traditional stock-in-trade only to bring it out again under a Christian label. With the aid of some very convincing biblical exegesis, however, the spiritualists claim they are reverting, not to traditional Kalabari beliefs and practices, but to early Christian beliefs and practices. As a spectator on the sidelines, I am inclined to think that both claims are correct, and that in their overriding concern for the explanation, prediction and control of worldly events, the spiritualists draw inspiration both from Kalabari traditionalists and from elements in the Bible that reflect early Christian ideas. Both traditionalists and spiritualists are able to adopt an amiable attitude toward the orthodox churches precisely because the latter abstain from this-worldly predictive and explanatory claims, and centre their work on the business of salvation. As several attenders at spiritualist prayer houses have put it to me: 'The prayer houses cure our sicknesses and the churches pilot [*sic*] our souls'.

Although this is only one example, it could be paralleled in many parts of Africa. It does, I think, serve to bring home to us the fact that modern western Christianity, as a religion, is somewhat peculiar in its lack of concern with the explanation of this-worldly events. This characteristic, therefore, cannot be used to justify opposition to intellectualist analysis of other religious systems.

5 *If we are wrong-headed enough to treat them as explanations, we have to admit that traditional religious beliefs are mistaken. And the only possible interpretation of such mistakes is that they are the product of childish ignorance. Neo-Tylorians who take traditional beliefs at their face value therefore subscribe to the stereotype of the 'ignorant savage' and are illiberal racists. If on the other hand we treat them as having intentions which, despite appearances, are quite other than explanatory, we no longer have to evaluate traditional beliefs in the light of the canons of adequacy current in the sciences. Anthropologists who take this line are therefore not committed to the 'ignorant savage' stereotype. They are good liberals.*

The germs of this argument, if argument it can be called, are to be found in Lévy-Bruhl's early criticism of Tylor and Frazer[8]. Hints of it recur in many expositions of the orthodox anti-intellectualist position over the last two decades; and it has recently been given a highly explicit formulation by Leach[9]. My own feeling is that it is this sort of attitude that underpins and lends force to all the other arguments we have considered. In assessing its appeal, we shall do well to note its affinities with that other powerful offspring of Lévy-Bruhl's work, the militant ideology of Negritude.

There is a short and sharp answer to this whole line of thought. It is that, by all normal criteria of assessment, many of the religious beliefs of pre-literate cultures *are* primarily explanatory in intent; that by the criteria of the sciences, many of them *are* mistaken; and that to wriggle out of admitting this by the pretence that such beliefs are somehow not really what they obviously are is simply to distort facts under the influence of extraneous values. In this respect liberal anthropology is no better than Fascist anthropology, racist anthropology, or what-have-you.

So much for the straight case against the liberals. It seems unlikely, however, that a frontal attack of this kind will ever carry a position defended by irrational obstacles of the strength we are facing here. What we have to do is weaken the liberal position by persuading its adherents that the facts do not really come into conflict with their most cherished values.

Let us start by asking: what is so very dreadful about holding theories which later turn out to be mistaken? The liberals, of course, are very put off by Tylor's contention that the mistaken theories of pre-literate peoples are the outcome of a childish mentality. But surely we do not have to follow Tylor in thinking that childishness is the only possible explanation for mistaken theories. On the contrary, it seems the least plausible of all conceivable explanations. In recent articles, I myself have explored what seems a fairly convincing interpretation of such mistakes, and one that casts no slur at all on the mental capacity or maturity of the peoples concerned (HORTON 1967a).

For those who will not easily see the point when it is made about pre-literate peoples, let us move over to the history of European ideas, and more specifically to the history of the sciences. Contrary to the view of many social anthropologists, science, though progressive, is not in any simple sense cumulative. It progresses through the overthrow of a goodish theory by one that gives wider coverage of the data; through the overthrow of this better theory by one that gives still wider coverage, and so on [10]. Under this system, today's intellectual hero is inevitably tomorrow's mistaken man. But the quality of his achievement will still stand tomorrow. Indeed, it is his achievement which was made possible the further advance that proclaims him mistaken. Newton is no less a hero for the overthrow of classical physics. Heisenberg will be no less a hero for the overthrow of quantum theory.

The trouble with the liberals, as I see it, is the belief that although

554

their own theoretical framework may be elaborated by future generations, it will not be found radically mistaken. It is this belief which
makes them feel there is something illiberal about imputing mistakes
to pre-literate theorists. But if what I have said about the nature of
scientific progress is correct, their view of their own conceptual
framework is unduly optimistic. And if their own framework is
inevitably going to be tomorrow's mistake, what is illiberal about
imputing mistakes to preliterates?

From here it is but a small step to my final piece of persuasion. I
should like to suggest to the liberals that in certain fields the dichot-
omies 'wrong/right', 'mistaken/correct' are in fact far too strong to
do justice to the relation between the beliefs of pre-literates and those
of modern Westerners.

One of the things that makes the liberals see pre-literate explanatory theories as totally wrong-headed is the fact that they characteristically feature invisible personal beings. Here the positivist background of so many of them obtrudes itself. As positivists, they view
themselves as revolutionaries in action against the old, pre-scientific
order. And like most revolutionaries, their besetting error is that, in
trying to liquidate the old order, they throw out the baby with the
bathwater. Thus because many of the explanatory beliefs of pre-
scientific Europe happen to have been couched in personal terms,
they have declared any theory couched in such terms as *ipso facto*
beyond the pale of the rational. In so doing, however, they have
thrown out the basic canon of scientific method which lays it down
that no type of theory can be judged right or wrong solely on the
grounds of its content.

A very vivid exposition of this canon is to be found in the astronomer Fred Hoyle's science-fiction novel *The black cloud*. Here we find
an internatioational committee of scientists trying to explain the
nature and behaviour of a terrible opaque cloud which, coming between the earth and the sun, threatens to freeze up the planet. In
what is clearly intended as a sermon on scientific method, Hoyle takes
as his hero a gruff, monosyllabic Russian. All the others laugh at this
man because, whenever they ask for his views, he simply repeats
'Bastard in cloud!' – thus showing himself to be either a joker in poor
taste or a deluded animist. Later, however, it is the animist who has
the laugh; for his theory and his alone covers the various puzzling
aspects of the phenomenon, and provides a basis for the prediction of
its behaviour.

Animistic explanations, then, have nothing *prima facie* unreasonable
about them; and the liberal has no cause to blush when he meets
them in pre-literate cultures.

The liberal can, of course, concede all that has been said so far, and still object that when it comes to accounting for the facts, the animistic beliefs of pre-literate cultures, considered as theories, make a very poor showing alongside the impersonal theories of the West. This is certainly true enough where we are dealing with inanimate matter, with plants, and with lower animals; but the nearer we come to the 'higher' activities of man, the more dubious it becomes. Traditional beliefs have very little of interest to say to the physicist, the chemist, and the biologist; but they have a surprising amount to say to the psychologist and the sociologist.

The truth of this contention is well illustrated by Evans-Pritchard's classic *Witchcraft, oracles and magic among the Azande* (1937). This monograph was the first to document in detail the way in which members of a traditional African culture used a corpus of explanatory 'mystical' theory to make sense of and cope with the vicissitudes of their everyday lives. In particular, it highlighted the connexion made by Zande theory between human misfortune and disturbance in the social fabric – a connexion which later research showed was typical of traditional thought. When this book came out thirty years ago, both the author and his readers talked on the assumption that, judged by the criteria of the sciences, Zande ideas on this subject were mistakes. Today, I think many commentators would be hesitant about making such an assumption. In an age where social disturbance, operating via psychological disturbance, is recognised as a probable contributor to a whole spectrum of human misfortunes ranging from high blood pressure to falling under a bus, it is no longer so easy to say that the Zande thinker is just mistaken. Now what brought about this change in Western beliefs? One factor at least seems to have been inspiration by just those pre-literate beliefs that once were considered so erroneous. It is not for nothing that Walter B Cannon, commonly acknowledged as 'the father of psychosomatic medicine', called one of his early articles on the subject 'Voodoo death' (1965).

Another book which is likely to be seminal in this respect is Fortes's *Oedipus and Job in west African religion* (1959). This book deals with what may be called Tallensi social psychology. It reveals a system of concepts in many ways uncannily similar to those of Western psychoanalysts, but with certain significant differences. Notably, Tallensi concepts postulate a somewhat different distribution of motives as between conscious and unconscious sectors of the mind (HORTON 1961). In a decade in which psychiatrists are becoming increasingly aware of the culture-bound nature of Western psychodynamic concepts, this and other west African social psychologies clearly merit a respectful hearing.

556

If the reader feels tempted to smile patronisingly at the last two paragraphs, he should ask himself the following question. After all the sound and the fury and the self-congratulation have been discounted, just how far have psychoanalysis, behaviourism, structural-functionalism, and other basic Western theories of higher human behaviour really advanced our understanding of ourselves? If he answers honestly, I think he will stop smiling.

Let me sum up on all this. Behind the liberal's concern to play down the explanatory aspect of pre-literate religious beliefs lies a strong streak of patronage. Basically, he believes that, so far as explanatory value is concerned, his theories are in some absolute and final sense right, whilst pre-literate theories are in some equally absolute sense wrong. What I have tried to point out here is that the rightness of the current western belief-system is in the nature of things transitory; and that in the sphere of 'higher' human behaviour, at least, pre-literate belief-systems may from time to time be the source of insights that seriously shake some Western foundations. In reminding the liberal of these things, I hope I have done something towards removing the sentimental obstacles which have hitherto prevented him from considering the intellectualist approach on its merits.

I should like to end this rather polemical article on a note of reconciliation. Social anthropologists often talk as though one had to choose between an intellectualist and a sociological analysis of pre-literate beliefs. In fact, however, such a choice is neither necessary nor desirable.

Tylor's intellectualism, it is true, was innocent of any sociological overtones. To the question of why some cultures had 'animistic' and others 'scientific' world-views, his ultimate answer was that members of the first lot of cultures had a childish mentality, whilst members of the second lot had an adult mentality. Whatever else this was, it was certainly not a sociological explanation. But, as I said earlier, we can be intellectualists without following Tylor in other respects.

As I see it, the only thing the intellectualist is entitled to ask is that we begin by analysing pre-literate belief statements in terms of the overt explanatory ends they serve. After this, he should welcome all comers – sociologists, psychoanalysts, the lot. In point of fact, it is almost impossible to make an intellectualist analysis of belief statements without doing some sociology in the process. This was borne in upon me most forcibly when I embarked on a generalised comparison of African and Western thought-traditions. I was driven to an intellectualist approach to this task by the singular failure of the anti-intellectualist establishment to make any headway with it. In trying to make intellectualist analyses of various traditional African religious theories, however, I came up against the fact that they were above all theories of society and of the individual's place in it. Hence it was impossible to gain understanding of them without taking detailed account of the social organisations whose workings they were concerned to make sense of. Much the same thing happened when I tried to understand why African traditional cultures favoured person-alised models for their explanatory tasks, while Western culture favoured impersonal models. In tackling the question, I started out with the intellectualist assumption that both the gods and spirits of traditional Africa and the ultimate particles and forces of the Western world-view were alternative means to what was basically the same explanatory end. This assumption led to the further question of why the theoretical models of the two sets of cultures were founded on such very different analogies. And in trying to answer this second question, I found I had to take into account such unambiguously sociological variables as stability and complexity of social organisation, and the relation between society and its non-human environment (HORTON 1967a: 64–5).

On the basis of my own work, then, I regard the intellectualist approach as a healthy corrective to certain current fashions in social anthropology. I do not regard it as an alternative to sociological analysis.

Notes

[1] Complaints about a 'Neo-Tylorian' or 'Back to Frazer' movement seem to have been touched off by a number of recent challenges to the anti-intellectualist establishment in British social anthropology. One of the first of these was made by Jarvie (1964), in a colourful plea for a return to intellec-tualism roughly as practised by Frazer. Later came provocative articles by Geertz and Spiro (1966) in a volume resulting from a confrontation of British and American social anthropologists. At a more particular level, the return to intellectualism was advocated in Young's (1966) paper on the Jukun king-ship. Three of my own recent papers have taken much the same intellectualist line (Horton 1964; 1967a; 1967b).

The response to these intellectualist views has been a grumbling one. Jar-vie's book got a generally ill-tempered reception, typical of which was Ardener's (1965) review. Among more concerted statements of opposition, one may single out Beattie's (1966) programmatic paper, which puts very strongly the thesis that pre-literate magico-religious beliefs are 'not what they seem'. One may also note the anti-intellectualist injunctions in ch 5 of Douglas's brilliant *Purity and danger* (1966) – injunctions which come a little surprisingly from the author of a revolutionary intellectualist interpretation of pollution behaviour. Finally, there is Leach's strongly worded condemnation (1967), which contends that the intellectualist approach to pre-literate beliefs is not only wrong, but symptomatic of vicious prejudice.

[2] For good account of the intellectualist assumptions of modern historians of science, see the 'Introduction' to Kuhn (1962).

[3] Douglas (1966: ch 5) warns against intellectualist approaches to those cultures which, as she puts it, have not developed a 'conscious reaching for objectivity'.

[4] This again is implied in Douglas (1966: ch 5). See for instance p 89: 'It is a practical interest in living and not an academic interest in metaphysics which has produced these beliefs . . .' For an earlier formulation, see Gluckman (1963), especially p 141: 'They had elaborate theologies, but these were developed in social relations, rather than in intellectual speculations'.

[5] Richards (1967: 291) remarks on the general reluctance of British social anthropologists to make the striving for consistency the starting-point of their analyses. This reluctance is exemplified by Douglas (1966: ch 5).

[6] Richards (1967: 291) comments: 'Sceptical British anthropologists have also suggested from time to time that such consistent and logical systems as those described in the case of the Dogon must be the product of a single mind and a philosophical one at that – an Ogotemmêli in fact.'

[7] This is one of the arguments in Leach (1967). For instance: 'An alternative way of explaining a belief which is factually untrue is to say that it is a species of religious dogma; the truth which it expresses does not relate to the ordinary matter-of-fact world of everyday things but to metaphysics.'

[8] See the critique of 'L'Ecole Anglaise' in the introduction to Lévy-Bruhl (1910).

[9] The whole tone of Leach (1967) is one of strong moral disapproval of the intellectualist approach. Thus he accuses Spiro of being 'positively eager to believe that the aborigines were ignorant' and says that intellectualists 'seem to gain assurance from supposing that the people they study have the simple-minded ignorance of small children'. Since submitting this article, I have read Spiro's rejoinder to Leach (Spiro 1968). Although his argument is very similar to my own, I have left the text of the article unamended as I think it carries the argument somewhat further than he himself has taken it.

[10] For a very clear picture of this process see Kuhn (1966), especially the closing chapter on 'Progress through revolutions'.

References

c ACHEBE, *Arrow of God*. Heinemann, London, 1964.

E ARDENER, Review of *The revolution in anthropology*. *Man* **65**, 57–8, 1965.

J BEATTIE, 'Ritual and social change'. *Man* (NS) **I**, 60–74, 1966.

W B CANNON, 'Voodoo death'. In *A reader in comparative religion* (eds) W A LESSA and E Z VOGT, Harper & Row, New York, 1965.

M DOUGLAS, *Purity and danger*, Routledge and Kegan Paul, London, 1966.

E E EVANS-PRITCHARD, *Witchcraft, oracles and magic among the Azande*, Clarendon Press, Oxford, 1937.

R FIRTH, 'Religious belief and personal adjustment'. *J R anthrop Inst* **78**, 25 43, 1950.

M FORTES, *Oedipus and Job in west African religion*. Univ Press, Cambridge, 1959.

C GEERTZ, 'Religion as a cultural system'. In *Anthropological approaches to the study of religion* (ed) M BANTON (Monogr Ass social Anthrop 3). Tavistock Publications, London, 1966.

M GLUCKMAN, *Order and rebellion in tribal Africa*, Cohen & West, London, 1963.

R HORTON, 'Destiny and the unconscious in west Africa'. *Africa* **31**, 110–16, 1961.

—— Ritual man in Africa. *Africa* **34**, 85–104, 1964.

—— African traditional thought and western science. 1, *Africa* **37**, 50–71, 1967a.

—— African traditional thought and western science. 2, *Africa* **37**, 155–87, 1967b.

F HOYLE, *The black cloud*, Penguin, Harmondsworth, 1960.

I C JARVIE, *The revolution in anthropology*, Routledge and Kegan Paul, London, 1964.

T KUHN, *The structure of scientific revolutions*, Univ Press, Chicago, 1962.

E R LEACH, *Political systems of highland Burma*, Bell, London, 1954.

—— Virgin birth. *Proc R anthrop Inst*, 1966, 39–49, 1967.

L LEVY-BRUHL, *Les fonctions mentales dans les sociétés inférieures*, Paris: Presses Universitaires de France, 1910.

J MIDDLETON, *Lugbara religion*, Oxford Univ Press, London, 1960.

A I RICHARDS, African systems of thought: an Anglo-French dialogue. *Man* (NS) **2**, 286–98, 1967.

M E SPIRO, Religion: problems of definition and explanation. In *Anthropological approaches to the study of religion* (ed) M BANTON (Monogr Ass social Anthrop, 3), Tavistock Publications, London, 1966.

—— Virgin birth, parthenogenesis and physiological paternity: an essay in cultural interpretation. *Man* (NS) **3**, 242–61, 1968.

M YOUNG, The divine kingship of the Jukun, *Africa* **36**, 135–53, 1966.

Further Reading

General

J BARTHOLOMEW, 'The Teacher as Researcher – A Key to Innovation and Change', *Hard Cheese*, **1**, 1973.

J BARTHOLOMEW, 'Sustaining Hierarchies Through Teaching and Research', P M FLUDE and J G AHIER (eds) *Educability, Schools and Ideology*, Croome-Helm, 1974.

B R COSIN ET AL (eds), *School and Society*, Routledge and Kegan Paul in association with the Open University Press, 1971.

J D DOUGLAS (ed), *Understanding Everyday Life*, Routledge and Kegan Paul, 1971.

P FILMER ET AL (eds), *New Directions in Sociological Theory*, Collier-Macmillan, 1972.

M GREENE, *The Teacher as Stranger: Educational Philosophy in the Modern Age*, Wadsworth, 1973.

Hard Cheese – a Magazine of Education, Editor: Ted Bowden, 95a Shooters Hill Road, London SE3 8RL, 1975 onwards.

C JENKS (ed) *Rationality, Education and the Social Organization of Knowledge*, Routledge and Kegan Paul, 1976.

J O'NEILL, *Sociology as a Skin Trade*, Heinemann Educational Books, 1972.

G J WHITTY, 'Sociology and the Problem of Radical Educational Change: Notes Towards a Reconceptualization of the "New Sociology of Education"', P M FLUDE and J G AHIER (eds) *Educability, Ideology and Society*, Croome-Helm, 1974.

M F D YOUNG (ed) *Knowledge and Control – New Directions For The Sociology of Education*, Collier-Macmillan, London, 1971.

Section 1: Childhood as a Social Construct

C ACHEBE, *Arrow of God, African Writers Series*, Heinemann Educational Books.

C ACHEBE, *No Longer At Ease, African Writers Series*, Heinemann Educational Books.

C ACHEBE, *Things Fall Apart, African Writers Series*, Heinemann Educational Books.

A DEARLING, 'The Theory and Practice of Youth-Work in One Large Youth Centre', *Hard Cheese*, **2**, 1973.

C EKWENSI, *Burning Grass, African Writers Series*, Heinemann Educational Books.

M GORKY, *My Childhood*, Foreign Languages Publishing House, Moscow.

J HOLT, *How Children Fail*, Pitman Publishing Corporation (1964),

Penguin Books 1969.

D INGLEBY, 'The Psychology of Child Psychology', *Hard Cheese*, **1**, 1973.

D H LAWRENCE, *Sons and Lovers*, Penguin Books.

R MACKAY, 'Conceptions of Children and Models of Socialization', H P DREITZEL (ed) *Recent Sociology* No 5: *Childhood and Socialization*, Macmillan Publishing Co, Reprinted in *Ethnomethodology*, Turner R, (ed) Penguin Books.

M MERLEAU-PONTY, 'The Child's Relations with Others', in *The Primacy of Perception*, (ed) J M EDIE, North Western University Press, 1964.

J MIDDLETON, *From Child to Adult: Studies in the Anthropology of Education*, The Natural History Press: New York, 1970.

J MURONYE, *The Only Son, African Writers Series*, Heinemann Educational Books.

I PINCHBECK and M HEWITT, *Children in English Society*, **1**, Routledge and Kegan Paul, 1969 (and **2**, 1974).

K A PORTER, *The Old Order*.

P S WILSON, 'Plowden Children', *Hard Cheese*, **2**, 1973.

R WRIGHT, *Blackboy*, Harper & Row, 1951.

L WYLIE, *Village in the Vaucluse*, (esp ch 4), Harvard University Press, 1961.

Section 2: Social Pathology Models and the Sociology of Education

S S BARATZ and J C BARATZ, 'Early Childhood Intervention: The Social Science Base of Institutional Racism', *Harvard Educational Review*, **40**, No 1, Winter; 1970, Reprinted in *Language in Education*, A CASHDAN ET AL (eds), 1972, Routledge and Kegan Paul in association with the Open University Press.

B FISHER, 'The Reconstruction of Failure', *Social Problems* **19**, No 3, 1972.

P M FLUDE, 'Sociological Accounts of Differential Educational Attainment', P M FLUDE and J G AHIER (eds) *Educability, Schools and Ideology*, Croome-Helm, 1974.

C FRAKE, 'The Diagnosis of Disease Among the Subanum of Mindanao', *American Anthropologist*, **63**, Feb 1961; reprinted in *Tinker, Tailor ... the Myth of Cultural Deprivation*, N G KEDDIE (ed) 1973, Penguin Books.

E FUCHS, 'How Teachers Learn to Help Children Fail', *Trans-action*, Sept 1968; reprinted in *Tinker, Tailor ... the Myth of Cultural Deprivation*, N G KEDDIE (ed) 1973, Penguin Books.

T GLADWIN, 'Culture and the Logical Process', in W H GOODENOUGH

562

(ed) *Explorations in Cultural Anthropology: Essays in Honour of George Peter Murdoch*, McGraw-Hill, 1964; reprinted in *Tinker, Tailor . . . the Myth of Cultural Deprivation*, N G KEDDIE (ed) 1973, Penguin Books.

J HORTON, 'Order and Conflict Theories of Social Problems', *American Journal of Sociology*, **71**, No 6, 1966.

N G KEDDIE (ed) *Tinker, Tailor . . . the Myth of Cultural Deprivation*, Penguin Books, 1973.

W LABOV, 'The Logic of Non-Standard English', in *Language and Poverty: Perspectives on a Theme*, F WILLIAMS (ed) Markham Publishing Co: New York, 1970; reprinted in *Tinker, Tailor . . . the Myth of Cultural Deprivation*, N G KEDDIE, (ed) 1973, Penguin Books.

A Consultant, 'Cultural Deprivation: a Case in Point', in *Sorting Them Out: Two Essays in Social Differentiation*, Open University Press, 1972.

N POSTMAN, 'The Politics of Reading', *Harvard Educational Review*, **40** No 2, May, 1970; reprinted in *Tinker, Tailor . . . the Myth of Cultural Deprivation*, N G KEDDIE (ed), Penguin Books, 1973.

M L WAX and R H WAX, 'Formal Education in an American Indian Community', *Social Problems Monograph*, Spring, 1964.

M L WAX and R H WAX, 'The Enemies of the People', in *Institutions and the Person*: Essays Presented to E C Hughes, H S BECKER ET AL (eds) Chicago: Aldine Press, 1968.

D WRONG, 'The Oversocialized Conception of Man in Modern Sociology', *American Sociological Review*, **26**, 1961.

Section 3: Ability as a Social Construct

B BECK, 'Welfare as a Moral Category', *Social Problems*, 258, 1968.

A V CICOUREL, *Language, Socialization and Use in Testing and Other Educational Settings*, Seminar Press, 1973.

A DAVIS, *Social Class Influences Upon Learning*, Yale University Press, 1951.

J D DOUGLAS, 'Deviance and Order in a Pluralistic Society', in *Theoretical Sociology: Perspectives and Developments*, J C MCKINNEY and E A TIRYAKIN, (eds), Appleton-Century-Crofts, 1970.

R E EGERTON, *The Cloak of Competence: Stigma in the Lives of the Mentally Retarded*, University of California Press, 1971.

G M ESLAND, 'Teaching and Learning as the Social Organization of Knowledge', in *Knowledge and Control: New Directions for the Sociology of Education*, M F D YOUNG, (ed), Collier-Macmillan, 1971.

E GOFFMAN, *Stigma: Notes on the Management of Spoiled Identity*, Prentice Hall Inc 1963, Penguin Books, 1968.

E J GOODACRE, *Teachers and Their Pupils' Home Background*, National

563

Foundation for Educational Research; extract pp 14–25 reprinted in *School and Society*, B R COSIN ET AL (eds) Routledge and Kegan Paul in association with the Open University Press, 1968.

A H HALSEY, 'Genetics, Social Structure and Intelligence', *British Journal of Sociology*, **IX**, No 1, 1958.

N G KEDDIE, 'Classroom Knowledge', in *Knowledge and Control: New Directions for the Sociology of Education*, M F D YOUNG, (ed), Collier-Macmillan, 1971.

Section 4: Teacher–Pupil Relations

H S BECKER, 'Social Class Variations in the Teacher–Pupil Relationship', *Journal of Educational Sociology*, **25**, No 4, 1952; reprinted in *School and Society*, B R COSIN ET AL (eds) Routledge and Kegan Paul in association with the Open University Press, 1971.

Y BEECHAM, 'The Making of Educational Failures', *Hard Cheese*, **2**, 1973.

E BITTNER, 'The Police on Skid Row: A Study of Peace Keeping', *American Sociological Review*, **32**, 1967.

C CASTENADA, *The Teachings of Don Juan: A Yaqui Way of Knowledge*, University of California Press, 1968; Penguin Books, 1970.

A V CICOUREL, *The Social Organization of Juvenile Justice*, John Wiley, 1968.

A K DANIELS, 'The Social Construction of Military Psychiatric Diagnoses', in *Recent Sociology No 2*, H P DRIETZEL (ed), New York: The Macmillan Company, 1970.

P FRIERE, *Cultural Action for Freedom*, Penguin Books, 1972.

B G GLASER and A L STRAUSS, 'Awareness Contexts and Social Interaction'; *American Sociological Review*, **29**, 1964; reprinted in *Symbolic Interaction*, J MANIS and B MELTZER, (eds) New York: Allyn and Bacon, 1967.

E GOFFMAN, 'The Moral Career of the Mental Patient', *Psychiatry: Journal for the Study of Interpersonal Processes*, **22**, No 2 1959; reprinted in *Asylums: Essays on the Social Situation of Mental Patients and Other Inmates*, Penguin Books, 1968.

J GUSFIELD, 'Moral Passage', *Social Problems*, **15**, No 2, 1967.

D HARGREAVES, *Social Relations in a Secondary School*, Routledge and Kegan Paul, 1967.

J HENRY, *Essays on Education*, Penguin Books, 1971.

J HOLT, *How Children Fail*, Pitman Publishing Corporation, 1964; 1969 Penguin Books.

K JOHNSON, 'Expectations in Classroom Interaction, a Case Study', *Hard Cheese*, **1**, 1973.

R M KANTER, 'The Organization Child-Experience Management in a

Nursery School', *Sociology of Education*, **45**, No 2, 1972.

C W MILLS, 'Situated Actions and Vocabularies of Motive', *American Sociological Review*, **5**, No 6; 1940, reprinted in *School and Society*, B R COSIN ET AL (eds), 1971, Routledge and Kegan Paul in association with the Open University Press.

M NANDY, 'Social Studies for a Multi-Racial Society', in *The Multi-Racial School*, J MCNEAL, and M ROGERS (eds), Penguin Books, 1971.

R C RIST, 'Student Social Class and Teacher Expectations: the Self-Fulfilling Prophecy in Ghetto Education', *Harvard Educational Review*, **40**, No 3, August, 1970.

J A ROTH, *Timetables*, Bobbs-Merrill, 1963.

A SCHUTZ, 'The Stranger', in *Collected Papers II: Studies in Social Theory*, Martinus Nijhoff: The Hague; 1964, reprinted in *School and Society*, B R COSIN ET AL (eds) 1971, Routledge and Kegan Paul in association with the Open University Press.

R STEBBING, 'The Meanings of Disorderly Behaviour', *Sociology of Education*, **44**, No 1, 1970.

J TORREY, 'Illiteracy in the Ghetto', *Harvard Educational Review*, **40**, No 2, May 1970; reprinted in *Tinker, Tailor . . . the Myth of Cultural Deprivation*, N G KEDDIE (ed) 1973, Penguin Books.

M WATKIN, 'The West African Bush School', *American Journal of Sociology*, **48**, 1942.

Section 5: Perspectives on Learning

H S BECKER, 'Becoming a Marihuana User', *American Journal of Sociology*, **59**, November 1956; reprinted in *School and Society*, B R COSIN ET AL (eds), Routledge and Kegan Paul in association with the Open University Press, 1971.

H S BECKER ET AL (eds) *Boys in White: Student Culture in Medical School*, University of Chicago Press, 1961.

H S BECKER, 'What Do They Really Learn in College?', *Trans-action*, May, 1964.

H S BECKER ET AL (eds) *Making the Grade: the Academic Side of College Life*, John Wiley and Sons Inc, 1968.

P BOHANNAN, 'Field Anthropologists and Classroom Teachers', *Social Education*, 1968.

A V CICOUREL, *Cognitive Sociology*, Penguin Books, 1972.

G E DAVIE, *The Democratic Intellect*, Edinburgh University Press, 1961.

F DAVIS, 'Professionalization and Subjective Experience', in *Institutions and the Person: Essays Presented to E C Hughes*, Chicago: Aldine Press, 1968.

H GARFINKEL, 'Passing and the Managed Achievement of Sex Status in an "Inter-sexed" Person, Part 1', in *Studies in Ethnomethodology*,

Prentice-Hall, 1967.

J GAY and M COLE, *Cultural Contexts of Thinking and Learning*, Basic Books, 1972.

B G GLASER and A L STRAUSS, *Awareness of Dying*, Chicago: Aldine Publishing Co, 1965.

J LOFLAND and R STARK, 'Becoming a World Saver', *American Sociological Review*, December, 1965.

J G MANIS and B N MELTZER (eds) *Symbolic Interaction*, Allyn and Bacon, 1967.

V OLESEN and E WHITTAKER, *The Silent Dialogue*, San Francisco: Jossey-Bass, 1968

M SPIER, 'The Everyday World of the Child', in *Understanding Everyday Life*, J D DOUGLAS (ed), Routledge and Kegan Paul, 1971.

A L STRAUSS, 'Transformations of Identity', in *Mirrors and Masks*, The Free Press: Glencoe, 1959.

Section 6: Knowledge as a Corpus

P ANDERSON, 'Patterns of National Culture', in *Student Power*, A COCKBURN and P ANDERSON (eds), Penguin Books, 1969.

R BLACKBURN *Ideology in Social Science: Readings in Critical Social Theory;* Fontana, 1972.

A BLUM, 'The Corpus of Knowledge as a Normative Order', in *Theoretical Sociology: Perspectives and Developments*, J C MCKINNEY and E A TIRYAKIN, (eds), Appleton-Century-Crofts, 1970; reprinted in *Knowledge and Control: New Directions for the Sociology of Education*, M F D YOUNG (ed), Collier-Macmillan, 1971.

P BOURDIEU, 'Systems of Education and Systems of Thought', *International Social Science Journal*, **19**, No 3 1967; reprinted in *Knowledge and Control: New Directions for the Sociology of Education* M F D YOUNG (ed) Collier-Macmillan, 1971.

P BOURDIEU, Intellectual Field and Creative Project, *Social Science Information*, **8**, No 2; 1968 reprinted in *Knowledge and Control: New Directions for the Sociology of Education*, M F D YOUNG (ed) Collier-Macmillan, 1971.

T BOWDEN, 'The Transmission of an Educational Ideology', *Hard Cheese* **1**, 1973.

N CHOMSKY, *American Power and the New Mandarins*, Chatto and Windus, 1969.

P FILMER, 'Literary Study as Liberal Education and as Sociology in the Work of F R Leavis', in *Rationality, Education and the Social Organization of Knowledge*, C JENKS (ed), Routledge and Kegan Paul, 1976.

A GRAMSCI, *The Modern Prince and Other Writings*, New World

566

Publishers, 1957.

A GRAMSCI, 'In Search of the Educational Principle', *New Left Review*, **32**, 1965.

F L KAMPF, 'The Trouble with Literature', *Change*, May 1970.

H KEARNEY, *Scholars and Gentlemen*, Faber and Faber.

J KENNETT, 'The Sociology of Pierre Bourdieu', *Educational Review*, **25**, No 3, 1973.

H KLEIBARD, 'The Structure of the Disciplines as an Educational Slogan', *Teachers' College Record*, **16**, 1964.

D LAYTON, *Science for the People: The Origins of the School Science Curriculum in England*, Allen and Unwin, 1974.

T PATEMAN, (ed) *Counter Course*, Penguin Books, 1972.

T S POPKEWITZ, 'The Craft of Study, Structure and Schooling'. *Teachers' College Record*, **74**, No 2, 1972.

N POSTMAN, 'The Politics of Reading', *Harvard Educational Review* **40** No 2; reprinted in *Tinker, Tailor . . . the Myth of Cultural Deprivation*, N G KEDDIE (ed) Penguin Books, 1973.

T ROSZAK, *The Dissenting Academy*, Chatto & Windus and Penguin Books, 1969.

A SCHUTZ, 'On Multiple Realities', in *Collected Papers* **I**: *The Problem of Social Reality*, The Hague: Martinus Nijhoff, 1967.

M SEGRE ET AL 'A New Ideology of Education', *Social Forces*, **50**, No 3, May, 1972.

A SHUTTLEWORTH, 'People and Culture', *Working Papers in Cultural Studies*, University of Birmingham, 1971.

C STANLEY, *Literacy and the Crisis in Conventional Wisdom, School Review*, **80**, No 3, May, 1972.

D WALSH, 'Science, Sociology and Everyday Life', in *Rationality, Education and the Social Organization of Knowledge*, C JENKS (ed), Routledge and Kegan Paul, 1976.

J D WATSON, *The Double Helix*, Weidenfeld and Nicholson; 1968, Penguin Books, 1971.

M F D YOUNG, 'An Approach to the Study of Curricula as Socially Organized Knowledge', in *Knowledge and Control: New Directions for the Sociology of Education*, M F D YOUNG (ed), Collier-Macmillan, 1971.

M F D YOUNG, 'Taking Sides Against The Probable: Problems of Relativity and Commitment in Teaching and the Sociology of Knowledge', in C JENKS, *op cit*, 1976.

Section 7: Education and Rationality

A BLUM, 'The Sociology of Mental Illness', in *Deviance and Respectability: The Social Construction of Moral Meanings*, J D DOUGLAS (ed), New York: Basic Books, 1970.

A BLUM, 'Methods of Recognizing, Describing and Formulating Social

Problems', in *Handbook on The Study of Social Problems*, E O SMIGEL (ed), Rand MacNally, 1971.

A BLUM, 'Theorizing', in *Understanding Everyday Life*, J D DOUGLAS (ed), Routledge and Kegan Paul, 1971.

A BLUM, *Theorizing*, Heinemann Educational Books, 1974.

C CASTENADA, *A Separate Reality*, Penguin Books, 1971.

C CASTENADA, *Journey to Ixtlan: The Last Lessons of Don Juan*, Simon & Schuster, 1972.

H GARFINKEL, *Studies in Ethnomethodology*, Prentice-Hall, 1967.

H GINTIS, 'Towards a Political Economy of Education: A Radical Critique of Ivan Illich's "Deschooling Society",' *Harvard Education Review*, **42**, No 1, 1972.

R HORTON, 'African Traditional Thought and Western Science', *Africa* **37** 1969; reprinted in *Knowledge and Control: New Directions for the Sociology of Education*, M F D YOUNG (ed), Collier-Macmillan, 1971.

C JENKS, 'Powers of Knowledge and Forms of the Mind' in C JENKS (ed) *Education, Rationality and the Social Organization of Knowledge*, Routledge and Kegan Paul, 1976.

N G KEDDIE, 'Education as a Social Construct', in C JENKS (ed), *op cit*, 1976.

T KUHN, *The Structure of Scientific Revolutions*, Chicago University Press, 1970.

H MARCUSE, *Industrialization and Capitalism*, *New Left Review*, **30**, March, 1965.

P MCHUGH, 'On Positivism', in *Understanding Everyday Life*, J D DOUGLAS (ed), Routledge and Kegan Paul, 1971.

M MERLEAU-PONTY 'Phenomenology and the Sciences of Man', in *The Primacy of Perception*, J M EDIE (ed), North Western University Press, 1964.

N MORRIS, '*State Paternalism and Laissez-Faire in the 1860's*', History of Education Society, Methuen, 1970.

J NYERERE, 'Education for Self Reliance', in *Essays on Socialism*, Oxford University Press.

J O'NEILL *Making Sense Together*, Heinemann Educational Books, 1975.

A SCHUTZ, 'The Problem of Rationality in the Social World', in *Collected Papers* **II**: *Studies in Social Theory*, The Hague: Martinus Nijhoff, 1964.

D SMITH, 'Theorizing as Ideology', R TURNER (ed) *Ethnomethodology*, Penguin Books, 1974.

R TURNER (ed) *Ethnomethodology*, Penguin Books, 1974.

Also published by Collier Macmillan, London

KNOWLEDGE AND CONTROL:
New Directions for the Sociology of Education

Edited by Michael F D Young

Table of contents

Introduction **Michael F D Young** University of London Institute of Education

PART 1 Curricula and Teaching as the Organization of Knowledge

1 *An Approach to the Study of Curricula as Socially Organized Knowledge*
   Michael F D Young

2 *On the Classification and Framing of Educational Knowledge*
   Basil B Bernstein University of London Institute of Education

3 *Teaching and Learning as the Organization of Knowledge*
   Geoffrey M Esland The Open University

PART 2 Social Definitions of Knowledge

4 *The Corpus of Knowledge as a Normative Order*
   Alan F Blum New York University

5 *Classroom Knowledge*
   Nell Keddie Goldsmiths' College, University of London

6 *Intellectual Field and Creative Project*
   Pierre Bourdieu École Pratique des Hautes Études, Sorbonne

PART 3 Cognitive Styles in Comparative Perspective

7 *Systems of Education and Systems of Thought*
   Pierre Bourdieu

8 *African Traditional Thought and Western Science*
   Robin Horton University of Ife, Nigeria

9 *The Management of Knowledge; A Critique of the Use of Typologies in the Sociology of Education*
   Ioan Davies Queen's University, Ontario